THE STORY OF
CINEMA

VOLUME ONE
From the Beginnings to Gone with the Wind

THE STORY OF CINEMA

AN ILLUSTRATED HISTORY

VOLUME ONE
From the Beginnings to Gone with the Wind

DAVID SHIPMAN

Preface by Ingmar Bergman

HODDER AND STOUGHTON
LONDON SYDNEY AUCKLAND TORONTO

By the same author

THE GREAT MOVIE STARS:
  Volume 1 – The Golden Years
  Volume 2 – The International Years

British Library Cataloguing in Publication Data

Shipman, David
    The Story of Cinema (Volume One: From the
      Beginnings to Gone with the Wind)
Shipman, David
    The story of cinema.
    1. Title
    1. Moving-pictures – History
    791.43'09'04   PN1993.5.A1

ISBN 0 340 25587 0

Contents

Preface

IT WAS CHRISTMAS and I was nine years old. A wealthy old lady who was a friend of the family used to give us children rather expensive presents. Two days before Christmas Eve her servant arrived with the gifts, which together with the other packets were placed in a large laundry basket under the stairs up to the attic. I saw at once that one of the packets (big and angular, wrapped in strong brown paper) contained a film projector. I nearly fainted with joy. For several years I had wished for a projector; now the dream was to come true. I went about in a trance, unable either to sleep or eat.

The great moment turned out to be a terrible disappointment. The film projector went to my brother, who was four years older than me; I was given a bear that could growl. My grief was agonising. My brother, who had never shown the slightest interest in cinematic art and was moreover a clever businessman, seized the opportunity. He sold me the apparatus at a price of two hundred tin soldiers, that is to say, my entire army. Two days later he declared war and invaded my country, defeating the few gallantly fighting troops that were left, despite our agreement that no war was to break out until I had a chance of building up a new armed force. I fled into the nursery's dark and spacious closet with my 'cinematograph', as the toy was called. Although simple it was a fine little machine, but more dangerous than a bomb.

It consisted of two spools for sixty metres of 35-mm film, a steady feeding mechanism (Maltese cross and crank), a sector and a fairly large lens in shining brass. The lamp-house was of black lacquered tinplate with a reflex mirror, paraffin lamp and a backward curved chimney. In addition there was a holder for slides. A blue box (with a pretty picture on the lid of a young man in a sailor suit showing moving pictures of fighting lions to an impressed family) contained a film loop about four metres long, an everlasting film. The loop was brown and had a pungent, rather sweet smell; like all film at that time it was made on a nitrate base and was frightfully inflammable. Nitrate film, paraffin lamp, dusty closet, a nine-year-old projectionist – no grown-up knew just how dangerous the whole thing really was. During the next few years I spent all my pocket-money and savings on film. I must have kept thousands of metres of film in the closet, where I established my cinema in the flickering light of the paraffin lamp. The fact that the family and the old rectory survived must be put down to the constant vigilance of guardian angels.

Sometimes I have wondered at the child's wild and inexplicable excitement. It was all a mechanical process. A little machine which rattled loudly as it fed in sixteen frames a second. If I cranked frame by frame nothing, or almost nothing, happened – the frames hardly changed. If I went faster, movement was born. The shadows acted, the faces turned towards me, eyes opened, lips formed inaudible words. The darkness, the rattling, the smells, the lighted rectangle on the wall . . . I made up stories about the small, mysterious figures, they sent out magic signals, they took part in my dreams. I remember these pictures with a clarity and focus which they no doubt lacked in reality.

The rectangle of light in the dark, the shadows' unceasing movements controlled by me. Unaccountable courses of events, secret relations that extended far into the boundless twilight land of dreams. Hypnosis and magic – the nine-year-old touched the little finger of a giant's invisible hand. Today, fifty-five years later, in the murk of the cutting room I can feel the same excitement, the same tension, in the presence of the endless and the unexplored.

Fårö, 25 July 1981
© Ingmar Bergman
Translated by Alan Blair

Introduction

IN 1972, out of the blue, I received a letter inviting me to write a history of the cinema. It was a project which I had previously considered as too vast for one person, but I needed no persuasion once a concrete offer had been made. Even compressed, I realised it would have to be a very long book, and if at first I was unsure of my approach I wanted it to be as factually accurate as was within my power.

I had already discovered how few reliable books were available on the subject. For instance, researching *The Jazz Singer* has proved a hazardous task. As the first Talking picture and therefore of great importance in the development of the medium, it is a title to be found in the indices of all cinema histories, yet not one agreed on what was actually spoken from the screen. Some were vague, some had apparently made up the facts to suit the author's beliefs and some were inaccurate – as I discovered when I had the opportunity to see the film. The first requirement, therefore, was that I should view every film to be discussed – not at that time, however, foreseeing that that, plus further research and actual writing, would take more than ten years.

During that period the cinema's past has become available as never before, with literally hundreds of lost or forgotten films emerging from archives and dusty corners. These films in themselves called for a reinterpretation of cinema history, while the accepted classics had begun to offer meanings quite different from those accepted by their original audiences. Many valuable films, recording their times with honesty and accuracy, had been ignored or forgotten, while some much-admired films turned out to be of minimal interest. The first commentators on cinema had tended to praise any movie which raised the medium above its primary purpose – as mass entertainment – and thus a proportionately large number of experimental and avant-garde films had been welcomed beyond their intrinsic worth. From its humble beginnings, the cinema gained in respectability whenever connected to other art forms, and the earliest films publicly approved were adaptations of plays and novels, especially those with a religious or historical basis. Thus Griffith made his inflated reputation, and thus matters rested till the Soviets experimented with film form in the Twenties. In the interim the most admired movies were those of the German Expressionist movement, with their juxtaposition of an old art – the theatre – and a new science – psychiatry. Today these films provide merely a footnote to the cultural climate of the time, while those which with hindsight have become the really important films (because they show us what Germany was like then) were ignored or derided, and consequently not exported.

Very few critics or film historians were prepared to view unknown films – or so declared James Card, the curator of the Eastman House archive, in an attempt to explain why Griffith and Von Stroheim are still regarded as the best directors then working. To me, it was not only clear that Griffith had never advanced beyond a basic level of competence, but recent researches had shown his claims to innovation to be false. Similarly, *The Great Train Robbery* is still described as the most influential film in early cinema, despite the revelation, in 1959 in the Eastman House magazine, *Image*, that it was copied almost frame by frame from another film, just then rediscovered.

Such misconceptions were significantly not corrected in Paul Rotha's 'The Film Till Now', the ancestor of all serious writing on the subject. First published in 1930, this work has always been regarded as definitive, so much so that when Rotha declined to update it Richard Griffith did so, both in the Forties and the Fifties, giving it a new lease of life. Rotha's text is revealing as a guide to what constituted cinema culture at the time, but otherwise is no longer of value. He had, for instance, difficulty in concealing his contempt for all American cinema except for Griffith, Chaplin and Flaherty; and his enthusiasm for the German cinema was, as I have implied, both partial and misjudged. Yet his influence was such that his favoured films formed the basis of most of the world's film archives, thus perpetuating the myths by making those particular films alone available for study. He is sound only on Eisenstein and Pabst, though Richard Griffith's additions recognise the importance of the French directors of the Thirties and of Capra and Lubitsch. If in the post-war period we add the names of Rossellini and de Sica, together with John Ford, Minnelli and the British documentarists, we arrive at the total cinema pantheon as enshrined in the most prominent of Rotha's successors, 'The Penguin Film Review' of the late Forties and *Sight and Sound* in the early Fifties. Clearly this is an impoverished pantheon, and one may wonder what Rossellini and the British documentarists – with the outstanding exception of Humphrey Jennings – were doing there in the first place. Nowhere was there to be found any comment on the brilliant and immensely influential early Swedish cinema, virtually dismissed by Rotha. Even Arthur Knight, in his more authoritative 'The Liveliest Art', published in 1957, confines his discussion of early Swedish cinema to one of its lesser efforts, *Gosta Berling's Saga*. Meanwhile, with the possible exception of the 1939 'Rise of the American Film' by Lewis Jacobs, the most readable and informative study of early cinema continued to be Benjamin B. Hampton's 'A History of the Movies'. But that was never mentioned in 'The Penguin Film Review' or *Sight and Sound*, since it concerned the movie *industry*.

Yet the cinema is first and foremost just that – an industry – and since any motion picture is a manufactured product film cannot be profitably discussed only with reference to its highest endeavours. Were I to confine myself to the revelatory and influential films I should be limited to about one thousand, and were I to deal only with the enduringly entertaining I should probably reach the same figure: and few would duplicate the other. Some films are now of interest for the manner in which people moved, spoke, dressed or decorated their homes, and we can therefore add two further categories of films deserving attention: those which faithfully reflected their times and those which – since this is an entertainments industry not inclined towards sociology – made no attempt to do so.

Trying to say so much to so many, often in the simplest terms, film had, or had until recently, the advantage of its presentation: on a gigantic screen in a vast, darkened auditorium seating sometimes thousands; and these circumstances enabled it to become the most powerful of all means of expression. At its peak, in the Thirties and Forties, the entire populations of most civilised countries were regular cinemagoers, and it was then that films replaced literature as a principal after-dinner topic, not yet superseded in that role by television. For the purposes of this book I saw again the films of youth and childhood, and it was clear that from them as much as from any other source were derived my values – on such matters as public spirit, courage, romantic ardour, humour and the other qualities with which movie heroes were naturally endowed. Some of these films had lodged so deep in my consciousness that despite my having forgotten, I thought, everything about them, each sequence unrolled anew with vigorous familiarity. Obviously I have not restricted myself to films with a personal significance, and as far as possible I have tried to include those which were very popular. The latter have often been the industry's own favourite artefacts, and for the same reason I have usually detailed the leading awards of the American Motion Picture Academy of Arts and Sciences – though certainly not because its Oscar is any guarantee of merit.

Since the Hollywood film has been dominant in every country with which the United States has a trade agreement, often keeping local product from theatre screens, I have devoted to it the largest share of the text, certain that what has emanated from Paramount, M-G-M or Warners is as familiar in Bombay or Helsinki as in New York or New Orleans. In fact, my dissatisfaction with most previous cinema histories is that they have ignored the worldwide exposure of American films and their consequent social significance. As far as the other national industries are concerned, I began with those films which crossed frontiers and added little-known ones of such quality that they had to be included, if only to demonstrate their superiority to others which have gained attention in the international market. Except when American-financed, the odds against foreign distribution are very long indeed. 'Winchester's 1948 Screen Encyclopedia' lists approximately 250 foreign-language films publicly shown in Britain from 1920 to that time – less than the number of American films shown annually. The listing is not entirely accurate, for in the Silent days a number of European films were passed off as British or American, but it is significant that over fifty per cent of the films listed is from one source, i.e. France (a comparable listing for the United States would be difficult to compile, since many more European films were imported, but often were shown, without subtitles, only in cinemas catering to specific ethnic populations). The 'failed' German films I mentioned earlier were denigrated by the critics and shunned by the public because their subject matter was poverty – and though that could be an advantage in the eyes of foreign critics the producers concerned made little attempt to find buyers abroad. Japanese producers from the start never considered that there would be foreign interest in their films, despite the fact that by the mid-Thirties they were as technically advanced as those in the West and often more mature in treatment. That changed in 1951 when *Rashomon* was shown at the Venice Film Festival, and from then on 'World Cinema' was no longer confined to a handful of countries. The existence of international film festivals has become crucial to the history of the cinema, since they provide a market-place for film-makers: I have tried to see the early films of those who did not gain international prominence thereby till comparatively late in their careers – for example, Ingmar Bergman, who made at least a dozen remarkable films before achieving world renown.

Nevertheless, even he worked in an industry motivated by profit, but these films may be ascribed to him – as creator or prime mover – and the same may be said of most directors working outside America. In Hollywood more than anywhere else the story of cinema has been a prolonged battle between those who have regarded it as a means of achieving fame and wealth and those for whom it is a medium for communication and/or personal expression. Few Hollywood directors have been allowed to be creative in the sense that Bergman and, say, Antonioni are, so that for each Capra and Wilder there are dozens of honest, interpretative craftsmen, as well as many more whose work has been skilfully assembled in the cutting-room till it becomes acceptable entertainment. I regret being unable to credit all the individuals – writers, designers, photographers, editors – who make decisive contributions to any film, but as it is the text is sufficiently burdened with names. Complete cross-referencing would have made the text even longer than it is, and the use of q.v. refers only to items later in the text (including those in Volume Two): I have tended not to use this abbreviation in cases where it is obvious that there is a later discussion of the item concerned or within brackets when members of any film's cast are listed. I have assumed that the reader has some knowledge of technical terms, and have included the dates of birth and death only of leading figures – usually at that point when the individual concerned has come into prominence. Similarly I have assumed familiarity with the players and films of recent years, so that the illustrations in the early part of the book have been selected mainly as a guide to appearance, while those in the latter section represent either films which are interesting or important.

On the studios, I have the film historian's usual dilemma as to whether to refer to them in the singular or plural: the reader may take it that the plural implies the executives, 'the front office' or the production team, the singular either the corporate identity or the building itself. (In the case of 20th Century-Fox, I have in general used the more clumsy '20th' rather than the customary 'Fox' after their amalgamation, in order to avoid confusion with that operation as controlled by William Fox.) I have taken the opportunity when appropriate to discuss American cinema in terms of producer, director or star – which means that for the most part the text is divided into parallel chapters on Hollywood, that is on individuals and on the studios. I have hesitated to use the director's possessive unless convinced that it was either recognisably his work or that he was the driving force behind it.

The classic case is *Casablanca*, since it may be everyone's favourite Hollywood movie. It was produced and directed by two knowledgeable and skilled craftsmen, respectively Hal Wallis and Michael Curtiz; the former contributed to the often memorable dialogue, credited to some otherwise undistinguished veterans – but what is probably the secret of its popularity is the teaming of Humphrey Bogart and Ingrid Bergman. She has said that she barely knew Bogart, and since she has attested to the constant confusion and dissension during shooting we must conclude that the end result is the product of a team. Other popular films of that time – *Les Enfants du Paradis* and *Ladri di Biciclette* – clearly owe as much to their writers as to their directors, but they are not studio films and we credit them to their directors for convenience.

I hope that I have obtained the right balance between Hollywood and the other national industries in selecting five thousand films to tell the story of cinema; their titles are printed in the text in bold face. Among those omitted are early films which, alas, have not been preserved, and those of once-important film-makers whose later work dwindled into insignificance – and in this case I trust that I have made it clear why I stopped persevering. The dates I have given the films are not those when copyrighted, but the completion date – i.e. when they were first shown to other than studio employees and were therefore deemed to be fit for public consumption. I have assumed some knowledge of the chief European languages in keeping the original titles of French, German, Italian and Spanish films, adding the English title only when the original is likely to be unknown. In the case of all other foreign titles I have used the best-known, whether in English or not – and all of these are cross-indexed at the back of the book. Films are discussed in chronological order whenever possible, since the cinema has been particularly susceptible to influence and indeed plagiarism, and every study of it should take into account what was being done just a few months earlier. Since, however, the cinema is a volatile industry/art form I have been able to vary my approach; and since this very long text required two separate volumes I hope the reader will agree that we made the right break at the beginning of the Second World War – that as far as Hollywood was concerned *Gone with the Wind* marked the end of one era and *Citizen Kane*, released sixteen months later, the beginning of another.

Of all the films I expected to see, beyond those irretrievably lost, less than a handful were unavailable. Doubtless archivists are making further discoveries, but if I take as a starting point the two hundred 'Outstanding fiction films, 1914–48' listed as an appendix in the Rotha-Griffith book, I have seen all but twenty, of which some are officially lost and the rest – all Soviet Talkies – unheard of since that list was compiled. (An additional seventy-eight documentary and experimental films are also listed, of which I lack perhaps a dozen – and cannot be more precise since many of the titles, e.g. *Chang*, *October*, *Roma Città Aparta*, do not belong in either of the appointed categories.) This brings into question my own standards of excellence, and the plural is necessary since the cinema encompasses Eisenstein and Buster Keaton, Marilyn Monroe and Kurosawa, Bergmans Ingmar and Ingrid, Jean Arthur and Gene Kelly, Satyajit Ray and David O. Selznick, Capra and Méliès, Antonioni and W. C. Fields. Some of these contributed to entertainments which after several viewings still seem fresh, while others created films attempting to illuminate aspects of the human condition in terms which are intrinsic to themselves.

Introduction

Everyone in films hopes their product will reach the widest possible audience, but there are nevertheless different publics – and it is easier for me to define my ideal audience than my idea of the perfect film. The text that follows includes qualitative judgments on most of the films discussed, but those are not judgments made in isolation. If I am happiest with audiences in the cinémathèques and repertory theatres, asking to be entertained and stimulated by the cinema's past, I have also sat with other audiences: the art-house or student audience sitting reverently through one-half of a double-bill and barracking the other; and the circuit audience, sitting through *Gone with the Wind* in almost as much awe as those for whom it was originally intended, or talking noisily – vast sections of it – through *Star Wars*, which rivalled the earlier film in popularity, or so it seemed. Perhaps I seize on popularity when it supports my own taste and deplore it when it doesn't; I hope at least that I have always been able to chart the undeserved successes and the undeserved failures inevitable in a product which demands mass support.

Unfortunately many movies which were designed to wile away an idle hour are subjected to analyses undreamt of by their progenitors – which is not to say that the most commercial or mechanical artefacts cannot incidentally tell us something of the culture which gave them birth. The matter was neatly put by Robert F. Moss in the *Saturday Review* (23 June 1979): '"I'm not sure film is an art form," said Lionel Trilling one day in a seminar at Columbia University. "Certainly most film scholarship is hardly worthy of the name." Indeed, to anyone trained in an orthodox academic discipline, film studies is apt to look like a primitive outpost of intellectual activity, a mining-camp of critical anarchy and wild-eyed artistic judgments. There are marvellous exceptions of course, but even allowing for them most film criticism is a do-it-yourself undertaking in which the critic remoulds the films of his favourite director closer to his heart's desire, investing jaunty melodramas and cowboy epics with some hidden motifs and subterranean profundities that would never have occurred to the directors themselves.'

If I have found few differences of opinion on what are the cinema's highest achievements, there is equal agreement on those at the opposite end of the scale: amateur films, and I do not mean 'home movies'; cheap horror films and, indeed, all exploitation product; movies which are overlong – a proliferating species because their makers are now more in awe of their own talent than respectful of audiences; and works of no intellectual content which aspire to festival exposure by the wilful confusion of narrative – thought by their makers to provide 'enigma'. Then there are the cultists, ranging from those who find feminist messages in old Hollywood junk to self-confessed 'Marxist' theorists who only approve of films intended to bring down a bourgeois culture.

The most pernicious of the cults is the 'auteur' theory, which in the last twenty years has wrecked any rational interpretation of the cinema's past. The film historians of the early Fifties held to the same beliefs as the first writers on film, partly because they needed 'classics' and partly because there were few opportunities to see old movies without that status (thus the great films of Sjöström were unseen outside Sweden for more than a generation). Since it was accepted that such films were made by one man – Eisenstein, Griffith, Chaplin, Murnau, Lang – the auteur theorists of the late Fifties decreed that the only worthwhile films were those that were clearly the work of individuals. Thus film-makers of authority within the industry, like William Wyler, who prided himself on changing his subject matter, if not his approach, were derided in favour of journeyman directors. Few of these had any individual style, and their admired consistency was due to their inability, either from lack of talent or lack of opportunity, to do other than make variations over again of the same film – except, obviously, Hitchcock, who was too commercially canny to do anything else. Thus arose a fallacy which has bewildered or bored even the most hardened movie buffs, who have in this period taken to avoiding the often second-rate directors favoured by the theorists. At the same time many excellent films have fallen into neglect because their work confuses those unable to understand creative activity of a various nature, whether of subject or quality. I have thus been particularly anxious to point up in the text both once-influential films by directors who did little else of interest and those made by talents which moved into – often spectacular – decline.

No other visual art form is so dependent on the written word. The more a film is discussed the better it is known; so that if it is new it is the more likely to earn back its investment, and if old the more likely to recover the cost of bringing it from the vault. It is therefore necessary for writers on film to be well versed in the opinions of their confreres. I have restricted myself in the text to the most influential critics working in London and New York, and when I have not quoted in admiration it is to explain why some terrible films have been accepted. It is not that cinemagoers themselves are particularly gullible, but many believe in the infallibility of critics, as if it were conferred by the distinction of having their opinions in print. The two most influential New York critics during the past thirty years have been, to say the least, erratic. The situation improved as one retired and the other, more recently, lost credence, but in the summer of 1981 Fassbinder's routine *Lili Marleen* received American notices better than those for Rosi's *Cadaveri Eccellenti*. Admittedly among European critics there is no unanimity on Fassbinder, an uneven film-maker, but throughout Europe Rosi is regarded as a master and that particular film a major work. In these cases posterity may have much to say – and it is one of my themes to show how recent reviewings have so wholeheartedly overturned past judgments. But to be just, the film historians of the past were attempting to interpret an art form in the light of their own cultural values. The reason that they have been proved wrong is because we now regard the cinema in a different light.

As a means of communication the film has been overtaken by television. In historical terms the age of cinema was minute; many of the early pioneers were still living when I began this book – and a few are still, happily, with us. The Silent cinema lasted just over thirty years. Thirty years later, movies bowed to the power of television – which is where, now, most people watch them. As a record of the twentieth century – certainly the last part of it – posterity will look to television. But that is another story.

1
Beginnings

THE CINEMA began in Paris, in 1895. The first moving pictures – and they are no more than that – are not in themselves rewarding, unless you imagine yourselves there that evening, 28 December, having paid one franc admittance to the basement of a café in the boulevard des Capucines, its one hundred serried seats occupied by only thirty-three people, watching a show lasting twenty minutes: if you can, these half-minutes of images will haunt you.

We know from artefacts that the Ancients had wanted to tell stories in pictures – which was more than the cinema did at first. The optical principles of the camera were known to the Greeks, but it was not until the early nineteenth century that efforts were made to fix images by mechanical means. Photography was invented in 1835, but the cinema film did not become possible till 1888, when George Eastman (1854–1932) devised, among other photographic products, the celluloid roll film. In the meantime, in 1873, an English-born photographer, Eadweard Muybridge (1830–1904) had been commissioned by the Governor of California to take action pictures of a favourite race-horse. He experimented to the extent that later, working with the University of Pennsylvania, he took over one hundred thousand exposures – of speeds of up to 1/2000th of a second – of people and animals in consecutive action, intended to interest art lovers and students of anatomy. Among others interested was Thomas Edison (1847–1931), who had already invented the phonograph, and when he met Muybridge in 1888 he was impressed by a machine the latter had invented, the zoopraxiscope, by which

drawings of his photographs were projected. He envisaged something similar to accompany recorded sound, and two years later his assistant, W. K. L. Dickson (1860–1935), using Eastman's new roll film, began to produce sequences of images. Edison was the first of many in the history of cinema to take credit for the work of others, and since he was the boss it was only right that the Kinetoscope be patented in his name. It was fashioned like a peepshow; the viewer peered into a box to watch mechanically operated strips of action film. In 1893 Edison constructed a work-shop near his laboratory to take pictures for the Kinetoscope; called the Black Maria, the studio could be turned, and the roof opened, to take the greatest advantage of the sun. The first film made there, reputedly, was **Fred Ott's Sneeze**, which as *Record of a Sneeze, 7 January 1894,*was the first film copyrighted. **Fun in a Chinese Laundry** (1894) was more ambitious, part of a vaudeville skit; and **Execution of Mary, Queen of Scots** (1895) offered the gruesome spectacle of that lady's headless body – effected by a dummy put in place while the camera was halted.

What was needed was to combine these strips with the principles of another toy or gadget, the magic lantern, and in February 1895 two brothers, from their father's photographic factory in Lyon, patented an 'appareil servant à l'obtention et à la vision des épreuves chronophotographiques' – in other words, a projector. August Lumière (1862–1954) and Louis (1864–1948) were only two of many scientists experimenting with film – the ability to reproduce nature on a continuous piece of celluloid – and

17

pioneer claims have been registered most notably on behalf of William Friese-Green (1855–1931) in Britain, and Etienne-Jules Marey (1830–1904) in France, as well as Edison and Dickson. If Edison himself merely regarded the Kinetoscope as a profitable toy, Dickson, Friese-Green and Marey were among those trying to find a way of projecting moving images on to a screen. In Britain the partnership of Birt Acres (1854–1918) and Robert William Paul (1870–1943) – having counterfeited a Kinetoscope – patented a camera to take pictures for it in May 1895, and it is clear that they were giving private projections before the end of the year. On 1 November, almost two months before the public presentation in the boulevard des Capucines, a German showman, Max Skladanowsky (1863–1939), offered his Bioskop at the Berlin Wintergarten in a programme of novelties, but his machine 'was an elaborate affair using two parallel film strips and two lenses, and so hardly qualifies as a film projector in the sense we have come to understand it' (David Robinson). The Lumières did make the first film, both publicly registered and projected, if by publicly we mean to people they hoped would buy the novelty, on 22 March 1895, at 44 rue de Rennes, Paris – **Sortie des Ouvriers de l'Usine Lumière**. Among those uninterested were the Musée Grévin (whose wonders were mainly waxworks) and the Folies-Bergères, so in December they rented the 'Salon Indien' of the Grand Café, 14 boulevard des Capucines, with posters outside announcing the attraction. After the *Sortie des Ouvriers* came such tidbits as *Le Goûter de Bébé, Le Demolition d'un Mur, L'Arroseur Arrosé* (a gardener looks into the nozzle of a hose-pipe and gets a faceful) and, most sensational of all, *L'Arrivée d'un Train en Gare de la Ciotat*.

The press took little notice: only two reporters from the forty-odd Paris newspapers showed up for the first performance. 'With this new invention,' wrote one of them in *La Poste*, 'death will be no longer absolute, final. The people we have seen on the screen will be with us, moving and alive after their deaths.' Without thoughts of immortality, the public began to flock to the Salon, and one among them who asked to show these 'animated photographs' because of their scientific interest was Quintin Hogg, founder of the Regent Street Polytechnic in London. Seen there, on 25 February 1896, they immediately attracted the attention of the Empire Music Hall, which borrowed them, and soon had to put them at the top of the bill, adding 'animated photographs' of such London landmarks as Marble Arch and Piccadilly Circus. Two months later Edison's Vitascope process was unveiled to the American public at Koster and Bial's Music Hall, on the site now covered by Macy's. Edison had purchased and patented a projection device, one of several that appeared simultaneously. The first projected film that those New Yorkers saw was of a music hall act, the Leigh Sisters in their umbrella dance, followed by a shot of waves breaking. 'Some of the people in the front rows seemed to be afraid they were going to get wet,' went the report in *The New York Dramatic Mirror*, 'and looked about to see where they could run to,' going on to note that 'the Vitascope is nothing more than an enlarged Kinetoscope.' The Lumière programme followed two months later, at Keith's: vaudeville and variety had found a new attraction.

The craze to see moving-pictures had started, and by the end of the year had spread throughout the States. Theatres projected them; carnivals and penny arcades had to make do with peepshows, but as these were cumbersome and uneconomic, with only one customer able to view at one time, their proprietors looked longingly at projectors. A fierce battle ensued between those who owned, or had patented projectors, determined to retain their exclusivity and those who wanted them; but just as rivals to the Kinetoscope came thick and fast, several companies began to market projectors. Fairgrounds began to provide both projection and peepshow, and the proliferation of tents for the former received only a temporary setback in Paris in 1897, when 140 people perished in a fire started in the cinema tent of a charity bazaar.

Despite legal injunctions, Edison's rivals multiplied. The chief competitor of the Kinetoscope had been the Mutoscope, and its owners developed the Biograph for showmen who preferred to project their pictures. Indeed, the Muto-scope, a book of pages of consecutive images which might be flicked through manually or mechanically, had been devised by Dickson with Herman Casler; Dickson had resigned from Edison and with Casler and others formed the American Mutoscope and Biograph Company, whose product was introduced in Pittsburgh in September 1896, in turn to move into Koster and Bial's two months later, and to take up what was to become a ten years' residence at Keith's the following year.

The films of both companies were still sketches – *Burning Stable, Feeding the Chickens, Easter Parade on Fifth Avenue* – but at least two were thought to be scandalous, and were much imitated: from Edison, **The Kiss** (1896), a discreet middle-aged embrace, a scene from the play 'The Widow Jones', and from Biograph, **Fatima** (1897), part of the act of a Coney Island belly-dancer. **Tearing Down the Spanish Flag** (1898) also proved sensational, appealing to the current mood, and its success caused its maker, J. Stuart Blackton (1875–1941), a former journalist and vaudeville artist – and like Dickson, British-born – to set up as a rival to Edison and Biograph; with his partner Albert E. Smith, he founded Vitagraph in 1899.

By this time, films were more likely to be projected than viewed through a peepshow. They became a popular item at smoking-concerts and church socials, and their value was proved to theatre-owners when they replaced vaudeville during a performers' strike in 1900. At the St Louis Exposition the following year one of the most popular exhibits was 'Hale's Tours and Scenes of the World', in which audiences sat in a simulated railway coach and watched the world – or some of it – flash by. Local fairgrounds were the logical venue of the novelty, along with performing seals and wax-works; eager audiences watched films in improvised auditoria behind partitions. In the U.S. the cinema, as such, did not exist till the owner of one Los Angeles amusement arcade threw out the 'amusements' and installed seats and a projector. That was in 1902, but five years earlier the Lumière brothers had opened a building in Paris for the specific showing of films. The peepshow began to die: throughout the world, stores and then theatres were converted into cinemas. In the U.S. the price of admission determined the name – the nickelodeon – and that became the generic name for the makeshift or purpose-built show places for some years.

The films remained simple. They were sold outright to exhibitors for a few cents per foot and as most of the trading was done by mail-order, more money went into the preparation of the catalogues than into filming. Alongside such early categories as 'Views' and 'Vaudeville Acts' there appeared 'News Events'. Films purporting to show action in both the Spanish-American and Boer Wars brought in wide audiences, and 'staging' became an accepted part of the game. Edison, Biograph and Vitagraph began to offer brief sketches and burlesques of stage productions, but they were no more imaginative than their 'Views'. It was a Frenchman who turned it into an art: Georges Méliès (1861–1938).

In Méliès' own opinion (as expressed in his memoir), 'in the development of the cinema I have played a more important part than Lumière', and in considering *development* this is certainly true. The Lumières photographed nature; Méliès photographed a reconstructed life. The public would have tired of watching factory-workers leave their building; Méliès offered them a realisation of their fantasies. He discovered, or invented, the fiction film.

He was thirty-four when he went into films – a designer, actor, magician, and director of the Théâtre Robert-Houdin. A visit to the Salon Indien transformed his life. When the frères Lumière would neither rent nor lend him their equipment, he purchased a camera from London; and showed his first film in April 1896. Later that year he built the first studio in Europe (at Montreuil-sous-Bois), and he made an interesting discovery: his camera jammed while filming a street scene, and when the film was projected a carriage miraculously became a hearse. Edison had been aware of this trick when recreating the decapitation of Mary Stuart, but to Méliès it offered magical opportunities: immediately he made **L'Escomptage d'un Dame**

The Magic of Méliès

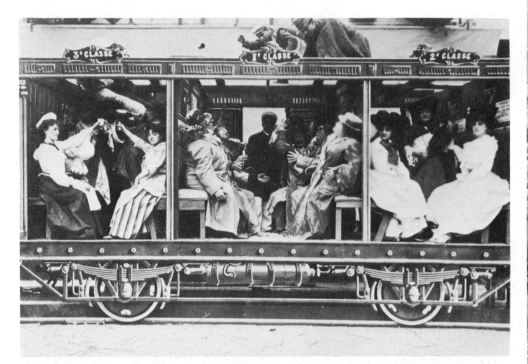

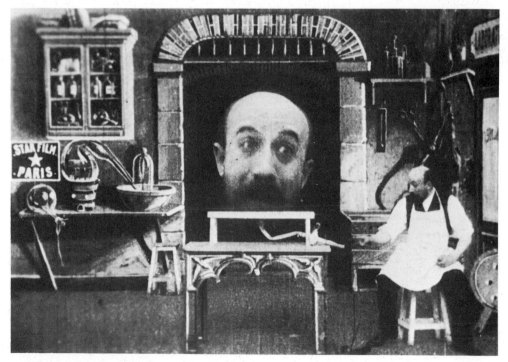

More than any primitive films, the brief pieces put together by Georges Méliès continue to enchant. Remembered best for his science fiction tales, such as *Voyage à Travers l'Impossible*, ABOVE LEFT, and his joke fantasies, such as *L'Homme à la Tête de Caoutchouc,* LEFT, he also made reconstructions of actual events and of stage spectacles.

Here are two more
facets of Méliès:
allegory, as in
*Civilisation à Travers
les Ages*, ABOVE and
fairy-tale, as in *Barbe
Bleue*, RIGHT.

(1896), in which a woman temporarily becomes a skeleton. From photographing 'anything that moved' he experimented ceaselessly. In **Nouvelles Luttes Extravagantes** (1900) women wrestlers become men, and the sexes continue to rotate amidst much dismemberment; in **L'Homme Orchestre** (1900) chairs and men multiply and disappear as if by magic. Ghosts dance at the top of the screen in **Le Chaudron Infernale** (1903), and in **L'Homme à la Tête de Caoutchouc** (1902) a real head grows smaller and larger, an effect made by careful superimposition and an advancing and receding camera. Méliès hand-tinted his films, in the manner of contemporary photography, but he was reluctant to use other photographic techniques, such as the close-up. It has been claimed that the pioneers refused to use the close-up because audiences would not accept people shown chopped off at knee or waist, but indeed close-ups were common from *Fred Ott's Sneeze* onwards – at least, with those initiators who regarded the new art form as allied to photography. Méliès in fact saw it rather as a branch of the theatre, enabling him to rival the spectacles of the Théâtre du Chatelet, which he had been unable to do on the small stage of his theatre. Hence his camera in general is rooted in the stalls, and thus the meticulously painted scenery. His use of narrative, as in **Barbe Bleue** (1901), is to chop it into segments of approximately one minute each, each of which is little more than a tableau in motion; but in fantasies such as **Rêve de Noël** (1900), a sequence of pictures on Christmas themes, he is already using the dissolve.

However, if his favourite subject was not a magician on a stage, it was a scientist in a laboratory; he turned inevitably to the works of the still-living Jules Verne. His first Verne-inspired film was *Le Voyage dans la Lune* (1902), which, with his *Cendrillon* (1900), established him throughout the world – to the extent that at a time when the production cost of one reel was confined to mere salaries and a limited expenditure on costumes or sets he spent the equivalent of $7,500 on **Voyage à Travers l'Impossible** (1904). It does last for two reels, probably the first film to do so, and audiences of the day, con-vinced that they were at the dawn of an age of marvels, responded with enthusiasm; but today the odd, imaginative tricks and the endearing details of the short subjects tend to pall when the material is stretched out to twenty minutes. His savants, viewed satirically, tend to gesticulate like clowns, but that is also true of his characters in his reconstruction of real-life events, such as **L'Affaire Dreyfus** (1899), an elaborate, one-reel effort in nine sequences. The trial finished on 9 September 1899, with the verdict that shocked Europe, that Dreyfus was guilty 'with extenuating circumstances'; and in the light of the furore caused by *L'Affaire* it is possible to say that Méliès' final sequence, showing Dreyfus returning to prison, is inflammatory. The aspects of the case he chose to show were not so much informative as designed to play on audience emotions – and we may well wonder how many spectators thought they were seeing actuality. Some rushing across the camera by the cast indicates that Méliès did not understand the importance of action, and during the next decade his films remained inert while the medium moved on. He made fewer and longer films, but lost his pre-eminence as piracy and plagiarism ran rife in the industry; and just as the unit he set up under his brother in the U.S. collapsed under the onslaught of more important companies, so he found local conditions difficult with the industry dominated by the Pathé company (q.v.).

He was also unable to change in the light of innovations by others. By 1912 French film-makers were out in the streets of Paris shooting the chase comedies which had become so popular, but Méliès was offering *A la Conquête du Pole,* which was similar to the films he had made ten years earlier – animated tableaux set against painted sets, each of them explained in an introductory intertitle. The film is pleasing, with a suffragette determined to go on a trip of Polar exploration and its voyage among the signs of the Zodiac – represented by scantily-clad maidens holding painted stars. Once at the Pole they discover a giant, who gathers the explorers into his icicled arms, occasionally popping one into his mouth. But such matters were no longer novel to audiences and Méliès gave up making films in 1913, having made over five hundred, and some titles indicate his range: *Le Château Hanté, La Vengeance de Bouddha ou la Fontaine Sacrée, Les Sept Péchés Capitaux, Le Barbier de Séville, La Tour de Londres et les Derniers Moments d'Anne de Boleyn, Hamlet, Jeanne d'Arc, Le Tsar en France, Le Juif-Errant, New York-Paris en Automobile* and *L'Eruption du Mont-Pélé.* He was rediscovered, not long before his death, selling toys, not the first of many creative artists to find the cinema an ungrateful mistress, since virtually all the pioneers were driven out or ruined by it. His work may be primitive, but audiences of the time were enchanted; and the enchantment lingers.

Méliès was the first to make publicity films for other companies, in 1898; and he may have been the first, for the sake of publicity, to put his name on another's film. The British-based American entrepreneur, Charles Urban, engaged him to make a version of the Coronation of Edward VII, but it was in fact made by George Albert Smith (1864–1959), whose Warwick Trading Co. was financed by Urban. Smith was a follower of Méliès, but more interested in his *jeux d'esprits* than in his longer films. He had been a portrait photographer, which may be why his films are rich in close-ups; double exposure was known to photography, but Smith patented it for cinematographic use in 1898 – though others, including Méliès, were using it by 1900. Smith's films show a delight in trickery, and his **The Kiss in the Tunnel** (1899) is the earliest surviving example of action put together without intervening titles: a couple in a railway carriage embrace, framed at beginning and end by shots of a train. There is something prurient about the kiss, and Smith seems to have been a pioneer in the matter of sex. In **Let Me Dream Again** (1900) an older man is drinking and smoking with a girl, but as he leans to kiss her he finds himself in bed with his wife; the **Things Seen Through a Telescope** (1900) includes a couple embracing and a woman undressing – as are the objects seen through a keyhole by *Peeping Tom* (1901). Apart from the impish humour, there is an attempt to get audiences to accept close-ups by suggesting that they were watching objects enlarged mechanically; and

there are close-ups cut into innocent little frolics like *Grandma's Reading Glass* (1900) and *The Little Doctor and the Kitten* (1900), not to mention **Mary Jane's Mishap, or Don't Fool with the Paraffin** (1903), in which a slovenly maid blows herself up and appears as a ghost with a paraffin can.

The British were adept at trick films, and from the Hepworth company the output included *How it Feels to Be Run Over* (1900), **The Jonah Man or the Traveller Bewitched** (1904), with its disappearing coats, trolleys and trains, and **What the Curate Really Did** (1905), in which the curate's true adventures are superimposed above a number of gossiping ladies. James Williamson, also associated with Urban, offered **An Interesting Story** (1904), in which a man's absorption in his book causes many a mishap including dismemberment.

The British pioneers were indeed at one point – 1902 – the most innovative, but the French took the lead the following year, mainly due to the enterprise of the Pathé brothers. Charles Pathé (1863–1957) had become successful importing Edison's phonograph and records into France; when offered the franchise of Edison's films and the accompanying equipment he realised the importance of the new medium, observing that it was school, newspaper and theatre all combined. He was also to claim that though he did not invent the cinema it was he who industrialised it; in 1901 he left the phonograph business in the hands of his brother Emile and opened a studio in Vincennes. The following year he opened a branch in London, the beginning of a world-wide network, and it was estimated that by 1908 he controlled at least half of the movie business in the U.S., also selling in that market twice as much product as all the local companies combined.

At the time of his first expansion, in 1901, he was fortunate in appointing Ferdinand Zecca (1863–1947) to ensure a regular supply of films. Both men had worked originally in fairgrounds, and Zecca had originally been commentator for the Pathé films. He borrowed ideas and innovations from his contemporaries, and duplicates of most of Smith's films may be found in the Pathé catalogue – though it could not now be established

23

that Smith did not plagiarise in return; but when Zecca uses a dissolve in his version of *Let Me Dream Again* instead of Smith's clumsy shift of focus, that is probably because the dissolve had not yet crossed the Channel. Zecca improved upon Méliès by disposing of the proscenium effect, and his early experience of popular taste enabled him also to widen its subject matter. He made the first French crime film, *L'Histoire d'un Crime* (1901) and the first movie religioso, *La Passion de Notre Seigneur* (1902). He also made a *Quo Vadis?* (1901), an *Ali Baba et les 40 Voleurs* (1902) and *La Conquête de l'Air* (1901), while his re-enactments of true events include another on Dreyfus and the equally popular assassination of President McKinley; some titles suggest more weighty matters – *Les Victimes de l'Alcoolisme* (1902), *La Grève* (1904), *Les Executions Capitales* – but under Zecca's leadership Pathé were most adept at fantasy. The tricks, for instance, in **Marionetten** (1904) and **Japonaiserie** (1904) are really quite extraordinary, two of a series built round acrobats in which nothing is impossible, from living people being pulled from paper cones to magic boxes forming a child's – real – face. In **L'Ingénieuse Soubrette** (1902) the lady of the title walks up walls; in **Rêve à la Lune** (1905) a drunk sees dancing champagne bottles, and there are miraculous transformations and vases with faces in **Aladin** (1906).

Zecca followed Méliès in believing that what the cinema did best was fantasy. It was by no means certain at this time that it would adopt the narrative habit, for the film-makers realised that that was something that the stage could do so much better. However, the public began to tire of magical tricks and began to favour the more narrative films, and these became possible with the invention of editing. The fantasy films prove that within a few years of the Lumières' first showings the technical vocabulary of the new medium was immense, and also that audiences were not so reluctant to accept innovation as has been pretended. The wholesale piracy of ideas and techniques is such – and the preservation of early films and cataloguing so rare – that the film historian treads a minefield in allotting credit to anyone, but we may certainly challenge the accepted view that Edwin S. Porter (q.v.) was the inventor of editing, i.e. the creation of narrative by joining pieces of film together. With Méliès the film became an art, but it is with editing that the art of the film begins. Somewhere among the dozens of 'fire' movies listed in the catalogues is the first edited film, probably **Fire!** (1901) made in Britain by James Williamson. Warwick's **Fire Call and Fire Escape**, first shown in March 1899, suggests some sort of staged action, since a man is seen giving an alarm; but Williamson's film is longer and more sophisticated, in five scenes: 1. Policeman sees burning house; 2. Hove Fire Brigade leaves its HQ; 3. Engines rush down street; 4. Man in bedroom is rescued by fireman; 5. Fireman descends ladder with another man. Unlike, say, the narratives of Méliès, each scene depends on the one before, and Williamson had earlier made **Stop Thief** !, which in three scenes follows a thief from theft to apprehension. Among the many subsequent films on this theme is one directed by Frank Mottershaw for the Sheffield Photo Company, **A Daring Daylight Robbery** (1903), a quite elaborate affair involving a burglar, several policemen, the Sheffield Fire Brigade and, most significantly, a finale in which the burglar is apprehended as he steps off the train, as the result of a telegraph message. Clearly Williamson and Mottershaw had reasoned that if a narrative could be constructed from pieces of film, the logical progression was to decide beforehand what, beyond the props, was needed. Thus, if not the screenplay, screen-planning was born, as opposed to Méliès's meticulous preparations.

Edwin S. Porter (1869–1941) worked for the Edison Company, a projectionist-turned-cameraman who by this time was production head; the influence of Méliès (whose films Edison distributed) can be seen in **Uncle Josh at the Moving Picture Show** (1902), a little joke on the principle of what we now call 'the film within a film', and that of G. A. Smith and his imitators in **Gay Shoe Clerk** (1904), which includes a close-up of a lady's ankle. Porter was merely another plagiarist in an industry now founded on that principle, and indeed one of his jobs was to study imported film for ideas; it is generally conceded that he had *Fire!* in mind when he made **The Life of an American Fireman** (1903), but he increased audience interest by showing a woman and child in danger, heightened by cutting back to the galloping fire-engine. He does not use this discovery in an exciting way, and though in **The Great Train Robbery** (1904) he cuts from dance-hall to telegraph office to the robbers escaping, he never cuts from pursuer to pursued – so clearly this standard device of almost every Western ever since did not occur to him. The film, though based on an actual event, owed its existence to *A Daring Daylight Robbery*, which in fact the Edison Company as distributors had put into circulation some months earlier.

In the interim, Porter had directed a pet project of Edison's, and reputedly the most expensive film made in the U.S. to that time, a version of *Uncle Tom's Cabin* (1903) – and he had made it in the style current for 'classics', i.e. the moving tableau. Many American manufacturers were resisting close-ups and cutting because they thought they would bewilder and distract audiences, but audience acceptance of *The Great Train Robbery* paved the way for much livelier films. Porter himself was not carried away, and indeed, *The Seven Ages* (1905) is deliberately a series of tableaux, while *The Dream of a Rarebit Fiend* (1906) continues his copies of Méliès.

Audiences did not merely accept *The Great Train Robbery*: they went wild about it. It was copied and imitated, but its popularity was such that it was almost always the opening attraction of the nickelodeons now springing up – as a result of its success. The chase, literally, was on, and Biograph came up with **Personal** (1904) and **The Lost Child** (1905), both directed by Wallace McCutcheon Sr, respectively about a French nobleman who advertises for a wife and is pursued by the candidates, and a child kidnapper pursued by a number of passers-by, including a policeman. The latter was photographed by Billy Bitzer, later to work with Griffith, and it includes the interpolated close-up which four years later was claimed by Griffith to be his own invention.

Audiences the world over clamoured

for action, but in Britain, at least, the influence of *The Great Train Robbery* was slow to be felt – though **Raid on a Coiner's Den** (1904) is more elaborate than the little crook pieces that preceded it. Sheffield followed their *Daring Daylight Robbery* with a companion picture, **The Life of Charles Peace** (1905), which in terms of popularity far outshadowed the earlier film, and locally rivalled Porter's film – to the extent that it was also widely plagiarised. The ingredients are once more a crook, a train and the police, but in this case it was 'Taken on the Exact Spot' and the engine-driver was the same man who had driven the train taking Peace to jail. Such factors doubtless added to the thrill of being so close to crime, and the exploits of Peace, the most famous of Victorian criminals due to his daring burglaries and innumerable escapes, were still fresh in the mind of the British public. The cinema was still akin to the Chamber of Horrors, appealing to the millions who devoured the crime stories in the Sunday papers: it is not coincidental that the first hugely popular American and British 'features' were both about criminals – though neither, unlike later films, glamorises them.

Rescued by Rover (1905) is also about crime, and may well have been inspired by *The Lost Child*, since it also concerns a stolen baby – and a dog with apparently

Rescued by Rover was so popular that it was remade twice – the negatives of the first two versions wore out. Its original cost was £7.13s.6d (unnaturally low, since it was mainly a family affair); which became £10.12s.6d for positive prints sold outright.

extrasensory perception. It was made by Cecil Hepworth (1874–1953), the most successful of the British pioneers, from his 'Animated Photography', in 1897, the first book on the cinema, to his second version of *Comin' Thro' the Rye* (q.v.) in 1923. Though at this time it is unwise to attribute anything innovatory to any one person, *Rescued by Rover* may have owed its success to its cross-cutting which increased audience tension as it slipped back and forth between the baby's fate and its parents' agitation.

Certainly Porter, who had tentatively cut back and forth in *The Life of an American Fireman*, uses it to illuminate **The Kleptomaniac** (1906), telling simultaneously the stories of a rich woman caught shoplifting, and a poor woman who steals from desperation. He had done an earlier tract on social injustice, *The Ex-Convict* (1904), and **The White Caps** (1906) indicates the perils that can befall a wife-beater at the hands of a group of social do-gooders – who, since they are hooded, may be based on the Ku Klux Klan. This latter film, only attributed to Porter, is a particularly messy one, as it meanders over its fifteen locations; and the later famous **Rescued from an Eagle's Nest** (1907), a re-working of *Rescued by Rover* which is also attributed to him, was in its time greeted with particular scorn by the trade press. Another version was McCutcheon's **Her First Adventure** (1908) from Biograph, a virtual remake, even to the close-up of the dog at the end; it is more elaborate, especially in the cross-cutting at the climax – another invention which Griffith was to claim as his own. We know he saw this, because he is, in fact, its leading actor – and his first film as a director, made a few months later, **The Adventures of Dollie** (her Marvellous Experience at the Hands of the Gypsies), is another version of the same subject.

Griffith's rise as a director did nothing to improve the generally appalling quality of the American film, though the attention he attracted to himself and his supposed innovations reminded other film-makers of the diverse gifts the medium had acquired for its purpose – which was, since *The Great Train Robbery*, the telling of a story. The fact is that the industry staggered along, even retro-

gressing to the tableau-form when it found itself inadequate to stuffing a long story into one reel (Vitagraph's 1909 *Oliver Twist* is a good, or rather bad, example). Between the two landmarks, Porter's film and *The Birth of a Nation* (q.v.), further requirements for narrative came into being, be it an imaginative camera set-up or the fade between scenes or the travelling camera. The latter did not become common till more than a decade later, and the fade only became extensively used *circa* 1912. These American film-makers were as enthusiastic as the more fastidious Europeans, but they lacked finesse – as, they thought, did most of their audience. There remained, too, the rivalry of the three major companies as a barrier to progress, though by the end of the decade Edison was limping behind Vitagraph and Biograph; significantly, as the public began recognising their players, for there was no 'Edison Girl' to rival 'The Biograph Girl' and 'The Vitagraph Girl'.

The subjects they chose to film ranged from the classics and Shakespeare through nineteenth-century melodramas to popular novels of the day – the latter literally stolen without acknowledgment. The historical films and literary adaptations are today very dull as stories, though the lavishness of costume, if not setting, can sometimes surprise; but it is the contemporary dramas which are exciting to watch, trite though many of them are. Here are a number of favourite themes: infidelity, which invariably means a mild flirtation on the part of the husband and the wife's discovery of it; courtship, often of a middle-aged widow by a no-good johnny; abduction, usually of children, by gypsies, Red Indians, and other untrustworthy people; seduction, or rather attempted seduction, often of a friend's wife or a pretty employee engaged to another man; deception, which may mean posing as a swell to raid a wealthy home or planting jewellery on an innocent man; revenge, perhaps on some hapless victim supposed to have wronged mother or daughter; and just about every form of crime. A vast army of young girls discovered that they didn't love the men they thought they did; a number of diabolical schemers went mad; assorted animals, but usually dogs, found themselves quicker at detection and rescue than human beings; many unfortunates accused of larceny turned out to be innocent or to have what is called extenuating circumstances; and a great many villains, invariably moustached, perished in horrible manner, often crazed with lust at the time.

These people emoted, sometimes much more naturalistically than is supposed, whether before painted scenery, on which was printed the company's insignia to prevent duping (the intertitles with the company's name or insignia had proved ineffectual, since the pirates simply incorporated new intertitles) and also in an increasing number of natural settings. Porter used fourteen scenes to tell *The Great Train Robbery:* eight years later, in 1912, D. W. Griffith used sixty-eight scenes, including intertitles, close-ups, etc., for *The Sands of Dee* – a proliferation that was not always welcome, since some cinemagoers spoke of 'confusion'. The changes in the industry from 1910 onwards are so enormous that we will trace through them carefully in a separate chapter. We move from the American industry when two of its three leaders left it – Wallace 'Old Man' McCutcheon of Biograph and Porter of Edison. The survivor was J. Stuart Blackton of Vitagraph, and as heads of production of the three companies we may regard them as the three founders of American film production. But the new maverick companies which had sprung into being were filching the assistants of these three men to turn out their own films, and even Porter left Edison in 1909 to form his own company, Rex; then in 1915 he decided that the industry needed younger blood and turned to technical experimentation till drifting away altogether from films. Adolph Zukor (q.v.) and Blackton remained with Vitagraph till 1917, but McCutcheon left Biograph in 1908 to return to the theatre – which is when Griffith took over as head of production.

Since Blackton was among those responsible for the development of the animated film, we might look at it briefly before turning to the situation in Europe. The Kinetoscope and the other machines had utilised drawings; in 1906 Blackton produced **Humorous Phases of Funny**

Max Linder's clowning was as elegant as his appearance, but he could do masterly things with his cane, twirling it to express satisfaction, or knocking his hat with it to express surprise.

Faces, the first animated cartoon done in the single frame method. This series of metamorphosing faces was followed in 1908 by *The Haunted House,* which mixed drawings with live objects. It was Blackton's experience as cartoonist which prompted his interest; and it was another newspaper artist who created the most famous early film cartoon, Winsor McKay, with **Gertie the Dinosaur** (1909) – originally to accompany his vaudeville act, though a filmed prologue (showing him accept a wager that he can make drawings move) was later added for cinema showings. In France the firm of Gaumont from 1908 onwards encouraged Emil Cohl in animation, and the inventiveness of his little films still astonishes.

In France, in keeping with the attitude of the Belle Epoque, the cinema was mainly

27

devoted to frivolity, and in 1905 Pathé engaged a music hall star, André Deed, to make a series of comedy films built around a character called 'Boireau' – and Deed therefore takes credit as the first screen performer recognised by the public. It was perhaps the French who most widely appreciated the cinema as a vehicle for action, and if Britain invented the chase film, and the U.S. the chase comedy, it was France which turned the latter into high art. Something moved: it fell, or began to run, and the utmost havoc was created in the streets of Paris. Chase comedies were turned out by the thousand, and in the midst of them appeared the cinema's first great performer, Max Linder (1883–1925), who joined Pathé not long after Deed. He had had some success as an actor in the 'boulevard' theatre, but like the great American Silent comics later, it took some time for him to develop his silk-hatted screen persona, though the titles of his early films – *La Première Sortie d'un Collégien*, *Les Débuts d'un Patineur* – indicate that he soon hit upon the idea of a young man innocently causing chaos, not least to himself. He quickly discovered that the higher the young man the harder the fall, and thus became the impeccably-dressed man-about-town. Within three years of his debut, the titles of most of his films indicate his presence in them, proof that he was the first movie performer to be an attraction in his own right. From 1911 he wrote and directed most of the films in which he appeared, and here are just a few of these later titles: *Max est Distrait* (1911), *Max et son Chien Dick* (1911), *Max Professeur de Tango* (1912), *L'Anglais tel que Max Parle* (1914) and *Max Devrait Porter les Bretelles* (1915). Starting as a sketch or a situation, his films begin to tell a story, if a rudimentary one: for instance, in **Max Pédicure** (1915) – based on one of his stage sketches – the lady he has called upon passes him off as a chiropodist, and her father insists that Max treat his feet, complications which lead eventually to the real chiropodist being thrown through the window and landing on Max emerging below.

Other Linder films confirm the importance of the final gag, and he seems to have first used the comedy 'coda', as taken on later by Keaton and Lloyd. Chaplin once admitted that Linder was his master, and when he left Mutual that company invited Linder to replace him; a year later he did go to the U.S., to join Chaplin's earlier employers, Essanay, but the three two-reelers he made there did not encourage him to stay. Two successful features in Europe tempted him back to Hollywood, where he preceded the American comics into feature-length films, going further than they in that he not only wrote, produced, directed and starred, but also financed. That each had a different distributor indicates the bumpy road at the box-office – which is ironic, since both **Seven Years' Bad Luck** (1921), and **Be My Wife** (1921) are not only funnier than the first features of Lloyd, Keaton and Chaplin, but have more sustained and 'building' narratives. The misadventures of fiancé and prospective bridegroom are inventive, visually witty and endearing; his most brilliant sequence is the false mirror image – and because he is hungover it is funnier than the version done by Groucho Marx in *Duck Soup* (q.v.). After a comic spoof of Dumas. **The Three Must-Get-Theres** (1922), he returned to Europe, and after making a film in Vienna he and his wife committed double suicide in a Paris hotel room. In 1963 his daughter collected his three American features into *En Compagnie de Max Linder*, to re-establish him among his peers; his unfortunately little seen one- and two-reelers give evidence of his astonishing superiority over the cinema's other first clowns.

It was his success which caused Itala Film of Italy to filch André Deed from Pathé, and rechristen him Cretinetti – or 'Gribouille' in France and 'Foolshead' in England: his is primitive slapstick, and it is surprising to find that he had a host of imitators within Italy, including Polidor, who is even worse. These were larcenous times: in England there was Pimple ('Flivver' in the U.S.) and Winky, the latter a round, cheery fellow whose habit of glancing at the camera for approval is remarkably successful. He played put-upon tramps and husbands for Bamforth, a Yorkshire company, and disappeared during the War because of public feeling towards his real name, Reggie Switz: with the French Onésime ('Simple Simon' in Britain) he is, after

Beginnings

LEFT: *La Mort –* or *L'Assassinat– du Duc de Guise* was much admired and influential. What actually impressed were the names of those engaged – Saint-Saëns wrote an accompanying score, the Académie Française supplied a writer for the scenario, and the Comédie Française the cast and co-directors, André Calmettes and Charles La Bargy – the latter also in the lead. The film tempted Sarah Bernhardt to put on screen her Dame aux Camélias BELOW.

Beginnings

Gli Ultimo Giorni de Pompei was a popular subject with the early Italian film-makers, since Vesuvius had erupted four times since the beginning of the century. Caserini's second attempt at the subject was plagued by smoke which did not always come from the top of the (painted) volcano; perhaps a rival version, directed by Enrico Vidali, was more convincing.

Linder, the most accessible of the early clowns. Onésime was played by Ernest Bourbon, but he is simply a peg on which to hang the gags: one reason the Onésime comedies are so far ahead of Cretinetti is that the plot is the all-important element but another is that there is a specific point of view. Jean Durand (1882–1946) was the man who looked, for Gaumont, and he saw things in a very funny light; his editing is very tight, and his one-reelers should be much better known than they are.

It was in France that the theatre first embraced the film, when the frères Lafitte, financiers, founded the Société du Film d'Art to provide material worthy of the new medium – that is, films dealing with 'elevated' subjects. Their first film, **La Mort du Duc de Guise** (1908), overwhelmed contemporaries, as can be seen from this notice in *The New York Dramatic Mirror*: 'Its superior quality in photographic excellence, superb acting, rich settings and costumes and skilful dramatic handling of a carefully constructed picture narrative distinguishes it as one of the masterpieces of motion picture production' – none of which is today readily apparent in what is the usual series of tableaux. Sarah Bernhardt was persuaded to immortalise her *La Tosca* (1908), and then in two reels another of her stage successes, **La Dame aux Camélias** (1912), which André Calmettes also directed. Lack of close-ups prevents comment, except to say that she is coquettish and vivacious, and that she moves awkwardly (her leg had not yet been amputated). The story, not a complicated one, has been much simplified, and yet requires lengthy intertitles despite its length.

Les Amours de la Reine Elizabeth (1912) was twice as long, and the longest film yet made: two alumni of the Film d'Art, Louis Mercanton and Henri Desfontaines, produced it – in London – with the former directing. Again adapted from one of Bernhardt's popular vehicles, it is not about her 'loves' at all (in English it was known simply as *Queen Elizabeth*), beyond her relationship with Essex. It is not, to put it mildly, historically accurate, and Bernhardt's performance, again without close-ups, is no more impressive than the earlier one: her poses are not to our taste, though I can imagine that they thrilled live audiences.

The Lafittes set up their company in

defiance of Pathé, who retaliated by starting a rival, the Société Cinematographique des Auteurs et Gens de Lettres, which they put in the hands of Albert Capellani, a former actor with André Antoine's 'Théâtre Libre', many of whose members joined him – and from which he took its creed of literary 'naturalism' as exemplified by Zola. Unfortunately, Capellani, like his rivals, believed that the elevated subject was the historical one, and though he tried for realism in his crowd scenes and a multiplicity of (painted) sets, his films are no more watchable than other primitive historical spectacles. Pathé, meanwhile, handled the Lafittes' films abroad, taking credit for them, and they finally succeeded in putting them out of business at the time the Bernhardt-Elizabeth was filming. Pathé not only dominated the industry in France, but their tentacles were long, and in 1908 they took the 'art' film to Italy with the foundation of the Film d'Arte Italiana. There, however, the historical spectacle was already a staple of the industry.

The first important Italian company was that founded at Turin by Arturo Ambrosio (1869–1960) and named after him. The first pioneer of the Italian industry, however, is Filoteo Alberini (1865–1937), who snatched the leadership of the industry when his Cines company made the first spectacle, *Il Sacco di Roma* (1905). Ambrosio retaliated with *Marcus Lycinus* (1907). In the same year, at Cines, Mario Caserini made an *Otello*, and among other subjects to his credit are *Catalina*, *Macbeth*, *Siegfried*, *Parsifal* and two versions of Bulwer-Lytton's novel, *Gli Ultimo Giorni de Pompei* (1908 and 1913) Apart from Shakespeare and the Romans, the most popular sources plundered were Dante and the Greek heroes. Giuseppe de Liguoro's two-reel **L'Inferno** (1909) is ambitious: a quick tour of hell, with Virgil conducting Dante, and pictorially faithful to the Doré illustrations to 'The Divine Comedy'. De Liguoro was a member of the aristocracy who ran his own company, Milano, and the superiority of his productions was recognised by contemporaries. This one indicates a tremendous amount of preparation: locations range from mountaintops to the sea, and hell is most imagina-

tively done, with a huge number of Méliès-like tricks – and hundreds of nude men, which, given the prudery of the times, suggests the poverty of the participants.

These were times of great advances: the falling pillars of Troy in Giovanni Pastrone's **La Caduta di Troia** (1910) look very much the real thing, but the Wooden Horse, awesome in long-shot, turns up in close-up to be a cardboard cut-out. The unknown director of Cines **La Sposa del Nilo** (1911) keeps the screen buzzing with people – which was one reason it was widely influential. Such spectacles found a market abroad, and with that in mind – and simultaneous with the Bernhardt-Elizabeth – Cines put into production an eight-reel version of Henryk Sienkiewicz's popular novel about Romans and Christians, **Quo Vadis?** (1912). Caserini should have directed, but defected to Ambrosio, and the job went to another pupil of Alberini, Enrico Guazzoni, whose output included an *Agrippina* (1910) and a *Brutus* (1911). 'Direction' in this case is a relative term: contemporary opinion considered that the spectacle swamped all else, but the

The 1912 *Quo Vadis?* was not the first screen adaptation of this oft-filmed tale. Like at least one later version, the spectacle was relieved by witty impersonations of Nero, right, and Petronius.

burning of Rome is mostly a matter of smoke(-screens), and the scenes in the arena show almost nothing crucial of the action. 'Two hours fifteen minutes to project,' said the announcements in the New York press when it opened there in May 1913; in Britain it was premiered at the Royal Albert Hall.

But as happens in films, the 'greatest' was soon superseded. The moment it was clear that *Quo Vadis?* would return its investment, Itala Film put into production **Cabiria** (1914), directed by Pastrone. It opened in New York exactly a year after *Quo Vadis?*, was two reels longer, and lasted three hours. Unlike the earlier film, it is still worth watching. The sets, designed by Camillo Innocenti, range from the magnificent – the Temple of the Moloch – to the functional and false; the venues from the Alps to the Sahara: all of them are always an integral part of the film, and there can be no doubt that the storming of Carthage was copied by Griffith for the similar scenes in *Intolerance* (q.v.). It was to convey the size of the sets that Pastrone invented the tracking-shot, which refined the occasional camera-shift by moving at an angle. His other achievement was to persuade Gabrielle d'Annunzio to write the scenario – the first major literary figure to be involved directly with films: at least, he was credited, but he merely donated the names of the characters and re-wrote Pastrone's intertitles – and very florid they are. The story, concerning the Punic Wars, includes elements from a dozen sources, and the best that can be said for it is that it never flags: this is a teeming world, but it is its carpentry and not its characters which really interested Pastrone. If I quote *The New York Dramatic Mirror* again, it is not only because that was one of the few papers to notice films, but because its rapture was tempered by caution: this was 'the summit,' it reasoned, 'but the climb upward during the last decade has been so persistent, who could venture to declare that the top has been reached?' The paper considered, however, that though it might be a nine days' wonder, 'it is going to convince many doubtful people that high art and the motion picture industry are not incompatible.'

In fact, it was a summit for the Italian industry: *Maciste*, which Pastrone made the

following year was a kind of sequel; inasmuch as its eponymous hero was the popular and huge negro slave of *Cabiria* (played by a former Genovese docker), but the industry was not inclined to top it. There were modern dramas as well, surprisingly many of them managing to incorporate a troupe of lions – not then needed in arenas with Christians. We may also be surprised by the popularity of the 'divismo' dramas, so-named after the style of their leading actresses, which was based on the declamatory style of Bernhardt – and which can be seen, in aspic as it were, in the posters of Mucha. These were all dramas of high society – perhaps appropriately, because many of them were showcases for the mistresses of the aristocrats so much involved in Italian films. Among these ladies were Lyda Borelli, whose *Ma L'Amore Mio Non Muore* (1913), directed by Caserini, concerns the fatal love of an exiled primadonna and the heir to the throne, and Pina Menichelli, whose *Tigre Real* (1916), directed by Pastrone, concerns the fatal love of a Russian countess and a diplomat – though after her husband's death in a spectacular fire she recovers from consumption for a happy finish.

The acknowledged leader, however, was Francesca Bertini, who in the remnants available of *Serpe* (1919) may be found in the classic position of the vamp: exultant on a huge divan, pearls round her brow and one shoulder graced with feathers, while her victim lies below, white tie and tailed, so overcome by lust that he has drunk himself into impotency. When, earlier, the vogue for such tales had waned for a while, Bertini had made **Assunta Spina** (1915) directed by Gustavo Serena from a play by Salvatore di Giacomo (reputedly inspired by *Sperduti nel Buio* now lost, also based on a play and said to mark the beginning of realism in the Italian cinema). The plot has no new slant on the old tale of the woman who commits an indiscretion for the sake of her lover, but the details of Neapolitan life are completely integrated into it and the location photography by Alberto G. Carta is extraordinary. Its producers, Caesar, combined with Ambrosio to make **Cenere** (1916), directed by Ambrosio himself and Febo Mari; Mari wrote the scenario with Eleanora Duse, and plays her son in the picture. It is a tale of mother-love, not to our taste, but a cut above others of the genre; it is adapted from a novel by Grazia Deledda (later a Nobel prize-winner) and since hitherto Duse had refused movie offers we may assume she thought this one worthwhile; as with *Assunta Spina*, there is a delight in the minutiae of daily life, and there is Duse herself: almost alone among stage-performers of the time she doesn't disappoint. At fifty-eight, she was still beautiful; her movements are slight, but cinematically highly expressive.

If the longer film was the result of a taste for historical spectacle, it was the serial which helped to make movie-going a habit – and with both had arrived the two enduring complexes of this industry, the conjunction of size and length, and their confusion with quality, with the attendant worry of winning and keeping audiences. The serial sprang from the detective film, and that is reckoned to begin in 1908, when Victorin Jasset filmed the Nick Carter series, set in Paris. The most famous exponent of the early serial, Louis Feuillade (1873–1925), began directing in 1907, and was best known for his series with the child Bébé, for Gaumont, when he published a manifesto which claimed that film could exist on its own terms, without recourse to other media, and that above all it should be visual. He began a series of family dramas, *La Vie telle qu'elle Est*, and a series of comedies, *La Vie Drôle* – the whole point of the series being that they ensured a public for the next change of programme. The detective serial evolved from a suggestion at the end of the reel that this was not the end of the story, by leaving the hero in such a predicament that the spectator was compelled to return to find out how he gets out of it. Feuillade made his first essay in the genre in 1912, *Le Proscrit*, with René Navarre as detective Jean Dervieux – and Navarre became Fantômas, l'Empéreur du Crime, whose exploits were originally issued in thirty-two parts between 1911 and 1913. Like almost all the later master criminals, he was based on Maurice Le Blanc's then enormously popular fictional thief, Arsène Lupin. Fantômas dressed in skin-tight black, with a mask, and was adept at disguises. His enemies were Inspector Juve, of the Sûreté, and a journalist, to whom he offered a baffling series of crimes – which meant occasionally capturing and always outwitting the two of them. I have seen only one of the *Fantômas* films, **La Mort que Tue** (1913), and it is antiquated, simple penny-plain stuff, moving so fast that you have to pay the closest attention; knowing, in fact, that you will be little rewarded by its hooded criminals, real and bogus policemen, stolen jewels, false fingerprints, hidden doors, secret chambers and mysterious spiritings-away.

Within two years the serial was established as a feature of cinema programmes throughout the world. The Nick Carter series had already had its imitators, and we may find it telling that in Britain the most popular was an intrepid naval officer, Lieutenant Rose, RN, in Germany a superman, Homunculus, and in the U.S. a young woman – as produced by the Selig Company under the title *The Adventures of Kathlyn,* although all of Kathlyn's adventures were complete in themselves and did not end with the ubiquitous 'continued next week'. The most famous of the serials proper followed Kathlyn two years later, *The Perils of Pauline* (1914) and *The Exploits of Elaine* (1915), and they starred a former trapeze artist, Pearl White, as their trouble-prone but dauntless heroine. Her producers absolutely understood the importance of the visual thrill, and we may call them French-American, inasmuch as the films were made by Pathé's American subsidiary.

Meanwhile, the Danes were making the best films, and it was due to the popularity throughout Europe of both *Afgrunden* (q.v.) and *The White Slave Trade* (q.v.) that the two-reel film was adopted there much earlier than in the U.S. Both concerned sex, but Denmark's first world-wide success had been **The Lion Hunt** (1907), which sold a total of 259 copies – and its hopeless attempt to re-stage the event of the title suggests that to that time there had been few (wild) animals in movies. The producer was the Nordisk Film Company, founded by Ole Olsen, an amusement park proprietor; his director was Viggo Larsen, who had been the barker at one of his nickelodeons, and the photographer was Axel Sørensen, who had been the fairground's engineer.

Urban Gad's sex drama, *Afgrunden*, had an astounding effect on world audiences. His then-wife, Asta Nielsen, was the star, and at this point an old beau is about to discover that she has sunk even further than, as he thinks, singing in a beer-garden. Will he pay for her favours? Reject her? Or rescue her?

Looking for another sensational subject, Olsen had come up with a one-reel abduction story, and he remade it three years later in a two-reel version, **The White Slave Trade** (1910), reasoning that Feuillade's real-life series for Gaumont and Vitagraph's similar series (q.v.) in the U.S. had created a demand for truth. The market for the white slave traffic was enormous, since these were respectable words for marquees where the word 'whore' clearly wasn't; and if to our eyes the bordellos look equally respectable – men and women drinking, smoking and dancing to a piano – they must then have seemed the height of daring. Since, however, the ways of getting young girls into the clutches of the traffickers were dramatically limited, later films concentrated on the mechanism of escape – since no heroine, of course, could submit to what was offered. Both this film and **The White Slave Trade's Last Big Job** (1911) were directed by August Blom (1869–1942). They are fascinating examples of the early exploitation movie.

Blom was as accomplished as any film director then working, and **The Shop Girl** (1911) is another good example of the early sex drama: both the boy and girl are treated sympathetically, but whereas in American films the pregnant waifs, if any, had always been 'deceived', this boy merely turns out to be too weak to remember true love when confronted by his parents. Consequently he suffers considerably, but the fact that her fate is much worse – she dies – indicates the harsher penalties allotted to young girls who give in to their carnal instincts.

However, the most famous example of 'the wages of sin' drama was **Afgrunden** (1910), or *The Abyss*, devised by Urban Gad as a vehicle of his wife, Asta Nielsen (q.v.), to display her abilities to the theatre managers who neglected her. One might speculate as to why, throughout movie history, so many writers/directors have cast their wives as whores or loose women, but certainly at this time the subject was a favourite of the working class who were then the most enthusiastic audiences for films. In this particular version a music-teacher prefers a circus-performer to her hard-working fiancé, which indeed starts her on the road to the abyss.

The Danish cinema had another huge success with **The Four Devils** (1911), directed by Robert Dinesen (who also played one of the leads), Alfred Lind (who also photographed) and Carl Rosenbaum, and one of the reasons, again, was sex; in one particular scene the woman guiltlessly follows the man into the bedroom. In most cases the only form of impending sex allowed to be shown was rape; in *The Shop Girl* and *Afgrunden* it is simply not shown at all – or even later in such American films as *A Fool There Was* (q.v.) – so that the suggestion here of mutual enjoyment is very rare indeed. Otherwise this version of Herman Bang's novel is crude. But there is proof that European film-makers were in advance of the Americans in realising that audiences wanted spectacle, be it circuses, wild animals, battles – or shipwrecks. The demand for the latter followed the sinking of the *Titanic*, and Nordisk's *Drama at Sea* (1912) is an early example and *Atlantis* (1913), directed by Blom, the best known. The former was directed by his colleague, Eduard Schnedler-Sørensen, whose output that year also included one of the manifold copies of *The Four Devils*, **The Great Circus Catastrophe**, whose hero, Valdemar Psilander, is chased by a pre-Hollywood attempt at a vamp. Actually, this team, with the same writer, A. Kjerulf, offered a fairly sophisticated comedy, **The**

Strongest (1912), a title that refers to putative lovers, she the pursuer and he the pursued.

At this time Nordisk was second only to Pathé in its output, and continued to be a force in Denmark long after the international demand for Danish film had ceased. Olsen's directors were trying to do too much from too few resources, and they simply did not have the visual imagination of Benjamin Christensen (1879–1959), an actor in their company who left and turned director when Olsen refused to back **The Mysterious X** (1914). Both this and **The Night of Revenge** (1916) have complicated and deftly melodramatic plots of, respectively, a wronged officer caught up in espionage and a wronged ex-convict, and in both roles Christensen himself gives performances of considerable vivacity; but his films are most remarkable for their demonstration of the care taken in camera set-up, lighting, location and editing. They are, in fact, technically adventurous, and though his later films (q.v.) demonstrate the same care they would indicate little advance in characterisation.

The Danish cinema declined with the defection of many of its leading talents to Germany, and chief among these was the actress who immediately after Max Linder became the best-known screen performer, Asta Nielsen (1890–1972). 'She is all,' wrote Guillaume Apollinaire after seeing *Afgrunden*. 'The vision of the drunkard and the dream of the hermit.' After that film she made three with Blom, and then went with her husband to Germany, where he did a variation of *Afgrunden* called **Die Arme Jenny** (1912) in which she sinks from scullery maid, betrayed by a swell, to soliciting with a cigarette in her mouth, and finally walks into a snow-drift after learning that her seducer is to marry. Less risqué, but as much in keeping with the taste of the time, is **Mädchen ohne Vaterland** (1912), about a gypsy persuaded to steal secrets – something she does without hindrance – from the barracks where her lover is stationed. A tentative statement is made about inter-racial love, and certainly the title, and the ending, make it clear that the displaced have no patriotism. *The Moving Picture World* waxed enthusiastic when the film reached the U.S. two years later: 'A more finely finished production . . . it will be hard to find. All the elements of a great and striking success are present in happy and harmonious combination.' They are not; but in Europe at least this infant art form was growing so fast that it would mesmerise even sophisticates like Apollinaire – whose view of Miss Nielsen was shared by this particular critic: her performance was, he said, 'a masterpiece'; she already knew more about screen acting than most Hollywood stars a decade later. Her skill may be compared with Mary Pickford's, since in **Engelein** (1913) she played the sort of role Miss Pickford often undertook, a sixteen-year-old – one who has to pose as a child, and suddenly grow up when the uncle who falls in love with her has qualms about being a Humbert Humbert. She is furiously inventive, whether ogling a guardsman, or smoking, or deciding that the lake is too cold for a suicide attempt – and very droll indeed.

Engelein was one of the feature films, five reels long, now common in Europe. Of the three forms open to the cinema, documentary as offered by Lumière, fantasy as promulgated by Méliès, and the narrative as (probably) developed by the British, the new medium had opted for the last named though its now multi-reel form was likely to be supported by one reel of the other two – since programmes were increasingly including the newsreel (first offered on a regular basis by Pathé in 1908) and an animated cartoon. Cinema developed faster in Europe, because most of its exponents saw it primarily as a means of expression: so far those involved in the infant American industry saw it best as a means of making money – and they had not progressed yet to the quality offered by Pathé or Nordisk. But with Europe committed to the Apocalypse, the U.S. would take the lead in film production, and from then to the present its films would predominate throughout the world.

2

The Rise of the American Industry

IT WAS not only the cutback in production entailed by the War which caused the European film industries to fall behind the American one – because, War or not, the latter was already poised to push ahead. The new medium suited the new country: it was an entertainment understandable to the new immigrant population, and it was the first complete means of communication to scattered townships in a vast country. It is doubtful whether the managers of the three pioneer companies, Edison, Biograph and Vitagraph realised what powerful potential the cinema possessed, though at Biograph D. W. Griffith did, to the extent that he was determined to ride with it to glory. There is no doubt that he realised the boundless artistic possibilities, and since he was, in his own view, an artist, it was a comparatively simple matter to make his name as synonymous with cinema as was that of Dickens with literature. Another so minded was Thomas Ince, less well-remembered, since he died in mid-career and did not have propagandists to keep his name alive as his films became forgotten. When film appreciation started, roughly at the time the Silents died, the only American authority was the poet and essayist Vachel Lindsay, and the only American director he appreciated was Griffith (significantly, he later wrote poems inspired by Griffith heroines). But if Griffith and Ince saw in the cinema a means of self-aggrandisement their achievement in drawing attention to it, in making it respectable, cannot be underestimated – and they were perhaps more honourably motivated than the new entrepreneurs, who saw in it a means to wealth. The achievement of the latter is by no means despicable, since they founded an industry which was to overshadow all other means of mass communications for the next thirty years, and which was to remain almost unchanged for another twenty.

It began in 1905, when films left the penny arcades and saloon backrooms for specially equipped premises. The practice was facilitated by the formation of film exchanges – distribution centres which bought from the manufacturers and rented to exhibitors at a quarter of the purchase price. The first was started by a cameraman, Harry J. Miles, in 1903, and within four years there were over a hundred exchanges throughout the country. Easier access to a greater number of films meant that some exhibitors could change their programmes more frequently, even daily; if they could pay bigger fees than their rivals they could get new products and advertise 'first-run' pictures; or if they owned several sites, they could pass the print from one to another – usually carried by boys on bicycles (so that 'bicycling' remains the industry term for shipping to a nearby theatre).

What is regarded as America's first cinema was opened in Pittsburgh by John P. Harris and his brother-in-law, Harry Davis – who coined for it the name nickelodeon, to suggest both the cheapness of entry and its aspirations to respectability. They had converted a disused store with trimmings from a defunct opera-house (the opening film was *The Great Train Robbery*, of course); within three years there were 10,000 nickelodeons in the U.S., their programmes usually consisting of a melodrama, a comedy and a novelty – probably a film of an actual event – each, of course, still one-reel long. The pit pianist arrived on the scene, to accompany the films, and so, sometimes, did a singer to lead the community singing in the intervals. Popcorn, candy and peanuts were hawked in the aisles – such goodies the essential accompaniment to movie-watching for years to come. In time, the price of admission might also include an orange or a toffee-apple; in lean times, admission might be obtained on presentation of a token fee and some lowly object, i.e. a jam jar. The entrances, plastered with posters, proclaimed a haven of sensational but simple entertainment; and, in the early days at least, it was not a haven found on the more elegant thoroughfares. Inevitably opposition arose to an entertainment so enthusiastically patronised by the more humble people: newspaper editorials thundered on the 'immorality' to be seen at nickelodeons, but the most strenuous agitators were those · people feeling the pinch – saloon owners, vaudeville entrepreneurs and clergymen.

To meet criticism, the industry's trade magazine, *Views and Film Index*, began to clamour for a self-instituted censorship board, and in 1909 the National Board of Censorship of Motion Pictures – later the National Board of Review – was set up by the People's Institute of New York, in conjunction with the Motion Picture Patents Company (q.v.) but the Board was never very effective because the Patents Company did not embody all the producing companies. In Britain, the film-makers set up the British Board of Film Censors (in 1912), which always acted as an official body – though its findings could be challenged by local authorities. In the U.S. only a handful of States passed legislature controlling movies, and it wasn't till 1922 that more stringent censorship was exercised, with the formation of the Motion Picture Producers and Distributors Association – usually known as The Hays Office, after its first president, Will H. Hays, recruited from President Harding's cabinet. Again, the impetus for this came from within the industry, as a result of some scandals, and some noisy legal squabbles between theatre owners, distributors and manufacturers – many of whom were then

one and the same – attempting either to monopolise the industry or to drive competitors to the wall. Many independent producers were indeed forced out, but it should be noted that the industry was never so united as when business was poor – as happened after the War.

An earlier crisis had precipitated the foundation of the Motion Picture Patents Company. As nickelodeons multiplied, so did manufacturers to fill them with product. Legally, only Edison, Biograph and Vitagraph had patents to manufacture motion pictures but in an attempt to stifle competition they combined in 1909 with the best-established of their rivals – Selig, Kalem, Essanay and Lubin, and the French-owned Pathé and Méliès. Pooling their patent claims, they were licensed to manufacture films; they arranged with Eastman Kodak, the largest supplier of raw film stock, to supply only them; and with Edison himself within their fold they charged exhibitors $2 a week to rent his equipment – a tax which was much resented. Despite it, over ten thousand exhibitors signed with them to show only their films. Those producers left outside the trust protested, and arranged underhand deals; bootlegging of films became common – and associations were formed to fight the monopoly. In a further attempt to strengthen its hold, the Patents Company established a national film exchange, the General Film Company, in 1910, and in less than two years – by revoking licences – it had absorbed all fifty-seven of the leading exchanges. But there was one hold-out, the Greater New York Rental Company, headed by William Fox, who owned sufficient theatres to oppose the trust: he instituted a lawsuit against it, invoking restraint of trade, and though the matter was not legally resolved till 1916, the monopoly began to crumble almost immediately.

Fox (1879–1952) himself became one of the independents – a manufacturer of films – in 1912, and in 1915 he formed the Fox Film Corporation, which he headed till it amalgamated with Twentieth Century in 1935. The founders of the great Hollywood studios all came from similar backgrounds. In Fox's case, he was an immigrant, at the age of nine months, with his German-Jewish family; as a boy he worked in the garment industry, and entered the film business by acquiring a penny arcade in Brooklyn which expanded into a chain of fifteen cinemas.

The other leading opponent of the Patents Company was Carl Laemmle (1867–1939), who also would eventually establish one of the great, continuing, production companies, Universal. He too was a German Jew, arriving in the U.S. to work with his brother in 1884; he worked as a book-keeper and store-manager in Oshkosh, and in 1906, instead of opening his own store, as intended, he started a nickelodeon, in Chicago. He soon had a chain of cinemas and his own distribution company – the Laemmle Film Service, notably active against the trust. To compete additionally, he formed a producing company, the Independent Motion Picture Company, or I.M.P.

It was I.M.P. and Laemmle who instigated the movies' two abiding fantasies, Hollywood and the American film star – though to be exact the 'discovery' of Hollywood was accidental, and I.M.P. was only one of several companies which found themselves in that part of California at the height of the war with the trust. By 1912 it was imperative for these independents to get as far from the Patents Company as possible: California offered sunshine, a variety of landscape, and a welcome from workers and real-estate dealers, both of whose financial demands were lower than those in the East. Los Angeles was more attractive than San Francisco, because it was nearer the Mexican border if the Patents Company sent writs or injunctions; most of the companies settled in a suburb of L.A. known locally as Hollywood – a name which was formally adopted in 1913.

The institution of the film star also arose from the anti-trust war. In Europe theatre-players had begun to work before the cameras, but in the U.S. film performers were likely to be propmen or their wives or visiting relatives. As actors arrived from the stage – usually because they couldn't get work on it – the manufacturers refused them publicity because they believed it would create a demand for higher salaries: they were slow to seize upon the possibilities of personality cults on celluloid, but exhibitors were soon aware of them: a buzz of recognition

in the audience, and then increased business as word of mouth spread. Laemmle was determined to get that lady known as 'The Biograph Girl' to I.M.P. In 1910 at Biograph she was getting $25 a week; he offered her $1,000 a week and she, not surprisingly, accepted. His war with the trust had taught him the value of publicity, and he planted a story in the St Louis press to the effect that she, Florence Lawrence, the Biograph Girl, had been killed in a streetcar accident. Then I.M.P. took an ad in *The Moving Picture World* to the effect that the story was an invention of I.M.P.'s enemies: 'We nail a lie'. And Miss Lawrence visited St Louis with I.M.P.'s leading actor, King Baggott: they were mobbed.

After I.M.P. had become Universal, in 1913, it advised exhibitors to book films with familiar faces, but by then all the companies, on both sides of the war, were advertising the names of their players. The last of the Patents group to give in to the advertising of stars was Biograph, which had twice lost the most valuable star property of them all, Mary Pickford (1893–1979), dubbed by exhibitors 'Little Mary' and 'The Girl With the Curls' during her first spell with the company. She had also been filched by I.M.P. in 1910, and did equally brief stints at Majestic, at Biograph again and in the theatre before returning to Biograph – though that company was not particularly enthusiastic about her popularity, reasoning that what mattered was the product itself – and Biograph's films were the most favourably received by those newspapers that took note of movies. In charge of production, and making most of them, was D. W. Griffith.

David Wark Griffith (1875–1948) came to dominate the American film industry in the second decade of the century. His achievements so mesmerised his peers that for a brief while it looked as though the director – rather than the producer or financier – would have control over what actually went into movies. He is said to be the great innovator – it was certainly said by himself. When he broke with Biograph he advertised himself thus in *The New York Dramatic Mirror*: 'D. W. Griffith: producer of all the great Biograph successes, revolutionising the Motion Picture Drama, and founding

Of the early Griffith two–reelers, the 1910 *An Arcadian Maid* is among the most pleasing – partly because of the rustic locations for its story of a washerwoman (Mary Pickford) persuaded to rob her employer by a handsome pedlar.

the modern techniques of the art. Included in the innovations which he introduced and which are now generally followed by the most advanced producers are: the use of large close-up figures, distant views, as reproduced first in *Ramona*, the "switchback", sustained suspense, the "fadeout", and restraint in expression, raising motion picture acting to recognition as a genuine art.' No one seems to have been concerned that these claims were false – probably because the industry was moving so fast, probably also because it didn't seem to matter ; the fact that some film-writers till the present have accepted them simply indicates that they do not know any pre-Griffith material. James Card, the curator of the Eastman House archive – and the man who has perhaps seen more antique movies than anyone living – believes that Griffith's reputation began with the advertisements he placed in the trade press.

Griffith was born in Kentucky, the son of a doctor impoverished by the Civil War, and he became successively theatre critic, dramatist and actor. Unemployed in New York, he approached the film companies with scenarios – which were refused by Porter of Edison, who nevertheless offered him the role of the brave woodsman in *Rescued from the Eagle's Nest*. Biograph, however, were prepared to use him in both capacities, paying him $5 a day to act, and up to $15 for any ideas contributed. From the time he took over as production head, in the summer of 1908, till the end of the following year, he was Biograph's sole director, turning out in that period 131 films, a one-reeler and a half-reeler each week, at a salary of $50 per week plus a weekly commission of not less than that amount. The cost of each film was approximately $200, and since the company was clearing over $5,000 a week in profit, against the competition of its dozen rivals, it is clear that the industry was growing.

Altogether, in his six years with Biograph, Griffith made just under 450 films, working so well with his photographer, Billy Bitzer, that the latter left

The Rise of the American Industry

Two of Vitagraph's popular leading men, Earle Williams, and FAR RIGHT, Maurice Costello in the 1911 *A Tale of Two Cities*. Williams often sported a monocle, but that and his lordly manner were suitable for the heroes he played. Costello was older, and seems even less approachable, but audience fondness for such favourite players hastened the arrival of the feature–film: for this version of Dickens, released in three parts of one reel each, was played by enterprising exhibitors in one programme. Also, the insertion of 'It is a far, far better thing...' advanced the use of dialogue intertitles, for the latter to this point were invariably descriptive.

EARLE WILLIAMS

61.

with him in 1913 and moved with him from company to company till they quarrelled in 1924; it is recorded that they worked together so closely that it is impossible to distinguish their contributions. Given the available shooting time, it is not surprising that the quality is variable, from a family charade like **They Would Elope** (1909) to the earlier, well-achieved **The Drive for Life** (1909), respectively a comedy about an abortive elopement and a thriller about a man (Arthur Johnson) hurrying to his fiancée to prevent her eating the poisoned chocolates sent by his ex-mistress – a good example of the 'switchback' or cross-cutting which Griffith was now developing for his climactic situations; but he does not seem to have realised the value of the mobile camera (placed here on another motor car), since he seldom used it again. **Gold is Not All** (1910) is a morality tale paralleling the lives of two couples, poor and wealthy, and a shot of them divided by a wall shows a vivid sense of location; **Ramona** (1910) is an ambitious version of Helen Hunt-Jackson's popular tearjerker about a girl (Pickford) who marries an Indian (Henry B. Walthall) : the characters rush on from one side of the screen and off the other, gesticulating wildly, and the photography for which Griffith claimed credit consists only of a few shots of foreground action played against a valley and mountains beyond. **Wilful Peggy** (1910) concerns a hoyden (Pickford) who refuses a lordly suitor and runs away with his nephew who, despite or because she's in male attire, makes advances ; it does demonstrate that Miss Pickford had more vivacity than her rivals, but she was more likely to be found in roles like 'The Little Slavey' in **Simple Charity** (1910), helping a penniless couple and finding a handsome young doctor in the process.

By this time, halfway through his Biograph period, the evidence does suggest that Griffith understood the medium better than the other American directors ; his climactic cross-cutting was so much admired that he began to stage these sequences in two different settings – even when unnecessary to the plot. He had certainly realised that it was cutting which gave his films mobility – there are ninety separate shots in the fourteen-minute length of **The Voice of a Child** (1911), where most films of the time have one-third to one-half that number. The story, a favourite one of Griffith's, concerns a neglected wife (Blanche Sweet) who almost runs off with a bounder, while the unusual **Fate's Interception** (1912) tells of a rejected Mexican girl who tries to gas her American lover. 'Loneliness' is the reason given for his involvement in the first place, and the film is particularly vicious towards Mexicans: but the wooing is sympathetically done, with one long-shot, from above, with the couple framed among leaves, which is remarkable for the time. **The Musketeers of Pig Alley** (1912), like much of Griffith, has a spurious reputation – as the first gangster film. In fact it is just another cops-and-robbers' tale, and a confused one at that, apart from the central situation: the poor girl (Lillian Gish) and her musician lover (Walter Miller) caught in the crossfire. It cannot be compared to a Reliance two-reeler of the following year, *Detective Burton's Triumph*, made in the semi-documentary style which the American film industry eschewed till after the Second World War.

The industry was discovering that the transition from one- to two-reeler could be achieved only with difficulty: in Europe the longer running time was smoothly utilised, but in the U.S. the plot of the second reel tended to be convoluted and repetitive. Technically, this was a time of great change. Angleshots were becoming common, being first used in Denmark to indicate Point-of-View; the Americans would take much longer than the Danes to rid themselves of this *raison d'être*. The language of the cinema was also enriched by the discovery of the time-shift, and **Just a Shabby Doll** (1913) – a rags-to-riches production, typical of the Thanhouser Company, in which the boy finally marries his now-impoverished childhood sweetheart – dispenses with intertitles to denote past time. The future was usually a matter of dreams, as in Majestic's **The Warning** (1914), in which an indolent country girl (Dorothy Gish) thus learns of her future with 'The Drummer from the Big City', but dreams were very big anyway – in Selig's **The Devil, the Servant and the Man** (1910), a marriage grown cold is restored by some dreams and by Christ, all superimposed on the original image. The close-up came into common use, and location shooting was more rigorously exploited, as in Kalem's **A Race with Time** (1913), in which a station-agent's daughter saves a train from sabotage, and Kay-Bee Broncho's **In the Nick of Time** (1914), in which the put-upon heroine flees to a deserted railroad station and saves it from a posse of train-robbers. The cutting speeds in both films were adjusted to their subjects, and when the latter was reissued ten years later it would not have seemed, technically, too dated : but the films of 1912 could not have been passed off as new even two years later.

In Vitagraph's **The Right Girl ?** (1914), the heroine studies a movie poster, and it lists a dozen items, including Mary Pickford (whose films could be endlessly reissued), 'Song Contest' and 'Amateurs' : the rest of the programme – now running to about two hours – consisted of comedies, melodramas, and novelty tales like

this, about a 'bach' (i.e. a bachelor) who takes his friend's advice and follows the first pretty woman he sees, who turns out to be the other's wife. The stars are Earle Williams and Anita Stewart, frequently teamed – and notably in **His Phantom Sweetheart** (1915), built around a clubman's dream. The director of both is Ralph Ince (1887–1937), brother of Thomas H. Ince ; he was also an actor, and in **His Last Flight** (1913) he saves a shipwrecked honeymoon couple from a brutal crew (for which, at the end, the bride thinks of him in flashback). The three films are so accomplished as to make one want to see more of Ince's early work. He continued into the Talkie era, though abandoning leading roles for character parts – and ended his days directing quota quickies in Britain, one of many early directors who later tried their chance across the Atlantic (others included Vitagraph's Larry Trimble and Kalem's Sidney Olcott). Earle Williams was a stalwart of Vitagraph for most of its existence, tall, dark and handsome and possibly the prototype of all movie heroes. Type-casting began early – before 1911, when the practice of identifying players became accepted – and in both **Love's Awakening** (1910) and **Coronets and Hearts** (1912) he played impoverished milords who marry American heiresses ; the former was one of Vitagraph's series 'Scenes From True Life', which Victor Sjöström acknowledged as an influence on him.

In the same vein are **The Spirit of Christmas** (1913) and **The Man That Might Have Been** (1914), directed by and starring another pillar of Vitagraph, William Humphrey, and both very sure in their mixture of melodrama and high-flown sentiment. The former concerns a poor mother tempted to steal, but forgiven and passed on to an eccentric millionaire who doesn't like the 'usual' Christmas, and the latter a man who spends his life dreaming of his dead wife and child, till re-united with them by his own death. Both were novelty items, but Vitagraph also made melodramas – such as **Conscience** (1912), about a cop's sister who elopes to marry a brute, and years later, after separation, finds herself in a wax-works where for a bet he is spending the night, and **The Fire Escape** (1915), in which a boy and girl romance is over-shadowed by some crooked politicians in the same apartment block . . . But the people who saw these films when they first came out remember Vitagraph best for their comedies with the rotund John Bunny and Mr and Mrs Sidney Drew. Bunny joined Vitagraph from the stage in 1910 and stayed till he died in 1915 – usually playing the exuberant and long-suffering husband of pinch-faced Flora Finch. The Drews also did domestic comedy, of a somewhat more urbane nature – as befits a man who was uncle to the Barrymores – but neither their films nor those of Bunny that I have seen give an indication of why they are so fondly remembered.

Among the important early directors is Sidney Olcott (1873–1949), a Canadian actor who was briefly at Biograph before joining Kalem at its inception in 1906 – a company founded on $400 cash by George Kleine, Samuel Long and Frank Marion. Writers at that time were mainly ideas men, but Olcott, invited to direct, had had experience enough to prepare a scenario, and since he liked to shoot on location this preparation proved both economical and useful for smoother continuity. His **Ben Hur** (1907) was a huge success, opening the way for more American costume films as well as clarifying the matter of screen rights: Kalem were sued by the publishers, the author's estate and the producers of the dramatised version, and though the matter wasn't settled till 1911 (for $25,000) it at once became the policy of the film companies to pay for properties of recognised value. In 1908 Olcott was working in Florida when Kalem, acknowledging his success with location-shooting, decided to send him to Europe, with a troupe including Jack Clark, the leading man, and Gene Gauntier, who also doubled as writer. Olcott made some films in Ireland, including **Rory O'Moore** (1911), a silly tale of a rebel and the redcoats which Kalem considered politically controversial (which it almost certainly was, at that time) – and moved on throughout Europe to the Middle East. I have also seen his **Captured by Bedouins** (1912), mainly notable for some shots of the garden of Shepheard's Hotel and of the Sphinx before its paws were uncovered. In Jerusalem he made *From the Manger to the Cross* (1912), which so infuriated Kalem that he was forced to resign: but instead of the public staying away, as his bosses had thought, it flocked – thus justifying its high cost (the controversy over it in Britain helped to bring about censorship), and establishing Olcott as one of the leading directors. He was active as a director till 1927, when he became production manager of British Lion, but he left the industry two years later.

The first important woman director was Lois Weber (1882–1939), who with her husband, Phillips Smalley, acted in Edwin S. Porter's first independent pictures. Porter left Edison when a former carpet-dealer was placed in charge of production there ; he joined the non-Patents producers, forming the Rex Picture Company. One of his first productions was *A Heroine of '76* (1911), in which a tavern wench (Weber) receives the assassination wounds intended for George Washington (Smalley). When Porter was lured from his own company by Zukor, Laemmle absorbed Rex, and his Universal distributed their films. Rex eventually disappeared, but Weber and Smalley were involved in some big Universal productions, such as *The Merchant of Venice* (1914) and *The Picture of Dorian Gray* (1914). They wrote, produced, directed and acted, sometimes in tandem; as a director, solo, she had a success with *Where Are My Children?* (1916), which touched upon abortion, and as a result Universal offered her a producer contract. She continued to direct, and made one Talkie, in 1934, at the time when Smalley's career as a character actor was beginning to falter. Among their early films, worth noting are **An Ill Wind** (1912), a familiar anecdote – used, among others, by Mrs Henry Wood in The Channings – about a young man falsely accused of stealing a cheque, and **Suspense** (1913), about a young wife alone in a lonely house, and a tramp trying to break in. Most films of this period – Westerns excepted – could as easily have been done on the stage, but the latter depends on the situation of the house, a telephone, and the husband's rush to the rescue; it also has a number of imaginative touches, including a split screen.

The first major name connected with the Western is Gilbert M. Anderson (1883–1971), born Max Aaronson and known as 'Broncho Billy'. He had been a newsboy; at seventeen, he went on the stage, and just three years later started in films – in *The Great Train Robbery*. In 1907, with George K. Spoor, he founded Essanay, which began the 'Broncho Billy' series with *Broncho Billy and the Baby* (1908), based on what would be an oft-filmed play, 'Three Godfathers'. The film Western, in fact, grew not from Edwin S. Porter's film, but from the popular melodramas of the West – and the early Broncho Billy films are as much domestic comedy as Western. Despite a Durante-sized nose, Anderson himself is rather fetching – comely, with a thatch of hair : usually a shy man winning the girl from his more dashing rival, or unexpectedly besting the robbers, he was probably the inspiration for Will Rogers's stage personality.

The popularity of the Western was such that it was the sole product of some companies; it was also attractive because location-shooting kept the company far from the battles with Essanay and other members of the Patents Company. Important in this field was the American Manufacturing Company started in 1910 when a Chicago distributor filched most of Essanay's leading staff, including Allan Dwan (b. 1885–1982) who had been an electrician. Successively scenario editor for American and production manager with the California stock company, Dwan became a director in May 1911, and before the year was out had made sixty-eight films – at the rate of two a week, filming side-by-side on Mondays, Tuesdays and Wednesdays, and processing them on Thursdays and Fridays. Ideas were made up on the spot: thus filming by the sea at Santa Barbara meant involving smugglers with cowboys – as in **The Fear** (1912); and a handy flume suggested an odd revenge when a cowpuncher's marriage proposal has been refused – **The Poisoned Flume** (1911). Dwan was one of the talents poached by Laemmle; most of his company went with him, including the leading man, J. Warren Kerrigan, who became one of Universal's biggest stars.

Also purveyors of Westerns were the subsidiaries, under various names, of Kessel and Bauman (q.v.). **An Apache Father's Revenge** (?1911) concerns an heroic Indian so besotted with a handsome Anglo-Saxon that she dons Western clothes, and when her father attacks the fort she lights the signal – for the earliest surviving example of the Cavalry riding to the rescue. The film's attitude towards the Indians is vile, a good enough expression of prevailing opinion in the U.S. at the time. **The Wheels of Destiny** (1911), mainly the tale of a baby adopted by a drunken father, starts with an Indian massacre; and there is only one good Indian among the many treacherous ones in **Blazing the Trail** (1912), a story of attacks and counter-attacks among the covered wagons. The star and director of the latter is Francis Ford (1883–1953), elder brother of John Ford, and his vigorous handling at this time remains a pleasure. However, the best of Kessel and Bauman's directors would seem to be Reginald Barker (1886–1937) – and *The Wheels of Destiny* has been attributed to him on account of its fluidity: a lone cowboy rides across the hill and down to the camera, and the Indians pour into battle from behind the camera. Barker is credited on **Bad Buck of Santa Ynez** (1914), the tale of a man so mean and bad that he is driven out of town, but pauses to befriend a widow and her small daughter, for whom he sacrifices his life when the latter is bitten by a rattlesnake. The story is credited to Bret Harte, and it was remade as *The Toll-Gate* (q.v.), by Lambert Hillyer, who like Barker was a protégé of Thomas H. Ince. The star of both versions is William S. Hart (1870–1946); a former trailhand and stage actor, who had come into films in 1913 as a result of his friendship with Ince. Roles like this earned him the designation, 'The Good-Bad Man', and among the early stars only Asta Nielsen surpassed him in intensity – though in his case his acting is bare to the point of impassivity. *Bad Buck*, like *The Wheels of Destiny*, indicates a director's joy in the medium : it may well be that the exigencies of the Western did most to liberate movies from the techniques they took from the stage.

Another liberating factor was the feature-length movie, and in the United States that was a long time in gestation. It grew from the habit of filming the classics in multi-reel versions, of which the first may well have been a two-and-a-half reel version of *Les Misérables*, issued by Edison in 1909. There is no evidence that any enterprising exhibitor screened them together, nor Vitagraph's four-reel version of the same subject issued over a two-month period at the same time ; but Vitagraph's five-reel *The Life of Moses*, issued over a fourteen-month period, 1909–10, was shown in one New Orleans cinema in April 1910 – to what *The Moving Picture World* called 'record business'. The same company's three-reel *Uncle Tom's Cabin* (1910) was de-signed to be released in three weekly parts. Almost certainly that had been shown in one programme before two multi-reel Italian films were imported in 1911 – as *The Crusaders* and *Dante's Inferno*; and quite certainly there were a number of American features before July 1912, when the success of the French four-reel *Queen Elizabeth* at the Lyceum, New York, is reckoned to have reconciled exhibitors towards the longer film. In January 1912 Atlas advertised a four-reel *Ten Nights in a Bar Room*, but the other contributions were all from the 'classics' – a five-reel *Oliver Twist* and a four-reel *Hiawatha*, while two actresses followed Bernhardt's example of immortalising herself, Blanche White in a five-reel *Resurrection*, and Helen Gardner in a six-reel *Cleopatra*, which she also produced. Adolph Zukor's Famous Players (q.v.) lured Edwin S. Porter away from his own company, Rex, to direct a five-reel *Monte Cristo*, to star James O'Neill (the father of the playwright, Eugene) – but by the time it was ready Selig had a three-reel version on the market. Zukor therefore persuaded Porter to make *The Prisoner of Zenda* in five reels, which had its premiere in February 1913. There followed a slew of European imports, including a six-reel *David Copperfield* from Britain, and the eight-reel Italian *Quo Vadis?* – which, like the Bernhardt film, was shown in a Broadway theatre, the Astor : that was in May 1913, and it cost $1.50 a seat instead of the customary fifteen cents. Thus the feature film reached America only as an adjunct of theatre and literature.

The excitement over *Quo Vadis?* reached D. W. Griffith in California, nearing the end of his winter season : Biograph refused to let him come East to see it, just as they had refused to sanction a feature after his two-reel spectaculars of 1912, *Man's Genesis* and *The Massacre* (a recreation of Custer's Last Stand), passed unnoticed. Biograph, however, were discussing a deal with Klaw and Erlanger to film their stage productions in the Famous Players manner, and Griffith, furious and without authorisation, began his own feature, **Judith of Bethulia** (1914). The company was startled by both length and cost – $36,000 – and determined to withdraw him from direction : he was offered the job of supervisor, which he countered by demanding autonomy as a director. They refused and he left. He himself in his memoir claimed of the film that 'the bosses rather liked it', but that seems unlikely, as they delayed release for eight months. 'It remains,' said Iris Barry in her Museum of Modern Art monograph (repeating Lewis Jacobs's gaffe that it was the first American feature), 'both in [Griffith's] own career and in the memories of those who saw it at the

time a real landmark.' Such, of course, has been said about such contemporaries as 'Le Sacre du Printemps', but film was an infant art and this film is a shambles – much rushing about and barnstorming, amidst which may be discerned the Bible story of Judith (Blanche Sweet) and Holofernes (Henry B. Walthall). Miss Barry's assessment of Griffith's innovations is equally absurd, and we are reminded that it was at this point that he began to advertise himself – almost certainly influenced by his association with Miss Pickford : if a mere player could achieve world-wide fame, how much worthier was a director and dramaturge!

From Biograph Griffith went to Mutual, to supervise production and direct five films – and to plan an even longer epic than *Judith*. He wanted a

subject from America's past, and a member of the company, Frank Woods, recommended 'The Clansman' by the Reverend Thomas Dixon, a novel of the Reconstruction – and, as dramatised, a popular road-show attraction: Woods had done the continuity for a film version abandoned by the Kinemacolor Company. Harry Aitken was the backer of Mutual, but as the film outgrew his resources he and Griffith formed a new company, Epoch, to market it ; its eventual cost was in the region of $91,000 – which included $30,000 for publicity – and its profits around $5 million. After the West Coast opening under the original title, it opened in New York, at Dixon's suggestion, as **The Birth of a Nation** (1915), at an unprecedented $2 top – and it was immediately clear that the gamble had paid off. This was the first time in

So much legend surrounds America's first 'epic', *The Birth of a Nation* – as, for instance, that its profits were incalculable, perhaps as high as $50,000,000; but even if recent research has found them to be about one–tenth of that, that is still good money for the period. Both its plot and ethics make it difficult to sit through, but the panoramic scenes of battle remain impressive.

45

The Rise of the American Industry

As late as 1973 the forty most prominent American critics voted *Intolerance* the second greatest American film of all time – *Citizen Kane* was first – and *The Birth of a Nation* the third. Can any of them actually have seen it? Certainly *Intolerance* was big. As with a great many other matters, Griffith falsely claimed credit for Walter L. Hall's magnificent sets. Some survived on various backlots into the Twenties, but most were dismantled at the request of the Los Angeles Fire Department.

American cinema that a movie-maker who thought big and acted big found himself appropriately recompensed – and indeed the film was for years considered a 'great' one.

Historically important, it has today virtually no entertainment value. Its admirers point to the cross-cutting at the climax, by then a cliché in Griffith's work; they praise the famous panning shot which concludes with Sherman's army in the valley, but most sequences are as static as the view of Lumières' workers leaving their factory. Indeed, much of the film is a throwback to the days of animated tableaux – admittedly often elaborate – introduced by explanatory intertitles. The story, like most Civil War tales, is about divided families: a Northern boy (Robert Harron) falls in love with a Southern girl (Miriam Cooper), and his sister (Lillian Gish) falls in love with her brother, 'The Little Colonel' (Henry B. Walthall). Their war is a dull affair: the film is not offensive till the aftermath, with uppity Negroes shoving people off the sidewalk and putting their bare feet on the desks in the legislative chamber. Before, a white had led them raping; now they do it on their own initiative, and it's the attempted rape of his sister which causes 'The Little Colonel' to devise the Ku Klux Klan. 'In agony of soul over the degradation of his people, [he] thought of a secret army – the organisation that saved the South from agony. But not without more blood than was spilt at Gettysburg.' At the end this army rescues both the family, besieged with some Union soldiers by berserk blacks, and Miss Gish – from the lecherous clutches of the mulatto governor.

So the birth-pangs of this particular nation are reduced to 'Will Lillian be saved?' The film is, at best, an hysterical poke at a confused period, and, when it might have been balanced, as in the matter of the rapist's guilt, we're offered the shortest trial in the history of movies. Griffith's later apologists have explained away his prejudices by claiming them typical of a Southerner of the time; but if the film is not libellous to blacks (if they were uncivilised that was because education was denied them) it is manic and rabble-rousing. Movie-makers constantly made clear their contempt for

46

people of different skins, certainly a retrogression from enlightened nineteenth-century opinion; but as a study in racial intolerance, this film far outclasses those which used the dusty-shoed and the slant-eyed as their villains. Originally it was worse. There was no shooting script, so no record remains, but we do know that in response to criticism Griffith snipped and cut, and prepared new intertitles. There were riots in some towns; in New York, the Mayor and the Licence Commissioner insisted on the removal of the more inflammatory scenes. Griffith responded to the accusations of bigotry in a pamphlet, 'The Rise of Free Speech in America': 'Intolerance martyred Joan of Arc' he claimed, and what he considered his all-embracing theory of history transformed his next film. Based on a recent case, the killing of nineteen industrial workers by their employers' self-appointed militia, he added to it three stories from history to emphasise his sympathy for the oppressed: **Intolerance** (1916), 'A Drama of Comparisons' – with its subtitle changed to 'A Sun-Play of the Ages' for its New York opening, and 'Love's Struggle Through the Ages' for its 1933 revival. It was also described as 'A Drama in Two Acts and a Prologue' to explain the interval and confer respectability.

At just under three hours (and fourteen reels) it is a sight longer than *The Birth of a Nation*, having to accommodate its four stories: the modern one, originally called *The Mother and the Law*; the fall of Babylon; the famous events in Judea in AD 33; and the Massacre of the Eve of St Bartholomew in 1572. They would begin, declared Griffith, 'like four currents looked at from a hilltop. At first the four currents will flow apart, slowly and quietly. But as they flow, they grow nearer and nearer together, and faster and faster, until in the end, in the last act, they mingle in one mighty river of expressed emotion.' That is true up to a point, for one story – Judea – is merely a trickle, and another – the French one – no more than a stream; for long periods both are ignored, but the very lack of symmetry can only add surprise to a film which needs every bit of help it can get. This simultaneous unfolding of parallel stories however remains attractive, and

technically the film is a clear advance on its predecessor. It was much studied by the Russian masters, fascinated by the variety of shots – infinitely greater than in any film yet made; close-ups, medium-shots and long-shots intermingle, exactly judged and whipped away before interest is exhausted. There are some trolley-shots and an occasional shift of the camera – but not enough to suggest that Griffith really understood camera movement. The film does race along, appropriately, with the chariots which will destroy Babylon: the real triumph is in the editing.

The spectacle, also, was something to stun contemporaries. Griffith went further than any of the Europeans in construction: the walls of Babylon were 300 feet high, and the cost of Belshazzar's feast alone more than twice the total cost of *The Birth of a Nation*. Since the success of that was regarded as a fluke, the final cost of this – including, reputedly, 250 chariots on call, and 15,000 extras – was a wanton $1,900,000. (Within six years, Douglas Fairbanks would exceed that sum, but by that time movie investment was no longer considered a risk.) In a way, the money was misspent, since spectacle swamps everything: in the Babylon story Mountain Girl (Constance Talmadge) has a crush on the King, but is unable in time to warn him of the downfall of the city; but plot interest loses out entirely to effects. The two assaults are strikingly done, as based on the works of John Martin (the more colourful nineteenth-century illustrators and writers influenced all of Griffith's work); and the man whose head is struck off shocked audiences at the time. The French story is equally gory, and one might wonder – at least for the first two hours – what intolerance has to do with any of this: it is, at best, a simplification to suggest that that is what caused the Crucifixion. The modern story is explicit on the evils done by do-gooders, but it is wildly dishonest to suggest that they create the particular conditions to be overcome here – 'The Boy' wrongly convicted of murder, 'The Dear Little One' deprived of her child. In fact, the characters in all four episodes are either pure-white or jet-black, so that the audience's attitude towards intolerance is never tested – until the epilogue, which more modestly implies that intolerance caused the War in Europe (before the whole thing ends with 'us' on earth being united with 'them' in the sky). Griffith himself spoke of 'a protest against despotism and injustice in every form', but his ambitions outran his conceptions by light-years; and though few regarded this film as being of deep philosophy, he has been taken at his word by some – though even admirers concede 'absurdity' and 'sentimentality' in the telling.

The disparate stories are held together by the famous device of Lillian Gish rocking a cradle and the words 'Out of the cradle endlessly rocking' – its purpose obscure without the source, Walt Whitman's 'Endlessly rocks the cradle, Uniter of Here and Hereafter.' To the suffering audience, however, the word 'endlessly' is all too appropriate. Audiences of the time were thin, no matter how often critics confirmed its creator's genius, and it was soon clear that the film would not begin to recoup its costs. Its failure limited Griffith's independence, but did not lessen his standing, for *The Birth of a Nation* had proved something for which the powers of the industry had dared not hope – that the potential audience for films consisted not only of the more humble members of the community but of every single person in it. Less to the understanding and liking of the moguls, the two films proved that some people considered the new medium to be an art form.

With the rewards now proved so great, the in-fighting and competition were conducted with even less scruple. Laemmle and Fox were typical of the new entrepreneurs, Jewish immigrants, of little or no education, and in some cases unable to speak the language properly. This industry was an extension of familiar territory; like them, it was brash and new and not quite respectable. They wanted to make a fast buck, and as the bucks came faster than anticipated, they rose on the crest of a wave. Those who survived became the rulers of Hollywood – characterised later by S. J. Perelman as 'a dreary industrial town controlled by hoodlums of enormous wealth, the ethical sense of a pack of jackals, and taste so degraded that it befouled everything it touched'. Their taste and cultural values touched most people in the world for at least two generations, albeit that as filtered through writers, directors and players it was in happy concurrence with what the world wanted anyway.

The war boom and the feature film helped to change the structure of the industry. The once-mighty Biograph discontinued production not long after Griffith left, and Edison called it quits in 1918, so that the only survivor of the original Patents Company was Vitagraph – and that tottered, managing to cling on by combining in 1915 with Lubin, Selig and Essanay to form a distribution company to handle their product jointly – V.S.L.E Kalem gave up the ghost around the same time, and the failure of its Max Linder films in 1917 signalled the end of Essanay. Then V.S.L.E. crumbled: Vitagraph absorbed Selig and then Lubin, to be itself swallowed by Warner Bros. in 1925 – so that the sole survivor of the companies which joined the trust in 1909 (since Méliès had folded almost immediately) was Pathé.

If the two most aggressive opponents of the trust were Laemmle and Fox, not far behind were H. E. Aitken and the team of Adam Kessel and Charles Bauman – not that any of them were allies, or if so, not for long. It was Aitken who had poached Mary Pickford from Laemmle's I.M.P. for his newly-formed Majestic, and as that increased the enmity between him and Laemmle he allied himself with John R. Freuler, a former colleague from his exchange days, to form Mutual. In retaliation, Laemmle founded Universal, comprising a number of independents, including his own I.M.P., Rex, Pat Powers and his Powers Picture Plays, and Kessel and Bauman's exchange, the New York Motion Picture Company. Kessel and Bauman had been exhibitors who, balked of getting films for their exchanges had decided to make their own: after two (in which they both appeared), they founded Bison Life Pictures, which became successful when Thomas Ince applied to them for a job.

Thomas H. Ince (1882–1924) came from theatrical stock, and began in films in 1910 acting with I.M.P. and then Biograph; he returned to I.M.P. to direct (and was briefly in Cuba filming, out of reach of the trust's agents) before going to Kessel and Bauman. They wanted him to take over the Bison Life company in California, and there he hired the Miller Brothers' 101 Ranch Wild West Show, renaming the company 101 Bison. The popularity of his Westerns enabled his bosses to start Reliance to make dramatic subjects – for which they stole Biograph's popular star, Arthur Johnson. Meanwhile, they found that they could not get on with Laemmle, and bought themselves out – leaving Universal with the name '101 Bison' to add to the other names under that umbrella. Their Western unit was renamed Broncho (later Kay-Bee Broncho), and both the Broncho and Reliance pictures were put in the hands of Aitken's Mutual, together with those of their new company, Keystone – backed for Mack Sennett, whom they had encouraged to leave Biograph. Ince moved over from Broncho to Reliance, and stayed with that company when its picture-making activities were amalgamated with those of Majestic – and it was at this point that Griffith also worked for Majestic-Reliance.

Then there was a split in Mutual – between Aitken and Freuler. Freuler was also a partner of Samuel S. Hutchinson in the American Film Company. These two made, in Europe, *The Quest* (1915), and shipped it, as was normal with American's films, to Mutual to distribute – but Mutual, in response to the presence of Griffith and Ince and the industry vogue for theatre-players, had started a policy of 'Master Pictures', and Aitken did not consider *The Quest* accorded with that policy. He shelved it, and when finally released, American's advertising stressed Hutchinson. 'The Master Producer'. More seriously, Freuler managed to oust Aitken as president of Mutual. Aitken thereupon withdrew the Majestic-Reliance product from Mutual, and persuaded his co-owners of that company, Kessel and Bauman, to withdraw Keystone; Aitken then, with the co-operation of Kessel and Bauman, formed Triangle – so named after its three directors, Griffith, Ince and Sennett, all of whom were much in the public eye. Triangle's chief aim was to solve the industry's most pressing prob-

lem, the growing power of the new company formed by the amalgamation of Adolph Zukor's Famous Players with Jesse Lasky. If the chief asset of this rival was Mary Pickford, Triangle had something comparable in William S. Hart, but in emulating Zukor by contracting stage stars, Triangle had only one success – Douglas Fairbanks – which was one reason for its quick demise, especially when, at the end of his contract, Fairbanks accepted a better offer from Zukor, which included his own production company. It was because Mutual had Chaplin that that company survived the defection of Aitken's people (and Kessel and Bauman's), but it did not last long after his departure. Soon after that Triangle began to collapse, and Famous Players–Lasky, which had already added Ince to Fairbanks, hastened to grab Griffith, Sennett, Hart and Wallace Reid.

The fact that some sources claim that Triangle was founded by its three directors seems due to the exaggeration which surrounds most writing about Griffith, but also to the fact that both he and Ince were powerful enough to have real independence. From the moment when Ince had gone West to join Bison Life his energy and imagination had astounded the industry; and his films were successful enough for his employers to purchase 18,000 acres of land in Southern California for a studio christened Inceville. Unlike Griffith, he enjoyed supervising. Of the hundreds of films turned out under his aegis, it is difficult now to sort out his contribution; even when credits survive it is unwise to believe that Ince's actual work on any particular film was very great. He liked taking credit, and we may be sure that when he is said to have collaborated on direction or authorship that his contribution was minimal. I have seen two of his Triangle films, said to have been directed by him, **Civilization** (1916), which certainly was – and which deserves a paragraph of its own – and *D'Artagnan* (1916), a version of Dumas of absolutely no interest.

Civilization was meant to rival *Intolerance*, and, like that, was built on the base of an existing and completed film: it took the War in Europe not as its epilogue, but as its whole subject. There had been a number of pro-war and anti-isolationist films, of which the most notable was J. Stuart Blackton's *The Battle Cry of Peace*, based on Hudson Maxim's 'Defenseless America'. *Civilization* was Ince's rebuttal, and its success may partly have been due to timing: its $100,000 cost (*D' Artagnan* cost $15,000) made a profit seven times over. Its popularity is surprising, for there is no identifiable hero, and all is flat-out propaganda. For the box-office, there is a power-mad demagogue – the king who makes war; there is a secret league of women who desire world peace; and there is Christ coming to earth (in the body of the husband of one of them) to make the king see the error of his ways.

Directors who served under Ince at this time include Henry King, Frank Borzage and Fred Niblo; the best Ince films of this period are now attributed to Reginald Barker. We have noted his flair in his two-reel Westerns, and that is a quality to be found in **The Typhoon** (1914), a study of the Japanese community in Paris and how it protects the young doctor (Sessue Hayakawa) who has strangled a taunting showgirl. It is based on a Hungarian play by Melchior Lengyel which had been a success in New York and London – but it is far more cinematic than any of Zukor's 'Famous Plays', and it was to that company that Kessel and Bauman (presumably in a moment of truce) sold it. Even better is Barker's **The Italian** (1915), a plea for compassion in semi-documentary style on behalf of New York's immigrant community. The hero (George Beban) is a boot-black and he does suffer unusual hardship; but the incident of the politician who buys his vote, via the underworld, remains a chilling comment on public life. The writer was C. Gardner Sullivan, and the same directness of plot may be found in both **Hell's Hinges** (1916) and **The Return of Draw Egan** (1916), both of which, as it happens, have the same story. The second is directed by William S. Hart, who stars in both, and the first by Barker, with his strong visuals – the marvellous use of dust and fire in this small Western town puts it way ahead of most movies of its era. Both films were made under Ince's supervision, and Hart's film, if polished, is not as technically expert as Barker's. In both Hart is the

Thomas H. Ince's *Civilization*, as sold to audiences tired of reading about the War in Europe: its influence is reputed to have helped Woodrow Wilson in the 1916 election, campaigning with similar ideals. Note the description 'An Ince Masterpiece' – untypically small. Ince, like Griffith, was fond of taking credit where none was due – and was thus the object of a shaft in Buster Keaton's *The Playhouse*, in which a poster credits all creative functions to one man.

bad man who for love of a lady keeps the law between the rowdies and the churchgoing folk. It is equally pleasant to see him in city duds in Barker's **Between Men** (1915), a knight errant bugging the villain's office, thought in this context to be an admirable thing. House Peters is the bully-boy businessman villain, out to ruin a father and marry the daughter.

Ince left Triangle after a year to found his own company, with facilities provided by Zukor; after three years there he formed Associated Producers with some other directors, who included Allan Dwan, Mack Sennett, Marshall Neilan, King Vidor and Maurice Tourneur, but within months they had moved into the First National fold. Ince's death, incidentally, was for years one of Holly-

51

William S. Hart was the first movie actor with a perfected image. Audiences knew what to expect of his best–known predecessor, Broncho Billy, but Hart, having established himself as the Good–Bad Man, had to work harder at being reformed, especially when there were temptresses around like Louise Glaum. The film concerned is *The Return of Draw Egan*, and as in the very similar *Hell's Hinges* her natural habitat is the saloon.

filming Broadway plays – and undoubtedly, the fact that they commanded higher admission fees as well. Among the plays filmed by Triangle was **Pillars of Society** (1916), directed by Raoul Walsh, which, like Majestic-Mutual's earlier **Ghosts** (1915), directed by George Nicholls, was supervised by Griffith. Both featured Henry B. Walthall, as Karsten and Captain Alving respectively – and the presence of the Captain in *Ghosts* indicates that what interested Triangle were the melodramatic events to which Ibsen merely referred. His actual plays are confined to the final reels, but if *Ghosts* is reduced to a simple tale of retribution, complete with orgy, *Pillars* is considerably more fleshy and convincing than most films of the period. **Old Heidelberg** (1915) was one of several stage properties offered by a subsidiary, Fine Arts, starring Wallace Reid as the student prince and Dorothy Gish as the tavern maid: the direction is credited to John Emerson, and the film is notable for the violent anti-militarist stance injected into the material – and also as an example of Triangle's re-working of plays. Let Famous Players, they decided, bask in reflected glory: they would emphasise the fact that cinema was an independent art. The elevation of Sennett to stand with Ince and Griffith might be considered far-sighted were it not for the fact that he was acknowledged a master – though he, 'the king of the comic cut-ups', regarded his own work as trivial.

Mack Sennett (1880–1960) was born in Canada, and entered films as an actor at Biograph. He became a writer, and subsequently director, specialising in slapstick – much of it influenced by Linder and the French chase comedies. He added elements of the circus and vaudeville, using every trick device of which the camera was capable; and though today some of the chases he engineered may lack variety, it is a stony spectator who remains unamused by the car which doesn't quite go over the cliff or the bus that makes it over the level-crossing a split-second before the train. These vehicles would almost certainly contain the Keystone Cops, that band of unfailingly energetic policemen which joined his repertory when Kessel and

wood's biggest scandals: he was taken ill aboard the yacht of William Randolph Hearst, the newspaper magnate, and died two days later. Because he didn't want rivals printing stories about wild drinking parties, Hearst tried to hush up the matter – which was why speculation started as to the true cause of death. Ince's legacy to Hollywood was his policy: a complete and detailed script, constructed individually but under his supervision, directed as written, and edited by himself. The studios adopted it because the responsibility for expenditure did not devolve upon the director – an animal which, given its head (as Griffith with *Intolerance*) was inclined to lose it.

Triangle was founded because its owners sought position and respectability, having noticed the extent to which Famous Players-Lasky commanded respect by signing stage-players and

Bauman gave him his own company in 1912. Joining him from Biograph, from vaudeville or just by wandering in the door, were the Sennett troupe: Mabel Normand, prettiest of comediennes; Roscoe or 'Fatty' Arbuckle, melon-headed comic of immodest girth; Chester Conklin, with the forlorn moustache; Ben Turpin, of the swivelling and meeting eyes; Ford Sterling, the heavy with fuzz on his chin; and Mack Swain, most lugubriously stout of evil-doers – nor must we forget Sennett's Bathing Beauties, frowned on by some, and the nearest equivalent for the troops of World War One to the leggy pin-ups of the Second.

Sennett's films were often improvised, under various directors, utilising every prop within sight : sticks to hit with, doors to be chased through, stairs to be fallen down, water to be fallen into, walls to collapse, custard pies to be thrown, cash registers to be stolen from, sausages for dogs to steal, dogs to tear holes in pants, pants to be lost, pretty girls to be kissed, fat ladies to be sat on, soup to be spilled, dishes to be broken, and, above all, cars to chase and be chased: small cars to disgorge a score of cops; cars to proceed after being sliced in half, to pass unharmed through brick walls, to proceed without wheels, engines or sometimes drivers, always emerging triumphant and unscathed. In Sennett's world everything went to extremes – absurd, illogical and surrealistic; his films survive as entertainment, even in the form we – unfortunately – know them best, chopped-up for compilations with relentlessly jokey commentaries. Some of them, it is true, mistake energy for invention, and flounder, but parts of most of them survive the years with ease.

It was Sennett who brought Chaplin into pictures, and it was while with him at Triangle that Douglas Fairbanks emerged as the most popular male screen star after Chaplin. Both actors moved on, and in 1917 Sennett signed a contract to make two-reelers for Paramount: in 1921 he was one of the Associated Producers who moved to First National, during which time he made a number of features, with his stock company, for release by other distributors. He did not adapt to the less robust shenanigans demanded by audi-ences towards the end of the decade, but went on to the Sound period, when he employed both Bing Crosby and W. C. Fields. The two-reel comedy remained a staple of film programmes till the Forties, but for at least a decade had lost its popularity to Mickey Mouse and his breth-ren.

Sennett made the first feature-length comedy, **Tillie's Punctured Romance** (1914), which sought respectability by being based on a stage play with its original star, Marie Dressler. As a coy spinster she has to be seen to be believed: her expressions provide amusement, but the slapstick is of the most rudimentary kind – much kicking, falling over, cavorting, bumping into. Chaplin, as her money-grabbing suitor, is almost totally unfunny. Theodore Huff, in his monograph on Chaplin, calls it: 'Not merely crude slapstick, however; it is brilliant satire', one of the manifold over-assessments from which Chaplin's reputation is now suffering. Sennett never went in for satire, though he liked spoofs – such as **Down on the Farm** (1920), which has a wicked landlord threatening to foreclose, and Louise Fazenda as another hopeful and heavy heroine. The enormous success of *Tillie* – confounding its backers and the re-viewers, who were unsure whether the public would accept a six-reel comedy – did not encourage Sennett to move over for good to the longer film. *Down on the Farm* is a good indication of the care he took with the few he made: it has a complicated plot, a sub-plot, a chase, and a number of fights and drubbings.

Neither Sennett nor Chaplin should be judged on the shorts Chaplin made for Keystone. Charles Chaplin (1889–1977), a London-born music hall comic, became one of the best known men in the world while with that company. He moved on to Essanay, where he made fourteen films in thirteen months. Reviewing one of them, *His New Job* (1915), *The Bioscope* wrote: 'There is probably no film comedian in the world more popular with the average picture theatre audience than that famous funmaker, Charles Chaplin. . . The art of Charles Chaplin defies analysis, and disarms the critic. Just *why* he is so funny, it is impossible to say, and very probably he could not tell you himself. He possesses a naturally comic personality and his humour is accentuated by the originality of the innumerable bits of "business" with which his work is so profoundly interspersed. Scarcely a moment passes while he is on the screen, but he is up to some wild piece of mischief or committing some ludicrous folly. And perhaps the funniest thing of all is his own complete imperturbability'.

Chaplin's clowning was already spoken of as 'art': one of the problems confronting the cinema historian is the praise showered on Chaplin – certainly not justified by the silly, improvised knockabout of the Keystones and Essanays: but he *is* imperturbable. Audiences liked his pluck, his self-reliance, his cocking-a-snook at authority. He begins to be funny towards the end of the Essanay period, in **A Night in the Show** (1915), a version of one of his music hall sketches, as a drunk swell, using an expression of immense hauteur in the hope of disguising his condition. In **Police** (1916), his penchant for pathos is beginning to show, and as he adds motivation to his gags we can see him maturing. He did grow to meet the praise: almost every film he made at Mutual was an improvement on the one before. There is much less thwacking and bum-kicking, and he is able to get beautiful meaning into his expressions – the mingled admiration and horror with which he regards Eric Campbell eating spaghetti in **The Count** (1916), or the disappointment at finding the girl prefers his rival in **The Vagabond** (1916). He is learning to use props at length, and build routines round them, as in **The Pawnshop** (1916), and in which he first perfected the precision and balletic grace of his movements.

Easy Street (1917) is his first masterpiece. The earlier Mutuals had been churned out at the rate of one every three or four weeks: but this was six weeks in gestation, and there would be three to four months between the later ones. It is episodic, shifting from incident to incident in no particular order, but it hews mainly to the relationship between Chaplin and Eric Campbell. Up to this time Campbell had certainly menaced Chaplin in the Mutuals, as nemesis and rival: but the pairing of the diminutive Chaplin and the towering Campbell had never been as effective as here – Campbell had never been so fearsome a villain, so tough that a dozen police truncheons on his head go unnoticed. He is, of course, the king of Easy Street; Chaplin is a policeman. In **The Immigrant** (1917) Campbell is a waiter whose carelessness is matched only by his fierceness; Chaplin is in the title-role, delicately judging the pathos. This is a rich comedy, but **The Adventurer** (1917) – Charlie in high society – is merely a return to slapstick, with such devices as ice-creams falling into ladies' cleavages. Shortly after this Chaplin moved to First National – without Campbell, who had been killed in a car crash.

Chaplin's phenomenal popularity gave pause to those who would dismiss the movies as a visual equivalent of the penny-dreadful, as well as having a galvanising effect upon the industry. His female equivalent was Mary Pickford, and the two of them engaged in a purely private rivalry as to which could earn the most – which went at high as $10,000 a week plus bonuses (at a time when the average annual wage in the U.S. was about a thousand dollars). Undoubtedly, however, Miss Pickford was the prime factor in building the fortunes of the biggest company of the period – though the 'Divine Sarah' and the first Queen Elizabeth also had a hand. The U.S. distribution rights of the Bernhardt-Elizabeth film were owned by Adolph Zukor (1873–1976), a Hungarian who had arrived in the States just before the turn of the century, and who had moved from the fur business into nickelodeons. He merged his cinema interests with Marcus Loew, a fellow-furrier – and later, via Loews Inc., owner of M-G-M – but parted from him to handle the Bernhardt film, in which he had a financial interest. Its success led to the formation of his own production company, to feature 'Famous Players in Famous Plays' – and though he operated outside the trust, he was able to function in New York: because he also had the support of the veteran showman Daniel Frohman, who after three years of Broadway failures was looking for a way of re-establishing his once mighty prestige. He had offered to show Bernhardt's Elizabeth film in one of his theatres, an action which alone gave respectability to the film industry: he conferred respectability on Zukor by fighting the Patents Company, pointing out to its members they would do a disservice to culture by preventing showings of the film – thus helping the importation of other European films and hastening the end of the Patents monopoly. Frohman's partnership with Zukor also ensured the latter in getting the co-operation of stage players of the calibre of Minnie Maddern Fiske, Bertha Kalich, Cecilia Loftus, John Barrymore, Gaby Deslys and Pauline Frederick. The public, however, found their vehicles stuffy, and Zukor realised that his profits were from the less prestigious efforts being made in Hollywood by Mary Pickford.

It is difficult now to see why she was so much more popular than her rivals (and imitators), but undoubtedly her traditional image – gingham and golden curls – was reassuring at a time when women were asserting themselves equal to men. It is a paradox that she was not only the most famous actress who had ever lived, but also the most successful career woman: her astronomical salary demands were inevitably met by the grumbling Zukor. A further curiosity is that the public indicated a preference for those films in which she played a child. **The Poor Little Rich Girl** (1917), directed by Maurice Tourneur, finds her lonely in an ivory tower till father decides to devote himself to her and her mother after an illness – done as an extended pre-Freudian dream sequence, with Death in a long black veil carrying lilies, and Life prancing about an Arcadian meadow in white lace. In **Rebecca of Sunnybrook Farm** (1917) she is an orphan who puts a good face on adversity and wins over her mean old aunts, despite having, literally, turned their barn into a circus. She also wins the rose-gathering bachelor with the bow-tie – despite her first greeting, 'Are you the lady of the house?' – growing up miraculously in the last few minutes to achieve this happy ending. Marshall Neilan directed both this and the rather more cunning **Stella Maris** (1918), which offers two Pickfords, one to admire and one with whom to identify – thus audiences got a wilting heroine and a mischievous one, a sad one and a happy one, with endings to match. Stella is a radiant,

wealthy cripple, and Unity Blake a cockney orphan and slavey, plain if not actually deformed, and a born sufferer: both are in love with the same man (Conway Tearle) and Unity sacrifices herself to save him from his drunken and drug-addicted wife – which makes it rather unfeeling for him and Stella to be so happy at the fade-out.

It was a lady at the other end of the scale who founded the fortunes of William Fox's studio: Theda Bara (1890–1955), an obscure stage actress whose name became synonymous with all that was daring and luxuriously sinful. Copying the Italian 'divismo' films, he put her into a series of melodramas in which she flaunted herself till death, conscience or reformation caught her in the final reel. The only film to survive is the first and most famous, **A Fool There Was** (1914), which included nothing that you'd see on Main Street in a month of Sundays. It includes nothing that had much to do with life, either, but audiences were thrilled to the nth degree by this tale of a respectably married man who falls helpless prey to a designing woman. For once, his downfall does not include drugs, but as ever adultery is equated with drunkenness, and neither is found to be remotely enjoyable. She exults in his disgrace, and Fox revelled in his profits, reckoned to be a million dollars. As directed by Frank Powell, this was muck-raking, revelling in the thing it pretends to condemn, but its vague source – a poem by Kipling – is quoted extensively in the intertitles to give the thing respectability. Miss Bara, described as 'a notorious woman of the vampire species', is the only thing that links this to the twentieth century – she is more ruthless than her predecessors, and does not have to atone for her sins. She is pretty, but her acting is as incredible as her behaviour, moving from petulance to gloating triumph in a glance. From then on, American films did not have to relegate sexual misdeeds to historical subjects only.

If Zukor and Fox rode to success on the coat-tails of Pickford and Bara, Laemmle had been unlucky with Florence Lawrence, whose popularity soon faded; however, it might be said that it was another aspect of fornication which formed the basis of his success – the white

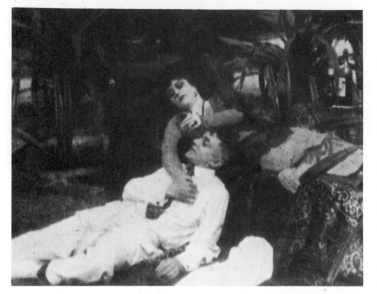

Edward Jose succumbs to Theda Bara's charms in *A Fool There Was*. He is a social reformer and diplomat, no match for this American cousin of *les Grandes Horizontales*, who even lures him in front of his child. They meet on an ocean crossing – after she has had a deckchair put over the spot where her last lover shot himself – and he will soon echo an earlier lover (now a bum), 'See what you have made of me and still you prosper, you hellcat!'

slave trade, as practised in New York. And if *A Fool There Was* owed everything to the Italian Cinema, **Traffic in Souls** (1913) was clearly inspired by the Danish films. Its instigator and director was George Loane Tucker, who shared its cost – $5,700 – with several other Laemmle people. Indeed, it was made against Laemmle's wishes, but since it was made on his time it became his property, and a pawn in his many fights with his co-directors – since it was of feature-length. Most features to that time had been the 'prestige' pieces, playing at opera-houses and legitimate theatres, but as none of these would touch this subject, the Shubert theatre chain arranged for it to be shown in a leading vaudeville house – having liked it enough to pay $33,000 for a one-third interest, thereby making a profit even before its public screening, when, advertised as 'a $200,000 spectacle', it played to 30,000 in its first week. On its profits, the following year, Laemmle built Universal City, where, mainly eschewing features for the time being, his subsidiaries turned out one- and two-reelers to be rented together to exhibitors as complete programmes.

Thus, by 1914, amidst the internecine strife, there were already in business three of the eight film companies which would dominate Hollywood in its heyday – the third being Paramount, which grew from the combination of Famous Players and Lasky. Jesse Lasky (1880–1958) was a third-generation American and former vaudevillian, who in 1913 had launched Jesse Lasky Feature Plays, in association with his brother-in-law Sam Goldwyn (q.v.), Arthur S. Friend and Cecil B. de-Mille, an actor and playwright. Lasky had in fact wanted the co-operation of a young Broadway dramatist, William deMille, but had to settle for his less successful younger brother. Their aim was to photograph plays, and Cecil deMille arranged with David Belasco for the rights for his productions; he also persuaded Belasco's chief designer, Wilfred Buckland, to work with him, thus introducing art direction to the American film. Buckland's careful work, and the directorial experience of Oscar Apfel, helping deMille in his debut at that task, got the company off to a flying start on their first film, **The Squaw Man** (1914), based on a popular play, about a wrongly-disgraced English nobleman who flees to the West and falls in love with an Indian princess. 'The touches of great beauty,' said *The Moving Picture World*, 'contain a secret of success known only to screen presentation – they cause us to surrender ourselves more completely to the story . . . and to love this new art form for its own sake.'

For his second film, *Brewster's Millions*, Lasky hired a legitimate theatre, and Zukor, impressed with this attempt to emulate his methods, invited Lasky into partnership. They soon joined forces with H. V. Hodkinson, who from one cinema in Utah had developed his own circuit and had subsequently become manager for the Western operations of the Patents Company. Foreseeing the demise of the Trust, he was looking for product for his own distribution company, which he called Paramount. Two years later, in 1916, the three companies merged, though the production company remained 'Famous Players-Lasky' till virtually the end of the Silent period. Hodkinson was forced out in 1917, whereupon he founded another distribution company, under his own name, which he ran till he started P.D.C. in 1924. From the merger of the three companies, Paramount dominated the industry, and just as surely Mary Pickford dominated Paramount. Her popularity enabled Zukor to institute block-booking, an iniquitous system by which exhibitors bought blind a block of films in order to get one or two they knew would do sensational business – a practice denounced and officially outlawed but still occasionally used today. Miss Pickford put a stop to it, at the time, as far as her own films were concerned, in order to get more money from 'special' bookings; and it was when she left him, in 1919, that Zukor concentrated his energies – and helped by a ten million dollar bank loan – on the acquisition and construction of theatres. He had already boasted of building the first national circuit, his growing power so alarming competitors that they formed themselves into a cooperative group which in retaliation they christened First National: and in view of his renewed aggression in the field of exhibition First National started a studio to challenge him in the field of production (q.v.).

The in-fighting of the industry at this time is exemplified by the story of Lewis J. Selznick (1870–1933), a Russian-born Jew who quit the jewelry trade for the hazards of the film business. He hitched his wagon to a star, namely Clara Kimball Young, persuading her to move from Vitagraph to World to his own organisation, set up within Universal by virtue of voting a friend's stock. Her popularity and his methods attracted other stars, enabling Selznick to use the slogan 'Features With Well-Known Players in Well-Known Plays'. As with Lasky, Zukor decided that this imitator was safer as partner, and he invited Selznick to join him as partner in a company called Select Pictures, with complete freedom but under the aegis of Famous Players-Lasky. One condition was that Selznick films could no longer be prefixed 'Lewis J. Selznick presents' but soon 'Selznick presents' preceded the titles of films ostensibly produced by another company headed by Selznick's son Myron, seventeen years old at the time. After a court battle, Lewis J. Selznick was free, and Zukor revenged himself by stealing Clara Kimball Young. The industry declined to forgive Selznick, especially when he copied another slogan, 'Mutual Movies Make Time Fly', changing it to 'Selznick Pictures Make Happy Hours'; and he was not forgiven for signing Olive Thomas against all competition when her Triangle contract finished. Miss Thomas, a former

Ziegfeld beauty, was expected to be the biggest star in pictures, and Selznick's career faced its biggest reversal when she, at the age of twenty, was found dead of drug-addiction in a Paris hotel-room. Fox and Laemmle joined Zukor and Lasky in taking Selznick's other stars, and Selznick's son David (q.v.) always believed that their vindictiveness drove him from films.

After Miss Pickford, Paramount's biggest asset was Cecil B. deMille (1881–1959), whose technical skill was equalled only by his knowledge of what the public wanted. **The Cheat** (1915) was so popular that the scenarist, Hector Turnbull, turned it into a play – the first scenario adapted for the stage. A flighty Long Island wife (Fannie Ward) misappropriates club funds to pay her debts, and turns for assistance to the Burmese playboy (Sessue Hayakawa) with whom she has been dallying, and he, later, cheated of his prize, brands her with the stamp he uses for his goods and chattels. He is clearly the villain, but deMille realised that the public would not have sympathy for the callow couple at the centre, and offered instead high society in sumptuous settings. The heroine (Cleo Ridgely) of **The Golden Chance** (1915) aspires to such settings, and is sheltered from her drunken husband by a society couple. While deMille pondered as to which sort of heroine fitted best into such sumptuousness, he was asked to guide the screen career of the prima diva Geraldine Farrar – signed at $20,000 for eight weeks' work, and the culmination of the policy of getting renowned stage performers into the studio. After a *Carmen* (1915), with Wallace Reid and Pedro de Cordoba, she did the similar **Maria Rosa** (1916) with the same players, and also based on a popular play, a tale of fatal loves and vendettas. Her true love leaves jail to find her just married to a murderer, but unsullied, and indeed earlier she had avoided being raped by that gentleman – which makes this film an early example of deMille's (and Hollywood's) devious attitude towards sex. Miss Farrar is more like a Catalonian peasant than you'd expect – plump, ageing, and not very pretty; and her simple emoting includes a good deal of throat-clutching. Her stolid presence is the major drawback to **Joan the Woman** (1917), which (since the

The Rise of the American Industry

OPPOSITE:
Cecil B. de Mille was associated all his life with sex and spectacle, though at first he hardly combined the two. After being advised by the front office to do 'modern stories of great human interest' he embarked on a series about adultery – assumed, intended, and occasionally real. In *Don't Change Your Husband,* BELOW RIGHT, Gloria Swanson, a neglected wife, is tempted by Lew Cody, playing a bishop's nephew, no less; and in *The Affairs of Anatol* she has every reason to look unhappy, since she is married to Anatol – played by Wallace Reid. The freshness of both films will surprise anyone who knows de Mille only from his later work.

others are all terrible) manages the interesting but not considerable feat of being still the best film about Joan of Arc. The courtroom images indicate that it influenced Dreyer's film (q.v.), and it confirms deMille as a director of force and imagination, be it in the vigorous battle scenes, the numerous superimpositions, or merely in the compositions. It makes analogies with the concurrent conflict in Europe – which gets some footage – and as it progresses towards its climax it gathers, despite the liberties of the script, a degree of complexity hinged with real tragedy. Nothing in Griffith indicates that he gave as much thought as deMille (at this time) to the business of telling a story through images, and for sheer power and beauty the immolation sequence stands alone in the Silent period.

Miss Farrar was lured away by Goldwyn, now independent, for $10,000 a week, and deMille returned to melodrama, finding the high society formula he sought in **Old Wives for New** (1918), and matching it with an ironic tone. As the middle-aged husband (Elliott Dexter) leaves his frumpish wife (Sylvia Ashton) for a pretty modiste (Florence Vidor), a contrast between the wife then and the wife now is indicated by dynamic cutting. **Don't Change Your Husband** (1918) examines the same situation from the wife's point of view, and in acquiring Gloria Swanson (b. 1898) deMille found the heroine he sought – one who found that boredom with her first husband was preferable to the philandering of her second. She suffered in luxury – the girl who had everything but wasn't happy with it, bridging the gap between Bara and Pickford and their imitators, and establishing a screen type more lasting than either, the woman who was both sophisticated and sympathetic.

She, and these films of deMille's, were exactly what a restless, post-war generation wanted to see: a more relaxed attitude towards sex and a more liberal attitude towards women; a hint of corruption among the rich, of effeteness among the older generation; and a touch of the exotic – something the returning doughboy thought he had left behind in Paris cafés. **Male and Female** (1919) offers a bizarre scene with Miss Swanson

in a marble bath, as well as a quite extraneous sequence set in luxurious ancient Babylon – neither episode can be found in the play on which it is based, Barrie's 'The Admirable Crichton'. The impression of such trappings was to complement Swanson's sophistication: of going to the opera and the best resorts, of drinking cocktails to the sound of the gramophone – and indeed when the soulful wife (Swanson) loses her husband (Thomas Meighan) in **Why Change Your Wife?** (1920) to the girl (Bebe Daniels) who prefers the Follies, she takes up smoking to win him back, learns to shimmy, and dons the once-disputed negligée. This, presumably, was the pattern of behaviour employed by the wealthy – a pattern that included the infidelities, shown as explicitly as possible, which in fact means glimpses of ankle and silken beds featuring prominently in the decor. Happy endings were vitally important, however, so that audiences might aspire to such married bliss, and the smartness and spuriousness of the pieces are indicated by the aspiring cynicism of the intertitles, e.g. a husband pondering 'the difference between his wife and the girl he married' (*Why Change Your Wife?*) and the vamp claiming 'I'm not the type of girl for a little boy like you to play with. The place for you is home' (*The Affairs of Anatol*).

The attitudes reflected are certainly not those of Barrie – but are hopefully those of the marital comedies of Somerset Maugham and the plays of Schnitzler. DeMille's version of **The Affairs of Anatol** (1921) indicates how little his Massachusetts soul understood the spirit of the Viennese dramatist. We may overlook the fact that staying to formula Anatol (Wallace Reid) is no longer a bachelor but a bored husband; but after three episodes of dalliance – notably in the Oriental boudoir of Satan Synne (Bebe Daniels), the wickedest woman in town – he is not (as in the original) as far from his ideal as ever, but happily reunited with his wife.

DeMille, in fact, was an opportunist, but his muddled theories do not blind us to the fact that he was also technically more adroit than any of his contemporaries, notably in the matter of continuity and lighting. More genuine sophistication is to be found in the work of his brother,

58

On the basis of his very few surviving films, we are, however, more likely to admire Cecil's brother, William deMille, a former Broadway dramatist who took to film directing with ease. This is Thomas Meighan in *Conrad in Search of his Youth*. The proud mother is Sylvia Ashton, once his childhood sweetheart: he had not been prepared for the change, or the squawling brats.

William C. deMille (1878–1955), and especially in **Conrad in Search of His Youth** (1920). Conrad (Meighan) is an Indian Army officer who tries to relive his past. A reunion with his cousins in their childhood holiday home is a several-pronged disaster, and further disillusion follows when he seeks out his first love and the magical older woman who once gave him a good night kiss. The final sequence, in which he does find happiness, is a betrayal of the original novel (by Leonard Merrick), but it still has the sort of 'civilised' humour which appealed to the ladies who belonged to the lending libraries. **Miss Lulu Bett** (1921) also suffered on the journey from page to screen, via a Pulitzer-prizewinning play by the original writer, Zona Gale. I say 'suffered' because where *Conrad* remains a rare delight among films of the period, *Miss Lulu Bett* relies, like too many of them, on coincidence and omission. However, like the earlier film, it offered audiences identification rather than escape, and a notable portrait of family life with its squabbles and fears of what the neighbours think; the advance of Lulu (Lois Wilson) from drab skivvy to attractive wife is well done, and I'm sure audiences cheered when she smashed those dishes and marched out. William

deMille's strength was in matters of characterisation, by which he hoped to transform rather mundane subjects like these; when he could no longer interest producers in such subjects he quit directing.

Among the other directors· of the period, Maurice Tourneur (1876–1961) was one of the most admired. Born in Paris, he began in films as an actor, but turned director in 1913, and crossed the Atlantic with art director Ben Carré, when their employers, Eclair, started an American branch, at Fort Lee, New Jersey – which was the major production centre for the industry until it ceded its place to Hollywood. Indeed, New Jersey recognisably doubles for Britain in **The Wishing Ring** (1914), 'An Idyll of Old England'. It is not to be expected that the 'Cranford'-like charm it seeks is achieved, but the story – the reformation of a ne'er-do-well by the daughter of an impoverished parson – is of little interest anyway. As indicated, *The Poor Little Rich Girl* is hardly better, but **A Girl's Folly** (1917) is worth notice: concocted by the director and Frances Marion, it is one of the first movies about movie-making – and like many later ones, about a film-struck girl (Doris Kenyon). Her folly is not in leaving the New Jersey fields for New York, but in staying after flunking her chance, dazzled by movie people; like a vast number of early films before the moguls' tastes began to impinge, the satiric strain is very strong – which also tells us much about the people who made them. There is nothing of this Tourneur in **The Blue Bird** (1918), a lavish production of Maeterlinck's play for Paramount, with over fifty sets, designed by Carré, which are varied and within the limitations of the time, exciting: but the film itself is a matter of staging rather than direction. It is easier to admire Tourneur for **Foolish Matrons** (1921), three stories of marriage, told simultaneously: the actress who traps an ageing doctor into matrimony, only to find that the demands of her career have turned him into a drug-addict; the woman reporter who marries the nice, promising young poet, and watches him turn into an alcoholic because he cannot get published; and the young wife from the country who succumbs to the blandishments of her husband's boss, losing both in time but achieving a sort of tarnished wealth. Victorian melodrama hangs heavily over all three tales, but the approach is ironic and the treatment entirely fresh. It is, however, New York which gives the film its distinct flavour: the many, impressive locations, separately directed by Clarence Brown, make you suddenly aware that you never before saw a convincing restaurant or bar in a movie. For such things this film is both more convincing and more entertaining than Von Stroheim's similarly-titled *Foolish Wives* (q.v.), and not a good deal less cynical or outspoken. It was a product of Associated Producers, the group of independent directors led by Ince, and on the strength of it we must regret that the company was so short-lived.

Another Frenchman, Léonce Perret (1880–1935), was also one of the superior directors of this period. A former actor, he started the 'Léonce' series, in which he also starred, for Gaumont in 1911, and they reveal both a sprightly wit and a smooth technical skill. Pathé sent him to Hollywood in 1917, and during his four years there he made a number of melodramas, including **Twin Pawns** (1919), which starred Mae Marsh in a double role. Perret himself wrote it, several removes from its acknowledged source, 'The Woman in White', and apart from the villain (Warner Oland) who lives by his wits it is very silly: but beyond the always imaginative and still-fresh intertitles it holds evidence that Perret wholly understood the shape of the screen, and how it could be filled: the composition and lighting are superb, and the strong images of the factory scenes are matched by the narrative hold.

Raoul Walsh, in **Regeneration** (1915), offers a portrait of the times to stand with *The Italian* and *Foolish Matrons*. Walsh (1892–1981), a former actor with Griffith, had hitherto co-directed shorts, and he manages with accomplished ease this portrait of New York low life, moving from beer hall to mission picnics. It is not, as Walsh and others have claimed, the first gangster film, since it has more in common with the early counterfeiter tales than, say, *Little Caesar* (q.v.); it does attempt to analyse the mentality of the layabout – not the hoodlum – and is, alas, a little too pious, as the title indicates.

Rather that, though, than **Hawthorn of the U.S.A.** (1919), directed by James Cruze for Paramount, one of a number of post-war films to reiterate faith in American-style democracy. Being Hawthorne, says the star (Wallace Reid), 'that's got every king in Europe backed off the map'; he helps the foolish king rid the country of a number of vile revolutionaries, transforming the country 'with Yankee gold and ginger'.

The haughty, tall Reid and burly Thomas Meighan were Paramount's leading male stars, and in the case of Reid it is difficult to see why; both pale in comparison to William S. Hart – by the time he arrived at Paramount one of the cornerstones of the industry. That strange face, blinkered and hard, was surely like that of Marley's which Scrooge found on the knocker, haunted and hunted, and not needing intertitles like 'Realising that the road of the outlaw closes all others'. The episodic nature of **The Toll Gate** (1919) indicates that neither he nor his director and co-writer, Lambert Hillyer, was yet at home with the feature-length movie, but his knowledge of the frontier was never better expressed: the film is harsh, raw and unexpected, and because of what must surely be its authentic look and spirit, the most valuable example of the

William S. Hart was one of the actors who reached near-autonomy at Triangle – as jealously watched by Adolph Zukor at Famous Players-Lasky, who regarded himself as the leader of the industry. In fact, he helped to bring about the eventual collapse of Triangle by poaching Douglas Fairbanks Sr, with the offer of his own production company. When Thomas H. Ince quarrelled with his bosses at Triangle, Zukor offered him a haven – though what mainly interested Zukor was Ince's personal contract with Hart. When it ended Zukor broke with Ince, but kept Hart – with, of course, the offer of his own company. Its first film was *The Toll Gate*, one of the finest films Hart made.

genre extant. Its title is a reference to the soul, the difference between today and yesterday, or so an intertitle tells us, but **The Testing Block** (1920) is a wife: 'Along the ladder of life every man finds a rung that is his testing block, and writes his future as he climbs' – a phrase which accurately indicates that this film goes further than its predecessor in moralising, and it is even more overplotted. Hillyer was again Hart's collaborator, but this is less a portrait of the wild and rugged West than a weepie which could just as easily have had gangsters as its desperadoes. Since the old codes had been superseded, Hart had difficulty in finding subjects.

The lawless regions he had known as a youth were now settled, which was why he played an outlaw, the 'Good-Bad Man', only able to function outside that settled community. But now post-war audiences were more alive to social injustice: they wanted to see wrongdoing punished, and though settler and city-dweller alike could not obliterate the lawless past, they could however romanticise it, and in so doing destroy the authenticity of Hart's early films. His films were increasingly regarded as naif, and Zukor finally asked him to relinquish control and act under supervision. Earlier, Zukor had offered him $200,000 per film not to join United Artists (q.v.), and it was that company he now joined to retain his independence: but after one film, **Tumbleweeds** (1925), (in my opinion, a deserved failure) he retired.

Paramount's chief female player, after Miss Pickford, was perhaps Marguerite Clark, whose only film to survive is **Silks and Satins** (1916), directed by the then admired veteran, J. Searle Dawley. The title refers to the days of powdered wigs, but for all the references to 'the tap rooms of Paris' we may recognise the Palisades, a feature of every other film at the time. The star herself is merely another dimity heroine, dark, expressive and pretty: in 'The Movies in the Age of Innocence' Edward Wagenknect says that not to have seen her is tantamount to having 'never seen a silver birch or a daffodil', and in 1932 Sam Goldwyn listed her as one of the five greatest stars. She had retired in 1921: her husband had refused to let her kiss her leading man, and that was, in Lasky's opinion, the reason for her decline in popularity.

It was scandal which ruined another of Pickford's rivals, Mary Miles Minter, whose dimples may be examined in close-up in **The Ghost of Rosy Taylor** (1918), directed for Mutual by Edward Sloman, in which she suffers every misfortune but the wolves lapping at her heels. It is fast-paced, but dim, and the mystery promised by the title is notably missing. Miss Minter became implicated in the death of the director William Desmond Taylor, which was a mystery: and it also killed the career of the comedienne Mabel Normand, whose **Mickey** (1918) was astonishingly popular and is still fondly remembered. It was the first feature set up by her own company, as founded by Sennett (in whose one-reelers she had attained stardom) – and it was the only one, since she soon succumbed to a lucrative offer from Goldwyn. In fact, the film for that reason went unreleased for two years – a long time at that period – but its episodic plot did not deter audiences. That plot is literally 'Cinderella' rewritten for a modern tomboy, and Miss Normand's sharp reactions are occasionally funny as directed by Richard Jones.

Among the other players of this period must be mentioned John Barrymore, yet another of the over-age leading men. The line began with the genteel, kindly, Maurice Costello, but the more boisterous Barrymore was invariably cast as a reprobate who sobered up and showed his worth in the last reel. He was already the Barrymore we know from his Talkies – the quizzical stare, the jaunty self-confidence, the overall aura of a déclassé Don Juan. His films for Zukor are genial enough, but avoid **Raffles, the Amateur Cracksman** (1917), directed by George Irving, a confused account of E. W. Hornung's stories about a gentleman thief who plundered jewels at house parties. Another famous novel is just recognisable in **A Tale of Two Cities** (1917), directed by Frank Lloyd for Fox, and hardly an advance on the earlier Vitagraph version. The over-age hero in this one is William Farnum, as both Darnay and Carton (in fair to good trick work), and this portly, inexpressive actor makes one realise why audiences would soon fall for Valentino (q.v.).

Lon Chaney (q.v.), another name of the future, was at this time with Universal – not a star player, but one whose features, especially the whites of his eyes, made an indelible impression. He was one of Joseph de Grasse's stock company, along with some others left by Allan Dwan when he moved on from Universal: their scenarist was usually Ida May Park, who was the wife of director de Grasse, and the others in the company included Louise Lovely, who succeeded Gretchen Lederer as leading lady, and Hayward Mack. Their last two-reeler was **Dolly's Scoop** (1916), which offers the dilemma of a young reporter (Miss Lovely) who realises that the lady in the scandal she has uncovered is the wife of her editor (Mr Mack) – just retribution, of course, because he had threatened her with the sack if she didn't spice up her copy. The tone is light and lively, even the moralising; we forgive it its hypocrisy (the editor's wife is not really guilty), and it does indicate the level at which films might have worked had audiences not demanded sex, and producers not been determined to give it to them.

It was Universal that tried to make a film-star out of Anna Pavlova, and its solution was more sensible than making Geraldine Farrar a mute Carmen: she was put into a version of Auber's opera, **The Dumb Girl of Portici** (1916), in which by tradition the leading role – the lady of the title – was played by a ballerina. Looking haggard and intense, she does a tarantella or so, is seduced by the viceroy's son, and helps the Neapolitans to shake off the Spanish yoke. The action is as daft as most opera plots, and thus no sillier than most films of this era: but Lois Weber's direction confirms her position as one of the best directors of the time. Vigorous handling is also a feature of **The Virgin of Stamboul** (1920), and this other piece of exotic melodrama in fact made the reputation of a former vaudevillian, Tod Browning (1882–1962). The title-role is played by Priscilla Dean, one of Universal's most popular players, and part-clown in the manner of female stars of the time: as pursued by a dashing American officer and a sheik whose motives are much less honourable, the film conveys a fairly libellous account of the Levant at the time.

The preoccupation with sex was not accidental, and only the most popular players could get by with just a peck on the cheeks. A minor star like Molly King could be put in something like **The On-the-Square Girl** (1917), directed by Frederick J. Ireland for Pathé, a sexual version of *The Perils of Pauline* ; in such films titillation was provided by entirely double standards – the innocent seeming to be guilty, situations set up in which nothing actually happens, and the sinners paying for their happiness with entirely unconvincing reversals. Such was the major preoccupation of writers in the latter half of the second decade of the century : the arrival of the feature film confirmed that the cinema was not a passing fad, and sex was the simplest means at hand for hanging on to audiences.

On the other hand, films were achieving cohesion, and a number of filmmakers had demonstrated that the art of film narrative required far more than having actors emote before a camera. The most important technical development since the close-up was just a couple of years away – the moving camera: occasional cameramen had pushed it about, but its fluency had hardly been considered. As the decade turned, films seemed to have only two visual inadequacies: night-filming in exteriors remained difficult (a problem for audiences only when the stock was not tinted – dark blue for night, pink for twilight, yellow for sunlight) and parts of California stood in for the rest of the world. 'A tree is a tree is a tree' went the maxim, 'Shoot it in Griffith Park.' But it was a convention slowly losing credence ; the great era of set-building was about to begin, and technically the Americans would lead the world. Yet once again in ideas and imagination, the decade belonged to the Europeans – or so thought informed opinion of the time, including the American industry, which began to raid the studios of the Continent. The great era of purchasing talent had also begun.

3

The Screen's First Master

IT WAS not only the confidence and aggressiveness of the American industry which made it the most successful: chance also played a part, in the form of the War. With Europe in its apparent death throes, the leading producing companies – France, Germany, Britain and Italy – finished the War with industries diminished. Within a few years the film-makers of a defeated Germany would startle the world, and so would those of a new industry of a new country – the U.S.S.R. In Scandinavia the Danish industry declined, and Sweden continued to produce a few films of high quality.

Until quite recently the achievements of the German Silent film were thought to have been surpassed only by the Russians: to such an extent has Paul Rotha's 1929 survey of film influenced film historians that most major archives were based on his enthusiasms or those of such disciples as Iris Barry and Eileen Bowser of the Museum of Modern Art. Rotha's sole remark on the native work of Victor Sjöström is a passing reference to his 'Swedish masterpieces' and it has hardly been better documented elsewhere. It is ironic that Sjöström's most celebrated film, *The Phantom Carriage*, is also the most dated. It was the first Sjöström, says Ingmar Bergman, that he saw, and it was surely in his mind when he concocted *The Seventh Seal* (q.v.). If these two films were all that we knew of Swedish cinema, they would seem to confirm our notions of gloom and guilt, but in fact Sjöström is the only film-maker of the first three decades whose work can be considered as seriously as the major novelists and dramatists of the time. His situation has been admirably set by a contemporary French critic, Jean-Loup Passek: 'Towards Sjöström posterity has shown a singular ingratitude. It is almost indecent to see a creator of his stature relegated to the Purgatory of the Seventh Art. More perfidious than a perfectly planned assassination, for him has been reserved the lowest, most hypocritical, of contempt: oblivion.'

It has not been, of course, a blanket oblivion; due obeisance has been paid to the 'lyric' qualities of Sjöström and his contemporary, Mauritz Stiller. Iris Barry has noted their achievement more accurately: 'It was the Swedish film that first depicted individual human character with amplitude and truth, and taught the screen to suggest motive and mood. Both Sjöström and Stiller consciously and in original ways sought to make the film a vehicle for expressing by purely pictorial means subtleties hitherto unknown to it.' Sjöström succeeded triumphantly, though his films are technically barren; Stiller, the better technician, only sporadically. The gulf between them is enormous; but given Sjöström's admiration for his colleague, we may conclude that this has only become apparent with the years. Comparisons are inevitable, for they were not only contemporaries and colleagues, but collaborators – Sjöström acted in several of Stiller's films – and they filmed similar subjects, notably the novels of Selma Lagerlöf. One of these, Stiller's *Gösta Berling's Saga*, is the only one of their films to be discussed at length by Arthur Knight in 'The Liveliest Art'. It is a terrible film, described by Knight as 'the last great movie to come out of Sweden for many a year', one of those judgments, so common in discussing Silent films, in which boredom is equated with greatness. The films of Stiller are of their time, stilted and melodramatic: he imitated the Griffith movie. Sjöström in later life was not interested in discussing the films he had directed, but he conceded that some of them may have been before their time. The Museum of Modern Art note on *The Outlaw and his Wife* makes that point, also saying that Sjöström 'created effects not found outside the work of Griffith, yet more sophisticated and complex than anything even he had done'. It is not that Sjöström was before his time; his contemporaries in the industry were behind theirs.

The first credit for Sjöström's achievement should, however, go to Charles Magnusson (1878–1948), usually regarded as the founder of the Swedish film. In 1911 he built at Lidingö a studio reputed to be the most advanced in Europe. In establishing a distinctive native style – as opposed to the foreign

material flooding in – he turned to distinguished men of the theatre; in 1912 he persuaded both Sjöström and Stiller to join his team. Sjöström continued to work as both actor and director, and he wrote, or collaborated, on most of his screenplays. It was, he said later, 'a youthful desire for adventure' which brought him into films; but it was soon apparent, in the words of the film historians Bardeche and Brasillac, that 'here was a man really interested in what he was doing, loving the film as though it were one of the noble arts, and realising that it is, above all, a child of light'. The contribution to Sjöström's films of his cameramen cannot be underestimated: these were usually Henrik or Julius Jaenzen, brothers, who achieved for both him and Stiller images of breathtaking beauty. They photographed night and twilight, sky and landscape, sea and mountain, in a manner which astonishes even today.

Victor Sjöström (1879–1960) was born

Nothing else in early cinema can prepare us for the power of Victor Sjöström's *Terje Vigen*. In the title–role, Sjöström himself (with the white beard) breaks through a blockade, is captured, and returns to find wife and child dead. Years later, a lonely and terrifying old man, he is offered a strange chance for revenge.

65

The Screen's First Master

Sjöström's *The Girl from Stormycroft* is, for a movie of its time, honest about sexual mores. He knew that the choice was not always between a demure Gish–type maiden and a city vamp; the Other Woman is nice and sensible – as is the film's attitude to her, allowing her to confess that she still 'likes' her seducer. Here is Greta Almroth, as the wronged woman, with Lars Hanson, the man who has taken her in.

in Silbodal, a small town in south-west Sweden. He grew up partly in Brooklyn; back in Sweden, at seventeen years of age, he joined a troupe of actors touring Finland, and he mainly toured till Magnusson invited him to join his company, Svenska Biografteatern. His first film he made as an actor, with Stiller directing; and Stiller wrote the screenplay for Sjöström's first film as a director, a film which was banned by the censor and never shown in Sweden. Between 1912 and 1923 he directed forty-five features, of which only thirteen survive.

The earliest survivor is **Ingeborg Holm** (1913), much praised then for its realism or naturalism – interchangeable words in cinema theory and with a common meaning, that of depicting life in reproduction as it is. The source was a play by Nils Krook, evidently so eminent that a photograph of him precedes the story. Sjöström had directed it on the stage, and the leading role is taken by a stage actress, Hilda Borgstrom: but few films of any time, let alone then, are less theatrical. The melodrama of the story is disguised by a style of extreme simplicity, with nothing inessential to be seen, as derived from the Scandinavian literary tradition – which itself evolved from the simplicity of the landscape, with its plains, dense woods and luminous skies. To that landscape belongs this tale of a suffering woman, her children torn from her, descending into madness. Except for the coda – an unconvincing happy ending – the film is far from others on the same theme: the subject of impoverished widowhood, the poorhouse, of children parted from parents, was one then of universality – and that could be one reason why Sjöström tells it without ornament. That vexing movie question of the form for the content might here have had its earliest solution.

Twenty (lost) films intervene between it and **Terje Vigen** (1917), but these two were, at the time, the most highly regarded. The source of this one is a nationalistic epic poem by Ibsen, inspired by a local legend he heard when living in Grimstad, on the south Norwegian coast. Magnusson acquired the film rights for Svenska, and Sjöström decided to make it after a visit to Grimstad. It is set at the time of the Napoleonic Wars, when British ships were blockading that part of the Norwegian coast. It is not a strong plot, but masterly handling does make effective two passages: the pursuit and capture, and Terje's return. The desperation of starvation – the mainspring of the tale, and from his other work the thing we might have expected to most interest Sjöström – is treated in cursory fashion: nor does he, this once, make much of the spirit of the community. But the piece is imbued with the spirit of the sea – omnipresent, a source of wonder and livelihood, of danger and isolation, and a worthy opponent of Terje, played by Sjöström himself and looking the role absolutely.

This was a conscious effort to drag the film into the level of art; so was **The Girl from Stormycroft** (1917), and it was far more successful. The aspirations in this case were due to the fact it was based on a novel by Selma Lagerlöf (the first to be filmed by Svenska Bio), the most admired and acclaimed of living Swedish authors. The girl of the title is Helga (Greta Almroth), who bears a child out of wedlock. Called to court to accuse the

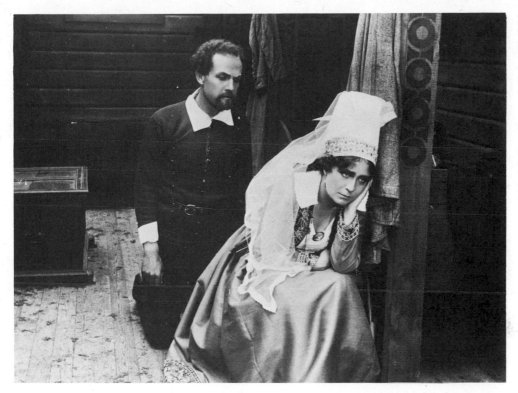

The composition of the pictures on these two pages indicates Sjöström's success in moving away from theatrical grouping and lighting. This is *The Outlaw and his Wife*, his second attempt – after *Terje Vigen* – at an epic. It fulfils all the definitions of that tough genre, while never moving towards the obvious. It is the man this time who is taken in – played by Sjöström himself; the woman is Edith Erastoff, who in life became his third (and enduring) wife.

father, she withdraws her plaint to prevent him perjuring himself, which so impresses Gudmund (Lars Hanson) that he persuades his mother to employ her as a servant, at risk to his relationship with his fiancée (Karen Molander). The plot has a gaping hole at the climax, if minimised by making Gudmund's guilt a fantasy which is his alone. There may well have been sexual attraction between him and Helga, and the point is that both girls are alike – blonde, pretty and of sunny disposition. But if the characterisation is stronger than the plot, it is the scenes from provincial life which make it the best film made up to that time: the wedding guests gossiping and drinking tea; the curious onlookers in the courtroom and the preening local bigwigs; the merry-makers in the tavern and its disapproving *patron*. Sjöström's touch is of the lightest: he merely sketches the families of the three young people, and they come alive.

The similarity with Griffith's *True-Heart Susie* (q.v.) brings that to mind, but there is nothing else like **The Outlaw and his Wife** (1917), though in power

and maturity it dwarfs all other film epics to that time. The public and critical acceptance of *Terje Vigen* caused Sjöström to attempt this tale, and if its actual source is a modern Icelandic play, by Johann Sigurdonsson, its spiritual roots are in the Norse sagas. With that in mind, it is easy to accept some tall moments in the second half, but its strength is in its marvellous portrait of a primitive farming community (if filmed in Sweden rather than Iceland) – and its essential point is the integrity of its wanderer hero. Sjöström himself plays that role, and Edith Erastoff is the widow who employs him, who declares him married to her, and who when his past catches up with him flees with him to the hills. Years later, locked in mutual loathing, she asks him in vain to recall their former happiness – but that may only be found in death, since they have, as they say, worked in the ways of God. 'Love is the only law,' she declares, and 'No man can escape his fate, though he run faster than the wind': these are the film's twin themes, with both the Norse gods and Freudian psychology elbowing into its Christian

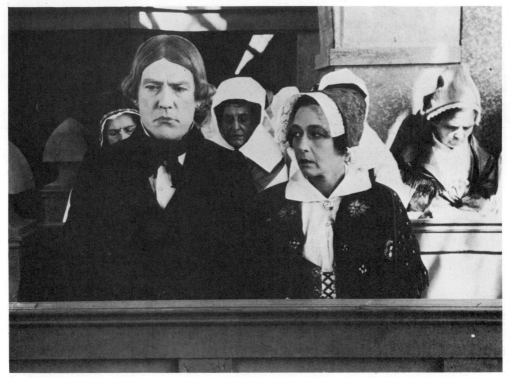

Since so many Silent films have disappeared, it may be rash to claim that *The Ingmarssons* was the greatest made till that time – but there is no better one extant. Sjöström's occasional heaviness requires the adjective 'great' rather than 'brilliant' – after which it may be said that he was as good an actor as he was a director; with him is Harriet Bosse, who had been Strindberg's third wife.

morality. The concept that deprivation can turn a happy couple into an embittered one, while not new, went wholly against the Victorian sentiment permeating all film-making in all countries; only a great film-maker would dare offer it.

As a picture of the past **The Ingmarssons** (1919) is even more valuable: set in a far province of southern Sweden in the nineteenth century, things could hardly have changed there by the time Sjöström went on location to make it. The source is again Lagerlöf – her two-volume novel 'Jerusalem', which provided Magnusson with five films in all: this one, shown originally in two parts; Sjöström's *Karin Ingmarsdotter* (q.v.); and the later *Ingmar's Inheritance* and *To the East,* both directed by Gustav Molander, at this time writer for both Sjöström and Stiller. This description of the novel – by Professor Bergmann of Gothenburg – equally applies to Sjöström's film: 'The first part makes an impressive study of a rural community and the often subtle underplay of the individual and the collective. With its hero, Ingmar Ingmarsson, and his

struggle for moral integrity Selma Lagerlöf has created her most memorable character, at once a rational being subject to impulses he only partly understands.' This is an introspective masterpiece, and very slow – taking almost two-and-a-half hours for what is hardly more than an anecdote. In the first part he (Sjöström) marries Britta (Harriet Bosse), against her will, and finds her dislike turning to hatred, to the extent that she kills their child; in the second, with her release from prison, he tries to solve the dilemma of them both – a tale of two basically decent people who have hurt each other and are, perhaps too late, trying to make amends.

In contrast, both **His Lordship's Last Will** (1919) and **The Monastery of Sendomir** (1920) are minor. The former is a comedy about a crusty old baron and his family, adapted from a novel by Hjalmar Bergman, with whom Sjöström would collaborate further; it is mainly notable for its sketch of life on a provincial estate, and the always entrancing Miss Almroth. The other is of the 'tales told to travellers' breed – and in this case the tale is of seventeenth-century adultery and revenge, as based on a play by Franz Grillparzer, a nineteenth-century Viennese dramatist who wrote a number of historical moralities. Sjöström has clearly tried to create a visual style to compensate for the loss of verse, but it remains primitive melodrama, occasionally enjoyable for its guilty Countess (Tora Teje).

Karin Ingmarsdotter (1920) takes up the story of the Ingmarssons with Ingmar (Sjöström) a widower and his daughter Karin (Miss Teje) sought in marriage by the worthy Halvor (Tor Weiden); because of his own mistake, Ingmar does not attempt to influence her, but she is influenced by the fact that Halvor's father drank and because he himself once succumbed – so that when she later finds herself married to an incorrigible old drunkard it is, as she says, a judgment on her. Although endorsing Lagerlöf's views on the evils of alcohol (a tradition which remains in Swedish society), Sjöström's film is not as harrowing as it sounds, and he plays his concluding scene for humour, spinning it out dangerously, calculating rightly that the audience is both in high good spirits and loath to say farewell to the Ingmarssons. Miss Teje's performance is as remarkable as those of Miss Bosse and himself in the earlier film. This film is less an achievement than that, and certainly less epic, a simple and straightforward account of a disastrous marriage. Its ending is happy, and the Ingmarssons, for all their self-righteousness, surely deserve that.

In **Mästerman** (1920) Sjöström is the gentleman of the title, a Silas Marner-like pawnbroker and the most loathed man in the small fishing port which is its setting; he takes as pawn the young Tora (Miss Almroth), always refusing to believe that her heart will ever belong to her ne'er-do-well fiancé. This performance is a study in depth, physically modelled on Ibsen, with his side-whiskers, stove-hat and voluminous cloak; despite his gruffness, kindness is not unknown to him, as when he relents to take in the budgerigars, and his loneliness is clear when he attempts to stroke the pig grazing with her litter. Like the villagers, we never get close – even physically. Tora has several close-ups, but he none. Sjöström, directing himself, has vast footage but never hogs the camera ; his Mästerman remains an enigma, and that is what makes this film so rewarding. We cannot foresee his actions; unlike other Silent villains he has dimension. He surprises us, and the same is true of Miss Almroth, with her quiet strength, her merriment and her youth, as well as the minor characters. The set-pieces are done with as much love and lack of self-consciousness: business in the pawnshop; the crowds waiting at the quayside for the sailors to dock; the open-air party to welcome them home; the boats crossing the water for Matins on Sunday. Hjalmar Bergman wrote the screenplay, one of the rare originals in Swedish films at the time. Looking then at the Scandinavian cinema, Carl Dreyer wrote in *Dagbladet*: 'It is not possible to mention Swedish film without mentioning Victor Sjöström's name in the same breath . . . he had the courage to go against the current. He was the first in Scandinavia to realise that one cannot *manufacture* films. . . Through Sjöström's work, film was let into art's promised land . . . the Swedish art film has acquired its distinctive character by becoming a medium for true and genuine human representation.'

Despite the melodrama and moralising required, some of these are great films by any standard – *The Ingmarssons*, *Karin Ingmarsdotter*, *The Outlaw and his Wife*, *Mästerman*, and I would add to them *The Wind* (q.v.), his best American film: yet Sjöström was technically uninventive, with moments of cinematic language so few and isolated as to give doubt that he really understood the medium. Sometimes the intertitles are so many and so lengthy as to obscure the action, but it is clear that his motivation was fidelity to the text and spirit of the authors whose work he adapted. It is perhaps by chance that he towers over his contemporaries, since he was allowed to work with better material – yet we have seen what happened to Ibsen in Hollywood, and we shall see what Stiller did with Lagerlöf. Later, Dreyer observed that Sjöström responded the better of the two to that writer, because he was Swedish in thought and mentality – 'Swedish to his very backbone', and he added, significantly in view of Stiller's failure, 'He put into the stylised figures of her novels the warm humanity and feelings of his own heart. Under his hands noble spirit was combined with noble form.' Ingmar Bergman, speaking of another Sjöström version of Lagerlöf, *The Phantom Carriage,* observed 'There are scenes in *Sons of Ingmar* [i.e. *The Ingmarssons*] and *Karin Ingmarsdotter* which with their precision, their genuineness and clarity, still have the same educative impression of being honest artistic products.' Sjöström was honest with his material, honest with himself, and honest with his audience: so perhaps was Griffith, but if his *Broken Blossoms* (q.v.) of this time was supposedly a film peak, we can only shake our heads. Native audiences so responded to *The Ingmarssons* that Magnusson was able to take over his rivals in the industry: he formed Svensk Filmindustri and built new studios at Rasunda. *Mästerman* was the first production made there, and the second of Sjöström's was the first Swedish film to have a large international success – after which things would never be quite the same again.

This was **The Phantom Carriage** (1921), again based on a novel by Lagerlöf, 'Korkarlen' i.e. 'The Driver', though the film has also been known by its British title, *Thy Soul Shall Bear Witness*, and it was originally shown in the U.S. as *At the Stroke of Midnight*. These titles indicate its theme, and Lagerlöf's starting point was a French legend claiming that anyone who meets with a fatal accident on New Year's Eve has to drive the carriage of death for a year. Lagerlöf's predeliction, as Dreyer observed, 'for dreams and supernatural events appealed to Sjöström's somewhat sombre artistic mind'. Contemporaries admired the film for its representation of the supernatural – in double images – and for its complexities, with flashback within flashback to depict the past life of the wastrel David Holm (Sjöström). And the moral then seemed relevant: drink is the root of all evil. In *Karin Ingmarsdotter* drunkenness was a reaction against repression, but here no reason is offered for Holm's descent into self-ruin, and the result is a moral tract, turgid and pretentious; it is a tribute to Sjöström that we take it at all seriously.

With world attention now turned towards the Swedish market, Magnusson, as so many subsequent European entrepreneurs, attempted to make films for the international market. Sjöström was encouraged to film an historical novel by Hjalmar Bergman, *Vem Dömer?* – a film known to us as **Love's Crucible** (1922). The setting is said to be Florence, but the titles do not indicate this – and nor, emphatically, do the settings. After a dull exposition, events come thick and fast, having to do with the eternal triangle, a phial of poison, a sudden heart attack, a miracle – possibly echoed by Ingmar Bergman in *The Touch* (q.v.) – and a trial by fire. The climax is imaginative, but overall it is a poor film. The Swedish title means 'Who judges?', to recall to us that both the Outlaw and his wife and the Ingmarssons preferred the judgment of God to man, but it is not, otherwise, recognisably a Sjöström film.

Its public and critical failure was fast and complete, but Magnusson, not discouraged, engaged two international names (both from Britain) for *The Surrounded House* (1922) and **Hell Ship** (1923), respectively Meggie Albanesi and Matheson Lang. The former, from a French play, with Sjöström in the leading male role, has not survived, breaking the run from *Terje Vigen* to what was to be his last Swedish Silent. Hjalmar Bergman wrote the original screenplay of *Hell Ship,* like all Sjöström's major films a study in obsession – the jealousy of a ship's captain (Lang) towards the former suitor (Sjöström) of his wife (Jenny Hasselqvist). These are protagonists of weight, neither all good and bad, so carefully worked out as to remind us how seldom Sjöström put colour into his female characters (the major exception is Karin Ingmarsdotter); it is also characteristic of him that they should be reconciled at the end. The attention to detail is as vivid as ever, with one outstanding sequence – the loading of the cargo at night, in a storm – but there is here and there a dot of contrivancy, a stroke of sentimentality. An uneasy story-line was not helped by an accident to the ship (it sank), and the need to improvise a new ending. Lang's performance is almost as good as Sjöström's – and very far from the scenery-chewing stints revealed in his British films; but the film moves towards the conventional movies of the period – the movies of Hollywood, Britain or France.

There is no record of Sjöström speaking of compromise, but he had been increasingly unhappy directing films, of which the last three were failures; and Magnusson was more than content to have him go to Hollywood to study film-making. His presence in the U.S. and the success elsewhere of *The Phantom Carriage* brought Hollywood offers, and he signed with the Goldwyn Company, on the point of merging with Metro and Mayer. It has been suggested that Magnusson wanted to distribute the films of the merged companies in Sweden, and used Sjöström as a pawn: certainly he did annul Sjöström's contract and he did handle M-G-M's films.

Sjöström's departure left him with only one film-maker of repute – Mauritz Stiller; and since there is no way of discussing him without reference to Sjöström, we might note the opinion of the director Jorn Donner, 'The film histories generally state that Sjöström was more powerful, if heavy; that Stiller was more elegant, if superficial. Ingmar Bergman puts Sjöström first, partly because of Sjöström's weighty Swedishness.' Stiller (1883–1928) was of Russian-Jewish stock, born in Helsinki, at that time capital of a Russian Grand Duchy. Orphaned at the age of four, he later gravitated towards the theatre, but fled to Sweden – like most Finns, he was bi-lingual – when conscription loomed. For some years he had no more success than in his native country, till a few good notices emboldened him to apply to Magnusson for employment; his enthusiasm for films was such that he was taken on not as actor but as director. He made his first film in 1912, but the first to survive is the thirtieth, **Love and Journalism** (1916), a comedy about a journalist (Karin Molander) who inveigles herself into the home of a famous explorer (Richard Lund) to get copy. Only Stiller's comedies survive from this period, and if far from the rollicking fun of the Sennett two-reelers they are swiftly-paced and notable in their frank approach to sex. Desire runs rampant: nice young men run after nice young girls, as do older men, unless

The Scandinavian cinema's preference for tales of sex found satiric bent in the comedies of Mauritz Stiller, with the lady often taking the initiative. The provocative miss on the left is Karen Molander, in *Thomas Graal's Best Film*.

too aged except to philander with the ladies of the town – while their wives support good works; even nice young wives dream of changing partners. **Alexander the Great** (1917) is a satire on small town morals, centring on an engagement between a penniless lieutenant and a hideous spinster. Her admonition that they must have single rooms brings a look of surprise and delight to his face – a typical Stiller touch. The film, however, is hardly worth seeing: all of Stiller's films are disjointed, and this one suffered further from censorship cuts.

Both **Thomas Graal's Best Film** (1917) and **Thomas Graal's Best Child** (1918) are blessed with the presence of Sjöström, playing a writer, and the witty and pretty Miss Molander. The first is a lighthearted tale about film-making; the sequel tells us what happens when they marry – or, rather, what doesn't happen, since a hasty quarrel precludes consummation. It is often amusing, more so than the similar but better-known **Erotikon** (1920), though it was the latter, Lubitsch said, which helped him form his style, along with the sex comedies of deMille; it can be said that Stiller's characters are somewhat more believable and sophisticated than those of deMille.

The first of his serious films to survive is **Song of the Scarlet Flower** (1918), the first of three film versions of a popular Finnish novel by Johannes Linnankoski – said to be a work of stature, but the film, though it plays well, is merely another melodrama about a headstrong dissolute youth (Lars Hanson) whose wayward experiences help him 'to find himself'. It is not dissimilar to *The Ingmarssons,* but whereas the supreme pleasure in Sjöström is his recreation of time past, Stiller hardly uses the brothels and taverns in which his films abound. Each of his surviving serious films does have one huge set-piece – here the log-rolling sequence, and in **Sir Arne's Treasure** (1919) the dash across the ice. That version of Lagerlöf, a tale of Scottish mercenaries and their plunder, only emphasises his inferiority, being virtually hysterical, clearly less considered than Sjöström's more naturalistic approach. Of his extant films, only **Johan** (1921) offers a valuable portrait of contemporary life – of life in a faraway place where people live off the soil and regard the opening of a canal as a momentous event. Its source is again a Finnish novel, by Juani Aho (who was much influenced by Lagerlöf), and its plain story concerns a wife torn between day-to-day drudgery and the romance offered by a stranger. She revolts against the loveless marriage, to the extent that the advent of the stranger puts her into a mood of sexual tension: having gone away with him, she again revolts, but from guilt. As with Sjöström's people, all options are open to her and her menfolk, and they grow before our eyes, taking on facets as so few characters did in films of this time. Stiller may not say as much as Sjöström, but he uses less intertitles and his cutting is always more imaginative.

After that high point, however, he returned to stark melodrama for his last two Swedish films, both versions of Lagerlöf. **Gunnar Hedes Saga** (1922) is the wan tale of a wealthy scion who goes mad and the waif who loves him, but **Gosta Berling's Saga** (1924) is saga indeed, lasting three hours and based on Lagerlöf's first and most famous book. If the film has several English titles, it seems to have two in Swedish, one that translates as 'The Cavaliers of Ekeby' – and it concerns these cavaliers, living in

The photography of the Jaenzon brothers was as beneficial to the films of Stiller as to those of Sjöström. The highly-lipsticked men and wild-eyed over-emoting that Stiller encouraged do not, however, make for naturalism, though neither factor exactly spoils the highly melodramatic *Sir Arne's Treasure.* Certainly at the time audiences were not bothered.

a remote part of Värmland, and their effect on the community. They are privileged retainers, idle and dissipated, their vices creating chaos till they take stock and return to order. Berling himself (Mr Hanson) is a drunken, unfrocked priest, and if his behaviour is as appalling as theirs, that is the fault of direction and adaptation, ransacking the piece for ersatz excitement. Lagerlöf herself, who loathed the film, commented that Stiller had seen 'too many poor serials'. There is a good fire sequence, a famous chase across the ice, and some scenes of revelry – but since the latter lack period flavour, pleasure in them is muted. Most people know the film from the cut-down versions, but the original – as restored by the Swedish Film Archive – reveals the whole to be no more coherent. The cut copies have, naturally, retained all

the footage of Stiller's discovery, Greta Garbo (b. 1905) – originally a subsidiary character till he grew so enraptured of her that he built up her role, which may also be the reason why she is given to Gosta at the fade-out, a complete distortion of Lagerlöf's ending. Garbo evinces little actual ability, and only once towards the end does she look attractive, as the light plays on her hair. Although she regarded the homosexual Stiller as her mentor, it is uncertain to what extent he moulded the magical figure that emerged at M-G-M, and he never directed her again. When their next project failed, he loaned her to Pabst for *Die Freudlosse Gasse* (q.v.). He insisted that M-G-M take her, when that company signed him to a contract, but as she flourished, he languished; he was removed from several films, and made

Because of the presence of Greta Garbo (seated) *Gosta Berling's Saga* – also known as *The Atonement of Gosta Berling*–remains the most famous early Swedish film. A concoction of domestic drama and gloomy social injustice, mixed with roistering, it was for years a warhorse of the film societies – despite being damply received when it came out.

73

only three American films, all on loan to Paramount. Assigned to direct her in *The Divine Woman,* he was replaced by Sjöström, and these two compatriots were the only two to see him off when he left Hollywood. He died in Stockholm a year later, of a lung ailment. His films have technical virtuosity and occasional sophistication, but are mostly ordinary: the point about Sjöström's is that they are extra–ordinary.

That adjective may be the one to apply to Benjamin Christensen's **Häxan** (1922) or *Witchcraft Through the Ages*, his first film since those two we examined earlier, and in fact made in Sweden under the auspices of Magnusson. It may be the first feature-length non-fiction film, this anticlerical study of necromancy, superstition and related matters, as told in old prints and some fantastical reconstructions, with Christensen himself appearing briefly as a grinning, tempting devil. Readers of Rattray-Taylor's 'Sex in History' would find these fat priests and possessed nuns fairly treated, and if the conclusion is superficial – that doctors have replaced the devils, and mental sickness is a descendent of witchcraft – psychology as a science wasn't that advanced when this film was made. The original had interminable intertitles, but the revised version, with a Sound commentary, is very taking.

Christensen went to Hollywood via Germany, and of these Scandinavians only Carl Dreyer (1889–1968) remained working in Europe – which is maybe why he acquired the most renown. Since his later films are uniformly terrible, it is pleasant to find the early ones so good. He began in films writing intertitles for Nordisk, and progressed via the writing of scenarios to directing. His second film survives, **Leaves from Satan's Book** (1920), an examination in four episodes of the compulsion of Satan to manifest himself as a representation of the State against the individual. It moves from the Passion to sixteenth-century Seville to Revolutionary France to

Helsinki just after the Russian Revolution, and if clearly influenced by *Intolerance* its great superiority is in its point of view, to be expected in a director who looked to Sjöström and Stiller for guidance: Satan's tools turn out to be good but sexually frustrated young men whose ambitions enable them to fulfil their sexual desires. Dreyer's debt to Sjöström is even clearer in **The Parson's Widow** (1920), in fact made in Sweden – for Magnusson – though set in Norway, a rather sweet but gallumphing comedy about the new parson (Einar Röd) and the elderly widow (Hildur Carlberg) he is required by tradition to marry. If Dreyer lacks Sjöström's insight into the tensions of a rural community, his picture of a drunken, lecherous priest is often funny, and there is much tenderness towards the end. **Once Upon a Time** (1922) is considerably less interesting than the German films (q.v.) he made on either side of it, though to judge from the hour-plus which survives it is not notably inferior to the Hollywood fairy-stories of the period. Dreyer's last Danish Silent (there was another in Norway) is **Master of the House** (1925), a study of a tyrannical paterfamilias, carefully and honestly done, but confirming that he was less interested in people than in strips of film – which is fatal to such slight domestic tales. It was a failure everywhere but France, which was why he was invited there to make *La Passion de Jeanne d'Arc* (q.v.).

He did not thenceforward have a lucrative career, and indeed by the beginning of Talkies the Scandinavian cinema was no longer a force in world cinema, and its achievements were already forgotten. Victor Sjöström can now be seen to tower over his contemporaries, holding at perfect balance the epic and the everyday; he had only images in which to express the thoughts, emotions, motivations and ideas of humanity, and he used them with genius. He left a tradition in Swedish cinema which, after a couple of bare decades, brought forth a worthy successor, Ingmar Bergman.

4

Germany in the Twenties:
Shadows, Poverty and Prostitutes

IT IS impossible to overestimate the effect of the post-war German cinema on the intelligentsia of other countries. The Swedish cinema was immediately overshadowed: only four of Sjöström's films were shown in the U.S., and of these *The Phantom Carriage* had to wait till *The New York Times* had lamented its absence from American screens. That journal did not review *Sir Arne's Treasure*, but did, after some weeks, print a eulogy by a lady troubled at its neglect, and described as 'instructor in photoplay composition at Columbia University'. Such films were not thought accessible to the great American public – which had, said D.W. Griffith, 'the mentality of a child nine years old': and it was precisely *not* for that mentality, said *The New York Times,* that Lubitsch was making films. Its critic was reviewing his *Anna Boleyn* (q.v.), and a few months later he expressed the general view in reviewing the 1920 version of *The Golem*, 'the latest motion picture to have come from the explorative innovators of Germany'. Swedish films were too slow for American audiences; later, fear of the propaganda content of Soviet films would prevent their reaching American screens; but Germany always had a hearing – thanks in the first place, to Lubitsch and *Caligari* (q.v.). The Lubitsch spectacles were popular; *Caligari* and the other wrongly-labelled 'expressionist' films were admired out of all proportion to their worth: the Lubitsch films were historical, and the others equally respectable, with their connections to the theatre and modern art movements – and certainly the German film-makers were both exploratory and innovatory. The German cinema thus offered in tandem biographies of historical figures and an enquiry into the nature of film and its possibilities for the fantastic, neither of relevance to a country deep in the grip of inflation – and both traditions were arriving at a dead end as the Soviet cinema exploded, and changed the concept of film. The German cinema reflected that change but slowly, though it eventually, towards the end of the decade, began to record contemporary life with vividness: Berlin of the Twenties, much written about, is also available on film.

In 1912, Berlin theatre managers had formally forbidden their artist to work in films, but the money and acclaim reaped by Asta Nielsen eventually caused the injunction to be ignored. The still-lively Danish and the equally thrusting Swedish cinema provided virtually the only foreign films available during the War, though the home industry had proved at least once able to make a film of serious appeal: *Der Student von Prag* (1913), directed by Paul Wegener, a tale of a young man who trades his soul with the devil, as borrowed from several sources. Wegener himself was a former Reinhardt actor with a strong sense of the fantastic; two years later, he made *Der Golem*, based on Czech-Jewish folklore, but this time owing something – the conception of the monster – to Mary Shelley's 'Frankenstein'. Neither film has survived, but we know them from their remakes: **Der Golem** (1920), made by Wegener and the same collaborator, Henrik Galeen, and **Der Student von Prag** (1926), directed by Galeen alone. In

Paul Wegener's second version of *Der Golem* was one of the first films to establish Germany as a force in the international cinema: one reason was its visual quality, and the photographer was Karl Freund, then at the start of his innovatory career – to end ignominiously in the U.S. as cameraman on 'I Love Lucy' for television.

this *Golem* the demand for magic is met at every occasion, due in part to the photography of Karl Freund: the *Student* is mainly notable for the performance of Conrad Veidt, ever-reliable as a haunted or obsessed creature – and in the title-role he is required to be both as so often in his career.

The first German film-makers came from the theatre, but unlike other early practitioners, they were successful theatre people – which is perhaps why they regarded cinema as an extension of that art form. Pre-eminent among them was Max Reinhardt (1873 – 1943), the dominant figure in German theatre, and though he directed only four films during this period his work in both mediums was the major influence for a number of years. Since he was renowned for his mounting of spectacles, the idea that the theatre was an arena for social realism was a long time catching on, at least south of the Baltic, and there was no urgency in applying it to films; but if the theatre was for drama and spectacle, well, that could best be expounded in films as fantasy – which

anyway seemed more suitable for an audience increasingly unhappy with reality. During the War the German government wanted the cinema for a third purpose: the effect of anti-German propaganda films made by the Allies had not been lost on the Kaiser's ministers, who in 1917 encouraged and part-capitalised the amalgamation of the leading companies as Universum-Film-Aktiengesellschaft, but known familiarly as Ufa. Thus this unexpected combination of official endorsement and intellectual responsibility created a cinema of competing interests, but they miraculously crossbred and coalesced – fantasy, realism and propaganda – to form a national school as strong and individual as that of Sweden.

The American cinema with its dramas of the West had created a 'national' image, but beyond a certain brash optimism, most of its product could have originated in London or Paris. For the first time in the history of the world, a popular 'literature' knew no boundaries – as the first film-makers had discovered; and for economic reasons their successors preferred to work with the international market in mind. Where there were fewer expectations of this market, as in Sweden and Germany, their films were more characteristic of their origin, and thus more highly valued – then and now. They reflected the native drama and literature, past and present; Faustian themes recur, and other echoes of the neo-Gothic, including the dichotomy of fate and chance; and a conception of the little man as a cog in the machinery of state. There was also the obsession with uniforms and/or authority, with policemen and/or cavalry officers as protectors of established order; in defeat, the government lost interest in propaganda, but the creative film-maker seized the chance to instruct and sway public opinion – and in the bewildering, changing political climate any reminder of authority was more welcome than ever. All these elements are to be found in the early films of Ernst Lubitsch, the most brilliant of the German directors, and the first to demonstrate to the world the vitality of his country's films. However, since his aim was to amuse and satirise, he cannot be said to be typical; but like his colleagues, he used at first frankly theatrical settings while exploring the plastic resources of the medium. By the time he went out into the streets and fields to shoot, he had conceived his film as an artistic entity, its visual quality balanced against the narrative. As basically theatre-people, the possibilities of decor absorbed this generation of German film-makers, and, filtered through such designs, the expressionist painters and their themes provided another influence. The themes of Dix, Schlichter, Beckmann, Grosz, Hubbuch, etc., had found their way into films before the reaction against expressionism – that movement called the *neue sachlichkeit* or the new realism; but it was the taste for theatrical excess which led to the Oriental subjects and the historical dramas. Those were the films which established the supremacy of the German 'art' film, regarded by contemporaries with far more awe and respect than the pure cinema of Sjöström or pieces like *Assunta Spina*. Art, history, literature: any film with a smattering of these – the more theatrically presented the better – could command attention, and it wasn't till the Russians worked exclusively within film that the intelligentsia 'saw' differently.

Ernst Lubitsch (1892–1947) had also worked for Reinhardt as an actor. Born in Berlin, he made a mild mark in films as a comic Jew – and if we find his beaked-nose craftiness unsympathetic, we must admit that that was the way Jewish actors edged into films and theatre at that time. His first two films to survive are both features, **Der Stolz der Firma** (1914), directed by Carl Wilhelm, and **Schuhpalast Pinkus** (1916), directed by himself, and they have virtually identical stories: in both by sheer *chutzpah* he rises from the most humble position in the store to the chief one, marrying respectively the boss's daughter and his benefactress. The former has a notable finale in which the Lubitsch of the first reel meets the Lubitsch of the last, underlining the differences in conduct and appearance and hence the advancement it is possible for a Jew to make; the second has what may be the first example of 'the Lubitsch touch', by which a narrative point is made both visually and wittily – in this case an idle

staff indicating the Lubitsch-character's (temporary) lack of success. He continued to play this character till 1919, admitting that it was its lack of success with the public which caused him to think of himself as solely a director. For the moment it was as comedy director: both **Ein Fideles Gefängnis** (1917) and **Wenn Vier Dasselbe Tun** (1917) are foreshadowings of the work for which he is remembered – witty examinations of the war between the sexes. The first of these is an adaptation of 'Réveillon', which he would film again as *So This is Paris?* (q.v.), with some of the same elaborate sight gags; *Wenn Vier Dasselbe Tun* concerns parallel romances between Ossi Oswalda – a rubber-jointed young lady who worked in many of his films – and a young poet, and between her father (Emil Jannings) and the poet's spinster boss. But Lubitsch's boss at Ufa, Paul Davidson, wanted him to try drama, and assigned him to **Die Augen der Mummie Mâ** (1918), to star Pola Negri (b. 1894), who had appeared with Lubitsch in Reinhardt's pantomime-ballet, *Sumurun*. Her forte was exotic dancing, and thus she played a temple dancer taken to Europe by a painter (Harry Liedtke), and pursued there by a vengeful priest (Jannings). According to Hans Kräly, its scenarist (and Lubitsch's chief collaborator from 1916 to the end of the Silent period), it was the first film drama taken seriously by the German press; but to us it is merely another daft melodrama, except for its glimpses of the salons and galleries of the era. It was another drama, **Carmen** (1918), which made the reputations of Lubitsch and Pola Negri throughout Europe, and though we may just see why contemporaries admired her Carmen ('wild, amoral, capricious, savage, brazenly independent, impulsive, cruel and passionate', said Theodore Huff, which is at least three adjectives too many), it is impossible to find the lightness of Lubitsch's other films of this time.

The first sustained, full-length demonstration of his skill is **Die Austernprinzessin** (1919), the tale of an American tycoon's daughter (Miss Oswalda) who determines to marry a prince and finds through a marriage agency a particularly bankrupt one (Liedtke). Lubitsch aims many a shaft at capitalists and royalty, and is particularly bright (as he would ever be) on court ritual; he is also funny but very much in favour of such matters as sexual attraction and nights on the town. **Die Puppe** (1919) is a companion burlesque, about a puppeteer's mischievous daughter (Oswalda) who impersonates one of her father's life-size dolls in order to marry a baron's nephew (Hermann Thimig). The theme is from Hoffmann, and its treatment heavy, but the humour is much less Germanic than the more acceptable **Ich Möchte Kein Mann Sein** (1919; released 1921), a farce about transvestism – and one which probably explores the subject more than any film hitherto. The spectacle of the tuxedoed heroine (Oswalda) being sick on a cigar or kissed by her guardian (Victor Janson) cannot amuse audiences as they once did, but the whole has an urbanity that we recognise by now as typically Lubitsch. Conversely, **Romeo und Julia im Schnee** (1920) and **Kolhiesels Töchter** (1920) are both bucolic romps, heavily dependent on their observation of (Bavarian) village mores and manners. Both themes are from Shakespeare, inasmuch as *Kolhiesels Töchter* is a part reworking of 'The Taming of the Shrew'. The success of that, however, is due almost entirely to Henny Porten in the dual role of the pretty sister and her plain, shrewish one – she was in the remake of 1930, and there was another in 1943, suggesting an abiding German amusement in ox-like farmhands, village idiots and their assorted frauleins. These still-delightful films were considered too parochial for foreign audiences, but then so was **Die Bergkatze** (1921), Lubitsch's one German masterpiece. It was also an anti-militarist satire, and the Germans were not in the mood for that, at least as it applied to them – which Lubitsch sensed, and therefore had Ernest Stern from the theatre design expressionist sets which beautifully mingled with snowy locations. But the film nevertheless was a failure. A robber's daughter (Negri) falls in love with a vain and dilettante lieutenant (Paul Heidemann), and vows to steal him from the fort and from under the eyes of the pompous commander (Victor Janson) who plans

to marry him to his daughter. The cavorting of the robbers has some funny knockabout, but is as nothing to the sharp portrait of the regimented ritual of the fort; and there is a marvellous example of the Lubitsch touch, inevitably with a door, when the daughter looks through the keyhole at the unclad lieutenant, and is pushed away by her mother, neither of them anxious to let the vision go. Alone, this film puts paid to any suggestion that Lubitsch was later bowled over by *A Woman of Paris* (q.v.) – responsibility for which rests with Herman G. Weinberg, who in his book on Lubitsch quotes Chaplin as claiming his 'was the first film to articulate irony and psychology'; Weinberg himself finds the remark only 'partly true', citing in exchange *Die Bergkatze, Die Austernprinzessin* and *Die Flamme* – which suggests that he hasn't seen any of them for years. Lubitsch's two extant films have far more irony and psychology than Chaplin's, and we may suppose as much of *Die Flamme* (1922), from the fifteen-minute fragment which remains. As a study of a marriage – in a Montmartre 'artistic' milieu – it would seem to be comparable to the films of Sjöström and Stiller which inspired it, and hence with irony and psychology much in advance of Chaplin's.

Certainly contemporary critics found these qualities in the historical films which were making Lubitsch very famous indeed. The European success of **Madame Dubarry** (1919) persuaded First National to buy it – for $40,000. Rechristened *Passion*, its origin hidden under the banner 'A European Spectacle', and the names of all concerned suppressed except that of Miss Negri, 'the famous continental star', it took the U.S. by storm, temporarily breaking the Hollywood dominance. 'One of the preeminent motion pictures of the present cinematograph age,' said *The New York Times*, also impressed by the way the Dubarry's 'simply sordid' affairs were 'weaved' into the setting, and by the handling of the Revolution, 'never so vividly portrayed'. The characterisations, if rudimentary, remain amusing: a Dubarry who wants to have her cake and eat it – the lot of all royal mistresses in cinema, always good-natured and guileless (which the original in this case was not); a Louis XV (Jannings) of fish-like complacency, which is as good a way as any of summarising the Bourbons; and a villain, Choiseul (Reinhold Schunzel), who happily recalls Tito Gobbi's Scarpia. It was the lighthearted treatment of these characters which so excited admiration, and we may think it civilised of the Germans in 1919 to take this view of their recent enemy: it was liked by Alfred Hugenberg not only because his huge investment in Ufa paid dividends, but because he was a fervent nationalist. So, since he considered it anti-French, he suggested an anti-English movie, also about the loves of a monarch: **Anna Boleyn** (1920), with Fraulein Porten in the title-role and Jannings as Heinrich VIII. It is at its best and worst with wholly invented matters: at its worst with Princess Maria publicly insulting Anna at her Coronation, and at its best when Heinrich disappears into the bushes with Anna to look for a tennis-ball. That's the Lubitsch touch for you, and surely the reason *The New York Times* wondered, 'Did he ever work in Paris or Vienna?' Today, there is virtually nothing to hold a modern audience, though it does have a point or two to make on the caprices of kings, and the viciousness of court life.

It has, however, more to it than has **Sumurun** (1920), Reinhardt's old (1908) Arabian Nights show, filmed by Lubitsch with visual elegance and very little else. We may wonder what audiences saw in all these Oriental junketings; this one did at least provide a vehicle for Negri, and a plum role for Lubitsch (his last acting job) as the hunchback clown in love with her. There was also for him, perhaps, the sense of competition, since Hollywood had already recently offered several similar films. With **Das Weib des Pharao** (1921) we had a scenario by Norbert Falk and Kräly that plunders from 'The Iliad' – though the setting is Egypt, with again a certain amount of borrowing (the crowd and battle scenes) from *Intolerance*. Jannings is the Pharaoh, and as with his other monarchs for Lubitsch he is a complete despot but not a complete tyrant, perhaps to be redeemed by love for the slave-girl

(Dagy Servaes). The film was in its time overwhelming; the only version now available is a reconstructed one, with some sequences curtailed or missing – yet it is much more impressive than any other primitive spectacle, including Lang's *Nibelungen* (q.v.).

Since the American press had freely referred to Lubitsch as a genius, it was only a matter of time before he went to Hollywood; meanwhile, his erstwhile colleagues laboured on in the historical literary field. Chief among them, in that respect, was the Russian-Polish Dimitri Buchowetzki, whose **Danton** (1921) and **Othello** (1922) were particularly admired: both simplify to a degree of absurdity, both use grandiose settings as if to reduce their characters to puppets, and both use a number of imaginative camera angles. They are notable for the acting partnership of Jannings, in the title-roles, and Werner Krauss, as Robespierre and Iago respectively. Jannings, inclined to give his all, is seldom effective in sympathetic or heroic roles – but since he could be seen to be acting, with 'weight' and with a number of disguises, he was the Twenties' idea of a great actor. Krauss managed make-up with genius, even suggesting changes in his flat moon-face via small twists in eye-brows, lashes and side-hair; he disappeared inside his characterisations,

The fame of Lubitsch's historical spectacles far overshadowed his other German films, a series of still-sparkling comedies. *Die Bergkatze* handled sex in that visually witty way which became known as 'The Lubitsch touch'; but its chief aim was to poke fun at the military, which it does with a mixture of wild slapstick and razor-sharp satire.

79

never chancing a bravura note. He was a consummate film actor, one of the wonders of the German Silent cinema – and his single-expressioned, single-minded villains are the best features of these two films.

Another Shakespeare, **Hamlet** (1920), remains one of the best known of this series, partly because Asta Nielsen plays the title-role. You didn't know Hamlet was a girl? There is more than that here to startle scholars, but to be fair the sources also include Danish legends and a German play, 'Fratricide Unpunished': for reasons of state the heiress to the throne has been brought up a boy, and she has conceived a hopeless passion for Horatio. Dying, she gets that longed-for kiss from him, as his wandering hand encounters a breast: 'Death reveals thy tragic secret,' he says. Sven Gade and Heinz Schall directed, for Miss Nielsen's own company. She is more interestingly employed in **Vanina** (1922), as the governor's daughter who plots against her father for the sake of her rebel-lover. As the governor, Paul Wegener goes beyond cruelty to sadism, and this doom-laden tale is also helped immeasurably by Walter Reimann's huge, dark craggy sets; the last, long, futile escape from the prison is one of the finest sequences from this era, as directed by Arthur von Gerlach and written – from Stendhal's novel – by Carl Mayer (1894–1944), the most imaginative of the German scenarists.

The literary and historical genres – never far apart – come together in **Carlos und Elizabeth** (1924), a version of Schiller directed by Richard Oswald with Conrad Veidt as an ambiguous but reasonably healthy Don Carlos. His quarrels with his father (Eugen Klöpfer) are set against huge flats, ornate only in detail, but Oswald otherwise worked in the *kammerspiel* tradition, usually reserved for emotional tales of the lowly.

Richard Oswald (1880–1963) was an eclectic film-maker. Born in Vienna and a former actor, his first films include a *Hoffmanns Erzählungen* (1916) and *Es Werde Licht* (1917), a study of syphilis, which achieved respectability by being sponsored by the official society organised to combat such illness. Venereal disease was a preoccupation of the War government, and Oswald was encouraged to add a second and third part to *Es Wirde Licht*; when the post-war government abolished censorship he added a fourth part. The German film industry accelerated its output on sexual matters, and Oswald made *Die Prostitution* (1919) and what was probably the first film on homosexuality, **Anders Als die Andern** (1919). The theme of the latter is spelt out in detail: unless Paragraph 175 of the Penal Code is repealed, there will be more suicides like that of the famous violinist (Conrad Veidt). It is a simple film: the acting is elementary and the set-ups obvious and few; homosexuality is denoted by a caress on the cheek, a hand on the hip, by men doing the two-step at a *thé-dansant*; and the story tells briefly of a chance-meeting at one such, the subsequent blackmail and hence ruin both of career and friendship with a student. The film was unpopular; today it strikes us as unremarkable, sympathetic, and a good deal more forthright than more recent films on this subject. The realities of life in the Weimar Republic may also be found in **Der Reigen** (1920), based on a play by Schnitzler that we know best as *La Ronde* (q.v.) – though you wouldn't recognise it from this version. Asta Nielsen has her familiar role, a girl wronged by society: up the ladder and down again, waifdom to kept woman, to mistress of the mansion, to prostitution, singularly unlucky in the men she meets (they include Herr Veidt), but when she pleads with the one man she loves to take her away, it is clear that she is a woman of her time, completely dependent on men. Without money, references or a man to support her she has only one way to support herself: that other alternatives do not immediately occur to the viewer is a measure of Oswald's persuasive handling. His Silents also include *Lady Hamilton* (1921), *Lucrezia Borgia* (1922), *Cagliostro* (1928), and a version of Wedekind's *Fruhlings Erwachen*; his Sound films, coincidentally, are mainly remakes: *Alraune* (1930), *Unheimliche Geschichten* (q.v.), a version of his 1919 horror story; *Tempête sur l'Asie* (1938), in France; and *I was a Criminal* (1942) in the U.S. as well as a version of Zuckmayer's *Der Haupt-*

mann von Köpenick (1931), which he made before fleeing the Nazis.

The Danish Carl Dreyer also attempted a film on homosexuality, **Michael** (1924) – though unlike Oswald's film, the word is never mentioned and we are left to guess the exact relationship of the painter (Benjamin Christensen) and his adopted son (Walter Slezak). The taste of the time may have dictated discretion, but the combination of subtlety and ambiguity, conscious or not, puts the film far ahead of its time, not least at the end, when the unexplained absence of protégé from the painter's deathbed is followed by an image of Woman as predator. The original novel was by Herman Bang, who was homosexual; and a knowledge of Berlin's artistic circles was clearly being utilised by the production team – Dreyer and Thea von Harbou (writers), Karl Freund (photographer) and Erich Pommer (producer). The stimulus of his co-workers must have contributed to Dreyer's making in Berlin by far his two best films – both made with an untypical passion, and committed to tolerance of minorities. **Die Geseichneten** (1922) means approximately 'The Marked Ones' and it refers to the Jews; it is taken from a long novel by Aage Madelung, and was filmed in Germany both because resources were not available in Denmark, and there was in Berlin a large number of Russian émigrés, many of whom play leading roles. By Dreyer's own admission the novel was too long, and the compression is inadequate: but like *Leaves from Satan's Book*, it also has ideas. It offers brief portraits of ghetto life and life in St Petersburg, and we learn much of motivation: snobbery, prejudice, envy, superstition – none of them well expressed, but comprising a wider spectrum than love, hatred and

Those who know Carl Dreyer only from his later work may be surprised at the excellence of his early films, including *Michael*, the study of a homosexual artist and his protégé. The artistic milieu of Berlin is such a strong feature of many German films of the early Twenties that we may suppose it a strong influence on them – as well as being the opposite, as here, of the accepted Bohemian conception.

81

Germany in the Twenties: Shadows, Poverty and Prostitutes

The coming to power of the Nazi party swept away most of the fine directors who were not already in Hollywood. Their fates would be various, and that of E. A. Dupont one of the saddest, to judge from the occasional poverty–row 'B' flicks he directed in the Fifties; in between-whiles he had owned a magazine and an actors' agency. He is remembered best for *Varieté*, but *Das Alte Gesetz* is altogether the more remarkable – a sensitive dual study of Jewish and theatrical life in the last century.

lust, the then-staples of movies. Both of Dreyer's films, like those of Oswald's, try for a whole range of human emotions set against a recognisable society.

As much may be said of **Das Alte Gesetz** (1923), directed by E. A. Dupont (1891–1956), a former film critic who entered films as a writer for Oswald, circa 1916. He directed his first film a year later, and though most of them are missing, this one – regardless of the later ones – establishes him as a master. It takes one Baruch (Ernst Deutsch) from the Vienna ghetto of the 1860s to supremacy as an actor, and whether dealing with Jewish life or life backstage, Dupont's evocation of the past is on a par with Sjöström's. It behoves me to say that films so bound to an ethnic cause did, eventually, prove dangerous. Did the Jews of the German film industry flaunt their Jewishness? At all events this portrait of what it was like for their parents' generation is an extremely valuable one.

Needless to say, it achieved nothing of the renown of a piece of theatrical arty-crafty called **Das Kabinett des Doktor Caligari** (1920), and, indeed, that is for many people *the* film classic. It was, says Lewis Jacobs, 'seen by comparatively few people, [but] it was nevertheless the most widely discussed

film of the time'. For a reviewer in *Exceptional Photoplays* it was 'a revelation and a challenge . . . a revelation of what the motion picture is capable of as a form of artistic expression. It challenges the public to appreciate it and the producer to learn from it.' Its producer, Eric Pommer (1889–1966), later said that he snapped up the scenario because mystery stories were popular, but its writers said they took it to him because he was a producer more adventurous than most. They were Carl Mayer, an Austrian, and Hans Janowitz, a Czech, who had based their scenario on a bizarre Hamburg murder case; to direct it Pommer brought from the theatre a man without film experience, Robert Wiene, and he gave the art direction to his own team, Walter Röhrig, Herman Warm and Walter Reimann. They used abstract sets as a matter of expediency, since there were government restrictions on power and lighting – but their distinctive style was not what the writers had had in mind.

The theatre was already tinkering with Expressionism, and thus, because of its sets, *Caligari* was linked both to culture and to the avant-garde. Within the film there is a cut-out of the somnambulist-villain which looks less like him than like Munch's painting *The Cry*: as Expressionism was a statement on emotional darkness, so was this film. It is, indeed, 'about' madness – and it arrived at a time when Freud's studies in psychology were required reading for the intelligentsia – but it is not Expressionist at all: it is Surrealist, and then only at an elementary level. Sets in the *manner* of the Expressionists cannot change the subject-matter, and perhaps only an animated cartoon could create a truly Expressionist film, i.e. one whose method of telling leads directly to its meaning, its central emotion. These sets and make-up reek disconcertingly of the theatre, and are not sufficiently imaginative to provide a lingering atmospheric charm. At its best, we are in the world of Poe – though we may feel we're watching a bad production of 'Petrushka' when Dr Caligari (Krauss) invites the crowd to watch the re-awakening of a dead man (Conrad Veidt, with black-ringed eyes and baggy black tights). The succeeding Grand Guignol events include pursuit into a madhouse, whose chief turns out to be Caligari, plus a final revelation that the whole thing is a tale told by idiots. The film is genuinely a Chinese cabinet, and it is easy to see why it was so much admired: but it was a one-of-a-kind thing, since there would only be one film which turned out to be the ravings of a madman – though there have been many films which turned out to be dreams.

That other ways than painted sets were needed to take us into private worlds was apparently proved by Wiene's *Genuine* (1920), an immediate failure. Despite their reservations about the *Caligari* sets, Mayer and Janowitz had provided the story, about a bloodthirsty vamp who drives men to ruin. Andrei Andreyev designed the sets for **Raskolnikov** (1923), and they are not inappropriate to the guilt-haunted fantasies of Dostoevsky's hero, though the film as a whole is dusty. In Vienna, still involved with horror, Wiene made **Orlacs Hande** (1924), based on a novel by Maurice Renard about a pianist (Veidt) who wakes after an accident to find that the donor of his hands-transplant was a convicted murderer, and suffers consequent twitchings whenever he holds a knife. This promising idea is indifferently handled, with a disappointed denouement as Orlac's behaviour becomes increasingly imbecilic; and as Fritz Kortner's acting is as absurd as Veidt's we may blame the director, a good example of the 'one-film' man.

The success of *Caligari* spawned a hundred imitations – that is films with weird, painted sets. Mayer wrote **Torgus** (1921), directed by Hanns Kobe, a sad tale of a weak young man who allows his aunt (Adele Sandrock) to separate him from his true love, the mother of his baby: the Icelandic setting and the Golem-like presence of the coffin-maker Torgus (Klöpfer) help the mood of gloom, but the sets neither add nor detract from the story. In fact, the public tired so quickly of expressionism that many of these films were not released, and until recently **Von Morgens bis Mitternacht** (1920) was seen only in Japan: from one point of view, it is the most important of the series – more important than *Caligari*, since both its writer and director were established expressionists before that film was even thought of. Indeed, Georg Kaiser was considered the foremost expressionist dramatist, and as a play this had been done in 1918; the film's director and co-scenarist was Karl-Heinz Martin. Like *Caligari*, it is depressingly determined to be art: there are unreal sets, a complete absence of intertitles, and all the female roles are played by the same actress, Roma Bahn. The original was worth telling in straightforward manner – a portrait of a man (Ernst Deutsch) at the end of his tether. His symbols are those of the graphic artists – champagne-bottle, lamplight, whore, lurking death – and his odyssey from embezzlement and flight to the maelstrom of the night-city would be echoed by every other German film to the end of the Weimar Republic.

Meanwhile, the industry continued to deal with the grotesque and fantastic, and since the current mood for escapism was of pessimistic turn a number of interesting talents were attracted. Fritz Lang made **Der Müde Tod** (1921) – ennobled into *Destiny* in its English version, and in fact the struggle against destiny would be a recurring theme in his work. This primitive, operatic work concerns a woman (Lil Dagover) who consults Death when her lover (Walter Janssen) disappears, and is offered him back if she can prevent three deaths – in old Baghdad, Renaissance Venice and Ancient China. The film is enhanced by a compendium of camera tricks (Douglas Fairbanks bought the rights, in order to use them in *The Thief of Bagdad*, q.v.); and F.W. Murnau offered several in **Nosferatu, Eine Symphonie des Grauens** (1922). Some of Fritz Arno Wagner's images still startle, and the fearsome Count (Max Schreck) follows the tradition already set for movie monsters, grotesque-pathetic; but overall this tale of demonic possession – it is a pirated version by Henrik Galeen of Bram Stoker's 'Dracula' – remains powerful.

Wagner also photographed Arthur Robison's **Schatten** (1923), an attempt to tell a psychological tale entirely in terms of shadows, reflections, lights, silhouettes and what-have-you. The story concerns a jealous husband (Kortner), his wife's admirers, and the mesmerist (Alexander Granach) who makes them act out their thoughts: amidst ponderous direction and absurd acting it arrives at a banal ending. Its supernatural reasoning is entirely in keeping with others of its kind, and, like them, it is set in the past: this may be because the mesmerist is culled from the tales of E. T. A. Hoffman, but confirms an obsession with the neo-Gothic.

To Siegfried Kracauer, in 'From Caligari to Hitler', it was 'this extraordinary drama', but then to him one of 'the greatest achievements of film art' was the final sequence of **Das Wachsenfigurenkabinett** (1924). This film of Paul Leni (1885–1929) is in three parts, as dreamed up by a poet (Wilhelm Dieterle) in a carnival waxworks. The first is a lumbering comic anecdote about a lecherous Haroun al-Raschid (Jannings) and a baker's wife; the second is a sinister, inconclusive yarn involving Ivan the Terrible (Veidt) and a young bride; and the third a bit of brimstone about Jack the Ripper (Krauss). Money had run out by the time they reached the Ripper, and Leni, a former designer, abandoned Galeen's script to improvise – with superimpositions, multiple images, shadows and back-lighting. It is still effective, and proof of Leni's talent for the medium: but hardly worth enduring the rest of it for.

Leni's film, along with some of these other grotesqueries – *Caligari*, *Der Müde Tod*, *Nosferatu* and *Schatten* (rechristened *Warning Shadows*) – helped establish the artistic supremacy of the German cinema among foreign cineastes. *Nosferatu* is the only one amongst them to use wholly natural settings, and is indeed the least tainted by the shadow of the theatre. F. W. Murnau (1889–1931) was an alumnus of Reinhardt, but from the evidence of his few surviving early films he was immediately aware of the cinematic possibilities of his medium; among contemporary German critics, he was more widely regarded than any of his colleagues, and often called a poet. His inspiration was avowedly the cinema of Sjöström and Stiller, as we may see from his seventh film, and the first to survive, **Der Gang in die Nacht** (1920). Carl Mayer wrote it, from a treatment by Harriet Bloch, a popular writer of the Danish cinema, and it concerns an eminent doctor (Olaf Fonss) who abandons his fiancée for a dancer, only to lose the latter to a blind painter (Conrad Veidt) after he has retired to a seaside village. The plethora of shots of the sea suggest the Scandinavian models, and Willy Haas, the critic of the *Film Kurier*, observed that the film reminded him of Ibsen; Haas also paid Murnau the great compliment of observing that he was unable to see where the director took over from the writer. Haas helped write **Der Brennende Acker** (1922) for Murnau, made after an indifferent thriller, *Schloss Vogelöd* (1921), and here again the Scandinavian influence is very strong. The protagonist is a proud, ambitious man (Wladimir Gaidarow), who becomes secretary to a Count and moves his affections from the Count's daughter (Lya de Putti) to his young, second wife (Stella Arbenina) when he realises that the latter will inherit the greater fortune, a field under which lies a huge petrol reserve. The film begins dully, but becomes involving as the young man's machinations become clearer: as in Sjöström, however, motives may remain a matter of conjecture.

Unanimous praise greeted this film, but the much superior **Phantom** (1922) was not liked: based on a novel by Gerhard Hauptmann, it was released to coincide with his sixtieth birthday celebrations and was generally considered superficial. To an extent it is just another Silent melodrama, with over-gesticulated acting and a plot founded on impossible situations. The hero (Alfred Abel) is, like so many in German films at the time, haunted and buffeted by fate: yet in the midst of clichés and conventions is a quite remarkable film. Murnau is no longer under the influence of Sjöström, and though he lacks the latter's penetration, he is far more imaginative. Lorenz is taken by a dual fancy, of becoming a famous poet and marrying a wealthy girl in the town: obsessed by her, he meets her double (Lya de Putti), daughter of an impoverished Baroness, and in paying suit to her he is financed by his aunt (Grete Berger). The interesting characters are this aunt, and her fancy-man (Anton Edthofer) – and it is he who manipulates Lorenz, leading him to his doom – and the little town itself, with its cabarets and wide squares. Murnau's use of figures in his settings is more advanced than any of his contemporaries, and his fantasies – notably when Lorenz dreams of his beloved or imagines that the town is literally falling on him – remain extraordinary.

Die Finanzen des Grossherzogs (1923) pleased contemporary German critics as being one of the few domestic films without pretensions to signficance, but Murnau himself disliked it, and we would certainly side with him. Photographed along the Dalmatian coast, it tells of a penniless Grande Duke (Harry Liedtke), the moneylender who helps to overthrow him and the Russian Grand Duchess (Mady Christians) who elects to marry him. It is clear that Murnau intended burlesque, and the piece indicates an extension of his talent: but it is no preparation for the film which made his international reputation, **Der Letzte Mann** (1924). It also made the reputation of Mayer, who wrote this story of a hotel porter (Jannings) stripped of his livery and demoted to lavatory attendant – a fact that he manages to keep from the neighbours – until rehabilitated by a wealthy American who has used the facilities: an epilogue which has been disowned by certain admirers and improbably explained away as a satire on happy endings. The critical réclame was due to the absence (again!) of intertitles, but its chief achievement is Murnau's virtuoso balancing of three rare enough elements – the authoritative (if monotonous)) performance of Jannings, and, more importantly, the probing cinematography of Karl Freund and Mayer's simple scenario. As a team, they seemed unmoved by the film's reception the world over, since **Tartüff** (1925) breaks new ground neither in subject-matter nor style – unless we include setting Molière's play (or what is left of it, since most of the characters have gone) as a film within a film. The framework – a disinherited heir shows his grandfather a film to point out the hypocrisy of his housekeeper – is dark, harsh, realistic; the 'flashback' is light and fanciful, with visual effects such as the extinguishing of the wasteful candles and the repeated image of the bulky but thin-legged Tartuffe with

a book to his nose. In that role Jannings comes close to genius, never venturing beyond the pious and haughty till transformed into a grinning drunken lecher, when he's very funny. As Orgon, Krauss has little to do but look fond and/or credulous. Contemporary reception centred on these two performances, but since *Der Letzte Mann* had made Murnau one of the world's most eagerly watched film-makers, he planned and came up with **Faust** (1926). The opening and the first thirty minutes are the most triumphantly visual of all Silent movies, as the forces of light and darkness argue and look down on our earth. Later it moves to, shall we say, the level of Gounod. In Germany it was unappreciated; the country at that point was not interested in 'Faustian problems' says Kracauer, dismissing it as 'another Ufa superproduction': but abroad its magic was recognised.

Dupont's **Variété** (1925) was also photographed by Freund, and also based on a simple premise: a small-time trapeze artist (Jannings) is stung to revenge when he discovers that his wife (Lya de Putti) is unfaithful with the star (Warwick Ward) they have taken into partnership. Dupont had embraced the *neue sachlichkeit*, and the film is flawlessly done, from the razzmatazz of the music hall milieu

85

to the details of the couple's squalid little room; and he used these with the appurtenances of the expressionists – the superimpositions, the camera-angles, the lighting. The combination was a winning one for foreign audiences; retitled *Vaudeville* its success abroad eclipsed even that of *Madame Dubarry*.

Faust was of such prestige that it was initially shown in Britain at the Royal Albert Hall, 'presented' by C. B. Cochran and 'edited and titled' by Arnold Bennett. During the same season, Pommer's first American film was shown – and the ads for *Hotel Imperial* (q.v.) featured his name in equal size to that of the star, adding, 'Germany's greatest film genius of *Vaudeville* fame'. As the fame of these films echoed round the world, their makers followed – as far as Hollywood. Lubitsch had been there for some years: Murnau went, and Dupont, Freund and Pommer, as well as Jannings, Negri and Veidt. It has been claimed that Pommer was the great force behind this burst of creativity, which may be true; but there was also much inter-stimulation and discovery between a group of people who cared for the medium; there was 'something in the air' (as George Cukor said of Hollywood at the time of *Citizen Kane*), and certainly it did not die with the defection of the leading artists. Pommer's sojourn in Hollywood was brief, and he returned to produce some more notable films for Ufa – but not again to any degree either influential and seminal; and if his were the creative juices which fed this period, they were drying up by the early Thirties. The most immediately influential was Freund, and the distinctive Ufa-style lighting was a commonplace in movies for at least ten years.

Ufa itself was in a bad way. Its films may have achieved international fame, but many – *Der Letzte Mann* and certainly *Metropolis* (q.v.) – lost a great deal of money. In 1925 the company approached Hollywood for support, and Zukor of Paramount and Marcus Loew both loaned $2 millions. Ironically, the American companies were at the root of the trouble, since with the re-establishment of the gold standard they had opened distribution offices and cinemas in Germany, swamping local competition: to counteract this, and to stem the flow of money from leaving the country, the quota system was introduced, similar to those to operate later – for the same reasons – in Britain and France. Fox used the situation to establish Fox-Europa, using blocked capital to make quota films, but Paramount and Loews were smarter – from their point of view: the Parufamet agreement (so named from the three companies) gave them the use of Ufa's quota certificates and an entrée into its theatres. These new obligations – plus old debts and internal mismanagement – only worsened the situation, and in 1927 the company was in a drastic state; it was solved by Hugenberg, who had expanded his communications empire since he had pressed Ufa to make *Anna Boleyn*, and he was able to acquire the whole company. His conservative, reactionary views were said to impose a threat to those major film-makers who were left – but there were probably only three of these: Lamprecht, the humanitarian, whose work did decline; Pabst, whose career owes little to Ufa; and Lang, who seems to have been unaffected.

Fritz Lang (1890–1976) studied art in his native Vienna, and entered the industry as a writer. His first scenario filmed – *Die Hochzeit in Ekzentrik Klub* (1918) – disappointed him, but he felt 'something great, a new medium, something which I usually call the art of our century'. Pommer, then head of Decla-Film, made him story-editor, and allowed him to direct *Halbblut* (1919), from his own scenario; on the next, *Das Wandernde Bild* (1920), he was joined by Thea von Harbou, who became his collaborator and wife for more than a decade. His only film to survive till *Der Müde Tod* is the two-part **Die Spinnen** (1919), conceived in fact in four parts, i.e. as a serial at a time when longer films were in vogue. 'I simply wanted to film adventurous subjects,' said Lang. 'I loved everything that was exuberant and exotic' – but adventure in this case meant a couple of locations on the Baltic Sea and a minute budget. On the evidence of this imitation-Feuillade about a secret organisation called 'The Spiders' and their involvement with an Inca priestess the cancellation of the last two parts is no deprivation.

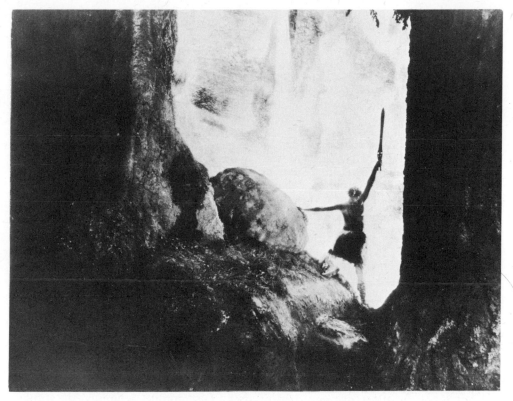

Influenced by Sjöström, Fritz Lang did his own version of the German saga, *Die Nibelungen* – of which this is the first part, *Siegfried*. Years later Henry Fonda explained that he had disliked working with Lang because he cared too little for the performer and too much for the plastic, and it is obvious here, to the film's detriment.

The success of *Der Müde Tod* whetted Lang's ambition, and he and von Harbou came up with **Dr Mabuse der Spieler** (1922) – also a two-parter, but a long one, and much too long for the sort of thing you wouldn't give five minutes to on television with Sound and colour; though I must say for those who like this sort of thing, this is the sort of thing they like – the adventures of a mastermind (Rudolf Klein-Rogge) seeking to dominate the world. Again Feuillade-inspired, the source was a novel by Norbert Jacques, but with 'much of the social criticism eliminated' (Liam O'Laoghaire). Its narrative strength and visual boldness almost compensate for the convolutions and ramifications – the sheer amount of which finally gets through to the most restless spectator; we file out at the end of the second part, numb, but satisfied with our final view of the mastermind – sitting on the floor, mad-eyed and despairing, counting his useless money, the image of Germany in defeat. Kracauer maintains that this film, with *Caligari*, 'attempts to show

how closely tyranny and chaos are interrelated', and that it portrays a society 'fallen prey to lawlessness and depravity'. But the only chaos is that projected by the tyrant; and the behaviour in the gambling parlours is exceptionally decorous. True, a doorman asks 'Cards or cocaine?', and the unremarked-upon presence within of the State Attorney does suggest a level of corruption; but one intertitle biography of a den-owner hardly qualifies as social comment among all the disguises and dropped notes and confrontations and coincidences.

That audiences sat through *Mabuse* on successive nights caused Lang to embark on another film so 'big' that it would be shown at two sittings – and though the word 'epic' is often misused in movie terms, it certainly applies to **Die Nibelungen** (1924). The cinema, he decided, was an ideal medium for the sagas, and having experimented with spectacle and fantasy he was tempted to the thing itself; the Wagner score was rearranged to accompany what was a different arrangement of the same thirteenth-century poem. In *Siegfried*, that warrior inherits the treasure of the Nibelungen, and with magic powers helps the Duke of Burgundy win the hand of Brunhild, gaining for himself the Duke's daughter, Kriemheld; but he is murdered by the aged, jealous Hagan, goaded by a Brunhild aware of the deception. In *Kriemhelds Rache* Kriemheld marries Etzel, king of the Huns (the English version calls him Attila) whom she tricks into killing Hagan and the Burgundians while ostensibly entertaining them. There is no magic here, but bleakness and horror, the very stuff of – primitive – epic; the final scenes of immolation are powerful. Yet, as with *Mabuse,* the experience is tiring. The trickery used to convey the fantastical is more developed than in *Der Müde Tod,* but the film is static. The dragon encountered is patently papier-mâché, though that instant when his eye is gouged is still not for the squeamish. Precedence was given to the costumes (those of the Huns were copies of those in the Hamburg Folk Museum) and to Otto Hunte's sets, based on the paintings of Altdorfer, Elsheimer and Böchlin – the latter not the most distinguished of painters, but like the others the most Germanic. If German audiences were encouraged to escape into fantasy, this particular film was, in the manner of the legend, a reassertion of the country's faith in itself; and though Mabuse and Siegfried are defeated, both correspond to the Nietzschean theory of a superman, always able to rise again.

Significantly the film was a great encouragement for the tyros of the Nazi party, unable to find much cheer in other German films; its huge sets and those of **Metropolis** (1927) would provide the conception of the stadium at Nuremberg, and though one film was set in the past and the other in the future, vastness – like the pyramids – was bound to last. In the city of Metropolis the gilded youth are at sport in a vast arena; and the Nazis noted with satisfaction that its mad inventor lived under the star of David.

Metropolis was made for Ufa (who had taken over Decla); for Frank Vreeland in *The New York Telegram* it was 'a sardonic Ufa dissection of our mechanical age . . . so towering and overwhelming and unique'. Rotha noted 'a brilliant *filmic* conception' and reasoned that the abuse it invoked was due to the version shown in Britain (and the U.S.), which had five reels cut. H. G. Wells called it 'quite the silliest film' and years later Lang referred to it similarly, blaming himself as much as von Harbou. At over two million RM, it was Ufa's most expensive picture to date – in Lang's own words, 'A battle of modern science and occultism, the science of the Middle Ages.' The Krupp armaments factory in Essen, with its regimentation and 'ideal homes' and hierarchy, had undoubtedly been studied; Capek's *R.U.R.* and Wells' novels were among works poached, as were two films (q.v.) *The Four Horsemen of the Apocalypse* and *The Hunchback of Notre Dame* – and the inventor is a variation of Dr Mabuse. The result you might imagine to be a bastard, and that's a good word for it: suffice to say that it chiefly concerns the tyrannical boss (Alfred Abel), his rebellious son (Gustav Frölich), the mad inventor (Klein-Rogge), and a sort of Miss Messiah, Maria (Brigitte Helm), who has a false double, whipping the zombie-like workers into revolt and finally chaos. Lang later referred to the denouement as 'fairy-tale', and he was clearly less interested in the struggle between capital and labour than in machines and magic (much of this was cut, which is why the film is so choppy) – so that whenever things get humdrum, something comes along to stun: the huge furnace which turns into Moloch; the electronic transformation of the robot; the building of the Tower of Babel; the flood; and the city of the Future. As opposed to these – and the architectural constructions – the blunting naivety is relieved only once, when Lang intercuts the shimmy of the false Maria into the hero's dream of the Seven Deadly Sins, so that she becomes part of the dream, nudging him into a realisation of the strangeness of his beloved: *that* is a brilliant filmic conception.

With **Spione** (1928) Lang returned to the man who wanted to master the world, played again by Klein-Rogge, the tale now set in the land of political intrigue and espionage – territory later

mapped out by writers like Greene and Ambler, spurning the masterminds with dungeon palaces beneath the respectable frontage of a bank. The piece swarms with idiocies, like the vamp who casually murders as a way to meet the hero, or the spy who pretends to be a waif in order to be picked up by a diplomat (we know politicians aren't always fussy about their bed-partners, but this one carries the safety of the world in his attaché case); however, there is a sense of fatality, of ups and downs and pains and rewards: almost for the first time one recognises the later Lang. And in **Die Frau im Mond** (1929) Lang returned to the early film-makers – in this case Méliès, though a small boy's Nick Carter comics provide a clear reference. This boy has smuggled himself aboard this moon-rocket, whose daft adventures on that planet contrast with those of the international financiers who backed it. I have to report that it is liable to drive

contemporary audiences into hysteria.

Fate, as we have seen, was writ large in all these films, and a whole series of films was built round the tragedies that resulted when the bourgeoisie encountered the underworld. The prototype is *Von Morgens bis Mitternacht*, the play if not the film, and it is certainly the starting point for Karl Grune's **Die Strasse** (1923) – and Grune lifts direct from the earlier film (because it wasn't shown publicly?) the device of the women's faces which turn to skulls. Karl Grune (1890–1962) had worked with Reinhardt, and during the War had lived with foreign soldiers, whose language he didn't speak: his experiences aroused his desire to develop on the screen 'a pictorial language as communicative as the spoken one', writes Kracauer. *Die Strasse* certainly speaks; there are only a dozen intertitles, mainly to clear up the plot at the end – and the speech is in the movement. Everything

Karl Grune's *Die Strasse* was probably the most influential German film of the Twenties, standing midway between some films whose fame has been more enduring: adopting the so-called 'expressionist' motives as carried into films by *Caligari*, it started its own movement towards more realistic subjects like *Die Freudlose Gasse* and on to *Asphalt* and *Der Blaue Engel*. The gentleman in front is Eugen Klöpfer, and Aud Egede Nissen, behind, has designs on his virtue – and pocket.

The greater social inequalities of half a century ago attracted many of the best film–makers, but since the public has never cared for films about poverty few of them were popular. Gerhard Lamprecht made a number of such films – which foreign importers did not want; nor were they showy or theatrical enough to impress local reviewers to the degree that they might attract attention abroad. Lamprecht, in fact, tells more of Berlin in the Twenties, and more entertainingly, than some writers whose name we more readily associate with it. This is a scene from *Die Verrufenen* – literally 'The Discredited' – with Bernhard Götzke, Aud Egede Nissen and Arthur Berger.

moves, from the opening onwards, when the hero watches on his ceiling the shadows of a woman picking up a man; when he dreams, it is in montage with superimposition (which gave Dziga-Vertov an idea or two). The film is not particularly good, and Grune's ideas are not original: a respectable husband rejects the monotony of middle-class life for a night on the town – till the prostitute (Aud Egede Nissen) he fancies and her cohorts frame him for the murder of another of their victims. With its mostly stylised sets it belongs absolutely to its time, along with *Schatten* and *Raskilnikov*, but its success gave rise to that much healthier school – the tales of prostitution and the underbelly of society. Grune was in the forefront of those who rejected expressionism to embrace the *neue sachlichkeit*. **Die Brüder Schellenberg** (1926)

is no more entertaining than *Die Strasse*, but it sets its melodramatics against a Germany founded on fate, money and sex – a recognisable Germany, in fact. It begins with a factory holocaust (which influenced *Metropolis*, just as the scenes in the stock exchange found their way into *L'Argent*, q.v.), and that changes the life of two brothers, both played by Conrad Veidt. The suave, handsome one rises high in the world of finance and becomes a playboy and seducer; the grey-bearded bespectacled one becomes a philanthropist, and eventually 'saves' one of his brother's victims. He runs a rehabilitation centre for the poor, and it is clear that the film was intended as a comfort aga013nt the inflation then rampant in Germany; in the same way **Am Rande der Welt** (1927) is Grune's tract against war – but with a narrative so bizarre as to be . . . well, let us say, surrealistic. It is set in a mill near the border of two warring territories – a mill which in Robert Neppach's art direction and Fritz Arno Wagner's photography is even more fascinating than the similar setting in *Der Schatz* (q.v.) – and has one vital sequence, on the declaration of war, prefiguring *All Quiet on the Western Front* (q.v.) Grune, disillusioned, later turned to conventional historical melodramas and after the coming of the Nazis made one half-notable film in Britain, *Abdul the Damned* (q.v.).

By far the best of the *neue sachlichkeit* directors was Gerhard Lamprecht (b. 1890), another one-time actor who had come under the influence of Reinhardt, and who had entered films as a cameraman. He has left a portfolio on Berlin quite as valuable as Ozu's of Tokyo – and if he has been underrated it is because his films were overshadowed by the Berlin cartoonist who inspired them, Heinrich Zille. Zille's stories and drawings were the basis of a number of films at this time – and novels, such as Alfred Döblin's 'Berlin Alexanderplatz'. Like Döblin's book, Lamprecht's first film, **Die Verrufenen** (1925) – adapted from Zille, whose drawing of down-and-outs sets the tone at the outset – concerns the difficulty of an ex-convict (Berhard Götzke) in finding again his place in society. Since he had been both wronged and rich, we are near to Hollywood's later bromides on the subject, and indeed the story is banal, moving eventually towards contrivance and sentimentality. But it is told in modern fashion, without the 't's being crossed and the 'i's being dotted – often at the most important points; and the 'dialogue' is also ahead of its time in carrying wit, such as the prostitute-heroine's jeer to a shocked passer-by, 'What do you think I'm doing, dressed like this? Advertising a choral society?' or the hero's apology to the boss, after fixing the machine after-hours, 'I'm sorry I had to stoop to doing it in romantic fashion.' What faults of narrative there are absent from **Menschen Untereinander** (1926), and since it adds great gusts of humour, it is an even better film. This is a collective portrait of life in an apartment-house, in the genre we know

as *Grand Hotel* (though Vicki Baum's novel of that name – in German 'Menschen in Hotel' – was written three years later, in the tradition of cross-section stories like this one), and it succeeds marvellously in juggling its half-dozen stories. The tenants are introduced to us by an inmate gossiping to the new concierge, and we mostly become involved with the desiccated lawyer (Alfred Abel) who finds it hard to forgive his wife (Aud Egede Nissen) for a fatal automobile accident, and – more than making amends for the stickiness of that – the mean, vain landlady 'caught' by an Australian adventurer met at one of her high-priced introduction parties.

Lamprecht's simple titles were indication to his audience that they were not to be offered escapism. He followed Oswald in demanding open discussion of and sympathy for those wronged by society. If it was the Americans who discovered, during the War, the cinema's ability to sway mass opinion it was the Germans who put it to social use: and **Die Unehelichen** (1926) demands thought for illegitimate children. Peter (Ralph Ludwig) is exceptionally unlucky in his foster parents, feckless and drunken – just as he is equally lucky, later, with the wealthy, generous lady who takes him under her wing; but Lamprecht neutralises his sentimental excesses at the end, when Peter has gone reluctantly to his own father (Götzke), a tough bargeman whose only relaxation from his labours is the solace of the bottle; the cross-cutting between boy on deck with dog, and father getting drunker, is as touching as it is elementary. The first and third of this trio – trilogy? – demanded not only attention from the public but the lawmakers; and **Unter der Laterne** (1928) makes great play of the fact that there is not enough work to go round, following as it does former sweethearts, he to a nice suburban home and she to the profession and death of Marguerite Gautier. In fact, her downfall began when she stayed out all night – innocently – with him, and the film is a conventional account of a whore's rise and fall. We may note some staples of the films of the period: a stunning montage when she's most successful, of lingerie, diamonds, etc.; the visit to the businessman in his apartment; and the situation *à trois* which would be copied less innocently in the Lilian Harvey musicals (q.v.). But as a whole the film is unremarkable, and we may suppose – did the same thing happen to Grune? – that Hugenberg would not permit Lamprecht to continue on his conscience-stirring path. This film does, however, have one sequence in a low-life bar to set beside the wealth of such sequences in the earlier ones, ranging from penny arcades and skittle alleys to huge boozy music halls. In Lamprecht's films there is a panorama of the times: the ballet school, the little Jewish photographer's bare apartment, the flophouse, the cellar where piece-work is paid for in schnapps, the bureaucrats' dusty office, the mansion in Lugano, the dime-a-dance cabaret or the bars where the sexes don't separate to dance . . . for in the end, there are always the bars, the dives, the cafés. At the end of *Die Verrufenen*, the hero has a tirade: 'Poverty and suffering, vice and alcohol make people what they call the Fifth Class . . . They cannot escape their fate. You can fight against it, but you cannot change it': and that was the sort of moralising that the self-righteous wanted to hear. Sjöström did it too, and next to him the Silents have no more honest observer. Lamprecht may be, in the fashion of the time, sentimental towards his hero-victims, but he never is to the poor.

His films had no great success outside Germany, or indeed within it, since audiences only liked poverty when dealt with in the manner of Pollyanna. Nor were critics immune: Pabst's **Die Freudlosse Gasse** (1925) had far more success than *Die Verrufenn*, and since Pabst is the greater film-maker, this particular film is much deeper in melodrama than Lamprecht's, though perhaps, in its mordant portrait of a divided society, it possesses more edge. It is a profoundly socialist film: the rich recklessly inflate mine shares at the expense of the middle class, disporting in cabarets while the inhabitants of the joyless street queue for bread. The irony in the cutting was influenced by *Strike* (q.v.); Pabst so admired Eisenstein that he planned a film on a German mutiny

after seeing *Potemkin*. The background is post-Hapsburg Vienna under inflation, and here is Asta Nielsen, the corrupted one, and Garbo (in her second film), about to go the same way. The latter is a silly goose, in straitened circumstances getting into the toils of Frau Greifer (Valeska Gert), and then not being nice to her 'client' – the butcher (Krauss): whereupon the hideous Greifer throws herself at him in desperation and is accepted – a touch that is absolutely Pabst, and the sort of thing that makes his work at this time so much more mature than Lang's. The butcher is presented as the immediately capitalist enemy of the people, though there are certain ladies prepared to bargain with their bodies: he is killed by the hungry mob, and Garbo is 'saved' – the moral of which is reputed to have caused the film its two year run in Paris. It played for over a year in Berlin, but censorship in other countries resulted in mutilation of the material. These included the U.S., which imported it, in 1927, on the strength of Garbo's participation. In Britain it was banned absolutely for some years.

G. W. Pabst (1885–1967) was born in Czechoslovakia and raised in Vienna; he began his career as an actor, but after one film he turned to writing scenarios for Carl Frölich's company, and Frölich gave him the chance to direct. **Der Schatz** (1924) was adapted from a novel by Rudolph Hans Bartsch, which clearly provided what was then thought para-mount in the German cinema: a moral melodrama played out against bizarre settings – in this case a mill, brilliantly designed by Robert Herlth and Walter Röhrig. The plot is conventional stuff about buried treasure and greed with the miller's daughter (Lucie Mannheim) as the pawn. It is understandable that with the treasure at stake, both parents and the brutish handyman (Krauss) should forget her – but then so, momentarily, does her true love, and that is Pabst the social realist in his true voice. *Der Freudlosse Gasse* was his third film; his fifth was a psychological study, **Geheimnisse einer Seele** (1926), for its time an incredible achievement, and one of the most sober and imaginative of Silent films. With two former colleagues of Freud, Pabst

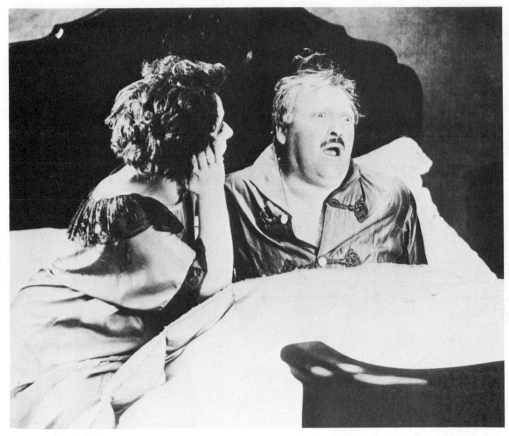

Perhaps the German directors who most consistently impressed their contemporaries were Murnau, Lang and Pabst: the Silent output of Murnau and Lang often looks dated, but the work of Pabst remains strong and vivid: *Geheimnisse einer Seele* or *Secrets of a Soul* is still a remarkable study of a mentally sick man, played by Werner Krauss. Freud disapproved of the enterprise, but gets a nod in the foreword to the effect that he, 'the university professor', had found a cure for such illnesses.

worked out a case in which a neighbourhood murder and the gift of a knife by a cousin bring out a phobia in a chemistry professor (Krauss): he cannot pick up a knife, a razor, a letter-opener, till he consults a psychiatrist, who urges from him fantasies from his past and the dreams that we have already seen. The front-door key soon becomes symbolic: the doctor finds the key – the cousin's tacit reference to the professor's *kinderlosigkeit* or impotence – and dredges from the professor's memory the moment that scarred. It is too simply resolved; but the symbolism of the dreams impresses, and the surrounding narrative envisages moments of sexual frustration.

The only other director who might – *just* – have treated the subject was Von Stroheim, and Pabst acknowledged admiration in the opening sequence of **Die Liebe der Jeanne Ney** (1927): a military orgy which surpasses any of the former's in probability and beastliness. It

was easier to be more explicit in Germany; but Ufa did force upon Pabst a bowdlerised version of Ehrenburg's long novel. Briefly, it concerns the pursuit to Paris of Jeanne Ney (Edith Jehanne) and her Bolshevik lover Andreas (Udo Henning) by the scheming Khalibiev (Fritz Rasp); the latter manages to get himself affianced to her – blind – cousin (Brigitte Helm), and to pin one of his murders on Andreas – to unpin which Jeanne agrees to go away with him. In the book she becomes both his mistress and that of Andreas; gone too are the moral and political implications – replaced by a sub-plot about Bolshevik subversion in Paris, plus a hint that Andreas will see the error of his views. The film is complicated rather than complex, but Pabst constantly offers relishable details – above all, the greedy, unshaven private detective and his book-lined warren of an agency.

His interest in the darker side of man's

nature led him to his two masterpieces, **Die Büchse von Pandora** (1928) and **Tagebuch einer Verlorenen** (1929), so much a pair that we may stretch the word 'unique' to describe the experience they make. The former was taken from two plays by Wedekind which had shocked audiences two decades earlier, and the latter from a moralising novel by Margarete Böhme which Oswald had filmed in 1918. In *Pandora*, Lulu threads her amoral way from the conquest of a respectable doctor (Fritz Kortner) to death in London at the hands of Jack the Ripper; in *Verlorenen*, Thymian moves from seduction by her father's assistant (Rasp) to a bordello, then to marriage to a wealthy old man. Pabst subjects his players to a battery of close-ups, carrying events forward in glances and nuances; he offers a decadent wedding party and some fine, flaunting backstage scenes with the same panache that he brings to reform-school gymnastics or a family conference, cutting brilliantly to find detail. In both, Louise Brooks is not a femme fatale but a child – so delighted with everything, unable to be regretful for long, pleased to be admired. In response to the doctor's

Pabst's *Die Buchse der Pandora* and *Tagebuch einer Verlorenen* are, because of the incandescent Louise Brooks, something more than a girl's odyssey into the world of sin and luxury. LEFT, in *Pandora*, with Franz Lederer, son of her lover, and ABOVE, in *Verlorenen* with Fritz Rasp, just before embarking on that odyssey.

hopeless, eyes-open passion, Lulu exults without a thought in her head; when the lesbian countess hugs her on her wedding night, she gives a glimmer of a smile, aware of a new conquest. Twice Thymian knows she is going to be ravished – once by the assistant, and later by her first client in a brothel – and she closes her eyes, her head thrown back in a trance; she had already submitted, a fragile plaything and not a partner – and the ecstatic stance indicates more than willingness, since she is no longer mistress of her fate. Even without the luminous presence of this actress, we might say that there is no other *fille de joie* quite like her: in the brothel, looking at the men about her, or preparing to sip a glass of champagne (her first?), her reaction, beyond sheer delight, is unfathomable. Consequently, because of her, Pabst's two films have a deeper resonance than the other German prostitute films. They are all moral tales – finally; but Pabst comes down firmly for 'sinning' as vital to the life force. The men are all dry-throated and wet-lipped with anticipation: they are also unpersonable to a degree. Wedekind's original producer, Karl Kraus, described the plays' matter as 'the revenge of the world of men . . . for its own guilt', but Pabst feels no guilt: since sex is so much to be desired, prostitution is not to be deplored.

Prostitution in the other films of the period, including *Der Freudlosse Gasse*, is linked to poverty and inflation; it brings disease, unhappiness and death – as it does, indeed, in *Pandora*. But for Pabst it is not so easy: his clients are as likely to be in the usual image – fat, old and gross – and in the brothel it is an aged man who sweeps into the bedroom the youngest and most innocent-seeming of the girls. He is not, finally, a social realist like Lamprecht, but a satirist; the others find faults in the German haute bourgeoisie, but he concedes nothing. *His* people are not rotten because of present economic conditions: they have been rotten for generations – but they are not fixed, because humanity is capable of shifting. 'A little more love,' says Thymian's benefactor, 'and no one would be lost.'

That is a message implicit in **Das**

Gefahrliche Alter (1927), another of the prostitute or 'street' (from *Die Strasse*) films, directed by Eugen Illes. Unlike the girl who falls from grace in *Unter der Laterne*, this one – Miss Nielsen again – is a middle-aged lady, and she falls in love with one of her husband's students (Walter Rilla). For a while, this is like one of Hollywood's Florence Vidor vehicles, as much smartness as sadness, about a woman trying to retain her youth; but under the lantern she is a pathetic figure. **Dirnentragödie** (1927) was directed by Bruno Rahn, who died shortly after it was finished: alas, for on this evidence he might have been a master. The English title was *The Tragedy of the Street*, but the original means 'Whore's Tragedy'. It is the whore this time who falls – Auguste (Nielsen), first glimpsed applying a toothbrush dipped in bootblack to the roots of her hair. She has an amiable pimp (Oskar Homolka), but when she meets young Felix (Werner Pittshau) he is bribed to leave and she abandons her 'client'. To hold Felix, she uses the rest of her money for a down-payment on a grocer's shop, but the pimp returns and manoeuvres Felix into the arms of the party-girl roommate: and as tragedy sweeps away three of these people, Felix weeps in his mother's lap. I do not think experienced whores give up all at the first glimpse of a youth from a nice family, but this film suggests that this is the one act of foolishness of which such ladies are capable. Miss Nielsen, hunched now and smiling without mirth, makes us believe absolutely; and Rahn's people move furtively through the shadows, in the stylised sets still sometimes used in such films.

You might suppose, film-makers being what they are, that there would be a film combining the 'street' genre with the fantastical – and there is: **Alraune** (1927) – though to be fair, Alraune (Brigitte Helm) is femme fatale rather than street-walker. The daughter of a whore and a hanged criminal, as 'manufactured' in the lab by a scientist (Paul Wegener), her discovery of her origins leads from bad to worse, and the same can be said of the film, since its motive – her revenge on her creator – is handled in dim fashion. Or so it seems now:

at the time *The Kinematograph Weekly* spoke of 'the genius of H. H. Ewers's story and Henrik Galeen's directorial genius'. The posturing of Fraulein Helm is a distinct demerit; she played the same role in the first of the two Sound remakes.

The wholly commercial directors may be represented by Alexander Korda (1893–1956), since his films reflect the period as accurately as more famous titles. They deserve to be better known because Korda was a man of intelligence, and that quality is reflected in them; he was also an opportunist, a necessity in Weimar then and the movie industry always. He was born in Hungary of an impoverished Jewish family, and made his way into the industry via film criticism; he had directed twenty-five films there before arriving in Vienna, where he made *Seine Majestät das Bettelkind* for Sascha Film, a version of Mark Twain's 'The Prince and the Pauper', of no interest whatsoever. His second film for Sascha (it was in fact made simultaneously, on the same locations, as *Herren der Meere*, which hasn't survived) was **Eine Versunkene Welt** (1922), somewhat better, and with a subject of passionate interest at the time – indeed, it won a Gold Medal for best dramatic film at a Congress in Milan. The subject is that of a Grand Duke who embraces socialism – after, that is, embracing a dancer. In films such relationships usually lead to self-sacrifice or suicide; but the Grand Duke's suicide is due to his beliefs, he and the film having decided that socialism is a good thing in theory but unworkable in practice. There is also a political reference or so in **Samson und Delila** (1922), inasmuch as the strange young man found aboard the prince's yacht is thought to be an anarchist. He appears in the modern part of the film; the rest of it is the Biblical story, the two tied together by the notion of a *diva* about to sing Delilah. The ancient-modern device was not new in films, and this precedes the best-known one, deMille's first *Ten Commandments* (q.v.); Korda's co-writer was Ernst Vajda, who later became a writer for Lubitsch. The international success of the Mark Twain film had given Korda a taste for more, and the example of *Sumurun* had proved that spectacle films sold throughout the world – and

this particular subject offered spice from an unimpeachable source. The sets are splendid: the cost of them, despite the film's relative success (it never played the U.S.) bankrupted the backers – which was and would be the fate of most people who financed Korda.

Fleeing Austria, he gained Berlin, where he found a compatriot to back **Das Unbekannte Morgen** (1923), written with Vajda, and derived from both *Der Müde Tod* and *Schatten* – and more entertaining than either. It is an examination of the past, present and future of a potential suicide (Maria Corda, then the director's wife). Korda attacks the subject with energy, and his Teutonic London is more menacing than in other, comparable films – which would include many with bogeymen: in that role again is Herr Krauss, diabolical once more, with longish hair and monocle, developed (as an intertitle informs us) from musician to maniac, insanely plotting for carnal purposes against our poor heroine. The film's reception enabled Korda to buy his way into a distribution company, but that went into liquidation; after a film for Ufa, he obtained backing from another Hungarian for a film which Ufa released, **Tragödie in Hause Hapsburg** (1924). Lajos Biro (who would work with him in Britain) wrote it, and it is the first film on the Mayerling affair: perhaps because audiences would have been familiar with the Crown Prince, Koloman Zatony is the only one of

The incomparable Asta Nielsen continued to act up to the Sound period (she made just one Talking picture), playing, as she always did, sad ladies of unfortunate virtue. Here she is (right) with Hilde Jennings in *Dirnentragödie* – a young lady to whom she has foolishly offered a room. The looks of Miss Jennings make her a popular girl at parties of old bachelors, while Miss Nielsen's haunt is more likely to be the street – where, of course, the other will eventually end up.

several screen Rudolphs to look like him – and he also gives a tremendously affecting performance. Frau Corda is Maria Vetsera. Wrote Dorothy Gies McGuigan in her marvellous book on the Hapsburgs: 'So completely, so painstakingly, was every shred of truth, every concrete piece of factual evidence hurried out of public sight that even today, nearly eighty years later, the full truth of Mayerling continues to elude the searcher.' We must therefore admire Biro's script, keeping to the known facts – including the accepted opinion that the Prince killed himself for reasons other than love. The result is fair entertainment: Korda was never good at narrative strength, but as the film lurches on, it does so, impressively, in Schönbrunn and other locations associated with the principals.

Eine Dubarry von Heute (1927) is further reminder of Korda's abiding interest in the amours of kings – though it was designed to exploit the charms of his wife, now considerably glamorised and thus expected to be his passport to international acclaim. As written by Biro, it attempted to combine two popular film genres, royal romance and the rise of a Paris coquette. The latter, at least, is of interest – to a degree not far short of Miss Brooks's progress in Pabst's films (we may suppose Pabst saw this, since he chose an actress identical in appearance to Frau Corda here) – and we find, rare in such films, a genuine feeling between the king (Alfred Abel) and this woman of the world. It is pleasant to find that feeling in a film which borrows so much – whether it be the shots of revolving, multiple faces, or walking legs on the sidewalk: the abiding clichés of the German Silent film.

For the Germans, as for most other film-makers, Paris was the very best setting for escapist movies, since there, as everyone knows, high society and the bohemians could mingle and indulge in *l'amour* to their hearts' content: though the starting-point of films like Richard Eichberg's **Die Keusche Susanne** (1926) was surely emulation of Lubitsch's Hollywood films, even to the extent, in this case, of a huge finale – cf. *So This is Paris?* (q.v.) – in the Moulin Rouge. Adapted from a French operetta, the farcical complications are not entirely served by a cast including Ruth Weyher in the title-role, the not-so-chaste Susanne, Willy Fritsch as a gay young blade, and Lillian Harvey.

Wilhelm Thiele's **Die Dame mit der Maske** (1928) is on its own merits of little account, but it is completely of its period, absolutely representative of a Berlin crippled by inflation, and it has an opening montage on inflation (designed by Hans Richter) that is so strong that it colours all that follows. Alexander Esway and Henrik Galeen wrote the scenario, which concerns the daughter (Arlette Marchal) of a writer who goes into a scantily-clad revue rather than tell him she couldn't find a publisher for his book – and today it's very difficult to feel sympathy for a man who hopes to make a fortune from a book about his hunting days in Africa. It is all here: the Russian émigré hero and his cab-driver friend; the Jewish pawnbroker; the impresario's girlfriend who fancies herself a star; and the impresario himself (Heinrich George), who takes a shine to our heroine. Will he ravish her? Will she shoot him?

There are no such problems in **Der Geiger von Florenz** (1926) since the heroine (Elisabeth Bergner) dresses up as a boy and meets the nicest Italian artist (Walter Rilla), who has no qualms about the consequent palpitations in his breast. This version of 'As You Like It' was written and directed by Paul Czinner to perpetuate the winsome charms of his wife, Bergner – and it must be quite the daftest variation on an already impossible theme.

Italy is much better served in **Das Haus am Meer** (1924): the story is sheer melodrama – the woman whose past catches up with her – but it is attacked with new conviction by the director, Fritz Kaufman. The *haus* is on the Sorrento peninsula, an inn kept by Enrico (Gregory Chmara) and his wife (Miss Nielsen) – who is recognised in due course as a notorious camp-follower by some conscripts bound for Morocco. 'So you mean to throw me back into the depths from which you saved me?' she pleads against Vesuvius in full smoke. There is one notable sequence: the wife's dilemma and her past presented in one

The young wife (Jenny Jugo) is encouraged by her spinster neighbour (Olga Limburg) to return the attentions of a local nobleman – without, of course, arousing the suspicions of her husband (Werner Krauss). Released abroad as *A Royal Scandal*, *Die Hose* was widely regarded as one of the best films of its time, but its director, Hans Behrendt, remains a shadowy figure. From the time of this film, 1927, to the coming of the Nazis, he was prolific, specialising in satiric small town comedy. His only recorded work after being expelled from the German film industry is a Spanish film made in 1934.

montage, cutting finally to her husband, and *thus* confirming his suspicions – technique at its most imaginative. The acting (Chmara was then married to Nielsen) is Silent acting of the most vivid kind and the locations – the rough and relentless sea, the land high, hard and rugged – are heady after the hermetic world of Ufa and its clever lighting.

Another remarkable film, also set away from the contemporary scene, is **Die Hose** (1927), directed by Hans Behrendt from a scenario by Franz Schulz: its source is Carl Sternheim's 1911 play, one of his small-town satires chronicling the rise to power of the Maske family. Werner Krauss is Maske, petty official, stuffing his belly into tight trousers, blinking pale-lashed eyes over a glorious splutter of a moustache. He has a young and pretty wife (Jenny Jugo), but his moustache and his job in the Prince's household are his chief claims to fame – not that he is seen to work, but he unwraps his lunch-time sandwich methodically, with as much mental effort as he'll use all day. He is convivial with 'the boys', irritable with his wife, obsequious with the Prince, and satisfied

before a mirror: Krauss might have made him more pitiable or more overbearing, and that he doesn't is because he was, quite simply, a wonderful actor. The film is not wonderful, but it is worthy of him: I like it better than any similar film I've seen, partly because it proves that the German sense of humour was not always lumbering – and partly because it is very well made. The sets and extensive locations are appropriately charming, and as the Prince's philosopher-adviser Rudolph Forster manages a comic portrait as richly amusing as that of Krauss.

The few historical films of the decade were usually based on plays or novels, and Friedrich Zelnik, usually a specialist in Viennese operettas, made a version of Hauptmann's drama **Die Weber** (1927), about the Silesian weavers' strike in 1844. Its confrontation between the bosses and the oppressed is uneven, and without being very dynamic it is nevertheless an incitement to mob violence – in emulation of its model, Eisenstein's *Strike* (q.v.). The Soviet films were changing the German cinema, and social realism became the cry of the remaining major talents – Lang excepted – of the German film industry. The influence of Reinhardt had long gone, and expressionism along with neo-Gothic horror belonged to the nursery days before the slump. Yet years of distorted images and fancy cutting leave their mark, and Ernö Metzner put them to service in his upending of German film tradition, **Überfall** (1927). Metzner was a studio architect (i.e. constructing sets from others' designs) and a Social Democrat; in this two-reeler he suggested a new set of rules. The accident of the title was the dropping of a coin, which leads the bourgeois hero into a spot of gambling. He is skinny, pop-eyed and unappetising, and the bar is not the usual friendly haven but a bare room of evil menace; the prostitute who saves him is no Asta Nielsen, but tough-looking, sexy, beautiful – and consistently vicious; and the policeman at the end, the symbol of law and understanding, proves ineffably dense and utterly indifferent as to whether our bourgeois hero lives or dies. The film was banned, but its influence was felt within the industry.

Berlin: die Symphonie einer Gross-stadt (1927) was made at the same time and was the brainchild of that child of expressionism, Mayer, who had come to the conclusion that there was more to cinema than scripting fictions. He had thought of it – the symphony as described in the title – while standing in traffic near the Palast am Zoo, and had enlisted the help of Karl Freund, and of Walter Ruttmann, who had until then only made abstract films. Ruttmann is the credited director, as Mayer withdrew his name since he considered Ruttmann's interpretation of Berlin too superficial – and it is too much an interpretation in the manner of Dziga-Vertov (q.v.) and his Kino-Eye group, montage and image for their own sakes, rather than an attempt to get beyond the surface of a city.

The influence of the film lies heavily on Joe May's superb **Asphalt** (1929) – or is it the *Asphalt* of Erich Pommer (one of his first films on returning from Hollywood) since May did so little else of note? The long, opening sequence is one of the most evocative ever filmed – the Potsdamer Platz, with store and traffic lights blazing, workers going home and late shoppers sauntering by;

and it is followed by another long sequence, in which the prostitute-thief heroine (Betty Amann) seeks to prevent the upright young cop (Gustav Fröhlich) from sending her to jail. It's clear enough he feels lust, and it's clear enough at the end that they'll marry – so the sort of film we expect from a city of legendary decadence by no means offended the moralities of provincial German audiences.

Nor were they offended by Leo Mittler's **Jenseits der Strasse** (1929), but the whore (Lissi Arno) lives on to steal again and tread the *trottoir* while her innocent young victim floats out, face downward, in Hamburg harbour. He (Fritz Genshow) is from the country, an *arbeitsloser*, and he is befriended by a bargeman, wealthy before inflation; and when he has to choose between lust/greed and friendship/loyalty, he chooses wrongly. Such then it was: a time of desperation, when lust and booze provided a temporary respite. Still, the film is more than a metaphor: it goes further yet in the depiction of the milieu. In *Die Verrufunen* we saw a whore continue to work despite true love; here, from the low-life bar with its same-sex couples we see the customer climb the stairs behind the silk-clad legs – we see, for the first time, a whore in bed with her client. As much as in Lamprecht's film, the masses struggle for existence on the edge of the underworld while the fat cats lap up their *café mit sahne*. The lucky ones all look like the capitalists in Eisenstein – and borrowed back from the Soviets are the flashy montages, handled with such confidence by Mittler. He left nothing else of note before fleeing the Nazis, but in *Razzia in St Pauli* (q.v.) Werner Hochbaum made a Sound companion piece – more gentle and, ironically, more optimistic.

The problem of sexual frustration is frankly discussed in an extraordinary film, **Geschlect in Fesseln** (1928), directed by the actor turned director Wilhelm Dieterle (q.v.), who also plays the leading-role, that of a young salesman, hit by the Depression, who is sent to jail after killing a man who pestered his wife (Mary Johnson). After a series of sexual fantasies, imaginatively conceived, on the part of wife, husband and fellow-prisoners, he begins a relationship with a cellmate, after which he cannot or will not return to his wife. This conclusion would have been unthinkable in any other national cinema at the time, and if the inevitable result is suicide, the homosexual issue is treated with both sympathy and subtlety.

Pessimism is the sole note of Carl Junghaus's **So ist der Leben** (1929) which follows the ill-fortunes from one Saturday to the next of one family living in Prague. I much prefer what is virtually the same story with humour, **Mutter Krausens Fahrt ins Glück** (1929), and certainly it was preferred at the time by audiences. Phil Jutzi, directing, offers a portrait of everyday life as fascinating as those of Lamprecht, and we find the hero's Marxist pal quoting Zille, 'Living conditions can kill as surely as an axe' – which allows the hero to forgive his girl the loss of her virginity elsewhere and let her join him in a people's demonstration that provides a rare healthy ending, with its indication that the remedy is at hand, that there are elements within society which will fight to push out the degradation and deprivation. The late German Silents may have borrowed from the Soviets, but few bothered with their message of hope. The Nazi party must also have taken hope, if not quite the same way: for all the glorification of the workers, the film stresses the unity of the family and the joys of sport, the open-air, and the community.

These last are celebrated in a slight piece, **Menschen am Sonntag** (1930), directed by Robert Siodmak (1900–73) and Edgar G. Ulmer, with assists on script or camera by Eugen Schüfftan, Fred Zinnemann and Billy Wilder – all of them then youngsters on the fringe of the industry. Literally a lighthearted Sunday version of *Berlin: die Symphonie einer Grossstadt*, with some fictional incidents borrowed from the Soviet *House on Trubnaya Square* (q.v.), it concerns two picnicking couples, played by amateurs who were encouraged to improvise. They were accompanied by only a music track and audiences delighted in them, ensuring a last success for Silent films as Talkies flooded German theatres. Doubtless the woods and lakes were refreshing after a decade of shadows and smoke-filled cafés, and the same was true of the mountain stretches of **Die Weisse Hölle von Piz Palü** (1929), co-directed by Pabst and Dr Arnold Fanck. During his brief spell at Ufa, Pabst had been commanded to direct in the Russian manner, and then – which he found much more difficult – in the American way. Left to himself by Nero-Film to make *Die Büchse der Pandora*, he determined to set up his own company to make *Tagebuch einer Verlorenen* – which was why, between the two, he agreed to co-operate with Fanck. Fanck, a geologist, had specialised in 'mountain' films since *Das Wunder des Schneeschuhs* (1920), their emotions and actions as awesome as their scenery. Pabst was able to cool the emotions, and for the first time one of Fanck's films was regarded as more than 'fringe' entertainment – indeed, it was a worldwide success. The visuals were then as remarkable as they still appear to be – which include the aerial shots used in the rescue attempt at the end. You must not think from that that this is just another disaster movie, but it is relatively simple: what happens when a honeymoon couple (Leni Riefenstahl, Ernst Petersen) run into a famous mountaineer (Gustav Diessl), still searching for the wife he lost in this white hell a year ago.

There is a quest, often as obsessive as this one, throughout the German films of this decade: for lost loved ones, for self-knowledge, for economic survival, for information on the forces of darkness and disillusion. They are a reflection of the prevailing gloom of a Germany in defeat, where paper money has no value and consequently little else has: it is the open-air and the mountains which offer hope that the spirit will soar, a polarisation similar to that in the American cinema and its conflict between the old, as represented by the heroes of the West and the gingham-clad heroines, and the new – the flappers, gangsters and smart-talking reporters. The two conflicts would be resolved in very different ways.

5

The U.S.S.R: Montage and Message

IN SWEDEN, the particular nature of Sjöström's genius led him to concentrate on specifically Nordic material; in Germany, the emphasis on similarly indigenous matter was dictated by the mood of the time, at first reinforced by a government aware of the advantages of a nationalistic cinema. In Russia, the new Soviet government was quick to recognise the cinema's potential as propaganda. When that country, after the Revolution, opted out of the War, the film industry was virtually non-existent. The first studio had not been built till 1907, and the cinema for years had shown the French, British and Italian burlesques, or copies thereof. In 1913 some artists had banded together to make a film considered avant-garde, but the feature films were comfortable bourgeois subjects permitted by the Czarist regime. Under the freer conditions of the Kerensky government, Yakov Protazanov did a version of a Tolstoi short story, *Father Sergius* (1918), said to be well in advance of most Russian production. With the Civil War following the Revolution, what production equipment there was was dispersed, but its re-assembly was considered a priority – to record the activities of the Red Army for exhibition to the public. Lenin declared: 'The cinema for us is the most important of the arts,' and the world's first film school was established.

There was not, however, enough raw film stock to do much more than theorise, and chief among the theorists was Vladimir Majakovski, one of the leaders of the Futurist movement; he believed passionately in film, and with a group of fellow Futurists had been responsible for that 1913 experiment, *Drama in Futurist Cabinet 13*. When the War was over he joined the Czarist film company, Neptune, but survived to co-operate with the Revolutionary authorities. He managed to make three short films: *Creation Can't Be Bought*, adapted from 'Martin Eden' by Jack London; **The Young Lady and the Hooligan** (1918), adapted from 'Cuore' by Edmondo de Amicis; and *Shackled by Film*. The last of these Majakovski somewhat respected, but the first two he dismissed as 'sentimental commissioned rubbish . . . rubbish not because they were worse than others, but because they were not better.' The only one to have survived is *The Young Lady and the Hooligan*, and it is hard to disagree. An anecdote about the new schoolteacher and the lout (Majakovski himself) who cheeks her and then falls in love with her, it never amounts to much, though presumably to Russian audiences then, hitherto kept rigidly behind class barriers, the situation of a worker soliciting a lady had a certain piquancy; the sad ending must also have suited local taste. Majakovski, at first working for the government, became one of the great, influential voices of the Revolutionary cinema, but he never directed again; from 1926 until his suicide in 1930 he wrote a number of screenplays, only two of which – both stories for children – found their way to the screen, in much altered form. Other projects were cancelled, as he himself was increasingly critical of the shackles placed by the government on freedom of expression.

Meanwhile, at the State Film School in Moscow, without film stock, there were discussions; there were classes for acting in cinematic fashion; and there were study groups – taking apart the best-known films of D. W. Griffith, and re-editing them for different effect. What stock there was was used for what the French call *actualités*, and thus, via deprivation and the inability to practise the craft, the roots of the Soviet cinema were grounded in two qualities – immediacy and, more important, editing. Chief among the teachers was Vsevolod Meyerhold (1874–1940), a former theatre man who had directed two or three films before the Revolution; after it, he surfaced with a hundred and one ideas for allying the avant-garde with the revolutionary message – and though at this point no one was quite sure how far the cinema could be separated from the theatre, there was a wide belief that it should be, to the extent that 'plays' were attempted in 'cinematic', i.e. natural, surroundings. Lev Kuleshov (1899–1970) had had practical experience before the Revolution as film designer, and he had written extensively on the new art form. His great achievement – lacking raw stock – was the discovery that the emotions of the spectator could be shaped by the selection and juxtaposition of images: he transposed the same clip of an expressionless face with different images – a child, a plate of soup, a coffin – and found that audiences read the expression not as it was but as they expected it to be. He discovered the cinema's power to deceive; he realised that the arrangement of the material, and the length to which the image could be held, could create emotions quite opposite to those created when the same images were a series of still photographs. There is a striking example in **The Man with a Movie Camera** (1928), made by another of the theorists, Dziga Vertov (1896–1954): a ball hurtles towards the camera, an athlete lets fly a javelin, a goal-keeper defends his goal – and it is a relief when he catches the ball instead of the javelin. Vertov was still a young man when assigned officially to the task of assembling the Red Army news-reels in a three-hour film, *The Anniversary of the October Revolution* (1919). In a series of manifestoes he expounded the theory we now call cinema-*vérité*, believing deeply that the only worthwhile

form of cinema was the photographing of life-as-is. He started a newsreel called Kino-Pravda (Film-Truth), because he wanted to explain the new Russia to its citizens. But truth, of course, is relative: the Soviet film-makers put their discoveries of film deceit to the service of what they saw as the truth.

Not that Vertov held entirely to the line of the greatest propaganda; his obsessive interest in the visuals led in time to this *Man with a Movie Camera* in which man and camera are interchangeable – the I, the eye of the world. It is a film of vistas, of tricks, of artificially-heightened tension, of split-screens, of montage. Its very age offers slight compensation: an authentic snatch of old Russia, looking, with its shop-fronts and an occasional Peugeot, still capitalist. Perhaps if the selection of image was less arbitrary, or if there had been a theme – or related themes – or even a building of images, it would not have been made so completely obsolete (unlike *Berlin: die Symphonie einer Grosstadt*) by the myriads of feet of film shot since.

Even less from Kuleshov's films can we see that he was one of the founders of film theory: **Extraordinary Adventures of Mr West in the Land of the Bolsheviks** (1924) was the first film made by his Experimental department at the State Film School, a direct challenge to the theatre schools and therefore a statement by his pupils as to which direction film should follow. Pudovkin and he wrote the screenplay, and Pudovkin was assistant director, art director, and one of the leading actors. It concerns a naive American in the U.S.S.R., mainly involved – as he expected – with crooks; and as the title also implies, it is a free-wheeling comedy moving in directions both fantastic and satiric, hoping to make its points visually. Since Goskino put thirty-two prints into distribution we may suppose it popular – though it was not thought suitable for export. To sit through it today with an audience requires stamina, as the left-wingers present can be relied upon to laugh at any left-wing jokes, however unfunny – and these are either galumphing or smug: the fact that I still like the picture says much for its amiable high spirits. However, there is nothing to be

The films of Lev Kuleshov do not, on the whole, justify his reputation as a theorist on cinema; but despite a hint of self–parody *By the Law* is superb, one of several late Silent melodramas in which a small isolated group is subjected to the elements and their own emotions.

said for **The Death Ray** (1925), the second film of the Kuleshov collective, and like its predecessor designed to display American influence – it being Kuleshov's declared aim to captivate audiences as the Hollywood film-makers did. However, like *Strike* (q.v.) – which Eisenstein was making at the same time – it set out to make the proletariat its collective hero. Pudovkin wrote the scenario, in which between the propaganda may be discerned dim affinities with Feuillade and *Mabuse*; and it is here that the collective, for all their studies, fell apart – not realising that by this time the prime virtue of the Americans was their narrative clarity. Kuleshov, explaining the film's failure, had a number of theories for that – all failing to find the point: 'the ideological slander'

it created was 'utterly undeserved', he claimed, though he did admit that the film was 'inadequate' and elsewhere quoted a critic: 'You must be completely mad futurists – you show films made out of tiny pieces that to any normal spectator seem an incredible muddle – the pieces chase each other so fast that no one can possibly find out what's going on.'

As a result of this failure the collective was abandoned, and Kuleshov was unemployed for eighteen months; he finally interested Goskino in a low-budget film, **By the Law** (1926) – one interior set, a minute cast. It was an adaptation of Jack London's story, 'The Unexpected', set in Alaska, about three goldseekers – the Swedish Hans (Sergei Komarov), his English wife (Alexandra Khokhlova), and the Irish Michael

Dennin (Vladimir Fogel). It is the Irishman who finds the gold, leading to a murder, and months-long tension as the three of them are marooned by floods. As the captive, Fogel takes all our sympathy; he was never again required to give so much of his great gift for cinema acting. But the whole film is masterly. Kuleshov in his workshop had taught the importance of movement and facial expression, and instead of tripping over himself as in the other films, he lingers: the images, powerful or seemingly banal, add to the impact. It was not seen in English-speaking countries prior to 1939, but was influential on the Continent. In its refusal to take sides – in seeing the situation in shades of grey – it bears the influence of Sjöström, who may have seen it, returning the compliment in the not-dissimilar *The Wind*. My sole reservation concerns Miss Khokhlova, overdoing things as badly as in the other two films; despite its grimness and a hint of self-parody it is one to convert anyone to Silent movies.

Such is not the case with **Aelita** (1924), a science fiction tale which was probably the best-known Russian film abroad before *Potemkin* (q.v.). Directed by the aforementioned Protazanov, it moves clumsily from a resettlement centre to a space-ship, with excursions to a Mars constructed of parallel triangles and piano strings. Two points to note: a revolution on Mars as glorious as that of October 1917, and a superb ten minutes at the end when the images destroy chronology to leave us floundering, wondrously, between dreams and reality. Other examples of this technique, in the Twenties, include *Caligari* and *Das Haus am Meer*; there is no modern example till *Blow Up* (q.v.). **The Trial of Three Millions** (1926) shows Protazanov to have made as great an advance as Kuleshov. Adapted from a story by Umberto Notari which had as a play become popular in Russia, it attacks the standards and big business methods of a 'bourgeois kingdom' – and as such, said a contemporary review, in *Prim*, it 'should advantageously shake up the theme, mock a little less sympathetically, sting a little more . . . It is a soft film, with no spitefulness, completely inoffensive.' Certainly it is uneven; but

when in the middle the wife is entertaining in her room a handsome burglar, having speedily accepted him in lieu of her lover, and her fat old husband in his sock-suspenders is slobbering outside to be let in – well, that's in advance of Lubitsch at that point. We may laud it further: American comedy was innocuous, and wouldn't begin to bite till the following year, and in Europe only *Die Bergkatze* had had satirical thrust, eventually succeeded by *Der Liebe der Jeanne Ney*, again a year later than this film. These are not idle comparisons, since there is nothing specifically Russian about this film; the business of its three chief characters – three burglars – is far more 'American' than anything managed by Kuleshov.

Meanwhile, the teachings of Kuleshov and Meyerhold were coming to fruition in a pupil of genius. Sergei M. Eisenstein (1898–1948) had studied theatre with the latter and, once he had decided to move into films, he had looked in on the work of the Kuleshov studio. He had trained as an engineer, and had painted scenery at the Proletkult Theatre, a combination that led surely to films. He had made a short film sequence for one of his stage productions, and further experimentation led to the staging of a play – 'Gas Masks' – in a gas works, but the audience, expected to move about the premises with the actors, showed a reluctance to turn up in the first place. Eisenstein was persuaded that both the realism and freedom he needed could be realised only with film: after extended preparation and with the backing of the Proletkult collective he produced **Strike** (1924), a propagation of Soviet ideals – 'Towards the Dictatorship of the Proletariat' as the English copy is prefixed.

The argument is simple: a micrometer is stolen, and the man accused hangs himself; the workers strike, using the opportunity to demand reformed working conditions – and while management pretends to ponder, it brings in undercover men and *agents provocateurs* to create violence, and cavalry for the final massacre. However, we have not forgotten the words of Lenin quoted at the beginning, 'The strength of the working class is in its organisation.' The working

The three films Eisenstein made on the theme of Revolution remain among the cinema's greatest treasures. Supposedly without the trappings of fiction, they are in fact dynamic assemblies of highly emotive images. To see them, still, is to become as excited by the possibilities of the film medium as in the triumph of the 'People' which they are celebrating. ABOVE AND RIGHT, *Battleship Potemkin*, a tribute to the naval mutineers of 1905, and FAR RIGHT, both pictures, *October*, commissioned by the Soviet Government to commemorate the tenth anniversary of the Revolution itself. The young sailor is Eisenstein's representative of the proletariat, while the two pictures from *October* indicate the romanticised approach, ABOVE, and the documentary, BELOW – the invasion of the Winter Palace.

Eisenstein and the Image of Revolution

Sergei Eisenstein

class here behaves as nobly as individual appearance suggests; the stock-holders are fat and smug, cigar-equipped. It is a strip-cartoon, racing from image to memorable image, some of them simple (a child cleaning a boot, a cat pattering along a paper-strewn corridor), some ostentatious (a bank of fire-hoses, a shanty-town of barrels), all of them chosen for maximum emotive effect. People hurry and scurry, the rushing and hiding are overdone, but the result is invigorating: film had been freed from the narrative confines imposed upon it by the novel and the theatre. The Russians had recognised that *Caligari* had advanced from a pattern of pictures, but Eisenstein went further, for *Strike* proceeds *solely* from its selection and juxtaposition of images.

There was, further, no identifiable hero; the entire crew of a ship was the hero of **Battleship Potemkin** (1925) – originally designed as a section of a longer film (to have been called *1905*), but, with the addition of the Odessa Steps sequence and the shots of the harbour at dawn, considered by its creator to be complete. The theme again was the revolt of the oppressed: the crew mutiny when ordered to eat rotten meat, and when the men ordered

to the firing squad refuse to shoot them, there is no recourse but to attack the officers – and it is a measure of the director's skill that a meek, modern audience can exult at the consequent brutality: this film makes revolutionaries of us all. When it opened abroad, it was dismissed in some quarters as propaganda: if that were so, it would not be, still, an overwhelming experience. The government, which commissioned it, got, however, exactly what it wanted; audiences were rewarded with a reconstruction of an historical incident, as immediate as if pieced together from newsreel material (that species of film we call 'documentary' had till that time only *recorded*); and Eisenstein, often improvising, advanced the innovations of *Strike*. Each shot is held for only an instant, and most of them have movement: the sea below and the surface of the deck, great factors of life at sea, are insistently with us. The film is organised like a symphony: the mutiny – the first movement – is harsh and vivid; there is the interlude, the harbour at dawn, and then the response of the populace – a movement *con brio* – gathering on the Mole; the Odessa Steps sequence – the coda; and, finally, the ship steaming out to sea, unmolested by the other units of the fleet. The Cossacks moving down the Steps, bayonets lowered, must be the most anthologised of movie sequences: it marks the high point of the discoveries in the cutting-room, joining together for total effect – what Eisenstein himself called 'shock attraction' – the varied images of the aggressor and the defenceless. It lasts longer than it could have done in life (had it happened), and one is aware of this after seeing it too often: one is aware of the artifice – and that way terror does not lie. It does, however, contribute to the cumulative effect of the most rousingly emotional of all films.

October (1928) also harks back to past dissension, and its sometime sub-title – *Ten Days that Shook the World* – indicates the throbbing, explosive nature of its happenings. It starts with the demolition of a statue of Alexander III and the proclamation of the provisional government; and ends with the storming of the Winter Palace, pausing en route to illustrate the massing of the dedicated proletariat and the death-struggles of the ruling orders – while amidst the gilded paraphernalia of despots, the doomed government waits for the voice of the people. The political elisions serve only to emphasise the nature of the tract, but Eisenstein allows one surprising – and enlivening – comment: a young sailor in the room of the Czarina, ashamed and embarrassed when confronted with something he cannot understand. In the middle reaches the mechanism falters and the rhythm slows, till the crowds move towards the lighted Palace. The action then moves inexorably towards the triumphant close – the clocks of Petrograd and Moscow, then of the world, and hands applauding. At that point, as the images blur, Sound would be superfluous. The absence of Sound cannot date any of these three films of Eisenstein; *October* is romanticised history, but in its pain and passion it reflects the spirit of the Revolution. It is the desired record, eloquently revealing the hand of a man at that time inspired.

The Soviet authorities smiled benignly on Eisenstein's achievements, but they were not shown widely within the Union; abroad, although *Strike* was a success in France and Germany – and *Potemkin* made him world famous – showings were restricted to film societies, a movement born at this time in order to see just such films, those unwanted by commercial managements. Roger Manvell later recalled: 'I well remember the emotion with which I first saw films like *Potemkin*, *October* and *Mother* some twenty years ago – a kind of artistic awe which had no conscious connection with the social system which these films were designed to advocate. It was an excitement entirely derived from the artistic form they exemplified.' Certain industry people were impressed with the 'artistic form', but except for Germany the innovations of the Russians did not influence the other film industries as the German cinema had done – because, for one thing, style and content were welded, indivisible, and instigation to revolution was not what those industries had been founded to propagate. Dr Manvell might separate the two, but others saw only a threat to democracy; cinema-owners, aware of the enthusiasm of a minority, happily decided that the style was as alienating as the content. In Britain, when the furore created by the coterie began to attract the curious, the government stepped in: *Mother* (q.v.) was banned in 1929, *Potemkin* and *Storm Over Asia* (q.v.) in 1930.

The serious film student (i.e. the member of a film society – someone convinced that the cinema, given half a chance, could be an art) was so mesmerised by the Soviet cinema that he took it for granted that it could produce two young film-makers of genius at the same time. Attempting to differentiate, Lewis Jacobs wrote, 'Where Eisenstein is all mind, Pudovkin is mostly feeling'. There are identifiable heroes in Pudovkin, some glimpses of humanity and less caricature – but despite such evidence of 'feeling' he is, finally, more dependent on the medium than was Eisenstein.

Vsevolod Pudovkin (1893–1953), after his work with Kuleshov, co-directed a still-amusing two-reel slapstick, *Chess Fever* (1925), to celebrate the International Chess Tournament then being held in Moscow. At that point the government invited him to make a commemorative film on the revolutionary events of 1905; and where Eisenstein had chosen an actual event, he selected a story by Maxim Gorki. **Mother** (1926) bears the influence of *Strike*, each shot composed for the maximum effect – and Pudovkin also works rhythmically, cross-cutting to hypnotic effect: but whereas Eisenstein worked each image against those each side of it, he preferred a judicious linking of details. To create the impression of industrial unrest he accelerates the stock shots of the factory building – they're not stock shots in the accepted sense, but they are impersonal and repeated; towards the end, the images seem to dance upon the screen; but the hastening pace reveals a dependence on the 'gathering force' techniques of Griffith. And, alas, the opening stages – the hovel, the brutal father and the cowed mother – are much more Griffith than Gorki.

Except for some vignettes at the trial (the inebriated counsel, the uninterested judge) the film is too calculated to be stirring; its shortcomings are magnified in **The End of St Petersburg** (1927), commissioned, like *October*, to mark the tenth anniversary of the Revolution and covering the same events. Its chief dissimilarity is the presence of a particular hero, a peasant involved in strike-breaking prior to the October rising; the original plan had been to cover two centuries of history. The cause is, of course, propaganda – which means that we are shown a certain truth, life as the film's perpetrators would like it to be: here, manipulations to the plot (such as it is) are matched by the care given to 'construction' – to the extent that differing interpretations can be made; each image is 'composed' to within an inch of its life. This can be effective (a soldier huddled in a trench, writing a letter; the introduction to St Petersburg – a montage of reflections in water and parts of grandiloquent statues), but it need not bear any relation to the truth. The pictorial devices are somewhat tired: the boot, eternal symbol of the oppressor (over-used in all these films, but, to be fair, also strongly suggestive of Sound); the matching of massing workers to smoke from chimneys and waves; and the close-ups of faces screaming just above camera-range, most notably (if not first) deployed on the Odessa Steps.

This is already academic film-making – perhaps the prerogative of a young man. The attack on the Winter Palace lacks the sweep and incident of Eisenstein's version: *October* is no less propaganda, but its roller-coaster exhilaration transcends its purpose.

Storm Over Asia (1928) also has its redundancies and clumping ironies, but, moving from a study of revolt to one of imperialism, it has chances to take: it seems to me one of the most mature of Silent films. It was originally known in the West as *The Heir to Jenghis Khan*, which is more faithful to the Russian title. The setting is Mongolia, and the Caucasians have arrived on their usual business – exploitation and manipulation. A fur-trapper, Bair (V. Inkishnikov), flees from them, becomes a partisan, and is captured by the White Russians and forced to become the puppet-king, heir to the great Khan. But he is eventually aroused, and his partisan army appears miraculously behind him – which is demonstrably dishonest, but the miracle would not have been lost on the masses who rose in 1917.

Pudovkin made another thirteen films – in the Sound period – mainly in collaboration; none of those shown in the West achieved any degree of recognition. It is a pity, however, that his fame and that of Eisenstein should have eclipsed some engaging minor talents. The late Russian Silent cinema is, in fact, a fine flowering, a result not only of Kuleshov and his Experimental school in Moscow, but of the Eccentrics in Leningrad – FEKS, as they called themselves – who were also great theorisers and experimenters. The most important of the FEKS are Grigori Kozintsev (1905–73) and Leonid Trauberg (b. 1902), who worked in tandem for most of their careers. They had worked together in Kiev in the theatre, and as a result of their experience with a touring studio theatre founded FEKS – the Factory of the Eccentric Actor – with Sergei Yutkevich. In 1924 they were invited by Sevzapkino to make a short comedy. Two years later they moved to Leningradkino to make **The Devil's Wheel** (1926), which was deeply indebted to the German cinema; but their commitment to the Moscow school is evident from Kozintzev's comment to the FEKS

Nikolai Batalov in Pudovkin's *Mother*, as the family is torn asunder by a strike: his father is killed and himself imprisoned, but he escapes to join the marching workers, reunited with his mother, a convert to the cause; and they die, martyrs, in mid–embrace.

group: 'All that we've been doing is childish nonsense, we must all see *Strike* again and again, until we can understand it and adopt its power for our own.' So the childish nonsense is behind them, and *The Devil's Wheel* is a story of ordinary folk. It is not, as Jay Leyda says in 'Kino' 'a drama of the gangster bands that preyed upon Petrograd during the Civil War': the town is clearly called Leningrad, and since the hero is a Soviet sailor, we may take the time to be the present; he does become involved with crooks, but they are petty hoods rather than gangsters. The sailor, a country boy, also gets involved with a girl, and booze: he goes back to his ship contrite and prepared for the worst, but the friendly smiles of his escort suggest that he'll be let off because he's only young once. Undoubtedly that is propaganda – of the sort that would eventually stifle the Soviet cinema: but at least the sailor is more human than most Russian movie heroes, and since later movies refused to allow that there was anything rotten in Russia, it is good to have a fairly comprehensive portrait of the Leningrad underworld. It is apparent throughout these early Kozintsev-Trauberg collaborations that they were fascinated by vice; they are most at home in smoke-clouded bars and bordellos – though careful not to make such places attractive to their heroes. Their cleverness here is in making their comment on the underworld in 'Eccentric' style, letting the camera go ape in the fairground or whenever there are crowds. Turning for the first time to 'everyday life' – which had never interested Russian film-makers – they have put it on the screen in a way that is honest both to the subject and to their own principles of style. Visually, the film is lively, but it seems a little trivial when set beside Pabst's more melodramatic *Die Freudlose Gasse*. The girl's butcher father more than resembles Werner Krauss in that film: and did Pabst in return study this girl for his own portraits of women who are neither whores nor virgins but, like this one, what we'd call a good-time girl?

With **The Cloak** (1926), Kozintsev and Trauberg turned to Gogol – and it may be said to be a tale of everyday life a century earlier. Kozintsev explained later that the Leningrad cinema was dominated by historical films of stultifying stiffness: Gogol, with his grotesques and ironies, provided a counter-balance – and also a chance to be true again to the principles of FEKS. Leyda is right in seeing the central character as kin to both the somnambulist in *Caligari*, because of his appearance, and the doorkeeper in *Der Letzte Mann*, because of his pathos and isolation. The style and content have been worked out with as much thoroughness as with *The Devil's Wheel* – too much so, since the joint directors couldn't see the wood for the trees. The images may spill across the screen, but for the first half at least it is impossible to follow the narrative without a knowledge of the original novel plus some of 'The Nevsky Prospect', purloined to pad out a thin anecdote. As the clerk, Andrei Kostrichkin overplays with intelligence. In all these Russian films there is too much 'acting': the heroes and heroines are always naturalistic, but when anyone has anything half-villainous to do, they start to over-indulge – but in this case they're justified. The decor by Yevgeni Enei and the camerawork by Andrei Moskvin are in both cases superior to that on the earlier film, and they surpassed even this work in **The Club of the Big Deed** (1927). A contemporary study of the FEKS – by V. Nedborovo – calls this 'the most cinematographic' of their films, and he quotes another critic as saying that it was 'the smartest film yet produced by the Soviet Union' – by which I take it he means the most handsome. It is possible that Kozintsev and Trauberg sought historical subjects because they had these two brilliantly talented men in their team . . . but this was an historical subject in fashion with Eisenstein and Pudovkin, celebrating a revolutionary period of an earlier time – in this case the Decemberist movement of 1825. It has a collective hero, which here is an unsatisfactory device; and it has a villain who is villainous merely for the sake of it – which is hard to accept in a political film. Once again narrative clarity is not a strong point, but the sets – the gambling club of the title, the battlefield, a circus, a parade-ground – are used with great virtuosity. **New Babylon** (1929) was the only Kozintsev-

Trauberg film well received in the West; and was considered sufficiently important in the U.S.S.R. at the time for Shostakovich to write a score for it – surprisingly, not welded to the film in synchronised version after the coming of Sound. Although its title is that name given to Paris by the Prussian press of 1870, the subject is the subsequent Commune: the bourgeoisie (a theatre-owner and his actresses – the best representatives of decadence) retreat to the heights of Versailles as the Prussians advance, and the people, free of their bosses, find a new purpose in life – the Commune. The bourgeoisie can't bear to see them happy, and have the soldiers fire on them; a dying Communard shouts that they'll be back one day. For this trite tale, the French artists of the period have been ransacked, works by Doré and Daumier juxtaposed with those of Manet and Degas – for that same old purpose, irony: at the end, the film cuts back and forth between the defeated workers and corpses on the barricades and the same old effete faces swilling champagne – but with such bravura consistency that much may be forgiven. The medium is being used to its fullest extent, as putty, as a pliable toy – not as something recording the movements of actors.

The Kiss of Mary Pickford (1927) was directed by one of Kuleshov's pupils, Sergei Komarov, with due regard to his theories – the blending of fact and fiction; but since Komarov was a great admirer of the Eccentrics he gives much business to its hero, Igor Ilinskyi, one of Russia's favourite comics. The film is a satire on the local movie industry, incorporating newsreel footage of the celebrated European tour of Mary Pickford and Douglas Fairbanks; it is ironic that that tour should be best preserved via a film made in the Soviet Union – for the couple were, after all, two enormously wealthy people, major props of a capitalist industry. No one can doubt the charm and genuine pleasure of the couple, but one does notice them searching for the camera between smiles – just to make sure it's there. As with *Extraordinary Adventures of Mr West*, more might have been made of the subject, but the film is nevertheless a huge advance on that.

Another member of Kuleshov's workshop, Boris Barnet (1902–65), made **The Girl with the Hatbox** (1927), an almost perfect comedy – richer, indeed, with visual wit than the comedies that René Clair was making at the time. The girl is Natasha (Anna Sten), who comes from the country once a week with the hats she makes: her buyer, Madame Irene, claims to the tax-inspector that the girl has a room in her house, and the girl promptly marries a destitute student (Ivan Koval-Samborsky) to give him a roof over his head. The film is inventive and enchanting, be it in the odd relationship of the girl and her 'husband', or the vile bourgeois behaviour of Madame Irene and hers. Also airy and irresistible is **House on Trubnaya Square** (1928), although it does tend to go heavy on party propaganda – though one of the funniest sequences is an amateur theatre show at the workers' club, in which lots of hackneyed jokes come up sparklingly fresh. The heroine is again a country girl (Vera Maretskaya), and the piece mainly concerns her adventures in an apartment house, clearly influenced by *Menschen Untereinander*; the most entertaining of her fellow-tenants is the jumped-up hairdresser played in his last film role (he died in 1929) by Vladimir Fogel, the most human villain of the period.

He may also be seen in Abram Room's **Bed and Sofa** (1927), completing a *menage à trois* with Batalov and Ludmilla Semyenova, needless to say as the lodger who breaks up their marriage. In its acceptance of both adultery and abortion, the film might once have been shocking, but even allowing for the fact that Room was making a film for revolutionaries he was careful, for it's short on the necessary amorous activity. But if it is only mildly entertaining, it must be seen as another example of the Soviet film industry being ahead of any other. Like *By the Law*, the strongest influence seems to have been Sjöström, and the marriage here is not unlike that of the Ingmarssons, with no praise or blame for the trauma it undergoes. Others have seen this film as a comedy, since the situation is one of farce, and some of the devices used to indicate a marriage growing stale – husband ordering his tea

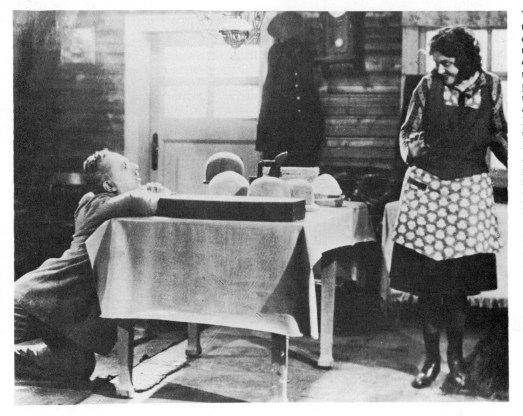

The achievements of the 'classic' Russian directors have cast too great a shadow over some lesser talents, but it is perhaps because of them that the comedies of Boris Barnet are such unexpected delights. In *The Girl with the Hatbox* the gentleman on the left is indeed proposing to Anna Sten: as her landlord he had not been particularly pleasant, but she has the winning lottery ticket – though she doesn't know it yet.

instead of asking for it – were typical of the comedy of the period. Let us say rather that it is drama treated lightly by one who finds absurdity in most human behaviour.

The same cannot be said of the Ukrainian, Alexander Dovzhenko (1894–1956), a painter who one sleepless night decided to start again in 'the one art which was fresh and new, with enormous creative potentialities and opportunities'. The first film he directed was a two-reel slapstick about a lost baby, **The Fruits of Love** (1926), a piece as inept as it is unfunny. When he turned serious, contemporary opinion placed him on a level with Eisenstein and Pudovkin, if not higher; as late as 1960 Ernest Lindgren wrote of **Earth** (1930): 'Its political moral is in its narrative framework, portraying the conflict between rich Kulaks and the collective farms which threaten to absorb their lands. But the film's more profound and more memorable content is its picture of the ever-recurring rhythm of pastoral life.

birth, love, death and sorrow following each other with the same inevitability as the ploughing, the sowing and the harvest.' Ah! there it is: peasants wresting their living from the soil – how much more worthy of attention than all those vamps, cuties, detectives and reporters!

It is the only one of Dovzhenko's pictures to enter the international repertory, but I have seen two of his preceding three features, and they are quite as dreadful. **Zvenigora** (1928) has some striking images, which is presumably why Eisenstein and Pudovkin recognised him as their equal. I find it unintelligible. Dovzhenko said, 'Do I hear the objection that some people in the audience may not understand my film? Well, I cannot help it . . . The reason you don't understand is within yourself. Maybe you are simply unable to think, whereas my purpose is to prompt your thinking while you see my film.' **Arsenal** (1929), supposedly a celebration of the Ukrainian people's struggle for liberty, plods on with pictures of armies, soldiers, peasants, fields, machinery, followed by more pictures of armies, soldiers, peasants, etc. Watching it is like going to an exhibition where the pictures move – posed, artificial pictures, meant to strike us all of a heap with their artistry. Even the contemptible *Earth* does at least have a story, and I beg you to bear with me.

'Seventy-five years behind an ox-drawn plough,' says someone about an old man who promptly dies. The village goes ecstatic: a big attraction is en route. A circus? Stalin? No, a tractor – driven by the deceased's grandson, Vassil; he strays on to the land of a kulak, Khoma, who later murders him. Vassil's father wants him 'buried the new way, and we'll sing new songs about our new way of life': the whole village turns out for the burial, singing new songs about our new way of life, and ignoring the now-demented Khoma yelling out his grief. The dead man's fiancée has also gone mad, and is rushing around her hovel stark-naked; while the priest, unwanted for this important funeral, sits and stares with apprehension. The film ends with Khoma doing a wild Cossack dance in imitation of Vassil. His guilt, I might say, is apparent from the start, and the posturing intrudes upon the film's only pleasure – the plain, unfussy faces. Neither they, nor any amount of shots of rain-pelted apples, can save it; but, Lenin be praised, it only lasts just over an hour. It was John Coleman of the *New Statesman* who in 1976 prevented me from attempting Dovzhenko's next

film, *Ivan* (1932): 'heavy and ludicrous' he dismissed it.

The sameness and self-consciousness of Russian cinema are reasons many avoid it: the films we have been discussing, even the comedies, are dedicated to one theme – the innate nobility of the worker/peasant. In the West, we have always preferred those concerned with revolutionary struggles, despite the over-use of irony, to those exalting the land; and when the greater of the two 'revolutionary' directors, Eisenstein, offers a study in the latter genre, we seldom programme it. **Old and New** (1929), also known as *The General Line*, co-directed with Grigori Alexandrov, was planned in 1926, but work was interrupted by *October* – and was further delayed when Stalin advised a more 'correct' ending: but all Eisenstein came up with was an epilogue – a montage, naturally – on the bond between Russian workers. The subject is the collectivisation of Soviet agriculture, via the study of one rural community. What makes the film unpalatable is that its message is simple-minded: tractors and bulls are lovely. I have to say that I am caught two ways by this film: by admiration for the images and editing – the language Eisenstein created for the cinema, so powerful that it is its own narrative; and by fatigue. All those smiling workers' faces, processions past enormous busts of Lenin, endless shots of fields and clouds . . . But then, this film wasn't made with us in mind.

6

The United Artists

IN 1919 the four most famous people working in films decided to pool their talents for their own greater financial advantage – Charles Chaplin, D. W. Griffith, Mary Pickford and her husband, Douglas Fairbanks. Despite the huge salaries they earned – particularly Chaplin and Pickford – their producers were making gigantic profits from their films, and they were in part reacting against persistent rumours that the studios would put a ceiling on star salaries. It was even said that Zukor was considering a merger with his arch-rival, First National, the more easily to achieve this; but it was an action of the latter company which triggered the foundation of the new association, when it casually refused Chaplin's request for an increase in his production budget. That talent should be its own boss was a policy the studios resisted – so strongly that all other attempts were killed until the Fifties, and then it was another long struggle before the studios bowed to the notion that talent demanded creative freedom – and as much money as it could command. The new company, United Artists, opened a distribution office, and its four principals either bought studios or hired space, relying on their reputations to have exhibitors demand their films. 'The lunatics have taken charge of the asylum,' went the industry quip, as it closed ranks against them: the cinema chains owned by the big companies refused to show United Artists' films – until they saw the profits being made by the independent theatres.

The concept, however, of United Artists was not started by one of its founder members but by a jobless executive determined to remain in the film industry. He was B. P. Schulberg (1892–1957), who in common with the other film moguls was Jewish, but unlike most of them was both American-born and literate. A former reporter, he joined Edwin S. Porter's Rex company as screenwriter and publicist, later moving with him to Famous Players. When Hiram Abrams, a New England distributor, succeeded H. V. Hodkinson within Paramount, Zukor began to realise that he no longer trusted Abrams: when he forced him out, Schulberg – by this time head of production – elected to go with him. Since the industry was controlled by Zukor, Fox, Laemmle and First National, the two men had three options open if they wished to continue in films: (1) apply to one of Zukor's rivals (2) join one of the still mushrooming minor companies, or (3) start up on their own. Schulberg believed that they could follow the last of these courses and overwhelm all competition if they gained the concurrence of the five most powerful figures in the industry. Thus Chaplin, Fairbanks, Pickford, Griffith and William S. Hart were each presented with a manifesto, '89 Reasons for United Artists'. Hart declined to join, and in the event United Artists was formed without Schulberg: for Fairbanks wanted the new company headed by William Gibbs McAdoo, a friend who was also an influential politician and son-in-law to President Wilson. McAdoo declined the offer, but proposed in his stead his press secretary, at the same time objecting to the financial arrangements to be made with Abrams and Schulberg. Abrams stayed; Schulberg left, to form his own production company (before rejoining Zukor in 1926, when Zukor coveted one of his stars,

Clara Bow. He resumed his position as head of production, till ejected from Paramount during that company's financial convulsions in 1932, along with Jesse Lasky – and like Lasky became an independent producer with only intermittent success.)

Once the experiment had proved successful, the four co-founders hired a production manager, Joseph M. Schenck (1877–1961), another immigrant and one-time theatre manager and producer; he joined them in 1924, and was virtually in control from 1926 onwards. He realised that more films were needed to feed the system of exchanges set up by Abrams as chief sales executive, and thus his own star (and brother-in-law) Buster Keaton joined the fold, as did others, including Valentino and Gloria Swanson.

Given their eminence at the time, it is not remarkable that the four founders of the company remain gigantic figures in cinema history. We can still admire and enjoy the star vehicles of Pickford and Fairbanks – certainly the later ones. The same is true of the comedies of Chaplin, but not to the same extent. Up to five

or ten years ago, as throughout his lifetime, he was regarded as a genius; since then his reputation has decreased, and continues to do so. For over half a century Chaplin's position was as unassailable as that of Shakespeare: our parents and our grandparents had loved him, and then, suddenly, audiences were no longer laughing. This struck me as so astonishing that I tried to see as much Chaplin as I could with as many disparate audiences. Those that roared through most of Keaton and much of Harold Lloyd evinced only intermittent mirth with Chaplin. The most serious blow, however, to his reputation was the re-showing, in the last year of his life, of his one serious film, *A Woman of Paris* (q.v.), reputedly a masterpiece. For over fifty years he had refused requests from students to view it, and there was no copy in any Western archive; revealed, it was of appalling banality even by the standards at the time.

But though the contemporary reviews were ecstatic, what of the case of Griffith, who continued to have his admirers through the years? Aside from his false

D.W. Griffith at work: The lady to whom he is giving last minute instructions is Lillian Gish, while behind them is Robert Harron, his usual leading man. With the advent of Richard Barthelmess he was demoted to comic, or romantic lead in less important projects like *The Greatest Question*. When he shot himself it was said to be accidental, but it was after the New York premiere of *Way Down East,* which promised to be a triumph for both Griffith and Barthelmess. The film Griffith is directing in this picture is much earlier, *The Battle of the Sexes,* made in 1914.

claims to innovations, he has at least the achievement of 'bigness' with *Intolerance*; but his later films are sentimental and contrived melodramas, with virtually identical endings, as the heroine is saved from death, or a Fate Worse Than, amidst much cross-cutting. *Orphans of the Storm* (q.v.) was described by Robert E. Sherwood, in the old *Life* Magazine, as better than any previous Griffith film, and 'immeasurably better' than the two German films which had inspired it, *Danton* and *Madame Dubarry*: 'There is scarcely a moment,' Sherwood said, 'that is not charged with intense dramatic power,' and Lillian Gish in her memoir quotes another contemporary: 'A great work of art. It has the sweep of *The Birth of a Nation,* the remarkable tragic drive of *Broken Blossoms,* the terrific melodramatic appeal of *Way Down East . . .* ' It is difficult today to find these films any less dreadful than those which Griffith's admirers deplored. *Dream Street* (1921) was 'a low point' in his work, said Iris Barry, but 'too early to be considered the beginning of decline', and her colleague, Eileen Bowser, dismissed Griffith's three First National films as 'potboilers, and one suspects them to be the work of not very competent assistants'; but since she describes *The Greatest Question* (1919) as 'the usual melodramatic Griffith story' I fail to see why she could not accept that the usual Griffith was directing it.

A clue to the mystery may lie in Rotha's 1929 assessment of *Broken Blossoms* (q.v.), that its 'simple, human story [was] without the box-office attractions of silk legs and spectacle.' James Agate, writing in 1922, found 'this little picture as arresting as ever' and ten years later he bracketed it with *Way Down East* as films of which he 'personally can never tire'; another ten years on he listed it as one of the ten best films ever made. How little, you see, was expected of the cinema: would Agate as theatre critic have accepted a drama as barren and emotionally naïve?

After *Intolerance* Griffith had accepted an invitation from the British government to make a propaganda film, **Hearts of the World** (1918), which it financed together with Zukor (against Griffith's future services). Griffith, under two pseudonyms, provided the scenario – about a boy (Robert Harron) and girl (Miss Gish) divided by war but reunited in the heat of battle, in an inn where there are Germans (literally) coming out of the woodwork. The film was eventually of little purpose, since the U.S. had entered the War by the time it was shown – but it quickly made half-a-million dollars' profit. Some of the film was shot in England, where it gathered Noël Coward as an extra, but most of it in California; the battle footage left over was incorporated into **The Girl Who Stayed at Home** (1919), which contrasts a French heiress (Carol Dempster) and her American soldier suitor (Richard Barthelmess) with two effete New Yorkers (Clarine Seymour, Mr Harron). It is a particularly shapeless film, cutting inanely between these couples and a German soldier, whose presence is finally explained when he saves the heiress from the inevitable Fate Worse Than. Griffith's work on it was supposedly perfunctory because his attention was taken up by **Broken Blossoms** (1919), a tale of miscegenation in Limehouse rendered the more excruciating by its intertitles (e.g. 'Into the dark chambers of her frightened, incredulous little heart comes warmth and light'). Agate was right to praise the performances of Barthelmess as the Yellow Man and Miss Gish as the girl who runs away from her brutal stepfather (Donald Crisp); he also liked the settings – photographed throughout, appropriately, as a stage-set, and disastrously influential: when other producers learnt that this film was shot in eighteen days at a cost of $88,000 they drew away from location shooting. It was made for Zukor, who thought it 'too poetic' and sold it to United Artists, since he knew they needed product, for $250,000: it made a profit for the new company of $700,000.

Griffith dedicated **True-Heart Susie** (1919) to all the girls who wait vainly for a husband – presumably by staying pure: the intertitles emphasise that paint and powder constitute traps of a devious nature, but the film is attractively ambivalent. We are supposed to admire the artless, plain Miss Gish, and despise the hussy Miss Seymour, but though the pure one eventually triumphs and her rival becomes slatternly and dies, we may sense the division in Griffith himself between Victorian sentimentalist and Hollywood

The photography of Billy Bitzer and the acting of Lillian Gish are virtually all that make Griffith's films watchable today. The most pleasant is *True–Heart Susie*: Miss Gish (right) sells the family cow to pay secretly for the college education of her sweetheart (Robert Harron), to lose his good opinion by taking the blame for the infidelities of his new love (Clarine Seymour).

party-man. It does, therefore, offer an accurate reflection of the changing attitude towards women, and contains also a clear and well-judged portrait of a small rural community. It was Griffith's last film for Zukor, and he reputedly signed the First National contract in order to buy his own studio – at Mamaroneck, New York. *The Greatest Question* has the hideously abused Miss Gish as an orphan skivvy, and in **Way Down East** (1920) she is seduced but abandoned. Griffith paid $175,000 for the rights to this already dated barnstormer, and it was his biggest commercial success after *The Birth of a Nation*. Readers, after all, still wept at the death of Little Nell, and the borrowings from Dickens in this film are many: that author, however, would surely have loved Miss Gish, playing a waif but with such spirit that you know she will denounce her seducer before rushing out on to the ice-floes. **Orphans of the Storm** (1921) was based on an even more venerable melodrama, reset at the time of the French Revolution because the two previous German films had such acclaim in New York; an introduction spells out the dangers of Bolshevism and

anarchy when one iniquitous government is replaced by another, while the portrayal of Danton, as an intertitle has it, makes him 'the Abraham Lincoln of France'.

When the public failed to respond in sufficient numbers, Griffith tried a mystery story, *One Exciting Night,* and another attempt to present rural America coping with the Jazz Age, *The White Rose;* but without Miss Gish to furnish her beauty and talent his films looked more old-fashioned than ever. Although he had experimented with synchronisation at the time of *Dream Street,* he advanced in no other direction. Indeed, he regressed, and in **America** (1924) attempted to do for the War of Independence what his most successful film had done for the War between the States. Also, he returned to the animated tableaux of old, and claims to historical accuracy were derided when the plot has George Washington playing Cupid to a plough-boy poet (Neil Hamilton) and a highborn lady (Carol Dempster). Stung by such criticism, Griffith tried a contemporary story, of conditions in post-war Germany, **Isn't Life Wonderful?** (1924), about childhood sweethearts (Hamilton, Dempster) who can marry if they can surmount poverty. The film does flicker to life with a sequence about queueing for meat as the Reichsmark rises by the millions, but was no better liked by press or public. Griffith was an expensive worker, and because he had given United Artists only failures since *Way Down East* his quarrels with his partners now became public. He signed a contract with Zukor – which, announced before he had severed that with United Artists, caused the latter to claim his first Paramount film, **Sally of the Sawdust** (1925) – a version of a W. C. Fields stage vehicle which foolishly shifted the emphasis from Fields to the heroine (Miss Dempster), a circus-girl finally reunited with her 'real' grandparents. Griffith's loss of independence found compensation when, after another Fields vehicle, he was assigned to an expensive project, *The Sorrows of Satan,* abandoned by deMille when he left to form his own company. But when, after costs had further mounted amidst much dispute, it too was a disaster at the box office, Griffith's lingering reputation within the industry was finally annihilated.

Nevertheless, Schenck brought him back to United Artists, inasmuch as he signed him to make five films for his Art Cinema Corporation, releasing through U.A. – for which privilege he voted Griffith's remaining stock (which Griffith hung on to till 1933) and exercised control over script and budget. Only four films were made, and **Lady of the Pavements** (1929) is at best mediocre, the story of a Parisian countess (Jetta Goudal) who revenges herself on a reluctant suitor (William Boyd) by making him fall in love with a trollop disguised as a lady. There is more to be said, however, for **Abraham Lincoln** (1930), his first Talkie. 'Shucks,' says a small boy, looking at Baby Abe, 'he'll never amount to anything'; but nothing that follows is quite as bad. The script, credited to Stephen Vincent Benét, was apparently much disregarded – which is perhaps why the Civil War consists of bitty battle scenes, punctuated by Mr Lincoln receiving news of varying import – but in the title-role Walter Huston (q.v.) has the strength and sincerity to make such badly conceived scenes seem consequential. During production, Griffith was, in his own words, in 'a nightmare of the mind and nerves', but this is a reasonably polished piece of work. It is difficult to offer more credit in view of the all-round incompetence of **The Struggle** (1931), made without studio control and as a gesture to prove that his failures had been due to 'interference'. It was made possible by a bank loan, some backing from United Artists, and a 1929 tax refund to his old company, luckily invested. There are just two good sequences: the prologue, set in 1911, in a beer garden; and an engagement party done with a more reasonable view of the proletariat than was usual in films of the era. The rest is a tract on the Evils Wrought by the Demon Drink, from the husband getting rolling drunk after being taunted for ordering a sarsaparilla, through broken marriage and vagabondage, to an attempt to murder his daughter during the last throes of D.T.s – followed by an epilogue in which he is regenerated and gets his job back, together with a raise, because the factory has adopted his invention. Griffith's own 1909 *A Drunkard's Reformation* could not have been less sophisticated – or less topical: despite the modern costumes, there is no reference to Prohibition. The staging is clumsy, the sound as primitive as in the very first Talkies – and audiences at its few showings, in Philadelphia, roared with laughter while Griffith cowered in his hotel room. His company went into receivership, and he lived on another sixteen years, earning enough from occasional reissues, occasional consultant's fees and the remake rights to *Broken Blossoms* – made in Britain in 1936 – to pay for a hotel room and booze. Writers on film who castigated Hollywood for not using him had presumably not seen *The Struggle* – or examined his record of failures. Hollywood, for once at least, knew better than its critics.

Mary Pickford's last film for First National was **Daddy Long Legs** (1919), in which she leaves an orphanage because of an unknown benefactor. At a time when workhouses were a prominent part of the urban scene, the orphanage must have terrified audiences, till they could relax with the pre-Raphaelite countryside of the second half; and they must have been happy that she preferred the old-world courtesy of the unknown benefactor (Marshall Neilen, who also directed) to brash young Jimmy, who almost certainly liked jazz. The difficulty with Miss Pickford today is that her interpretation of childhood varies between the kittenish and the grotesque; in the midst of tall supporting-players and sets made to scale, she pouts and grins, walking with legs wide apart and toes turned out – and it is a parody of childhood. The public's insistence that she play children was surely due to the fact that though it had taken her to its heart, it found her pallid in grown-up roles; as a child, her spirited and merry personality must have endeared her to spectators who cherished their childhoods more than we do today: there was authority to be flouted, there were crusty hearts to be melted, the poor and deprived to be cosseted. She was Cinderella in a different dress, usually in stories that adolescent girls had wept over on the printed page. She apparently loathed such tales, but chose one, **Pollyanna** (1920), for her first United Artists film because she wanted to protect her investment. 'This is really not a story,' says the foreword, but 'the rainbow born of the sunshine of a

The World's Sweetheart

ABOVE: Mary Pickford in a double-role in *Little Lord Fauntleroy*: it was her gifted photographer, Charles Rosher, who – in this film – first used double-exposure for such effects, and they are still impressive. RIGHT: After the insipidity of most of Miss Pickford's films, *My Best Girl* is a delightful surprise. In one funny sequence, the boss's son takes her home – only she thinks he's merely a store apprentice and is uncertain about this supposed dinner for two of the workers. He is played by Charles 'Buddy' Rogers, whom she married after her divorce from Fairbanks.

On the set of *Rosita*, from left to right: Charles Chaplin, Ernst Lubitsch, Mary Pickford and Douglas Fairbanks. Miss Pickford had invited Lubitsch to direct her because of his historical spectacles – and this was another. It was the critical success of Chaplin's *A Woman in Paris* which caused Lubitsch to return to the sophisticated comedies which he most enjoyed making.

little girl's smile.' The little girl learns the 'glad' philosophy from her father and imparts it to all and sundry till felled by an almost fatal accident, while trying to save a baby, of course: 'God wouldn't let those little feet be destroyed when He needs them to run His errands,' says an intertitle. **Suds** (1920), directed by Paul Powell, is more palatable both because it is short and because Miss Pickford's role is similar to the skivvy in *Stella Maris* – a cockney laundress who dreams of romance with a masher but finds love with the delivery boy. The source was a one-act play that Maude Adams used to perform, but Pickford returned to the 'classics' with **Little Lord Fauntleroy** (1921), directed by Alfred E. Green and Jack Pickford, her brother. She plays both the little lord and his mother, Dearest; he is not actually a lord, but the American heir to an earldom – melting his grandfather's heart, besting a rival claimant and introducing American democracy into an English castle. The success of the film – and of Frances Hodgson Burnett's novel – was partly due to the tingling thought that American red

blood was intermingling with British blue; what today repels is that it was thought to be the height of human ambition to be a lord.

In her other films at this time – e.g. *Tess of the Storm Country* (1922) – Miss Pickford, at that time almost thirty, plays an adolescent of uncertain age. The apparent acceptance of her Dearest encouraged her to try adult roles, but the public responded to neither **Rosita** (1923) nor *Dorothy Vernon of Haddon Hall* (1924). The former was directed by Lubitsch, after he had rejected the latter – for which Pickford had brought him to the U.S. As Rosita, a fiery street-singer whose virtue is threatened by the Spanish king, she fails to supply him with the sensuous appeal of Negri; and if it is surely the most enjoyable of her extant films, it was a regression for Lubitsch himself. In the pages of *Photoplay* Miss Pickford asked her fans what roles she should play, and the overwhelming response was Cinderella. But that would have been too easy; like her husband – and as 'king' and 'queen' of the American film industry it was befitting –

she wanted to offer her public both the best possible production and herself in a new role. The challenge, however, was never extended beyond the bounds of reasonable investment, so virtually all that is new in **Little Annie Rooney** (1925) is the milieu – she's the daughter of Officer Rooney, a New York cop. Again, she is an urchin, again she almost dies, and again she grows up miraculously at the very end for a romantic fade-out. William Beaudine directed, as with **Sparrows** (1926), where she mothers a group of orphans in the middle of an alligator-infested swamp, her resourcefulness unquestioned – to the extent that one wonders why the owners of this baby farm haven't fed her to a quicksand. They are excellent villains (Gustav von Seyffertitz and Charlotte Mineau), and the film undoubtedly has thrills of a far-fetched nature.

The Cinderella aspect of **My Best Girl** (1927) is so strong that Pickford advanced to adolescence, as stockgirl in a department store. In this last of her Silent films she proves an adept comedienne, sharing some delightful scenes with the boy (Charles 'Buddy' Rogers), the boss's son learning the business. Sam Taylor directed this almost perfect romantic comedy, a good example of the Pickford and Fairbanks films, co-operative efforts not factory-packaged. The stars were the controlling forces, assisted by the director, and, in her case, Charles Rosher (according to his own word), who photographed her films so handsomely – and probably by her mother, watching on the side of the set. The 'Elton Thomas' who wrote most of the Fairbanks films is his own pseudonym, but Allan Dwan, who directed two of them, has said that it referred to the Fairbanks crew, since every one chipped in.

The energy of Douglas Fairbanks (1883–1939) was prodigious, and it is said that his exuberance alienated his co-workers at Triangle: Anita Loos, then a scenario writer with that company, managed to harness him and present him to the public as the all-courageous, always optimistic all-American boy; her stories for him* often found him as basically

*They are credited to her and her husband, John Emerson, often also as director: but Miss Loos later insisted that Emerson's creative contribution was nil.

decent playboy or wronged black sheep of the family. He made four such films for United Artists, but only one after he started his series of swashbucklers: **The Nut** (1921), directed by Ted Reed. In this, he is a wealthy scion whose attempts to aid his fiancée's philanthropic schemes end in chaos – the same role that Keaton played in *The Saphead* (q.v.), as recommended a few months earlier by Fairbanks, who had done it on the stage in New York, borrowing in return the fantastic household gadgets from *One Week* (q.v.), to remind us how frankly dependent were these artists on each other. But he was no more a comic than he was an ardent romantic hero, and he didn't find his real screen identity till he took sword in hand. His comic sense was always apparent, however, deliciously so in his Spanish dance as Don Q, all heel-taps and bum-wriggles; his bragging and his dashing, always a mite self-mocking, took on an extra edge in his swashbucklers; and his balletic agility was entirely suited to leaping parapets, shinning walls and tackling a dozen assailants while protecting the heroine with his free arm. 'When life was life and men were men' runs an intertitle in **The Three Musketeers** (1921), and one loves this enlivening and sometimes magical performer for believing it.

He had wanted to play d'Artagnan for years, and took the chance when he decided that the troops returning from France were not in the mood for his usual optimistic subjects. First he made **The Mark of Zorro** (1920), from a magazine story about a Spanish-educated Californian don who poses as an effete buffoon by day and is by night the daring swordsman who rights the peons' wrongs. It is, alas, a throwback to the early features, since you could shuffle the incidents without harm and no character but the don has individuality; and there is little more to be said for anything other than his stunts in the Dumas film, also directed by Fred Niblo, or for **Robin Hood** (1922), directed by Allan Dwan, or for **The Thief of Bagdad** (1924), directed by Raoul Walsh. His Robin Hood finds him rather Robin Goodfellow; and not so parenthetically, his followers are not so much 'merry' as 'gay'. This has something to do with the way they were choreographed, but indeed the reverence accorded comradeship in the Fairbanks films goes beyond the buddy-buddy attitude of many American films; however innocently meant, surely only one interpretation is possible of that scene where Robin is found romping on the floor with a friend, and the king (Wallace Beery) observes, 'At a time like this 'tis befitting he shows his love for a maid.' It is the nature of such against-all-odds tales that their heroes are renegades or outlaws, a tradition that goes back at least to Hereward the Wake: Fairbanks contrived to be outside the law, either pretended or wronged, from the start, but with *Robin Hood* he found his formula. The exposition is painfully slow (to modern eyes) till the halfway mark, when the tempo will quicken, then dull till the all-out action of the final sequence. The pastiche of *The Thief of Bagdad* – inspired, incidentally, by the German spectacles – finally explodes into the marvellous final sequence with the carpet whizzing above Bagdad, its shadow over the towers to prove that it wasn't a simple matter of superimposition.

For Fairbanks believed in giving value for money. *The Three Musketeers* was by the standards of the time a 'super-production', and Edward Knoblock was engaged to handle the adaptation; also Fairbanks sensibly believed that his films had to be visually exciting, importing on occasion designers from Europe to achieve this. The famous castle set in *Robin Hood* still takes the breath away. The upper reaches of the great hall were achieved with glass-shots, i.e. backcloths painted on glass before the camera-eye or sometimes on the lens itself, an established device to enhance the spectacle at minimum cost, but the exteriors brought the budget to $2 million, the highest for any film till that time and provided by Fairbanks himself when faced with his financiers' doubts. The industry was in crisis, for it had begun to repeat itself, and the public, not then as movie-orientated as it would be during the first decade of Talkies, had begun to stay away from all but the exceptional film – and though this was, it hardly recovered its costs. *The Thief of Bagdad,* also expensive, was hugely profitable, encouraging Fairbanks to use Technicolor for **The Black Pirate** (1926)

directed by Albert Parker. Keaton the previous year had been the first to use this colour system, for the prologue of *Seven Chances* (q.v.), and until the arrival of three-tone Technicolor it was more commonly used for one-reel sequences in otherwise monochrome films – due, clearly, to its limitations. In choosing to make the first movie wholly in colour Fairbanks selected a subject and setting to suit the limited colour palette then available – for sea and sky and what was literally a desert island. The effect is other-worldly, and the fact that the film is visually satisfying owes much to the paraphernalia of sails and rigging designed by Carl Oscar Berg. It is against those sails that Fairbanks performs one of his most celebrated stunts, sliding down the sails with his knife in the canvas. Not till long after Fairbanks's death was it disclosed that he had done few of his own stunts – 'the best kept secret of the time', as Eileen Bowser puts it. (The other famous stunt – sliding down the curtain in *Robin Hood* – was done with a concealed slide.)

The Black Pirate, however, has its longueurs, but I have no reservations about the other late Fairbanks Silents. **Don Q, Son of Zorro** (1925) is a great advance on its predecessor, an adventure set in old Madrid, with the ageing Zorro crossing the Atlantic to help his son out of difficulties – Fairbanks in a double role, well supported by Donald Crisp (who also directed) as the villain, and Mary Astor as the heroine. There is a superb villain in **The Gaucho** (1927) – Gustav von Seyffertitz as Ruiz the Usurper; and instead of the usual anaemic leading lady there is a fiery senorita, Lupe Velez, a shrew to be tamed; there also lurks 'The Victim of Black Death', a figure as terrifying as any created by Lon Chaney. Fairbanks himself is head of a band of outlaws pitted against a fascist regime, and as directed by F. Richard Jones the whole film has sweep and imagination; it is ingenuous but not naïve. The duels, escapes and last-minute rescues take place in settings by Berg even more impressive than those in *The Black Pirate*, and the piece is wrapped in a religious mysticism that isn't cloying. At a time when virtually all films carried morals, the principals of United Artists were particularly strict about this, doubtless because their

The Great Swashbuckler

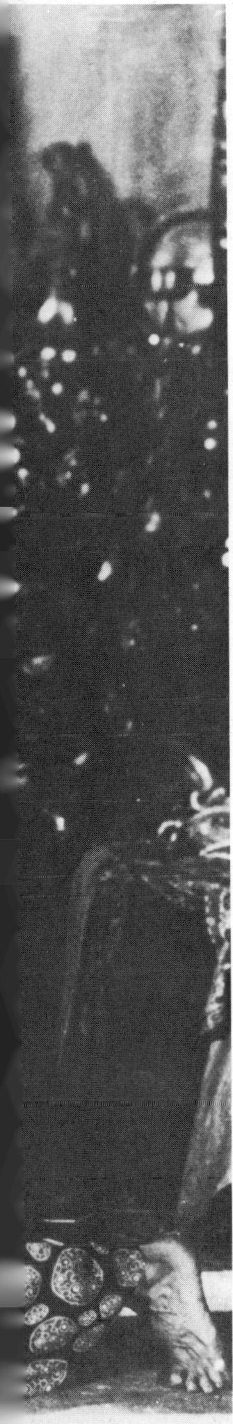

FAR LEFT: Douglas Fairbanks about to embark on one of his space-defying leaps in *The Thief of Bagdad* and, ABOVE, as lover with Lupe Velez in *The Gaucho* The latter is later and better, since it was a challenge to Fairbanks to make each vehicle more colourful and more exciting than the last. His final Silent is shown LEFT, in an advertisement for a reissue.

eminence decreed it; Griffith's and Pickford's moralities were fundamentally of the Sunday school, and so were those of Fairbanks. However, **The Iron Mask** (1929) is suffused – albeit in an elementary way – with a feeling of defeat, of time passing, of death and change. All the Fairbanks swashbucklers exemplify the days when movies were young and fun, but he was growing older and was conscious of it: Dwan directed this d'Artagnan to go about his derring-do with greying locks. And movies themselves were growing older: the jazz singer had sung, and now Fairbanks spoke – prologue and epilogue, and just for a moment in the middle.

The fame of Chaplin was greater even than that of 'Doug' and 'Mary' and the acclaim virtually unanimous, his 'genius' an accepted fact. Probably no film of its time was as much loved as **Shoulder Arms** (1918), in which he represented all those 'little men' who didn't want to fight the Kaiser and who endured the blitzkrieg of trench warfare. **The Kid** (1921) was an even bigger triumph, acknowledged, as Chaplin says in his autobiography, a 'classic' immediately after its New York opening, and going on to repay its $300,000 cost many times over. First National had insisted that the public did not want to see Chaplin in features, despite the success of both *A Dog's Life* (1918) and *Shoulder Arms* in three reels each and the comparative failure of the two two-reel successors, *Sunnyside* and *A Day's Pleasure*. *The Kid* was six reels long, and only released after long battles with the company, which proposed to release it as three two-reelers. Chaplin proved to be justified, for the world laughed and cried at these adventures of the tramp and the ragamuffin (Jackie Coogan), a miniature version of himself. The slapstick is particularly inventive in a sequence where the kid breaks windows and Charlie turns up as a glazier, and the pathos is well judged; however, the fantasy sequence is horrendous, and it is difficult to justify Chaplin's reputation as a social satirist by such rare, nudging touches as the shot of the hospital crucifix after the mother has been turned away from its door. Certainly he took his reputation seriously, attempting a satire on the rich in **The Idle Class** (1921). However, although that film contains some superb comic invention (which has little to do with satire) more to be preferred is **Pay Day** (1922), which is indeed an extended music-hall sketch: in it the Little Fellow has a wife for the first time since *Getting Acquainted* in 1914, played by the same actress, Phyllis Allen. After those two-reelers he went to four for **The Pilgrim** (1922), effortlessly filling them as he is mistaken for the new preacher and thus exposed to new temptations (the collecting box; the urge to show off during his sermon), to a ghastly family and an inconvenient colleague from his convict days. The film, like *Easy Street,* is a masterpiece, throwing into relief the pretension of much of his later work.

A Woman of Paris (1923) was his first film for United Artists, written, produced and directed by him, but a vehicle for his usual leading lady, Edna Purviance – playing a demi-mondaine caught between her country sweetheart (Carl Miller) and the wealthiest bachelor (Adolphe Menjou) in Paris. As a piece of film-craft it is no better or worse than most American features of the time, though certainly inferior to the Keaton and Lloyd films released the following month; as a film about 'sin' it is in the simple-minded tradition of *A Fool There Was*, and its vaunted sophistication is not to be compared to that in the films of the brothers deMille. However, Chaplin (after commissioning Josef von Sternberg to make another film with Purviance, which he apparently destroyed in a fit of professional jealousy) was back on form with **The Gold Rush** (1925), making the Tramp a prospector in the frozen North, giving him at least three fine sequences: a hilarious one where the tramp and Big Jim (Mack Swain) are in a hut which unbeknown to them is on the edge of a precipice; and two pieces of mime, both of pathos, both at the dinner-table – the boiled old boot, its laces eaten like spaghetti, and the dancing rolls, stuck on forks, with which he entertains his girl in fantasy. But Chaplin's glances at the camera indicate his increasing self-consciousness, and the commentary he wrote and added for the 1942 reissue only confirms the mediocrity of his thought, viz. 'A city grew, and humanity warmed it, with living, loving, desiring.' **The Circus** (1928) strives to comment on humanity, as the Tramp – a clown to his employers and to the girl he vainly worships from afar – suffers the ill-will of others in the cause of goodness; and when he finally offers some slapstick on the high wire, the laughs come stumblingly. Chaplin was aware that the film was lacking, for he did not mention it in his memoirs and it was the only one of his features he did not reissue during the Fifties, when in 1970 he did allow it to be shown, the reviewers were dismissive – and indeed several of those in London recommended their readers to go instead to the Academy Cinema to see Buster Keaton.

The original reviews, however, of **City Lights** (1931) – and of its first reissue in 1950 – are unanimous in saying that it hardly falls short of perfection; Chaplin's 'genius' was confirmed by his daring to make a Silent – then regarded as the pure form – among the Talkies. Even the maudlin ending was admired, though like that of *The Kid* it dithers between his early good endings, complete rejection by society, or walking off with the Girl into the sunset, as in *Modern Times* (q.v.). Here, the Tramp has fallen in love with a blind girl and is befriended by a millionaire who recognises him only when drunk – a hugely manipulative film, bearable only for a boxing-match in which Chaplin confirms that he was a great clown. His own treacly score (poured over all his films thereafter) and the tenth-rate sets reinforce a feeling that he believed his own 'genius' was enough.

Buster Keaton (1895–1966) was liked and admired, but critically often got the crumbs from Chaplin's table. Or not even that: *The New York Times* commented – incredibly – of *Steamboat Bill Jr* that 'Buster Keaton's latest attempt to make the millions laugh is a sorry affair'. His decline and disappearance were not marked by the attention which would surely have been paid to Chaplin. When Lewis Jacobs wrote 'The Rise of the American Film' in 1939, he devoted a chapter to Chaplin and one line to Keaton. The former lived long enough to see his work decried – at least in some countries; and Keaton died not long after finding himself reinstated. The fact that the reputation of the one was inflated during the forty years in which the other was in almost total eclipse has caused all sorts of snap-judgments as to Keaton's superiority. John Crosby was right, however, when he said, in 1975, that Chaplin 'clearly considered himself to be the clown for all ages – and that's why the stuff creaks a bit today. Buster Keaton holds up much better – and Keaton had no idea he was playing for posterity.' The truth of the matter is that Keaton is more in tune with modern taste; he was not before his time – for audiences laughed at him then – but his appeal is timeless. That Chaplin's one-man-band talent awed his admirers cannot be doubted; because Keaton worked with directors and writers, his own work with them uncredited, may be one reason he was undervalued. Our view of the cinema is different from that of their contemporaries: Chaplin never mastered the medium, Keaton did. Long after Chaplin's films had moved from a confined set, he was incapable of doing any chase or piece of action except within the equivalent of stage confines; his scenarios remained narratives with intertitles taking the place of dialogue. He never learnt to use the medium as Keaton did, using space and detail: Keaton understood the limitations of the Silent screen, and he *used* them. Not all his shorts reveal his capabilities, but the totality of his Silent films reveal him unmistakably as the screen's supreme genius of the Silent era.

He was born into a vaudeville family of acrobats, and went into movies by chance, when Roscoe 'Fatty' Arbuckle, directing and acting in **The Butcher Boy** (1917), invited him, an onlooker, to participate. Here, he is a grave young man in a flat hat wanting molasses, but he is absent-minded: before he knows it he is deep in molasses, not to be freed till a struggle reminiscent of the wrestlers in the Palazzo dell' Signoria. Keaton had fallen in love with movie-making. He continued to support Arbuckle in his two-reelers, gradually getting more of the action; when Arbuckle accepted an offer from Paramount, his producer, Joseph M. Schenck, gave Keaton the chance to replace him as his prize comic. Schenck made an agreement with Metro to release, and that company engaged Keaton independently for a feature, **The Saphead** (1920), directed by Winchell Smith, to play a foolish young man who saves the

The Little Fellow

'The Little Fellow' was the way Charles Chaplin usually referred to the character he created, seen RIGHT, at his most outrageous and engaging, in *The Pilgrim*. The slapstick *Pay Day*, BELOW RIGHT, is one of his last two-reelers and again one of the most enduring: he is a hén-pecked husband and Phyllis Allen was clearly excellent casting as the wife. He had by this time begun to inject pathos into his work, most notably in *The Kid*, BELOW FAR RIGHT, with Jackie Coogan. Chaplin's most successful blend of comedy and pathos is probably in *The Gold Rush*, ABOVE FAR RIGHT: the lady standing on the bar is Georgia Hale, to whose heart he will aspire, without, at first, much encouragement.

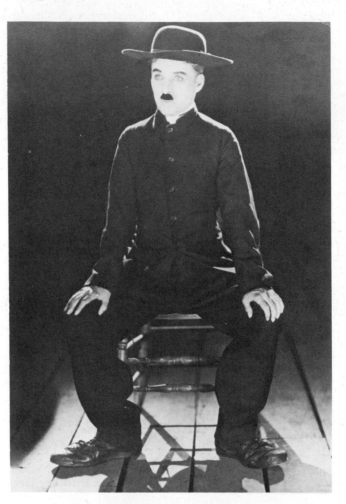

family fortunes by dabbling on the stock exchange. Though he returned to this figure – the solemn-faced, silk-hatted dummy whose meddling inadvertently saves the day – the film is by no means as funny as his later ones. The constant was his unsmiling face; unlike his rivals, the roles he played varied; where Chaplin's screen romances were yearnings for the unattainable, and Lloyd's directed towards nice eager girls, Buster's were exasperating and soppy. He moved through slapstick, satire, fantasy and black comedy, otherwise consistent only that he matched nimble wits and an athletic body with overwhelming odds. In his first-released starring two-reeler, **One Week** (1920), he follows tradition by wearing a clown's clothes but, free of Arbuckle, he triumphantly attacks the world of gadgetry, with a Do-It-Yourself house of which a rival has switched the numbers on the containers. **The High Sign** (1921), made first, also has a house – the home of a secret society; it is even more crazily animated, with swivelling doors and panels useful not only as escape routes but as weapons. It is less inventive, but an intertitle offers the best introduction to Keaton: 'Our hero came from *nowhere* – he wasn't going *anywhere* – he got kicked off *somewhere*.' This rootlessness is the only thing Keaton owes to Chaplin: he will attempt to earn an honest living – or at any rate a living – but misfortune and misunderstanding dog his footsteps.

In **The Goat** (1921), his eighth two-reeler, he is an innocent man thought to be a desperate criminal – he had simply been watching a prisoner being photographed, and the prisoner had ducked. **The Playhouse** (1921) also finds him at his peak, busily filling the playhouse and the screen with myriad Busters; but **The Boat** (1921) is bleak, his ingenuity so little called into play that the normal balance of adversity and eventual triumph is lost: the elements win, and with home and boat gone, the family trudge off into the darkness. In **The Paleface** (1921) the pursuer becomes the pursued: an innocent lad, blithely chasing butterflies, disturbs some Red Indians and barely escapes scalping. In **Cops** (1922), the pursuers appear to be the whole of the Los Angeles police force. It is their day for parading,

and Buster, in an odd number of manoeuvres, has acquired a horse and cart not his own, loaded with furniture not his own, and setting out for no destination. He has accepted good luck and ill, hoping for a deal and thus to marry the Mayor's daughter – the American dream, as Rudi Blesh points out in his book on Keaton. Having magnificently outwitted every single cop, Keaton is ignored by her, so he unlocks the prison door and goes inside: if you're going to be lonely and unloved, what price freedom? It was in the nature of Chaplin's tramp that society rejected him, but in Keaton's case it was actively hostile – for no good reason. Chaplin's upbringing might have brought from him a similar view, but after the amorality of his shorts he poured such affection on his character that beyond the moralising no actual philosophy is discernible. Keaton was very modern in that he never moralised; the black vision of his shorts suggests that he accepted defeat equally fatalistically in his later battles with M-G-M and alcoholism. **Daydreams** (1922) is a cry of despair, its title referring to the lies told by Buster in his letters to the girl back home of success in the city. One daydream becomes a nightmare as one cop, again, becomes an army of cops: Buster takes refuge on a ferry-boat – but it is only manoeuvring, and he finds haven in the paddle-wheel. Blesh thinks that the movie ends with him falling into the water, but in another version he is deemed to travel for ever between two shores, beyond the barriers of the law; unfortunately the most complete version concludes tamely with him returning to the girl – but it is still pessimistic, since her father throws him out.

The view of **The Three Ages** (1923) is that success, power, wealth and brutality go hand in hand, and that if the little man achieves anything against those odds, it's not going to be with elegance or panache. This is the first of the Keaton features, a look at the one thing that stays eternal – love. As he himself pointed out, it is really three two-reelers stuck together: Buster in prehistoric times, in the Roman era, and in the present day, in each outwitting his rival (Wallace Beery) to win the girl, the stories interweaving and the parallels not enforced with rigidity. **Our Hospitality** (1923) is a return to the standard of the best shorts. The title is ironic: the story was inspired by the Hatfield-McCoy feud, and Keaton is a New York boy travelling South to take up an inheritance, unaware that the girl (Natalie Talmadge, his wife at the time) on the train has brothers who have sworn to kill him on sight. How he stays alive is accomplished by a profusion of brilliant, indescribable visual gags; and it is difficult to write about **Sherlock Junior** (1924) because it is so completely magical – and since Keaton knew that magic wears off, he made the film shorter than his other features. He starts with an ordinary story, and moves into fantasy as his hero, a cinema-projectionist, walks into the screen and becomes a man-about-town detective. Keaton never threw custard pies or lost his pants; the bad men pursue and heroines doubt, but after he left Arbuckle he seldom used a conventional joke – or if he did, he built on it, ending ten steps in front. He ends thus there; and as he finishes, his look is as enigmatic as Garbo's at the end of *Queen Christina* (q.v.).

In **The Navigator** (1924) he is a rich boy, 'living proof that every family tree must have its sap'. The reason for his pedigree seems to be to emphasise his uselessness when stranded on a deserted liner – the usual Buster would have been as immediately inventive as he later becomes. By mischance the girl (Kathryn McGuire) is with him on these acres of floating iron; after learning to cook for two in a kitchen meant for hundreds, they are beset by cannibals. This climax is suspenseful rather than amusing; that in **Seven Chances** (1925) contains his most sustained brilliance. A prologue establishes his inability to propose to his girl in any of the four seasons; and then he desperately needs a bride to inherit a huge fortune – before seven o'clock on this particular evening. His first proposal is maladroit, and he is refused; he tries the ladies at his country club, and by the end of the afternoon 'had proposed to everything in skirts, including a Scotchman [*sic*]' – and a joke involving the female impersonator Julian Eltinge is done with equal delicacy. The dilemma has been offered to a local newspaper, armed with which brides descend upon the appointed church – by foot, horse, tram, bicycle. And when

Buster, inevitably, flees, brides converge from all directions, as many, as menacing, and about as pretty as his old enemy, the cops.

Seven Chances, with *Sherlock Junior*, are the only films on which he takes sole directorial credit – and since both are so beautifully made we need not look at his collaborators; but it is worth noting that Clyde Bruckman and Jean Havez are credited among the writers of his first five features, and neither seems to have worked on **Go West** (1925) and **Battling Butler** (1926), the weakest films of his great period. He was attracted to the former, for he wanted to see how far he could take the gag of having a cow for heroine – and one who evokes the same single-minded passion as the others; and *Battling Butler* offered the chance of a serious climax – a brutal boxing-match. It is certainly funnier than *Go West,* but not to be placed with **The General** (1926), for which Bruckman returned, also co-directing. The title refers to an engine, and the film remains the cinema's happiest exercise in playing trains; if the gags are not Keaton's most brilliant or most sustained, on no other occasion did they spring so easily from the narrative and blend with it. The girl (Marian Mack) is notably dim: she throws away a log (fuel) because there is a hole in it; she uselessly sweeps the floor of the engine's cabin; and she stokes up the fire with a twig. Buster mocks her by handing her a chip: more than Chaplin, his innate chivalry towards women dissolves when they become dangerous or *de trop*.

College (1927), possibly the greatest of the features, was inspired by Lloyd's *The Freshman* (q.v.) – but the campus is absolutely of Keaton's world. He is the school swot who, rejected by the Girl in favour of the hearties, turns up at college with every item of sporting equipment known to man: an odd man out in this athlete's world, he perseveres. He attempts the long jump, the high jump, putting the shot (it puts him), ignominiously ignored by his fellows till his antics menace their safety. As a sportsman, he gets just one thing right – and it's the one thing that doesn't matter: the stance at the starting-post. Then, strained and quivering, his unchanging face is at its most eloquent, as it is again when failing miser-

The shorts of Buster
Keaton are among
the greatest pleasures
the cinema has to
offer – even if the
woes in *The Boat,*
RIGHT, with Sybil
Sealey, are a little
too relentless. Those
in *Daydreams,* BELOW
CENTRE, are varied: In
this particular scene
the cop is too dumb
to recognise an actor
in costume, but sees
only a guy in a skirt.
The features are
miraculous –
certainly so in the
case of *Sherlock
Junior,* ABOVE FAR
RIGHT, in which
Buster is a cinema
projectionist. Unlike
Lloyd or Chaplin, he
moved about the
social scale, and in
College, BELOW FAR
RIGHT, he is a student.
His mother was
Florence Turner,
'the original Vitagraph
Girl', who had spent
more than a decade in
England, attempting
to prolong her waning
career; when it
finally halted there,
she managed to find
a few small roles in
Hollywood before
retiring.
Incidentally, as against
the possible evidence
of these stills,
Keaton's unvarying
expression was able to
convey a wide range
of emotion.

The Great Stone Face

ably as a soda-fountain clerk, his every gesture a witness to whether or not he's being watched. If, at the end, he wins both the Girl and the race (instead of the traditional football-game climax, Keaton chose a boat-race because only two mishaps can occur – the boats can collide or sink, and thus audience anticipation is keener), the consolation is temporary. Despite the film's title, no one is seen studying; it is natural to Keaton that brawn should dominate over brain.

He is again an effete young man in **Steamboat Bill Jr** (1928), the despair of his sea-dog father (Ernest Torrence). Unhappily bereft of college togs and moustache, he finds unexpected consolation in his natty naval togs; and as he saunters along, a friend suggests to his father, 'No jury would convict.' He becomes, when pressed, as stoic and enterprising as ever: and it is perhaps this that makes him so endearing, since it is always by accident that he discovers his heroic self. The adversary to be overcome this time was to have been a cyclone, and Keaton resented till he died the substitution of a flood. Starting with *The General,* Schenck had appointed a supervisor, and Keaton unhappily deferred to him; when he complained, Schenck made it clear that without supervision there would be no more Keaton films.

He lacked the courage to strike out on his own. His last three films had been made for United Artists, and he was happy to be with the company that included Chaplin; he did make one timid attempt to be independent of Schenck, but when Schenck contracted him to M-G-M, with all powers of autonomy lost, he began to sink. He produced **The Cameraman** (1928), suggested the idea, and worked out the gags with Bruckman; Edward Sedgwick directed it, but, unlike his later Metro pictures, Keaton always regarded it as his own. He is a tintype photographer determined to get a job with the M-G-M newsreel company and win the girl (Marceline Day, the prettiest of his leading ladies) who works there; his determination, and gestures, are often zombie-like, and thus half of Buster is missing – his skill, and we are surprised by his lack of ingenuity in the Tong War. It has half as many laughs as its immediate predecessor, and there are half as few

again in **Spite Marriage** (1929), in which he is a pants-presser whose dream comes true when his favourite star (Dorothy Sebastian) marries him on the rebound. The story was foisted on him, he was denied the use of Sound, his incredible athletics were forbidden as being too risky, and he had to fight to keep what he correctly thought was the funniest sequence – trying to get a tipsy bride to bed. Keaton believed that he was destroyed because M-G-M considered that they knew better how to make a Keaton film than he did, but the simultaneous deterioration of his marriage and his relationship with the once-protective Schenck – who was married to his wife's sister – may have weakened his creativity. In these two studio-controlled films, there are a number of routines clearly his own, but apart from the tipsy bride none is very good, harking back to his days in vaudeville. Is it not possible that his imagination was wearing thin? He had made twenty shorts between 1920 and 1923, and ten features in the subsequent years: the limited number of masterpieces among them suggests, on average, that he could not have gone on for ever.

The third great Silent clown, and the second best of them, is Harold Lloyd (1893–1971), though at the time both he and Keaton agreed with and accepted, at least publicly, the world's opinion that they were a rung or so below Chaplin – though Lloyd led the others at the American box office. Chaplin was unique, and copied only by blatant imitators, while all the other two-reel comics borrowed from each other. Lloyd's fascination with movies was a contributory factor to his success; he became an extra before he was twenty, and was invited by Hal Roach (b. 1892) to join him when the latter, a former Universal cowboy, founded his own company. Roach emulated Sennett: Lloyd was star and gagman, attempting to rival the other funny-clothes clowns with enthusiasm and hard work – but to little appreciation. Where others fell by the wayside or moved to supporting status, Lloyd pressed on, changing from Willie Work to Lonesome Luke to Winkle, whose spectacles and mild appearance belied his ability to flout authority and make fools of those around him. After a while the name was dropped, the silk hat gave way to the boater, and as the character evolved he became respectable, the Galahad of the college set, fighting adversity and winning the girl. Lacking the pungency of Chaplin at his best, he towered above his other rivals in the sheer inventiveness of his gags – a challenge to Keaton, starting his own two-reelers as Lloyd moved into features. Keaton eluding Red Indians in *The Paleface* was emulating Lloyd in *Take a Chance*, fleeing prison warders, while Lloyd learnt from Keaton how to deepen predicament into disaster. Both were possessed by some deep inner fantasy, though Lloyd's was probably only that of the average American male. Although he was once miscast as a doctor, the point of Lloyd's industry and invention was that it was never for the good of the community but to satisfy a girl or a dream. Silence created the movie clowns, from Max Linder onwards; if movies had talked from the beginning, their physical action might still have been confined to what was possible behind a proscenium arch. But that Lloyd deserves to stand with Keaton is made obvious when we realise that as Chaplin was putting the finishing touches to his visually stodgy *Gold Rush* they were offering the magical chases of *Girl Shy* (q.v.) and *Sherlock Junior*.

It was public response which encouraged Roach to add a third reel to the Lloyd films – something which till then only Chaplin had dared attempt; and of the many comics only they, Linder, Arbuckle, Keaton and later Harry Langdon (q.v.) made the transition to longer films. But even with his last three-reeler, **Never Weaken** (1921), Lloyd was having the usual difficulty in sustaining a theme, and it falls into three separate but prolonged gags: employing a circus contortionist to attract customers to an osteopath; trying to commit suicide because he thinks his girl is planning to marry another; and being trapped high on a building site. The first two find him often contrived and mechanical, but once trapped on that girder he becomes immortal. This extraordinary climax he tried to live up to, and though some of the gags from his shorts found their way into his features, later gags were never repeated: the sheer variety of his spectacular climaxes is one reason audiences adored

him. In **A Sailor-Made Man** (1921) he is a rich man playing at sailor who finds courage battling a sheik, and in **Grandma's Boy** (1922), a parody of *Tol'able David* (q.v.), a shy village lad who finds courage battling his uncouth rival. Discussing the latter in 'The Best Moving Pictures of 1922–3', Robert E. Sherwood noted that Lloyd 'constructed each scene as carefully as though it were the mainspring of a watch . . . There is nothing haphazard about his methods; he puzzles over every episode and situation, working it out first in his mind and then in the action itself. He had a remarkably clear vision and an acute sense of risibility; he knows instinctively what will be naturally funny, and what will be merely forced.' His collaborators included Sam Taylor and Fred Newmeyer, who singly or together directed all of his pictures till 1926; the two later Silents were directed by Ted Wilde. A small number of writers and gagmen, including Clyde Bruckman, worked for both Lloyd and Keaton. The two clowns also had in common a desire to change both comic formulae and the film itself if preview audiences did not respond, as with *The Freshman* (q.v.), when Lloyd returned to the set to lose his pants as well, because preview audiences had not laughed at what he had hoped was a new gag, a disintegrating jacket. Unlike Keaton, he was an astute businessman, and after parting amicably with Roach he left Pathé for an extremely advantageous deal with Paramount, which guaranteed complete autonomy.

The Lloyd on screen is, as James Agee observed, 'funny from the inside' – which is why his skyscraper stunt in **Safety Last** (1923) works so well. This sequence should only be seen in context (i.e. never in excerpt) for we must know his reasons for climbing, which are accidental – though he would surely have done it to please a girl. It is justly famous: and to see it today with an audience alternately roaring with laughter and gasping is one of the great experiences of cinema. Lloyd admitted, 'This sort of thrill comedy was dangerous but it wasn't as dangerous as it looked' – for once they had established the location, it proved possible to build a 'safe' portion of the 'dangerous' building with the same view beyond. He used a double in the long shots, a fact not

Master of the High and Dizzy

Harold Lloyd in *Why Worry?*, RIGHT, as a young American involved in a South American revolution – a situation reprised fifty years later by Woody Allen in *Bananas,* which has probably one–fifth of the laughs. For that matter, *Speedy,* BELOW, has a number of car chases funnier than those ubiquitous in the movies of the Sixties and Seventies; he played a cab–driver, here on his day off at Coney Island with Ann Christy, temporarily replacing Jobyna Ralston as his leading lady. The other two pictures are from *Feet First,* FAR RIGHT, discussed later, but included here to show that it wasn't only in *Safety Last* that Lloyd scaled a skyscraper – and that as long as movies are shown people will be watching Lloyd on high buildings.

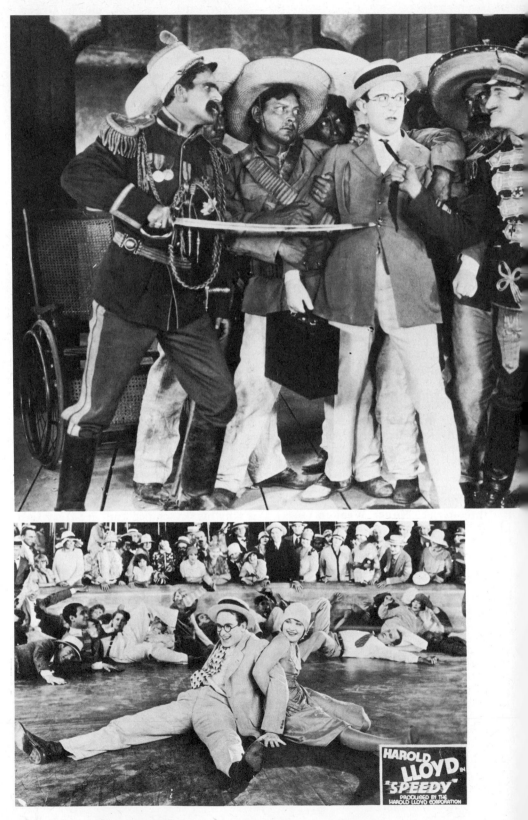

HAROLD
LLOYD IN
"SPEEDY"
PRODUCED BY THE
HAROLD LLOYD CORPORATION

revealed till after his death, and wore a harness; also, there were wide platforms just out of camera range. Yet we might still like to think of his task as Herculean, for he worked with a hand that had a false thumb and forefinger (because of an accident), and 'it took us sometimes over a month to make one of these sequences, because we could only work between about eleven o'clock and one o'clock, otherwise shadows would come up in the street and it wouldn't match the other scenes.'

In **Why Worry?** (1923) he is an innocent trapped amidst Latin-American revolutionaries; in **Hot Water** (1924) the possessor of both a new car and new in-laws; and in **Girl Shy** (1924) he is a country boy who from complete ignorance writes a treatise on love, and loses his girl to a bigamist. If in this case he had telephoned to stop the wedding we would have lost a climax as thrilling as that of *Safety Last*, as he employs every means of land transport to get him to the church on time – a masterpiece of precision ill-served by the copies currently in circulation, which run it at sound speed, i.e. faster, in order to accommodate a music-track. Chases also conclude both **For Heaven's Sake** (1926) and **Speedy** (1928); a football match ends **The Freshman**; and a fight of particular violence, aboard an abandoned hulk, provides a brilliant climax to **The Kid Brother** (1927). There is also a brutal free-for-all in *Speedy*, involving greybeards, and it is clear that Lloyd equated violence with the cities, changing for the worst. The screen Harold may have set out to be the all-American go-getter, but his ideals were Victorian – and it is only too typical of him that in this particular film he experiences empathy with a horse-drawn trolley. Perhaps only an old-fashioned man would indicate that the end of the world is nigh as those trousers fall apart, or be so enchanted by the crooks reformed in 'his' mission in *For Heaven's Sake* – not to mention his joy in *Speedy*, hurtling from one side of town to the other, because he has Babe Ruth in the back of his cab (thus allowing Americans to watch two current idols at the same time). Unequipped except in ingenuity to cope with the dangers of the modern world, his final emergence into triumph

might well be transitory, but it is often a great deal less precarious than Buster's.

Any of the other Silent comics, in whatever garbled form they now reach us, are worth seeing – especially Charley Chase, in his two-reelers for Roach, often a hen-pecked husband, but in his funniest film, **Limousine Love** (1928), a prospective bridegroom hampered by a naked lady on his way to the church. Then there is Roach's superb **A Pair of Tights** (1928), with its vain attempts by a girl to get her ice-creams to the car and its climax when men crash to the ground because those already lying there whack their calves. Like the trouser-tearing finish to *You're Darn Tootin'* (1929) and the pie-throwing of *The Battle of the Century* (1927) – both made by Roach with Laurel and Hardy (q.v.) – this wholesale combination of heartlessness and loss of dignity has something to say about the human condition.

Other American artists of the Twenties live on, if only in legend, and we shall look at their work in the next chapter: but there is one film-maker who should be considered at this point, because his work was so strikingly individual. Erich Von Stroheim (1885–1957) was born in Vienna of Polish Jewish parents, and had arrived in the U.S. in 1906; after collaborating on a play he drifted into films in 1914, acting and writing for Triangle, and since he claimed – falsely – to have been an officer in the Imperial army, he was much in demand to advise on the many films dealing with the European military. When the Armistice made such subjects unfashionable, he approached Carl Laemmle with a screenplay that he had written – saying that to film it would cost only $5,000, but that he must direct it himself; he also claimed that it was based on a novel by him, supposedly called 'The Pinnacle'. Laemmle agreed, and the result, actually costing $100,000 and retitled **Blind Husbands** (1919) – and now sporting a happy ending – was the biggest success that Universal had had up to that time. Its mixture of the eternal triangle and mountaineering was as opportunistic as its creator's approach to Laemmle had been fraudulent. DeMille's stories of erring wives and husbands were all the rage, and as with deMille the film has a foreword asking us to look freshly at the situation – specifically whether the husband is as guilty as the other man. But whereas de Mille had taken the characters of Schnitzler and made them into simple-minded Americans, Von Stroheim offered a mentality closer to that of his countryman. The character he himself played, an aristocrat dedicated to seduction, was clearly influenced by Schnitzler – and portrayed in such detail that he was more fascinating than most screen rakes. The fact that he was European and the couple were Americans indicated the dangers and/or delights awaiting Americans daring or wealthy enough to travel abroad. The clash of old world decadence and new world purity may have been borrowed in turn from Henry James: it became a staple in American cinema from then on, though already touched upon in the war films. The new world was full of Europeans, but none like this particular gentleman; if it was Von Stroheim's past as a penniless immigrant which attracted him to the role, he was to maintain all his life the fictions of his birth and upbringing.

The reviews immediately justified his confidence. *The New York Times* found it 'superior to most of the year's productions' because 'its outstanding pictorial quality indicates that Mr Stroheim, unlike many directors, grasps the fact that the screen is the place for moving pictures' and if 'some of the scenes are continentally frank, they are not offensive, nor more suggestive than is necessary.' This 'pictorial quality' would include the close-ups, almost wholly concerned with Von Stroheim's fetishistic interests: a woman's ankle, the details of his own uniform, the voyeurist spying of the maid, the amorous couple whose kisses emphasise the wife's neglect. Von Stroheim understood lust and eroticism, and he understood, as no other Hollywood film-maker at the time dared to, the distinctions between marriage, love and lust. His characters were as mercenary as they were sexual, with the stronger gulling the weak – a view he would have seen expressed in the theatres of his native city, if not in the seventeenth-century satirists. It was a view novel only to the cinema.

The same attitudes were propounded in *The Devil's Passkey*, which no longer exists, and in **Foolish Wives** (1922): the setting has moved from the Alps to Monte Carlo and this time Von Stroheim is supposedly a Russian count. The prey remains an American woman – though once again she is not the only one. Whether he has also had 'relations' with his cousins is not clear – if they are his cousins – and they certainly are revealed as anything but the princesses they claim to be; he has, moreover, compromised the maid (Dale Fuller), whose suicide puts an end to both her pregnancy and pleas for marriage. As retribution begins to mount, his conduct is revealed as increasingly ignoble, till at the height of his troubles he decides to ravish a half-idiot girl. He is killed by her father, who stuffs his body into a manhole. Von Stroheim had intended the Count to be even more dastardly – and by far the best thing in the mutilated copies which remain are the indications of his ruthlessness. The film originally extended to at least twenty-one reels (though Von Stroheim claimed that there were as many as thirty-four) but had been reduced to fourteen by the time of the New York première, after which four more were removed to appease censors and critics. The re-written intertitles not only covered the gaps in continuity but softened the text, so that the American husband was demoted from Ambassador to mere business functionary. The film, despite its moral, still revels in its world of cafés and casinos. There is an odd moment when the American woman discovers that the soldier whose manners she has deplored is in fact armless – not an incident at odds with the tone of the film, but too isolated to place the film with Von Stroheim's later attempts at social realism. As it was censored the world over for its *sexual* realism, so it was praised: Harriett Underhill in *The New York Tribune* declared that Von Stroheim was a genius – a view in which he concurred – adding that she had seen 'many motion pictures and *Foolish Wives* is the best photoplay I have ever seen without any exceptions whatever.' Since *Intolerance*, it was also the most expensive, and Universal's publicists, with the short memories which mark many in the industry, advertised it as 'The First Million Dollar movie'. The company soon realised that it would have to settle for a prestige hit, for vilification kept audiences away. 'An insult to every

'The Man you Love to Hate'

Von Stroheim – the above soubriquet was coined by publicists and used extensively throughout his career – was not allowed to play the lead in *The Merry-Go-Round*, RIGHT, so he dressed Norman Kerry in the uniform he had designed for himself. He was taken off the film, and most of it is an anodyne affair; some of his ideas for it he later transferred to *The Wedding March*, BELOW. Playing his mother is Maud George, who had been his 'cousin' in *Foolish Wives*. His role was the same, wearing uniform, using perfume, smoking cigarettes six inches long breakfasting on caviar and drunk in the evening. Few men have so indulged their fantasies on the screen.

The Merry Widow hardly impresses as a version of Lehar's musical frolic, but it is unique among American films of the time in that Von Stroheim managed to set most of it in a *maison close* – and its hero, John Gilbert, was, in seeking comfort from older ladies, supposedly still a typical American male. BELOW: Gibson Gowland and Zazu Pitts in Von Stroheim's *Greed*, in one of their happier moments. She has already won the lottery prize which, with his drinking, will lead to the disintegration of their marriage – the film's true subject, rather than that indicated by the title.

American,' declared *Photoplay,* and Thomas Quinn Curtis in his book on Von Stroheim quotes a Methodist minister as denouncing 'a disgusting story of lust. Not only is gambling shown, but men and women are seen brazenly smoking cigarettes.'

For the premiere, Sigmund Romberg had composed a special score, an extra expense to add to the full-scale construction of a Monte Carlo square on the Universal lot. Elated by the notices, the studio reproduced what it called 'the Coney Island of Vienna', the Prater, for **The Merry-Go-Round** (1923). Irving Thalberg, Laemmle's new assistant, had suggested a circus picture to Von Stroheim, who decided to use a carnival background for the tale of an aristocrat in love with a pure maiden. The budget was set at $100,000, but it was soon clear that Von Stroheim had no intention of keeping to it (this was the film for which he required the military to wear silk monogrammed underwear – not, of course, to be seen on the screen); and due to his arrogance, there had been tension between him and Thalberg since Laemmle had left for a European trip. After five weeks' shooting, with only one reel completed, Von Stroheim was replaced by Rupert Julian, the sole credited director of the completed film. Since Von Stroheim shot in sequence, the first twelve minutes indicates how he spent those five weeks: an aristocratic officer (Norman Kerry) is awakened by his valet after the previous night's debauch, and the Countess, his mother, treats her servants sadistically, having them slavishly pull off her boots and massage her silk-stockinged legs as she lolls on a divan. The first sequence would be repeated in *The Wedding March* (q.v.), and the attitudes of the Countess borrowed for *The Merry Widow* (q.v.) – while the heroine (Mary Philbin) is observed with the same harsh pathos that would characterise Zazu Pitts in *Greed* (q.v.). As the film proceeds these characters lose their interest, and it is a dull thing except where some Von Stroheim touches remain, as in a party sequence with the officers and girls all with vine-leaves in their hair.

Turning from European high life to American low life, Von Stroheim made **Greed** (1924), based on Frank Norris's popular attempt at a Zolaesque novel, 'McTeague'. The Goldwyn executives backed it, having announced their hostility to the factory system and their plans to give their directors freedom; they were also on the verge of amalgamating with Metro. By the time the film was finished, the new company – M-G-M – was headed by Thalberg and Louis B. Mayer, whose idea of entertainment was not *Greed* and certainly not at this length, forty-two reels. Von Stroheim himself reduced the number to twenty-four, and the released print was of ten – or two-and-a-half hours, exactly the duration of the deleted account of McTeague's early years, reduced to a seven-minute prologue. *Greed* was not Von Stroheim's title, and the film is not, as it has been said to be, a study in miserliness: McTeague (Gibson Gowland) is a thick-witted dentist who courts and weds Trina Sieppe (Zazu Pitts), but banned from practising, he fails to hold other, demeaning jobs. He drinks because he is bored, and because they are living in increasing squalor, if held together by bouts of affection; but as he realises the extent to which her obsession with money has taken over her life, he regards her with indifference. It has been claimed that her hoarding is due to the experience of the wedding night, but the film (as it now stands) does not support that view. Her primness always indicated that she would be careful; the money becomes an obsession because they have little and will soon have less. This is the best part of the film: sober, convincing, and of concern – before the descent to melodrama.

Von Stroheim's reputation as a realist rests on *Greed*, but, said Herman G. Weinberg, 'he was essentially a romantic. The theme of loveless marriage runs through all his films' – and since we know that the most profound examination of a loveless marriage then available in film terms was *The Ingmarssons* we may assume that Von Stroheim saw it. There are numerous echoes in *Greed* of *The Phantom Carriage*, notably in its handling of the demon drink, but it has more in common with Sjöström's greatest film: both are melodramas taking on the mantle of tragedy; both are meticulous recreations of past times made chiefly on location; and apart from the common subject, both are very long or were intended to be. Norris's book provided Von Stroheim with the detail he needed for an exercise in European culture somewhat different from his earlier achievements; but once placed beside Sjöström's films the much-praised originality of *Greed* is in fact slight, and indeed Von Stroheim is revealed again as opportunistic, since he has managed 'realism' but to no discernible end. There is no point of view to be found in the film, other than that people are not very nice – the opposite of Sjöström's – and it lacks the complete cynicism of Von Stroheim's other films, with its hints of sympathy for McTeague. Realism, in Von Stroheim's terms, means a farcical wedding feast, with everyone stuffing themselves and burping, or Trina's brother wanting to pee after a theatre visit, or the courting couple on the concrete sewer by the sea. There is certainly nothing wrong in this: Robert E. Sherwood in his review spoke of 'ferocity, brutality, muscle, vulgarity, crudity naked realism, and sheer genius', and all those qualities but the last are still apparent. How many other American Silents could be described as having ferocity and muscle?

Sherwood also mentioned the film's original length, and observed wryly that Von Stroheim would have to learn 'limitations': Von Stroheim is in fact the classic example of film-makers so in awe of their own talents that nothing was too expensive and no footage too long. His vanity was legendary; when towards the end of his life Billy Wilder said that he had been ten years before his time, Von Stroheim corrected him, 'Twenty'. He has been admired because he fought the system and lost, but he lost simply because he was too arrogant to work other than in a recklessly extravagant manner. That he made good films was recognised; but he was often praised for an approach to sex and marital relations merely in advance of his backward-looking colleagues.

Certainly his changes 'improved' **The Merry Widow** (1925), which, adapted from the operetta, was handicapped as screen entertainment; but he retains at length the famous waltz, which at best would have had orchestral accompaniment and at worst silence, if the piano-player was ill. The film is more than two-thirds over when the plot of the original begins to intrude, and most of that time has been spent examining the activities of the widow's three rival suitors, as they move in a haze of lechery and drunkenness: Danilo (John Gilbert) is a seducer of inconsiderable charm, given to saucy postcards; the horrible old baron (Tully Marshall) is also a foot fetishist; and the Crown Prince (Roy d'Arcy) seems prone to every depravity going. Alas, as the object of their attentions Mae Murray is vivacious but dull, though the uniforms, it must be said, give pause.

Thalberg, having inherited Von Stroheim on *Greed*, kept him for this film because he considered his 'European' approach ideal; but M-G-M was not prepared to suffer further, for the success of *The Merry Widow* did not atone for the miserable failure of *Greed* and the loss of most of its $750,000 cost. The independent producer Pat Powers listened to Von Stroheim's advances, and allotted him a budget of $700,000 for his next project, only to find that that had been exceeded by yet another half-million. The film lasted eleven hours, which Paramount, distributing, refused to handle: Von Stroheim and subsequently others reduced the material, cutting it into two separate films, **The Wedding March** (1928) and *The Honeymoon,* which was released in Europe only and of which there are now no surviving prints. *The Wedding March* announces itself 'in its entirety an Erich Von Stroheim Production' dedicated 'to the true lovers of the world', and its combination of debauchery and innocent, romantic love is merely a repeat of what was intended in *The Merry-Go-Round.* Von Stroheim plays the usual Von Stroheim hero, introduced to us via his clothing, strewed drunkenly on the floor; his first action on waking is to paw the maid, and his subsequent conduct is no improvement. His life-style must be paid for by a wealthy marriage, so he becomes engaged to the lame daughter (Zazu Pitts) of a corn-plaster magnate, despite the fact that he has fallen in love with the daughter (Fay Wray) of an innkeeper. This becomes an everyday anecdote as handled by Von Stroheim, and perhaps only he would have handled it at such length.

The United Artists

Von Stroheim moved on to Gloria Swanson, who had been impressed by his ability to turn Mae Murray into an actress and was curious to see what he might do with her own (and acknowledged) talent. **Queen Kelly** was based on one of his own stories, and a budget was set at $800,000 with a forty-week shooting schedule, for this was to be another very long film: shooting was closed down after ten weeks, thus effectively sealing Von Stroheim's American career as a director, though as with the later *Walking Down Broadway* (q.v.) he seems to have worked quickly and as economically as he knew how to be. The chief reason for the film being abandoned was that it was clear that it would not be ready till mid–1929 and already – before the end of 1928 – it was also clear that the public wanted only Talkies. It would have been possible to start again with Sound, or add Sound sequences, but Von Stroheim was disregarding the instructions of the Hays Office in respect of the script. In the film Swanson was supposed to go to Africa to manage her aunt's brothel: Hays had insisted that the establishment become a hotel, but Von Stroheim was filming material indicating the activities that went on inside it, as girls from the bar led clients upstairs. He was concentrating on the squalor of this particular part of Africa, and had, against Hays's advice, shown a black priest administering the last rites. Swanson's chief backer, Joseph P. Kennedy (1888–1969; future ambassador to Britain and father of President Kennedy), was also a prominent Roman Catholic, and he decided that he did not want to defend a film which seemed likely to be a complete box-office failure.

The film that now exists was originally the prologue, concerning an orphan (Swanson) who attracts the attention of a Prince (Walter Byron) when she loses her knickers. He, however, is contracted to marry a Queen (Seena Owen) who is not only mad but as depraved as he, and it is with these two that Von Stroheim is at his most typical, whether showing the Prince being forcibly fed by his servants after a night of debauch or the Queen in bed, the table beside her littered with a box of veronal, a copy of the 'Decameron' and a cluttered ashtray. When the Queen discovers the Prince with the girl she horse-whips her, and the girl attempts suicide. In the ending shot for this version – probably directed by Edmund Goulding (q.v.), who directed Swanson's next film, *The Trespasser* – the Queen relents and allows him to marry the girl, but the suicide attempt has been successful. At ninety minutes, the film was exported to Europe and South America, on the assumption that in both continents were many cinemas not wired for Sound. It has been said Von Stroheim used a clause in his contract to prevent the film being released in the U.S., but it is more likely that Miss Swanson's distributors, United Artists, felt that it had no market value. Finally, it was Von Stroheim's arrogance and his penchant for length and eroticism which wrecked his career as a director. When he acted in France projects were announced by enthusiastic producers but none came to pass, apparently because producers decided that he did not well support the daily bottle of whisky stipulated in his contracts.

The ousting of Von Stroheim, though undoubtedly deserved by industry standards, was a blow to the freedom of the individual artist; and although the importance of Griffith in the Twenties has been exaggerated by historians, the same may be said of him. The ideals, other than financial, which had caused the foundation of United Artists were by the coming of the Talkies in disarray – and that was due as much to the personalities of the founders as to their eminence. Within a few years the public had deserted both Pickford and Fairbanks, and the stars who replaced them had no wish to double as executives, preferring the comfort of the studio contract. Keaton, who had had no business sense, was gone as well; Lloyd and Chaplin made only occasional films, the former regarded as a character from the past, the latter stationed on his lone pinnacle. The producers releasing through United Artists had the same mentalities and motives as those of the other major companies, and none of them wanted to employ artists with an inflated idea of their own importance, with budgets to match. Success henceforth depended not on reputation, but on profitability – though, as the idea of independence floundered, a number of people arrived, like Lubitsch and Garbo, who could with docility provide both.

7

Hollywood in the Twenties:
The Studios

TECHNICALLY, the late American Silent film is often close to perfection. The luminosity of the photography and an imaginative but unshowy use of composition were welded into narrative by editors whose understanding of rhythm and dramatic tension remains extraordinary. Intertitles were reduced to the minimum, and not only had the barnstorming histrionics gone, but players were able to convey with only slight gestures a whole range of emotion – though whether, given the subject-matter, the expertise was worthwhile is debatable. It was certainly taken for granted, as critics rushed to admire the new artistic event from Europe.

One American film was much admired at the beginning of the decade, **Nanook of the North** (1922), which as the first travel-picture of feature-length eclipsed its few predecessors. This study of Eskimo life was made by Robert J. Flaherty (1884–1951), who as an amateur film-maker had taken a motion-picture camera with him when working in Hudson Bay. His first effort was destroyed by fire, and he obtained backing from Revillon Frères, the furriers, for this second attempt, taking eighteen months simply to gather the material. Both Paramount and First National passed up the chance to distribute, and it went to Pathé, which was owned by the same parent company as the fur company. Even then it stayed on the shelf till it fired the enthusiasm of S. L. 'Roxy' Rothafel, the impresario. Today its effect compares badly with modern documentaries made for television, and unlike them it offers a fictionalised climax (when, hunting far from home, the Eskimos seek refuge in a deserted igloo); but contemporaries were enraptured, including Frances Taylor Patterson in *The New Republic*: 'We are excessively weary of adaptations from the other arts. . . Here at last begins our native screen language, as original in concept as *The Cabinet of Dr Caligari,* yet as natural as that is fantastic.'

Nanook was hardly the dead end that *Caligari* was, but by the time the industry had recognised its achievement, the hold of the German film had grown stronger: most of the admired American films were those showing the Teutonic influences – till the lessons of the Russians were assimilated. Both pushed the American film towards realism, but it was a movement as short as it was sweet; the public and the industry were seduced by Sound.

By the end of the Silent period virtually every man, woman and child in the U.S. went to the cinema at least once a week; whole populations elsewhere grew up with a detailed knowledge of American life. The tastes of audiences everywhere coincided with that of the Hollywood moguls, which was fortunate for their stock-holders. If in Europe directors often took the credit for an entire film, the fall of Griffith and Von Stroheim convinced the Hollywood moguls of the foolishness of giving power to the man who directed the action on the studio-floor. The flirtations with Flaherty proved him equally expensive and unamenable to commercial considerations; Ince was approved of, since he was able to supervise several productions simultaneously, but he died young. Replacements could be purchased from Europe, often less with enthusiasm than in the competitive spirit of ten years

Nita Naldi and Rudolph Valentino in *Blood and Sand*: she is 'the widow of an ambassador [sic] who has turned the heads of half the kings and diplomats of Europe' and he is a matador. This bite comes after a kiss, as she cries, 'Snake – one moment I love you – one moment I hate you – serpent from hell.'

earlier – to prevent rivals from profiting from possibly important talents; and the European director, enticed by the available money, could be bent to the moguls' will. Scenarios could be imposed on him, and decor, and players. Any freedom given to directors was the result of success with studio-imposed material, and that freedom was studio-controlled. Yet a Lubitsch survived; a film as close to its director's heart as *The Crowd* (q.v.) could emerge – but do not look for consistency among American directors of the Twenties, other than that, for most of their time, they were forced to support the star system.

Everyone loved stars: since the emergence of Mary Pickford, the necessity of stars was recognised by everyone, from the merest studio stock-holder to the most egotistical of directors. Though that lady, and her star-colleagues at United Artists, had proved capable of holding power, they were the exceptions among players: Gloria Swanson proved no more successful at business than Keaton, and Rudolph Valentino, offered a degree of

autonomy, proved a singularly inept producer. The studios kept under contract a stock of lesser names, for the factory system and the star system went hand in hand. 'Answering your letter,' wrote David O. Selznick to a contract writer in 1929, 'we are in need mostly of stories for Nancy Carroll and for Dick Arlen. Carroll's vehicles should be rather on the emotional side, with a little comedy of the precious type, if possible . . . I think that Carroll and Arlen are our most serious needs in that we have only one story ahead for Nancy, and none for Dick . . . We are in splendid shape on William Powell, and fairly well off on Clara Bow, Evelyn Brent, Ruth Chatterton, and Gary Cooper. We have two stories ahead for Buddy Rogers, but could use a couple more very nicely.' These people were, of course, commodities, as Selznick makes clear in a later memo: 'At one time, when [George] Bancroft and Bow were strong, we discussed co-starring this pair; but you felt that we would be losing a picture by it, and that subsequent pictures starring these players individually would suffer through a seeming comparative weakness after a co-starring picture. But now, with Bow on her way out, and with Bancroft certainly not as strong as he was a year ago, I think that a Bancroft-Bow picture would assume real importance; that we would be extracting the last ounce of value out of Bow before letting her go . . .'

Today we may well feel that a star's presence is a mixed blessing: certainly it is a pleasure to watch a player of accomplishment and it is painful, often, to watch a nonentity, but the presence of stars in the fictions which movies tell is almost as deleterious as if novels began with a list of characters and their functions in the plot. Consequently few films of this time hold any surprise for the modern viewer – nor did they at the time to the sophisticated filmgoer; but the mass audience, it seemed, so wanted to watch their favourite players repeat themselves that even the smallest variation came as a surprise.

'Who is the real maker of a film?' asked Jean Renoir in 1974, answering the question himself. 'In the heroic age of the American cinema it was generally the actor who put his stamp on it. As the industry prospered it became a medium for the manufacture of stars.' Earlier, Raoul Walsh had concurred: the real auteurs, he had said, were the stars. The auteur theory, started by the French in the late Fifties, and posited on the director as sole creator, has been rejected by most of its cult-figures – Walsh himself, William Wellman and Vincente Minnelli among them. Film-making, its practitioners agree, is a collaborative effort. We may notice that the films of Walsh move faster than those of James Cruze, that the comedies of LaCava are lighter than those of Clarence Badger; we may find John Ford drawn to open-air stories or Frank Borzage preferring those with sentiment; but while the star system predominated, American films, with rare exceptions, took their complexion from the looks and personality of the leading players* – a complexion even stronger when Sound brought voice – as we may see from the various versions (q.v.) of, say, *The Prisoner*

of *Zenda* and *A Star is Born*, or the tests for *Gone with the Wind*.

'Under Zukor's management and guidance some of the most famous stars of the screen were developed,' boasted 'The Motion Picture Almanack', and Paramount for a while owned the most famous star of his time: Rudolph Valentino (1895–1926), fresh from his success in *The Four Horsemen of the Apocalypse* (q.v.). In *The Sheik* he had set a whole generation of girls dreaming of being carried off to a desert lair by a romantic Arab – though we may feel that the secret of his appeal died with him. He moved awkwardly, but in **Blood and Sand** (1922) he gives a performance of sorts – a boy-man, loving his fame, unused to his dandy's clothes, amused as he smokes his mistress's candy-striped cigarettes while she plays the harp. His chameleon-like changes from clodhopping naivety to burning intensity were utilised in relentlessly exotic situations: these particular ones were provided by Ibañez' popular novel of the bull-ring and directed by Fred Niblo. The film, like *The Sheik*, was influential in creating the taste for the more florid interior decor popular over the next decade.

Dependence on stars was sometimes waived for 'big' pictures, though **The Covered Wagon** (1923) had been bought for Mary Miles Minter (who refused it); Paramount, anxious to recoup the large sum paid to acquire Emerson Hough's novel, turned it over to James Cruze, and then poured more money into the project, hoping for an authentic American epic. The film has genuine sweep: Cruze was thought to have struck a blow for a return to the omnipotence of the director, but from his later work it is clear that he was much indebted to the cinematography of Karl Brown (working with stationary cameras and stock film insensitive to blues). In 1923 there were still alive many who had been on that particular landrush starting out from what became Kansas City. Films in the preceding years had developed entirely different ways of treating the gunfighters and pioneers whom William S. Hart had regarded as virtually his enclave. This film, however, became the prototype for the prestige Western, and for two generations Hollywood blurb-writers linked it

*Perhaps the best example is *Casablanca* (q.v.), which surely would have been quickly forgotten had it starred Dennis Morgan and Hedy Lamarr, as at one time planned.

with a later film for effective copy: 'There was *The Covered Wagon* . . . and then *Cimarron* . . . Now, Greatest of all –' Four years later Cruze was put in charge of **Old Ironsides** (1926), a 'true' adventure of the Revolutionary War, in which Esther Ralston went to sea for love of Charles Farrell, an interpolation regretted by some critics, who otherwise did not spare their superlatives. At specified city premieres the image was enlarged at one point to reveal a huge replica of the *Constitution* itself, done by a magnifier in the projection-box; but the film's failure put an end, for the moment, to wide screens – and to Cruze's career at Paramount, despite the reviews.

Paramount's other leading director, deMille, continued his modern morality tales with **Manslaughter** (1922), about a rich girl (Leatrice Joy) who believes that 'modern girls do not sit by the fire and knit': when she is involved in an automobile accident we are told 'These over-civilised, mad young wasters must be STOPPED – or the nation will be destroyed as Rome was destroyed,' which leads to an 'ancient' sequence as gratuitous as that in *Male and Female*. This led to the retelling of Exodus in **The Ten Commandments** (1923) in which the parting of the Red Sea was shown by photographing two bowls of water as they emptied, then playing the shots backwards and magnified. This is followed by a fable of two brothers, a good one (Richard Dix) and one (Rod La Rocque) who doesn't believe in the laws of Moses; using cheap concrete he builds a church which collapses on their mother, and La Rocque is seduced by a Eurasian vamp (Nita Naldi) before being hounded to death by the Furies, presumably representing the Almighty. As flatly made as they are opportunistic, these two films indicate deMille's decline as well as his predilection for the grandiose; he was exceptionally budget-conscious, and found that the greater outlay for spectacles was rewarded at the box office. Curiously the public considered the second film as Hollywood's atonement for the scandals which had led to the

Ronald Colman, left, in the title–role of *Beau Geste*, with Ralph Forbes as his brother John. For audiences, this was *the* Foreign Legion story, and they would also have recognised that the final sacrifice of the other Geste, Digby, was based on that of Captain Oates.

creation of the Hays Office (an event that was followed, incidentally, by another shock, the death from drug-addiction of Wallace Reid, one of Paramount's most important stars).

In **Beau Geste** (1926) divine justice is British and therefore more absolute, as adapted from P. C. Wren's story of three brothers who join the Foreign Legion when a precious stone disappears, each fleeing to protect the others. From the arresting opening – the deserted fort and the dead garrison – the film seldom falters: and if the direction by Herbert Brenon is imaginative, it owes as much to the performance of Ronald Colman, graceful and replete with aristocratic charm. That the director Brenon, like Cruze, also depended on his photographer is apparent from the two films for which he is best remembered, **Peter Pan** (1924) and **A Kiss for Cinderella** (1925) – and since these plays by J. M. Barrie had enchanted audiences for two decades Brenon seems to have taken the decision not to tamper with them. The result is a plethora of intertitles and talking-heads which is a drawback if the audience is not convinced by the story. Watching Paramount's equally poor *Alice in Wonderland* (q.v.) I felt a surge of affection for the original, but with the other two I merely wondered at Barrie's psychology – at least, as translated here, e.g. when the London bobby writes to his Cinderella, 'There are thirty-four policemen in this room but I would rather have you, my darling.' The *Peter Pan* is the more bearable, despite a Peter with a distinct shadow and the Lost Boys sporting the Stars and Stripes (though that became the Union Jack for the British version); it has a vile Captain Cook (Ernest Torrence), a jolly Nana and a crocodile, both humans in skins, and no apparent strings on the flying children. Betty Bronson's Peter, approved by Barrie himself, has sprightliness and boyishness, but her waif in the second picture is as tiresome as any of the child-women of Silent movies, with their primping and coyness and ringlets.

These two Barrie films, though they were praised by the urban critics, were aimed at less sophisticated audiences – and those who might have been tempted to stay at home with radio, which had recently become a serious competitor for after

working-hours entertainment. Such films were also offered to those who wanted traditional entertainment rather than the 'continental' tales which had started with Von Stroheim and had become entrenched with the success of Lubitsch's *The Marriage Circle* (q.v.) in 1924. Adolphe Menjou, star of that film and of *A Woman of Paris*, made some similar films for Paramount, including **Open All night** (1924), directed by Paul Bern from stories by Paul Morand, and **A Gentleman of Paris** (1927), directed by Harry D'Abbadie D'Arrast. The former is an odd combination of sex-comedy and slapstick, wherein Thérèse (Viola Dana) gets herself taken to the Cirque d'Hiver for a bicycle race because she thinks she prefers a 'cave-man' to the courtly Menjou; the latter is an examination of a roué who frequents high-class brothels and seduces a number of ladies, including the wife of his faithful valet. In two different roles, the character remains the same, ambivalently regarded; in the second film he proves himself a man of honour when not tempted by the flesh.

The British Clive Brook played similar roles, that of the basically decent cad, and if his role of the gentleman clown in **You Never Know Women** is not quite

Viola Dana and Adolphe Menjou in *Open All Night*, one of a great number of films in which he played the eternal cad – usually, for easier acceptance, set in Paris. The films nevertheless had much to say about traditional values since the War had shifted the balance of male–female power – and they always concluded with an assurance that things hadn't really changed after all

149

typical, the film is notable since it made the reputation of its director, William A. Wellman, and is one of the many imitations of Sjöström's *He Who Gets Slapped* (q.v.). The clown is afraid to tell the leading lady (Florence Vidor) that he loves her; the title refers to her realisation that it is reciprocal, after he has been dropped in the Hudson as a stunt and she has escaped rape by his playboy rival (Lowell Sherman). Also 'European' in feeling – specifically German – and also directed by an American, in this case Victor Schertzinger, **Forgotten Faces** (1928) mixes crime, *crime passionnel* and father-love. Brook is a silk-hatted crook, William Powell (q.v.) his accomplice, and Olga Baclanova the unfaithful wife – for whom Howard Esterbrook wrote a couple of memorable scenes: one of crazy passion at the piano with her paramour, as she bangs his head upon the keys, and another, later, when her way of life is indicated not by the usual row of bottles but the moue of disgust she makes as her hand encounters a cigar-butt by the bed.

Paramount's sophisticated lady – the female equivalent of Menjou and Brook – remained (till she left for United Artists) Gloria Swanson, the epitome of glamour to millions; and to the millions of working girls who dreamed of emulating her, she repaid the compliment by occasionally eschewing pearls and satins to impersonate one of them. Thus she is in her two best films of this period, **Manhandled** (1924) and **Stage Struck** (1925), both directed by Allan Dwan and demonstrating her superiority as a comedienne; she is particularly delightful in the former, whether enduring a rushhour subway ride to her place behind a Macy's counter, or impressing society with her bogus Russian countess – whose mannerisms were based on her new rival at the studio.

This was Pola Negri who had been transported across the Atlantic after her successes with Lubitsch: since these had included the Dubarry, she was typed as an adventuress, but when the public evinced little interest Lubitsch was borrowed from Warner Bros. to find a suitable subject. He chose an old play by Lajos Biro and Melchior Lengyal, 'The Czarina', and rechristened it **Forbidden Paradise** (1924): reviewers of the time were delighted at the concept of turning Catherine the Great into a contemporary ruler, but she is merely another movie vamp – with a passion for guardsmen. Chief object of her attention is Rod La Rocque, and Menjou is the wily chancellor who connives at the liaison. There are typical situations, and Lubitsch describes the putting-down of the Revolution in just three close-ups (the general's hand upon his sword; the proffered foreign bank account book; the general's hand loosening). Mary Pickford's dictum that Lubitsch was obsessed with doors is borne out: we see more of them than of the actual intrigues. When the public again proved indifferent, Negri was put into the hands of Mal St Clair, for a story of small towns more typical of him, **A Woman of the World** (1925). The reaction of a back-woods populace to a real-life countess in its midst was a popular theme at the time, and this one humanises the image of the star which the studio had so carefully built up. The D.A., a reform-addict, leaps about in fury at a glimpse of her cigarette-holder, and for that she horse-whips him in public – after which we find them sharing a wicked cigarettes as they leave for their honeymoon.

These two delightful comedies still did not endear Negri to American audiences, so she was entrusted to Erich Pommer during his brief spell at Paramount. He cast her in two war stories, **Hotel Imperial** (1927) and **Barbed Wire** (1927), in plebeian roles – hotel-maid and farm-girl respectively. The former is set in a hotel in Galicia in 1915, and concerns the relationship between its staff and the Russian troops in occupation; the latter concerns the effect of German P.O.W.s on a French rural community – and is as fully perceptive on the uneasy relations between the two nationalities. *Hotel Imperial,* primarily a spy story (when Billy Wilder remade it as *Five Graves to Cairo,* q.v., he sensibly kept the hotel looking very much the same), is the more enjoyable today: Mauritz Stiller directed, from a story by Biro, a Hungarian, and these European talents were almost certainly stimulated by the Americans around them, if only in the inevitable tensions. An American, Rowland V. Lee, directed the second film, and apart from Negri and Pommer a name common to both is

Jules Furthman (1888–1966) – and since he became one of the masters of screen-writing, their exceptional quality may be due to him.

Paramount's major contribution to the war film cycle – triggered off by the success on Broadway of 'What Price Glory?' in 1924, with its emphasis on disillusion – was **Wings** (1927), directed by William A. Wellman (1896–1975), an ex-flyer. He staged his action beautifully, be it the craft in flight or the humans milling on the ground – in both respects superior to the later *Hell's Angels* (q.v.), his screenplay is by John Monk Saunders (1905–40), whose individual and acrid view of the Great War and its aftermath would be the basis for a number of even more pungent pictures (q.v.). In a conventional tale about two student pilots (Richard Arlen, Charles 'Buddy' Rogers) are moments still fresh: the realisation by the students that their cadet elder (Gary Cooper) will not return to finish his Hershey bar; a dying pilot scratching his neck; the RFC flyer who flinches as the medal is pinned on his chest; and all the scenes in Paris, where the men on furlough are going beyond the pursuit of loose women – including a lesbian or so – and drinking themselves into oblivion. These scenes shocked puritan America – while titillating those to whom drunkenness was supposedly a memory; and worse was to come when the nice American ambulance driver (Clara Bow) allows herself to be taken to a hotel room.

The war films were much praised – and did little to disturb the Hollywood equilibrium. This one won the first Best Picture award presented by the Academy of Motion Picture Arts and Sciences (founded by Louis B. Mayer in 1927 in an attempt to prevent unionisation of actors and studio-workers) – and it is symptomatic of almost all those films associated with the Academy's prizes, subsequently called Oscars, being serious, prestigious, entertaining, spectacular and artistically above average. The war films also brought sex back across the Atlantic, having shown the doughboys indulging in Europe's old fleshpots. Until then Hollywood had found it prudent to set stories of sin and adultery in the Old World, thus emphasising the more homely and democratic virtues of the native land. Towards the end of the decade, however, newspaper headlines made it plain that sex was as common in the U.S. as bootleg gin – and the continental hooker made way for the college flapper, with Europe again relegated to the favoured setting for period romance.

This is not to say that American stories were about contemporary problems: until the advent of the gangster film, a concerned and shriven U.S. was only

From left to right, William Austin, Clara Bow, Jacqueline Gadsdon and Antonio Moreno in *It*. Miss Bow sells gloves in Moreno's store, and in reel One she sets her cap at him – which is more difficult than Mr Austin will believe. 'She's a ripping sort really,' he says, 'She's absolutely heavy with "It"!'

reflected in tales of flappers and jazz-babies – and they were innocuous enough. Social problems came with a laugh – as with **Are Parents People?** (1925), directed by Mal St Clair, one of the first films about divorce; and we know when the daughter (Betty Bronson) gets to work on Mum and Dad (Florence Vidor, Adolphe Menjou) what the result will be. The subject of a young couple (Lois Wilson, Warner Baxter) saddled with an appalling widowed father would seem to require more nerve, and the old boy does go into a home: but **Welcome Home** (1925), directed by James Cruze, had already been a successful Broadway comedy, by Edna Ferber and George S. Kaufman – and that was why Paramount wanted to film it.

Clara Bow (1905–65) was the quintessence of what the term 'flapper' signifies, according to F. Scott Fitzgerald, and since she was fully developed as such

before she arrived at Paramount, we may look at an enjoyable earlier film, made for one of the independent companies, **My Lady of Whims** (1926), directed by Herman Raymaker. It embodies the same myths as other flapper films – that, for instance, Greenwich Village is sinful, and peopled by sculptresses with names like Wayne Lee and lecherous artists who smoke Turkish cigarettes. A party is 'a rumpus' – and though described as 'wilder than an old maid under the mistletoe' it looks most decorous to the modern eye. It would be too much to claim that the sculptress is keen on Miss Bow, but hints are laid in that direction; she is rescued, anyway, from the triple temptations of literary aspirations, the Village and vice.

'Why, she'll flirt as long as she lives' says Ernest Torrence of Bow in **Mantrap** (1926), the sole subject of which is Bow flirting. Reputedly based on a novel by Sinclair Lewis, the title in fact refers to a small mountain town: when Joe (Torrence) leaves it for Minneapolis, the first one he notices is Bow, tripping from a taxi to a swell hotel. She's manicurist in the barber shop, but in no time she's Mrs Joe, and making eyes at a vacationing lawyer. Photographed entirely on location by James Wong Howe, and directed with a fine disregard for its implausibilities by Victor Fleming (q.v.), this enterprise considerably entertains. Bow is delightful. At the beginning as she moves towards the hotel she turns and winks; she primps her hair whenever a man hoves into view. Even when bored, insulted or misused, she is never woebegone for long, since she knows there's a new man round the corner. There is nothing subtle about her: she's attractive and she knows it. She wants to give a man a Good Time, in its most ample and admirable sense. Watch her when the lawyer arrives, or when Joe is preparing a party: she is hither, thither and yon, restless and eager to go. She's still primping at the end, incorrigible: reunited with Joe and in his arms, a new young Mountie appears and her eyes light up.

The quintessential Bow film – if only because of its title –is, inevitably, **It** (1928), directed by Clarence Badger. Madame Elinor Glyn (as she is billed) appears, to define 'it' – 'a quality possessed by some which draws all others with its magnetic force'. 'If ever I saw It, that's It,' says one male on sight of Clara. 'Hot socks, here's our new boss,' says her chum, at once sarcastic when Bow says she plans to marry him. 'Let's have a double wedding. You and him, and me and the Prince of Wales,' – to which Bow retorts, 'I'll soon take the snap out of your garters.' Because she has It, she does marry him, but not before some misunderstandings on a yacht – and since a yacht also provided the climax for *My Lady of Whims*, it was presumably the right place for girls of this kind.

Miss Bow's fame lives on. Raymond Griffith (1894–1957) has only recently been recognised as one of the great screen clowns, perhaps because audiences were spoilt then, and partly because so few of his features survive – and in none of those is he, like the other clowns, the whole show. His gags are not as individualistic as those of Keaton or Chaplin, and his

dude outfit is modelled on Max Linder; but he is inventive and endearing – and because he signals his irrepressible optimism with such glee he is more likeable, even, than Lloyd. He started with Vitagraph in 1914, and worked with Sennett as gagman and direct, but seems to have made his acting debut as a supporting actor in features – he has a small role in *Open All Night*, as a permanently drunk New Yorker hoping to be the next screen sheik. We note a cad's mannerisms but an eagerness to please (not the audience, but the suckers in the film), button-bright eyes and the physique of a mouse. **Paths to Paradise** (1925) is an enjoyable crook comedy, a forerunner of that staple of the Thirties, the elegant couple in uneasy alliance to con someone – and ending up in love. She (Betty Compson) poses as a maid and he as a detective, and there is some inventive business trying to steal a jewel, and a final slapstick chase. Clarence

Raymond Griffith, right, with Betty Compson in *Paths to Paradise*, one of his few extant films. Griffith has only recently taken his place with the great Silent clowns – though not because, as has been suggested, others overshadowed him. Except for Chaplin, they were all forgotten or half forgotten till James Agee's famous essay in 1949. The fact that Agee did not mention him can only mean that he had not seen him.

Badger directed both this and **Hands Up!** (1926), in which Griffith is an inefficient but nimble Confederate spy. He's ingratiating when smiling to hide his guilt, or doing a double-take at realising one of his own mistakes; but the fun is up and down till a roaring climax. In this film Robert E. Sherwood considered him ahead of the other comedians 'in point of ingenuity, imaginativeness and originality'. Talkies were difficult for him because he hardly spoke above a whisper (among those he made was *All Quiet on the Western Front*, playing the dying French Soldier); he later became a producer.

Paramount's other Silent comic (if we except Lloyd) was W. C. Fields (1879–1946), whose greater fame in Talkies has obscured the merit of his early films. These are just as disorganised as the Talkies, indicating on the studio's part a consistent tolerance towards the eccentricities of a particular talent. They also include many sequences and gags subsequently found in several of the Sound films. **It's the Old Army Game** (1926) trades on his old sketch, 'The Pharmacist' (filmed as a short by Mack Sennett in 1933) and has two sequences carried over intact into *It's a Gift* (q.v.). Since from his later films we know his clowning as a combination of misanthropy and a sense of damnation we may most treasure his delicate movements, to the extent that we may be tempted to place him with Lloyd and Keaton, though in the end his work is – inevitably – more improvised. Eddie Sutherland directed, lacking the firmness of Gregory LaCava (1892–1952) on **So's Your Old Man** (1927). The latter is rather thin, about a mild man who changes under hypnosis, but the earlier film finds him on form as Samuel Bisbee, glazier: 'See the world through Bisbee's windows'. Amidst bouts with his drinking colleagues, he invents an unbreakable windscreen – but mishap brings ignominy till a Spanish princess arrives to impress the snobs of the town in his favour. There also arrives a senator and a policeman, at the sight of whom he runs – for, like Keaton, he always expects to be outside the law. At the end, successful, he waves wife and princess goodbye, settling down to two weeks' vacation, drinking with his cronies. This is absolutely the Fieldsian universe – he remade it as *You're Telling Me* (q.v.) – and the original lacks only his murmured epithets. He is a very great man indeed, though contemporary audiences did not appreciate it. Paramount partnered him in his last three Silents with Chester Conklin in the hope of repeating the popularity of their teaming of Wallace Beery and Raymond Hatton.

Paramount also had a female droll, Bebe Daniels (1901–71), making strictly formula comedies. She had once been Harold Lloyd's leading lady, and had also played sultry ladies for deMille. She doesn't, in fact, seem funny so much as game. In **She's a Sheik** (1927), directed by Clarence Badger, she is chieftainess Zaida, rejecting the advances of wicked chieftain William Powell and kidnapping Foreign Legionnaire Richard Arlen for a strictly pure amour. As slapstick or parody it is tame. Better – because of La Cava's lighter touch – is **Feel My Pulse** (1928), in which she plays a molly-coddled, hypochondriac heiress who learns that her private sanatorium is being used as a base for rum-runners. Arlen is the sympathetic smuggler who is also a reporter, and Powell (b.1892) the gang boss. In both ventures William Powell's facial expressions are the best thing: though not yet immaculate, he has that eye to the main chance which he so well displayed in his Talkies' role of sauve charmer.

Richard Dix, who succeeded Wallace Reid as the studio's leading leading man, alternated comedy and drama. Jowly, even as a young man, he was suitably dressed in white tie and tails, high on bootleg booze until inevitably the right girl comes along to make him settle down. As such, he was in the tradition of the youthful John Barrymore, and **Let's Get Married** (1926) was a remake of Barrymore's 1914 *The Man From Mexico*. The 'right girl' is Lois Wilson, and by far the best performance in the film is Edna May Oliver's portrayal of a hymnal-seller with a taste for racy speakeasies. Dix is an Indian boy brought up as white in **Redskin** (1929), an action-filled tract made mainly in Technicolor, directed by Victor Schertzinger, from a story by Zane Grey; 'the greatest gift is not oil but tolerance' proclaims a worthy intertitle at the end.

Not then, or later, was Paramount interested in social problems, but the company made a notable move in the trend towards gangster studies with *Underworld* (q.v.) – which is also significant in the career of Josef von Sternberg (1894–1969). He was Viennese-born, Jewish, and an immigrant at the age of seven. More or less self-taught, he drifted from one job to another till he realised his capacity as an artist, which brought him into films. His first picture, **The Salvation Hunters** (1925), was the result of an arrangement with George K. Arthur, a British comic having difficulty repeating his native success in the U.S.: they made it for only $4,800, filming among the derelicts of the San Pedro waterfront. Its visual style is as unpretentious as the story is not. Each image is held until the significance of what is happening is properly understood; and the foreword makes it quite clear that: 'There are fragments of life which have been ignored by the motion picture because they concern the Thought and not the Body.' This Thought, or concept, is poverty, being down, out, despairing: but the story is trite in the extreme. It is one of the first 'arty' American films (contemporary with Nazimova's *Salome*, though that is arty in a theatrical way), and much impressed Fairbanks and Chaplin – it being seemingly impossible then, as now, for Hollywood to make the distinction between the arty-honest and the arty-phoney. They appreciated affinities with the German cinema. Suggestions that von Sternberg had worked there were not denied by him; they also arranged for United Artists to distribute it. Then he was engaged to direct Mary Pickford. She had second thoughts when he proposed another picture on poverty, perhaps because she took a second look at *The Salvation Hunters*. Chaplin also had second thoughts: he not only suppressed the film von Sternberg later made for him, but repudiated him by saying that he had only wished to test public acceptance of his opinions.

Despite the commercial failure of *The Salvation Hunters*, and two aborted films for M-G-M, B. P. Schulberg of Paramount took on von Sternberg, and put him on a story by Ben Hecht (1894–1964), which was troubling another director, Arthur Rosson. Hecht was a newspaperman, the first of many to flourish in Hollywood as audiences demanded contemporary stories. He had worked in Chicago, and his script for **Underworld** (1927) incorporates not only the killing of Dion O'Bannion in a flower shop in 1922, but a police siege and shoot-out of the sort he had often witnessed – though the film is less about what we think of as gangsters than derelicts, a couple of whom happen to be armed. This deliberate deglamorisation means that these robber chiefs dispute not so much over hooch or territory as over the plan of one to rape the girl of the other (George Bancroft) – a lady called 'Feathers' (Evelyn Brent). The film was much admired, and three years later the National Board of Review said that it had substantiated its director as 'an experimentalist whose work would sooner or later parallel in its creative aspect the work of artists in other fields and mediums of expression.' Its influence was strongest among the young French directors, but except for the shots of George Bancroft asleep among the carnival streamers, it has little of von Sternberg's visual flair.

The Last Command (1928) was also written by von Sternberg, from an incident told by Lubitsch of a movie director looking over the extras for a Russian officer 'type'. This one (Emil Jannings) had been a Russian general, and the director (William Powell) had been a revolutionary; the film flashbacks to their earlier activities, till, as an intertitle puts it, 'The backwash of a tortured nation had carried still another extra to Hollywood.' The Russian sequences are melodramatic, but the Revolution is imaginatively sketched in, and the Hollywood scenes are rightly frenetic, with some viciousness. Neither *The Dragnet* (1928) nor von Sternberg's last Silent, *The Case of Lena Smith* (1929), are known to survive. The latter was a Viennese story about a peasant girl's fight to regain her son from her husband's aristocratic family; and the former was a follow-up to *Underworld*, with Miss Brent and Bancroft – 'an emphatically mediocre effort' according to *The New York Times*. If so, **The Docks of New York** (1928) is at the other end of the scale. These docks are permanently wreathed in fog, and the clapboard houses look like anywhere but New York, but the story must be typical of any dockside at any time – if one overlooks the old fiction of the drunken night-time wedding, forgotten or regretted the following morning. Jules Furthman wrote the script from a story by John Monk Saunders, and they are entirely accurate on the violence, the casualness and licentiousness of the milieu; while the settings – the dark, crowded bar, the bare apartment-rooms – indicate that von Sternberg was approaching his peak as a visual stylist. Bancroft is the ox-like stoker and Betty Compson the frail he marries, bedraggled and all apprehensive glances, with an underlying hardness foreshadowing Dietrich in *Der Blaue Engel*.

Paramount's last Silent was **The Four Feathers** (1929) – last, because it took so long to make that it wasn't ready till every other screen was all-singing and all-talking. Its instigators were Merian C. Cooper (1893–1973) and Ernest B. Schoedsack (1893–1979), who had been, respectively, a flyer and a cameraman. Backed by Paramount, they went to Iran to make a film in the manner of Flaherty, *Grass* (1925) a 'vivid record' (Rotha) of the Baktyari tribe's twice-yearly migrations in search of grazing land. Its reception encouraged a further expedition – to the jungles of Northern Thailand, from which emerged *Chang* (1927), a story of a Lao tribesman and his battles with the jungle. However, little of the ethnic material brought back from Africa found its way into this version of A. E. W. Mason's novel, and the presence of a third director, Lothar Mendes, suggests that Paramount had no faith in their ability to handle fiction. The film is almost rousing: the shots of the Fuzzy-Wuzzies and the climactic battle are as good as in any Hollywood movie about the British Empire – proof always of how much Americans were in awe of that mighty, mystical concept. Like *Beau Geste*, the story begins in an English country house before moving to Africa, where the hero (Richard Arlen) redeems himself after accusations of cowardice: his bravery is super human, and if, also, so is his way with a dagger, all was permissible for Queen and Empire. Two intertitles are of interest: 'I promise you help is coming. Has a British officer ever failed you?' and 'Steady, men. Remem-

ber that all Ney's cavalry at Waterloo could not destroy the British square.' The film follows the book in its awe of military mystique, and that has dated far more than reverence for the Empire.

At Fox, the theatrical demise of Theda Bara brought them to tales of home-spun virtues, mostly set in the West or mid-West. These films are notable mainly for their indication of change, as the wagon-trains gave way to the Model-T Ford and the great trains rushing through; most of them starred the company's two biggest stars, Buck Jones and Tom Mix.

Jones (1889–1942) was a man of the West, who liked fishing and idling: 'the idol of youths, the bane of the elders' as one intertitle has it. Both **Just Pals** (1920) and **Lazybones** (1925) show him winning gloriously over suspicion and distrust. In the former, directed by John Ford, he befriends a rootless boy and is suspected of stealing the school funds; in the latter, directed by Frank Borzage, he risks opprobium by bringing up Zazu Pitts's son as his own – and, incidentally, the sequence where that lady is horse-whipped by her mother remains shocking.

Tom Mix (1880–1940) was described as 'that gun-toting cyclone on horseback' and another intertitle referred to 'The fastest gun, horse and smile of any man in the West'. He wore a skin-tight white outfit with gloves to match, but unlike the similarly accoutred cowboys who followed, he was the real thing – a former Texas Ranger, U.S. cavalryman, rancher and deputy marshal. As to his qualities as an actor, there is little evidence, but as a stunt performer he was a marvel: he jumped on and off horses, trains and stages; he wrestled beneath them and battled on top of them; on ropes he forded rivers and ravines, moving from precipice to valley and back again. His horse, Tony, was as enterprising as he – as swift as an eagle and as accurate as a homing pigeon. In **The Great K and A Train Robbery** (1926), the huge expresses are manoeuvred as easily as a toy, and just as easily Mix rounds up the gang, single-handed. In **The Last Trail** (1927), also directed by Lewis Seiler, he

The Last Man on Earth is one of those films so freakish that one can only question the mentality and motives of its makers. Earle Fox is the man, and, as an intertitle put it, 'There hasn't been so much interest in a man since the late King of England visited New York in 1924 – when he was Prince of Wales.' Clearly, this was science–fiction – of sorts.

brings up his pal's orphaned son, taking over from him as sheriff of the town, and defeating the dastardly outlaws in both battle and a chariot-race for the local Express concession.

Away from such sure-fire stuff, the Fox films faltered. In **The Silent Command** (1923) Edmund Lowe gets publicly disgraced in order to infiltrate a foreign power planning to blow up the newly-built Panama Canal. J. Gordon Edwards directed, and his film has two moments worth contemplating: the crew refusing to abandon ship, 'Beg pardon, sir, we'd rather go down with colours' and Bela Lugosi listening to a conversation miles away with a bugging device. Henry Otto directed **Dante's Inferno** (1924), which begins with both an imaginative evocation of Gustave Doré's illustrations designed for the text and a foreword claiming that much thought has gone into this version of a classic, implying that we would all enjoy it more because of the modern section – though that turns out to be a rehash of 'A Christmas Carol', with Dante and visions of hell replacing the visitations of the Christmas ghosts in the Dickens story.

Even more bizarre is **The Last Man on Earth** (1924), directed by John G. Blystone, which starts in 'the flip-flappering summer of 1940' with the men in dinner-jackets and jodhpurs, and the women in brief hooped-skirts and frilly pantaloons. Hattie (Derelys Perdue) tells Elmer (Earle Fox) that she wouldn't marry him if he were the last man alive – which is what he is about to become: the world is swept by a mysterious disease called 'masculitis' – fatal to males over fourteen years of age', as Dr Lulu Prodwell puts it. Ten years later, the women go around hand-in-hand, pantaloons abandoned for sequinned shorts. Only Greenwich Gertie of the Teahouse Gang knows where Elmer is – among the redwoods of California, and how her plane gets down in the midst of them is something only Fox could explain. Elmer is put up for auction, 'the most momentous sale in history', but it attracts only eight people, plus Dr Prodwell, who bids on behalf of her government. In her clinic, invalids

Reunion in the trenches: in *Four Sons*, two brothers (James Hall, left, and George Meeker) are fighting on opposite sides, and one hears the other, dying, cry 'Mutterchen'. He *hears* it, for the synchronised score is interrupted by just this one line of dialogue, an experience found 'disquieting' by *The New York Times* – whose only experience of Talkies hitherto had been *The Jazz Singer*.

throw away crutches to chase him – though the chief pursuer is the doctor's daughter, now a raging nymphomaniac. The aim is presumably Swiftian satire, and if the achievement is unsettling, it is for different reasons.

It is a relief to return to the Western, and it was **The Iron Horse** (1924) which made the reputation of John Ford (1895–1973), former propman and stuntman. He later suggested that a 'simple story' was stretched when Fox saw the location shots, but it is far more likely that Fox sought to emulate the success of *The Covered Wagon*. A foreword promises accuracy, and Ford has precisely caught the pioneering spirit: there is real pride in the statement that due to the enthusiasm of the workers the two transcontinental lines met seven years earlier than Congress had anticipated. This makes for a marvellous ending – as in deMille's *Union Pacific* (q.v.), in which the construction of the railroads is a backdrop to an equally trite story. In this case it concerns a buck-skinned leader (George O'Brien) who wins the boss's daughter (Madge Bellamy) from his treacherous aide. The Indian attacks against plains and distant mountains (photographed by George Schneiderman, assisted by Burnett Guffey) are handled in a way we recognise as Fordian, and **Three Bad Men** (1926) is even more stuffed with themes to which this director would return in film after film. Its images of the

Dakota Gold Rush of 1877 are even more consistently impressive than those of Cruze's film, as three desperadoes (J. Farrell MacDonald, Tom Santschi, Frank Campeau) adopt a fatherless heroine (Olive Borden) and find for her a husband (O'Brien). This couple could be John Wayne (q.v.) and Maureen O'Hara, and aficionados will also welcome the masculine camaraderie (tough old buzzard in tears after a farewell), slapstick (the dude getting a going-over to see whether he's a suitable husband) and sentiment (the prayer in the chapel).

Ford remained under contract to Fox till well into the Talkie period, occasionally getting his teeth into subjects that interested him: the reiteration of favourite themes suggests alternately playing it safe and a degree of independence not granted to his colleagues. **The Shamrock Handicap** (1926) has moments of hilarity – an Irish baronet so changed by U.S. democracy that he digs ditches till his horse can enter the big race; and one of meanness – the black valet who holds a razor-blade, just in case, during a changing-room fight. Two other films reflect Ford's Irish antecedents: **Hangman's House** (1928), a thriller with some horse-racing, a number of Celtic crosses, and Victor McLaglen as a local patriot bent on revenge; and **Riley the Cop** (1927), the adventures of an Irish cop (J. Farrell MacDonald) both on his beat and among the fleshpots of Europe. The latter manages a minor variation on an old theme: young America vs. old Europe, with a decided attempt to make boozing (then, of course, outlawed in the U.S.) attractive.

Sentiment also rides high in Ford's **Four Sons** (1928) – less an account of the four brothers involved than of Mother Bernle (Margaret Mann), the most lovable, most smiling, whitest-haired *mutter* of all. Three sons fight for the Kaiser; the other, remembering a slight by a German officer, leaves his New York delicatessen to fight against him. A hideously sentimental epilogue concerning Mother's arrival in New York is accompanied by the relentless grinding of two songs, 'Little Mother' and 'The Sidewalks of New York' – and as a whole the film sticks to the stereotypes of Griffith's war films.

Fox had already managed a more realistc view of the War in **What Price Glory?** (1926), though that had not been filmed till well after the Broadway success of the play by Laurence Stallings and Maxwell Anderson – and then only because *The Big Parade* (q.v.) had cleaned up for M-G-M. The play itself had not been produced till a year after completion, for not until rehabilitation was somewhat complete was it possible to look back at that mudbath of slaughter and suffering, and reflect that it had actually happened – and, even more incredibly, that some had survived it. Remarque in 'All Quiet on the Western Front' was the first to question its values and motives, and the Second World War was to come and go before a flood of books examined it: the tenor at this time was expressed in this film – 'What price glory now?' as the dead and dying are brought in. Another inter-title runs, 'The world must be in a bad way if the earth has to be wet down by the blood of boys like these every thirty years,' and others refer to the stench of death: but the piece mainly concerns the comic feud between Captain Flagg (Victor McLaglen) and Sergeant Quirt (Edmund Lowe). The front-line sequences have little to do with them, and indeed of all the war films from *Civilization* to the version (q.v.) of Remarque's novel only *The Big Parade* tackles the battles head on. The rest, overwhelmed or under budgeted – the Marne taxis in *Seventh Heaven* (q.v.) are particularly unconvincing – settle for montage; passion here is dissipated in the antics of Quirt and Flagg and their pursuit of Charmaine (Dolores del Rio) – who, like most of the ladies in these films, is no better than she should be.

The director was Raoul Walsh, who had come to Fox from Triangle and stayed, except for a brief spell at Paramount, for twenty years – though he made his best-known Silents elsewhere, e.g. *The Thief of Bagdad, Sadie Thompson* (q.v.). **The Red Dance** (1928) is, however, a good example of Hollywood influenced by Europe, with an orgy borrowed from *Die Liebe der Jeanne Ney*, and indications of sexual variety including lesbianism – which suggests more sophistication in Fox films than in the hayseed audiences for which they were usually intended. It was considered essential to stress the decadence of Europe, but also by this time the American film, having reached technical perfection, was trying to translate the complex temperament of mankind. Unfortunately the plot is a simple-minded thing about the pure love of a Grand Duke (Charles Farrell) and a peasant girl (Dolores del Rio); the Imperial family is sympathetically portrayed, and the Revolutionaries are the stereotypes of the Soviet films themselves – from which are copied a number of the action shots. Ben Carré's art direction is elaborate. Walsh's direction is fluid, and the film easily reflects America's attitude to Soviet Russia – a mixture of fear, wariness and grudging admiration.

Also handling a number of Fox's more worldly products was another director destined to be one of the long-serving craftsmen of the American screen, Howard Hawks (1896–1977), a former racing-driver whose occasional ventures into the industry had led him to the scenario department of Paramount. Two years later Fox gave him the chance to direct – a film now lost, and no deprivation if we judge it by his second, **Fig Leaves** (1926), which he also wrote, yet another facetious look at primitive times, plus a hackneyed modern story about a mannequin (Olive Borden), her jealous husband (George O'Brien) and her employer (André de Beranger). It is hard to sit through today, though the vestigial reward of all early movies is an indication of the way people lived then – best exemplified in the work of directors considered 'great' at the time, like Henry King and Frank Borzage, because they were allowed freedom of interpretation. Setting out only to divert, a minor industry director like Hawks is especially dependent on this material. **The Cradle Snatchers** (1927) is a light-hearted romp about three unfaithful husbands, three neglected wives, and the students they employ to make their husbands jealous. **Paid to Love** (1927) is a drama about an apache dancer (Virginia Valli) employed by an American financier (J. Farrell MacDonald) to attract a penniless Crown Prince (George O'Brien) away from his automobiles. **Fazil** (1928), an adaptation of a French play which was one of the many imitations of *The Sheik,* concerns a French girl (Greta Nissen) who marries an

No matter what critics thought of the imaginative powers of the German directors, Hollywood tended to think of them only in terms of their best–known films: so Paul Leni was called upon by Universal to recreate the sinister aspects of the film we call *Waxworks*. Here is Laura La Plante being menaced in perhaps the classic 'old dark house' tale, *The Cat and the Canary*: the disguised gentleman has claims to the same inheritance.

Arab prince (Charles Farrell) and finds, imprisoned in his harem, that never the twain shall meet; but she still loves him, and they die together like Romeo and Juliet. That *Paid to Love* is actually enjoyable is probably due to one of its three scenarists, Seton I. Miller, who would contribute to some of Hawks's best Talkies. Its deliberately risqué title is justified by the plot, which also includes a rape by the Prince – permissible, as it turns out, since love is mutual and democracy permits its victim to become Queen. **A Girl in Every Port** (1928) is said to be seminal, because Hawks later made several more films in which male friendship proves more enduring than fickle heterosexuality – but the presence of McLaglen reminds us that the situation had already been used in *What Price Glory?* Robert Armstrong is the other merchant seaman, Louise Brooks the girl, and the piece is boisterous and amicable. **Trent's Last Case** (1929) is the second of three film versions of E. C. Bentley's 1913 detective story (the other two were British), and it captures some of the book's ingenuity; Donald Crisp is the millionaire who plots his own death, and Raymond Griffith is the amateur detective. (A Sound version was made, but now appears lost.)

The acquisition of Frank Borzage (1893–1962) strengthened Fox's roster of directors. A former stage actor, he had worked with Ince and had directed for Triangle. By the time he joined Fox in 1925 his films were billed 'A Frank Borzage Production' in letters as big as the stars' names. The best of those extant is **The First Year** (1926), based on Frank Craven's play about newly-weds, played here by Kathryn Perry and Matt Moore; that it is diverting for half its footage is due to the couple's disastrous dinner-party. Borzage's *Seventh Heaven* was once described as 'the Silent picture which nine out of ten people recall with most pleasure' and I shall recall it at the end of this chapter. However, it might be mentioned here that a barrier to present appreciation is the synchronised score, consisting almost wholly of a refrain we know as 'Diane', and clearly sister to the equally omnipresent 'Charmaine' of *What Price Glory?*

Like Fox, Universal lagged behind in the race to acquire theatres; there was greater financial acumen at Paramount and M-G-M. The rivalry between them was intense, and if exhibition was now considered far more profitable than production, it behoved studio chiefs to shore up exhibition with films the public wanted to see. Universal's founder, Laemmle, remained supreme, though briefly he handed the reins to the producer boy-wonder, Irving Thalberg (1899–1936), whose tenure of office coincided with Von Stroheim's battles; and if the latter's extravagance virtually impoverished Universal, he was also to an extent responsible for its remaining a major force. Apart from his films, almost the only ones the studio made which are still remembered – and the only ones greatly successful in their time – were two historical-horror stories with Lon Chaney; ironically, Chaney's best work was for M-G-M, with whom he was associated for most of the decade.

Lon Chaney (1883–1930) was the son of deaf-mute parents; he had done almost every job in the theatre when he started in films as an extra. An extraordinary facility with make-up brought regular employment, but he did not begin to achieve his great popularity until he played a sham cripple in *The Miracle Man* (1919) at Paramount. Often bereft of features or limbs, he became known as 'The Man of a Thousand Faces', a Caliban-like creature, more to be pitied than feared. Under contract to Universal, he played Fagin in *Oliver Twist* (1922), as well as cripples, crooks, mad scientists and those eternal bogeymen, Orientals. His burning eyes and the humps and limps make his Quasimodo in **The Hunchback of Notre Dame** (1923) a pathetic figure, but you may feel the make-up is excessive. The film is also notable for its replica of the cathedral itself, though the backlot construction did not go much above the doors; Wallace Worsley directed this simplification of Hugo's novel, but Rupert Julian was put in charge of **The Phantom of the Opera** (1925) – though replaced during the shooting by an uncredited Edward Sedgwick. This one reduces Gaston Leroux's nineteenth-century thriller to the relationship between a singer (Mary Philbin) and the mysterious creature (Chaney) whose obsession with her brings him up from the catacombs where he hides his hideous face from mankind. Prima donnas are noted for vanity rather than common sense, but it is hard to know why this one insists, when her life is in danger, on singing Marguerite and going to the *bal masque* – a sequence, incidentally, photographed in Technicolor.

As works to chill the bone, neither film can compare with **The Cat and the Canary** (1927) Paul Leni's first film in the U.S. John Willard's old play about the reading of a will is not as funny as the 1939 version (q.v.), but it has Laura La Plante as the pretty victim, and Creighton Hale as the cowardly cousin who helps to unmask the murderer. The director's work can be described as follows: 'By an ingenious use of shadows, lights and photographic angles Mr Leni has created the eerie atmosphere necessary in a house where sudden death and sinister happenings occur' – that is *The New York Times*, in fact discussing *The Chinese Parrot*, which no longer exists. In contrast, **The Man Who Laughs** (1928) is merely another historical, with Universal hoping that both this version of Hugo would repeat the success of *The Hunchback of Notre Dame*, and that it had

acquired another Chaney in the imported Conrad Veidt – who on this occasion is just another clown-hero of the time. **The Last Warning** (1929) returns Leni to his shadows, a thriller set entirely inside a theatre – and no one ever had so much fun with the sinister aspects of an empty theatre. After a flat exposition, the tension mounts: indeed, this is one of the most accomplished and enjoyable of all Silent thrillers – its small reputation due to its advent just as cinemas were wired for Sound, and possibly also to Leni's early death.

Universal's other prize European acquisition was E. A. Dupont, who retired to Europe after just one film, *Love Me and the World Is Mine Tonight*. The liaison between the studio and the Hungarian Paul Fejos (1897–1963) was more profitable but little more agreeable. He had studied medicine, but after contact with the theatre during military service took it up full-time, and made his first film in 1920. In the U.S. he found independent backing for *The Last Moment* (1927), now lost; it caused Laemmle to offer a contract and give him freedom on *Lonesome* (q.v.), the critical reception of which encouraged Universal to put him on one of their first big Talkies, *Broadway* (q.v.). Indeed, to make that Fejos and Hal Mohr, the cinematographer, were taken off **The Last Performance** (1929), which limped into cinemas a year later, its added Sound sequences of no benefit among the all-Talkies. The Fejos flair is always apparent in this tale of a stage illusionist (Veidt) and his obsession with his ward (Miss Philbin), but audience indifference may also have been due to over-familiarity with these black-rim eyed and sinister supermen. Fejos moved, after some uncredited work, to M-G-M, where he was removed from one film and otherwise kept idle. He returned to Europe, to make at least two interesting films (q.v.); but it is because of *Lonesome* that he has an honourable place in film history: it calls for separate discussion, which you will find at the end of this chapter.

Universal's most skilful native director was Clarence Brown (b. 1890), formerly assistant to Maurice Tourneur – and their *Foolish Matrons* we have already admired. Two of his Universal films are

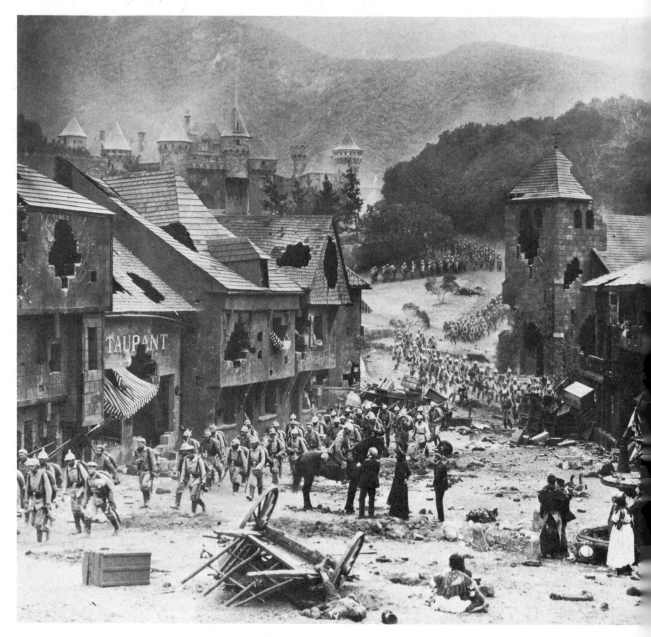

directed by Albert Parker, with John Barrymore in the title-role, Roland Young as Watson, Gustav von Seyffertitz as Moriarty, William Powell, Reginald Denny, some location shots of Baker Street, and complicated plot which has little to do with either Conan Doyle or William Gillette. Goldwyn was no luckier with *Caligari,* which he imported: few exhibitors would book it after New York audiences booed and demanded their money back. He learned the satisfaction – of inestimable value for the future – of having an artistic success, but his stock-holders were less happy and he was ousted; later in 1922 Loew took over the company in a stock exchange deal. Goldwyn started again as an independent, leaving as legacy for the new Metro-Goldwyn company a roaring lion

wanted, to manage a motion picture studio, he looked around for a surrogate. His eye alighted upon Louis B. Mayer (1885–1957), a former exhibitor and distributor whose fortunes had started with the local franchise of *The Birth of a Nation*. Mayer had been briefly involved in the founding of the Metro company, then called Alco, in 1915, and had started his own production company three years later, when he enticed the popular Anita Stewart from Vitagraph on an exclusive contract. Like all the moguls, he had a reputation for ruthlessness and double-dealing. Filching major stars from rivals remained a major activity among them; but from Miss Stewart's point of view it meant a higher salary and the proposition that the new company was devoted to her popularity and abilities. Mayer made an agreement with First National to distribute, and at a time when a good gross for a film was $250,000 that company offered a guarantee of $125,000 –and though Mayer's films usually cost more than that, they were profitable. Consequently Metro approached him with a request to make four films a year for them, in addition to his commitment to First National, and that brought him into contact with Loew, who was to find himself saddled with two failing companies – for Metro had begun to flounder when June Mathis left for Paramount with Valentino, indignant that the latter's salary request had been refused. Loew and Mayer signed an agreement for Mayer to manage both studios, in April 1924, and Metro moved to the Goldwyn lot at Culver City. The name Metro-Goldwyn-Mayer was not used till a year later; for the moment Louis B. Mayer – prominently – presented Metro Goldwyn pictures.

Mayer was production chief, but the brains of the outfit was Irving Thalberg, recruited from Universal a year earlier, and who with the merger became second vice-president and supervisor. Within the industry, during his lifetime and for some time after, he was regarded as a 'genius' – even by the normally sceptical scenario-writers. That he had drive, ingenuity and a far-sighted commercial acumen there is no doubt, but the verdict on the films he produced and supervised cannot be so positive: most of them can

'The world was dancing. Paris had succumbed to the mad rhythm of the Argentine Tango,' says an intertitle in *The Four Horsemen of the Apocalypse*, but the film soon proved that it had other matters than tangoes on its mind. The war–torn French villages may not look so convincing to modern eyes, but audiences at the time were stunned.

(then mute) and a slogan, '*Ars Gratia Artis*', which, except for a brief spell of 'modernisation' in the Sixties, have opened every M-G-M film from then to the present.

The Goldwyn company was deeply in debt, but its assets included the studio at Culver City – built by Ince, and purchased from Triangle by Goldwyn – and since Loew neither knew how, nor only be judged in commercial terms. It is impossible to admire Mayer even to that extent; he may have made decisions which made the accountants happy, but his creative demands were, in Lady Bracknell's words, 'of more than usually revolting sentimentality'. He was a bigot and a hypocrite, once described thus by *Variety*: 'One does not remember his achievements so much as his monumental pettiness, his savage retaliation, the humiliations he heaped on old associates.' If his name is synonymous with that of M-G-M in its heyday it is because he loved publicity – while Thalberg eschewed it; and because the creative team built up by Thalberg was to remain at Culver City till long after his premature death.

The relationship between the two men was to be an uneasy one, developing into a complete rift during the Thirties. At this point they were too busy solving the two major headaches willed them by the Goldwyn company. One was *Greed*, which we have already discussed, and the other was **Ben-Hur** (1925), also taken on by the company as a prestige item after Sam Goldwyn's departure. General Lew Wallace's novel about a Jewish nobleman at the time of the Roman Occupation of his country had been the biggest-selling book since the Bible – from which it purloined a number of its episodes; the theatrical firm of Klaw and Erlanger had presented a stage spectacle based on the book in 1889, and as its popularity never dimmed the film rights were eyed longingly by the movie industry from the 1907 pirated version by Kalem onwards. In 1921 Erlanger arranged with the Wallace estate to offer those rights for $600,000, and then formed a consortium with two other impresarios, Ziegfeld and Dillingham. which bought them for that sum and offered them to the industry for $1 million. The Goldwyn company could not afford that, but it offered the syndicate fifty cents from every dollar earned by the film: that the film would be hugely profitable neither side had any doubt, for Lubitsch's German spectacles were currently proving again that huge expenditure was justified at the box office – as was, also, *The Four Horsemen*. And June Mathis, having now defected from Paramount (without Valentino), would

also be in charge of *Ben-Hur*. It was she who decided that the film must be made in Italy, that the director should be Charles Brabin and the star George Walsh: in conditions of chaos, caused partly by the Italians – both the authorities and the crew – and partly by an inadequate script, filming proceeded. After viewing the rushes, Mayer and Thalberg replaced Brabin with Fred Niblo and Walsh with Ramon Novarro; Mathis was also dropped, and after further erratic shooting, production was transferred to Hollywood, with only about ten per cent of the Italian footage retained. The final cost was just under $4 million, and the worldwide gross around $9 million; that it went into the M–G–M ledgers at a loss of $700,000 was due entirely to the percentage paid to Erlanger's group – however, reissued in 1931 with a synchronised score and sound effects it took somewhat more than that figure, which was a very good gross indeed.

That may seem surprising, since the Silent film was then dead, but the world had loved *Ben-Hur* – and it is easy to see why. Like all good Silent spectacle, it moves ahead with conviction and aplomb, and neither the sea battle nor the chariot race disappoints. The intermittent use of Technicolor and the groupings in such sequences as the Birth of Christ and the Last Supper (after da Vinci) indicate the care taken; and if the film not unreasonably takes its pictorial quality from nineteenth-century religious painting it is still much less Victorian in image and sentiment than the 1959 remake (q.v.). It is much more entertaining, and therefore a far better film: its qualities were certainly recognised by the makers of the new version, which uses identical set-ups in the chariot race and for Christ carrying the Cross.

Thus *The Four Horsemen* and *Ben-Hur*, neither of which had originally anything to do with Mayer or Thalberg, created the M-G-M image – of uplift and literary origins, of larger-than-average budgets (approximately one-third higher than at other studios) and, following Valentino and Novarro, of 'more stars than there are in heaven'. That was one boast of the publicity department, which more consistently than that of other studios maintained superlatives – and we can

The wicked Roman, Messala (Francis X. Bushman), hardly plays fair with his former childhood friend, Ben-Hur (Ramon Novarro), in the 1925 film of that name. There were several uncredited directors, and it was Reeves Eason who was responsible for the still-exciting chariot race, for which forty-two cameras were used. Though clearly they did not construct the whole stadium above ground level, the sheer size of what we see on the screen still takes the breath away.

agree that M-G-M product was the classiest. Later, it was often the most pompous, but as long as Thalberg was alive Leo the Lion had both teeth and guts. Two other films of M-G-M's first year – both instituted and shown as the company struggled with *Ben-Hur* – helped it take the industry's crown of leadership from Paramount. Both cost above the average, were commercially and artistically successful, and starred John Gilbert (1897–1936). One was Von Stroheim's *The Merry Widow*, and the other **The Big Parade** (1925), commissioned by Thalberg from Lawrence Stallings, co-author of 'What Price Glory?' – the Broadway success of which proved that the public was ready for another war subject, more realistically treated than *The Four Horsemen,* but not, finally, less romantically. It is structured like a symphony: the opening – the wealthy dilettante (Gilbert) who is so taken by a patriotic tune that he joins the army; the long middle section, the coda – the frolics of the hero and his buddies in the French village, and his wooing of a local Marianne (the aptly-named Renée

Adorée); and, finally, the battle. The actual plot emerges in an epilogue, when the hero, now crippled, returns to search for his beloved in an impossibly sun-drenched countryside. The facts of army-life and duo-national romance are glossed over, but the more important war scenes are handled by the director, King Vidor, with a skill that remains astonishing. He also ensures that Gilbert, for all his charm and authority, retains till the end some of his initial arrogance: unlike Valentino's earlier soldier hero, this is no cardboard toy.

Star and director, with Lillian Gish, shared another success with **La Bohème** (1926), quite rightly described by *The New York Times* as 'virtually flawless', before adding 'and one that will do its share to bring the screen to a higher plane.' Such could not be said of **Bardelys the Magnificent** (1926), based on a swashbuckling novel by Rafael Sabatini, but it is great fun. If all three films confirmed Vidor as one of the most accomplished of directors, posterity may give equal place to Monta Bell (1891–1958) – at least on the strength of **Upstage** (1926) and

Sjöström's *He Who Gets Slapped* was based on a popular play, 'a circus allegory', in Brooks Atkinson's words, 'that no one understood but everyone loved.' The film is only too understandable: the rejected scientist (Lon Chaney, right) who becomes a clown, the bare-back rider (Norma Shearer) he secretly loves, and the partner (John Gilbert) she loves but cannot marry. It made the reputations of Shearer and Gilbert, and enhanced that of Chaney.

Man, Woman and Sin (1927), among his few films to survive. He had been one of Chaplin's assistants, and had directed his first film in 1924, *Broadway After Dark*; apart from producing *West Point of the Air* for M-G-M in 1935, he retired after the conventional *The Worst Woman of Paris?* (q.v.) two years earlier. Contemporaries never placed him with Vidor, nor were his films the sort to elicit exceptional attention – simply conventional tales of love and melodrama. Bell was able to apply both wit and tension to every sequence; he used imaginative but not arty set-ups, and was marvellous on the detail of the milieu – the vaudeville theatres and offices of *Upstage,* and in *Man, Woman and Sin* moving from newspaper-office to embassy-ball to suburban bordello. In the latter film Gilbert is the adoring cub-reporter used by the paper's society editor, played by an already legendary stage actress, Jeanne Eagels, with a natural ease and elegance. Gowned in chiffon, slightly bored and irritated, and occasionally amused, she treads her way through life with casual indifference to those around her. Bell cannot elevate this to tragedy, but his mixture of romance and realism makes this one of the best Silent dramas of them all.

Hardly inferior is **Laugh, Clown,**

Laugh (1928), directed by Herbert Brenon, who only three years earlier had been offering *A Kiss for Cinderella*. In that film, the camera of James Wong Howe had simply recorded the action, but now it contributes to it; so does the editing, and the sets and locations really look like Italy. And the acting is naturalistic, even if one hesitates before the mellifluent style of Lon Chaney. This version of 'Pagliacci' is based on a 1923 play by David Belasco and Tom Cushing, and the clown (Chaney) has melancholia: he is assigned to a Count (Nils Asther), whose 'spells of uncontrollable laughter are due to a life of self-indulgence', for a mutual cure, but it is still a question of *cherchez la femme*, a bare-back rider (Loretta Young) – whose attentions to the lascivious Count are further evidence of the increased sophistication in films during these years.

The films of Lon Chaney are a footnote to the taste of the Twenties, but merely as a thriller **The Unholy Three** (1925) is remarkably accomplished – and it is not to be judged by the 1930 Sound remake, also with Chaney, directed by Jack Conway. The trio of the title are a dwarf, a strong man, and a ventriloquist (Chaney) who is disguised as a dear old lady; their business is burglary and their cover a parrot shop. It is an ingenious story, economically and tensely told by Tod Browning, an old acquaintance and frequent director of Chaney, whose career had been bedevilled by drink up to this time. Brought to M-G-M by Chaney, together they embarked on a series of grotesqueries, usually involving the star as a pitiable-ghastly outcast of society bent on revenge for some past wrong, real or imagined. At its worst, the formula resulted in **The Unknown** (1927), in which Chaney is a supposedly armless knife-thrower who has his arms amputated in a scheme to destroy the lover (Norman Kerry) of the girl (Joan Crawford) he adores; and at its best, in **West of Zanzibar** (1928) in which he is a severely crippled trader whose revenge on his enemy (Lionel Barrymore) includes the use of voodoo and the reduction of the latter's supposed daughter to a drink-crazed whore. There are, of course, degrees of acceptability, and Browning, always (at this time) a vivid storyteller, works best when he can gloat over the whole paraphernalia of evil, as opposed to exploring the byways of sado-masochism.

Chaney's first film for M–G–M had been the amalgamated companies' first success, **He Who Gets Slapped** (1924), based on a popular play, and 'a shadowy drama so beautifully told, so flawlessly directed, that we imagine that it will be held up as a model by all producers' said *The New York Times*. Chaney is supported by John Gilbert and Norma Shearer, and the role is also that of a clown; however, Leonid Andreyev's variation of 'Pagliacci' offered the director, Victor Sjöström, only tentative opportunities for the sort of group portrait – i.e. the circus – which had been so taking in his Swedish films. An earlier film of Sjöström's, made before the amalgamation, has not survived, nor a number of the later ones, but **The Scarlet Letter** (1926) and **The Wind** (1928) are glowing testaments to his happy collaboration with Lillian Gish. The former begins with a sequence Sjöström had made notably his own – going to church on Sunday morning; the interiors of the cottages and the images of meadow and stream have the calm beauty and authenticity we expect of him – but also of the superlative M–G–M art direction of the period. It is clear that it is not his *Scarlet Letter,* but that of Frances Marion, who did the adaptation, scenario and intertitles. For one thing, the protagonists simply do not have the complexity of those of his Swedish films, but Lillian Gish, as Hester, has a directness about her emotions, and an ability to project thought and feeling through the camera to the audience which is miraculous. It is not an easy role. The most interesting aspect of the affair is the conception of the child: the father is, after all, a priest – and she knew she could not marry him. All we are allowed to see is a discreet kiss, but Gish manages to suggest a decent woman so deeply in love that she gives way to one indiscretion.

Nathaniel Hawthorne's novel had been filmed before – there were two versions in 1917 – but by this time it had become a proscribed book; the Hays Office gave in to Miss Gish's pleas, partly because she was Miss Gish, and partly because she pointed out that it was a classic. She also initiated *The Wind,* a story by Dorothy Scarborough, and she says that Thalberg,

Miss Marion and Sjöström all shared her enthusiasm. She describes it thus: 'Its main character is a wind which constantly blows sand, indoors and out, and finally drives the heroine to madness. It is the story of a gently bred Southern girl who goes to Texas, marries a Texan, is violated by a man she met on the train, murders the man, and goes mad.' With that ending, everyone concerned 'thought it was the best film we had ever done.' But the company shelved it: 'Irving explained that eight of the largest exhibitors in the country had seen it and insisted on a change in the ending . . . The heart went out of all of us, but we did what they wanted. Marion told me that it was the last film to which she gave her heart as well as her head.' The ending is the least of the faults today – all of which have to do with the character of the vile seducer. At first the husband is one-dimensional, but Lars Hanson – so wild-eyed in *The Scarlet Letter* – is soon giving a performance to match the marvellous one by Miss Gish; we begin to feel an understanding between this couple after their disastrous beginning. Sjöström offers the set-pieces which were his speciality – the town dance, the cousin's dinner party – but also reaches his best

Lillian Gish and Lars Hanson in *The Wind* – with William Orlamond, right, glimpsed admiring Miss Gish, the mail-order bride. Sjöström directed, and Miss Gish herself said that she never worked with anyone she liked more – probably because they were very much at one in wanting honesty on the screen, that is, not only truth, but dimension and the wholeness of life.

The success of *Our Dancing Daughters* led to two sequels, of which the first, surprisingly, was Silent – since the most effective moment in the synchronised score and sound effects of *Daughters* was its one line of dialogue, a yelled invocation for Joan Crawford 'ti strut her stuff.' In *Our Modern Maidens* she (centre), Josephine Dunn (left) and Anita Page (right) are resting from the charleston and their manifold marital problems – which, as in the earlier film, are caused by their desire to have as wild a time as possible before the long married twilight.

level with the two most difficult scenes, the wedding night and the killing. This couple, on their wedding night, simply do not know how to react, and we are reminded of the relationship between Ingmar Ingmarsson and Brita. The film is the only one of Sjöström's surviving American work to stand with his native masterpieces, but, said Lewis Jacobs in 1939, his refusal to compromise and his 'propensity for psychology, realism and the rendering of the characters of people close to the soil' mitigated against either influence or popularity. And, he went on, quoting Robert Herring, that though Sjöström's films may not be true, pure cinema 'the cinema there in them is pure, and their own, which is why they breathe a nobility unlike any other films' nobility.' We may suppose that in this respect Sjöström found Miss Gish his ideal interpreter; and since she had taken over from himself as his problem-beset protagonist, we may further suppose that in this gifted woman he found an extension of himself. The film's complete failure

with the public resulted in her leaving M-G-M – and the virtual end of her screen career.

Miss Gish was an old-fashioned heroine; Norma Shearer (b. 1904), then married to Thalberg, was acceptable as both ginghamed heroines and silk-clad sophisticates. Her most notable Silent is probably **The Student Prince** (1927), for which Lubitsch went to M-G-M, nobly orchestrating: the romance between her, the tavern wench, and the prince; the massed choruses of the students, to be accompanied by the pit orchestra; and the scenes of palace protocol. And there was Joan Crawford (1906–77), M-G-M's answer to Clara Bow – after they had starred her as a flapper in **Our Dancing Daughters** (1928), directed by Harry Beaumont. Crawford was to prove remarkably consistent throughout her long career – for here she is already Misunderstood, all glitter and glamour on the surface, but suffering underneath. She is 'wild' or 'dangerous' Diana, and she can't even stop dancing the charleston as she pulls on her panties. The result, said a British trade paper, the *Kinematograph Weekly*, is 'entertainment of the smartly scandalous kind', though, it warned, 'sympathy is impossible for anyone, and the tone will always brand this type of film as a foreign one by its treatment; there is not a lady or a gentleman in the story as understood by British people' – which is doubtless why it was so popular, in Britain as well as the U.S. The freer morality of the young jazz set is both questioned and exploited, albeit always in euphemism: 'Before I met you – and knew what love means – things happened.' The speaker (Dorothy Sebastian) thereafter has a marriage whose happiness will be always clouded in doubt; the girl (Anita Page) who uses her virginity to win the man (John Mack Brown) is finally exposed and falls to a drunken death; and 'decent' Diana eventually triumphs. The plot, withal, is over-familiar, but Crawford's vivacity impresses: suffering, she looks fierce rather than noble, suggesting a better actress than she subsequently became.

Marion Davies (1897–1961) is a rather different case: virtually forgotten even before she quit films, she was remembered during later years, if at all, either as a joke or as the original of the mistress in *Citizen Kane* (q.v.) – a fact indeed which has restored her to fame. That film, and most comment on her relationship with William Randolph Hearst, the millionaire newspaper proprietor, is unsympathetic, but on his side at least this was a case of great devotion. She was merely acquiescent towards his belief that film stardom was the ultimate achievement, but he found an unexpected ally in Mayer. Although no newspaper even hinted at her position as Hearst's mistress – though it was a known fact in the industry – Mayer had noticed that her name appeared with monotonous regularity in each issue of Hearst's twenty-two newspapers, invariably accompanied by superlatives. Hearst was persuaded to move his Cosmopolitan Productions – then releasing through Paramount – to Culver City, to be financed by M-G-M, which would also pay Miss Davies the immense sum of $10,000 per week: in return for which the Hearst press was expected to pay similar

attention to other M-G-M players. To those *au fait* with the situation, regarding Davies as a joke played on a gullible public, Hearst offered fuel when he cast her in films like **Zander the Great** (1925), as a demure, ringleted orphan, if also a playful one. George Hill directed, with a number of Arizona locations, and the plot concerns a Mary Pickford type meeting a William S. Hart type. It is not, however, a scenario-writer's concoction, but a Broadway imitation of such, since it had seen service first in New York. The Hollywood-Broadway borrowings were not all one-way.

The Patsy (1928) had its source in a popular Broadway play of the period, and Davies is delightful in it – as she is in **Show People** (1928), though that is partly because her tendency to mug was in both cases checked by King Vidor. After his films with Gilbert, Vidor made *The Crowd* (q.v.), and perhaps it was because he wanted to make further 'uncommercial' subjects like that that he decided to put his then immense prestige at the service of Hearst, who had Mayer's ear. Certainly between these two comedies and another with Davies he did another risky subject, *Hallelujah!* (q.v.); and he showed no interest in comedy during his long Talkie career. *Happiness*, however, had indicated a flair for comic situations, and those in these two films were clearly promising before he set to

Donald Crisp in *The Viking* (1928), a box-office failure, despite
being one of the very few pictures of the time in Technicolor –
and the first in the 'improved' process. Technicolor, the supreme
colour system for at least two decades, from the inception of the
three-tone process in the early Thirties, was the only one
extensively used by Hollywood during the Silent period. It was
the invention of a former college professor, Herbert T. Kalmus
(1881–1963), who formed the Technicolor Company in 1912. In
1918, he produced his first film, a one-reeler, *The Gulf Between*,
to no great acclaim; in 1922 he tried again, with the full-length
The Toll of the Sea, a Chinese 'Madame Butterfly' with Anna
May Wong and Kenneth Harlan, which Metro distributed; the
following year deMille filmed the prologue to *The Ten
Commandments* in colour, and in 1924 there were two films with
Technicolor sequences, *The Uninvited Guest*, made by Metro-
Goldwyn, and Sam Goldwyn's *Cytherea*. That year, also,
Paramount made a feature completely in the process, *Wanderer of
the Wasteland*, with Billie Dove and Jack Holt; in 1925 that
company inserted Technicolor sequences into *The King on Main
Street* and *Stage Struck*, while Universal used it for part of *The
Phantom of the Opera* and M–G–M for sections of *Seven Chances,
The Big Parade* and *Ben-Hur*.

Douglas Fairbanks made the third wholly-Technicolor film,
The Black Pirate, but the system, despite the success of that film,
was still confined to a handful of single sequences and shorts –
for the simple reason that Technicolor reels tended to buckle
when projected. Kalmus had developed in 1919 a practicable
system, by which a beam-splitting device was fitted into the
camera, allowing two negatives to be made – which were then
printed on to positive film, coated with gelatin and cemented

together. An advance was made in 1928, whereby the dye
images were transferred from a matrix film, with a relief image,
to the final print. Joseph Schenck felt that Technicolor was
finally feasible for the industry and advised Kalmus that if the
latter would produce a feature M-G-M would undertake to
release it: in the event Thalberg liked the result so much that he
persuaded the company to buy it. It proved to be one of his few
poor commercial decisions, for the public decided that it was not
interested in Vikings – at least, not in this manifestation.

The subject had been sensibly chosen, for it disguised the
limitations of the Technicolor palette under the two-tone
system, being strong on the reds and browns of the Vikings'
costumes, and not too noticeably inaccurate on the hues of sea
and sky. The trouble is the story, concerning internecine strife
and a hellcat princess (Pauline Starke), and the direction, by Roy
William Neill, who quite rightly spent most of his subsequent
career making low-budget films.

Kalmus later blamed the film's failure on the public's
preference for Talkies, but it was first shown in November 1928,
before the rush began. Certainly its failure retarded the extensive
use of Technicolor, which except for Warners did not begin till a
year later when that company had a big success with *Gold Diggers
of Broadway*. Warners had entered into an agreement with
Technicolor, having decided that the company which had led the
way into Talkies should do the same with colour, and had earlier
released *On With the Show* – often cited, so complete was the
failure of *The Viking*, as the first Technicolor feature since
Fairbanks's film. All the same, industry acceptance remained
guarded, even after the first three-tone Technicolor feature,
Becky Sharp (q.v.) in 1935.

work – with what is equally clearly great affection. *The Patsy* is domestic comedy with Davies as a Cinderella pushed into the background by her mother (Marie Dressler) in favour of her prettier sister; in *Show People* she plays a Hollywood hopeful who forgets her dreams of drama when given a chance in slapstick – till signed by another studio, when she goes high hat and forgets the top banana (William Haines) who has given her her first chance. This is satire without cynicism, featuring a number of Hollywood personalities of the time, with a number of in-jokes, and in fact based loosely on the career of Gloria Swanson – whom Davies mimics at one point, as in the earlier film she had done devastating impersonations of Gish, Pola Negri and Mae Murray. At such times she justifies her stardom; but if in *Show People* she is warmly matched by Haines as the faithful swain, it must be said that *The Patsy* is taken by Dressler, vinegary as the ghastly snobbish mother.

The girl who became the greatest star of the era – and indeed of all eras – was not only acquired by chance, but they did not know what to do with her: Norma Shearer had turned down the role, and Greta Garbo was cast, since as she was both European and naturally girlish it was considered that she could encompass both aspects of the role, that of a peasant who becomes a famous diva. The film was **Ibañez's Torrent** (1926), the title indicating the studio's respect for the original writer. As it happened a novel by Ibañez was the source of Garbo's second American film, **The Temptress** (1926), which even more strongly indicates why he provided almost perfect silent-screen material, offering many intrigues that can be illustrated visually, so that audiences were completely involved by the time the explanations came in the intertitles. The first film, directed by Monta Bell, has a plot not unlike those of the Italian 'divismo' movies, its mid-way spectacle – a flood – merely one of those popular at the time; its significance is that it permits its sophisticated, scandalous heroine to become playful again – on being reunited with her childhood sweetheart (Ricardo Cortez) – and there was no doubt which aspect of Garbo M-G-M felt was most commercial. She was rushed into *The*

Temptress, with Mauritz Stiller directing, till replaced by Fred Niblo after a few days of shooting. It begins with a masked ball, two lovers in the garden, love – undying love – at first sight, and an idyll at dawn. The she (Garbo) is revealed as married, and he (Antonio Moreno) as an old friend of her husband: repulsion, and then expulsion, when she is further revealed, *à la* Theda Bara, as one who has ruined her husband and driven her host to suicide before his guests. Haughty still, she follows Moreno to South America to distract him from dam-building; two men die of love for her, his rival shoots her husband, and in a storm the dam collapses. He will rebuild: at the gala reopening she returns to claim him as he talks about the woman who inspired him. That, at least, was the American ending; for European audiences she walked the streets of Paris. It is curious now to reflect that M-G-M could only see Garbo as a scarlet woman. She was incredibly beautiful, which meant that she must break hearts; and it was a beauty both sensuous and angelic, hence enigmatic. She could be all things to all men. A limited acting range was at its best with anguish: hence, she must suffer.

During the period of her first contract – the customary seven years, with options in the studio's favour – she was to play virtually the same role, and her first fifteen minutes in **Flesh and the Devil** (1927) are almost a recapitulation of the opening of *The Temptress.* Clarence Brown directed, from a story by Sudermann, one of his tales of adulterous passion in provincial society, and the film is a splendid example of Hollywood apeing the German cinema to recreate Germany. Garbo plays Felicitas, who deceives her husband with a young officer (John Gilbert), eventually wrecking all around her when, married to yet another officer (Lars Hanson), she attempts to get him back. Growing as an actress, she plays the woman as completely self-absorbed except when in love – and the love scenes, with Garbo hungrily kissing Gilbert, were considered sensational at the time. That is why they became lovers again in *Love* (1927) directed by Edmund Goulding (1891–1959), which is 'Anna Karenina' modernised and reduced to 'Love Conquers All' – but on that level intelligently

If Garbo herself remains endlessly fascinating, so does the image that M-G-M created of her – usually making this slip of a girl into the most passionate of courtesans. RIGHT, she is adulterous with John Gilbert in *Love*, and, FAR RIGHT, unmarried for once, she still flouts society by running away with Nils Asther in *The Single Standard*, because she wants 'life to be honest – and exciting.' Audiences interpreted that, as they were meant to, as meaning that she wanted sexual freedom.

set up to satisfy audiences whose main object was to see Garbo loving Gilbert. As he, Vronsky, attempts to compromise her, her lack of anger suggests temptation; dancing together, their animation attracts attention. Her husband (Brandon Hurst) asks her to be mindful of her reputation, and as she looks at him she is comparing him unfavourably with Vronsky. The matching is inevitable with Gilbert's smouldering looks and flashing grins alternating: no member of the audience could blame her for preferring him. She refuses to see him till the races – and when he falls, she flails her arms in anguish, as if trying to swim to him through the crowds, or to duplicate his pain. It is at such highly-charged moments that Garbo's instinctive ability shines; throughout her performances

there are such gestures – which other actresses dared not attempt and no director taught her. Half the time she was using herself, using what she knew to be effective on the screen, 'inventing' herself; for the rest, her directors simply let the cameras catch the simplicity and spontaneity of her personality – that unforced and yet often huge response to any situation, frequently tactile. She needs less intertitles than any other Silent player. In this film, Vronsky does not tire of Anna, but she has resolved to leave him for the honour of the regiment. As he prepares to leave her, summoned by the Grand Duke, they are both emotional: 'Even death cannot part us,' he tells her, and her suicidal intention is startlingly clear. She can suggest fatalism better than any other tragedian. Their parting, as she wipes away

tears, is without intertitles – an exquisite, indescribably subtle piece of acting. All, perhaps, in vain: a tacked-on ending for the American version has Anna, a recent widow, discovering that her son's riding-master is none other than Count Vronsky.

The Divine Woman is among the missing films, which is sad, for it was the only time during the Silent period that she worked with an indisputably great director, Sjöström. The plot reads no better than that of **The Mysterious Lady** (1928), in which she is Tanya, a Russian spy, but this is directed by Niblo with not only fine regard for matters military but the language of the Silent screen. Indeed, the events do not seem too egregious after a superb opening in which she, encountered at the opera, invites into her apartment a young officer (Conrad Nagel): her magic never dims, but this is one of the sequences which allow it full rein, so overwhelming audiences that it follows them from the cinema. Since she was the screen's supreme exponent of eroticism, perhaps we should not complain that she did not take on the great parts, or the varied parts she asked in vain to play. What she does with these *soignée* but suffering *femme fatales* has to be experienced, since she gives mood, emotion and vitality where surely none existed in the script. Because of her **A Woman of Affairs** (1929), then considered unworthy, is an exceptional entertainment. The source was Michael Arlen's 'The Green Hat', as play and novel so notorious that M-G-M tried to conceal the fact; and the original cause of the heroine's shame – syphilis – has become embezzlement. The idea is attractive, concerning a woman who prefers dishonour to shaming her dead husband, and Garbo is moving. Looking correctly English county, in cardigans and tweeds, she had become not only intuitive but clever, as in the scene where she is reunited with her true love, Gilbert. Clarence Brown directed, and Sidney Franklin did an equally impeccable job on **Wild Orchids** (1929), one of the will-they, won't-they seduction stories of the time. Garbo, because she dominated her leading men, was seldom as girlish, partly due to the costumes designed for her on this occasion by Adrian, partly to the effective

performance of Lewis Stone as her elderly husband. Also, she does not react to the attentions of her would-be lover, a Javanese prince (Nils Asther), as the worldly woman of her other films, but what she does do with the flimsy sexual psychology makes it seem real and even startling.

The elderly 'protector' (or husband)– young aspirant formula was temporarily abandoned for **The Single Standard** (1929), though the title indicated that Garbo would, as usual, challenge the rules governing society. Like Norma Shearer in *A Free Soul* (q.v.) her idea of excitement is driving at 70 mph; other women cannot see what men find in her. This film, in its way, offers something more than her, and something more than a feeling for its time: there was a general mood of restlessness – Noël Coward wrote 'World Weary' in 1928 – and the film embellishes it. The lights of ships in the harbour, the sun-baked Southern shore; the urge to travel, to get away. Moments of tranquillity and moments of speed; the urge to escape. There is an urgency in this film consciously put there by the director, John S. Robertson, and by Josephine Lovett, who adapted the novel by Adela St John Rogers.

Long after other stars spoke, Garbo remained mute: M-G-M were afraid that Sound might destroy their most precious asset, as it had done other accented actresses. As late as November 1929 appeared her last Silent, **The Kiss** – in which she played a murderess and an adulteress. 'The kiss' was bestowed on her by an amorous schoolboy (Lew Ayres), and how could she, the Garbo, amused and flattered, refuse him so small a moment of happiness? Her husband, elderly once again, arrives suddenly, and in consequence she finds herself in court, defended by her lover (Conrad Nagel).

The director was Jacques Feyder, to whom she felt sympathetic because he was European, but she also liked Brown, and was to work with him again. Perhaps all of them helped her towards making these films seem more adult than they basically are, but it is also a matter of her vibrancy, grace and talent.

The end of the Silent film coincided with that of one of the major studios, First National, which had been founded in

1917 by a conglomerate of exhibitors in resistance to the policy of block-booking – objections to which were so widespread that there were no fewer than twenty-seven representatives of the circuits on its board. It was originally a distribution organisation, inviting independent producers to co-operate; Triangle was the first important company to join, and Paramount, alarmed at the growing strength of First National, began to buy its own theatres. First National countered by buying and running its own studios, but the real struggle was for the control of distribution, which could govern both production and exhibition – without the responsibility to either. Eventually most of the other production companies owned their own cinemas, and as the three branches of the industry aligned, block-booking was again forced on both the circuits and the few exhibitors who remained independent.

One of the purposes behind the formation of United Artists had been to control distribution – as it was for Ince and his Associated Producers, whose merger with First National brought to that company a store of talent, though significantly the general manager now appointed was Richard Rowland, who had had considerable experience of distribution. He had been one of the founders of Metro Pictures, and by claiming 'personally' to have produced *The Four Horsemen of the Apocalypse* was deemed able to run a studio; he was not however, able to hang on to much of the talent. Already, Chaplin and Pickford had passed through; a lesser coup was the acquisition of Charles Ray (1891–1943), defecting from Triangle, where he had established his perpetual role of country boy – the male equivalent of all the heroines in gingham. The most popular of his films was **The Old Swimmin' Hole** (1921), directed by Joseph de Grasse among sunny streams and meadows, and detailing the misadventures of Ray, the coquettish, beribboned Myrtle (Laura La Plante) and the pig-tailed girl (Marie Prevost) who worships him. The one flaw in its almost total charm is Ray, who acts delicately, but could not hide his years. Audiences soon tired of him; in 1922 he began to move from company to company, and in the Talkie era he worked

mainly as an extra.

One reason for his decline may be the comparisons made with other rustic heroes – like Lloyd Hughes, under contract to Ince and remaining with First National after Ince's death. He plays a Cajun in **Scars of Jealousy** (1923), one of the vastly complicated rural melodramas reinstituted after the success of *Way Down East*, and produced by Ince himself in an attempt to recover his fallen stock. Its director was Lambert Hillyer, who really fails to get much sense into it. Easily the best of such films is **Tol'able David** (1921) and the best of the barefoot boys was Richard Barthelmess (1895–1963), despite his 'city' face. He had left Griffith at the instigation of a businessman, Charles H. Duell, to form in partnership Inspiration Pictures, under the aegis of First National – and for their first film they were indeed inspired to choose Henry King (b. 1892), recently come to prominence after a decade as actor and director. Joseph Hergesheimer's then famous novel was a variation of David and Goliath, the 'Goliath' being the escaped convicts who have billeted themselves on David's sweetheart and her grandfather, family honour depends on young David, and one cares enormously what happens to him. Ernest Torrence is such a villain as to make Gustav von Seyffertitz seem like Prince Charming, bringing a look of congenital idiocy to a fearsome mug; and the film is a compendium of exquisitely-wrought moments, as when David's sweetheart pulls down her hat to hide her tears, or he surveys his home as conveyed in the intertitle, 'A wave of love swept over David – a love for everything and everybody that made his home.' King also directed Barthelmess in *Sonny* and *Fury*, both of comparable quality; and when Inspiration collapsed – due to Duell's chicanery – Barthelmess remained with First National, the company's leading male star for the rest of the decade.

Its chief lady star was Colleen Moore (b. 1900), at her worst and best respectively in **Irene** and **Ella Cinders**, both directed in 1926 by Alfred E. Green. The former had been the longest-running Broadway musical in 1919, and that, plus the seventeen road companies, could have been its only recommendation: without

Irene, with Colleen Moore and George K. Arthur. You might call Mr Arthur a prehistoric Franklin Pangborne, but Mr Pangborne was around at the time; you would certainly call Miss Moore a deft comedienne, but like all her breed she had an obligatory scene where she's left alone and whiles away the time by miming the sort of heroine she isn't, i.e. a vamp. At such times it is clear why audiences turned with relief to Garbo!

the music the story is thin, making us wonder today why audiences never tired of romances between rich boy and poor girl. Miss Moore's unstoppable cuteness mitigates against any enjoyment, but George K. Arthur is funny as a couturier, all bright eyes and quick movements – with a fashion-show in Technicolor. The star, however, gives a delicately-shaded performance in *Ella Cinders*, and Mr Hughes, flat-footed in *Irene*, is fine in the combination role of Buttons-godmother-Prince. Its motivation is not an invitation but a movie-talent contest, and Cinders ends not in a palace but on the spacious lawns of Hollywood – the appropriate end to a modern fairy-story: indeed, the film is deftly funny both about the small town thralldom to movies and movieland itself.

Playing himself in a guest role is Harry Langdon (1844–1944), First National's first clown. Vaudeville-trained, he made a number of shorts and one feature for Sennett, from whom he brought Harry Edwards and Frank Capra (q.v.). Edwards directed, and Capra helped to write, **Tramp, Tramp, Tramp** (1926), a quite funny film about a cross-country race. Capra had been appalled when he learnt that Sennett intended to make Langdon a star: 'Only God could help this creature'

he decided – and that became the basis for Langdon's screen character, whey-faced, titchy, gracefully birdlike, a child who hasn't discovered the rudiments of coping with the world; at one point he's discovered throwing rocks at a cyclone in an effort to persuade it to go away. He shows courage, rescuing the heroine from a wavering house, but not for him the flights of invention of Lloyd or Keaton. His best film is **The Strong Man** 1926). due less to him than to Capra's manipulation of the audience and his direction of an inventive screenplay by Arthur Ripley. Langdon is a Belgian ex-soldier looking for his pen-pal, Mary Brown. When in New York a thief, Broadway Lily (Gertrude Astor), drops some money into his pocket she has to take him to her apartment to retrieve it, and a succession of exceptionally detailed gags has him eventually fighting for his honour and she for the coat. He finally finds Mary, and we are not told whether he knows that she is blind – which leads to a shot of the blind leading the blind, when *he* falls over the stone in their path. By the time shooting started on **Long Pants** (1927), Capra loathed him, which is perhaps why he made him both a creature of lust and homicidal, which with his hopeless idiocy and no hint of character is an appalling combination. He is neither funny nor pathetic – and pathos was now what Langdon wanted to do. The acclaim for these three films convinced him that he was a genius, and he dispensed with Capra and Edwards on *Three's a Crowd* (1928) and the two that followed, after which First National annulled the contract. Hal Roach took him on for two-reelers, and he worked occasionally during the Talkie period.

First National's most famous film remains **The Lost World** (1925), directed by Harry O. Hoyt and the brainchild of Willis O'Brien, who had already featured models of prehistoric animals in a couple of movies. Unhappily these models are now derisory, as are most of the special effects – though the climax, a dinosaur at loose in London, has its moments; the situation would be reprised in *King Kong* (q.v.) on which O'Brien also worked. Wallace Beery is excellent as the Professor in what is not, withal, a typical First National product.

The company's pictures were stylish and well-crafted, but in general too slight to have great success. Typical are **Heart to Heart** (1928), directed by William Beaudine and ringing some pleasant changes in its theme of a princess (Mary Astor) in a small American town; and **Yellow Lily** (1928), a romance between a cold but lecherous archduke (Clive Brook) and the village doctor's noble sister (Billie Dove). The director was Alexander Korda, working from a story by Lajos Biro which would certainly have appealed to both Lubitsch and Von Stroheim, respectively the most successful and notorious of Hollywood's European directors – as Korda was surely aware. He had had one success with the company, **The Private Life of Helen of Troy** (1927), based on a novel of that title by John Erskine, and Robert Sherwood's play 'The Road to Rome' – though its real source is surely Offenbach's 'La Belle Hélène'; however, the treatment of ancient people in modern idiom needs spoken dialogue, and First National is not, in any case, as economic as other studios in its use of intertitles, which could be a reason its films found disfavour.

For eight years the other companies had nibbled away at its theatres; at its inception, Zukor had bought stock in the hope of killing it from within. In 1928, Warner Bros., riding high with Sound, negotiated a bank loan which enabled it to buy a controlling interest, and in 1929 the remaining circuit owner, Fox West Coast Theatres, sold Warners its own shares for $10 million. For ten years Warners produced pictures under the First National banner (literally: a flag was its logo) but they were Warner pictures in all but name.

Ironically, First National had released the first attempt at film production by the Warner Bros., *My Four Years in Germany* (1918), based on a bestseller by a former U.S. ambassador to the Kaiser. The Warners were the sons of an immigrant Polish-Jewish cobbler, and, starting with nickelodeons, were established with their film-exchanges before the battles with the Trust. The four brothers who entered the film business edged into distribution and then production, often writing and acting themselves. After the profitable *Four*

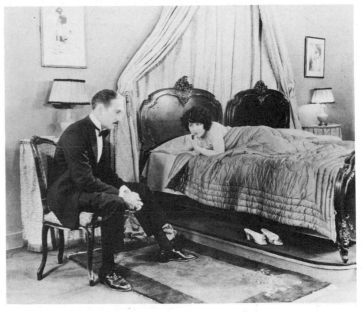

Years in Germany, they restricted themselves to serials till 1922, when they began to produce on a regular basis. Jack L. Warner (1892–1978) was in charge of the West Coast studio, and within two years he had been joined by the two men who would eventually be most responsible for that special quality of Warner Bros. movies, Hal B. Wallis (b. 1899), originally in the publicity department, and his predecessor as production chief, Darryl F. Zanuck (1902–79), a former salesman and writer who in 1924 was engaged to write the films of the studio's first star, a dog called Rin-Tin-Tin.

But if it was 'Rinty', as the dog was fondly called, which put Warners on the map, it was Ernst Lubitsch who first gave the company prestige, when it astutely offered him a contract after his experience with Mary Pickford; and since he·was far more famous than the Warners he was able to forgo the historical spectacles which had brought him U.S. renown, to return to the marital comedies he had so enjoyed making in Germany. He had not made a comedy since *Die Bergkatze*, and he had not then seen deMille's *Forbidden Fruit*, with a sequence he always claimed influential, in which a social climber hesitates as to which fork to pick up: his own refined visual skill is apparent in the opening sequence of **The Marriage**

Adolphe Menjou and Marie Prevost as husband and wife in Lubitsch's first American success, *The Marriage Circle* – at least, the critics liked it, and though the public stayed away that didn't prevent it from being much imitated – by Lubitsch himself, among others.

Circle (1924), when Adolphe Menjou finds his sock-drawer empty but his wife's stocking-drawer full. Clearly this is a Lubitsch summary of a marriage, its source a play remembered from his Berlin days.

The film's reception caused other studios to pour forth imitations, and Lubitsch imitated himself: **Three Women** (1924); *Kiss Me Again* (1925), now lost; **Lady Windermere's Fan** (1925); and **So This is Paris?** (1926). They are much of a muchness, whether set in Paris, Vienna, London or New York; they reflect the interplay between the sophisticates of the *beau monde* (Menjou, Irene Rich, Pauline Frederick, Monte Blue, Florence Vidor, Lew Cody) and the more playful younger generation (Marie Prevost, Mae McAvoy), all of them both mendacious and flirtatious – and if any of them had told the truth at the beginning, there would have been no plot. The scenarios were usually based on well-known European plays, and most of them are the work, partly or wholly, of Hans Kräly, Lubitsch's old collaborator. In the Talkie era, Ernest Vajda and Samson Raphaelson would replace him, but by that time he had helped formulate the famous 'touch'. Here is another example: the night one lover defects, Catherine the Great is consoled by another, and as was customary, he is promoted; later he has a chance to plead for the other man's life, 'Spare this boy! Thanks to him' – cut to Catherine anticipating the next words – 'I became a general'; and as that was not what she expected to hear, she signs the warrant. The sexual innuendo is what Lubitsch used so brilliantly in his Talkies, but which is largely absent in his Silents – and indeed this instance is not from his Catherine film at Paramount but *The Eagle* (q.v.), which Kräly wrote for United Artists. In fact, the American Silent comedies of Lubitsch lack the sparkle of both the earlier and later ones. The critics raved, the public was indifferent, and both reactions stemmed from the source material: the critics were favourably disposed towards the sort of respectable risqué plays which Lubitsch used, and the public disliked lengthy explanatory intertitles and talking heads. The visual points in *Lady Windermere's Fan*

have mainly to do with society's curiosity about Mrs Erlynne; Lubitsch wisely eschews the epigrams in the intertitles for a light, bantering tone; but he still has to tell a rather soppy story of a mother's sacrifice. In *Three Women* he tantalises us by omitting the intertitles in what is clearly an important conversation: but he still has a lot of plot – as much as deMille in his similar comedies of a few years earlier.

A European director who fared less well in Hollywood is Benjamin Christensen, brought over on the strength of *Häxan*, when the mood was for the weird and Lon Chaney was beginning to hold sway. After three films in that vein for M-G-M, none very successful, he turned up at Warners-First National for one last one before returning to Denmark, **Seven Footprints to Satan** (1929), a banal creepy-house tale which runs out of steam after the tenth or so trick. However, Michael Curtiz (1888–1962) remained to become Warners' most prolific director during their great period. Hungarian-born, he had been a colleague of Korda's at Sascha-Film in Vienna, making his name with two ancient-and-modern tales after the manner of Korda's *Samson und Delilah* – *Sodom und Gomorrha* and *Die Slavenkönigin*. Warners brought him to the States for another, though he directed several other films for them before it was ready – **Noah's Ark** (1929), from a story by Zanuck; either inspiration or money ran out, since it ends abruptly with the information that both ancient and modern goodies lived happily ever after. The modern part is set during the War, and concerns an Austrian dancer (Dolores Costello), a Russian agent who wants to rape her, and two American youths who befriend her; and if nothing much happens in the other part, the relevant disaster is eminently watchable – and a tribute to the co-operation of the Los Angeles water-board. Miss Costello is also in peril in **Old San Francisco** (1928), as a senorita fancied by a Barbary Coast boss (Warner Oland) who has betrayed his Chinese blood by affecting Christianity. Alan Crosland directed this anthology of San Francisco mythology, including its Spanish past and the earthquake, whose first tremors are felt just as things are blackest for hero and heroine. It had a synchronised score and sound effects – and, indeed, *Noah's Ark* was also available in a part-Talkie version: for during this period Warners had completely changed the dimension of film.

On the subject of spectacle, deMille was by now the acknowledged suzerain, and in **King of Kings** (1927) he gave the dying Pathé a last whopping success – and, indeed, it was still touring the church-hall circuit till comparatively recently. It was then important enough to open in London at the Royal Opera House and for *The Times* to give it a leader, but the mooted 'controversy' was mainly in the minds of the publicists. The religious advisers to deMille were on one occasion closeted with some new footage from the Holy Land (not that any is discernible in the film) when the actor playing Christ, H. B. Warner, was found *in flagrante delicto* with a young lady whose object was blackmail. This episode, though hushed-up, seems to me symptomatic of the whole hypocritical enterprise: 'This is the story of Jesus of Nazareth' says an introduction, whisking us to a Roman banquet modelled on one of the more worldly paintings of Alma-Tadema. Mary of Magdala, as she is called here, has become the mistress of Judas Iscariot, who has become ambitious – joining Jesus because he thought he would be king 'and reward him with money and high office'. Thus the most enigmatic figure in history has become just another Hollywood villain, but what astonishes is that, with its phoney provenance for quotations, the film should have received the endorsement of the clergy.

Its success justified deMille's departure from Paramount, after complaining of front office interference. From Ince's widow he bought the Producers Distributing Company, which amalgamated with Pathé in an attempt to keep both afloat; as the Sound revolution rocked the industry, and Pathé was absorbed in turn, he accepted an offer (q.v.) from M-G-M – but found that he disliked Mayer even more than Zukor, and returned to Paramount with a guarantee of autonomy. However, at P.D.C. and Pathé he did sponsor a number of other directors, including Donald Crisp,

Paul Sloane and William K. Howard. Crisp's **Dress Parade** (1927) is a genial comedy about the cocky newcomer (William Boyd) who learns to love West Point traditions; and Sloane's **The Blue Danube** (1928) is a Von Stroheim-like tale, with some sharp touches, about a baron (Nils Asther) whose passion for an innkeeper's daughter (Leatrice Joy) does not run smoothly. Howard's **White Gold** (1927) – the title refers to sheep – was another familiar story, about the woman (Jetta Goudal) marooned in a man's world: threatened with the inevitable seduction or rape, the extent of her complicity is withheld by the intertitles – which caused the piece to be critically acclaimed, though it flopped so badly that for years no print was thought to survive. The one that did proves it lacking the intensity of the Soviet *By the Law* and the honesty of the even more similar *City Girl* (q.v.). Pathé at this time gave refuge to another Paramount alumnus, James Cruze, whose **On to Reno** (1928) is an engaging marital farce with Marie Prevost and Cullen Landis as young marrieds whose hopes for a reunion are more cheerful than those of an older couple, Ned Sparkes and Ethel Wales.

Under Joseph Schenck, United Artists also provided a haven for other players anxious, like its founders, to escape the tyrannies of the big studio moguls. In 1925 he was joined by Sam Goldwyn, who had been releasing through First National since his break with the Goldwyn Co., and the three to four annual Goldwyn productions were to be extremely important to the distribution arm. Both Schenck and Goldwyn were ardent believers in stars, though the stars under contract to them did not have the freedom of Pickford and Fairbanks. Films were made committee-style, so although **Stella Dallas** (1925), directed by Henry King for Goldwyn, displays the director's usual sympathy and lucidity, its dual purpose was to exploit the personality of its star, Belle Bennett, and the narrative qualities of Olive Higgins Prouty's original bestselling story. As such, it was marvellously successful: advertised as 'The Greatest Mother-Love Picture Ever Made' it was indeed loved more than other mother-love movies, as Miss

Marceline Day and John Barrymore in *The Beloved Rogue* – who was François Villon. Of all the screen Villons, there was not one less attractive: forty–four at the time, equipped with ill–fitting wig and two whiffs of up–pointed moustache, Barrymore really appals, but atones somewhat with his agility, especially in a Rumpelstiltskin-like dance.

Bennett, acting superbly, snaps up a man (Ronald Colman) from a higher social sphere and is too foolish to change – slatternly at home, over-dressed in public but always good-hearted. **The Winning of Barbara Worth** (1926) bases its appeal on Goldwyn's 'love team', Colman and Vilma Banky, and Harold Bell Wright's 'famous' novel – according to the credits – for which Goldwyn paid the record sum of $123,000. It was also Goldwyn's bid in *The Covered Wagon* stakes, beginning with a desert sandstorm and concluding with a flood; but King's direction cannot disguise the clumsiness of the screenplay by Frances Marion, who, nevertheless, was on the way to becoming the industry's highest-paid scenario writer. In the original novel the lady of the title, played by Miss Banky in the film, does not appear till the end: here she is sought throughout by Colman, as an engineer out West, and Gary Cooper, the local man – till the latter is summarily dropped. Ronald Colman (1891–1958), English-born, and Cooper (1901–61), of English parentage, became two of the most enduring of stars.

If the appeal of both remains strong, that of Valentino again proves elusive in the two films he made for Schenck before his sudden death. However, **The Eagle** (1925) is probably his best film, as directed by Clarence Brown, taking his tone from Kräly's buoyant scenario, based on a story by Pushkin, about a Queen's guardsman who is loved by her (Louise Dresser) but prefers to help his beloved (Vilma Banky) by adopting a Zorro-like existence. **Son of the Sheik** (1926), directed by George Fitzmaurice, is as much like its predecessor as to be indecent, reminding us that nothing emphasises the gulf in taste between then and now than Valentino's two sheik films.

The constant reiteration of themes, scenes and situations is apparent in the three films John Barrymore made for Schenck. He played François Villon in **The Beloved Rogue** (1927), already filmed in this romanticised fashion in 1920 as *If I Were King,* with the addition now of the 'Court of Miracles' sequences as copied from *The Hunchback of Notre Dame.* Alan Crosland directed, and Conrad Veidt's gleeful, satanic Louis XI outclasses Barrymore's athletic hero. In view of the latter's reputation, it is perhaps a pity that he only once played a weighty role in films before drink impaired his capabilities: that was Captain Ahab, but of the rakes and roués whom he did play, his Beau Brummel, also for Warners, is splendid in his moments of pride. He is certainly well cast in **The Tempest** (1928), as a peasant-born dragoon who rises from the ranks, responds to the princess's whipping with a kiss, and goes to sleep drunk on her bed. One of his colleagues likes to stub out cigarettes on the necks of rankers, and another likes girlie magazines – in which touches we note the hand of Von Stroheim, who wrote it, but was contractually prevented from playing the lead and directing. The film is credited to Sam Taylor who, working again with photographer Charles Rosher, has made a film as technically good as *My Best Girl,* with superb art direction by William Cameron Menzies. If Schenck vacillated over the leading lady before settling on his own close friend, newly arrived from Germany, Camilla Horn, so he did on the director, and several eminent names are reputed to have worked on it. Lubitsch had been approached, and he did direct Barrymore and Miss Horn in another portrait of old Europe, **Eternal Love** (1929), in which they are Swiss patriots and lovers during the Napoleonic Wars. Kräly wrote it, his last film for Lubitsch, and there are echoes of their two Bavarian comedies; but in returning to a serious subject Lubitsch has emulated Sjöström. He uses snow as Sjöström used sand in *The Wind*; the affectionate interiors recall the latter's Swedish work, and the portrait of the prejudiced community is similar to that of *The Scarlet Letter*. Its climax apart, it is to be regretted that it got 'lost' in the rush to Talkies.

Gloria Swanson's most successful film with United Artists was **Sadie Thompson** (1928), based on Somerset Maugham's short story, 'Rain'. Although a dramatised version had been a wild success the world over, the Hays Office refused to sanction a movie till confronted with the determination of Swanson, and probably also that of her backer and lover, Joseph P. Kennedy. Sadie, the whore, still seduces the preacher, but so much else has been bowdlerised as to make it a distinctly foolish piece of fiction. Attention has shifted from the preacher, less hypocritical than smug, to Sadie, and though she has become a cipher, Swanson inevitably attempts to fill in the gaps – laughing with the marines, listening eagerly to the phonograph, or cheeking the preacher and his prim wife. She is immeasurably aided by Raoul Walsh's fluid direction, and William Cameron Menzies' art direction is again one of his best, a dark and storm-swept Pago Pago. The film is one more witness to the accomplishment of the American Silent screen as it was about to die.

Though critics lamented, audiences couldn't have cared less about its death. *Eternal Love* was not the only film lost in the crush, and there were others – among which were some which might have changed the course of American movie entertainment. The moguls demanded exoticism and melodrama, but Frank Borzage was one director esteemed enough to withstand demands, and his preference for dramas of plain people led eventually to **Seventh Heaven** (1927), and a follow-up also with Janet Gaynor

and Charles Farrell, **Street Angel** (1928). The first film is part *Broken Blossoms,* part *The Big Parade,* with a chunk of 'La Bohème' and the ending of 'Jane Eyre'. As usual, the girl is a *poule* – if only by wicked chance – and the boy a sewer-rat who leads her to true love, which means grinding his coffee or snuggling under the quilt: what *Picturegoer* called 'their unspoken need for each other and their unquenchable spirit' was something that appealed mightily to cinemagoers, as well as to the industry's Academy, which voted Oscars to Gaynor, Borzage and Benjamin Glazer for his scenario, based on a play by Ernest G. Palmer. *Street Angel* is based on a play by Monckton Hoffe, and though its borrowings are less eclectic, its subject is that old favourite, the Price Paid for a Moment of Sin. Equally sentimental, there is a new element to the Great Love – sexual obsession, and its presence is as traceable to German influences as are the settings. Equally stylised in both films, the Paris of *Seventh Heaven* is merely cardboard,

Gloria Swanson and Raoul Walsh, who also directed, in a version of Maugham's short story, 'Rain', rechristened *Sadie Thompson*, since the Hays Office refused to sanction the original title – which didn't matter, since everyone knew who Sadie was. The Rev. Davidson was no longer allowed to be a man of the cloth, and in all printed sources has been renamed Oliver Miller (but in the only extant copy – at Eastman House, with the last reel missing – he is Davidson in the intertitles, suggesting that it was never publicly screened).

while the Naples of *Street Angel* is the city of any of the German *street* films.

Both are far from realism, but that *Street Angel* is a mite rawer and tougher is due to Murnau's **Sunrise**, made at the same studio in the interim. Murnau had arrived in the U.S. with a copy of *Der Letzte Mann*, but the Hollywood companies had ignored him till that and then *Tartüff* were praised by reviewers; Fox then wanted him so badly that it accepted both the scenario – by Carl Mayer, from a story by Sudermann – and the set designs for a film he was about to start shooting. Consequently *Sunrise* was Germanic, causing Fox to add a foreword to the effect that the tale could take place anywhere and *The New York Times* to observe that Murnau could 'do just as fine work in Hollywood as he ever did in Germany.' Murnau's ability with narrative in images was at a new height, if marred by artiness – just as the tale becomes too melodramatic when 'The Man' (George O'Brien) becomes so sexually enslaved on a trip to the big city that he attempts to murder his wife (Janet Gaynor).

That city adventure brought a new vitality to American cinema, and the film's success encouraged two other studios to sanction tales of ordinary folks without star names. At Universal Paul Fejos directed **Lonesome** (1928) and at M-G-M King Vidor **The Crowd** (1928), both showing the German influence in such matters as montage and mobility of camera; both are about New Yorkers and include long Coney Island sequences. *Lonesome* is simplicity itself: a lonely factory-worker (Glenn Tryon) meets a telephone operator (Barbara Kent), loses her and meets her again. Vidor's film is more ambitious, taking its hero (James Murray) from birth onwards, his life is motivated by a conversation on the Staten Island Ferry, 'You gotta beat that crowd,' to which he replies, 'Maybe. All I want is the opportunity.' He loses a job, a child, and suffers a deteriorating marriage – matters not to be seen again in American movies till 1939 in *Made for Each Other* (q.v.) and then in 1952 in *The Marrying Kind* (q.v.), both influenced by Vidor's film. Audiences for it were enthusiastic, and its above-average cost, $551,000, made a small profit, but neither Vidor nor

Fejos was on principle encouraged to undertake another immediate 'personal' film.

At Fox, however, both Borzage and Murnau were allowed to try again; unlike Fejos and Vidor, but like Sjöström and von Sternberg at this time, they were after an amalgam of reality and romance, of the everyday and the erotic, but once again the people are supposed to be us – the audience. Borzage's **The River** (1928) and Murnau's **City Girl** have pulsing, realistic accounts of the daily grind, and work and sex go hand in hand, man's prime motivations. All other national cinemas followed this rule, even the British and the unknown Japanese: it was only in Hollywood that pretty little stories existed in a vacuum. In this group of films there are degrees of frustration and deprivation, and in these particular two the frustration is partly sexual. The girl in both is the strong-willed Mary Duncan, and the boy Charles Farrell; in *The River* she is a flirt, possibly a whore, who fritters away her time with a besotted country boy while her man is away for the winter; in *City Girl*, he brings home a Chicago waitress, to face the hostility of his family. From the fragments of *The River* that remain (almost an hour), Borzage clearly intended a documentary account of dam-labourers, and Murnau as surely intended something similar in his account of the lonely farm in the wheatfields. With one reel dubbed with Sound, *City Girl* was belatedly released, in 1931, to perish instantly in the All-Talking world. *The River* simply disappeared, though its banning by several states may be one reason why there is also virtually no written record of it. Borzage was permitted by Fox to do another realistic drama in the Sound period, *Bad Girl* (q.v.), since he still trailed the glory from *Seventh Heaven*; but Murnau quarrelled with Fox before *City Girl* was finished and departed with Robert Flaherty for the South Seas.

Flaherty's own quest for realism belonged to the same side of the coin. Since *Nanook* the studios had courted him, and Jesse Lasky told him that he would back him to the hilt if he could make another film equally interesting. Flaherty chose to go to Polynesia, as a nice place to take his family, and he spent three years

Scenes of Daily Life: Barbara Kent, looking at the camera, in *Lonesome*, ABOVE, and Mary Duncan and Charles Farrell on their way from Chicago to country in *City Girl*. Both these films were part of a movement away from nightclubs, newspaper offices and marble halls towards the actual environment of the ordinary joes in the audience. It was a feeling shared by directors in other countries around this time, but even when tarted up with a little sex the films found audiences sparse.

making **Moana** (1926). Since the Samoan people were contented with Western ways, and were ruled over by a New Zealand-appointed German governor, Flaherty had to recreate the idyllic past, though the film is supposedly set in the present. The subject is the coming of age of Moana, played by Ta'avale, who required a huge sum to submit to the tattooing of the initiation ceremony – a practice long obsolete on the island. It is ironic therefore that the word 'documentary' (from the French *documentaire*) was coined by John Grierson (q.v.) to describe this film, which is otherwise only important because Flaherty used Kodak's new panchromatic stock, resulting in glowing blacks and whites.

Despite a publicity campaign directed at the most prominent citizens of each town where the film was booked, it flopped, unhelped clearly by the naked breasts on view. Nevertheless Thalberg decided that M-G-M could market a similar film, though he insisted on Flaherty accepting W. S. Van Dyke (1889–1943) as co-director, to prevent the squandering of time and money, and to ensure a more commercial product; in 1931 Murnau interested Flaherty in an independent production to be made in the South Pacific, to be released by Paramount. Flaherty quarrelled with both Van Dyke and Murnau, and departed, thus receiving no credit on Van Dyke's **White Shadows of the South Seas**, and only a writing credit on Murnau's **Tabu** – which does not make either, as has been suggested, inferior to *Moana*. *White Shadows* has white traders, and an unconvincing story; and Murnau's native lovers are much to be preferred. The three films remain very beautiful and their approach is more paternal than patronising, but though one cannot doubt the sincerity of purpose, there is something

anomalous about high-priced talents making films about the 'simple' life; at all events none of the three is very riveting. *White Shadows* in particular was successful enough to cause M-G-M to send Van Dyke to Africa for the fictional *Trader Horn* (q.v.), and then to North Alaska for **Eskimo** (1933), a considerable film in its own right and a huge advance on *Nanook*. John Lee Mahin wrote this tale of a huntsman and the wife who is raped by a drunken white crew, and the Eskimo's dialogue has been turned into intertitles, but since the language has no first or third personal pronouns these become 'One' – and 'One leaves his wives in the same kramit' must be the most obscure intertitle in film history. There are difficulties with ethnological films, not the least of which is doubt of audience response – which in this case was minimal, thus causing Hollywood to turn to the things it better understood.

Murnau died in a car crash before they premier of *Tabu*, which had only a music-track and therefore went as unnoticed by mass audiences as *City Girl*. The public, after all, wanted excitement, and except for a coterie their needs were backed not only by the moguls but most journalists of the period, claiming that people did not go to the cinema to see themselves or their neighbours and workmates. This brief flirtation with realism does leave a partial record of the life of the average American in pre-Depression days, but it is otherwise a footnote to the era of wonderful nonsense. To an extent both realism and the ethnological films continued the cinema's experimentation – both as to what the medium could do, and what the public would pay to see. By the time the furore of Talkies was over the studio factories were confident of the answers, and for the next thirty years provided only entertainment.

8

The Twenties:
Britain and France

IT WAS AMERICAN films that cinemagoers preferred the world over. Neither the British nor the French industries recovered from the War, losing the dominant positions they had held in the world market. In Britain the influx of American films was strengthened from an odd source, the antagonism of the wartime government and the military authorities towards the home industry, which curtailed production and resulted in a placatory spate of patriotic dramas – with titles like *Boys of the Bulldog Breed, Boy Scouts be Prepared* and *A Munition Girl's Romance*. The films that were made had difficulty getting shown, for the American companies, now opening distribution offices in London, had foisted the system of block-booking on British cinemas, many of which booked product for a year ahead. In 1921 the industry called a meeting to decide whether to abandon production – during which William Friese-Greene, the pioneer, was found to have died, some minutes after making a plea for its continuance. In the same year the British National Film League was formed, campaigning ineffectually till 1927, when the Cinematograph Act – usually known as the Quota Act – was passed, decreeing that cinemas must show 5% of local product, rising to 20% ten years later. The effect on production was immediate.

Under the prevailing conditions, most of the films, not surprisingly, were of poor quality – since the entrepreneurs were not in cut-throat competition as were their American counterparts. They were mainly dilettantes and theatre showmen, including both managers and actors, though there were sound businessmen behind the most successful companies, which were Stoll, Ideal, G. B. Samuelson, Gaumont, the team of Thomas Welsh and George Pearson – the latter an alumnus of both Samuelson and Gaumont – and Hepworth, the sole pioneer to be still a force in the industry.

Hepworth, however, was forced out of business as he prepared to meet American competition, his last film ironically a remake of his greatest success, **Comin' Thro' the Rye** (1923), a Victorian tale of the sort popular in the lending-libraries – with a tomboyish heroine (Alma Taylor, the only one of the Hepworth stock company to play the same role in both versions), a handsome wealthy hero (Shayle Gardner), and the scheming rival who wants to take one from the other. The plot depends on the convention that a woman once kissed can only appeal to what the intertitles call man's 'worst part'– which becomes so enflamed after a glass of wine and the sight of some lovers embracing that its owner goes a-ravishing. This combination of tears and lust is no more retarded than in other films of the time; Hepworth's decision to remake it was prompted by a forthcoming film festival, but illness delayed production and by the time it was completed he had been declared bankrupt, as a result of trying to enlarge his Walton-on-Thames studio. He directed one more film, as an employee of Arnold Nettlefold, and spent the rest of his life making trailers, i.e. previews of coming attractions. As his stock of films was melted down for chemicals at the time of his bankruptcy, too few survive to make any assessment of his contribution to the medium, but this particular one is technically as good as any of the era. The single most important development in films at this point was the progress from illustrating a dramatic situation to the telling of it in images: few in Britain were aware of this, but Hepworth is one who was.

We may not say the same of the also-prolific Adrian Brunel – to judge from **The Man Without Desire** (1923), considered, he says in his memoir, a masterpiece by the critics – though he himself didn't agree. A dopey piece about a lover (Ivor Novello) who wakes after two hundred years to face the sexual predicament of the title, it was admired because some of it was shot in Venice (unimaginatively) and authentic costumes were borrowed from private collections, which would explain why costumes in British historical films seemed to be falling apart with age. Although there were contemporary subjects, usually concerned with love or crime, the preponderance of costume romances indicates a dependence on novels and the West End stage rather than an attempt to emulate the German spectacles. In 1923 alone, the studios offered Novello as Bonnie Prince Charlie, Fay Compton as Mary Stuart, Lady Diana Manners as Elizabeth I, Henry Ainley as Oliver Cromwell and Sir Frank Benson as Becket.

Such subjects were thought more exportable than local comedies of manners, and among their most enthusiastic promoters was Herbert Wilcox (1892–1977), a former film-renter whose ruthlessness and drive would not have disgraced an American producer. Turning director, he began a long career, and also like deMille, his early films are by far his best. He was innovative for he thought in international terms, as a producer bringing from Hollywood Mae Marsh, even if her popularity was fading; as a director he went to Berlin, co-producing *Decameron Nights* (1924) with Erich Pommer. The stars were Werner Krauss and Lionel Barrymore, though the latter's box-office appeal was insufficient to attract an American distributor – Ufa handled the film in the U.S. four years later, when for a brief period it had its own American company. Undeterred, Wilcox negotiated with First National's London office to handle *The Only Way* (1925), a version of the celebrated stage adaptation of 'A Tale of Two Cities' with its original exponent, Sir John Martin-Harvey. The American distributing companies in Britain were not otherwise involved in production, but First National's local success with this caused United Artists to pick up the American rights. Emboldened by this, Wilcox engaged another American star, Dorothy Gish, to appear in *Nell Gwynne* (1926), again made in conjunction with First National; but when money ran out, an American producer, J. D. Williams, helped to complete it. Adolph Zukor was so impressed that he offered one million dollars for three more films with Miss Gish – *London, Tiptoes,* which co-starred Will Rogers, and **Madame Pompadour** (1927), the first film to be made at Elstree Studios, built with optimism and Paramount money by Williams and Wilcox for their company, British National. It was also the last under this regime, since Williams' ways with money were chaotic, and Wilcox left to set up his own British & Dominions company.

He had engaged eminent foreign help on *Pompadour*: Frances Marion was the scenarist, E. A. Dupont, at a fee of £1,000 a week, was the 'Supervising Director', and Antonio Moreno crossed the Atlantic to co-star. Since popular tradition has made of royal mistresses – except Mistress Gwynn – painted harpies, dramatised editions have to reconcile that view with a sympathetic heroine; a formula had been found to satisfy audience expectations, whereby the lady is haughty at court, but simple-hearted and generous when her fancy is caught by a handsome peasant or guardsman. This screenplay does manage to surprise, but it is aided by Miss Gish's vivacious performance; and there is a good villain by Gibb McLaughlin, in the Restoration tradition of effeminate lechers.

With such exceptions, British films were not of the standard required by American audiences – or, indeed, those at home. American domination, financial crises, poor quality – these were the bugbears of the British industry, as they have been ever since. Another producer who survived them over the years was Michael Balcon (1896–1977), who also fought back by raising quality and looking realistically to the American market. Undeterred by the current industry crisis, he moved from making advertising films into production, with two partners, one of them Victor Saville (who later became a director). They hired space – alongside Wilcox – in Islington Studios, just vacated by Paramount after a short-lived attempt at local production (the films proved unsaleable in the U.S.); and they engaged as director Graham Cutts, formerly with Wilcox, and widely believed to share with him something of the American know-how. Emulating Wilcox, they brought over a popular American star, Betty Compson, at £1,000 a week, and gambling further they purchased a popular play, *Woman to Woman* (1923), the film of which got the new company off to a flying start. But when a second film with Miss Compson failed, their distributor refused an advance, and Balcon founded a new company, Gainsborough Pictures, whose product would be released by Gaumont-British. The first venture starred another American, Alice Joyce, and for the second, *The Blackguard,* Balcon obtained a co-production agreement with Ufa. Otherwise, he proceeded slowly and cautiously until **The Rat** (1925) provided the company with its first huge success. The star was Ivor Novello (1893–1951), whose signing was a coup for Balcon, since Novello had hitherto been his own producer, and was known in the U.S. by virtue of a starring role in Griffith's *The White Rose*; renowned also as composer, playwright and matinee idol, this was probably his finest hour, as the only British film star of international fame. This particular film was based on a play written by himself and Constance Collier, under a pseudonym, and he has the title-role, an apache king of ravenous sexual appetite – except for the girl he truly loves (Mae Marsh), queen among waifs. Comes slumming a rich man's mistress (Isabel Jeans): 'I gave in because you are nevertheless a child and irresponsible', to which his response is 'You smell nice.' 'I am bothering to talk to you,' she says, 'because you are my sort . . . In your world you rule. In my world I rule,' but when they quarrel the intertitles become disappointingly prosaic, 'I wish I'd thrown your rotten note out of the window.' Her lover, impatient, selects a new mistress, the waif, and when she refuses his advances he decides upon rape . . . The film's popularity was such that there were two sequels, *The Triumph of the Rat* and *The Return of the Rat,* and I count myself fortunate in not having seen them.

Balcon's chief screenwriter, sharing his predilection for contemporary subjects, was Alfred Hitchcock (1899–1980), who had entered films writing intertitles. From *Woman to Woman* onwards, he was one of Cutts's small unit, sometimes doubling as art-director; but as Cutts's professional jealousy increased, Balcon determined to promote Hitchcock to director. In so doing, he found someone not only able to enhance the value of his stars, but capable of drawing attention to himself as director – by virtue of an exceptionally flashy technique, and a number of other devices, all borrowed from Germany; fortunately Hitchcock's studies had also taught him how to make the narrative move compulsively forward. He had watched Murnau on an adjoining set while working with Ufa, and he returned to Germany for another co-production, **The Pleasure Garden** (1925), with the obligatory American star, Virginia Valli. She plays a chorus girl who marries a Britisher (Miles Mander) from the East; joining him there, she finds him with an under-age mistress and a bad case of D.T.s The husband's true character is withheld for a while, and the theatre scenes are lively, but Hitchcock did not find his way – there was an intervening film, now lost – till **The Lodger** (1926). Rushing from image to image, largely eschewing intertitles, he creates a portrait of London racked by a series of murders. 'A Story of the London Fog' is the film's subtitle, and as the lights of the Embankment fade, a girl is murdered: there is a montage of headlines and shocked people listening at their crystal-sets, while all the time a sign flashes, 'Tonight – Golden Curls'. The rest, however, is trite and unconvincing, neither faithful to Mrs Belloc-Lowndes's novel about a middle-class, middle-aged couple who come to suspect that their lodger is Jack the Ripper, nor to the facts of the case. In the title-role Novello acts suspiciously, beyond the call of reason, though always making sure that he is

Alfred Hitchcock came into prominence directing star vehicles for such popular British figures as Isabel Jeans, Betty Balfour and Ivor Novello. In *Downhill*, as the sweetshop cutie (Annette Benson) accuses Novello, right, of being the father of her child, the true culprit (Robin Irvine) stays mute. Novello stands by the schoolboys' code – though at thirty–four much too old for the role – and stays silent. After that, he goes from chorus boy to gigolo to unnamed degradation in Marseilles, and Hitchcock couldn't resist a symbolic 'downhill' to start it all off, as Novello goes down an Underground escalator.

photographed well; June, the heroine, is far less pretty than he, an early instance of dreadful leading ladies. However, it is presumably not his fault that at the last minute his mysterious behaviour is explained while the real murderer is arrested off-screen. Hitchcock, who did the adaptation with his then regular collaborator, Eliot Stannard, himself explained later that it was impossible at that time to cast a star as a killer; and the distributor had apparently demanded revisions.

The film's reception established Hitchcock, encouraging him to more batteries of arty shots in **Downhill** (1927) and **Easy Virtue** (1927) – though neither is remotely static, like most British film versions of plays. *Downhill* was another from the pens of Collier and Novello, and its U.S. release title, *When Boys Leave Home*, gives an idea of the plot, which is heavily misogynist. Its best sequence finds Novello as a miserable dance-partner in Paris, gradually aware that the motherly lady talking to him has sexual designs – during which, in Ufa fashion, her make-up gradually becomes more garish. Isabel Jeans, as a stage star, is

another who uses this unfortunate young man, and *Easy Virtue* was a vehicle for her, as hacked from Noël Coward's Pineroesque play. By removing the sub-plots and offering more of the heroine's life it emerges as bland nonsense, though still having to do with a family's hostility to the son's new wife. Coward's plays were shocking to West End audiences, and the idea doubtless was to let them be seen by the less sophisticated in Wigan or Dumfries. Balcon also bought **The Vortex,** and admitted later that he had been wrong: 'We followed trends and did not try to make them. It was doubly a mistake to lean on stage plays because we were making Silent films . . . both were financial failures.' As directed by Adrian Brunel, *The Vortex* makes incomprehensible Coward's tale of drugs and sex among the smart set, but the failure is also one of nerve: to make Miss Jeans sympathetic in *Easy Virtue,* she becomes ill-treated, wronged, and unjustly accused, a glamorous innocent in the mould of Irene Rich or Pola Negri – and this was the age of Clara Bow. British censors passed both Miss Bow's antics and the equally bold behaviour of Coward's stage characters, but here the latter have been handled – and it is true also of *Downhill* – with a sense of morality both smug and, compared with American films at this time, outdated.

Hitchcock left Balcon for British International Pictures, newly formed by John Maxwell, an exhibitor, in light of the Quota Act; Maxwell shortly afterwards allied the company and its studio (Elstree, not long vacated by Wilcox and Williams) to the Associated British circuit; and about the same time Gainsborough was absorbed into Gaumont-British, also developing its circuit interests – so in fact Hitchcock moved from one to the other of what were now the two biggest film companies. **The Ring** (1927) he regarded, after *The Lodger,* as the second 'Hitchcock picture', and the influence of *Varieté* is again all over it, even to the story (written by himself), which concerns the rivalry between two boxers over the same woman. **Champagne** (1928), however, was 'probably the lowest ebb in my output,' though he neglected to add that it was a vehicle for Betty Balfour, whom the readers of the *Daily Mirror* had recently voted their favourite British star – probably the reason it apes the Hollywood vehicles of such as Colleen Moore, the story of a tomboyish heiress who toys with the advances of a roué (who, as with *The Lodger,* turns out to be not at all as we'd thought). The acquisition of Hitchcock and Miss Balfour indicates Maxwell's ambitions, and he also filched from Gainsborough two popular players, Jameson Thomas and Lillian Hall Davis; Hitchcock directed their second co-starring effort for B.I.P., **The Farmer's Wife** (1928), but it is less a vehicle than a straightforward version of Eden Phillpotts' long running play about the Devon widower who woos three spinsters before realising that his house-keeper is the ideal mate. For the mainly West country aphorisms, Hitchcock has tried to substitute visual humour, but if there is a satirical edge it is more Shaftesbury Avenue than Yelverton, and the film is certainly not to be compared with contemporary Hollywood comedies of small town life. **The Manxman** (1929) is another rural tale, based on Sir Hall Caine's old novel: 'What shall it profit a man if he gain the whole world and lose his soul?' is the foreword to this tale, as to many others – all to be preferred to this intense triangle drama, with its particularly tedious trio, Carl Brisson, Malcolm Keen and Anny Ondra. Dully made, it proves that as he curtailed his tricks Hitchcock was less interesting than in his derivative days. Like many other film-makers more interested in celluloid than people, he passed by every opportunity to comment on his era – except in *The Ring,* which, like its prototype, is rich in its portrait of its milieu.

Except perhaps in that film, Hitchcock's borrowings do not arise naturally from the situations but are imposed upon them: and the same is true of the films of Anthony Asquith (1902–68), the only other British director of the period to attract serious critical attention – though it helped to be well connected, and indeed he was the son of a former prime minister. He was able to study filming in America and Germany, and was taken on by British Instructional, a company which specialised in documentary reconstructions of battles. On his first film, **Shooting Stars** (1928), he was associate producer, editor, writer and director – though John Orton and A. V. Bramble (the latter a veteran of the industry) are respectively credited with the last named functions. This is yet another derivation of *Varieté,* with the triangle drama set this time in a film studio, and ending on an ironic note, with the rejected husband (Brian Aherne) becoming famous and the unfaithful wife (Annette Benson) a nobody. Asquith had not sloughed off the German influence by the time he made **Underground** (1928), this time credited as director – and indeed he brought over Karl Fischer to do the lighting. More than the earlier film, it is an exercise in style, which is just as well in view of the plot – about the rivalry of an underground guard (Aherne) and an electrician (Cyril McLaglen) for a shop-girl (Elissa Landi). It is affectionately done – though it is clear how little Asquith knew of the lower orders, supposedly living in drab little rooms and going for picnics on Hampstead Heath. At the time, however, it was much praised – since most other films on British working-class life were either patronising or comic.

The director of *Varieté,* E. A. Dupont,

was also at B.I.P., having fled Hollywood after his disastrous film for Universal. His five-picture contract included two Silents – and both follow *Varieté* in being triangle dramas with show business backgrounds; and though both were photographed by an old collaborator, Werner Brandes, and the second of them was designed by Alfred Junge, both brought to Britain from Germany (Junge remained, to become the doyen of British art directors), neither film is as derivative as the Hitchcock or the Asquith. **Moulin Rouge** (1928) is set in a Paris night club (despite Paris locations, a London night club was used), and concerns a star (Olga Tschechowa) who discovers that her daughter's fiancé has fallen in love with her; **Piccadilly** (1929), set in a London night club, is about a star (Gilda Gray) who discovers that its owner, her lover (Jameson Thomas) has fallen for the new attraction (Anna May Wong). Her dilemma is that she does not know whether or not she has committed a murder, a situation common in movies at the time, and on this occasion devised by Arnold Bennett, one of the very rare major writers to accept a commission to write an original screenplay. The polish of both films belies their origin, but they also reflect Dupont's uneasiness away from his native land; with the advent of Sound, he directed three Anglo-German dual language films: **Atlantic** (1929), based on the sinking of the Titanic; **Two Worlds** (1930), a story of Jewish life in Vienna during the War; and, more disappointingly, **Cape Forlorn** (1931), a heavy triangle drama set in and around a lighthouse. He then went back to Germany, and by the time he returned to Hollywood in 1933 was regarded as a spent force.

Another German director, Arthur Robison, was at Elstree making **The Informer** (1929), which unlike John Ford's later version (q.v.) is merely a tale of doom and atonement. We may be sure Ford saw this, since his studio-created Dublin is identical, but Robison of course had been one of the major influences of the Ufa style, as copied abroad for 'art' movies. His stars here are Lya de Putti and Lars Hanson, the latter in his usual pursuit of being haunted and hunted, a figure of destiny. These were not the only

Continental artists in British films, since the local entrepreneurs had begun to raid European studios both to increase their export market and to improve the quality of their product – while the artists themselves saw Britain, because of the common language, as a step nearer Hollywood. The period was brief, and ended when British studios wired for Sound.

In France, those film-makers who believed in the film as an art considered that it should deal with real life – by which was understood the artisan class. Their leader was Louis Delluc (1890–1924), a young aesthete who was among the first of his countrymen to give the film more than serious consideration; he founded a magazine called *Cinéma*, whose every issue carried the injunction, 'The French cinema must be *cinema*; the French cinema must be French.' This conviction was the result of his enthusiasm for the three leading national cinemas, the American, the Swedish and the German.

Unhappily, the French cinema of the Twenties – far richer than the British – is far from accessible, its lack of representation in archives outside France serving to confirm how little impression it made, though enough is available for us to note its respect for its audiences. For instance, **L'Agonie des Aigles** (1921) is eloquent demonstration that historical subjects were free of the conventions imposed by Hollywood – and effortlessly superior to such as *Orphans of the Storm*, not an inapt comparison since the period featured is close enough, in this case the aftermath of Napoleon's reign. There is no love affair, beyond the machinations of a conniving dancer (Gaby Morlay); and the hero is an ageing duellist, played by Maxime Desjardins with all his Comédie Française expertise. The director was Dominique Bernard-Deschamps, who made just a few commercial films during a twenty-year career, being otherwise collaborator with Henri Chrétien on scientific films (a pattern not uncommon in the French film industry), and the source was a novel by Georges d'Esparbes, 'Le Demi-Solde'. The commercial cinema was happiest with literary adaptations; Delluc and his followers made their working-class-films; and the avant-garde artists went their own way.

The set-up of the industry was very much as it is today: there were the studios and the distributing companies, and between them the producers or production companies who rented space at the former and hired the completed film to the latter. The only major companies with a hand in all three branches remained Pathé and Gaumont, though known by the end of the Silent period as Pathé-Natan-Cineromans and Gaumont-Aubert-Franco-Films respectively. Ownership in each case shifted, as financiers from time to time considered that either company or both could, or should, monopolise the industry. It never happened, and one reason was that the industry was bedevilled with fly-by-night or dilettante producers – though many of these were not averse to finding backing for the eclectic works of the directors.

Chief of the film-makers grouped around Delluc was Marcel L'Herbier (1890–1979), a former poet and dramatist who arrived in films as a scenarist; his early films were experimental – and are now lost. The Silent films which survive are poor entertainments, but witness to a talent absolutely obsessed with the medium. **L'Homme du Large** (1920) follows Delluc's taste for working-class tales and has a number of good sequences, including a town fête and an evening in a low dive, complete with fondling lesbians; but this free adaptation of a story by Balzac, 'Un Drame au Bord de la Mer', about a father's grief over his wastrel son, is too much like *Terje Vigen* for its own good. In emulating Sjöström at every turn, L'Herbier simply fails to understand his purity; and by using artifice in theatrical manner, i.e. framing, fretworks, maskings, his overall images are in violent disharmony with the Breton settings. Even more does **Eldorado** (1921) represent the cinema aesthete thinking and working overtime, with great care given to set-ups, cutting, the use of people in landscapes, distorted images to express emotions: but as L'Herbier bundles in the whole paraphernalia with no sense of style, it is also clear that he confused the pictorial possibilities of film with those of the theatre and the decorative arts. He was certainly trying to find a route for the medium, and his ingenuity is often fascinating. However, ludicrous emoting and confused narration help neither this film nor his most famous one, **Feu Mathias Pascal** (1924), based on Pirandello's novel about a man (Ivan Mosjoukine) who begins a new life when reported dead. It organises a number of Pirandellan themes, including a dream sequence which disdains to make apparent what is truth and what is fantasy, as in *Aelita*. The locations, Rome and San Gimigniano, are refreshing, but L'Herbier makes little of Granada in the earlier film, which mainly concerns the tribulations of a dancer (Eve Francis, the wife of Delluc, and leading actress for the films of his group) over her sick bastard son.

Between the two, L'Herbier made *Don Juan et Faust*, now lost, with designs by Claude Autant-Lara influenced by *Caligari;* and with **L'Inhumaine** (1924) L'Herbier experimented again with decor, employing with Autant-Lara also Fernand Leger, Cavalcanti and Mallet Stevens (and Darius Milhaud also composed a score). The idea behind the film was to show the advances France had made in modern design – thus like a great many later French flop-movies, it was made to impress the Americans. It was commissioned and partly financed by its star, the singer Georgette LeBlanc – who plays a diva with an entourage of admirers, very much in the manner of the Italian 'divismo' films of a decade earlier. Indeed, L'Herbier, like Hitchcock and Asquith, was so besotted with the medium that he borrowed and copied slavishly. **L'Argent** (1928) is plundered from the Soviet films, from *Greed,* from *Dr Mabuse* – and in filming Zola's novel, now modernised, L'Herbier was probably emulating Renoir's *Nana* (q.v.). This film is even longer, running over three hours, telling mainly of the rivalry between two financiers (Pierre Alcover, Alfred Abel). The decor is again often extravagant, but the film is frequently striking to look at, notably the scenes in the stock exchange: you may prefer the cool, perfected, visual interpretation by this time in force in Hollywood, but L'Herbier's work is often dynamic – and in its turn was influential, certainly the inspiration for Feyder's *Les Nouveaux Messieurs* (q.v.). L'Herbier's Sound films (q.v.) would move towards

The Sound films of Marcel L'Herbier are stolid affairs, but in the Silent period he was forever experimenting – ceaselessly borrowing, and being borrowed from. This is Brigitte Helm in *L'Argent*, and it is almost certainly from her that von Sternberg got the idea for his Hollywood Dietrich.

conservatism, and indeed *L'Argent* spelled the end of the Delluc movement dubbed 'impressionist': the intellectuals who had originally praised the attempts at experiment had gradually cooled – and they had in particular disliked *L'Inhumaine*.

The accomplishment of Jacques Feyder (1887–1948) is much more sound. Belgian-born, this former actor with Feuillade directed his first film in 1915, and had his first commercial success with **L'Atlantide** (1921), Pierre Benoît's story of exploration in Atlantis – and ludicrous today as the Queen pounces on her romantic prey with wild eyes, flailing arms and golliwog hair; but of the two films which established him abroad the only surviving one has not dated at all – **Carmen** (1926). The medium had advanced since *L'Atlantide*, but this revitalisation of *Carmen* is vastly superior to Renoir's contemporary *Nana*. No one since Merimée, nor in later versions, has tried to interest us in the *characters* of Carmen and Don José, as opposed to their

fates, and Feyder does this by presenting them as thoughtful people. Louis Lerch, overall too boyish, does suggest a man buffeted by fortune; Raquel Meller (whom Feyder used against his will) does some of the conventional poses but is not the customary cardboard. Despite the meticulous detail throughout and the inclusion of more Merimée than we usually get, the vigorous approach makes this long *Carmen* seem short – Spain, for instance, has never been better used, and even today some of the shots are breathtaking. It is one of the glories of the Silent screen, which makes all the sadder the loss of *Thérèse Raquin* (1928) – especially as it was the more admired at the time. Particularly praised in this similar tale of obsessive love was the performance of Gina Manès and the evocation of atmosphere, indicating Feyder's primary allegiance to his source material. **Les Nouveaux Messieurs** (1929) has dated somewhat, since we are no longer shocked to find that ballerinas have elderly, rich protectors, or that they prefer them to idealistic young workers; we are familiar with the view that such idealists on attaining power may become as corrupt as those they denounce. With Charles Spaak, Feyder adapted this satire from a popular boulevard comedy by De Flers and De Croisset ; the title refers to trade unionists getting into government; but though the three leading characters offer chances in the matter of their morals, mores and motives, the film takes none of them. But it does confirm Feyder's mastery of the Silent language – now to be transferred to Hollywood; angered by local reaction to *Les Nouveaux Messieurs* he signed a contract with M-G-M.

By this time, the fame of René Clair (1898–1981) had eclipsed that of both L'Herbier and Feyder. The son of a wealthy soap merchant, he moved from journalism to acting in films which included two of Feuillade's serials. He also became film editor of *Le Théâtre et Comoedia Ilustré,* which published this manifesto on the occasion of his first film as director: 'If the cinema has any aesthetics of its own, they were discovered at the same time as the camera and the film, in France, by the Lumière brothers. They are summed up in one word: movement. The external movement of objects perceived by the eye, to which we will now add the internal movement of the action.' The film was **Paris Qui Dort** (1924), and it certainly looks back – not to Lumière, but to Clair's boyhood idols, Méliès and Zecca: a sardonic trifle about an invisible ray which, turned on Paris, immobilises life and movement – to the glee of some people safely beyond its effect, on the Eiffel Tower. **Entr'acte** (1924) was commissioned by the Ballets Suédois to accompany one of their ballets, to music by Satie and a 'book' by Francis Picabia – who also designed the decor. Picabia was a Dadaist, and appears in the film with other members of the group, including Marcel Duchamp and Man Ray: as with their aims, it is bizarre, inconsequential, designed to shock. Clair, though this is the only one of his French films for which he did not provide his own screenplay, took his chance: imagery, super-imposition, quick cutting and some 'in' jokes; but he was not really drawn to the avant-garde.

On neither film was the equipment more than amateur; and neither was destined for more than a limited public. His first full-length film and the first destined for commercial cinemas was **Le Fantôme du Moulin Rouge** (1925) – and the title, while not dishonest, was clearly meant to appeal at the box office. A man, disappointed in love, meets at the Moulin Rouge a doctor who can separate spirit from body: while his spirit haunts Paris, the doctor is accused of his murder. Clearly, this plot suits Clair's own dictum that a film should be above all visual; in his own words, this is 'a fantastic story based on superimposition' – but the superimpositions are poor, and the jokes (stealing clothes from a cloakroom, driving away in an empty taxi) both schoolboyish and scanty. **Voyage Imaginaire** (1925) is again *un homage à Méliès*, concerning a bank-clerk's dream: unlike the *Fantôme*, it was not successful, nor was *La Proie de Vent* (1926), an adventure story with a number of visual effects. For Clair's gift lay not in impish fantasy but in delicacy of comic situation, where the joke absorbs the plot or vice versa, coalesced, inseparable, as at the end of *Le Fantôme*: as the police prepare an autopsy, the ghost, now wanting to live, desperately needs to get back into the body before the first incision; and when he comes round, he glares at the surgeon for having nicked him.

Clair's flowering was **Un Chapeau de Paille d'Italie** (1927), based on a farce by Labiche and Michel which first saw the light of day in 1851; since he was among those who believed that adaptations from the stage and the novel had no place on the screen, he accepted the project only for the opportunity it gave to recreate the chase comedies of his youth, and thereby changing from a scientist with a camera to a puppet-master. To his existing skills – for balletic movement, for swift and pointed editing, for visual wit – he added that of satirical comedy, with a portrait of a wedding group of quite awesome awfulness. His plot, in fact, is ideal: a young man (Albert Préjean), on his wedding morn, has the misfortune to cross a ferocious army officer and his mistress, when his horse eats her hat; and needs must that he haplessly replace it before, during, or after the ceremony, whichever is soonest. Though the film was not popular in France, it made Clair's name with the metropolitan critics and internationally, and he stayed with Labiche and Michel for **Les Deux Timides** (1928), which he modernised, extending the original one-act play with some themes from a serious scenario, abandoned when the Censor refused to pass it because it was based on a recent crime. The gentlemen of the title are a meek lawyer (Pierre Batcheff) and the father of the young lady he would like to marry, both in frequent confrontation with the bigger and bullying fellow suitor. The two films run as merrily as a clockwork train, magically re-wound after losing speed on a bend; and though the visual tricks remain original and brilliantly funny today, much of the rest is derivative. Perhaps because these were not the sort of comedies Clair *wanted* to make, he borrowed – in *Chapeau de Paille* from Sennett, Zecca, Chaplin and Linder; in *Timides* from Lloyd and Keaton – and, indeed, its hero even looks like Buster. Clair's own genius would not be revealed till his Sound pictures, and it should be noted that he loathed the thought of a Sound cinema even more than most creative people in film at the time.

If, however, his reputation was already

made, that of Jean Renoir (1894–1979) had already settled on that seesaw where it was to remain till universal acclaim greeted him in old age. The son of the painter, his profession was ceramics and his passion the American cinema – a passion he shared with his wife, who had been a model of his father's; she looked, he considered, so much like the great American female stars that he was determined to make a film star of her – a project she regarded with indifference. He intended to be only the financier (his wealth, such as it was, was inherited from his father), but he could not resist collaborating with the friend whom he had commissioned to write the scenario, Pierre Lestringuez. The plot of **Une Vie Sans Joie** (1924) is obviously inspired by some of Mary Pickford's films, having to do with a waif (Catherine Hessling, as Madame Renoir had been rechristened) loved by a tubercular youth, and a former benefactor who risks scandal for her sake; and the influence of the American cinema may be found in its portraits of local dignitaries and – direct from *Intolerance* – do-gooders. Successful as a satire on small town life, it is otherwise ineffective, as Renoir – like Clair – started with one purpose and found himself better at another: his talent was not for the star vehicle (though he tried again later in his career), but for the by-play of society – never obscured by his dislike of the bourgeoisie. The director was Albert Dieudonné, who found his interference intolerable; and Renoir could not wait to be in sole charge. Their quarrels were in vain: the film was not publicly shown though, re-cut by Dieudonné – who also played the invalid – it achieved a few showings three years later, retitled *Catherine*.

Undeterred, Renoir embarked on **La Fille de l'Eau** (1924) – the title-role to be played by Miss Hessling; and though he may have entered films for her sake, he said that he became intoxicated by the medium after seeing Chaplin: 'For Catherine and me the cinema was a medium of expression that deserved a life of its own . . . [We] dreamed of developing a French cinema free of all theatrical or literary encumbrances. We also hoped to foster an American style of action, derived more from the direct observation of nature than the French style was.' Accordingly, this film was born 'of the strange juxtaposition of Catherine Hessling and the Forest of Fontainebleau' – and, we might add, other juxtapositions: his love of improvisation and his loathing of being dependent on a story, plus his belief that filming was merely technical and actors only machines. In the case of Miss Hessling, he was right, and her story – the tribulations of a parentless barge-girl – is banal; but its glimpses of village and village life are worthy of Sjöström. It was filmed entirely on location, and had it been unsigned you would still know that it was by the same hand as *Partie de Campagne* (q.v.).

It was also rejected by exhibitors, because of a dream sequence, but that – unknown to Renoir – had been extracted by Jean Tedesco to show with some avant-garde films at the Vieux-Colombier; his indignation dissolved when the audience, recognising him and his wife, applauded – which gave him the courage to try again. 'I stopped foolish criticism of the public's so-called lack of comprehension, and contemplated the possibility of reaching them by treating authentic subjects in the tradition of French realism' – and he chose to do Zola's story of the courtesan **Nana** (1926). As with Clair, he had earlier refused to contemplate an adaptation from another medium, but this one – selected partly because of the general enthusiasm for *Foolish Wives* – would allow him to change direction *and* make a 'commercial' film, thus enabling him to enter the industry proper. Of that change of direction, he was to say much later: 'The consistency that I hate so much – and which film critics are always demanding, because otherwise they get confused – also causes people who are creative at the beginning to start copying themselves,' and he may have been thinking of François Truffaut (q.v.), who claimed for him 'characteristic themes . . . the love of spectacle, the woman who chooses the wrong vocation, the actress trying to find herself, the lover who dies of his sincerity, the distracted politician, the showman.' Continuing, Truffaut is on surer ground: 'In short, *Nana* rhymes with *Elena*'. *Elena et les Hommes* (q.v.) has been described by Renoir as 'un homage à la puissance de la femme et la faiblesse de l'homme' – and so

Jean Renoir went into films because he believed his wife, Catherine Hessling, deserved to be a big star. When his first efforts failed, he went for broke in an expensive and grandiose version of Zola's *Nana*. Miss Hessling is here being adored by Jean Angelo who, along with Werner Krauss, outacted her. Renoir had got the message; and the marriage didn't last either.

is *Nana*. Its major flaw – again – is Miss Hessling, playing, as he says, like a marionette – her posturing emphasised by the superb performances of Werner Krauss and Jean Angelo, both aware that loving Nana is no easy thing. Unlike the later Goldwyn version – or any other film about a courtesan that I know – Renoir brings out the curious aspect of the 'system', that men in high places were content to share these women, unconcerned that their motives were primarily monetary. There is, however, no sensuality, for in following Von Stroheim he achieved merely a coldness – and he was moralising, hoping that audiences would be, as with Stroheim and deMille, equally scandalised and satisfied. At the premiere, he was both hissed and applauded; the film failed, but it had been anyhow 'a mad undertaking', with a budget of of a then unprecedented million francs, due partly to the fact that to get Herr Krauss for the role the interiors were filmed in Berlin.

Again, he left films, and in 'a gesture of farewell' he took the unused footage from *Nana* to make a short, **Charleston** (1926), a celebration of dance so joyous that one hardly notices that the two dancers never get around to dancing together. For the second time, the reception to an 'avant-garde fragment' kept him in films, and he accepted a purely commercial venture, *Marquitta* (1927), offered by his sister-in-law and written by Lestringuez, who had deliberately loaded it with clichés. For that reason, perhaps, the result elicited no further offers, but he scraped up enough money to make a shortish version of a Hans Andersen story for one of Tedesco's avant-garde seasons; he chose **La Petite Marchande d'Allumettes** (1928) because of its opportunities for fantasy, but although no camera-trick is missed, it is today, like Clair's early fantasies, creaky. **Tire-au-Flanc** (1928) is also amateurish; compared with any American comedy of the time it looks like a home movie, and is surely the worst of the four versions of this old vaudeville (the last in 1961), chosen because of its presumed popular appeal. He had capitulated to the commercial cinema. in the expressive phrase of the film historian, Georges Sadoul, 'partly from necessity, and partly in an attempt to learn, by these despised methods, how the heart of the general public was to be won.'

For a company called Société des Films Historiques, he made **Le Tournoi dans la Cité** (1929), a melodrama of the days of Charles IX, and **Le Bled** (1929), intended by its sponsors to be an 'epic historical fresco.' The former – at least in the truncated version which is all that exists today – makes little of its

197

Carcassone locations, but *Le Bled* makes marvellous use of Algeria. In this case government money was involved, for the film was to celebrate the centenary of that country's annexation by France; but apart from one sequence emphasising the closeness of the two countries, this is an increasingly preposterous melodrama – in the manner of the early Douglas Fairbanks films, starting with comedy and moving on to romance and high adventure. Had Renoir stayed with comedy, he might have made a small masterpiece, and in the early part, too, he responds to the terrain and the people with his individual sense of wonder. He said that he took on these films as chores, but began to like what he was doing – which would suggest that *Le Bled* was filmed backwards; we can see that the best of this and of *La Fille de l'Eau* would be echoed in his later *Toni* (q.v.).

The French film-makers of this time, influenced by cinematic advances in other countries, copied and experimented, playing with film as boys play with Meccano or Plasticine; hence, Renoir and Clair flirted with what is called the 'avant-garde' – and we keep the name for those film-makers who never managed to appeal to the public at large. The art of the film owes something to these experimenters, but most of their films are now difficult to watch with pleasure. Perhaps the most tolerable is **La Chute de la Maison Usher** (1928), directed by Jean Epstein (1897–1953), a journalist of Polish origin who came to films encouraged by Delluc. His best film is probably *Le Coeur Fidèle* (1923), a triangle set among the criminal classes, representing for him the artisans; he was drawn towards natural settings, but it was with this version of Poe that he first claimed serious attention. It does boast a staggering number of superimpositions, strange juxtapositions and speeding shots, and there is an effective sequence of nails being hammered into a coffin inter-cut with frogs copulating; but it is theatrical, and with the impact made in Paris by the Soviet films Epstein's interest in trickery faded.

Also associated with Delluc was Germaine Dulac, whose **La Coquille et le Clergyman** (1928) was another admired warhorse among film societies: written by Antonin Artaud, its 'surrealism' is now – and probably always was – impenetrable. It was rejected by the British Board of Film Censors, as 'so cryptic as to be almost meaningless. If there is a meaning, it is doubtless objectionable.' Dulac gave up directing the following year to work in newsreels.

A similar progression may be noted in Luis Buñuel (b.1900), a Spaniard whose interest in films had brought him to Paris, where for a while he assisted Epstein. **Un Chien Andalou** (1928), a fifteen-minute short, was co-directed with Salvador Dali, a countryman and fellow-Surrealist. It is difficult to discuss perhaps because 'it is impossible to translate completely into ordinary language the complexity of this poem – for poem it is, and not a fable or an allegory' – or so wrote Freddy Buache in his book on Buñuel. Reading about it, however, is as interesting as seeing it, which can be true of few films – especially one with the inconsistency of a dream. This dream begins with a human eye being dissected by a razor-blade, the shock of which is to rid the mind of associations and therefore capable of accepting on its own terms the film that follows – one in which, in the words of its creators, 'nothing means anything.' Its purpose is clear, its meaning obscure, its images repellent: the priests being drawn across the road by donkeys, the dead horse on the piano, the crowd looking at the hand in the road, the man whose sudden beard is made of woman's arm-pit hair. It is too ugly to care about, to care what it means – if it means anything.

Another disciple of Delluc's was Abel Gance (1889–1981). He had started in films as early as 1911 and had had a success with his anti-war *J'Accuse* (1919) before coming under Delluc's influence. He continued to work until the Sixties, but is best known for his five-hour **Napoléon** (1927), whose ambitions included the use of a triptych of screens, which proved possible only on its premiere at the Paris Opéra and in a number of other major cities. M–G–M, which had bought foreign rights for a huge figure, experienced so little interest during its New York run that release was delayed for a year, when the film, now in a single-screen version, suffered its second American failure. The Talkie revolution had by then arrived, but it is only too easy to see why Anglo-Saxon audiences rejected this piece, since this is a banal run-through of the French Revolution and the life of the young Bonaparte, told with all the narrative finesse of D. W. Griffith, i.e. in primitive manner and completely without tension. Some twenty minutes are technically of interest: the opening sequence at school, with the camera at the heart of things in snowfight and pillowfight, tricked out with superimpositions and the screen split into multiple images ; and the intercutting of a storm at sea with angry scenes at the Convention – a sequence called by Gance 'Les Deux Tempêtes', and calling for the two extra screens and projectors, brought into use also for three later sequences. The raising of the siege of Toulon takes an hour, and further time is wasted with a fictional character – a girl whose passion for the Emperor exceeds that of Stendhal's Sorel; indeed your only moment of pleasure is likely to be when, as Napoleon embarks for Italy, you realise that the thing has come to an abrupt stop.★

Also delving into history was Carl Dreyer, who arrived in France to make **La Passion de Jeanne d'Arc** (1928) – with which we may conclude this brief catalogue of disasters. The mystery of its acceptance as the summit and one of the summations of the Silent film was finally cleared up by Penelope Gilliatt in her film column in *The New Yorker* in 1973. She did not mention it, but was expounding on the subject of Great Art – which, Leonard Woolf had apparently once told her, was bound to be a little boring: Bach and 'Hamlet' were both 'a bit boring' and 'War and Peace' was 'often very boring' – opinions unquestioned by Ms Gilliatt, who used the premise to prove that the film she is reviewing is 'not art, because it signally fails to bore.' The prevalence of this attitude must surely explain why so much rubbish has cluttered our screens (and theatre stages), enabling audiences to feel elevated after watching something

★ Mainly due to the exertions of the film historian Kevin Brownlow this film was shown for special performances in London and New York – at Radio City Music Hall – during the winter of 1980–1 with a full-scale orchestra, the presence of which virtually transformed the film as an experience. However, as Bruce Goldstein observed, with a symphonic orchestra playing the Marseillaise any entertainment is off to a flying start.

without a single intellectual fibre. *Jeanne d'Arc* aroused admiration because it was 'austere', because it was on a religious subject, because there was no last-minute rescue, and because, as Mr Rotha put it, it demanded concentration. Dreyer chose a subject, dear to the heart of every Frenchman (the last day of Joan's life, the final trial and the burning), and he filmed it – over an eighteen-month period – in that pompous ascetic way often associated with religious art. Falconetti *looks* tremendous, with big peasant bones and eyes, but you cannot call it a performance, because she has nothing to express but eminent thoughts, except for a moment of dementia before the taunts of her oppressors. The camera searches her face and theirs for revelation, but finds none because it is clumsily placed; instead, towards the end of the film, it begins to offer images of startling vulgarity – a close-up of a shouting mouth, soldiers viewed from overhead – and that is because Dreyer, denied his last-minute rescue, substitutes action equally emotive. Thus, the shaving of Joan's head is intercut with carnival performers and her burning with rioting soldiers – in slavish imitation of Eisenstein, which was another reason for contemporary enthusiasm. The subject is not very filmic, and Dreyer made it clear that he would have preferred to use Sound, one of the few film-makers to welcome the change. It is ironic that, in general, the directors who most understood and best used their medium dreaded the innovation and, at best, declared that Talkies wouldn't last.

An image of surrealism: *Un Chien Andalou*, prepared together by Salvador Dali and Luis Buñuel, with an eager desire to shock – though the opening image, of an eyeball being pierced by a razor–blade, was supposed to prepare us for everything that followed.

9

Talkies!

IN 1926, Warner Bros, made **Don Juan**, 'inspired by the greatest lover of all the ages,' and claiming to be based on the poem by Byron. It is not so much about love as about innocent maidens hounded by would-be ravishers, one of whom, the Don himself, is played as a college-boy tease by the ageing John Barrymore; as directed by Alan Crosland, these would-be seductions take second place to duelling, torture and Western-like posses, but the result is 'A Warner Bros. Classic of the Screen.' The film is, in fact, a landmark – the first feature to be issued with a soundtrack.

Both Edison in the U.S. and Gaumont in France had, during the first decade of films, experimented with Sound, and many others had also tried to find a solution to the two chief problems, synchronisation and amplification. Before World War One, Lee De Forest solved the latter difficulty, and sold the patent of his system to the Bell Telephone Co., whose engineers continued to experiment with Sound-on-disc, to be synchronised to the film. They had developed a new turn-table and accompanying long-playing records, of thirteen to seventeen inches in diameter, capable of lasting a reel, and Sam Warner agreed to try the system for *Don Juan*. Exhibitors had shown reluctance in booking Warner Bros. films, which accordingly played the smaller theatres: by encouraging these to wire for Sound, Warner hoped to attract patrons away from the large cinemas – while his exhibitors would be compensated by cutting out the orchestras deemed a necessity in any city theatre. Vitaphone was formed by Warners and Western Electric – Bell's parent company

– in co-operation, and in the Vitaphone process the New York Philharmonic recorded the score of *Don Juan,* to which were added the sounds of bells, of knocking, and (muffled and faint) the clash of swords. Its premiere in New York, in August 1926, followed a series of Vitaphone shorts – featuring Mischa Elman, Martinelli and Eddie Foy – and a spoken message from Will H. Hays.

Since the large theatres provided not only orchestral accompaniment but Sound effects, the public was not impressed, but as Warners instituted a policy to record scores for their important films, a number of theatres – and not only the small ones – wired for Sound. The shorts were another matter, and by the end of the year Warners had put a hundred into distribution – a figure they doubled in 1927. Lee De Forest had continued his experiments, evolving a system of photographing sound on the film itself, and for some time already he had been touring his Phonofilms – records of vaudeville acts. The only Hollywood mogul interested was William Fox, and then not until he knew that Warners were negotiating with Western Electric; Fox also bought the patent of a German system of Sound-on-film said to have pre-dated that of De Forest, and his engineers developed the system, eventually known as Movietone. With *What Price Glory?*, Fox began adding scores to their films, and as Fox Movietone shorts began to rival those of Vitaphone, it was noticed that theatres showing them were doing excellent business: Warners took a gamble, and **The Jazz Singer** (1927) was born.

Among the artists featured by Vitaphone had been George Jessel, a vaudeville player who was having a success in some of Warners' Jewish comedies, including *Private Izzy Murphy*: that was to have been followed by a film of his stage success, 'The Jazz Singer', but when Warners decided to add some songs – reputedly at the suggestion of Darryl F. Zanuck – Jessel demanded $10,000 in addition to his $30,000. When he insisted on written confirmation, the role was offered to Eddie Cantor (who declined, thinking it imprudent to follow Jessel), and then to another artist of the Vitaphone shorts, Al Jolson – who asked and got $75,000 for his services, plus Warner stock. The rest is history – though ironically the Sound-on-films proved more satisfactory than synchronised records, and Warners soon went over to it; *The Jazz Singer* that survives is a re-processed one. Seen today, the film is over-sentimental, as directed by Crosland, and so slight as to have difficulty achieving its 89 minutes. Its hero is a rabbi's son who prefers vaudeville to his father's profession, a dilemma captured in one intertitle ('The show must go on') and a transition from 'Kol Nidre' to 'Mammy'.

If we ignore the shorts the first voice ever heard from a screen is that of Bobbie Gordon, who plays Jolson as a child. After the lachrymose 'Dirty Hands, Dirty Face' Jolson speaks one line, 'Wait a minute, you ain't heard nothing yet,' and later, between two songs to his mother, he does a mother-love spiel, in both cases improvising as he did on stage – and it was Sam Warner who decided to leave in these impromptus. It has been said that the effect would have been less impressive with a less electric performer, and certainly Jolson's personality provided an additional crackle. The film took over $3½ million, and the fact that his next film took even more is indication that he and the Talking picture started out sensationally together.

Meanwhile, Fox had added Movietone to his newsreels, and equally extraordinary to audiences had been the sound of Lindbergh's plane taking off, in the spring of the year, and President Coolidge greeting him on his return from Paris; in November the Prince of Wales could be heard – and seen – speaking. In February an agreement had been signed between Paramount, M-G-M, First National, Universal and P.D.C. to disregard Sound till a common – and cheaper – system could be found, and they appointed a committee to investigate. The Warners themselves hesitated: *The Jazz Singer* ran on and on for months at cinemas which usually changed their programmes weekly, and it was not till the end of March, 1928, that the second 'Talkie' opened – *Tenderloin*, a rowdy melodrama, which had one reel of dialogue. Its star was Dolores Costello, considered by the studio a good speaker, and she was heard again a month later in an historical romance, *Glorious Betsy*. With the equally audible Lionel Barrymore – playing a financier – *The Lion and the Mouse* had two reels of dialogue, and in July Warners offered the first 'All-Talking' picture, *The Lights of New York*, intended as a short till its director, Bryan Foy, suggested he turn it into a feature for an extra $15,000. This tale of an innocent involved with Broadway gangsters was heralded by *The New York Times*, 'Seven Reels of Speech', and of *The Terror*, with Edward Everett Horton, it said 'A Titleless Talking Film'. The quality of speaking and recording was too clumsy to advance the cause of Sound, and of Warners' rivals only William Fox was preparing to add dialogue to films – till Jolson, in a part-Talking film, made them change their minds; the fact that **The Singing Fool** (1928) did not come along till almost twelve months after *The Jazz Singer* indicates the Warners' own caution.

The film itself manages the considerable feat of being even more maudlin than the earlier one, at unhappily greater length, with Jolson as a fond husband deprived of his child (Davey Lee) by an unloving wife; the child dies, and after a few bars of 'On with the Motley' Jolson sings 'Sonny Boy' – a song written for him in cod mood by Brown, de Sylva and Henderson, and the year's biggest hit. Both sexes were seen to shed tears listening to it, and partly because of it the film took more money at the box office than any hitherto, with a domestic gross of $5½ million.

The studio's profits rose from just over $2 million in 1928 to over $14 million the following year; on a bank loan it acquired a circuit of two hundred and fifty theatres

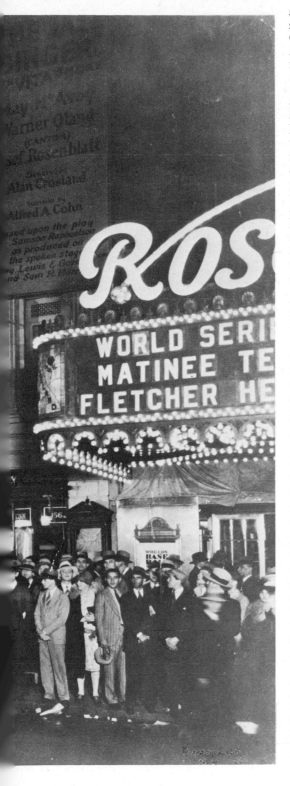

as well as the services of some of Jolson's stage colleagues – Fanny Brice, Texas Guinan, Sophie Tucker, Ted Lewis, Marilyn Miller – but none was to have more than a fleeting career in pictures; similarly, with *The Desert Song,* in May 1929, the company began a series of operettas but, despite Technicolor, each did progressively less business than the last. Jolson was on display again in **Say it with Songs** (1929), another tale of father-love, and **Mammy** (1930), a story of injustice against a minstrel show background; both were predicated on the idea that he was a great entertainer, and he does not miss an emotion familiar to the heroines of Victorian melodrama. As audiences tired of these screen-hogging antics, Warners tried to revive interest with **Big Boy** (1930), which he had done on stage: he is in blackface but hardly more entertaining, partly because the piece is no more than a filmed record of the original and, from the evidence, a third-rate original at that.

By this time, audiences were weary of movies which were little more than filmed plays or surfeited with talk. The early American Talkies are, indeed, extremely wearying; poorly staged, over-acted, and de-lib-er-ately spoken. We recognise them further by thuds which are too loud, gun-shots which are muted, and speeded-up action scenes, clearly filmed Silent. Footling little stories which might have passed muster in the perfection of the late Silent screen become, in such circumstances, insupportable. The first of them were made at panic speed, the accumulated skills of the cameraman subservient to 'king mike'; indeed, he and his equipment were installed in a sound-proofed booth, and freedom with the microphone only came with the invention of the boom. The confusion was apparent on the screen, as technical qualities fluctuated from month to month, from studio to studio.

During 1928 important pictures were increasingly released with synchronised score and sounds, but not till Jolson sang for the second time did the studios commit themselves to dialogue, amidst mutterings of it being a passing fad. The public proved otherwise: in 1927 there was an average 57 million admissions to

The Jazz Singer opened in New York on 6 October 1927. It could not be said that the movie business was never the same again, since most Hollywood studios thought the 'Vitaphone', as Warners' system was called, was only a passing fad. Alone, Fox and Warners persevered, and it wasn't until early 1929 that the industry decided that Talkies were here to stay. The most enthusiastic of the Warner Bros. for Sound was Sam, who died of a cerebral haemorrhage the day after *The Jazz Singer* was premiered.

Talkies!

U.S. movie theatres every week, which had risen to 110 million in 1930, despite the Depression. As lines formed for anything that spoke, dilatory theatre owners quickly ordered conversions, and dialogue sequences were added to films already in production. Throughout 1929, though the revolution had been accomplished by the end of the previous year, the 'part-Talkie' was much in evidence; for cinemas not yet converted, the studios prepared Silent prints of all their features, but the practice was gradually dropped during 1930.

Fox remained just a step behind Warners in the rush to Sound, and from that company emanated 'The First Outdoor All-Talkie', **In Old Arizona** (1929), for which cameras were hidden in bushes and which contains a celebrated close-up of sizzling ham and eggs. Raoul Walsh was directing and playing the lead when he lost an eye in an accident, relinquishing the former job to Irving Cummings and the latter to Warner Baxter – who won an Academy Award; he played the Cisco Kid, betrayed by the leading lady (Dorothy Burgess) to the law, as represented by Edmund Lowe. Such treacherous women were always of foreign extraction and usually of dusky skin, and an even more heinous example was to be found in John Ford's **The Black Watch** (1929), a glamorous female Mahdi (Myrna Loy) who dreams of conquering India. A sequence of the regiment leaving a London station was 'without a doubt the most realistic thing' achieved by Sound, said Mordaunt Hall in *The New York Times*, also noting 'giggles and chuckles' in the audience – which is not surprising since the film manages the amazing feat of combining the 'Arabian Nights' with *What Price Glory?*. A sequel to the latter appeared, **The Cockeyed World** (1929), commissioned from the same writers, and again directed by Walsh. Quirt and Flagg chase girls and fight in various corners of the globe, and those who had admired the earlier film (there would be several more sequels) were offered a sop in the form of a tame anti-war speech; the dialogue is shouted throughout, but audiences found its slang a welcome change from the theatrical speech of most current films. In fact they adored it, but they liked even more **Sunny Side Up** (1929), directed by David Butler, which has pretty tunes, the popular team of Janet Gaynor and Charles Farrell, and the standby plot of stage musicals for a decade – Long Island rich boy falls in love with poor girl from the East Side. Still today somewhat entrancing, the dance routines and soaring fountains would heavily influence Busby Berkeley. **Hearts in Dixie** (1929), directed by Paul Sloane, is also a musical, intended to capitalise on the popularity of spirituals – though introduced, all the same, by a gentleman explaining that people were the same the world over, regardless of the colour of their skin. The camera certainly moves, and the soundtrack erupts, but the public did not like this serviceable study of negro life.

The public queued to hear the voices of their favourite stars. Ronald Colman spoke in **Bulldog Drummond** (1929), and a few months later in **Condemned** – though the improvement in technique makes it seem like years; the difference may be that its director, Wesley Ruggles, was a real film man and his skill makes the tale acceptable – an unwilling love affair between a prisoner (Colman) on Devil's Island and the warden's wife (Ann Harding). Colman's microphone technique is the *only* virtue in the creaky Drummond film: he thus became Goldwyn's sole asset, as Sound had killed the career of Vilma Banky, with her thick Hungarian accent. The Brooklyn-Jewish accent of Norma Talmadge did not fit the public image of her, and she departed after two Talkies: the title-role in **Du Barry, Woman of Passion** (1930) would seem to have been a careful choice, for she was also somewhat older than studio biographies maintained – but the public would have none of her, or this historical nonsense, atrociously written and directed by Samuel Taylor. Newcomers poured in from the stage, and, also at United Artists, Roland West directed a batch of them in **Alibi** (1929) – though it had been made originally Silent and was hurriedly re-shot, at night, on the set of another film (*Coquette*). The story is a remarkably silly one about an open-faced young man (Chester Morris) who marries a cop's daughter (Eleanor Griffith) and is revealed halfway through as a paranoic killer; but it has a niche in film-history because it is the first film to use Sound imaginatively. In his only other Talkies, *The Bat Whispers* and *Corsair* (q.v.), made in 1931 and both thrillers, respectively of the genres creepy-old-house and gangster, West makes his casts seem even more amateurish than this one – but he makes much here of the noise made by criminals and cops, clanging truncheons, marching feet, police-whistles; he also seems to have been the first film-maker to realise that the public would welcome musical numbers to punctuate the action. A night club is also the setting of **The Great Gabbo** (1929) directed independently by the once-mighty James Cruze, a thin story about a ventriloquist (Erich Von Stroheim, in the only work he could get – as an actor) and the assistant (Betty Compson) he tries to win back. This tale – Ben Hecht, astonishingly, wrote it– serves only as a peg on which to hang the production numbers, filmed months after those in *Alibi* but less imaginatively: audiences undoubtedly wanted the sort of entertainment vaudeville offered, but Cruze's work is a good example of why the phrase 'All Singing All Dancing All Talking' was soon used so derisively.

Audiences no longer were served Clara Bow's speech in intertitles, but could hear her say 'She knows her onions', 'You dumb bunny' and 'You've got Gil on the beam' – even if she was a little developed to play a schoolgirl, a bad lot who is really a good joe and finally able to indulge her crush on the professor (Fredric March) – in **The Wild Party** (1929), directed by Dorothy Arzner. The film is technically way ahead of other Paramount films of the same season: **Chinatown Nights**, directed by William A. Wellman, about a society lady (Florence Vidor) who falls headlong for the boss of the Chinese underworld (Wallace Beery); **The Mysterious Dr Fu Manchu**, directed by Rowland V. Lee, about a wily Chinese philosopher (Warner Oland), carrying out vengeance on his enemies while his ward and dupe (Jean Arthur) falls for one of his victims; and **The Hole in the Wall**, directed by Robert Florey, about a gangster (Edward G. Robinson) operating a fake clairvoyant racket, with the aid of a nice girl (Claudette Colbert). Better than this tawdry trio is von Sternberg's melodrama about a miscarriage of justice, **Thunderbolt**, even if it is technically rough, with noises drowning out the dialogue, and its star, George Bancroft, enunciating thus: 'I've had . . . a lot of . . . time to think . . . *things* over.' Otherwise, the editor has lapped the Sound between sequences, a new sophistication. **Gentlemen of the Press** has Walter Huston (1884–1950), in his first film, as a dedicated journalist who finds that he has to make compromises when he takes on a job as publicity consultant: but this promising theme, as handled by Millard Webb, is too much a play and not much of a film. Huston and Gary Cooper shared the first famous exchange of Talkies: Huston (the villain): 'You long-legged-sonova –'. Cooper: 'If you wanna call me that, smile.' Huston: 'With a gun in my belly, I always smile.' The film is **The Virginian** (1929), the director is Victor Fleming, and it is a seminal Western if no longer an entertaining one.

Paramount's contribution to the craze for musicals was Maurice Chevalier (1888–1972), a Parisian of considerable and saucy charm. Ernst Lubitsch was invited to direct him, on the usual principle that they were both European – and he remained at Paramount for the next decade. A string of sparkling comedies began with **The Love Parade** (1929), and though Lubitsch subsequently made very few musicals, his delight in the form could have been predicted from the ballroom sequences of his early German comedies. **Monte Carlo** (1930) is indeed mainly notable for his staging of 'Beyond the Blue Horizon', sung by Jeanette Macdonald in a train, its music synchronised to the train's movements and those of the peasants in the fields – who join in with the singer. As the count who poses as a valet – to be near that lady – Jack Buchanan is no substitute for Chevalier, the ideal exponent of Lubitsch's conception of witty and charming male lust. *The Love Parade* was a critical triumph for both, and the director's visual sense particularly delighted at a time when words had taken precedence over pictures, as in the sequence where the Queen (Miss Macdonald) has to reprimand an officer (Chevalier) for a sexual indiscretion, and though she looks scandalised she rushes over to a mirror before receiving him. He becomes her husband, and deprives her of marital favours till she acknowledges that he is the boss – and since his satisfying the Queen is made of such concern, it might be imprudent to revive this film in countries prone to coronations and royal weddings.

An equally sophisticated view of sex was offered by the Russian-born Rouben Mamoulian (b. 1897) in **Applause** (1929), when an ageing burlesque queen (Helen Morgan) lets her men ill-use her, to the extent that she sacrifices herself rather than see her daughter suffer life upon the wicked stage. The magnificent Miss Morgan was one of the stage stars acquired by Paramount, but her puffy features, presumably, prevented a screen career. Mamoulian also came from the stage – one of several directors brought in to handle the new medium; some worked only as dialogue coaches, and others were forced on established film directors as assistants – but his reputation enabled him to study other film-makers, learning 'what not to do.' On the evidence of *Applause* he had also studied the most recent films from Germany and Russia (always seen in Hollywood, privately, but the New York cultural climate in which Mamoulian moved would have been far more receptive to their advances): it looks like a European film, with slanting shots, shadow shots, overhead shots and unexpected close-ups – indeed, it runs close to that line where innovation becomes pretension, and the fact that it doesn't is due to a flair for the apt image. Mamoulian is notably good on the theatres, offering a downbeat, nay, frowsy realism that is right for this particular story; the tragic ending is a European habit which Hollywood seldom allowed. The Sound is variable, and indeed the film is technically inferior to *Condemned*; but it has been held to be the film which got the cameras moving again.

Another claimant is King Vidor's **Hallelujah!** (1929). He reputedly borrowed the staging of the prayer meetings from Mamoulian's Broadway production of 'Porgy'; and certainly the story he wrote for it derives from that and the other famous white interpretation of negro life, 'The Emperor Jones'. Its sincerity and sympathy may not, however, be

doubted, and its assumptions about the connection between religious mania and sexual excitement are not offensive. The huge praise it invoked overlooked the stereotypes and concentrated on its documentary-like fervour, while its use of spirituals and jazz (Irving Berlin wrote two new songs) contributed, and still do, to its power as entertainment. It fared no better with the public than Fox's negro film, but M-G-M were compensated by **The Broadway Melody** (1929), which cost almost $380,000 and made a profit of over $1,600,000. It is the original backstage musical, of strife and heartache between a small time sister act (Bessie Love, Anita Page), and a hoofer (Charles King) who makes it to the Great White Way, but after an exhilarating opening – a montage of the lights of Broadway against the title-song – neither Edmund Goulding, who wrote the story, nor Harry Beaumont, who directed, were inspired. However, Miss Love's warm and vital performance remains a pleasure.

Several aspects of the plot, and that of many other early Talkies, could also be found where they originated, in **Broadway** (1929), a melange of bootleggers and show people which George Abbott and Philip Dunning had written for New York's prize director, Jed Harris. The popularity of the play had been such that Universal decided that people would want to see it again if lavishly done – hence Charles D. Hall's vast art deco night club set, with Hal Mohr's camera swinging around in it: here, Paul Fejos's direction is lively, but backstage it slackens, with Glenn Tryon a dull hoofer and Evelyn Brent surprisingly subdued as a chorus girl whose fiancé is murdered.

It was M-G-M who came up with **The Hollywood Revue of 1929**, in which most of its contract players appeared in sketches, or sang and danced, such activities being now *de rigeur*, even for artists not competent at either. Warners followed with their stars in **The Show of Shows** (1929), but it is memorable only for a brief appearance by Beatrice Lillie. Not bothered by what must have been intense audience irritation and boredom – now that the novelty had worn off – Fox offered its stable in *Happy Days* (1930), which was intrepidly followed by *Paramount on Parade* (1930). Universal,

Since Talkies came in with a song (one of Jolson's), that seemed to be what the public wanted, and every star had to open up and give vent to melody. 'All–Talking! All–Singing! All–Dancing!' was the come–on line, and Technicolor was in on the act, usually only for certain sequences. But the two–tone Technicolor of the time was not an audience attraction, and even the three–tone system would take some years to win approval. This scene is from *The Broadway Melody*, and the trio in the front are, from left to right, Anita Page, Charles King and Bessie Love.

having few stars of its own, bolstered its revue with Technicolor, and brought John Murray Anderson from Broadway to supervise it – **King of Jazz** (1930). The title referred to Paul Whiteman, and because of his contribution and that of his Rhythm Boys (who included Bing Crosby), it is marginally the most bearable of the group. Amidst all this frolicking, a little 'class' rears its head: in *The Show of Shows,* John Barrymore appears as Shakespeare's Richard III, and in the M-G-M effort, Norma Shearer and John Gilbert run through the balcony scene from 'Romeo and Juliet'. Audiences were indeed soon to be offered a whole film of a Shakespeare play.

For years fans had clamoured to see 'Doug' and 'Little Mary' together, but the illustrious couple waited till Sound – and then chose **The Taming of the Shrew** (1929), as much a token of their exalted status as a desire (on her part at least) to change their image. In both New York and London it opened on a reserved-seat basis, but flopped despite kind reviews. It is less Shakespeare than slapstick, and

Sam Taylor demonstrates again that he was no director for Talkies. Fairbanks' Petruchio, all thrust and swagger, is certainly more to modern taste than Barrymore's Crouchback, but Miss Pickford is probably as bad as she feared she would be. Filming was marred by quarrels between them, and the famous marriage would soon be over; neither would have a career in Talkies, partly because audiences associated them with the trivial, pre-Depression decade just gone.

However, if their only film together was not the event of the season, then **Anna Christie** (1930) was – and with Hollywood so soon following Shakespeare with Eugene O'Neill it did indeed seem that the industry was growing up. 'Garbo Talks!' said the ads – a phrase that lives on down the years, witness to the potency of her legend and the skill of the publicity department. Much rested on it, since she was M-G-M's chief asset, and the public was proving fickle – for instance dooming John Gilbert's career by responding with laughs and jeers to his light baritone. Garbo's voice was intelli-

207

Talkies!

gible and attractive, and O'Neill's heroine was of Swedish extraction. Audiences and critics were enthusiastic, not yet tired of tales of regeneration or questioning why sailors and whores were so bothered with pasts. Garbo's past this time is even less exalted than usual, but if uneasy with the slang she is good as a tired woman eager to start anew; she is prodigal with that frown – that crinkle between the brows – and also with that nervous half-laugh which unexpectedly ends in a chuckle: but Anna, in such circumstances, may have over-reacted. Otherwise, there is a superfluidity of acting; neither of the male leads does it engagingly, but Marie Dressler's old toper convinces, with her weird challenging stares and slurred speech. Despite its customary self-boosting, M-G-M were among the technically retarded of the Talkie era, especially in treating stage material; but under Clarence Brown's direction, William Daniels does compositions of ship, sea and dockside which are almost as much of an asset as Garbo.

A German version was made simultaneously, with Garbo, directed by Jacques Feyder. Hollywood had panicked at losing the various European and Latin American markets, and it became the practice for important films to be made also in French, German, Spanish, or any one or two of these languages – usually with different artists, many brought to Los Angeles for the purpose; but even in only two versions the scheme proved uneconomical and was soon abandoned – except in the case of Maurice Chevalier, warranted a big enough star to make French versions until he left Hollywood in 1935.

Amidst the traumas and flurries and soul-searching, one great film emerged: **All Quiet on the Western Front** (1930), directed by Lewis Milestone with visual disregard for the microphone – Arthur Edeson's fluent camerawork was a revelation after so many static films – but employing it to pick up natural sounds and overhead conversation. Erich Maria Remarque's novel had been read by millions, which was why Universal bought it – and the huge $2 million cost of the film was justified at the box office. It was reissued in 1939 with a commentary pointing up the horrors of war, and again in 1950 – when Campbell Dixon in the

(London) *Daily Telegraph* summed up Remarque's creed: 'that all the fury and the agony were meaningless, a tale told by an idiot signifying nothing.' The screenplay (by Maxwell Anderson, Del Andrews, Milestone and George Abbott) keeps this firmly in view: the waste and disillusion; all the dead, and nothing accomplished; the glory at home, the misery of the battlefield and the fatalism of the soldiers – boy recruits, accepting and then adopting the cynicism of the veterans. When the hero (Lew Ayres) visits his old teacher, still holding forth on military glory, his response is: 'We live in the trenches. We fight. Sometimes we're killed and sometimes we aren't . . . Up there we know we're done for whether we live or die. We've had three years of it now.' And the film offers no bravery to counteract the futility: the old sergeant (Louis Wolheim) dies when straffed on a foraging mission, the hero dies reaching from a trench for a butterfly, shot down by a lazy sniper. At the end, more recruits are marching, superimposed upon a vast field of crosses, and as each turns towards the camera their eyes reflect only bewilderment. The Russian-born Milestone (1895–1980) would never again make a film as good.

Among the first German Talkies was Pabst's similar **Westfront 1918** (1930) based on a novel by Ernst Johannsen, 'Vier von der Infanterie'. It lacks the impact of the American film, and must already have seemed dated. Zuckmayer's play, 'Der Hauptmann von Köpenik', which also dates from 1930, depicts prewar events in a way more representative of contemporary mood, and is much more scathing on the subject of German militarism; but this film gathers force, notably in the sequence when Karl (Gustav Diessl) goes home on leave to a populace not beginning to understand life at the front: the irony doesn't let up, and we, as much as Karl, are glad to get back to the camaraderie of the trenches and the graphic picture of life in a field hospital. After Karl has died, a Frenchman clutches his hand: 'Camarade . . . pas ennemis . . . de l'eau . . .' The film ends thus: 'ENDE?!'

Technically, the film shows its age with the explosions: the microphones picked up the bangs less well than the sound of falling earth nearer to them. When Pabst turned to a musical, **Die Dreigroschenoper** (1931), Sound techniques in Germany had not advanced sufficiently to do justice to Kurt Weill's score. The film is a synonym of Berlin at the time – though ostensibly set in Edwardian London – lit with a glare of desperate gaiety, and admitting to the principles of George Grosz while embracing the patterns of John Gay – for this is 'The Beggar's Opera', as adapted by Berthold Brecht, who unsuccessfully sued Pabst for misinterpretation. Weill might rather have sued over the removal of songs, less easily spared than elementary plotting and feeble attempts at humour, but those that remain are splendidly handled by Ernst Busch (as the streetsinger) and Lotte Lenya. As Mackie Messer, Rudolf Forster has the same sort of barbaric splendour as the London designed by Andrei Andreyev.

Pabst returned to the theme of 'All men are brothers' in **Kameradschaft** (1931), specifically addressed to French and German workers, and a co-production between the two countries, though the French version, *La Tragédie de la Mine*, is said to be considerably less radical. The setting is a small border town where a mining disaster causes the German workers to go to the rescue of Frenchmen – despite the frontiers, protocol, old wounds and international tension. The subject was a sensitive one, with the question of Alsace-Lorraine still in contention and when, because of the Depression, German resentment towards France was reaching a new peak. It is an uncluttered film, fresher than the majority of most subsequent mining dramas, but the people for whom it was intended were not interested, while its final note of warning – the authorities replacing the barriers – was removed by the distributors. Pabst learnt his lesson, and turned to escapism: **Die Herrin von Atlantis** (1932) or *L'Atlantide*, filmed on location in North Africa in German, French and English versions – all of them presumably superior to Feyder's old version of the tale, but it remains mumbo-jumbo despite Pabst's attempts to suggest a kingdom where all normal emotions are upended, from its Queen

(Brigitte Helm) downwards.

The film was surely too cynically undertaken to find a public, either, and it was not, in any case, the sort of escapism craved by German audiences who, after a decade of economic misery, were either basking in musicals or memories of the Prussian past – and indeed in a poll in 1931 they voted *Die Drei von der Tankstelle* (q.v.) their favourite film, and **Das Flötenkonzert von Sanssouci** (1930) third. This was the latest of the 'Fridericus' films, in this case directed by Gustav Ucicky but as usual starring Otto Gebühr, whose resemblance to Frederick the Great provided him with the means to a successful career. The series began in 1919, in the aftermath of the War, and this was the first Talkie 'Fridericus': the flag-waving apart, it is of the level of the George Arliss historicals (q.v.) which were its contemporaries – and a sad come-down for Ufa. It was exactly the type of film favoured by the company since its take-over by Hugenberg – even if, under his presidency, the new managing director, Ludwig Klitzsch, did persuade Pommer to return. Others also returned, since Ufa faced the problem of the American studios, of retaining its share of the markets in those countries which did not speak their language. The solution was held to be simultaneous ver-

Since the Silent picture was considered wholly international, it is curious that G.W. Pabst, hitherto a somewhat cynical chronicler of the malaise of society, should have chosen the coming of Talkies to preach international understanding. Both *Westfront 1918* and *Kameradschaft* (illustrated) are very fine, and if the propaganda in both is a little obvious, they remain remarkably realistic portraits of their time.

sions, but few of the English-language versions made headway in their intended countries, though the Germans continued to film in French throughout the Thirties. And the results are confusing, so that an international name like Conrad Veidt – who played in English versions in Hollywood and Britain – might turn up in both German and English, or in one or the other, in English sometimes dubbed and sometimes not. The engineers quickly became ingenious at combining dubbing and direct sound.

One such film overshadowed all the others, **Der Blaue Engel/The Blue Angel** (1930), marking a return to prestige for Ufa and a rare co-operation with an American company, Paramount, who were returning their German actor, Emil Jannings, and sending with him, to direct, Josef von Sternberg. The reputation of these two artists, and that of Pommer, was sufficient to cow Hugenberg, who disliked the socialist tone of Heinrich Mann's original novel, 'Professor Unrat'. It was Jannings's decision to eschew the latter part of it, in which the professor rises to become a pillar of society, in favour of his earlier lapse – when he becomes obsessed with a déclassée cabaret singer, Lola-Lola. This role was played by Marlene Dietrich (b. 1901), hitherto a minor star but immortal as this modern Carmen. Less entrancing than Louise Brooks in Pabst's two films, she is more her own mistress, not so much cruel as tough. We learn about her from her songs – 'Falling in Love Again', as haunting the thousandth time as the third, 'They Call Me Naughty Lola', 'Those Charming, Alarming Blonde Women', with its hints of bi-sexuality, and 'A Man, Just a Regular Man'. Sex is not only her business but her pleasure: the teasing, insolent smile will give way to open encouragement. Even her clothes tease. They conceal and reveal: a crinoline has no back, a skirt curls upwards to reveal a cancan panty and suspenders. For the professor, Lola-Lola's world is just out of reach, and her garters, which should be, are revealed to the world. She gives of herself, leaning back, hands on hips, white thighs gashed – and Dietrich was never more flesh-and-blood. The professor is the other paradox: the pleasure of her acceptance of him is the first step towards public humiliation and the straitjacket. They are not even man and wife, except in his eyes. His fate is the last thing he expected. Jannings is brilliant, too self-conscious to draw tears, but as he rampages around screaming 'Cock-a-Doodle-Do' he evokes a deep hurt.

The film was a success everywhere, for many people the definitive film portrait of big city decadence in the Weimar Republic – but that was mainly because foreign distributors rejected other contemporary stories as either too depressing or too left-wing; the film's theme was tried and true, it had an international name, Jannings, and Paramount backing it. Pommer was capable of returning to that theme – without similar success – but in making multiple language versions he wisely chose subjects likely to be of first interest in the home market. Widely successful throughout Europe – but not in the U.S. – was the musical, **Die Drei von der Tankstelle** (1930), directed by Wilhelm Thiele (1890–1975) with a popular team of the Silents, Lilian Harvey and Willy Fritsch. Pommer had chosen Thiele for the first Talkie of the pair, both because he was Viennese and because he had studied Sound techniques: but the success of both *Liebeswalzer* and its English version, *Love Waltz*, was only relative. It was an old-fashioned operette, but this second film looked rather to *Sous les Toits de Paris* (q.v.), moving its similar theme from the city to, literally, the open road – where three young men (Fritsch, Oskar Karlweiss, Heinz Rühmann) counter bankruptcy by opening a garage. Audiences adored it because the music counterpointed the mime of the players, any of whom, at any given moment, is likely to break into song and dance. It instituted a series of proletarian musicals, of which **Ein Blonder Traum** (1932), directed by Paul Martin, touched less obliquely on the Depression by putting its equally improvident heroes into a converted railway carriage, in a meadow outside the town – as we find also in *Kühle Wampe* (q.v.), and by implication in *A Nous la Liberté* (q.v.). Lilian and Willy were expected to be only gay and light-hearted, and on this occasion they were joined by Willi Forst, the other major German musical star, before he turned to directing. Miss Harvey, for me, makes

words like 'coy' and 'arch' inadequate, and watching her pulling her skirts to her armpits and literally kicking her heels, smiling all the while, is as resistible an experience as cinema has to offer. Both films are so packed with *gemütlich* 'charm' that it is a shock to find that the second one was penned by Billy Wilder (q.v.) and Walter Reisch. Both, of course, went to Hollywood, as did Miss Harvey, though she was quickly returned when the American public failed to respond. Born in England, she remained a favourite in Germany till war was imminent, when she retreated to France, and thence to Britain, where she retired.

A number of the English versions were co-produced with the British studios, such as *Sunshine Susie* (q.v.), but the operettes which Pommer continued to make found more favour in France. Ufa's biggest success of all was made with both English and French versions, reflecting Pommer's belief that the 'book' of **Der Kongress Tanzt** (1931) was stronger than that of most operettes. The Congress concerned is that of Vienna, where Metternich (Veidt) schemes while the Czar (Fritsch) dallies with a shopgirl (Harvey). Erik Charell directed, another example of a director who made his only notable film under Pommer, and we might have preferred Lubitsch, whose staging of 'Beyond the Blue Horizon' is echoed in the film's most notable sequences, a song passed from customer to customer in a *heurigen*, and *'Das gibt's nur einmal'*, taken up by villagers and children as the shopgirl's carriage takes her to her lover.

The optimism of the Willy-Lilian musicals may have been inspired by *Menschen am Sonntag*, but whose freshness is testament to Pommer's wisdom in signing its chief instigator, Siodmack, to a contract. Inasmuch as it was made

Emil Jannings in the grip of one of the cinema's favourite themes, sexual obsession – happily led downwards from the moment she – Marlene Dietrich – slips off her panties on the stairs and drops them on his shoulder. She laughs when he proposes, but is flattered; later, when he is reduced to rolling on her stockings, she enjoys his humiliation. The film is *Der Blaue Engel,* made simultaneously in English as *The Blue Angel,* and the lady on the right is Rosa Valetti.

211

by young enthusiasts, it has been called avant-garde: it was certainly an attempt to bring realism to the cinema, and at Ufa Siodmack continued so to do, in **Abschied** (1930), a resolutely simple tale of life in a Berlin lodging-house. The characters are often funny – the morose maid, the man who borrows on the strength of becoming compère at a cabaret, the sister dance-team longing either for work or a date, the young jazz musician whose piano-playing is virtually the film's only music; and Siodmack makes something touching of the salesman (Aribert Mog) whose love is genuine enough while seducing but unlikely to survive on transfer to another town. **Voruntersuchung** (1931) is the more familiar world of German realism, opening as it does, and brilliantly, in a tenement populated by whores, as the lover of one of them, a student (Gustav Frölich), is implicated in her murder – which brings him in time to the enquiry of the title as conducted by a friend's father; in that role Albert Basserman is in the massive tradition of actors who do little to achieve the utmost effect, and if at that point the plot is conventional, the film is infinitely superior to any contemporary American crime film. Indeed, it bears witness to the maturity of the German cinema at this point, soon to tumble as people like Siodmack and Pommer were driven away after the Nazi rise to power.

The predominant artist of the new regime had already begun to direct – the actress Leni Riefenstahl (b. 1902), who broke away from her mentor, Fanck, and used much of her own money to make **Das Blaue Licht** (1932). It calls itself *ein Berglegende*, and is splendid on that level – the tale of a peasant girl who fatally draws handsome young villagers to the mountain peak whenever there is a full moon. She in turn is destroyed by materialism in the shape of an idealist (Mathias Wieman); and since he is German and the setting is Italy the dialogue is minimal. The views are beautiful, but as in the lady's more celebrated films, grandiloquent.

Studying Thiele's methods at Ufa, and taking advantage of his knowledge, had been René Clair, who had earlier called the Sound film 'a redoubtable monster, an unnatural creation': in the interim he had taken a trip to London to see the monster, as shipped from Hollywood, and it was because he was particularly taken with *The Broadway Melody* that he incorporated songs into **Sous les Toits de Paris** (1930), originally designed for score and only occasional dialogue. He therefore relied, as of old, on visual means to tell his story, and though to him that seemed natural he was widely regarded as a genius. Writing in *The Nation*, Alexander Bakshy said, 'He has produced a picture that is in many ways a little masterpiece, and he is lucky enough to be the first artist in a field that has been dominated by Holywood robots. Indeed, so great is one's relief and delight at seeing a fresh mind, unencumbered with hollow conventions and equipped with taste, subtle wit, and imaginative insight, apply itself to fashioning a work of art that [its] shortcomings inevitably recede.' Clair's achievement – and he was the first to do it – was the welding of three elements, dialogue, music and image, each commenting on the other from the first delirious moment when the camera pans down from the chimney-pots to the streetsinger (Albert Préjean). It was not a success in Paris, but launched by Tobis in Berlin with attendant publicity it soon repeated its German triumph the world over. Today, the charm lingers: its chief shortcoming is a plot so wispy that it blows away as you watch it – but without the compensating high spirits of the Clair films which followed.

For him, it was a trial run; **Le Million** (1931), converts a play by Berr and Guillemaud into 'une comédie musicale' – which means, in Clair's case, not a narrative that stops occasionally for a song, but one to which song is so integral that everyone sings: creditors pursuing the hero, cops chasing a crook, inevitably the opera-singers who provide the climax – and if neither of the heroes sings, there are unseen choirs to advise, warn or berate them. Clair removed chunks of the original dialogue, replacing them with his own lyrics; he injected the rhythm and created a fantasy which is not only effervescent but very, very funny. **A Nous la Liberté** (1931) has the same insouciance though his purpose was serious – 'to attack the idea of the sanctity of labour when it is not interesting or serious.' He later said he regretted using the musical comedy form, but the songs are integrated, and the material moves gracefully from satire to fantasy to all-out farce. The message has dated – that the greed of capitalism reduces men to machines – or, rather, it seems more a fancy of the age than a philosophical conviction: but it is less self-consciously delivered than in Chaplin, whose influence may also be felt in the plot, about two little men, tramps, whose friendship eventually survives the brief and accidental period when one becomes a millionaire.

Quartorze Juillet (1932) is both a tribute to Paris and France's national holiday, and, quite appropriately, gaiety is all – a wonderful feeling of being alive and belonging to the human race, even if Clair's people are puppets, to be manipulated by him in the cause of heartbreak as well as happiness. There are grave moments, as if Clair felt the responsibility of being a world-admired artist, probably the reason he turned whole-heartedly to satire in **Le Dernier Milliardaire** (1934) – though in the event the result, despite felicities, is long-windedly facetious. The screenplay was originally about a banker and a casino, but as Clair developed it, it became a treatise on dictatorship and royalty. Hitler, of course, had come to power, and Tobis, to whom it was contracted, refused to produce it. French backing was found, and further events confounded production – or, at least, distribution – when the King of Yugoslavia was assassinated in Marseilles, hardly a suitable prelude to Clair's feeble jokes. The actual idea of the plot is brilliant: a bankrupt principality woos back its one successful expatriate, a banker, promising a royal marriage, and it has no option but to accept his absurd laws after an accident has turned him into a buffoon. The film's references to the Stavisky affair, by implication critical of the authorities, caused disturbances during the Paris run and the film's subsequent failure in France caused Clair to accept an offer from Korda in Britain. He would not make a film in his native land again until after the War.

Clair's connection with **Prix de Beauté** (1930), often said to be written by him, is slight. The scenario was submitted to Pabst, who thought it more suitable for Clair, but the latter liked only the final twist, and wrote a new script, incorporating it: for various reasons he never made it, and the idea passed to the Italian director, Augusto Genina, who wrote it and directed – memorably. Once again Louise Brooks is magical, this time as a stenographer who moves via a beauty contest to film stardom – but also to tragedy, as she lies shot by a jealous husband, and her image on the screen continues to sing, '*J'ai qu'un Amour, c'est Toi.*' The irony intended is representative of the film as a whole, but its lack of subtlety is matched by the pace and an astonishing variety of images – in such violent contrast to Genina's earlier work as to suggest that he was inspired by his star and the challenge of Sound, which he has mastered by ignoring it.

Typically, Marcel L'Herbier was drawn to that challenge, using the screams and bumps of an old dark house, and the winds howling round it, but **Le Mystère de la Chambre Jaune** (1930) is technically inept, and in this version Gaston Leroux's story is infantile to a degree; a sequel, **Le Parfum de la Dame en Noir** (1931), though pleasingly set in an art deco Côte d'Azur villa, shows only a mild advance in handling Sound, and the direction is hardly less amateurish. French cinema at this time, in contrast to the German, often seemed determined on puerility, and **On Purge Bébé** (1931) is only minor Feydeau, with jokes about chamber-pots and purgatives, bearable only for Michel Simon as a Feydeau man urbanely coping with the unexpected. Jean Renoir made it, to prove that he could work economically, since he wanted backing to film a novel by Georges de la Fouchardière – which the film's popularity obtained for him. **La Chienne** (1931) proved that when not working quickly and cheaply he could respond to the requirements of Sound, as with the piano being practised across the courtyard, or the gabbling of the crowd as the murderer slips away. The story does resemble that of *Der Blaue Engel*, at the same time more endearing and more misogynist, since *l'homme obsédé* is played by M. Simon, given both a nagging wife and

Almost alone René Clair brought a touch of springtime to the Talkies – for while all around stultified, he brought not only grace and gaiety but almost immediate command of the new medium. ABOVE, *Sous les Toits de Paris* – though its success also owed something to its haunting title tune, and to its portrait of one quarter of Paris. Orson Welles once observed that any fool could take a camera into the streets of Paris, but Clair created his own – as aided by his designer, Lazare Meerson. ABOVE RIGHT, *Le Million*, most Parisian of comedies, with a happy ending for René Lefèvre and Annabella, with, far right, Raymond Cordy watching them. RIGHT, *A Nous la Liberté* and what is perhaps the best-remembered scene in all Clair, when the wind scatters the money and then the silk hats of the nobs and nabobs, unable to resist the swirling bank-notes.

The Paris of René Clair

The Provençal charm of Pagnol's *Marius* trilogy remains strong, though the story of the first two films can be briefly put: Marius, the son of a saloon–owner, César (Raimu), dreams of faraway climes; he loves Fanny, daughter of Honorine (Alida Rouffe) who keeps the shellfish stall, but hesitates – and she, pregnant, marries Panisse (Charpin), a kindly, elderly widower. Raimu, right, in *Fanny*, with, from left to right, Robert Vattier, Mihalesco, Charpin, Paul Dulac and Mlle Rouffe.

a final joyous shot which is a prelude to *Boudu Sauvé des Eaux* (q.v.). These people are trapped in their environment – the pimps' bar, the commonplace flat of the fancy lady, the heavily draped apartment – and the film's producers found that they neither liked that nor Renoir's handling of Sound, so that he was initially barred from the cutting-room. Complicated wrangles followed before the film broke records in Paris, the one fact cancelling out the other so that Renoir had difficulty setting up his next project.

French producers, as unimaginative as any anywhere, were further stifled by foreign competition and foreign intervention, being forced to pay steep prices for Sound equipment – controlled by either Western Electric of the U.S. or Tobis in Germany. Tobis made French films in Berlin, and to their credit, opened a studio near Paris – as did Paramount, chief among the Hollywood companies unwilling to allow their French market to drain away. Its studio, said Sadoul, resembled a tower of Babel, as it

attempted as many multilingual versions as was economically possible. The majority of these were hardly more than photographed plays of appalling quality, but the distinction of **Marius** (1931) is immediately clear, as adapted by Marcel Pagnol (1895–1974) from his popular comedy-drama of life on the Marseilles waterfront. This ex-school teacher wrote with feeling, sly observation and great good humour, and, as on the stage, his interpreters were Pierre Fresnay in the title-role, Raimu as his father, and Charpin as his father's friend. Since its appeal was supposedly parochial, Paramount sanctioned no other language versions, though the director was one of the several Europeans returned from Hollywood for such purpose, Alexander Korda. Pagnol himself produced the sequel, **Fanny** (1932), choosing Marc Allégret to direct – though the direction of both films is as perfunctory as their contents are memorable. Pagnol himself directed **César** (1936), the only one of the trilogy written expressly for the screen, and it is not to be mentioned in the same breath – though that is because of the screenplay, mechanical and even more verbose. The characters have become bourgeois, and worst of all, César-Raimu (q.v.) has lost his magnificent rages and hypocrisies to become a powdered-hair cupid.

Owing to exhibitor indifference and censorship it was not until 1949 that Anglo-Saxon reviewers and audiences became familiar with the trilogy, falling in love with it and thus aligning themselves with the French public rather than the French critics, who had sneered – and it has remained a repertory item. Conversely, forgotten today is the one French Talkie – apart from Clair – to make a popular breakthrough abroad, **Le Rosier de Madame Husson** (1931), directed by Bernard-Deschamps and adapted from a story by de Maupassant (and the source, incidentally, of Britten's opera 'Albert Herring'). Its appeal remains apparent: a rollicking tale of small town hypocrisy, with those 'real' faces we associate with French movies. The town council, unable to nominate anyone to receive Mme Husson's annual cheque to the most virtuous woman ('*Ah non, elle habite tout près de la caserne*'). suggest a man, who, armed with cheque and new-found confidence, sets out to make up for lost time. Fernandel is this youth of divine imbecility, and Françoise Rosay (q.v.) is hardly less funny as the narrow-minded donor – with a particularly low view of the cinema.

Had she gone to it, she would have been incensed by Buñuel's **L'Age d'Or** (1930), which he said later was 'a deliberate seeking of scandal, dedicated to attacking the representatives of "order" and ridiculing their "eternal" principles.' The time, he thought, called for such a spirit; hence the ironic title, and it was 'the only film in my career conceived and created in a state of euphoria and enthusiasm' – which may be why it lashes out in all directions, anxious to hurt and shock as many spectators as possible. It has satire (mitres on skeletons), black comedy (a blind man kicked), eroticism (a girl sucks the toe of a statue while the Liebestod plays), heresy (Christ as the Marquis de Sade, or vice-versa) and a deep approval of lust. Audiences today, hipped-on to Buñuel's loathing of Church and State, laugh knowingly and applaud, in depressing contrast to his own after-thought, in 1965, 'How is it possible to shock after the Nazi mass murders and the atom bombs dropped on Japan? I feel today that the use of scandal is a negative action. L'Age d'Or, which in its day was a militant film aimed at raping clear consciences – and was therefore scandalous – is now a harmless work.' We might, however, still reflect on the responsibility of Church and State in regard to the concentration camps and nuclear warfare. At the time, many of its shafts found their targets, and their recipients retaliated: an alliance of the Jeunesse Catholiques, the Ligues des Patriotes and the Ligue Antijuive attacked the cinema, attracting the right-wing press, which promptly denounced the film. The censor stepped in with a complete ban – which was to remain in force in France for over twenty years.

Like *Le Chien Andalou*, it had been financed by the Vicomte de Noailles, whose money also permitted an indulgence to Jean Cocteau (1889–1963), swept away by Buñuel's experiments in putting surrealism on the screen. Made in 1930, **Le Sang d'un Poète** was not shown till two years later, because it was reshot when some of the relatives of the aristocratic performers objected to their applauding a funeral, and because the de Noailles family wanted the fuss over *L'Age d'Or* to die down. The title during filming was *La Vie d'un Poète*, but Cocteau thought up one with more reverberation, whose pretension he then had to justify: a fan of quite simple films, he could not bear to make one himself, and this one announces itself as dedicated to certain Renaissance 'painters of enigma'. A mish-mash of recollection, dreams and images, the film is only interesting as a forerunner for the later more responsible and organised films – *Orphée* (q.v.), with the same mirror through which the hero must walk, and *Les Enfants Terribles* (q.v.), though the snowball episode had already been used in the book of the name. 'Étonne moi', Diaghilev had said to him, but when a man says '*merde*' several times it is hardly in the same league as Buñuel's attempt to shock.

The Vicomte had thrown away his money to scandalise a few, and declined to do so again, while Buñuel discovered, as he said later, that surrealism had shown him that 'in life there is a moral direction man cannot but follow' – and thus returned to Spain to make a documentary study, **Las Hurdes** (1932), also known as *Land Without Bread*. He realised that the desperate lives of the Hurdanos did not need nor could suffer the indignity of 'interpretation'. 'Lack of nourishment, lack of hygiene and intermarriage' notes the commentary, as the camera settles on the face of a thirty-two-year-old woman who looks sixty. The region is not far from Salamanca, fifty-two villages with a population of 8,000, living on beans and potatoes except when supplies dry up and they go to the hills to forage for unripe cherries. The churches contain the wealth, and though Buñuel restricted his reference to one plain edifice, that was enough to have the film banned in Spain. Such conditions – the later commentary explains – brought the Civil War, and it was not till then that the film achieved its first public showings, in France. Buñuel had by then emigrated to the U.S., and when he eventually resumed filming, the plea for pity and care that is *Las Hurdes* would be more typical of his work than his two avant-garde films.

In Britain, the film-makers remained immune from such preoccupations, and just as certainly they were unprepared for Sound – despite a number of experimental shorts, starting with a sequence from Shaw's *Saint Joan*, produced by Lee De Forest, and featuring the play's first interpreter, Sybil Thorndike. That was available at the time of *The Jazz Singer*, but it was not till 1929 that the first Sound feature-length film appeared, **Kitty**, directed by Victor Saville and based on a novel by Warwick Deeping, about a tobacconist's daughter (Estelle Brody) whose romance with a soldier (John Stuart) is blighted by his war wounds and aristocratic mother. Trade-shown as a Silent, the reactions were sufficiently positive as to cause its producers, Saville and B.I.P., to send its principals to New York to refilm the last three reels with Sound, duplicating the interiors and replacing the Thameside locations with hastily painted back-cloths. Herbert Wilcox also hurried to the U.S., to produce for his own company the All-Talking *Black Waters*, a melodrama with an American director, Marshall Neilan, and a number of American players including its stars, James Kirkwood and Mary Brian. It had been predicted that the British would not understand American dialect, but Hollywood financial interests ensured that its films were shown, and when audiences indicated that, dialect or not, they continued to prefer them to their native product, British studios wired for Sound. At B.I.P., Alfred Hitchcock was preparing **Blackmail** (1929), and Maxwell agreed to convert the last reel to Sound – till panic hit the industry, and it was decided to re-film a number of the earlier sequences. Since certain scenes already filmed could be 'played' with only sound effects, the star, Anny Ondra, was retained; but as her Czech accent rendered her dialogue unintelligible, in reshooting she mouthed the words while another actress, Joan Barry, spoke them into a microphone behind the scenery. The combination of the heavy histrionics of the one and the 'refained' voice of the other makes this heroine one of the most

tiresome on record – though it is admittedly hard to sympathise with one who has agreed to pose for an artist late at night and then is surprised to find that the sight of her step-ins drives him wild. That she refuses to tell her Scotland Yard boyfriend (John Longden) that she has murdered, and that he, once arriving at the truth, behaves as suspiciously as she, is reason enough for Hitchcock to dismiss the story as 'rather simple' – but it is recognisably a film of this director: the chase through the British Museum, his first use of a famous building for climax; the blackmailer whistling 'The Best Things in Life are Free' as the detective hands over the cash; the camera swooping down on the knife during the struggle behind the curtains; and the famous scene as the heroine hears nothing but the word 'knife' as the silly neighbour gossips. The last of these is the Sound equivalent of the close-up of the mouth in *Sunrise*, and there are borrowings from *Geheimnisse einer Seele* (the recurring image of the knife) and *Varieté* (the off-screen murder): but they were, not unreasonably, much praised – though in the U.S. this could not persuade the public to sample them. In Australia, the public was denied the opportunity, presumably because the murderess did not pay the price.

The qualities of this confused melange of Silence and Sound helped to enshrine it as 'Britain's First Talkie', thus obliterating the claims of *Taxi for Two*, simultaneously on view, a Michael Balcon production directed by Alexander Esway, no longer available for verification – and which, incidentally, destroyed the career of its star, Mabel Poulton, who was found to have a harsh cockney accent. There is nothing cinematic about **Juno and the Paycock** (1929), as adapted from Sean O'Casey's play by Hitchcock and his wife, Alma Reville, a regular collaborator during the next decade. Filmed because the Abbey Theatre cast had recently been successful in New York, the players include a number from the original Dublin and London productions five years earlier – Sara Allgood, Maire O'Neill, Sydney Morgan and Barry Fitzgerald, the latter demoted to 'orator'; Edward Chapman, brought in to play 'Captain' Jack, is not of the same quality, and the piece which in the theatre can be exhilarating – cf. Laurence Olivier's National production in 1966 – is merely cramped and dowdy. Hitchcock had been handed the assignment as Britain's leading director but the impetus gained by *Blackmail* was lost in a number of atrociously directed films – photographed plays stagily acted, and occasionally intercut with arty shots. **Murder** (1930) is a whodunnit with a famous actor-manager (Herbert Marshall) turned amateur detective, and a trapeze-artist (Esme Percy) revealed as the murderer – incredibly misunderstood by François Truffaut to be transvestite, and therefore the film a treatise on homosexuality – on which Hitchcock didn't demur, since this made him a 'daring' director of the period. **The Skin Game** (1931) is indeed retarded, as adapted by the director and his wife from Galsworthy's play about a warring squire (C. V. France) and a nouveau riche industrialist (Edmund Gwenn); and although **Number Seventeen** (1932) is more of a film, with bumps in the night and a railway chase, it is also surely one of the silliest ever made. However, **Rich and Strange** (1931) is an exceptionally pleasing picture, about a bowler-hatted clerk (Henry Kendall) enabled by a kind relative to achieve his dream of seeing the world: he and his wife (Joan Barry, the first of Hitchcock's blondes) go to the Folies-Bergères and get drunk in Paris, enjoying a flurry of shipboard flirtations on the classic route to Empire – Port Said, Colombo and Singapore. Lacking in sophistication despite moments of irony, the piece nevertheless offered proof that Hitchcock might become a good director if he ever became as interested in people as he was in film-form.

Hitchcock was connected with one other disaster during his spell at B.I.P., **Elstree Calling** (1930), an all-star revue in which he directed a couple of sketches, and which was shot in twelve days at a cost of £13,000 – which doesn't explain why it is even worse than the Hollywood revues with which it hoped to compete. It may be endured, however, for the sake of the two songs by Lily Morris, the music hall comedienne. 'Shows Hollywood how to do it,' said Iris Barry, then film critic of the *Daily Mail* – and that is an early example of the xenophobic film 'criticism' which was to bolster the smug local industry through another thirty years of mainly dreadful product.

Michael Balcon's first Talkie, **Journey's End** (1930), was also made in the U.S. R. C. Sherriff's play about the trenches had, after an initial Sunday-evening performance, taken London by storm – to the extent that the film rights were sold for the then hefty sum of £16,000, an amount eventually shared by Balcon and his chief contender, Welsh Pearson. Since the latter had no studio and Gainsborough was not wired for Sound, a deal was done with one of the lesser Hollywood studios, Tiffany, with James Whale directing, as he had in London and New York, and Colin Clive from the West End production again in the lead. In Britain the film was a considerable success, but Tiffany were not too happy, despite *The New York Times* view that it was 'absorbing' and contained scenes 'undoubtedly far better than any other glimpses of warfare that have come to the screen.' These interpolated sequences on the battlefield are comparable to those in *All Quiet on the Western Front,* but the rest of it is a photographed play, despite Whale's attempt to provide visual variety; the acting is of theatrical intensity, totally unsuitable on film to this grim, purposeful slice of life.

Tiffany also provided facilities for Victor Saville, who wanted to do a quick Talkie remake of *Woman to Woman*: Balcon was also involved, and Saville returned to work with him after a last co-production with Maxwell, **The W Plan** (1930), an adventure story of startling fatuity, directed by Saville at snail's pace, and starring Brian Aherne as a British officer behind the German lines. It has often seemed that the British cinema has been dominated by war films, but those of this period were triggered off by the surprise success of Sherriff's play – thus very much paralleling the Broadway-Hollywood situation with regard to the genre. However, one company, British Instructional, specialised in reconstructions of the battles of the War, and could be expected to provide a good Gallipoli in **Tell England** (1931), as adapted from Ernest Raymond's novel – which had indeed been the most popular book on the War. The producer, Bruce Woolfe, had previously made *Zeebrugge* and *Mons*; he had also fostered the career of Anthony

Talkies!

Annabella and Gustav Fröhlich in Paul Fejos's comedy of the Depression, *Sonnenstrahl* – which translates as 'Ray of Sunshine', though we know it not by that title since there were no takers for the English version made simultaneously. Its view of the Depression is an often moving account of the era: and if its optimism is a little too facile it at least was what audiences needed.

Asquith, who wrote the script and co-directed with Geoffrey Barkas, writer of *The Somme* for this company. Their point of view is resolutely that of the 'officers and gentlemen', which makes absurd many of the scenes in the Mess and, more surprisingly, the earlier sequences of the public schoolboys and their tea-gowned mothers in the Grantchester-like calm of peace. Equally surprisingly, the film turns into a searing indictment of the fact of war. As one battalion dismounts, each man is mown down by machine-guns, and for them the counter-order came too late: 'It is inadvisable to send any more men ashore as conditions are unfavourable.' Asquith uses a dynamic Russian-style cutting and at least for fifteen minutes the film is as good as *All Quiet*. The (London) *Evening News* thought it 'one of the two or three outstanding British Talkies made so far,' but that, of course, is not saying much.

Other countries took longer to adapt to Sound, and for most of them dual-language versions, at least, became briefly a fact of life. As European directors returned from Hollywood, they saw their chances in charge of these films. Paul Fejos tried Britain, without success, and went to France to direct a new version of *Fantômas*; then in his native Hungary he arranged a Franco-Hungarian co-production, **Tavaszi Zápor/Marie – Legende Hongroise** (1932). English and German versions were also made, but in fact there is little speech, and the characters too often gesture when words would be more appropriate – in keeping at least with the embarrassing naivety of the story, concerning a pregnant maid cast out by her employers and her odyssey to an ending which recalls 'Liliom'. There are haunting images of white cottage and steeple, and the flower-like face of Annabella conveys the right sort of dotty passion: but it is not surprising that British and American distributors thought it unsuitable for their publics. However, it is sad that they turned down the English version of **Sonnenstrahl** (1933), made also in French and German, in Vienna, also with Annabella, who with Gustav Frölich forms a couple who meet at the point of suicide and survive the vagaries of unemployment in that city. Adolf Weith's photography, much of it on location, is sparkling, and the soundtrack is freshly used: indeed, it is a film of great skill and charm – too much so at times, as the couple mime in a travel-office, or join in the song at the cab-drivers' ball. The unlikely happy ending recalls *Lonesome*; and it is a pleasure after *Marie*, grimly facing the world, to find the world helping the young couple. Fejos would not be the only one to use a fairy-tale approach to help audiences through the Depression, and it is sad that his own career declined – that after moving from country to country in search of commercial projects he finally turned to anthropological films.

Victor Sjöström directed the first Swedish Sound film, **The Markurells of Wadköping** (1931), made also in German as *Vater und Sohn*. He had directed a Talkie at M-G-M, *A Lady to Love,* which hasn't survived, and was in fact planning to resettle in Sweden when offered an assignment because of his experience with Sound. He chose a novel by his old collaborator, Hjalmar Bergman, and wrote the screenplay together with him, an Ibsen-like tale of a proud man who learns that his beloved son is not his own. The man is both mean and exuberant, unloved by the townsfolk, completely wrapped up in both his family and vindictiveness towards a man who wronged him years before. Unlike the character in the original, Sjöström – also acting the role – makes him likeable enough for audiences, convincing us that the discovery of his son's real parentage is his greatest tragedy. The last section of the film is solely concerned with his anguish: at first, disbelief and doubt; then anger and bitterness. He takes off his coat and puts it on continually; when his anger and bewilderment have calmed he takes refuge in despair – until, like a true Sjöström hero, he finally finds compassion and adheres to the word of God. The performance is equal to the role, and though Sjöström remains an uninventive technician, he gives the film a sobriety rare for the time; it is not a film like those of his heroic period, but is equally uncompromising. Its timing was wrong, for it failed, and Sjöström retired from directing, apart from a British historical adventure in 1937, *Under the Red Robe,* which clearly didn't interest him. He returned to the stage and acted also in other people's films, an ironic fate for the greatest film director of his era.

In the Soviet Union, film-makers welcomed Sound since it gave propaganda a new dimension. At least, the first Russian Sound films indicate a turning away from social drama to outright propaganda, and it was the director of *Bed and Sofa*, Abram Room, who made the first one, *Plan of Great Works* (1930), albeit that it has a track of music and effects, with a few agit-prop speeches. Its subject was the Five Year Plan, told in documentary fashion, and Dziga-Vertov's **Enthusiasm, or Symphony of the Donbas** (1931) would seem to be a companion picture, though its peasants and coal miners do take time off to dance a measure or storm the churches. Vertov was clearly so pleased with the sounds of plant, mine and factory that music is secondary. The first Sound dramatic picture was *The Earth Thirsts* (1930), with a plot about canal construction, but the first Russian Talkie seen widely in the West was **Road to Life** (1931), directed by Nikolai Ekk. In his review, Forsyth Hardy quoted a friend who claimed 'There are two films and only *two*: the Charlie Chaplin comedy and the Russian propagandist films, no

matter if red as hell, fierce, exaggerated in method, unlikeable in aggression, but dammit, purposeful.' The rest, he thought, were rubbish, and I wonder whether he could have seen this film, purposeful to no purpose. It deals with a real problem, those children left homeless by the Revolution. Sent to a school for rehabilitation, they learn boot-making, till come the winter floods, and they are idle. Are they put to drill or gymnastics, theatricals or painting? No: they build a railway, a real railway – those, that is, who have not returned to the drinking-dens of the non-Soviets. One expects to find that camel from another Road film, *Road to Morocco*, who commented, 'This is the screwiest picture I was ever in.'

Western intellectual fervour for such Soviet movies may be seen in the context of those Cambridge undergraduates who later spied for the Russians; and presumably some indulgence towards naivety had lingered, ensuring a belated welcome, over forty years later, to **Happiness**, directed in 1934 by Alexander Medvekin. Medvekin, a former Red Cavalry officer, believed absolutely in the party dictum of the importance of film, and turned a train into a film studio, travelling throughout the country to film the people and show them the end product. None of these films survive, but the work, he said in 1971, inspired him to make this film, which is anti-capitalist propaganda so simple-minded as to be of interest only to those who believe in anti-capitalist propaganda for the simple-minded. It is a theatrical burlesque in the style of Méliès but lacking his inventiveness and wit. It is also Silent, and that perhaps had something to do with its kindly Western press reception. Now, as then, the Silent screen has its advocates. It was the general public which so decisively rejected it. When the Talkie revolution started, the medium retrogressed to the equivalent of baby-talk: by the time it was complete, cinemagoing was a habit far more ingrained than it had ever been before. For millions the world over, life was inconceivable without the weekly or twice-weekly visit to the cinema, and so it would be for the next two decades.

10

Japan: The First Masters

THE JAPANESE cinema, though as wedded to studio control and the star-system as any other, has always been reliant on a chain of directors, some of them among the greatest ever to work in the medium. One reason for the early excellence of Japanese films is the fact that, unlike most Western countries, the cinema was almost immediately respectable, accepted both by intellectuals and the groundlings. Its first films were the expected street scenes and records of the Kabuki theatre, and indeed for years Japanese cinema was dependent on the Kabuki, with female impersonators and the *benshi*, who narrated the Silent films as they unfolded. Nevertheless, occasional attempts were made to 'free' the cinema, and the pioneer Norimasa Kaeriyama both filmed on location and introduced women to play the female roles. The greatest changes, however, were brought about by the earthquake of 1923, which devastated the studios in Tokyo. By the time that production was, shakily, resumed in Kyoto (the other film-making centre), exhibitors had had to turn to foreign films as programme-fillers, and the popularity of these persuaded Japanese film-makers to modernise their product. Additionally, the shock of the earthquake caused audiences to demand subjects more relevant to the times than Kabuki tales.

Two great directors emerged during this period, Yasujiro Ozu (q.v.) and Kenji Mizoguchi (q.v.), though their work would remain unknown abroad for another thirty years. By chance, the only director known earlier in the West was Teinosuke Kinugasa (b. 1896), justly, perhaps, since he was one of those most susceptible to Western influences. He was particularly drawn to experimentation, to which he gave full vent in **A Page of Madness** (1926) – which by strange coincidence finally arrived in the West in 1973 concurrently with another aged curiosity, the Soviet *Happiness*. Such story as is discernible in Kinugasa's film concerns an old seaman now working in an asylum where his wife is incarcerated, and its inspiration is *Caligari* – about which Kinugasa had only read, since it had not been shown in Japan at the time. Kinugasa had been a female impersonator in the Kabuki and, as such, had entered films with Nikkatsu in 1917; when that company began hiring actresses, in 1922, he took part in the consequent strike and moved to another company, Makino, for whom he directed as well as acted. He was directing as late as 1967, but of the hundred films he made in just over fifty years only two are, or have been, widely known in the West. One is *Gate of Hell* (q.v.), one of the first Japanese films to arrive in the wake of *Rashomon* (q.v.), after the revelation provided by that film in 1951; the other is **Crossways** (1928), one of the few Japanese movies seen in the West prior to that. It is a typical Japanese 'family' subject, about a no-good rip whose adoration for 'a painted beauty' leads to his losing his sight, and his loving sister, who prostitutes herself in order to help him. As in *A Page of Madness,* a confusion between past and present is indicated by furious intercutting – a sophistication of expression unknown, or at least unused, in the West till the nouvelle vague in the early Sixties.

If we knew only these three films by Kinugasa, we might jump to many wrong conclusions. We would be correct in supposing from *Gate of Hell* that the Japanese make superb historical films, but we would be wrong in attributing a strong Germanic influence – also apparent in *Crossways,* gloomier and darker than many similar Japanese films and suggesting that Kinugasa was emulating such films as *Die Strasse.* Japanese directors were fascinated by foreign film-makers, and their films of the Twenties and Thirties abound with references, particularly to Hollywood: but their work does not seem to have been unduly influenced. A characteristic of the pre-war Japanese cinema is its neutrality. The traditions of the country's art and literature had decreed that it must be decorative, small-scale and civilised. It might move towards thundering melodrama or harsh social criticism, but it avoided the big gesture: there was no Eisenstein, no Griffith, Carné (q.v.), Dupont or Borzage. The films were divided into *gendai-geki,* or modern subjects, or *jidai-geki,* which in principle meant stories set before the abolition of feudalism in 1871. They could be divided then again into stories of the family, of the theatre, of the geisha, the samurai, the student and, occasionally, of the soldier or the criminal – with, as in *Crossways,* some overlapping. The contemporary dramas tend to be static, with little movement either of gesture or camera – in both of which respects the historical films go to the other extreme. Yet there is an overall modesty, certainly justified on those occasions when shooting seems to have started without an organised screenplay – a drawback of many of the period films. The modesty was not justified: many Japanese films of this time have a maturity of subject and viewpoint in advance of the movies of the West.

Even so, a number of the more placid dramas require from the Western viewer some degree of patience – and I am thinking of two Silents by two of the masters, Gosho's **Dancer of Izu** (1933) and Shimazu's **Okoto and Sasuke** (1935). The former concerns a spendthrift brother and his sister, the student who loves her and the mine-owner who is cruel to all of them; the latter, also slow and virtually incomprehensible, features a blind musician, her faithful servant and her playboy seducer. The story was filmed again by Kinugasa in 1961, to remind us how much the Japanese cinema, already repetitious in choice of subject, relies on remakes.

The *shomin-geki* (a modern working-class subject) is said to have been virtually invented by Yasujiro Shimazu (1897–1945), who made approximately one hundred and forty-four films during his twenty-five-year career, most of them for the Shochiku company; he was assistant director on one of the most celebrated early films, *Souls on the Road* (1921), and was the mentor for another generation of directors, including Gosho, Toyoda, Yoshimura and Kinoshita. (The traditional master-pupil relationship in Japanese art became axiomatic in the film industry – as, also, in France and Italy.) Heinosuke Gosho (1902 –81) made around one hundred films, and *Dancer of Izu* gives little indication of his capabilities – just as *Okoto and Sasuke* does not compare with Shimazu's earlier *Our Neighbour, Miss Yae* (q.v.), which is a Talkie. The coming of Sound to the Japanese cinema was a prolonged affair, and indeed Gosho had directed the first Talkie, *The Neighbour's Wife and Mine,* in 1931.

Clearly, no hard and fast conclusions can be drawn, but from out of the vastness of pre-war Japanese cinema unknown to the West the works of two great directors have fortunately been made available. Yasujiro Ozu (1903–63) studied at Waseda University and entered films as assistant to Tadamoto Okuba at Shochiku in 1923. He directed his first film in 1927, but the first to survive is **Days of Youth** (1929), the chief interest of which is its indication of a director of talent, but one still in search of a personal style. He admired Chaplin and Rex Ingram, and said once that he became a director because of Ince's *Civilisation.* His interest in Hollywood is apparent in his early films, invariably featuring American movie-posters as part of their interior decor; all of them reflect a fascination with the Westernisation of Japan, as for instance when girls in modern dress mock young men in traditional costume. His preferred subjects for study were petty crooks and students – the former basing themselves on the gangsters of Hollywood movies, and the latter looking to the West for enlightenment and entertainment. The student rituals in **I Flunked, But . . .** (1930) have been copied from *The Freshman;* and the hero common to both this film and *Days of Youth* – played by Tatsuo Saito – is indeed based on Harold Lloyd. Between the two films, Ozu developed his style – a combination of that of his master, Okuba, when he handled comedy, and of the Shochiku house style, which was formed from a belief that what the public wanted was to leave the cinema contented from an adroit mixture of laughter and tears.

This style of Ozu's is not that of his better-known later films. There are quick bursts of action, usually handled with a travelling camera, and the detail is more telling. All Silent directors had learnt to use what we may summarise as the 'guttering candle' image, to suggest the passage of time, but Ozu repudiated symbolism in favour of the banal, everyday object – a hand closing a briefcase, a doll abandoned on a chair, a stubbed-out cigarette, an alarm clock being switched off. In *Days of Youth* a student carefully hangs up trousers and socks by their supporters; in *I Flunked, But . . .* a shirt bearing the exam answers is sent to the laundry; in *The Lady and the Beard* (1931) a nervous student pulls the stuffing out of his chair during an interview. In images and anecdotes Ozu offers a portrait of Tokyo circa 1930 which is in itself an invaluable record.

Walk Cheerfully (1930) has a familiar plot – the man who reforms for a good woman – but it also has a vivid picture of a small section of Japanese society: the girl's mother, worried about her losing her job; the girl's boss, smug and dapper in a tail coat; and the *gens de milieu,* hanging out in boxing gyms and cheap bars, the girls with sulky painted faces, the men apeing American gangsters in their dandyish clothes. The contrast between this fringe of the underworld and the office workers of Tokyo is made again in **Dragnet Girl** (1933), also written by Takeo Ikeda, and Ozu's last film in the genre; a reformation is again effected at the end, and themes from other films recur, such as the girl who pays for her brother's education and the girl whose idea of goodness is to knit her boyfriend a pair of socks. With Ozu, only gangsters are allowed girlfriends, adding to their glamour; for students, women are either sisters or mothers or the idealised unattainable. He never married, and lived all his life with his mother. His work suggests that he was an amused and loving observer of the human race, as exemplified in **That Night's Wife** (1930), about the growing sympathy between pursuer and pursued – the man who has robbed a bank for the sake of his sick baby, and the detective who has chased him to his apartment.

Tokyo Chorus is Ozu's twenty-second film – the sixth to survive – and the third he made in 1931: his art is clearly deepening in this tale of a student, with a wife and children, who is sacked from college on a point of principle. The children do not understand, and if the relevent sequence is extraordinary in its insight into family life we may divine that for the director himself the break from college was one of the most profound of experiences. The next two surviving films, **I Was Born, But . . .** (1932) and **Where Now Are the Dreams of Youth** (1932), take up the same themes in deliciously comic manner, the latter made in an enforced delay during the production of the earlier film. It concerns a student forced to leave school and take over his father's company, and is a minor film but unique in Ozu's work by virtue of a sequence of physical violence – when the hero repeatedly strikes an old and unprotesting friend.

I Was Born, But . . . is about two small boys and their realisation that their father is not the 'big' man they thought. The underlying assumption that all men are not equal – which, as the mother says, is something with which they must learn to live – often recurs in Ozu's films about children. Though still a young man, he constantly strove to recapture his own past in his films. Of this one he said that he had hoped to make it cheerful but it turned out very dark and sad. Indeed, he now began to move towards studies of poverty, which to him – as to Renoir in the West – was neither ennobling nor sad. His people are cheerful and well-intentioned, often mistaken but resilient, with problems that are universal. The fact that in his own country Ozu was thought the most Japanese of their directors, unexportable long after *Rashomon,* would seem to indicate that they judged Western taste by the West's own films. The War with Japan would have happened regardless of whether or not we had known Ozu's work, but many Westerners would have found it difficult to reconcile his gentle characters with the view of the nation as then propounded in news bulletins.

Ozu's popularity with film goers had been assured by his first dozen films, but Shochiku was so uncertain of *I Was Born, But . . .* that release was delayed: however, it went on to win the country's leading film award, the *Kinema Jumpo's* first prize – which Ozu subsequently won for three consecutive years. There was no pressure on him, therefore, to turn to Sound; he wanted to explore the possibilities of Silents before they were discontinued. We can see now that his late, ossified style was beginning to evolve – he has just dispensed with the dissolve – but in brevity of expression he foreshadows Antonioni (q.v.). He is so contemporary in feeling that the films, were they in any degree 'bigger', would be astounding. As with Sjöström, he worked within the native tradition, which is why his achievement is so different – concise and delicate: together with Keaton, they understood the medium's capabilities and drawbacks more clearly than other Silent directors.

His additional reason for holding out against Talkies was that he had promised his cameraman, Hideo Shigehara, to wait until the latter had perfected the Sound system that he was developing. The suspicion that Ozu's art did not need Speech is borne out by the comparative dullness of his first two Sound films, **The Only Son** (1936) and **What Did the Lady Forget?** (1937), both badly paced, and with dialogue serving as verbal intertitles. *The Only Son* is a mother-love story, less effectual than his father-love stories, and it is no surprise to find that Ozu's exercises in this genre – known as *haha-mono* – were less popular than those which other directors made for Shochiku. *What Did the Lady Forget?* is a study of a bossy wife, her gossiping friends, her husband and his niece. The best that can be said of both is that they are honestly observed portraits of certain circumstances at a certain time.

Between 1937 and 1947 Ozu directed only two films. After finishing *What Did the Lady Forget?* he was drafted and sent to China; on his return he prepared a script based on this experience, but the censor rejected it. Instead, he made **The Brothers and Sisters of the Toda Family** (1941), avowedly influenced by McCarey's *Make Way for Tomorrow* (q.v.): instead of parents being shuffled between their children, Ozu has a mother and daughter in like predicament. The fabric of the family is minutely examined at the moment when it is disintegrating, and none of these good people knows how to prevent it falling apart. His spare story makes McCarey's seem like blazing melodrama, but unlike McCarey he could not resist a happy ending. Donald

Richie, in 'Ozu: His Life and Films', declares that every one of Ozu's films is about the disintegration of the family, which is demonstrably untrue: but this one is. The same book calls **There Was a Father** (1942) 'one of Ozu's most perfect films', but we are more likely to agree with the director himself that it could be improved. (He had started it before leaving for China, and had reworked it several times.) It deals once more with a father and son, from a well-to-do background, and how they get to know each other after years of separation. The father is played by Chisu Ryu, the gentle actor who might be said to be surrogate for Ozu himself in his films from now on, but although there are moments to savour – such as the men at the club playing games and drinking saki – the cryptic quality of Ozu's best work is absent. The film has neither melodrama nor life, and because of his now-rigorous style, it has no vitality either.

The other great Japanese director of the period is Kenji Mizoguchi (1898–1956). He was born into poverty and studied art and design, both Western and Eastern; he joined the Nikkatsu company in 1920, and got a chance to direct as a result of the 'actress' strike of 1922. His first fifty films are lost, and the first to survive, **White Threads of the Waterfall** (1933), indicates that while he had a body of work behind him similar to Ozu's he was not the master that Ozu was at this time. The film displays two particular characteristics – the restless, searching camera, and the concentration of isolated detail – and beyond those a few moments of passion such as we shall find again in his late masterpieces. It also embodies two favourite Japanese subjects – the adventures of a theatrical troupe and the woman who pays for her man's education. Played by one of the most famous of Japanese actresses, Takako Irie (who also produced), the woman is an actress, and her protégé a rickshaw man; later, he is defending counsel when she is on trial for murder, and there is a superb moment when their real relationship reasserts itself. Similar themes are covered in **The Downfall** (1934), not surprisingly since it too is adapted from a novel by Kyoka Izumi. The woman this time is mistress of a gangleader and the man the gang's runner, for whose tuition at medical school she pays. Mizoguchi himself thought the film 'failed to

The World of Ozu

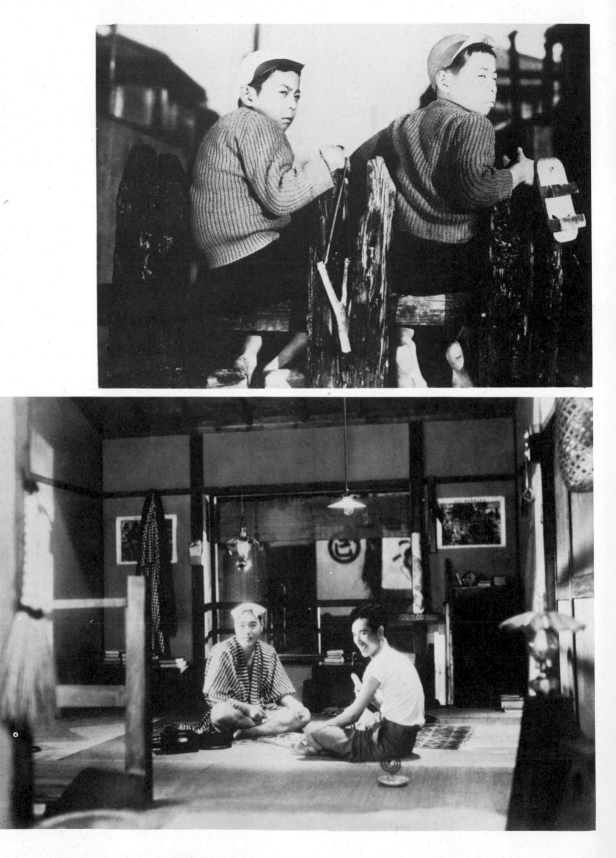

Hideo Sugahara and
Tokkankozo in *I
Was Born, But . . .* ,
one of his stories of
family life ABOVE
LEFT (and not a first
version of his later
Ohayu, as has been
claimed). BELOW
LEFT, Takeshi
Sakamoto and
Mitsuo Koji in *A
Story of Floating Weeds*,
(1934), which he did
remake, and his only
extant film of
theatrical life. ABOVE,
Yoshiko Okada and
Kazuko Kojima in
An Inn in Tokyo (1935),
one of his tales of slum
life. BELOW, Michiko
Kuwano, Sumiko
Kurishima and
Tatsuo Saito in *What
Did the Lady Forget?*,
in which Ozu moved
socially upwards to
what we call the
bourgeoisie.

When the British magazine *Sight and Sound* 'introduced' Japanese cinema in 1957. Mizoguchi's *Sisters of the Gion* was 'considered the best pre-war Japanese film.' Yoko Umemura and Isuzu Yamada as the geisha sisters with contrasting ideas on their profession, balanced against the attempts of the latter to keep away from the failed businessman that the other one truly loves.

evoke the quality of the original work', and indeed it never lives up to the promise of the opening sequence, on the platform of a suburban railway station, where the now-aged couple, not recognising each other, independently remember the past. This was Mizoguchi's last Silent, and was said to be his first 'pure' Meiji-period (1852–1912) film.

Oyuki, the Virgin (1935) goes further into the past, to 1878 and the Seinan War, taking as its starting point de Maupassant's 'Boule de Suif'. Two prostitutes are reviled by their fellow passengers, even though it is known that one of them (Isuzu Yamada) has offered herself to the foreign commander (Daijiro Natsukawa) in place of the young girl he coveted. Mizoguchi himself dismissed the film as 'badly written', but if the earlier sections are confusing it is also one of his most physically beautiful films (only one poor, mutilated print is extant), with excellent performances by the leads, his favourite players at the time. In the same year, as a change from the period films with which his name was associated he made **The Field Poppy,** a tale of young people's marriage prospects – very much a subject dear to Ozu and, like Ozu's own stories in his later period, seemingly drained of life.

Mizoguchi was thirty-eight when he made **Osaka Elegy** (1936), but according to the French film historian Georges Sadoul it was this film of which he was thinking

when he said, late in life, that he only found his true voice after he was forty. Sadoul adds that the main thread of his work then began to appear – 'the depiction of society and the condition of women within that society' – but it is truer to say that, working for the first time with Yoshikata Yoda, who would write most of his subsequent scripts, he found the voice he needed. All Japanese films depicted society, but Mizoguchi had been making films especially angled to women because, as he explained, his mentor at Nikkatsu had done the masculine films.

His training in art had led him to historical subjects and stories about the theatre. Though the only previous contemporary subject to survive, *The Field Poppy,* shows little concern for anything, the chief concerns of *Osaka Elegy* – the unity of the family, the exploitation of women – are to be seen in the earlier films, as they are in most Japanese films, but for the first time there is bitterness: a young woman, a telephonist (Miss Yamada), allows herself to be kept by the boss because her family is in financial difficulties. In **Straits of Love and Hate** (1937) a hotel maid (Fumiko Yamaji) is seduced by the master's son and, abandoned by him, sinks into prostitution. Both are stories from Victorian melodrama (though the former also surfaced in Britain at this time as a contemporary tale, 'Love on the Dole'), but what makes these films superior to the versions still being made in the West is their conviction: the combination of psychological truth and telling detail, done with an assured narrative drive which knows exactly what to omit – a quality still rare in Western cinema – constitutes masterly film-making. The theatre troupe of the later film (the heroine joins it to escape from harlotry) is engagingly observed, and I prefer both films to the more highly regarded **Sisters of the Gion** (1936). The Gion is the red-light district of Kyoto (and, like the *scena* of Mizoguchi's historical films, a world of narrow alleys and wooden houses), and Mizoguchi, a great frequenter of geishas, suggested the idea to Yoda – about the traditional, older geisha (Yoko Umemura) and her younger, more ambitious sister (Miss Yamada).

The struggle for economic survival is always near the surface with Mizoguchi's people, and indeed **The Story of the Last**

Chrysanthemums (1939) is the study of a career – that of the famous Kabuki actor of the Meiji period, Kikunosuke Onoe. Its sobriety compares favourably with the Warner Bros. biographical films of the same period, and its chief interest is Mizoguchi's increasingly inventive use of *decoratif*, foreshadowing his later masterpieces. Assisting him at this time was Kaneto Shindo (q.v.), who summarised Mizoguchi's career by observing that he had become good after a poor start, and 'in the middle of his career he became bad again for a long time. Just before his death he was so good he became superb.' Given that his work of this period can be only partly glimpsed – only four of the ten films he made between 1938 and 1946 survive, though his *oeuvre* is complete from then on – it is hard for a Western observer to agree that he was bad for a long time. Nevertheless, it is difficult to feel kindly towards the two-part **The Loyal 47 Ronin of the**

Genroku Era (1942), which we also know under its original title, *Genroku Chusingara*.

This story of the loyal samurai corps which eventually avenges the suicide of its master was a Kabuki favourite, and a perennial in the Japanese cinemas till the present, occasioning as many as two versions within a year – invariably long and expensive, with the purpose of this one partly political. Shochiku – to which company Mizoguchi had moved a year or two earlier – was in debt and had been promised government aid if it would come up with yet another version, to glorify the 'bushido' spirit. Mizoguchi avoided this – the piece consists of endless parleys and conversations – and indeed lost interest in the project on being commanded to make a 'loyalist' statement; his friends also thought him disheartened by the Japanese aggression in the Pacific and the further shock at this time of his wife's mental breakdown, apparently caused by syphilis – for which, despite

Mizoguchi's *The Story of the Last Chrysanthemums* is one of the many Japanese films based on theatrical people – many of them, again, based on fact. Shotaro Hanayagi as the Kabuke actor, Kikunosuke Onoe, and Kakuko Mori as his mistress – both charming players, but like some of their colleagues so bland that we long for some spirit.

Yasujiro Shimazu was the mentor for several of the best-known Japanese directors, and it is a pity that we know so little of his work. *Our Neighbour, Miss Yae* is as complete a record of a world long gone as anything in Ozu: the story of two families. Here is the son of one, Den Ohinata – according to the plot a dead-ringer for Fredric March – and the daughter of the other, Yoshiko Okada. It so happens that she is married, and has returned home when relations with her husband have soured: so her relations with this young student become a little complicated.

blood tests to the contrary, he blamed himself. Mizoguchi did not like action or violence – violence of emotion was something else again – and went unwillingly to work on two short samurai films intended by Shochiku as morale boosters, **The Swordsman** (1944) and **The Noted Sword** (1945). His distaste is apparent, but the genre required the restoration of his once-probing, gliding camera, and the settings, against a background of unrest and conflict, are again a portent of his greatest work. The eponymous warrior of *The Swordsman* is Miyamoto Musashi, also the subject of innumerable films: both films, however, have sword-wielding heroines – but less from a concern for women than as a statement on Japan's desperate condition at this late stage of the War.

Ozu and Mizoguchi were masters. Of some of the other directors we can only make a tentative statement. It is clear from the Silent films available that all of them regarded the camera as more than a mere recorder; moving on to the Sound period, we find in Kinugasa's interesting **An Actor's Revenge** (1935) and Mansaku Itami's **Kakita Akanishi** (1936) an aston-

ishing number of glides and overhead shots, not one of them pretentious or incorrectly juxtaposed. *An Actor's Revenge* is a version of the novel by Otokichi Mikami, most famously filmed by Ichikawa (q.v.), and its popularity is such that this three-part film was reissued, edited down to normal feature length, as late as 1952. Itami's film is also concerned with derring-do and righting wrongs, one of a series he wrote for their star and producer, Chiezo Kataoka, who plays an all-too-human hero – the comic samurai role which Toshiro Mifune (q.v.) would inherit. The two films also share, beyond their themes, the director Daisuke Ito, who wrote the first with Kinugasa and who was the mentor of Itami. Ito was also the mentor of Hiroshi Inagaki, whose **The Rickshaw Man** (1943) was written by Itami – an old-fashioned tale about a family retainer who brings up his yong master, and known to us best in Inagaki's own, better-developed remake of 1958, with Mifune.

Kajiro Yamamoto (1902–74), though best remembered as the master of Kurosawa (q.v.), also made a number of engaging films. Outstanding among them is **The Loves of Tojuro** (1938), a historical tale of an actor (Kazuo Hasegawa) who, challenged by a newcomer, tries to recapture his audience with a new play written for him by Chikamatsu: that play turns out to be about two lovers who had committed suicide a year earlier, and the actor only finds his way into the role after his leading lady (i.e. a female impersonator) has impersonated an old love. There are notions here of art being stronger than life, and of anything, even tragedy, being grist to the artist's mill: but Yamamoto's strength lies in his suggestion of psychological ambiguity – an ability he shares with Shimazu, whose **Our Neighbour, Miss Yae** (1934) is one of the best of all *shomin-geki* films. It is a gentle study of two families living in a grassy lane on the outskirts of Tokyo. The men drink saki together, their wives gossip, and a schoolgirl daughter and the boy next door may be in the process of turning friendship into love; an unhappily married daughter arrives but the disruption is only temporary. This is the world we know from Ozu, complete to the visits to American films, but Shimazu exercises more humour than Ozu in his family films, showing a faintly ironic detachment which

Sukezo Kuketakaya, Chojuro Kawarazaki and Kanemon Nakemura in *Humanity and Paper Balloons*, a remarkable film directed by Sadao Yamanaka – and the only one of his films extant. It is not unlike 'The Lower Depths', but perhaps both funnier and more powerful: since Kurosawa admired Yamanaka greatly, his later version of Gorki's play may be a homage to him.

almost recalls Jane Austen. Beside it, **The Whole Family Works** (1939), directed by Mikio Naruse, and former assistant to Shimazu, is lacking in spirit. The family in this case is lower on the social scale but, again, we join them at the point when one of the sons has to make the enormous decision between going to college or starting a career. The film is based on a novel by Sunao Tokugawa, a Marxist writer who took to writing about the poor when Marxism was proscribed in the Thirties; Naruse (1905–69) had been born poor, and had had no formal education; he made his name with slapstick comedies, but turned to serious themes as soon as he was able.

Akin to the family films were those centred on children, and the most successful director working in that genre was Hiroshi Shimizu – though he had been making films for fourteen years before his first notable one, **Children in the Wind** (1938). It is slight, but its virtue is that a situation of almost tragic gravity – the sacking from his job of a father and his (wrongful) imprisonment – is seen through the eyes of a child. Parental love is again propounded as a supreme virtue, but in

Children of the Sun (1938), directed by Yutaka Abe, we move closer to social melodrama – a film that may have been inspired by *Boys Town* (q.v.). The setting is a Roman Catholic orphanage in a remote part of Hokkaido, and the piece begins with the arrival of a certified delinquent; it changes with the introduction by one of the teachers of his new wife, formerly sold by her father into prostitution, who has feelings of inadequacy in this environment – but the stilted direction is unable to weld the two themes together.

On the evidence of **The Blossoms Have Fallen** (1938), Tamizo Ishida was not among the most inspired of directors – though the fault may lie with the screenplay of Kaoru Morimoto, at twenty too young, clearly, to tackle the complexities of geisha life. Outside, a rebellion or war is raging; inside the girls moon about their own and the others' problems, wondering what will happen when they are older. Though the film is admired by some, Ishida lacks both the humour and the emotion which Mizoguchi brought to his studies of geisha life.

Another favoured genre was the war film, and Tomotaka Tasaka's **Five Scouts**

231

Japan: The First Masters

(1938) is one of the pre-war Japanese films known in the West – though in view of the differing opinions pronounced it is doubtful whether, in fact, all the commentators have seen it. It is neither a defence of Japan's presence in China nor an apologia; the style is documentary without the fascination of authenticity, and the film seems to have no other purpose than to represent the Sino-Japanese conflict to a local audience, with no sympathy being shown either way. However, if neutrality were the keynote of most Japanese films of this time, **Humanity and Paper Balloons** (1937) reveals its director, Sadao Yamanaka (1909–38), as one of the most committed of film-makers, and one of exceptional talent. Of the twelve films he made, only this one survives (apart from a mutilated copy of one other), but his contemporaries were no less admiring than we. Since this particular film, though set in the eighteenth century, depicts authority as corrupt, uninterested and unjust, it is certain that he upset the military government, which, as a measure of repression, drafted him to the Chinese front, where he died. He was, in fact, a militant left-winger; he specialised in the *jidai-geki,* and was, according to certain commentators, a pessimist and a searcher for truth – either of which may have led him to the same conclusion. But although this film is about a working-class *quartier* of Edo, and the indignities inflicted upon the poor, it does not dwell on misery. It is a film of vivid life, portraying a community sharply divided between the privileged and the oppressed – among whom are Unno (Chojuro Kawarazaki), a *ronin* (i.e. an unemployed samurai) and Shinza (Kanemon Nakemura), who runs gambling parties against the wishes of the local 'Mafia'. Unno merely wants a favour from the local lord, but the same forces destroy both him and Shinza.

Yamanaka's co-producers were the Zenshin-za, a well-known progressive group, backed by the Toho company – at this time locked in bitter rivalry with the other giant of the industry, Shochiku. Toho and Zenshin-za were also responsible for **The Abe Clan** (1938), which sets out to show the life of a samurai at a feudal (1641) court. Life is a matter of honour, betrayal, poison, loyalty, carnage, and as the film builds from its – confused – beginnings to its powerful climax it does not hide its contempt for the samurai system. That must surely have been in defiance of the government, and it is significant that the film's director, Hisatori Kumagai, was among those named to the Americans at the end of the War as one of the industry's Class B criminals – among whom were a number of other prominent left-wingers.

On the evidence of this one film it is difficult to assess Kumagai as clearly as we can Yamanaka. What links Yamanaka, alone of his contemporaries, to the later, great generation of Japanese film-makers is his emotional power – though both Mizoguchi and Naruse would acquire this in time.

The abiding characteristic of the Japanese cinema of the Fifties and Sixties is the examination of both the feudal past and the nature of contemporary society – and both themes were tentatively present in the Thirties. The value of these older, lesser films resides in their portrait of the times, for which we have so few equivalents in the West that we perforce are reminded of Tchekhov, supreme chronicler of the everyday. If the historical films aspire towards the epic, the modern subjects tend to the reverse, and in contrast were filmed on location as much as possible. They demanded tranquillity of style, and the sudden interruption of that by a flurry of intercut montage almost always (and significantly) indicates change – the changing of the seasons or of a man's daily routine. The consistency of this style may not be remarkable, given the modesty and interdependence of these early film-makers, but perhaps when we can see more of their work we shall be able to attribute an individual style – as we can with Ozu and Mizoguchi. What we can already see is an abiding honesty and humanity, in complete opposition to the German film industry, which also was at work in a country preparing for war. In the aftermath of that war, and of the Japanese defeat, their cinema would rise to new heights – though, had we known these early films, its pre-eminence would not have so astonished us.

11

Sex, Crime and Booze: Warner Bros. in the Thirties

AUDIENCE enthusiasm for the Talking Picture was such that the Depression, arriving simultaneously, had little effect on cinema takings. Some producers felt it inappropriate to fill the screen with luxury, but as long as performers opened their mouths and sound emerged the public did not care whether they were in a palace or a hovel, on the prairie or the Place de la Concorde. There was a tendency, therefore, towards simple, cheap settings, the more so because at this volatile time Hollywood was unsure whether the good pickings would endure. There was also a halt to those large endeavours which have always bedevilled the progress of the American film – enterprises mainly characterised by their attempts at moral uplift and often also by their expense.

The films of this time are concerned, rather, with social realism and with gangsters, both subjects often interlocking and frequently described by the publicity department as 'Torn from Today's Headlines'. Not all these films are especially good, though they did recreate a recognisable world of second-rate people; their shortcomings are mainly due to over-haste – or they were made on two-to-three-week schedules in order to bring out more than one film a week. The directors scurried from film to film; the writers might be working on ten films at once, so that *six of them might be credited on any one project. They were not attempting to shake the world, nor did they strive for art; but despite their penchant for melodrama they

*In Hollywood, several names on the writing credit less often means a collaboration than that the project has been passed from one to the other till the producer is satisfied. In later years the credits were often determined by arbitration by the Screenwriters' Guild.

caught absolutely the ambience of their time. The War might not be mentioned, but one knew the men had been through it; the Depression made too obvious a background, yet there had to be a reason why a smart girl like Joan Blondell needed to make it rich before striking back to the mid-West. Everyone was making a fast buck, from the big-time racketeers and bootleggers to hoboes with loaded dice. It was a world of travelling salesmen, dance hostesses, show girls and con-men, each man mauling his mate – where the drinking is heavy and an advancing camera reveals that the singer of a song about 'our cottage small' is a raddled twenty-year-old. From time to time they showed soup queues, but there was no need to do so; one bare, dusty room told at once its tale of dingy passion. Points were made unobtrusively and with speed, and to their economy was added a vitality, a sense of reality and a feeling for the vernacular which make these films, as a body, unique in film history. The factory was humming, and none of the production lines worked more efficiently than that at Warner Bros.

If any one person deserves the credit it is not Jack Warner, who was in charge of production – or if so he was radical for only a brief period of his long tenure. The guiding force would seem to have been Darryl F. Zanuck, production chief from 1929 to 1933, and young and brash enough to have seen the virtue of reflecting the concerns of his audiences. 'Everyone,' said Joan Blondell later, 'got everyone else's juices going', and that probably started in the writers' department, where inspiration came easily and they worked fast (the synopses provided by Publicity often differed considerably from what was on screen). Sometimes credited with the original story and sometimes with the finished script were such as John Bright, Kubec Glasmon, John Monk Saunders, Joseph Jackson, Maude Fulton, Wilson Mizner (subject of a hundred legends), Kenyon Nicholson and W. R. Burnett. They were obviously people who had knocked around a lot: the one consistent quality of their films is their cynicism.

They were also down to earth. *One Way Passage* starts with a sedate trio, each irritated that one of the coins tossed to them has gone in the spittoon, and the soprano interrupts 'If I Had My Way' to hiss 'Third door on the left'; the hero, when arrested, observes to his captor, 'Still on the garlic?' In *Blessed Event* columnist Lee Tracy always refers to crooner Dick Powell as a 'pansy', while Humphrey Bogart says in *Big City Blues,* 'The old town ain't what it used to be. Cops pick up a man, got two guns and a butcher's knife in one pocket, and a powder-puff and lipstick in the other.' In the same film the one sober chorus girl assuages her obvious boredom with 'The Well of Loneliness'. As Dorothy Mackaill sashays through the lobby in *Safe In Hell*, the loungers move their legs to let their crotches 'breathe'; in *Three on a Match,* a magnifying mirror finds Edward Arnold pulling hair from his nostrils. Says Aline MacMahon in *The Mouthpiece,* 'Forget it, kid, it's all in a day's work, as the roadsweeper said to the elephant.'

Even so, a spade was not always called a spade. The girls were 'broads' or 'dames', but there were euphemisms for the words the Hays Office would not permit: 'You had her on a thirty-day trial offer' says James Cagney in *Blonde Crazy,* and 'She's been sister-in-law to the world' observes Mary Astor in *Little Giant.* The women sat around with cigarettes in their mouths, in scanties and rolled stockings, unnecessarily unfrocked, which didn't prevent their men from undressing them mentally and putting their hands in forbidden places. They could be heard squealing in the next room during some pre-breakfast sexual routine; they had grapefruit (memorably) stuffed in their faces, they were kicked and thrown on the floor, only to return for more – provided the pickings were good, the diamonds real. They were unashamedly grasping, and in their musical apotheosis they stripped for the delectation of their

men – if only in silhouette and with iron-clad scanties . . . and even then the men equipped themselves with can-openers. Nor was it a one-way traffic: Ruby Keeler could burst into Dick Powell's dressing room to find him in his B.V.D.s, and though this couple is not otherwise obsessed with sex – unlike their colleagues in this particular film, *42nd Street* – she neither withdraws nor does he grab his pants with undue haste. The end justified the means: Vivienne Osborne in *Two Seconds* bribes the J.P. who thinks Edward G. Robinson too drunk to get married, and that same lady, in *The Dark Horse,* suggests strip poker to Guy Kibbee in order that he lose the election. Death was the next best thing: Frank McHugh perches on a coffin in *I Am a Fugitive From the Chain Gang;* Lew Ayres in *Doorway to Hell* gets a plastic surgeon to work on the corpse of his kid brother for his debut in the morgue. Sex, crime, booze: in Prohibition America they went hand in hand, and Warners celebrated all three. In *Public Enemy* the passing of the Volstead Act is signalled by liquor stores besieged by staggering customers; a couple goes by, the woman carrying the baby since the pram is stacked with drink; and when a bottle is dropped from a limousine an evening-gowned beauty steps out and tries to gather up the pieces.

Then there were the players – those dear dames and those tough mugs. Outstanding among the latter are Edward G. Robinson (1893–1973) and James Cagney (b. 1899), both from the New York stage. Writers and directors were fascinated by their dynamism, and expected audiences to be: and they were. The two men played tough guys, good and bad, with little deviation from film to film, yet they interest us all the time. Watch Cagney after a successful flirtation, and note his cocky little dance step: he had airiness, and Olympian confidence and vitality. Robinson's screen character was more readily defined – vain, dandified and presumptuous. Both were fetching braggarts because they had style and wit. Both would prove themselves masters of many moods, but this was not what Warners asked of them. Their directors include a number of now well-thought-of names as well as some whose post-Warner work is without interest: none at this point shows an individual style, and Roy del Ruth was then the equal of Michael Curtiz. Thematically even the musicals blur into the underworld thrillers, and therefore the following films are discussed in approximate chronological order.

The Dawn Patrol (1930) was directed by Howard Hawks from a story by John Monk Saunders, based on incidents from the latter's own war service. The pair of British boots, from a dead pilot, dropped by the Germans; the gramophone with one record; the young pilot shattered when his friend is killed; the booze, the jagged nerves, the quick camaraderie: such matters were to recur in other films written by Saunders (q.v.). Sadly, the acting – Richard Barthelmess, Douglas Fairbanks Jr – is so much that of the poor early Talkies that the 1938 remake (q.v.) is possibly preferable.

Doorway to Hell (1930), directed by Archie Mayo, is based on a story by Rowland Brown (later a director), 'A Handful of Clouds' (when you are shot 'a handful of clouds grabs you'). Many of the guys *are* shot – by gangland boss Lew Ayres, who is obsessed with Napoleon, all things military, his kid brother and himself, in reverse order. This performance is hysterical rather than neurotic, and the film was completely overshadowed by a more accomplished variation on the same theme, released a few days later, **Little Caesar** (1930), directed by Mervyn LeRoy. The boss is again Italian, but the subject is gang warfare, so popular at the time than Robinson's rise to power from his beginnings as a grab-happy little tough with a preening love of ostentation. The Mafia is not mentioned, but the clues are there; and those who knew enough of Al Capone, the source of Edward G. Robinson's 'Rico', might guess at his homosexuality from the latter's attitude towards his former dancing partner (Douglas Fairbanks Jr). W. R. Burnett wrote the novel on which the screenplay was based.

Burnett and John Monk Saunders were responsible for the original story of **The Finger Points** (1931), directed by John Francis Dillon. Here Barthelmess, spectacularly miscast, is the crusading journalist who turns to his assailants when his newspaper refuses to pay his hospital expenses, and thus becomes the tool of the underworld – as represented by Clark Gable in spats and bowler hat. Before the year was out Gable (q.v.), together with James Cagney, would transform the accepted

The superiority of *Little Caesar* over other gangster pictures was explained by Richard Watts in *The New York Herald Tribune*: 'by pushing into the background the usual romantic conventions of the theme and concentrating on characterisation rather than plot, there emerges not only an effective and rather chilling melodrama, but also what is sometimes known as a Document.' And, he added, 'Chiefly it is made important by the genuinely brilliant performance that Edward G. Robinson contributes to the title-role.'

image of the Hollywood leading man.

Cagney has one of the most enlivening moments in all cinema when, directed by William A. Wellman, in **Other Men's Women** (1931) – also known as *The Steel Highway* – he arrives at a dance hall, sheds his oil skins, chats up the hat-check girl, and then moves across the foyer with a hop, skip and a jump, his arms in the air, grabbing his girl as he reaches the dancers. The film itself is an engaging marital drama, set among railroad workers, with Mary Astor as the suburban wife and Grant Withers as the lodger, a high-spirited and amorous drunk, both of them lying to her husband (Regis Toomey) as to their feelings for each other.

The Public Enemy (1931) was also directed by Wellman, who observed later, 'The thing that made it a success was one word – Cagney.' Written by Glasmon and Bright, formerly reporters in Chicago, the film detailed the rise of an all-American

The scene in *The Last Flight* where the four dedicated drinkers – John Mack Brown, Elliott Nugent, David Manners and Richard Barthelmess – meet Nikki (Helen Chandler). The champagne-glass contains the false-teeth of someone who said 'he was going out to biff somebody', which seems reasonable to them. Nikki's response to most things is 'I'll take vanilla' or 'It seemed like a good idea at the time.' They all agree on booze: 'It'll make you laugh or cry.'

gangster (Cagney) from his days as trouble maker at a boys' club. To Andre Sennwald in *The New York Times*, it was 'just another gangster film', a view seldom echoed now. For much is memorable: Cagney and his pal, Edward Woods, tiptoeing to peer into their friend's coffin; their fear when caught on their first job; Woods being gunned down, the noise of machine-gun fire being drowned by a coal delivery; the final image of Cagney, a corpse, swaying in the doorway before falling towards his beloved mother. Then there are their women including Jean Harlow (q.v.), who says, not altogether carelessly, 'Oh Tommy, I could love you to death', which tells us something about the women who loved these gangsters, and something about the audiences which went to revel in this new breed of anti-hero.

The Maltese Falcon (1931), directed by del Ruth and the first of the three Warner versions of Dashiell Hammett's detective novel, was much admired by contemporaries for its fidelity to the original.

Aficionados of the 1941 version (q.v.) will note that Sam Spade sleeps with Ruth Wonderly, and that his relationship with his partner's wife is equally unambiguous. Ricardo Cortez, with insolent smile and hooded eyes, is Spade; Bebe Daniels is brittle but clearly guilty as Ruth. As Gutman, Dudley Digges is seedy, but not as threatening as Sydney Greenstreet.

Smart Money (1931), directed by Alfred E. Green, concerns Nick the Barber (Robinson), a small-town gambler whose syndicate sends him to the city to take on the big boys: double-crossed and double-crossing, he soon owns half the gambling joints in town, half of high society, and all of the D.A. Cagney is in support, in the only film he made with Robinson, and it is a pleasure to see them together.

Night Nurse (1931), directed by Wellman, has Barbara Stanwyck (q.v.) in the title role, a Depression-hit girl who badly needs a job. She also tends bootlegger Ben Lyon, rooms with knowing and once-eager Joan Blondell ('I was afraid the

236

hospital would burn down before I got here. Now I have to watch myself with matches,') and who takes on the real villain, the chauffeur (Gable). She also, in this darkest of Warner films, nurses baby girls while their mother, drunk or drugged, lolls on a bed with her equally stoned lover.

The Last Flight (1931) was directed by William Dieterle (1893–1972), who, as we have seen, had moved from acting to directing; perhaps as it was his first film in English – under his Warner contract – the delivery is stilted, but that hardly weakens the superb screenplay by John Monk Saunders, based on his novel 'Single Lady' and identical with incidents in Hemingway's 'The Sun Also Rises'. Saunders's expatriate drinkers are led by Cary (Barthelmess), and there tags along with them Nikki (Helen Chandler), trading flippancy for flippancy, and Frink (Walter Byron), who, like Hemingway's Robert Cohn, is based on Harold Loeb. Except for the last-named – a member of the Wandering Hands Club, as they explain – their attitude towards her is asexual. On a whim they troop off to Portugal – the obvious choice, since they had so often wondered what was 'doing there tonight' – and one of them is wounded in the bullring: 'I'm glad I wore my new blue shorts. I'll be a big success in hospital.' Another is mortally wounded, still another shoots the unspeakable Frink and disappears. Left alone with Cary, Nikki makes what might almost be a declaration of love. 'Without them, nothing's left,' he replies. 'Comradeship. That's all we had.' The attitudes expressed would not find their way into films again till the Sixties, though the ineffable flippancy is echoed in *Laughter* (q.v.), written by Donald Ogden Stewart, who coincidentally was the prototype for another character – in 'The Sun Also Rises'. One can only speculate on how much is autobiographical. It is a portrait of people in a vacuum – and the most authentic study we are ever likely to get of the lost generation, infinitely more significant and enjoyable than the Hemingway novel. At the time its failure was complete: had it been a success the history of movies might have been very different.

Audiences undoubtedly found it easier to relate to **The Star Witness** (1931), about an ordinary family caught up with gangsters, and the film's throb of indignation concerning these innocents caught in the crossfire still seems genuine. **Love is a Racket** (1932) has a spendthrift nymphomaniac heiress (Frances Dee) throwing herself at an unprincipled columnist (Fairbanks Jr). She is encouraged by her aunt (Cecil Cunningham), and hindered by a gangster (Lyle Talbot), who hopes to muscle in. Wellman directed both films. His most sophisticated offering at this time is **Safe in Hell** (1931), from a play by Houston Branch which is one of several copies of 'Rain'. The loose, lost lady is Dorothy Mackaill, making a living, as she puts it, 'the only way I could', as the one white woman in a Caribbean hotel patronised by men as frustrated as they are crooked. Wellman also managed exotica – Chinese-style – in **The Hatchet Man** (1932), set in San Francisco at the time of the Tong War, and based on the old Belasco play, with Edward G. Robinson in the second of his usual two roles, the decent man driven to murder.

After *Little Caesar* Robinson's most famous early role was in **Five Star Final** (1931), as a newspaper editor, a tough old hand who claims that 'ideals won't put a patch on your pants'. He learns otherwise, of course, after victimising an innocent family: Mervyn LeRoy's sloppy direction foreshadows his later, sentimental work at M-G-M (q.v.). Nevertheless, Robinson has fun with the editor's cohorts: his secretary (Aline MacMahon), whom he has never thought of as a woman, let alone a sexual object; his unctuous handyman reporter (Boris Karloff), a one-time divinity student now as lecherous and as unprincipled as his boss; and a Jewish reporter (George E. Stone) of simple zeal.

The title of **Two Seconds** (1932), directed by LeRoy, refers to the amount of time Robinson has to relive his life as he sits in the electric chair – a mundane life till Shirley (Vivienne Osborne) comes between him and his buddy (Preston Foster). She soon drops claims to gentility and culture – 'Since when did you ask a dollar who was his father?' – and is the ideal denizen of the rooming houses and dance halls of this masterpiece of sleaziness. Robinson did a variation of the same plot in **Tiger Shark** (1932), directed by Howard Hawks, a film mainly notable for its setting – the San Diego waterfront – and its more forthright intimations of homosexuality, e.g. dying, Robinson has a caress for his pal (Richard Arlen), but none for the wife who has actually deceived him.

Cagney also strutted his stuff in vehicles designed for that purpose. **Blonde Crazy** (1931) and **Taxi!** (1932) were both directed by del Ruth. The former concerns a bellboy who moves from getting bootleg gin for guests to the shakedown game, making a bid for the big time by teaming up with one of its leaders (Louis Calhern): 'Honest men are scarcer than feathers on a frog' he says when double-crossed. The latter film concerns a cab driver whose marriage – to Loretta Young – is threatened when he becomes involved in a war between rival cab companies. In del Ruth's **Blessed Event** (1932) Lee Tracy replaced Cagney (currently fighting with his bosses over salary) in the role of a Winchell-like columnist who specialises in news of pregnancies and wages war against a crooner (Dick Powell) while a racketeer wages war against him. Like most Cagney vehicles, it is a ramshackle tale, notable for its minor characters, dovetailed in for laughs or thrills. The constant repetition of themes is best exemplified by Hawks's **The Crowd Roars** (1932), which thereafter Warners remade endlessly, with variations: in this original version a racing driver (Cagney) tries to keep his kid brother (Eric Linden) away from the horses and the dames which the tracks attract.

If Robinson and Cagney were the studio's most popular stars, its prestige actors remained John Barrymore and George Arliss. The latter, after a popular replay of an earlier stage and screen success, *Disraeli* (1929), continued in new versions of roles he had performed in his youth, and thus was sixty-three when he played the title role in **Alexander Hamilton** (1931), a gentleman who, at the time of the action actually was in his early thirties. The film is mainly notable for Alan Mowbray's performance as Washington, one of the few times the first President has been portrayed on the screen. Acting for Arliss consisted of twitching watery eyes to express cuteness – called for, its seems, at all times – and moving his mouth like a ventriloquist's dummy. He is fairly restrained in **The Man Who Played God** (1932), as a world-famous pianist whose sudden deafness takes him through atheism, philanthropy (towards Depression-hit couples in Central Park) and finally to reconversion to Christianity. Arliss's credited director on these and

most of his films was John G. Adolphi, but according to Bette Davis (q.v.), the intense young ingenue whose career began to flower when cast in this film, Arliss was really his own director.

Barrymore, too, had a success with an old melodrama, **Svengali** (1931), directed without inspiration by Archie Mayo. Michael Curtiz directed the superior follow-up, **The Mad Genius** (1931), and both films are notable for Anton Grot's extravagant decor. The early Warner Talkies owe much of their distinctive look to Grot. That look was predominantly sour, but sourness and extravagance, when applied to tenement stairs and attics, can be memorable. Curtiz's style is still basically European, very much at home in such settings, and he places his camera imaginatively – and too briefly to be considered pretentious. *The Mad Genius* is further notable in both rehashing the plot of the earlier film and using as its basis factual material – both favourite ploys in the Warner writers' department, and much approved of by their bosses. Though nominally based on a play called 'The Idol', its central situation is recognisably the relationship between Diaghilev and Nijinsky, in which role Donald Woods is far from convincing.

Union Depot (1932) is one of the forerunners of *Grand Hotel*, a dioramic study of a railroad terminus in Depression America. Passing through the terminus are two hoboes (Guy Kibbee and Fairbanks Jr), an inebriated gentleman (Frank McHugh), an out-of-work dancer (Joan Blondell), the aged, crippled sex maniac (George Rosener) who is pursuing her, and every ethnic group in the U.S. The film was directed by Alfred E. Green who that same year also made a bright political satire, **The Dark Horse**: after deadlock at the gubernatorial convention a man (Kibbee) of sublime stupidity is nominated, and his hustling campaign manager (Warren William) is sprung from jail to launch him. Not daunted by the choice, he declares of his candidate, 'Every time he opens his mouth he subtracts from the total sum of human knowledge . . . We're going to convince the voters that they've got someone of their own level.'

Ruth Chatterton (q.v.) was one of the former Paramount stars acquired by Warners via an underhand deal with an agent;

the others were Kay Francis and William Powell, and none of the three quite fitted into the Warner Bros. world. The studio decided to go into something with more tone – **Jewel Robbery** (1932), set in Vienna, with Powell as a thief and Francis as a (married) Countess. The director, Dieterle, was, however, no Lubitsch – a fact doubly proved when Lubitsch issued a similar tale a few months later, *Trouble in Paradise* (q.v.).

With the same co-stars, **One Way Passage** (1932) is the story of a doomed shipboard romance, he a convicted murderer and she dying of an incurable disease, drinking Paradise cocktails and leaving the stems of their broken glasses intertwined on the bar. This dotty idyll is directed with conviction by Tay Garnett, its stardust counterpointed by Miss MacMahon as a phoney Countess, formerly known as Barrelhouse Betty, and Frank McHugh as a larcenous drunk. The critic Kenneth Tynan once observed of the movies of this time that 'with the passage of time, the profundities peel away and only the basic trivialities remain to enchant us', and *One Way Passage*, never profound, is enchanting – along with *The Last Flight* and *Hard to Handle* (q.v.) the best of all the unsung movies in this group of films.

Also among the more relishable of these Warner offerings are **The Mouthpiece** (1932), directed by James Flood and Elliott Nugent, and **The Strange Love of Molly Louvain** (1932), directed by Curtiz. The former is one of the most immoral of these many moral tales, set in the usual milieu of deviousness, fraud, fooling and booze – and the story itself is the familiar one of the idealist who finds he can make it big once he compromises. Warren William is the assistant D.A. who finds that juries are less impressed by truth than by cajolery, as a consequence of which he becomes New York's most celebrated lawyer – with a strictly criminal clientele; Sidney Fox is his secretary, matching guile for guile as she wards off his attempts at seduction.

In the second film, the strange love of Molly Louvain (Ann Dvorak) is that for her illegitimate child. Deserted by his father, she accepts an invitation to try on some silk stockings, and soon she is soused on a combination of beer and champagne, her heart breaking as she bangs out a wild rendition of 'Penthouse Serenade'. How-

ever, she decides to enjoy her new status, reckoning without the medical student (Richard Cromwell) who dumbly worships her, and the reporter (Lee Tracy) who recognises her as his sort: 'You're one of the tinsel girls,' he says happily.

The critics of the time were less appreciative than we might be today: 'Tedious and distasteful', said Mordaunt Hall in *The New York Times,* in fact discussing **Three on a Match** (1932), which follows the fluctuating fortunes of three girls, Blondell, Davis and Dvorak. The latter leaves her stuffy husband (Warren William) for a gangster, takes to drink, and comes to her senses when her child is kidnapped. (Kidnappings were big news in 1932.) **Big City Blues** (1932), about the hick (Eric Linden) who learns about life fast on his first trip to New York, evoked no warmer response from the press, but the director of both these films, LeRoy, aroused widespread admiration with **I Am a Fugitive From the Chain Gang** (1932) – and certainly on this occasion, if no other, he was the equal of any director then working. Based on a novel by Robert E. Burns, in turn based on fact, the film caused sufficient outcry for Congress to revise the penal laws relating to chain gangs. A returning doughboy (Paul Muni), rather than go back to his routine job, decides to use the engineering skills he learnt in the army: but the job doesn't last. In a doss house he meets a man who makes

Paul Muni, right, in perhaps the best of the 'Social Concern' movies made by Warner Bros., *I Am a Fugitive From the Chain Gang* (1932). He has in fact just escaped, and is welcomed in Chicago by a former colleague on the chain gang, Allen Jenkins. The double bed was a standard fixture in Hollywood films of this period, and if it was never seen in use the dialogue made clear that it had been or would be: indeed, the blonde, Noel Francis, is a kindly gesture on Jenkins's part to a man in need of relaxation.

239

This aggressively eupeptic juvenile and this coy little chorine are not what one remembers best from Warners' Depression musicals: or are they? – their very awkwardness is part of the charm of the pieces, and an effective contrast to the very knowing show business types who surround them. Dick Powell and Ruby Keeler in *Gold Diggers of 1933*, and, yes, her outfit is made of metal: the solution to *that* is provided by a 'baby' (Billy Barty), who turns up with some equally lewd ideas in the 'Honeymoon Hotel' number in *Footlight Parade*.

him the innocent instrument in a stick-up: and that gets him twelve years on a chain gang. He escapes to become eventually one of Chicago's leading citizens, but though he has been promised a pardon he has unfortunately talked to reporters about the system . . . The script is very clear on the divisions of society, on the haves and the have-nots: the former are corrupt and the latter victimised. The film became a rallying cry during the Depression. It remains often subtle, and always powerful, to its unforgettable, hammering finish.

Cabin in the Cotton (1932) handles the same theme, the exploitation of the poor by the rich, but in this case the poor are the cotton pickers of the South. Barthelmess is the educated peasant who is both pawn and arbitrator till the corruption of the landowners becomes evident. Curtiz directed, and in **20,000 Years in Sing Sing** (1933) he handled a plea for prison reform, putting forward a case for humane and reform-

conscious wardens. Davis is the moll who kills in self-defence, and Spencer Tracy (in a role meant for Cagney) the guy who takes the rap – a miscarriage of justice which in real life even the most backward jury would never have perpetrated. Curtiz also showed gusto on **Doctor X** (1932), occasioned by the success of Universal's horror films, and **The Mystery of the Wax Museum** (1933). In both Lionel Atwill plays a mad professor in a pleasing mixture of Victorian gothic and gadgetry.

Employees Entrance (1933), directed by del Ruth, is a study of life in a department store, and of the manager (Warren William) who drives himself and his staff beyond reason, relaxing only to give a bed to a girl (Loretta Young) badly in need of a meal – thus bringing into the open the inference of all these films, that sexual favours may be traded for a full stomach; later, however, without that motivation – since she has married in the meantime – she elects to stay the night, even if, to appease the Hays Office, she is supposedly drunk.

This view of man as predator and woman as victim was sustained in Wellman's **Frisco Jenny** (1933), a typical Ruth Chatterton vehicle and in fact a rehash of her most famous film, *Madame X*. Warners, however, were finally prepared to admit that women might be as sexually motivated as men, and as the chorus girls assemble to audition in **42nd Street** (1933), directed by Lloyd Bacon, they gossip about such matters as the friend who earns $45 a month but sends $100 home to her mother. The studio had first put such young ladies on the screen four years earlier, in *Gold Diggers of Broadway*, but as they revived them, in this film and in **Gold Diggers of 1933**, directed by LeRoy, they were considerably more mercenary. In the interim Warners had virtually killed off the film musical with its series of operettas – but after an absence of a year or so the genre was resuscitated by these two immortal movies. Both concern the putting on of shows, the lecherous 'angels', the driving producers, the temperamental stars, and the boys and girls who hoof all day and night rather than join the breadline. *Gold Diggers* concludes with a mawkish but moving tribute to the ex-doughboys who had not avoided the breadline, 'My Forgotten Man' – one of the flamboyant, vulgar and enjoyable production numbers devised by Busby Berkeley in

Mary Brian, Ruth Donnelly and James Cagney with two unnamed actors playing detectives in *Hard to Handle* – a title that reflected Warners' relations with Cagney rather than anything in the film. The best thing in the film – better even than Cagney – is Miss Donnelly. Miss Brian is her daughter, and their similar costumes represent not only a common hedge against the Depression, but their like-mindedness in matters concerning money and Cagney: they are as covetous of the one as they are suspicious of the other.

conjunction with the composer, Harry Warren, and the lyricist, Al Dubin. The other songs may be read as invitations to sex – 'I'm Young and Healthy', 'Shuffle Off to Buffalo', 'You're Getting to Be a Habit With Me', 'Petting in the Park': but then in both films, sex is as much a preoccupation as money. However, as befits the demotic approach, the two films are also built round hard work, with attendant sourness and disillusion. The total effect is exhilarating: both films are sharply-paced, and one could not cut a line from either without spoiling them.

Apart from the occasional stock, we see neither 42nd Street nor Broadway – in contrast to the boardwalks and alleys where Cagney operates in **Hard to Handle** (1933). However, it is the same venal world. He runs (literally: to escape from his victims) from promoter of dance-marathons to New York advertising and P.R., all gall and guts, with a host of ingenious ideas as to how bright have-nots like himself can beat the Depression. To his prospective mother-in-law (Ruth Donnelly) he *is* the Depression, and her waxing and waning towards him, as his fortunes fluctuate, contribute towards virtual non-stop hilarity. LeRoy's direction emphasises both the satire and the sanity of the script. However, Roosevelt had been elected, and conditions were improving: Cagney became the crusading warden of a reform school in **The Mayor of Hell** (1933), directed by Mayo and inspired by the Soviet *Road to Life,* and in **Little Giant** (1933), directed by del Ruth, bootlegger Robinson decides to retire and acquire culture – only to find that Santa Barbara high society isn't quite ready for him. Prohibition was a dead duck, and this charming comedy begins with a montage of reactions to the new President.

Nevertheless, conditions in the country could not improve overnight, and like

241

In view of the plethora of money-grabbing heroines in the Depression era movies, we must assume that audiences found them at least half-admirable – though what Barbara Stanwyck was up to in *Baby Face* must have been in the mind of Will H. Hays when he strengthened the Production Code later in the year. Stanwyck, here in a factory-workers' speakeasy (with Nat Pendleton), is a part-time hooker to start with, and she has absolutely no intention of remaining in this milieu.

Cagney in *Hard to Handle* Barbara Stanwyck in **Baby Face** (1933) has a very personal way of overcoming them. Her method is to climb the ladder of success wrong by wrong – a not inappropriate expression, since her tale is the movie equivalent of the tabloid confession. She never stops to justify her conduct, be it the lie large or the look carnal – both of which are small weapons in her armoury. She ends back where she started, though she will surely try again: as directed by Alfred E. Green, this beguiling little tale deserved a sequel.

And yet these films are so much alike that they form a sequence. Their consistency is astonishing. Born out of star vehicles, the need to keep the distribution offices busy and the capitalist urge, they offer a pungent and mainly truthful account of America at a low point in its history. As we shall see in the next chapter, the other studios achieved nothing comparable. Warners did not set out to chronicle the Depression, nor did they ever quite abandon the concept of a varied batch of entertainments, but from their first Talkie successes – *The Dawn Patrol, Little Caesar* – was born a concern in accord with the editorials of most of the nation's newspapers. Consequently the studio gathered a group of writers able to give voice to that concern and a team of players more at ease in bar rooms than in marble halls. Success bred success, and since Warners throughout its history was prone to repeat itself, it was providential that it had perforce to abandon the gangster movie just when those same editorials accused Hollywood of glamorising crime. On behalf of the studios, the Hays Office pointed out that the films themselves proffered the message that crime did not pay; the leader writers retorted that Hollywood's only solution to the Depression was crime or fantasy, at which point most of the studios chose to forget the whole business. Warners, however, continued to look the matter squarely in the eye, be it in a modest entertainment feature like *Employees Entrance*, or in a self-confessed document like *I Am a Fugitive From the Chain Gang*; then, with something like genius, the studio made three further musicals designed to cheer patrons without letting them forget the soup kitchens round the corner. It was the success of *I Am a Fugitive* . . . and those three musicals which brought to a close this remarkable series; concern with social conditions the studio may have had, but it was also anxious, in a time of recession, to report good returns to its stockholders.

Heroes for Sale (1933) poses the problem of Tom Holmes (Barthelmess), an ex-doughboy with steel splinters in his back, an affliction which leads first to morphine addiction, and then to theft. Cured in hospital he is able to make a new start in a factory, and after many vicissitudes becomes successful; but there is labour unrest in the city, and this encourages the anti-Red squad, whose members recall Tom's Communist affiliations during previous agitation. He joins the freight-hopping, jobless, but combats pessimism: 'Did you read Roosevelt's inaugural speech? . . . It takes more than one blow to knock out twenty million people.' Because of this note of hope, the ending is the opposite of that of *I Am a Fugitive* . . . , but where that film indicted a system, but no individual and no class, *Heroes* accuses the capitalists, or what we now call the Establishment. The director, Wellman, and the writers, Robert Lord and Wilson Mizner, may have been *commercially* indignant, and they certainly hedge their bets on Communism by making Tom's Red friend (Robert Barrat) both 'daffy' and 'a maniac'; they also leave a large hole in the plot, but they are entirely honest in their depiction of the world of the dispossessed.

Wellman went on to make **Wild Boys of the Road** (1933), about children from good homes who take to the freights to avoid being a burden on their impoverished parents. He avoids melodrama, managing a portrait of the rootless, shifting stowaways, living in a world of rape, and easy murder, one in which no head is turned in protest, a world in which the youngsters search for that reward best expressed by Judy Garland (q.v.), when the Depression was over, in 'Over the Rainbow'.

Wild Boys was admired but *Heroes for Sale* was an outright failure. The history of the American film is littered with films which so much offended the right-wing, asking it to face unpalatable facts about itself, that they were thrown on the scrapheap – both adversely reviewed and unable to get bookings. Since so much in this particular film

still astonishes – the Establishment plotting to destroy a worker, the anti-Red squad shown as bully-boys – we may be sure that such was its fate. Barthelmess, moreover, had lost his popularity, and that fact could not have helped two further films concerned with injustice, **Massacre** (1934), directed by Alan Crosland, and **A Modern Hero** (1934), Pabst's only American film. The serious nature of Crosland's film is emphasised by the fact that it was shot almost entirely on location. Barthelmess plays an Indian-born rodeo star made suddenly aware of the ways of his people, and cruelly exposed to their exploitation by white officials; Ann Dvorak is the Indian girl he meets, educated at the Haskell Institute, and long resigned to such facts. In Pabst's film, Barthelmess is on the other side, a bare back rider in a circus who, by virtue of a lucky investment – and a number of compliant women – becomes a successful manufacturer. Both Pabst and Warners were fond of sexual frankness and adept at seedy detail; the basic subject, on this occasion as taken from a novel by Louis Bromfield, was typical of both, but the revised Hays Code was beginning to bite and Pabst, loathing the compromises, refused to work in Hollywood again. That subject was similar to Fox's *The Power and the Glory* (q.v.), and as that foreshadows

James Cagney, Allen Jenkins and Alan Dinehart in *Jimmy the Gent*, directed in 1934 by Michael Curtiz, with Cagney as enterprising as ever in the usual precarious job – in this case an entrepreneur who makes his money finding heirs to fortune. The girl, alternately loving and sceptical, is Bette Davis, at the start of her long career as one of the screen's outstanding actresses.

Sex, Crime and Booze: Warner Bros. in the Thirties

The Busby Berkeley girls in the 'By a Waterfall' number in *Footlight Parade*. Since the patterns that Berkeley made with girls are *sui generis*, there is every reason why his name above all should be associated with the Warner Bros. musicals of this time. However, since he merely copied – if sometimes elaborating upon – the routines he had already done for Goldwyn and M-G-M, the extent of his creative contribution may be questioned, as it has, indeed, by other Warners alumni, who have claimed that the numbers were the result of collaboration between the whole production team.

Orson Welles's first American film, so does this his second, *The Magnificent Ambersons* (q.v.): all four films concern the corrupting effects of power.

Warners' third Depression musical was **Footlight Parade** (1933), directed by Bacon, and where his *42nd Street* took its tone from Warner Baxter as the producer, driving and hard-faced, so this takes its tone from Cagney in the same role, driving but chipper, quippy and optimistic. There is Blondell as his neglected, ever-loving secretary ('You don't like *anybody*' he snaps. 'If only you knew' she sobs); Ruth Donnelly as the impresario's wife, promoting her latest gigolo ('He's waiting outside, ready and eager to start his career'); Claire Dodd as a scheming vamp; Frank McHugh as the hard-working dance director; and, again, Kibbee as the impresario and Ruby Keeler and Dick Powell as the ingenues. The film, like its predecessors, is alive to the glamour of show business, with a chorus for ever rehearsing in the background, a pianist trying out the songs, and someone – usually Cagney – barking out orders; there is the same approach to morals ('Outside, Countess – as long as there are sidewalks you've got a job'), but perhaps a heightened vulgarity in Berkeley's numbers. 'Shanghai Lil', a melange of opium dens, tinsel blondes, sailors and red-white-and-blue patriotism – not the least of it in Cagney's dance – is pop-art at its most enduring.

Wonder Bar (1934), directed by Bacon, stars Al Jolson in his stage role of night club M.C. – a venue, it seems, for tourists to rub shoulders with gigolos and dance hostesses, slipping in and out of melodrama. It is also a centre for various kinds of love – adulterous, unrequited, deviant, criminal

and, above all, purchasable. This one bypassed the new Code (though a blackface song, 'Goin' to Heaven on a Mule', offends taste), but **Dames,** directed by Ray Enright, did not. Warners advertised it as their 'Gold Diggers of 1934', but the new Code had drawn the studio's fangs. Since their movies had 'exposed' the same inequalities in the American system that the press picked upon, Hays could point to it as the most responsible of the studios, and he tightened the Code to curb the Misses Harlow and West rather than these gold diggers. Joan Blondell was the Warners' symbol of the Depression – never fazed, never down for long. She was a smiler and a soft touch, but clear-eyed. In *Dames,* as a scheming showgirl, her heartlessness has gone. The earlier gold diggers were motivated by mercenary considerations, but now they acted for society or 'the show'. Hugh Herbert is the puritan converted to boozing, gambling and showgirls, a consistent theme in these films; but where *Gold Diggers of 1933* offered such men as dupes, discovering a new life style, Herbert is merely a harmless clown. The Warner era of venality and venery was over.

It was not merely that the new Code was in force and that Zanuck had moved on to found 20th Century Pictures (q.v.); it was not merely that the studio bosses – the brothers Warner themselves – now looked towards the literary adaptations which spelt prestige at the other studios. Warner pictures would, indeed, retain demotic themes for many years yet. But the most notable thing about the Warner product between 1930 and 1934 is that no one knew at the time how good most of it was.

12

Hollywood before the Code

WARNER BROS. did not have sole prerogative on proletarian subjects during the Depression – they were simply the most insistent. Other studios continued with a mixture of wish – fulfilment and films which reflected the problems of their audience. The coming of Sound meant – words being a prerequisite – an even greater dependence on novels and plays, many of them written for a public more sophisticated than the old movie audiences. The stage players flooding into Hollywood were not geared to interpret the usual mindless entertainments, being in many cases too mature in age, and the new writers brought in were not interested in penning them. The Western and the swashbuckler, their spirit of adventure at odds with the mood of the time, went into decline. The young still went to the cinema, but, unlike later generations, *en famille*: while their parents waited for the latest gangster film, they were entertained by the increasingly diversified supporting programmes.

The only other studio besides Warners to show consistent interest in the working class was Paramount – even if their characters seldom stayed long at the counter or the work bench. An exception was Clara Bow in **The Saturday Night Kid** (1929), a remake of *Love 'em and Leave 'em*. She was meant to provide someone with whom all the footsore shopgirls of the world could identify; hence the title. As directed by Edward Sutherland, she is a clerk sacrificing everything for the sake of a conniving younger sister. Audiences had indeed increasingly identified with Bow, to the extent that her popularity fell away when headlines disclosed that she was in life much like the scandalous Clara of her early films.

Paramount saw the more mousy Sylvia Sidney as a replacement, defending her mobster father (Guy Kibbee) in **City Streets** (1931), directed by Rouben Mamoulian. 'What have your ideas got you?' she asks her boyfriend (Gary Cooper), who works in a funfair, 'Racketeers are smart, not dumb like some people.' Duly admonished, he joins the mob – not reforming till the fade-out.

Working Girls (1931) focuses on two out-of-town sisters (Judith Wood and Dorothy Hall) out to find jobs while fighting off men, and is set in one of the all-female rooming houses so common in films at this time; the director was Dorothy Arzner (b. 1900), to date the most successful of Hollywood's handful of women directors. Her **Honor Among Lovers** (1931) does have a heroine (Claudette Colbert) who keeps a maid on a secretary's salary – but she is an executive secretary. Her boss (Fredric March) is a philanderer, and the opening sequence – an office picnic lunch, with him advancing and her keeping him at bay, but both with mutual respect – is among the wittiest in films of this period.

Carole Lombard (q.v.) and Nancy Carroll also played working girls. In **No Man of Her Own** (1932) Lombard is a small town librarian, plucky but unlucky enough to marry a gambler (Clark Gable): 'A rather usual sort of melodrama,' Mordaunt Hall commented in *The New York Times*, but though without exceptional direction – by Wesley Ruggles – it is unusually entertaining today. In **Dangerous Paradise** (1931) Carroll is a woebegone singer with a particularly butch ladies' band and Richard Arlen is the lone trader who mistakenly believes her a whore. This very loose adaptation of Conrad's 'Victory' has direction by William Wellman which makes much of moonlit verandahs, low dives, desperation and a fine covey of villains. In **Hot Saturday** (1932), directed by William A. Seiter, Carroll is a suburban working girl torn between her hard-working geologist sweetheart (Randolph Scott) and the wealthy local representative (Cary Grant) of the post-jazz generation, spending Saturday afternoons picnicking with bootleg gin.

Fast and Loose (1930), a remake of *The Best People,* directed by Fred Newmeyer, indicates impatience with the irresponsibility of the young rich, and gold diggers are 'exposed' in **Girls About Town** (1931), in which two of them (Kay Francis, Lilyan Tashman) entertain visiting firemen for large fees. George Cukor (b. 1899), a Broadway director new to Hollywood, was unable to reconcile the comic and romantic elements, but he did better with **Tarnished Lady** (1931), about an impoverished member (Tallulah Bankhead) of the Four Hundred who marries for money and lives to regret it, through motherhood, street walking and store clerking before coming to her senses. And it might be said that **Devil and the Deep** (1932) also indicts the follies of the rich, as Miss Bankhead leaves her paranoid commander husband (Charles Laughton) to spend a night in the desert with his new second in command (Gary Cooper); Marion Gering directed.

Chief among the ladies who sinned and suffered for Paramount was Ruth Chatterton (1893–1961), who brought warmth and a degree of truth to the roles she was required to play – in what were then considered sophisticated entertainments by the trade, critics and audiences alike. However, **Sarah and Son** (1930) is merely a mother-love drama, with Chatterton as a German-born vaudeville hoofer who becomes a famed diva in order to fight for her son; in **Anybody's Woman** (1930), also directed by Arzner, she is an out-of-work chorus girl married to a drunken lawyer (Clive Brook). Dozens of films were predicated on this situation (the nuptials taking place while one of the parties is too drunk to comprehend) but this one does offer a convincing portrait of the subsequent marriage: two ill-suited people trying to adjust and making each other unhappier all the while. In John Cromwell's

Unfaithful (1931), Chatterton discovers that her husband is just that, so she drinks cocktails, sings 'Mama's in the Doghouse Now' in her frillies, and flirts with a nice artist (Paul Lukas). This film is unusual in that she starts wealthy and stays wealthy. Society had a remarkable mobility in Paramount's films, and, in general, the higher anyone moves the more venal the crowd. There were, in real life, stockbrokers on the dole and bootleggers in the penthouse, but if this portrait of a society in flux carries its own conviction that was not, necessarily, the prime motive: Paramount sold dreams, and it was *de rigeur* that the female star change her cotton frocks and cotton stockings for satins and silks. The Warner ladies often managed without – just as their movies sometimes managed without happy endings: in perhaps just a couple of these Paramount films is a happy ending actually justified.

A happy fade-out is not anticipated in **Behind the Make-Up** (1930), directed by Arzner and Robert Milton, an unpretentious story of two show business figures, the 'giver' (Hal Skelly, as type cast in his few films) and the 'taker', who makes off with wife, act and savings. The role of the taker was played by William Powell (b. 1892), who became a star in **Street of Chance** (1930), in which he is a big time gambler who sacrifices himself so that his younger brother shall not go the same way; in **For the Defense** (1930) he is a shady lawyer who prefers Sing Sing to seeing the woman he loves embroiled in a scandal. David O. Selznick produced both, Oliver H. P. Garett contributed to the screenplays, and Cromwell directed (q.v.); Lothar Mendes replaced the latter on **Ladies' Man** (1931), which ends with gigolo Powell thrown to death by the husband of one of his mistresses. If you mixed the reels of these films you would be mystified but not disconcerted – for you would recognise the same street corners, the same bars, the same hotel rooms and lobbies, both luxurious and threadbare; the leading ladies and the supporting players, when not the same, are interchangeable. Powell wears the same clothes, he plays the same role – the dapper, proper man of the world, whose connections, at the very least, are shady; to himself, however, and to his friends, his honour is as unimpeachable as his cravat. Audiences might let him die – he was too

247

suave, too flippant, to be allowed to live – but they could admire him along the way.

Fredric March (1897–1973) was less rigidly typed, but he was also the urban man of the time, decent but hard-drinking. He is a columnist-dramatist in Arzner's **Merrily We Go to Hell** (1932), which is also explicit on what Americans in the Prohibition era were doing behind closed doors. In this case, his wife (Sylvia Sidney) is trying to get as drunk as he, and when that fails, she matches him infidelity for infidelity. The film is sharp on manners and morals, and in that same manner **Laughter** (1930) is very nearly a masterpiece. It starts with an attempted suicide and, later, when another attempt is successful, it plunges into melodrama; but between whiles it operates on the same frivolous level as *The Last Flight*. Watching March and Nancy Carroll in this film is an odd experience, as if the characters of Evelyn Waugh or Coward had sprung back into life – American versions of the Bright Young Things, callous, deprecatory, bantering. Like Helen Chandler

in the Warner film, Miss Carroll is dry, acerbic, in full control of her wit and laughter Harry d'Abbadie d'Arrast (1893–1968), a director of few credits, made it, and Donald Ogden Stewart helped to write it.

The grimmer elements in *The Last Flight* may be found in **The Eagle and the Hawk** (1933), also written by John Monk Saunders – saluted by Mordaunt Hall in *The New York Times* for a screenplay 'devoid of the stereotyped ideas which have weakened most of such narratives'. Credit for the direction is divided between Stuart Walker and Mitchell Leisen (1898–1972), the latter just graduating from art direction, but if we look at the other films which Saunders had a hand in writing – they include *Wings* and *The Dawn Patrol* – we will find his the controlling voice, thus invalidating once again the director-as-auteur theory. Despite different directors, these films have an astonishing consistency, being based on Saunders's own wartime experiences, and he is more realistic than other writers on the night-time

Fredric March and Nancy Carroll in *Laughter*: she is the young wife of an ageing man (Frank Morgan), competing with her stepdaughter for the attentions of a suicidal sculptor – till March comes upon the scene, persuading her to return to the laughter of the past, in a relationship devoid of morals or emotion.

drunkenness and the death-or-glory philosophy. *The Eagle and the Hawk* is the blackest of the four films. March (who is tremendously good) plays a man bewildered and embittered, particularly savage on the question of 'citations . . . they're broken bones and flesh, and blood'; in London, he is disgusted by talk of tactics and bravery. It is as if Saunders compensated for the Hollywood gold by being more ruthlessly honest than any other writer of his time; and this film remains moving, even if the Hays Office ordered the removal of the most passionate antiwar scenes – as well as cutting the sequence with Carole Lombard, as the 'beautiful lady' who offers March a pillow during his furlough in London, and the original ending, which had Cary Grant (q.v.), the irresponsible colleague and now a hobo, looking at a plaque commemorating March's heroism. Saunders later went to Britain to work on a semi-documentary, *Conquest of the Air* (q.v.), for Korda, and he committed suicide in 1940, at the age of forty-four.

Most of these films were of medium budget, and when in 1932 Paramount went into receivership it was due not to failure or over expenditure but to the fall in value of its stock. The Long Island studio was closed, and production concentrated in Hollywood. Jesse Lasky, the overall production head, was ousted, and so was B. P. Schulberg, manager of the California studio: neither quite recovered from the blow, though both managed to produce independently at other studios. Despite attempts by creditors to relieve him similarly of his duties, Zukor survived, and was made chairman of the board in 1935.

The crisis year coincided with the release of two of the company's best-remembered pictures, both from much-read novels. Robert Louis Stevenson's **Doctor Jekyll and Mr Hyde** (1932) has a whopping climax to which, after a slow start, the director Mamoulian imaginatively works; but the leading players, including March in the title-roles, are colourless, thus pushing into abeyance the matter of Jekyll's dual sexuality – in the context of Victorian London the most interesting aspect of the tale. On the other hand, Borzage's **A Farewell to Arms** (1932) has a poor ending, with Death, Wagner's Liebestod and the Armistice all fighting for attention –

though we should be grateful that they did not use the alternative 'happy' ending which had been shot. Till that point, however, this adaptation of Hemingway is instinctively right, with a dreamlike intensity from the moment Lieutenant Henry (Gary Cooper) spots Catherine (Helen Hayes); the War recedes, as it did with them, and their love story is very touching. It is also quite outspoken (the love scenes were pruned on reissue, by decree of the Legion of Decency – the Roman Catholic watch committee set up just after the Hays Code was tightened), but we may recognise the film as one of the magic artefacts that the dream factory then threw up from time to time.

Modern novels of quality were of no interest to the studios unless (a) suitable for star players, (b) the public had indicated a predilection for the work in question, or (c) there was a high sex quotient – which meant, even at this time, battles with the Hays Office. A few years earlier Hays had refused to sanction the filming of 'The Constant Nymph', which led indirectly to the Authors' League getting an agreement that offending properties could be filmed provided that the title was changed and, in some cases, the names of the chief characters. The most famous fish to slip through this net was William Faulkner's 'Sanctu-

Gary Cooper and Helen Hayes in Frank Borzage's *A Farewell to Arms*. Cooper is allowed his share of mooning and, like other Borzage heroes, tears, but a movie hero who likes boozing and brothels can take us with him: Borzage knew that if the hard facts of life are there, audiences will swallow the rest.

ary', which became, under the direction of Stephen Roberts, **The Story of Temple Drake** (1933), about a girl (Miriam Hopkins) of good family who, imprisoned in a whorehouse, finds later that she has no regrets for the life she led. However, despite the atmospheric photography – by Karl Struss – lust becomes fairly risible with dialogue, viz. 'You, Temple Drake, in a place like this! Are you – ? Did he – ?' Another oddity derived from a notable novel is one of Paramount's contributions to the horror cycle, **Island of Lost Souls** (1933), messily directed by Erle C. Kenton; its source is 'The Island of Dr Moreau' by H. G. Wells , who disliked the film intensely – and was not sorry when the British censors refused to let their countrymen see this tale of a mad scientist (Charles Laughton) lording it over a menagerie he is turning into human beings.

All was not grim at Paramount, which had acquired the services of a popular radio singer, Bing Crosby (1901–77), taking a number of jokes at his own expense – he plays himself – in a scatty farce, **The Big Broadcast** (1932), directed by Frank Tuttle. The cast also included Burns and Allen, the Mills Brothers and the Boswell Sisters, and its success initiated the practice of guest appearances from radio and vaudeville, former enemies of Hollywood, throughout the decade. The company's best comedy of the period – Lubitsch apart – is **Three-Cornered Moon** (1933), directed by Elliott Nugent from a play by Gertrude Tonkonogy about a well-to-do Brooklyn family hit by the Depression. Coping with the situation, without sentiment, is an almost perfect cast: Mary Boland as the fluttery mother unused to nickels and dimes; Claudette Colbert (q.v.) as the sensible puss who saves them all from starvation; and Richard Arlen as the family doctor, waiting for her to see through the budding novelist she thinks she loves.

One director determined to say something on contemporary problems was Cecil B. deMille, with a film called **This Day and Age** (1933), in which the idealism of the young triumphs over the corruption of the old, or, rather, the high school gang beats the big racketeers: plagiarised are *Road to Life*, 'Emil und die Detektive', any number of gangster films and *M*, even to its camera set ups. **The Sign of the Cross** (1932) is the antithesis, a Roman story involving a sadistic, fiddling Nero (Charles Laughton), a nymphomaniac Poppaea (Claudette Colbert), an intense captain of the Guard (Fredric March), and a Christian (Elissa Landi). The subsequent fame of this film seems due to Poppaea's bath in ass's milk; it cannot even claim spectacular decor, and was not particularly successful in its time. However, it marked deMille's return to the company he had helped to found, and confirmed his bent for antiquity. A colloquial approach to Plutarch, **Cleopatra** (1934), contains some splendid lines, e.g. 'You took advantage of my uncle's body on the funeral pyre to win support for yourself – you with your "Friends, Romans, Countrymen"!' In the title-role Miss Colbert looks as if at a fancy-dress party, but the photography by Victor Milner won an Oscar, and there is a moment, when the giant oars of Cleopatra's barge move into action, worth the whole of the 1963 *Cleopatra* (q.v.).

DeMille, earlier, had been the company's most respected director, and he would later be its most commercial one: but in both regards it was Lubitsch who at this time dominated the Paramount lot – and the affections of the reviewers. 'All the shrewd delights that were promised in *The Love Parade*,' said Richard Watts in *The New York Herald Tribune*, 'are realised' in **The Smiling Lieutenant** (1931), which he went on to compare with *Le Million*; however, Clair's film is a lark, and *The Smiling Lieutenant* is an exercise in operetta, even if the evening's plot is founded on a wink. Maurice Chevalier has the title-role, forced to leave his mistress (Miss Colbert) for a princess (Miss Hopkins); he was reunited with his best partner, Jeanette MacDonald, in both **One Hour With You** (1932) and **Love Me Tonight** (1932). The former is a remake of Lubitsch's second American picture, its emphasis changed from the divorcing couple to the happily married one – happiness pointed up by the wife's whispered conversation with her girlfriend, whose sole comment is an incredulous 'He can?' The skill and grace of the leads are matched by Charlie Ruggles, who has designs on her, by Genevieve Tobin, who has designs on him, and Roland Young, who has designs on the maid. *Love Me Tonoght* is less sure-footed in its approach to matters sexual, of which there are considerably more: a young widow (MacDonald) has melancholia which can only be cured by marriage – to a tailor (Chevalier) made to masquerade as an aristocrat. The songs are by Rodgers and Hart, staged in over-contrived manner or derived from Clair, but the film is still a box of delights: its director, as any buff will tell you, is not Lubitsch but Mamoulian. The direction of *One Hour With You* is credited to Lubitsch 'assisted' by George Cukor, who has however said that he alone directed it and that he had to threaten a lawsuit to get his name on the screen at all – which suggests that Lubitsch was highly satisfied with his work.

The leads of both **Trouble in Paradise** (1932) and **Design for Living** (1933) lack the ebullience of Chevalier and Mac-Donald, but in the first film Herbert Marshall and Kay Francis have nonchalance to spare as a jewel thief and his wealthy dupe; in the second Fredric March and Gary Cooper are miscast as Bohemian rivals for Miriam Hopkins – a lady common to both films. *Trouble in Paradise* is Lubitsch at his most sophisticated, but the Hays Office clamped down on the *menage à trois* situation of *Design for Living* as it had been treated in Noël Coward's play. Now it is explained that the characters resist sexual temptation in order to save 'time, trouble and confusion', and Ben Hecht's screenplay famously rejected almost all of Coward's dialogue for weak jokes such as 'Let's talk it over quietly like a disarmament conference'; a further liability seems to be that Lubitsch misunderstood the English puritan tradition against which Coward was rebelling.

In the midst of these films Lubitsch made an antiwar tract, **The Man I Killed** (1932) – or *Broken Lullaby,* as it was retitled after its New York premiere, when the public, as the studio had feared, failed to respond to rave notices. Its power remains discernible, despite some poor performances – Phillips Holmes, Lionel Barrymore – and the phoney German setting; the source was a French play about a guilt-ridden soldier (Holmes) who infiltrates himself into the rabidly anti-French family of a soldier he has killed. Since Lubitsch's concern, if untypical of his work, is implicit in every line, he was perhaps pleased to contribute to a film which, influenced by current economics, is as pessimistic as any ever

made. **If I Had a Million** (1932) is built round a millionaire who gives his fortune to names picked at random from the telephone book; its later fame was due to the all-star cast and the rarity of episode films, but it was a failure at the time. It also suffered cuts, on moral grounds, and lost at one time was the episode where the whore (Wynne Gibson) takes a hotel suite and discards with fury the second pillow. Another sequence finds George Raft in a flophouse, but the harshest of them is the final one, with May Robson as the inmate of an old people's home. The dark vision may be that of the uncredited producer, or it could have been caused by the collective conscience of the eighteen writers and eight directors who, sitting on their California lawns, put it together.

Those eight directors do not include Josef von Sternberg, which may be deliberate, since Selznick, then a producer at Paramount, recognised that his forte was for artificial people in artificial situations. Von Sternberg apparently conceived his mission as creating the right ambience for Marlene Dietrich. Because in *Der Blaue Engel* she had driven at least one man to destruction, Paramount decided that her appeal was akin to Garbo's – more tawdry, a little brasher, but again in the tradition of

Jeanette MacDonald and Maurice Chevalier in the Lubitsch-Cukor *One Hour With You*: 'What a Little Thing Like a Wedding Ring Can Do' is a song they sing in the bedroom – and if their joy being in bed together is not apparent, Chevalier is inclined to share his directly with the audience. It is indication of his considerable charm that he gets away with it.

Marlene Dietrich prepares to face the firing squad in *Dishonored*, refusing the blindfold offered by the lieutenant (Barry Norton) in charge of the firing party. 'Death is only another exciting adventure. A perfect end to an imperfect life,' she says. The films she made with Josef von Sternberg are imperfect; see the early ones, before he turned her into a dummy.

sophisticated European vice. M-G-M's inability to see Garbo as other than a courtesan was favourable to Dietrich, who proved to be unconvincing in any other role; as an adventuress she was more likely than Garbo, and she could read a witty line with more equivocation. She played a cabaret singer again in her first American film, **Morocco** (1930), written by Jules Furthman, from a play by Benno Vigny, with a clear distinction as to the varying kinds of love. 'Every time a man has helped me there has been a price. What's yours?' she says to Adolph Menjou, artist and man of the world, prepared to marry her with the knowledge that she can never be his. She entertains his advances, but gives her key to legionnaire Gary Cooper, to prove that her promiscuity is tuned to looks rather than wealth. He goes to her room, but they do not even kiss – for if their passion is to be a lasting one they cannot do anything so cheap as to jump into bed. The extent, after that, of their relationship is unclear, but their individual independence prevents their love from running smoothly – an independence that is part of their sexuality, inseparable from his masculinity and her knowledge of where her body has led her in the past. In **Dishonored** (1931) she can be found plying her trade on a Viennese pavement, before being inducted into the Secret Service to seduce a Russian colonel (Victor McLaglen). She can therefore redeem herself by patriotism, if not love; and as the firing squad prepares to aim, a young lieutenant cries out against the injustice of killing beauty, to which she responds by applying a lipstick – an effect of crushing banality, entirely in keeping with what has gone before.

In contrast, von Sternberg made **An American Tragedy** (1931), abandoned by Eisenstein – lured by Paramount to Hollywood – after half a million dollars had been spent in preparation; the rights to Dreiser's novel had cost the corporation a huge $150,000 and von Sternberg was requested to achieve something on a reduced budget. He professed himself uninterested, but while never managing the resonances of the later version, *A Place in the Sun* (q.v.), his has both a stronger narrative drive and a more authentic feeling for the milieu. What is on screen hardly amounts to tragedy and is certainly not an indictment, as was the novel (Dreiser disliked the film, and unsuccessfully tried to sue); but it does make one wonder about the Clyde Griffiths of this world – this one a bounder (Phillips Holmes) who was lucky for a while. A former bell hop, he chances to meet a wealthy uncle, he chances to meet both the factory girl (Sylvia Sidney) he seduces and the rich girl (Frances Dee) who takes him up; by chance there is a newspaper headline about a drowned girl, but his downfall is not due to chance. He was not clever enough to start with.

Von Sternberg returned to Dietrich – and that breath-catching first moment of **Shanghai Express** (1932), when she advances along the platform trailed by Anna May Wong, 'and both of them rotten' as a bystander observes, 'Anyone can see they're out in search of victims . . . Why, she's wrecked a dozen men.' Among her fellow passengers is an old acquaintance (Clive Brook) who asks her tersely, 'Married?' 'It took more than one man to change my name to . . . Shanghai Lily' she replies. They are on the observation platform, she in feathers and he in full mess kit. Was the oldest profession ever so glamorous? It was certainly easy to make an entertaining 'train' movie with a writer like Furthman and a photographer like Lee Garmes – von Sternberg's invariable support – but it is the direction which provides the superb imaginary Orient, with its sinister face beneath the smile. Von Sternberg himself provided the story of **Blonde Venus** (1932), of a housewife who descends to whoring and 'uses man after man' before being a celebrity in a white satin tux in Paris; he later claimed that there was nothing of himself in the film, but at the time he fought the studio

for a happy ending – a reunion with the husband (Herbert Marshall). Paramount considered it immoral – not to say unconvincing – but gave in since star and director were ostentatiously preparing to leave. However, when box-office takings were disastrously below the $3 million earned by *Shanghai Express* – admittedly an outstanding amount – they were firm in separating director and protégée, putting her into the hands of Mamoulian, whose version of Sudermann's *The Song of Songs* effectively hides any quality in the original.

The Scarlet Empress (1934) is not only a demonstration of Selznick's comment on von Sternberg, but the latter's justification; it could only have been made by a vulgarian of genius. No writer is credited, but it lays claim to be based on Catherine the Great's diary, to which it stays close. It establishes her (Dietrich) as a virgin, out of her depth in the barbaric court, at odds with her imbecilic husband (Sam Jaffe) and her mother-in-law, the drunken Czarina (Louise Dresser); when the latter dies she succeeds to the throne because the army is on her side, she having, it is implied, taken a leaf from the old Empress's book and slept with most of its officers. Catherine thundering into the palace at the head of her army has such grandeur – despite or perhaps because of a soundtrack fusion of 'The Ride of the Valkyries' and the '1812 Overture' – that for a second one wonders whether it would have been a good film with a real actress; but then, without her, it wouldn't have been what it is. In one sequence, in a pique, she allows herself to be picked up by a young officer: given that it is instantaneous, that she is young and pretty and he magnificently caparisoned and handsome, the scene must rank high in erotic fantasy. The Hays Office would not have passed it a month or so later. In fact, the Code had been tightened before the film appeared, but that was because Paramount withheld it, fearing comparisons with Korda's British film about Catherine (q.v.). The comparisons were made, and were adverse; and it is possible to see, given the climate of the time, why that antiseptic piece was preferred to this carnival.

When few cinemas were prepared to book the film, Paramount permitted von Sternberg to try just once more: **The Devil is a Woman** (1935), based on 'La Femme et le Pantin' by Pierre Louys, later filmed by

Hollywood before the Code

It remains refreshing to experience Mae West's unbridled and luxurious enjoyment in men, sin and diamonds – not necessarily in that order. It is not difficult to see why she shocked so many.

Julien Duvivier with Brigitte Bardot, and later still by Buñuel. Despite that provenance, it was old-hat then – a triangle story in the manner of *Der Blaue Engel* and *Morocco,* concerning the obsessed middle-aged man (Lionel Atwill), his younger rival (Cesar Romero), and a trollop, if one may so describe the glittering but dummy-like *femme fatale* played by Dietrich. The public cannot be blamed for rejecting this film as completely as it did; audiences mistook plenty of synthetic blather for the real thing, but taken to this length it has all the excitement of a gift-wrapped bauble – which is often what it looks like. To achieve this sort of artifice is no mean achievement, but unlike the other great *décoratif* director, Max Ophuls, von Sternberg lacks heart and mind and gaiety; Ophuls's similar artificial stories are for adults, but von Sternberg's only intermittently – and then in cod fashion. He departed from Paramount, while Dietrich continued to hold her own in kitsch: once a breath of real air is let in, she withers and dies.

While von Sternberg turned this once-earthy fraulein into little more than a statue, Paramount was joined by the most glorious expression of the unabashedly amoral, Mae West (1893–1980). She arrived to play an old flame of night club owner George Raft in **Night After Night** (1932), directed by Archie Mayo, and in fact a Raft vehicle. It defines the Raft image: the backstreet boy who has made it to the top – legally, just. He is tough; he carries a gun when treating with rivals, but is loth to use it. He is a slick dresser and a ladies' man, but a nice guy at heart. As an actor, however, he is inexpressive, and it is a relief to turn to West, who, asked if she believes in love at first sight, replies, 'I dunno, but it sure saves time.' Her reception in this role proved to the studio that it might risk a starring vehicle for this actress associated with *risqué* stage plays, usually written by herself; such was the notoriety of her biggest success, 'Diamond Lil', that the film version was retitled **She Done Him Wrong** (1933). She first appears looking bored, but lights up when recognised and begins to purr as men doff their hats. Descending from her carriage, she pats a child on the head: 'You're a fine woman, Lady Lou' says the child's mother, and Lady Lou agrees: 'Finest woman who ever walked the streets.'. The film itself is a thrown-together thing, though directed by

Lowell Sherman with a fine eye for plush Bowery saloons; what matters is Mae, the honey pot round which the bees cluster. It remains refreshing to experience her unbridled and luxurious enjoyment of men, sin and diamonds – not necessarily in that order; it is not difficult to see why she shocked so many – for here was a lady who went after the men she fancied without a single inhibition. There were men in her past, and there would be men in her future; we never saw her in bed with one, but she had a habit of receiving in her bedroom. 'I'm meeting all comers this evening' she says in **I'm No Angel** (1933), adding, 'I like sophisticated men to take me out.' The man protests that he is not really sophisticated: 'You're not really out either.' she responds, and any way you consider the line its meaning is sexual. Her humour depends on a play on words to give that sort of meaning; it was outrageous most of the time, and sometimes witty. 'When women go wrong men go right after them.' she counsels in *She Done Him Wrong,* and her protégée (Rochelle Hudson) cannot wait to whip off her Quakerish dress and follow her advice.

This lady is virtually the only ingenue in a Mae West film. The star penned her own scripts, at least at first; she was not interested in writing for other women, and indeed disliked writing scenes in which she wouldn't appear. Hence the rickety nature of the vehicles; they are all quite short, and if they seem long it is because the material is often just enough for a revue sketch. The star's act – superb as it is – cannot sustain a full-length film: she merely sashays through it, throwing off remarks solely about sex, jewels and her easy going nature. The fact that the other characters are merely adjuncts further limits her, plus the insistence that she – invariably playing a vaudeville star – is 'the greatest star of the century'. It is remarkable that the films remain so entertaining, but they are progressively less so, and you may care to go no further than *I'm No Angel,* directed by Wesley Ruggles, and *Belle of the Nineties* (1934), directed by Leo McCarey (q.v.).

The Code proved almost fatal. The fury with which the custodians of the country's morals greeted *She Done Him Wrong* was only equalled by the public's curiosity. Paramount issued a formal statement to the effect that its profits had not only prevented

255

its creditors from selling out to M-G-M but the company's 1,700 theatres from closing – which only made it worse: she not only preached that sex was fun, profitably, but the country revelled in it. The far from silent majority directed their wrath against the Hays Office, and though other factors were involved in the tightening of the Code, Miss West was the chief one.

Her four subsequent films for Paramount are mainly notable for the bowdlerisation of her original character: she remains predatory, but now men come a good second to diamonds. The invariable sameness of her delivery becomes monotonous when the lines delivered are not funny; was she only capable of humour when it was a question of gender, or had the earlier films used up the jokes stored during the years on the stage? **Goin' to Town** (1935), directed by Alexander Hall, has her marrying for social position, singing Delilah in Saint-Saëns' opera, and getting her own back on uppity upstate New York society. In **Klondike Annie** (1936), she starts as San Francisco Doll, mistress of a Chinaman; deported, she sets her sights at the Captain (Victor McLaglen), but once in Nome gets involved in a Mission – but at least, as directed by Raoul Walsh, we have glimpsed the original Mae. The public lost interest, and we can only conjecture whether this was because she could no longer shock or, in fact, had been a nine days' wonder in the first place. Paramount was not inclined to renew her contract, but an independent producer, Emanuel Cohen, put her into two films for that company to release: **Go West, Young Man** (1936), directed by Henry Hathaway, in which she is a movie star who upsets a mid-West household when her car breaks down; and **Every Day's a Holiday** (1937), directed by Edward Sutherland, and only enjoyable for the performance of Walter Catlett, in a dry run for Disney's Honest John.

As it happened, Paramount had a monopoly of the great screen clowns of this period. W. C. Fields returned to play a king in **Million Dollar Legs** (1932), directed by Edward Cline. The title, as far as can be ascertained, refers to the athletes the king intends to enter in the San Francisco Olympic Games: but it is not a film in which to look for meanings. Fields headed a further cast of clowns in the also impenetrable but less hilarious **International House** (1933), directed by Sutherland, and was Humpty Dumpty in **Alice in Wonderland** (1933), as unrecognisable as were Gary Cooper as the White Knight, Cary Grant as the Mock Turtle, Edna May Oliver as the Red Queen, Edward Everett Horton as the Mad Hatter, etc. The Tenniel drawings were copied, but there is nothing of the mad but logical progression of the books, and even the most famous opening in English literature was turned inside out as directed by Norman McLeod in this pointless and rather nasty picture.

Paramount was returning to a vein they had mined in the Silent days, the children's classic, clearly intending a film with reissue potential. Conversely, Fields's other films were usually second features, designed to support the main attraction. Cinemas were more highly competitive than ever, offering comedy two-reelers, cartoons, a newsreel, general interest shorts, a theatre organ, live stage shows – and the competition had been intensified since the country capitulated to the Talkies. Then it was that the Hollywood companies began to oblige with supporting features, or B-pictures, approximately one-third shorter than the main feature – though in certain situations, notably the large cities, a Fields' film could top the bill. Anyway, **Six of a Kind** (1934), a factory-line Paramount B, directed by Leo McCarey, is a film for all time. It concerns a couple, Mary Boland and Charlie Ruggles, who decide to go West on a second honeymoon; to share expenses, she has advertised for a couple to accompany them, and they are landed with George Burns and Gracie Allen. Mr Burns had long learnt, if not to cope with Miss Allen, to accommodate her, but this was not something Mr Ruggles could do on such short acquaintance: thus, in disarray and confusion, they journey West. Mr Fields and Alison Skipworth do not appear till towards the end – to give the lie to the title, for they are as fly as the others are naive. It could not be said that with their entrance the film gets funnier: *that* would be impossible.

Nor does Fields appear till towards the end of **Mrs Wiggs of the Cabbage Patch** (1934), based on a sentimental old play about poverty and directed by Norman Taurog, with the mellifluous Pauline Lord in the title-role; but when he does, greeting his mail-order bride (Zasu Pitts) with

W. C. Fields in *It's a Gift*, with Kathleen Howard as his dragon of a wife, flanked by Tom Bupp and Jean Rouverol as their children. If Alison Skipworth made Fields a marvellous partner in duplicity, Miss Howard in this film and *The Man on the Flying Trapeze* was the ideal antagonist, magnificent in scorn and suspicion. A Prometheus sometimes – in stubbornness and cunning – he will always admit defeat when faced with this formidable lady.

'Madame, did you have dreams of connubial bliss?' and drinking without removing his cigar, the whole enterprise is redeemed. **It's a Gift** (1934), directed by Norman Z. McLeod, and **The Man on the Flying Trapeze** (1935), directed by Clyde Bruckman, are for those who want the man's genius neat and undiluted. In both, a thread of plot serves to support a series of calamities of which he is cause, butt or victim; with resignation and a touching awareness of inevitability he faces life's hardships. He alone is the good, kind man in a world peopled with nagging wives, rowdy children, inefficient assistants and rude neighbours – a good, kind man, with enough deceit to make life bearable and a flask to help when that proves deficient. He says yes and no to his wife's questions, offering for the explanations she demands the one she is (a) most likely to believe, (b) most eager to hear, or (c) least able to refute. It cannot be wrong to prefer Fields the put-upon paterfamilias to Fields the showman, as in *The Old-fashioned Way* and **Poppy**

(1934) – though in the latter he sells a talking dog which announces, as he exits the saloon, that it has given up talking. The film itself, a remake of *Sally of the Sawdust* directed by Sutherland, clearly reveals a double in some sequences; alcoholism kept Fields from films for two years, and he left Paramount after a rather tired appearance in *The Big Broadcast of 1938*.

Another survivor from the Silent era was Harold Lloyd, who scrapped the original, Silent **Welcome Danger** (1929) – at a cost of $400,000 – when he realised that the public wanted Sound, a challenge he met with typical ingenuity, staging a fight in almost total darkness, with the noises to amuse us. The public was sufficiently curious to hear him speak to make this spoof of Chinatown one of his more popular films, but when he returned to the top of a skyscraper, in **Feet First** (1930), it was not appreciative. Since he was a millionaire several times over, one can only marvel that he had chosen to do this again, but in his subsequent films he eschewed

257

such feats in favour of gags that any competent comic could have utilised; there are some good ones, however, in **Movie Crazy** (1932), an unacknowledged rehash of Harry Leon Wilson's novel, 'Merton of the Movies', the rights to which Paramount owned. All three films were directed by Keaton's former gag-writer, Clyde Bruckman. Lloyd's voice – high and slightly breathless – ideally suited the persona he had established, and he concentrated on character in the best of his Talkies, **The Cat's Paw** (1934), playing a dupe of the mob in this tale by Clarence Budington Kelland, who later provided the original of *Mr Deeds Goes to Town* (q.v.). Lloyd here might be cousin to Mr Deeds, and he is supported for the first time by a strong cast (Una Merkel, Grant Mitchell, Warren Hymer, Nat Pendleton, Alan Dinehart,

George Barbier, Edwin Maxwell); Sam Taylor directed, and the film was in fact made for Fox on a one-picture deal. Lloyd said later that he had been uncertain whether to play the story straight or use it as a prop for gags, and had only settled on the former after flipping a coin; uncertainty of approach is apparent in his last two films for Paramount, **The Milky Way** (1936), directed by Leo McCarey, and **Professor Beware** (1938), directed by Elliott Nugent. The latter is the more amusing, but its humour is of an earlier era: Lloyd, aware of this, retired from the screen, except for *The Sin of Harold Diddlebock* (q.v.).

The credits of **The Cocoanuts** (1929) are done over negatives, and it is entirely appropriate that the Marx Brothers should arrive on screen with everything turned inside out. They were a vaudeville team : Groucho (1890–1977), with the leer and fake moustache; Harpo (1888–1964), voiceless, larcenous, lecherous, an ensemble topped off with pink curls and a motorhooter; Chico (1887–1961), with his fractured vowels and misinterpretations; and Zeppo, the juvenile, who left the act when their Paramount contract expired. Like Fields and Mae West, their self-absorption permitted little consideration of others, and none at all for the mores of the time: 'I'm Against It ' is the title of Groucho's song in **Horse Feathers** (1932). Allowance was made for Margaret Dumont, the majestic dowager so often the object of Groucho's attentions, a relationship summed up by a line in **Animal Crackers** (1930): 'You've got beauty, style, money . . . You have got money, haven't you? – if not we'll stop right now.' In a deluge of puns good and bad, of malapropisms and innuendo, they insulted those about them; in a series of lunatic pursuits and misunderstandings they carried deceit to a new low; with sublime self-confidence they carried anarchy to the edge of destruction.

Paramount, understandably, approached them gingerly. *The Cocoanuts,* with direction credited to Robert Florey and Joseph Santley, is no more than a cameras-in-the-stalls account of a musical comedy of the period – on this evidence, a mediocre one – and no harbinger of Marxian antics to come. *Animal Crackers* they had also done on stage and as directed by Victor Heerman, little further effort had been made to open it out. Both plots have to do with larcenous activities, in hotel and country house respectively. **Monkey Business** (1931), directed by Norman McLeod, was written expressly for the screen, and casts the team as stowaways; their attempts to get past immigration by imitating Maurice Chevalier rank high in the annals of delirium. McLeod also directed *Horse Feathers,* set in a college, but like its immediate predecessor it suffers, in my opinion, from the absence of Miss Dumont.

In **Duck Soup** (1933), as the richest widow in the nation, Dumont chooses Rufus T. Firefly (Groucho) as its president – an appointment which no one thinks odd, least of all the gentleman himself, though he has fleeting doubts. Harpo and Chico are spies, changing sides so frequently that their competence – and interest in the job in

hand – is merely academic. Indeed, the plot-line is so cussed, so sheerly irreverent, that it is soon non-existent, buried under an avalanche of gags – including a number of parodies of Hollywood films of the period. Allen Eyles has called this one 'mint-fresh and almost timelessly funny', but it was not much admired at the time. Groucho blamed Leo McCarey, who directed, but as the years advanced and it became accepted as their best film, he did an about-face and credited McCarey for its 'political satire'. As Gavin Lambert observed, 'It was probably the only time the Marxes worked with a comic talent equal to their own' – his point being – 'and they didn't like it.' Many well-known names – Morrie Ryskind, S. J. Perelman, George S. Kaufman, Irving Berlin, Kalmar and Ruby amongst them – wrote either directly for the Marx Brothers movies, or had their stage material adapted for the screen, but Groucho, in later years, tended to denigrate the more famous participants. There can be no question but that the Marx Brothers were their own invention.

At M-G-M the emphasis was, as ever, on star vehicles and expensive properties. The tandem partnership of Thalberg and Mayer was deteriorating, but their films continued to take a larger percentage of the box-office than those of other studios – and, significantly, to attract more critical attention. With Garbo, that is understandable. Despite the success of *Anna Christie,* the studio made no plans to put her into 'contemporary' situations. **Romance** (1930) was based on Doris Keane's old vehicle, already filmed in 1920; the hoary plot concerns an opera singer (Garbo), her ageing 'protector' (Lewis Stone), and the young parson (Gavin Gordon) who refuses to believe the truth about them; his love brings to her a new morality, and she is thus disillusioned when he asks to spend the night with her. In **Inspiration** (1931), also directed by Clarence Brown, it is she who makes that approach – within minutes of the film opening, and within seconds of meeting the young student (Robert Montgomery) whom she desires. We cannot blame her: 'How *yong* you are !' she says wistfully when he tells her he is twenty-four, and what heartbreak is in her voice when she says to her friends, when he has left her, 'He was all my life'! The film,

though set in the present day, is a version of *Camille,* set in the Bohemian circles of Paris, where the men are all grey-haired and their women all very young. Love and lovers are their sole topics of conversation, and marriage is only spoken of in connection with the heroine and her unnatural preference for a young man.

If she transcends such material, as she did throughout her Silent career, the early sequences of **Susan Lennox: Her Fall and Rise** (1931) are as miraculous as she is, for the man is Clark Gable, protecting her after attempted rape by her intended fiancé. Since he is Gable and she is Garbo, his will towards something similar and her submission must follow after an idyllic day fishing and laughing: but consequent events will then keep them apart till the last reel. Once again more sinned against than sinning, she is found whoring – and for the record this is the only film in which she is; she rises to the world of the demi-mondaine – and once again everyone on view is bereft of morals – and must sink to the level of his degradation

before they both may be redeemed. In all the films they made together William Daniels never photographed her more brilliantly; and it would be a mistake to underestimate the direction of Robert Z. Leonard (1889–1968), of whom I have never heard a good word, or a bad one.

In view of M-G-M's attitude towards her screen personality, it is no surprise to find her in the title-role of **Mata Hari** (1932), a flickering effort which only rises at the end to the level we expect for her – high tosh, but tear-jerking. 'Here are your eyes,' she says to the blinded Ramon Novarro, pressing her hands to his face. George Fitzmaurice directed, and had better material in **As You Desire Me** (1932): in a bleached bob, Garbo is a cabaret entertainer in Budapest, drinking to forget an already amnesiac past and perhaps her protector (Erich Von Stroheim), whom she kisses with passion but without an iota of affection. This is her familiar role, and equally familiar is her longing for a new life – in this case achieved, when a Count (Melvyn

Of *Grand Hotel,* the English critic C. A. Lejeune wrote, 'I remember nothing to equal the curiosity, excitement and impatience with which London prepared to sample [it].' The reason was the all-star cast, which included Greta Garbo and John Barrymore.

261

Douglas) claims her as his wife. Von Stroheim schemes to get her back – which provides a 'third act' of some suspense, due presumably to the source, a play by Pirandello: in the matter of Garbo vehicles this is more mature than most. One constant about her is that – *Mata Hari* excepted – she is always better than she was before; she always surpasses expectations. Superb as the singer, she is breathtaking later, playing with keen humour a woman rid of the past and unexpectedly loved. There is a beautiful, erotic sequence when she goes to the Count's room for a light for her cigarette, and in the final scene she acts with a common-sense confidence which is miraculous.

Grand Hotel (1932) was based on a book by Vicki Baum, a study of some half-dozen guests in a Berlin hotel, in the manner of *Menschen Untereinander,* and it had become an international bestseller: but what caused unprecedented public interest was M-G-M's daring step of casting the five leads with five stars – at a time when it was exceptional to find a second star billed above the title, and in this case only Lionel Barrymore was not accustomed to solo top-billing. Garbo is unsuitably flamboyant as a Russian ballerina who falls for the (phoney?) baron who means to rob her – John Barrymore. Brother Lionel is Kringelein, a bookkeeper who has checked in knowing he has an incurable disease; and Joan Crawford is the 'fast' stenographer who decides to enjoy his last days with him. The best performance – and the only attempt at a German accent – is by Wallace Beery, as the industrialist who desperately needs a big deal. The sensitive Edmund Goulding directed, but it is typical of the M-G-M approach that it tries to graft on to an American product the rather brittle quality of German cinema, falling between both stools; however, then it was the year's highest grossing picture and an Oscar winner – as best Picture.

Anticipation was almost as keen when the Barrymore brothers were joined by sister Ethel for **Rasputin and the Empress** (1932). John, less twitchy than usual, is Prince Chegodieff, a character based on Youssoupoff; Lionel is Rasputin, and the familiar rasp emitted through all that hair would be risible in any case. Ethel is every inch a Czarina, but she cannot listen to a sentence of three words without raising an eyebrow. The director, Richard Boles-

lawski (1889–1937), was a Pole who had worked in the New York theatre, and had been a dialogue director since the inception of Talkies. He was chosen for this film because of his background, managing some striking effects within the rather bland decor and some drama from Charles MacArthur's flatly-written screenplay. The royal couple are portrayed as dignified and humourless, he (Ralph Morgan) care-worn and decent, she as caring only for her children. The film starts with news of revolt, moves swiftly to the time the Czarevitch falls and is helped by Rasputin, brought in by a disciple, Princess Natasha (Diana Wynyard). One M-G-M executive decreed that Rasputin would be a blacker figure if he attempted to rape this lady, and it was on that technical ground, since she could be confounded with his wife, that Youssoupoff sued for libel in the British courts – and was awarded £25,000 plus huge costs. Ironically, his surrogate in the film kills the monk in self-defence – gruesomely and convincingly, however, and the film further redeems itself with its vignettes of the Romanovs in captivity; honourably, it is Hollywood's first serious attempt to explain the motivations of the people of history.

Dinner at Eight (1933), as adapted from the play by George S. Kaufman and Edna Ferber, was another exercise for an all-star cast, in this case tracing the fortunes of some guests at a dinner party. The hostess (Billie Burke) is a vapid woman, unaware that her husband (Lionel Barrymore) is dying and that his business is failing. The other strands of the plot are equally contrived, but are redeemed by their protagonists, each a monster of selfishness or self-pity: the daughter (Madge Evans), neglecting her fiancé for a matinee idol (John Barrymore), himself ruined by Talkies and bent on self-destruction; the businessman (Beery), out to ruin the host, and locked in mutual loathing with his wife (Jean Harlow), who is amusing herself with their philandering doctor (Edmund Lowe); and the now-penniless actress (Marie Dressler), ditching the host when he cannot loan her money. This is a New York item, shrewd and cruel, unpopular at the time with audiences outside the big cities. This cast makes any revival of the play unthinkable, and even John Barrymore is superb – perhaps because the performance is autobiographi-

Hardly had London and indeed the world recovered from seeing so many favourites in *Grand Hotel* than M-G-M did it again with *Dinner at Eight*, whose stars included Marie Dressler and Jean Harlow, here in the famous closing sequence.

cal. Miss Dressler, dripping with foxes and pearls, sails through each scene like a galleon, mugging, and letting not a laugh escape her; and Harlow, in form-fitting satin, is mesmerising, nibbling on a chocolate and then diving under the bed for an even bigger box. The producer was David O. Selznick, Mayer's son-in-law, arriving unwillingly from R.K.O. Radio (q.v.) when Thalberg's protracted ill health suggested a replacement was needed, and Selznick borrowed George Cukor from R.K.O. to direct.

M-G-M's specialist in filmed plays was Sidney Franklin (1893–1972). **Reunion in Vienna** (1933) had begun with Robert E. Sherwood's view that the events of 1914–18 could not stop schmalzy plays about that city, so he had written one in which the old romantics were shown replaced by the new city of Freud, attempting to be flippant about both. On the screen John Barrymore and Diana Wynyard replaced that theatrical team known as the Lunts, whose thrall was such that even a film version persuaded critics that this material was better than it was. Thalberg had persuaded the Lunts themselves to record one of their stage successes, Molnár's **The Guardsman** (1931). 'It is a pity,' said Mordaunt Hall in *The New York Times,* 'that there are not more Fontannes, Lunts and Molnárs to help out the screen, for then this medium

of entertainment would be in a far higher plane.' Alfred Lunt is a resourceful light comedian, but Lynn Fontanne, as on the stage, is less actress than hostess. The film, long unseen, answers the once-debated question as to why they made no others. They were both approaching forty, and despite the soft focus in her case, it shows; but chiefly she was no match for established screen actresses like Ann Harding (q.v.) and Ruth Chatterton, and he, for all his briskness, cannot hide a touch of effeminacy. Hall is also wrong about the play, which emerges as a witless piece wholly concerned with marital infidelity.

Franklin directed another disputing couple in **Private Lives** (1931), a straight forward adaptation of Noël Coward's comedy, with Norma Shearer and Robert Montgomery. Shearer manages to approximate the quicksilver delivery of Gertrude Lawrence, but the magic of the original – distilled in the excerpts from it that Coward and Lawrence recorded – is entirely missed. Franklin also directed Shearer in a new screen version of an old Broadway tearjerker, **Smilin' Through** (1932), concerning the bride shot on her wedding morn, and the niece destined to fall in love with the murderer's son (Fredric March) in England to fight in the War: the least that may be said is that it is done with conviction.

Norma Shearer (b. 1904) was only a

'You're a new kind of man in a new kind of world,' Norma Shearer tells Clark Gable in *A Free Soul*, and he feels the same about her. He is a gangster and she the daughter of a wealthy daddy. After a trip in her roadster at the exhilarating speed of 60 m.p.h. she finds her fiancé, played by Leslie Howard, rather stuffy.

fraction lower than Garbo in the astral hierarchy of the studio, and that was partly because she was married to Thalberg, who in Silent films had caused her to alternate between demure virgins and women of the world. With Talkies, she settled mainly for the latter, and Thalberg sagely cast her as the post-flapper woman – or as the title has it, **A Free Soul** (1931). The story and Clarence Brown's direction are undistinguished, but the attitudes are more provocative than those in Warners' similar tales. Clark Gable kisses her and she says 'That'll be all, thanks', but when his sole response to her leaving their love nest is 'Your stuff's still hanging in the closet, baby' she quickly returns.

Miss Shearer, however, baulked (as did Joan Crawford) at playing the title-role in **Red-Headed Woman** (1932), such was

the notoriety of Katherine Brush's novel. According to Samuel Marx, at the time the studio's story editor, the book was considered too 'racy', but it had sold so well that no studio could afford not to bid for the rights; he also says that it was primarily responsible for the tightening of the Production Code, but in fact it only opened the way for the flood of similar tales which would eventually bring that about. Sex unsanctified by marriage had been advancing its cause since Clara Bow, but Harlow in this film is something else again. Anita Loos wrote the screenplay, and her first line has Harlow intoning 'So gentlemen prefer blondes, do they?': she dons a see-through dress, snaps a picture of a man in her garter and goes to put the theory to the test. 'A girl is a fool if she doesn't get ahead,' she says. 'It's just as easy to get a rich man as a poor man.' 'Love?' says her prey, Chester Morris, 'Why don't you call it by its real name?' As directed by Jack Conway, when she follows Morris into a telephone booth her appeal is that of a quick-time whore. She ends, the richest woman in France, with an aged 'companion' and a young 'chauffeur' (Charles Boyer). Loose ladies before had sometimes ended happily, but never triumphant, and in the year that followed several others suffered assault on their nether regions and lived to laugh about it – and it was in that climate that Mae West was permitted to transfer her stage persona to the screen.

M-G-M asked Miss West, vainly, to write dialogue for Jean Harlow (1911–37) – partly because they were not entirely happy at having a major star typecast as a sinner, and partly because she was inadequate as an emotional actress. It is as a comedienne that she is to be cherished, at her best with Clark Gable (1901–60), at this point her male counterpart. The ideal male of the 20s wore an Arrow collar and was comforting over the tea cups, but for the Depression he wore no tie and swore at his women over the whisky bottle. In **Red Dust** (1932) Gable yells at Harlow, 'I'm not a one-woman man, I never have been and I never will be', and he doesn't realise that she is his kind till she says 'Mind if I get drunk with you?' His sex appeal is emphasised when he is lusted after by both her and a very proper newly wed (Mary Astor), a problem he takes in his stride. The film plays safe by setting its melodramatics in the jungle, it being a recognised fact that in the steamy topics everyone gets steamed up about sex. Gable's initial reaction to Harlow is a bored 'I've been lookin' at her kind since my voice changed', but at the end his hand creeps up her skirt as she reads him a sick-bed story about 'Little Molly Cottontail' For its attitude to sex and for Victor Fleming's tick-tock direction, the film should be as vividly alive a century from now.

Also imperishable, also directed by Fleming and written by John Lee Mahin, in this case joined by Jules Furthman, is **Bombshell** (1933), still the wittiest satire on Hollywood. *The bombshell of the title

*I have seen this film in both New York and London and it plays better with native audiences. In New York, the laughter is virtually nonstop, perhaps because audiences are more relaxed, at ease with the crackling dialogue; in London the response was more hesitant, possibly because spectators feared they might miss something.

is Harlow, a poor little movie star, who supports: a drunken, cadging father (Frank Morgan); a moronic, cadging brother (Ted Healy); a conniving and graft-taking secretary (Una Merkel); a staff of servants including a maid (Louise Beavers), whose day off, in Harlow's words, 'sure is brutal on your lingerie'; the marquis she plans to marry; and, last but not least, three gigantic dogs. She also supports the studio, as represented by her director (Pat O'Brien) and publicity man (Lee Tracy), whose job it is to keep her on the front pages, while she attempts to escape and find freedom – the standard 'dumb blonde' plot, as used notably in *Born Yesterday* (q.v.).

Gable remained cheerfully amoral in his other films of the period, bedding women or slapping them around. He concedes his mistress (Myrna Loy) to the assistant district attorney (William Powell) in **Manhattan Melodrama** (1934), but then the latter had been a boyhood chum. This plot device, of two kids growing up together, one going to the good and the other to the bad, became a Hollywood perennial, and it is easily handled here by W. S. Van Dyke. Gable in fact becomes a casino boss and gangster, his several murders finally paid for in the electric chair at Sing Sing; but his charm and occasional gallantry make crime very appealing. Despite its later stately image, M-G-M at this time was as ready as any studio in Hollywood to portray the world as a place of fast boozing, casual sex and no morals in any direction – though both Mayer and Thalberg personally preferred the sort of movies which most appealed to the distaff half of audiences. In 1930 the studio offered **The Big House**, a conventional prison drama with an excellent performance by Chester Morris as the con who goes straight, and an interesting one by Robert Montgomery as a drunken driver whose prison term proves him to be despicable in every way. Under the direction of George Hill, it was a huge box-office success for the company, but there was no attempt to repeat it.

The Beast of the City (1932) is notable as one of the studio's few gangster pictures, though the emphasis is on the police force, as represented by Walter Huston. His brother (Wallace Ford) is also a policeman, but corrupted by a gangster's moll (Harlow whose conversation promises a number of unrefined pleasures. The direction

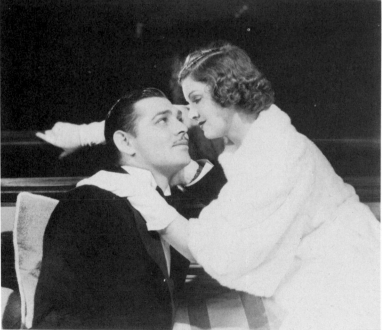

Moonlight was the *sine qua non* of Hollywood love scenes for over fifty years, but before the strengthening of the Hays Code, it could be – to quote Noël Coward – cruelly deceptive. In *Bombshell*, ABOVE, Lee Tracy is using romance to bring Jean Harlow into line. *Manhattan Melodrama*, LEFT, Myrna Loy is in the process of walking out on Clark Gable in favour of his best friend. It was a virtue of both films that audiences could not be sure who would end up with whom come the final clinch.

Walter Huston and Karen Morley in the final sequence of *Gabriel Over the White House*, a film which caused a rift among M-G-M executives. The ending originally shot was hardly suitable for U.S. audiences, with its cynical suggestion that any good done in the White House was due to temporary aberration and/or divine intervention.

by veteran Charles Brabin indicates why he would soon be moved to B pictures, and the plotting, by John Lee Mahin from a story by W. R. Burnett, becomes desperate; but the ending is curious, as a demoted Huston, despairing of police protection, gathers some like-minded vigilantes to take the law into their own hands, both sides being wiped out in the process. There is a foreword pleading for less glamorisation of crime by the then-president, Herbert Hoover, who was a crony of Mayer; but the impetus for the film may have come from William Randolph Hearst, whose Cosmopolitan outfit nominally produced the film.

A year later Cosmopolitan offered **Gabriel Over the White House,** which also propounded America's ills and offered its own solution. A completely corrupt president (Huston) is brought back from the dead – another popular plot device of the period – to have a complete change of heart, and by firm action solving (a) the unemployment caused by the Depression (b) the problem of the big-time gangsters, and (c) the situation of a rearming Europe. If not a profound film, it is prodigal with ideas, including the conception of the 'reformed' president taking on the physical aspect of Lincoln; it was also potentially uncommercial, since the public had shown no great

taste for whimsy, or for politics or the Depression. The producer was Walter Wanger (q.v.), brought from Columbia, and like Selznick an anticipated replacement for Thalberg; he had chosen the director, Gregory LaCava, and the writer, Casey Wilson, who was from Thalberg's team. When Wanger arrived at M-G-M, Thalberg had advised him to ignore Mayer; Wanger accordingly sent the story direct to Hearst, who loved it, and contributed to the dialogue. Mayer knew little about the film until the preview, when his objections were supported by Will H. Hays and Nicholas Schenck (brother of Joseph, and since 1927 Chairman of Loew's Inc.), also Republicans. Since the film by implication attacked those presidents now being criticised in his papers, it served to alienate him from Mayer; Mayer thereafter distrusted Wanger, so that the latter soon moved on. A new ending was shot, whereby the president dies while reverting to his old self; however, the original remained for Europe, impressing critics with its power – and it would not have done for American audiences, with its cynical suggestion that any good done in the White House was caused by temporary aberration and/or divine intervention. The film was finally shown in the U.S. not long after the inauguration of President Roosevelt, who reportedly loved it.

Hearst's actual departure from M-G-M came about when Thalberg managed to get two properties for Miss Shearer, *The Barretts of Wimpole Street* (q.v.) and *Marie Antoinette* (q.v.), which Hearst had coveted for Marion Davies. Miss Davies in Talkies seldom showed the nimble comic wit of her Silent movies, and was often terrible, as in **Going Hollywood** (1933), though the blame in this case may be due to Raoul Walsh, making every mistake of which a director is capable. She is certainly better as handled by Edmund Goulding in **Blondie of the Follies** (1932), a supposedly typical showgirl story commissioned by Hearst from Frances Marion, with dialogue by Anita Loos. People within the industry were amused because it was in fact a thinly-disguised account of the relationship between Davies and Hearst – except that she is rescued from a life of sin by a handsome young millionaire (Robert Montgomery).

Joan Crawford had become one of the studio's most important stars, and her early Talkies indicate why she fascinated audiences for so long: she had authority and intensity, with eyes like hard-boiled eggs stuck with black olives. She clearly believed in her roles, doing everything with them – indeed, overdoing everything, as in **Paid** (1931), a version of Bayard Veiller's play 'Within the Law', already filmed in 1917 with Alice Joyce and in 1923 with Norma Talmadge. It presupposes that a girl, wrongly convicted, will revenge herself on society by a series of confidence tricks, strictly within the law, plus marriage to the son of the man who sent her up; Sam Wood directs, for a sort of dotty conviction. If Crawford is ridiculous in **Today We Live** (1933), this is only partly because she is miscast as an aristocratic Britisher engaged to another (Robert Young) but in love with an American (Gary Cooper), helping them to fight World War I. Her role, made the chief one, was written into the script at Thalberg's request, but there is little consolation for admirers of William Faulkner, on whose story it is based, since he also contributed to the ludicrous dialogue. The director is Howard Hawks, currently acquiring a reputation with *The Dawn Patrol* (from which the only convincing details are filched) and *Scarface* (q.v.): the presence of Cooper may remind us that his previous film was also a war romance, *A Farewell to Arms* – and the two films underline the vast difference between a creative director and a hack like Hawks.

However, Crawford's best film of the period owes much to the unsung Robert Z. Leonard – **Dancing Lady** (1933), a musical, produced by Selznick, and quite the gutsy equal of the best shows over at Warners. Crawford's ambitions in later movies are strictly ersatz, but here she manages a nice, wry appreciation of her own aspirations, pleased when they like her singing and dancing – though the way she shrugs and turns down the corners of her mouth indicates that only mugs do not try for the big time. The cast includes Clark Gable as the harrying director, Robert Benchley, Franchot Tone and Ted Healy; Nelson Eddy makes his screen debut and so, more appreciated, does Fred Astaire, as 'himself' in a couple of numbers.

The career of John Gilbert was ending, reputedly due to the enmity of Mayer and an inadequate voice for Talkies – both certainly factors, though the timbre is merely light-tenored and uninteresting. As his face became lined, he became rather weedy – physically an absurd figure in **Downstairs** (1932) with ill-fitting double-breasted jackets. He contributed the story, which Monta Bell directed, about the new chauffeur seducing every lady in sight, including the ageing, plump cook – an idea perhaps borrowed from Von Stroheim. The film's main offering to the audience is a mild suspense – how long will it take him to break down the resistance of the butler's new bride (Virginia Bruce)? That also is the central situation of **The Barbarian** (1933), directed by Sam Wood (q.v.), one of the last vehicles of Ramon Novarro, whose career was also faltering with Talkies. In this case, the amoral hero is an Egyptian dragoman, and the lady (Myrna Loy) a British heiress. At one point he delivers her from peril in the desert to a more powerful and lecherous pasha (Edward Arnold), to whose silent handmaidens she gushes 'This is real hospitality' as they shepherd her into a massive pool filled with petals. She does not know what is in store for her, and the off-screen cries we hear seem to have been due to whips rather than rape; Novarro's seduction, after that, is more gentle, but the ending leaves us breathless, as she prefers sensuality on the Nile with him (obviously

t her own expense) to marriage with her tuffy fiancé (Reginald Denny). The role lisguises Novarro's inadequacy as a Talkie ctor, and clever direction, by Jacques Feyder, also does so in **Daybreak** (1931), rom a Schnitzler romance about a guards-man and a music teacher (Helen Chandler). Given Schnitzler's cynical view of love – hat it is never what it should be, especially s here, when it crosses class barriers – the appy ending seems unlikely. The film ontains an odd scene in which Novarro's alet clandestinely wears his undershorts nd coos 'Ooh, they are beautiful' when iscovered.

Such decadence cannot be found in the ilms of Wallace Beery, former comic and lent villain, who joined Gable in project-g for the studio a much more masculine ero – though in his case both bulk and looks prevented him from being a romantic lead. He originally came to M-G-M to take Lon Chaney's place as the toughest convict in *The Big House,* and he proceeded to win a Best Actor Oscar (tying with Fredric March's Dr Jekyll) for **The Champ** (1931), directed with understatement by King Vidor – wisely, since this is an old-fashioned, maudlin tale of a child (Jackie Cooper) yanked out of poverty into a life of abject luxury. Fighting over him are an ex-champ (Beery), hoping for a comeback, and his charming ex-wife (Irene Rich), so wealthy that she has her own private suite on the railroad; it is to the former, however, a drunk and a gambler, that we are sup-posed to extend our sympathies: but then this film, like many another, insists that poverty makes people loving, considerate, open-hearted and understanding. It must

Dancing Lady is not only a splendid musical but a magnificent demonstration of the talents of Joan Crawford (right). Ever determined, she plays a showgirl of steely will 'fed up with burlesque, I'm going up to where it's art' – i.e. moving from the Bowery to Broadway. She has a temporary set-back due to a misunderstanding by the police.

be said that ten-year-old Cooper, with his young-old face, is worth jerking a tear over.

Beery's most popular films were the two he made with Marie Dressler, **Min and Bill** (1930) and **Tugboat Annie** (1933), and they are most remarkable for the comic skills of that lady. Miss Dressler (1869–1934), her vaudeville fame long gone, had arrived at M-G-M after some years of hardship, rising quickly from supporting actress to leader of the popularity polls. She and Beery were instantly 'lovable', and equally given to twitching eyes, mouths and facial muscles to keep audience attention from the other; she wins with her swivelling, darting looks of disgust and suspicion, but also because she conveys a wondrous sense of love triumphing over her experience of his failings – which have mainly to do with the bottle. Directed respectively by George Hill and Mervyn LeRoy, both are set on the waterfront, cleverly blending comedy and sentiment; Miss Dressler is the equal in artifice of their writers, but she always suggests a real woman with real problems.

Success type-cast Beery, thereafter given cute Wally Beery scenes, usually including one to draw tears from the stoniest heart; there are other minor flaws in **Viva Villa!** (1934), but this is with reason one of Selznick's own favourites among the films he produced while at M-G-M. Despite his status as a folk hero, Pancho Villa was an unusual choice of subject for an American movie, joining the Romanovs as one of the few recent historical figures so treated, and one of the few not noted for either loves or scandals. The screenplay by Ben Hecht manages a number of ambiguities – again rare in films of this period; and the device of a fictional American reporter (Stuart Erwin) to act as commentator was used again, notably in *Lawrence of Arabia* (q.v.). The photography by James Wong Howe and Charles G. Clarke is impressive, but so much like that of other films set in Mexico that we may suppose that that country imposes its own style. Its virtue is in the location-shooting, but that was as fraught as it was costly, dissuading Hollywood from using far-flung locations except when unavoidable for more than a generation. A quantity of exposed film was destroyed when the plane carrying it crashed; Villa's own son was to have played his father as a

young man, but became ill, and the sequences had to be dropped; the Mexicans objected to the casting of Beery – and were additionally upset when he rejected local hospitality to fly back to the capital every night; and, worst of all, a drunk Lee Tracy urinated from a hotel balcony onto the Mexican army. The director, Howard Hawks, left Mexico to try to defend him from the wrath of Louis B. Mayer, who was instrumental in preventing Tracy from ever again playing the lead in an A picture; the actor was replaced by Erwin, and Hawks by Jack Conway.

Location difficulties also plagued **Trader Horn** (1931), begun in fact by Van Dyke as a Silent, not long after his success with *White Shadows in the Blue Seas*. He was sent to Africa to film this semi-autobiographical story, with microphones and generators sent on when Sound became necessary – though according to sources at the time, most of it was reshot on the back lot and in Mexico. That is not evident, and if it surprises today, what must the film have seemed like then? There is a rhinoceros charge, an escape down a crocodile-infested river, an operation to steal meat from a lion, all bound into a typical jungle tale of a search for a white girl (Edwina Booth) brought up by cannibals. It owes much to the relaxed playing of Harry Carey in the title-role, but we may feel as warmly towards the manifold writers and cameramen as audiences did at the time. Across the years, I salute them.

Its success encouraged the purchase of Edgar Rice Burroughs' **Tarzan of the Apes** (1932), with a former Olympic swimming champion, Johnny Weissmuller, as the tree-hopping, somersaulting, all-conquering jungle hero. Van Dyke directed, but the sequel, **Tarzan and his Mate** (1934), was directed by the studio's art director, Cedric Gibbons – appropriately, for it is so packed with back projections, glass-shots and rubber animals (the chimp, Cheetah, is at one point played by an actor in a monkey-skin) that the planning must have taken longer than the actual filming. Tarzan's mate (Maureen O'Sullivan) is a well-bred English girl, which may be why she treats him maternally. In one of the later sequels they were put through a marriage service to appease the puritans, and in 1942, when M-G-M dropped the series, it was picked up by R.K.O.

M-G-M's own further entries in the penny-dreadful stakes included **The Mask of Fu Manchu** (1932), directed by Charles Brabin from the characters invented by Sax Rohmer, already picked over by Paramount. Boris Karloff is the Oriental overlord who manages to have Nayland Smith (Lewis Stone) bound to a plank above an alligator pool filling with water; to have Smith's associate await death at the connivance of two slowly-closing spiked doors, and his daughter prepared for sacrifice; and to have the almost naked hero injected with the serum which will make him a zombie-like slave and the desired of Fu Manchu's daughter (Myrna Loy).

It was an M-G-M director, Tod Browning, who had revived the horror movie, when loaned to Universal for *Dracula* (q.v.); when its follow-up, *Frankenstein* (q.v.) also did spectacular business, Thalberg reputedly asked Browning to 'out-horror' it, and the result was the well-titled **Freaks** (1932), a tale of the circus world – of the pinheads, the bearded lady, the man-woman, the armless or legless or both. Even among the cheapjack horror movies of the present, you could not imagine anyone similarly using, say, thalidomide victims, and it is as well that much of the playing is amateurish, for it might otherwise be unbearable. The studio was not happy with it, and appended an apologetic introduction; their London office was not sorry when the censor banned it – till 1963. Browning's subsequent Talkies are negligible, with the possible exception of **The Devil-Doll** (1936), written by Garrett Ford, Guy Endore and Erich Von Stroheim, in which an ex-convict (Lionel Barrymore) revenges himself on his enemies by reducing them to two inches in height.

Another survivor from the Silents was Buster Keaton, whose first Sound vehicle, **Free and Easy** (1930), took in more money than any of his films in years – which convinced the studio anew that he should not return to creative control. Edward Sedgwick directed this and all Keaton's M-G-M Talkies except **The Sidewalks of New York,** when he was replaced by Jules White and Zion Myers. This was so bad that release was delayed for two years, and Keaton himself particularly despised it; but it has moments of clowning – such as carving the duck – reminiscent of his great

days. The other Talkies indicate no understanding of his qualities – and if a leap onto a train in *Free and Easy* was to demonstrate his agility, it is bungled, since the crucial action is not shown. Perhaps he was too drunk to do it; alcoholism, unreliability and increasing audience apathy caused his contract to be annulled in 1933, and he entered that dark period from which he would not really emerge for more than two decades, when his Silent work began to be appreciated.

Cecil B. deMille also failed at M-G-M at this time. He arrived at the studio after his period of independence, and made **Dynamite** (1929) and **Madam Satan** (1930), both starring Kay Johnson, an actress new to the screen. Her assets were an attractive voice and a brittle comedy style, the latter certainly needed but in fact wasted in the cheerless circumstances. As critics of the time observed, both films blended deMille's specialities – sex and spectacle, with both scripts indicating humorous minds at work. Unfortunately, the serious lines in both are even funnier than those intended to be, and *Madam Satan,* with its climax of fancy-dressed partygoers parachuting from a stricken zeppelin, redefines that quality called by a later generation 'camp'. When a remake of *The Squaw Man* also flopped, deMille returned to Paramount, never again daring to attempt the marital society comedies of which these are the last examples.

Madam Satan was also a musical, a genre so overworked in 1930 that this particular studio abandoned no less than four already in production. After Warners re-established it, Thalberg invited Lubitsch and Chevalier to M-G-M for a new version of **The Merry Widow** (1934), reuniting both with Jeanette MacDonald, now under contract to the studio. She replaced the Metropolitan diva, Grace Moore, who refused to take second billing to Chevalier – a fact for which we must be grateful, since the existing partnership was never more entrancing – nor, with barely a kiss between them, more erotically charged. It is a triumph even by Lubitsch standards, brilliantly designed in blacks and whites, and as light and insubstantial as a dream.

Like his previous film for the company, *The Student Prince,* the cost was so high that a profit was unlikely – but this being M-G-M, no one minded too much. With the exception of *Ben-Hur,* the company had never spent as much on a picture; *Trader Horn,* and more recently *Viva Villa!, Grand Hotel* and *Queen Christina* (q.v.) had all proved that a huge cost could be justified at the box-office – as would *Mutiny on the Bounty* (q.v.) in 1935. The budgets might be higher than at other studios, but when cinema attendances took a sudden tumble in 1932, M-G-M alone stayed in profit, with six of its productions listed in the *Motion Picture Herald* top ten grossing films. Warner Bros. lost $14 million, Paramount $16 million, and Fox exceeded both at $17 million, but M-G-M showed a profit of $8 million. That fall in attendances proved temporary; but if, in 1934, M-G-M remained the most lucrative of the studios, with a net profit of $7½ million, the losses at Warners, for instance, continued for the fourth year running – amounting to more than $2½ million, despite a paring of budgets.

Universal managed to stay afloat on the success of its horror fims – and like much in film history, that success was unexpected. In 1929 Carl Laemmle had appointed his son general manager – and it was Junior Laemmle (as he was usually known) who had instigated *All Quiet on the Western Front.* He had also bought a 1927 play, based on a novel by Bram Stoker, as a studio reunion for Tod Browning and Lon Chaney – but the latter died, and Browning had to substitute in the title-role of **Dracula** (1931) the Hungarian-born actor who had played it on Broadway, Bela Lugosi. With gleaming shirt-front and equally gleaming stare, he stalks through a fog-bound London in search of his prey – except when his bat-like cloak shelters him all too literally, and he flies. With Karl Freund on camera, the film bears witness to Browning's flair for the genre, but Universal gave the follow-up **Frankenstein** (1931), to James Whale, and a small-part actor, Boris Karloff, replaced Lugosi, who had quarrelled with the studio. James Whale (1896–1957) had successfully directed one film for the studio, *Waterloo Bridge* (q.v.), and as a European he was automatically, by the usual criterion, suitable for this version of an old but not classic novel, by Mary Shelley. It created an even greater furore than its predecessor, and remains the most viewable of vintage horrors – partly because of the masterly and famous make-up, and partly because Karloff contributes so much, such as the splayed walk and the animal groans. Nevertheless, the encounter between the monster and the child is somewhat embarrassing ('Who are you? I'm Maria. Will you play with me?'), but the sets, in which Whale took a special interest, are typical of his enterprise as a whole.

Freund himself was one of the Europeans recruited by Universal to direct these movies. **The Mummy** (1932) has Karloff in a double role, as the perfidious, hypnotising priest, and his own ancestor, the resuscitated 37,000-year-old mummy. 'Is there a view anywhere like this in the world?' asks someone, gazing on the Sphinx and the Pyramids from a Cairo nightclub. Freund directed a few other films, including *Mad Love* for M-G-M, a remake of *Orlacs Hände,* with Peter Lorre an outstanding villain, his head like a malevolent egg. Universal pitted Karloff and Lugosi against each other in **The Black Cat** (1934), directed by a new director from Germany, Edgar G. Ulmer, and including a Black Mass, which was not in Poe's original story and which caused the film to be banned in Britain and other countries. Alas, what had been allusive in his story **Murders in the Rue Morgue** (1932) becomes only too explicit as directed by the veteran Frenchman, Robert Florey. Also to this series belongs **The Mystery of Edwin Drood** (1935), directed (as was a version of *Great Expectations*) by Stuart Walker, in decline since leaving Paramount; one of its writers was the successful dramatist, John Balderston, a contributor to most of these scenarios, and among its players are Claude Rains, as a very wicked John Jasper, and Francis L. Sullivan (in training for his roles in David Lean's two Dickens films, q.v.) as Mr Crisparkle.

It was Whale who made the best of Universal's horror films, though these would not include **The Old Dark House** (1932), adapted by Benn W. Levy from a novel by J. B. Priestley about some stranded strangers subjected to the odd behaviour of its sinister inmates. Despite enjoyable performances from Charles Laughton (q.v.) as a newly rich Northerner and Karloff as a deaf-mute butler, lecherous and dangerous when drunk, the film seems to despise even those audiences who share its jokiness. However, **The Invisible Man**

(1933) is amusing and faithful to Wells, as adapted by R. C. Sherriff in a happy reunion with Whale. The effects are outstanding, and though the supporting performances are terrible, Claude Rains beautifully speaks the title-role – meant for Karloff, who had in turn quarrelled with the studio. **The Bride of Frankenstein** (1935) solves the knotty problem of a sequel by proposing that the monster was not, after all, dead, but living by an underground lake. Another curiosity is that this sequel, being discussed by Mary Shelley in a historical prologue, is nevertheless in modern dress. This time Frankenstein (Colin Clive again) is tempted to create a bride (Elsa Lanchester) for the monster, who, rejected by her, goes on a rampage and destroys, *inter alia,* all the scientific apparatus: but this time a way was left open for a sequel. It came, in 1939, as Universal relegated its horror product to the lower half of double bills; and Whale did not direct it.

His other early films are charming. **Waterloo Bridge** (1931) is a World War I anecdote about a prostitute (Mae Clarke) and a soldier (Kent Douglass), closely adapted from the play by Robert E. Sherwood and depending for its effectiveness on the boy being too naive and love-sick even to suspect her true profession. **The Impatient Maiden** (1932) disposes cleverly of another artificial situation, this time caused by the Depression, as a stenographer (Miss Clarke) allows herself to be kept by her boss (John Halliday) though in love with a student doctor (Lew Ayres). Nor is likelihood the strong point of **A Kiss Before the Mirror** (1933), but it is refreshingly matter-of-fact on marital relations: a lawyer (Frank Morgan) is defending a friend (Paul Lukas) for the murder of his adulterous wife when he has cause to suspect his own (Nancy Carroll). Morgan's innate goodness gives the film a centre, and the torment of the principals is thrown into relief by the relaxed playing of Charles Grapewin as his secretary – proof that Grapewin was later wasted, type cast as a yokel. Without losing his sense of realism, Whale moves easily into the world of the wealthy Viennese bourgeoisie, but that is not the only reason that *Motion Picture Magazine* found 'this delicately woven drama more like a foreign-made picture'. It remains extraordinary, far better than Whale's own, Americanised remake, *Wives Under Suspicion.*

Universal's horror films were part of the Laemmles, makeshift policy, which consisted of the churning-out of programmers, plus an occasional pre-sold popular novel or play. Thus their major comedy of the period, **Once in a Lifetime** (1932), is a literal transposition of the Kaufman-Hart play about the coming of Sound to Hollywood, with Aline MacMahon, Jack Oakie and Russell Hopton as a vaudeville team which takes itself to the studios to teach voice. As directed by Russell Mack, Oakie offers a portrait of stupidity unequalled in films for more than a generation, and Louise Fazenda is funny as a vapid gossip columnist: but the piece belongs to Miss MacMahon, cool-headed and conniving.

Not surprisingly, the Universal policy did not attract talent, which usually arrived on loan-out or short-term contract. Thus John Ford arrived to make **Air Mail** (1932), written by a specialist in such tales, Frank Wead, offering little new, even then, in squabbling flyers (Pat O'Brien, Ralph Bellamy) or in airfields with particularly bad weather conditions. However, the Laemmles did belatedly discover that they had under contract a front-rank director, William Wyler (1902–81), a distant relative, who had been turning out mainly two-reel Westerns for them since 1925. He established his mastery with **A House Divided** (1931), since the subject was the familiar – and artificial – one of the mail-order bride. He made it both touching and seemingly fresh, filming almost all the film in a small fishing village; and there has never been a more terrifying storm at sea on film than the one that forms the climax. Walter Huston gives his usual consummate performance as the groom and Helen Chandler and Kent Douglass are superb as the youngsters; Walter's son John (q.v.) gained his first screen credit for the dialogue. Wyler was further admired for **Tom Brown of Culver** (1932), approaching that institution with documentary vigour. His sheer intelligence in planning and execution is immediately evident in **Counsellor-at-law** (1932), after he had battled with the Laemmles to restrict the action to the lawyer's offices, as in Elmer Rice's Broadway play, using swift editing and a battery of close-ups to disguise the fact. His model was Capra's *American Madness* (q.v.), and the result, said *The New York Times,* was 'incisive and compelling' – not

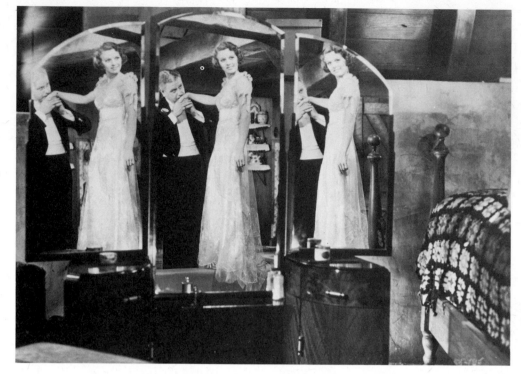

Frank Borzage's *Little Man, What Now?* is one of the formidable Hollywood romances of the Depression era, in which the hero and heroine suffer prettily, sometimes amusingly and without rancour. Their garret is picturesque, and she, Margaret Sullavan, is wearing a sequinned evening-gown the day he is sacked. However, she is a realist, and knows exactly how to cope with her mother-in-law's lover, Alan Hale, seen admiring her here.

adjectives automatically applied to Rice's work – with one of John Barrymore's more rounded performances.

John M. Stahl (1886–1950) had been directing for over a decade when he found his forte with **Back Street** (1932), showing justified confidence both in Fannie Hurst's sentimental bestseller about a woman (Irene Dunne) who elects to spend her life as the unacknowledged mistress of a prominent banker (John Boles); and Miss Dunne (q.v.), plays the role with that blend of grace and light heartedness which was her own secret. Both this and the 1941 version (q.v.) appear miraculous beside a later one, directed in 1961 by David Miller and throwing away every aspect which makes them admirable. Margaret Sullavan (1911–60), the star of the second version, is Stahl's heroine in **Only Yesterday** (1933), pert and 'forward', like Dunne reacting to her woes with levity and never asking for emotional charity. The screenplay is supposedly based on a book of the same name, 'an informal history of the Nineteen Twenties', and it starts on the eve of the Wall Street crash as Boles receives a 'letter from an unknown woman'. Anyone who has seen Ophuls's film of that name (q.v.) will recognise Stefan Zweig's story, here uncredited, and this version is the more faithful, despite the transposition of the setting to the U.S. and World War One.

Also directed for romantic intensity at full pitch, in this case by Frank Borzage, is **Little Man, What Now?** (1934), though it lacked the edge of the original material – the novel by Hans Fallada which had caught the imagination on both sides of the Atlantic and had in fact already been filmed in Germany. Universal remembering its success with another German bestseller, bought the rights, and cast as the couple coping with the Depression Miss Sullavan and Douglass Montgomery – the Kent Douglass of *Waterloo Bridge*. (That this actor reverted to his Broadway name while playing leading roles is indicative of the failure of his earlier films.) However, he is a prig, and his mother runs a bordello; the girl sees things clearly and there is a chill in the air, as in the other Borzage views of Europe, from *Seventh Heaven* to *The Mortal Storm*. (q.v.)Political unrest is represented by two briefly seen rallies and a starving couple who function as a Greek chorus, talking of people of 'our faith'. No one mentions the Nazis or Communists, but that, in view of the whole Hollywood schema of the time would have been superfluous. The best scene in the film is set round a huge satin-quilted double bed, as the couple chat with the lecherous lodger (Alan Hale); it was also, almost certainly, the last time a couple were seen in a double bed in an American film for many years.

At Fox, Winfield Sheehan ran the show, since the founder had been forced out in 1929 after an unsuccessful attempt to take over M-G-M – though the matter was complicated by the Wall Street crisis and William Fox's own incapacity as the result of a car crash. One of his last actions had been to endorse a wide-screen process, and his all-star revue, *Happy Days,* had been released both in that and standard gauge. So was **The Big Trail** (1930), and since there was also a German-language version each scene was filmed three times, at a total cost of over $4 million – though contributing to that figure was inadequate pre-planning for location-shooting, something which the industry coupled with M-G-M's troubles on *Viva Villa!*. The film was so long shooting that M-G-M's wide-screen *Billy the Kid* preceded it, but the public would have nothing to do with either. Its star many years later claimed that was because Fox withdrew the wide-screen version too quickly, but the truth was that the public had tired of endless versions of *The Covered Wagon.* The star concerned is John Wayne (1907–79), in his first leading role, gauche and inexperienced, doomed by the film's failure to spend the ensuing decade in B movies. The director, Raoul Walsh, responded more keenly to **Yellow Ticket** (1931), adapted from a play for John Barrymore had done in 1914, about a Russian Jewess (Elissa Landi) who procures the passport allotted to prostitutes in order to circumvent racial laws: her manifold adventures involve a British journalist (Laurence Olivier), a prince (Walter Byron), and the latter's uncle (Lionel Barrymore), motivated equally by lust and respect for the aristocracy.

Sheehan's interest in European affairs, however, was mainly concerned with repeating the success of the Fox war films of the Twenties; thus he elected to make **Surrender** (1931), already filmed by Universal in 1921, from a novel by Pierre Benoît about a French prisoner of war (Warner Baxter) and a German aristocratic family. 'What's Beethoven after the Big Berthas?' cries the only surviving son (Alexander Kirkland), as the old Count (C. Aubrey Smith) raves about the country's glories. The director is William K. Howard, moving his material at breakneck speed, as also in **Transatlantic** (1931), the usual shipboard potpourri – con-men, crooks and infidelity, and **Sherlock Holmes** (1932), a long way from Conan Doyle, with Clive Brook in the title-role, Reginald Owen, most masterly of character actors, as Watson, and Ernest Torrence stealing the piece as Moriarty.

The Power and the Glory (1933), was, in the words of C. A. Lejeune in *The Observer,* 'a courageous film, which has dared to break new ground in the very heart of the commercial cinema'. The funeral of the opening scene turns out to be that of the protagonist (Spencer Tracy), about whom there are divisions of opinion, and the film subsequently examines him as he changes from idealistic illiterate to ruthless autocrat. The thesis was not new even then – Tracy would do a later version in *Edward, My Son* (q.v.) – but the distinction lies in the fact that this man's life is not followed in chronological order. In that we recognise the genesis of *Citizen Kane* (q.v.): that this is not notably inferior is due less to Howard's direction than to the dialogue, by Preston Sturges (q.v.), then best known as a Broadway dramatist, and to Tracy's performance which, as gauche young man or unloved tycoon, always has an underlying humour. Colleen Moore plays the schoolteacher who becomes his – eventually embittered – wife.

Spencer Tracy (1900–67) is Fox's most interesting actor of the period. He came from the stage remarkably assured, but was too young – or so they thought at Fox – for the type of authoritative roles played by Walter Huston; since leading men were slotted into categories, he was cast tough and cocky like Gable and Cagney, though in his case resource and thought gave his roles more colour than was in the writing. He is superb as a confident, warm-hearted cop in **Me and My Gal** (1932), especially in his slanging matches with the girl concerned (Joan Bennett), which include a parody of *Strange Interlude.* It is an 'anything goes' tale, obviously, to do with racketeers; Raoul Walsh directed, with a certain zest,

The most enduring of the films directed by John Ford are probably those which he made for Fox in the early Talkie period – unpretentious studio productions, sometimes made with great feeling. *Pilgrimage*, OPPOSITE, features Henrietta Crossman, centre, a distinguished stage actress who made too few films, seen here with Robert Warwick. *Doctor Bull*, BELOW RIGHT, is one of the three films in which Ford directed another remarkable artist, Will Rogers – allowing him to rephrase the dialogue as he thought fit, which may be one reason why the actor's homely philosophising, difficult now to read, are delightful in practice.

but the blackness of the Warner films is lacking – the situation of the paralysed witness (Henry B. Walthall) seems to have embarrassed everyone but the actor concerned. However, as directed by Rowland Brown, **Quick Millions** (1931) is among the best gangster films. At the beginning Tracy is a truck driver but, as he says himself, he's a man with a ton of brain, too nervous to steal, too lazy to work; as a big-time racketeer, his life style is summed up by a statement to his moll (Sally Eilers), 'And before we get blotto, I'm gonna make another suggestion.' He falls for a 'high-class dame' but, double-crossed, attends the wedding only as a silk hat thrown from a limousine, whereupon a spokesman says that society has been cowardly, and blames the press for glorifying the dying words of gangsters. In fact, in this respect Hollywood and the press were locked in a mutual embrace of praise and rebuke. Thus, Tracy's first opponent in this film is in striking contrast to him, a contractor (John Wray) forced to pay protection money – ageing, bald, with wing-collar and pince-nez, a poor sap with whom no one in the audience would want to identify.

Born Reckless (1930) predates the Warner gangster movies. Edmund Lowe is a small-time crook who goes straight after becoming a war hero, but lets loyalty draw him back to crime – though as its victim. Unlike later examples of the genre, this one tries to suggest causes, but it is a minor film. John Ford directed, but was more at ease with **Seas Beneath** (1931), a conventional sea story which, without pitching and tossing, gives a more vivid impression of life at sea than any other film I can recall. Both films were written by Dudley Nichols (1895–1960), starting his long association with Ford. Their partnership is better exemplified by **Pilgrimage** (1933), about a mother (Henrietta Crossman) who enlists her son (Norman Foster) rather than have him marry the girl (Marian Nixon) she considers a tramp. The greatness of the film lies in its middle section, when she goes to France to see her son's grave, her guilt counterbalanced by the prestige of being the only bereaved mother in her county. Ford had caught beautifully the professional concern of social workers, and he manages well the sticky final sequence when the old lady in Paris, finds a surrogate son. Miss Crossman, keeping the woman's

humanity and odd humour dead centre, gives one of the screen's great performances.

Ford handled another consummate artist in three movies – Will Rogers, who had come into his own with Talkies and was now the studio's chief male star. In **Doctor Bull** (1933) he expresses the commonsense and homely wisdom expected both of a country doctor and himself, without pomposity and throwing away at least one line in six. He is a shy man, uncertain of his success with women; he has a quiff and the button eyes of Little Orphan Annie. He doesn't think he is a very good doctor – but he doesn't think much of the townsfolk either; his enemies are stuck up, intolerant, full of cant; and family audiences of the Depression welcomed his frank approach to such matters – not dissimilar from that of Marie Dressler, equally middle-aged and popular. His humour is different from hers, if just as sly, observing that he likes delivering Italian babies because he is given a glass of wine, or asking 'What you all doin' here ? Someone git out?' to a group looking into a grave. In this film Ford takes him close to emotion, but keeping him out of camera range or with his back towards us. **Judge Priest** (1934) is based on some memory pieces by Irvin S. Cobb, about small-town rivalries: it is a movie suffused with love and affection, as is **Steamboat 'Round the Bend** (1935), in which Cobb himself appears, as the rival riverboat captain. Appearing in both films, alas, is Stepin Fetchit, a black actor who epitomised the idle and thick-headed qualities supposedly found in 'niggers'.

By the time audiences saw the boat steaming round the bend, Fox had amalgamated with 20th Century Pictures (q.v.) and Rogers had died (like Miss Dressler, at the height of his popularity), killed in an air crash. Of his earlier films, **A Connecticut Yankee** (1931) based on Mark Twain, has him offering homilies to the dunderheaded knights of the Round Table, a one-joke film, neatly handled by David Butler. **Mr Skitch** (1933), directed by James Cruze, concerns a family dispossessed by the Depression, and though it is pleasing today to see this national hero with an eye to the fast buck, it could not have been of much benefit to audiences of the time. **Lightnin'** (1930) is an account of Frank Bacon's old vehicle (both as star and co-author), in its

The foreword to Henry King's *State Fair* notes that such fairs are ephemeral, which, together with the film's short running time, suggest only a diversion. That it is much more than that is due to these four players – Norman Foster, Louise Dresser, Janet Gaynor and Will Rogers. The movies have seldom offered a more convincing family.

time (1918) the longest-running Broadway play, at 1,291 performances, and already filmed by Ford for Fox in 1925; as rewritten by S. N. Behrman and Sonya Levien the role of the divorcees' hotelier makes for 'a really enchanting one man show', as the British *Film Weekly* put it.

The director was Henry King, starting that contract which would make him Fox's leading director for the rest of his career: during the Zanuck period he would be associated with many of the company's most important films. Unlike Ford, who was tempted towards 'statements' like *The Informer* (q.v.), King never believed in film as an art; and where Ford tended to like certain situations, e.g. those involving masculine camaraderie, King was content with any believable one. The more honest the writing, the more realistic his handling, as critics had noted with *Tol'able David* and *Stella Dallas;* he brings warmth even to **Merely Mary Ann** (1931), a popular waif tale, already twice filmed and this time chiefly a vehicle for the team of Janet Gaynor and Charles Farrell – now nearing its end, as Farrell's high-to-rasping voice would soon relegate him to supporting roles. **State Fair** (1933), based on Phil Stong's novel, is worth both the – musical – remakes (q.v.) put together; unlike the 1945 version it does not try for charm, but it has it effortlessly. King's imaginative touches are not in the remakes: pa (Rogers) placing a

rug round ma's shoulders as they drive to the fair; ma (Louise Dresser) pulling her ear lobes as she hears she has won the pickle prize; the son (Norman Foster) pulling the closet door to muffle his phone conversation; the daughter (Miss Gaynor) and her reporter in the doorway of his flat, examining each other in the light from the street.

Though the film re-established King's reputation, he was assigned to **Marie Galante** (1934) merely as a reliable handler of players – for the female lead was Ketti Gallian, a French girl who was Fox's entry in the Garbo-Dietrich stakes. Having cast her, like them, as a fallen woman in an exotic locale, Fox then lost nerve, for the crimson heroine of Jacques Deval's novel had become, said *The New York Times,* 'a virtuous and extraordinarily naive girl'. The story does not, therefore, make much sense. Spencer Tracy is convincing as a government agent trying to prevent the sabotage of the Panama Canal, but Miss Gallian, attractive at first, soon proves a lesser figure than Helen Morgan – whose two songs prove again that she was an immensely poignant interpreter of words and music.

One More Spring (1935) was more congenial to King, but perhaps because its conclusions are dishonest it is no more than pleasant – certainly a lesser work than Borzage's similarly-themed *Man's Castle* (q.v.). Everything, it says, following three lovable derelicts in Central Park, will be All Right if we only love one another; it – the Depression – was nobody's fault; the government is bound to help – but the best palliative is a convenient millionaire. Robert Nathan's novel had been published in 1933, and things had begun to look decidedly better by the time this film reached the world's screens. Bowdlerisation means that the musician Rosenberg (Walter Woolf King) is Jewish of feature and gesture only, and the hooker has become an out-of-work actress (Miss Gaynor): the appeal to Fox lay mainly in the co-starring chances for two of its biggest – but fading – stars. Miss Gaynor was finally becoming old-fashioned, but she could still put her imprint on a film; Warner Baxter was ever able to confront a desperate situation with fortitude, but one cannot but come to the conclusion that to be down-and-out at his age would not have permitted the least levity.

Edwin Burke wrote the screenplay and

With one exception, the extant Silent pictures of Erich Von Stroheim concern the *recherché* sexual practices of the European nobility or military set, with an occasional American victim from a similar social order. The answer to how he might react to an American urban working-class milieu is *Hello, Sister!* – and it is clear that at this stage Minna Gombell and Terrance Ray had nothing to learn from any European. Though Von Stroheim's name is not on the credits, they were surely tutored by him.

also that of Borzage's **Bad Girl** (1931), from a novel by Vina Delmar. Borzage won an Oscar for his direction, and *The New York Times,* not always so perceptive, included the film in its list of the year's best. Its critic, Mordaunt Hall, was understandably puzzled by the title – for Dorothy (Sally Eilers) is a good girl. Since the plot is much like that of *The Crowd,* it is not surprising that she meets the boy, Eddie (James Dunn), on a steamer returning from Coney Island. He works in a radio shop, and dreams of owning his own; when at the end he refers to the new baby as 'the future president of the United States' the remark is not risible but a further indication of the stubborn faith in democracy. Earlier, the goodnight conversations on the stairs have a truth seldom found in American pictures, and there is a remarkable study of the relationship between Eddie and the girl's best friend (Minna Gombell), moving from mutual dislike through bantering insult to respect. The film is also notable for the rare use of overlapping dialogue, sentences half-heard and slang (elsewhere usually restricted to gangsters and reporters); and if there are a few jarring notes, it is eloquent proof that Hollywood's flirtations with realism in the late Twenties subsequently bore at least one fruit.

Unlike its predecessors it was popular, but the only result was a series of films co-starring Dunn and Eilers; although he is

279

terrific here, playing unforcedly and with natural gosh–oh–darn ability, none of his other films with Eilers is worthy of note except one which we may consider a companion piece, **Hello Sister!** (1933), with direction credited to Alfred Werker. However, it had started out as *Walking Down Broadway*, directed by Erich Von Stroheim; and though said to have been completely re-shot, this seems unlikely from internal evidence. 'All you gotta do is walk down Broadway and act like you're not clean-minded' is the advice of the much-married Mona (Miss Gombell) for Millie (Zazu Pitts) and Peggy (Boots Mallory); but after they're picked up by Jimmy (Dunn) and Mac (Terrance Ray), nothing again is quite so simple. The bumpy road to love is complicated by sexual needs – not to mention some climactic street explosions, which would seem not to have been part of Von Stroheim's film. Gone from his original are a bawdy love scene between Mona and Mac, and the hero's seduction of the heroine, watched by the frustrated Millie; the tampering has made the lovers little more than ninnies, and Millie behaves oddly, even for her. Nevertheless Mona, a whore in the original, remains more convincing than most of the broads of the period, and Mac's crude approach is singularly believable: it is a typical Von Stroheim touch that he should attempt rape after a successful bout with another woman. We may be sure that this sequence is his, and the visit to the gynaecologist (with its religious symbolism), as well as the Coney Island swapping which sets the prevailing mood of cheap sexuality – quite unlike that of the other films of the period. The conversion, in fact, was clearly half-hearted: it was due to a producers' row within Fox , involving Sheehan, and had nothing to do with Von Stroheim's extravagance – yet it was regarded as another of his failures, sealing his career as a director.

It has in common with **Call Her Savage** (1932) hardly a thought above the navel. This was designed for Clara Bow, whose career Fox hoped to resurrect, playing a half-Indian heiress discovered whipping her pal Moonglow (Gilbert Roland) – practising, as she explains, for marriage. She does marry, after two headline-making years at finishing-school, a man who only wanted to get even with his mistress; disowned by him, she gambles away her

allowance till he tries to rape her while supposedly dying; in New Orleans, she takes to the streets, to buy medicine for the baby. There is a fire, a death and a legacy, all at once, and she returns to New York to 'get even with life', which means becoming betrothed to a gigolo: but he leaves her after she has a public brawl with her husband's mistress, whereupon she takes to drink in a skin-tight white lamé gown. Since two effeminate waiters have a fond duet about sailors, we may say that only female homosexuality is missing. Miss Bow, bright-eyed and plump as a squirrel, makes us wonder how she might have been with a great director – which John Francis Dillon certainly was not. The film did not succeed in restoring her to public favour.

Still exploiting the femme fatale, Fox offered **The Worst Woman in Paris?** (1933), directed by Monta Bell with none of his earlier brilliance, a lugubrious drama about a notorious beauty (Benita Hume) who is a real joe at heart, sacrificing her true love to help a friend (Helen Chandler). As escapism, you might prefer **Chandu the Magician** (1932), based on a nightly radio serial, and the studio's only contribution to the fantasy-horror fad. Under the dual direction of Marcel Varnel and William Cameron Menzies, poor Chandu (Edmund Lowe) finds his magicianship limited, unable immediately to defeat Roxor (Bela Lugosi), who is planning world domination from his underground palace high above the Nile: 'This death-ray in the hands of Roxor means the end of all that is good, all that is sane . . .'

Of similar innocence is **Zoo in Budapest** (1933), set entirely inside the *tiergarten* and telling of the idyll between animal-loving Zani (Gene Raymond) and orphan Eve (Loretta Young), hiding from the humans who are hunting them. The director, Rowland V. Lee, and the photographer, Lee Garmes, make pretty patterns with birds, beasts and leaves, and the screenplay is nicely against cages, orphanages, fur coats, the evil and the ugly. There never was a heroine more winsome than Miss Young, but one loses patience with Raymond and the whimsy both. Jesse L. Lasky produced, his first assignment on leaving Paramount.

Fox's most important picture of the time – and for years afterwards – was **Cavalcade** (1933), despite or because of its being

obstinately British in every respect. Notwithstanding its success at Drury Lane, Coward's play had not been seen in New York, so a Movietone News crew was sent to record the London production, in order that it might be faithfully reproduced in Hollywood. The film, therefore, preserves the exact nature of British theatre of the time, and if it is this which, by virtue of stiff acting, harms it, it is also what makes it enchanting – the inserts of the musical comedy and the end-of-pier show. It is a tale of 'upstairs and downstairs' – the Marryots and their servants, the Bridges. As the senior Marryots, Diana Wynyard and Clive Brook cope with every well-bred emotion which is their lot; as their children, Frank Lawton and Ursula Jeans skirt passages that sound like self-parody ('But it was *fun*, wasn't it?', 'Are you going to miss me *des*perately?'); as the Bridges, Herbert

Mundin is fine but Una O'Connor goes over the top. However, all that is maudlin gets forgotten in the care taken to realise the whole; all that is superficial – it is as accurate a picture of British life as 'Peter Pan' – is forgiven in the conception. The five-minute montage of the War is magnificent, given the emotive power of 'Tipperary' and 'Keep the Home Fires Burning': one strain of 'Yankee Doodle' is thrilling in its brevity. As a gesture of American friendship, the film is in itself moving; at the New York premiere the audience stood and cheered – a pattern repeated during its subsequent career. In the domestic market alone it took $3,500,000 – as much as any twelve Fox movies put together, and it won Oscars as Best Picture and for Frank Lloyd – whose replacement of Borzage early in the filming lost Fox one of its best directors.

Sheehan tried to repeat the success with

Cavalcade recaptures the heartbreaks of an era. Though its jingoism has now become quaint what remains regrettable is Noël Coward's opposing attitudes towards the upstairs and downstairs families – the Marryots, played by Diana Wynyard and Clive Brook, centre, and their servants, the Bridges, played by Herbert Mundin and Una O'Connor: he is in awe of the former, patronising towards the latter.

281

The World Moves On (1934), and was indeed so proud of it that he took producer credit (most Fox films of the time carry none). He commissioned Reginald C. Berkeley – author of a recent Broadway success, 'Lady with the Lamp' – to write a *Cavalcade* with an American slant. Berkeley's convoluted story begins with a New Orleans family in 1824, and mainly concerns its British, French, American *and* German branches in 1914, concluding in a dilapidated mansion just after the Wall Street crash. 'Everything's gone,' says Madeleine Carroll. 'Not everything,' says Franchot Tone, as the camera pans to a crucifix. John Ford directed: 'I pleaded and quit and everything else, but I was under contract and finally had to do it . . . It was really a lousy picture.'

At United Artists, Mary Pickford did her own version of *Cavalcade* – with a touch of *Cimarron* (q.v.) – called **Secrets** (1933) and based on a 1922 Broadway play by Rudolf Besier and May Edginton. A first version was scrapped, at a loss of $300,000, but after *Kiki* she returned to it, bringing in Borzage, who had directed the Silent version with Norma Talmadge, and a new leading man, Leslie Howard (q.v.). It opened, she recalled 'in twenty-five key cities on the day President Roosevelt declared the bank holiday. Very few people were spending money on entertainment in the weeks that followed, and while the film was well received, it was a financial disaster.' In any other circumstances it would still have been a disaster. The original is, obviously, a series of one-act plays concerning the same people, taking the heroine from elopement to distinguished old age via an ambush in a log cabin and her husband's infidelity. As a film from Borzage's richer period, it is particularly disappointing; he was adept at making romance both credible and touching, but he is handicapped by his star. She had a good speaking voice, but it is one without character – and that is true of her performance as a whole. In 'Act III' she plays a matriarch, the only time during her later career that she played her own age – and that is the closest she comes to being remotely interesting She did not film again.

In his role as American hero, Douglas Fairbanks decided to help vanquish the Depression, playing a stockbroker who loses his fortune in **Reaching for the Moon** (1931): but the suggestion that the solution is to marry an heiress (Bebe Daniels) is, if appealing, not very practical. Edmund Goulding directed, which may be why there are a number of misunderstandings concerning men embracing, less naively handled than was usual at the time. Distressed with the film's failure and his waning marriage, Fairbanks offered **Around the World in 80 Minutes With Douglas Fairbanks** (1931), co-directing with Victor Fleming, who also appears in it. He infuses it with his usual energy, whether clambering up Angkor Vat or doing a spot of calisthenics on deck. But he was no longer so lithe, and since Talkies were hardly the medium for his pantomime, he no longer knew what films to make. He did not care to return to Westerns nor invade the underworld, so he protected his image with **Mr Robinson Crusoe** (1932), directed by Edward Sutherland, jumping ship in the South Seas and playing at desert island, with mechanical devices as enterprising as anything in Disney.

Clearly, with Chaplin taking years to prepare one film, United Artists needed product, and since the only one of its producers supplying this with frequency was Sam Goldwyn, he assumed increasing importance within the company. When regarded by the press as either its head or its spokesman he was not inclined to contradict. His imaginative contributions were, as hitherto, confined to vehicles for his stars, but he did assign John Ford to direct Ronald Colman in **Arrowsmith** (1931), adapted by Sidney Howard from the novel by Sinclair Lewis. The direction, apart from some over-emphatic close-ups, is subtle, and Colman is at his Galahadish best as the young doctor who manages, just, to hang on to his ideals through indifference, quackery, official bungling and, most importantly, love of publicity. There are also good studies by Helen Hayes as the wife, and Myrna Loy as the New York sophisticate who comforts Arrowsmith when he is widowed.

It is the only interesting Goldwyn film of the period, unless you are addicted to the over-enthusiastic clowning of the vaudevillian Eddie Cantor (1893–1964). Certainly the black-face minstrel show in **Kid Millions** (1934), also with Ethel Merman, is invigorating as directed by Roy del

Ruth, and the musical finale – set in an ice-cream factory and one of the last instances of two-tone Technicolor – has a weird splendour of its own. The Busby Berkeley musical sequences of **Roman Scandals** (1933) contain only the five or six basic ideas and routines that he had been using for years, confirming later claims that his more elaborate later work at Warners was collaborative, but the film as a whole, if no more enterprising, indicates the Goldwyn approach – with George S. Kaufman and Robert E. Sherwood providing the story, and Sherwood and the equally well-thought-of William Anthony McGuire the screenplay. However, if they came up with anything beyond anachronistic jokes for Cantor – an old Goldwyn favourite – the direction by Frank Tuttle disguises the fact, though the chariot race was later plagiarised for *A Funny Thing Happened on the Way to the Forum* (q.v.).

Mention should also be made of Anna Sten, exquisite in European films but a failure for Goldwyn. When Garbo's appeal was found intensified by Sound, Hollywood's acquisition of continental beauties was stepped up and many embarked, never to be heard of again. Goldwyn, with greater belief than most in his own infallibility, persisted, and during the two years that Miss Sten laboured to learn English and whatever else was thought would make her the greatest star in the world, he announced grandiose plans. He finally settled on **Nana** (1934), to be directed by von Sternberg, supposedly experienced in the ways of accented glamour, but in the event it was directed by Dorothy Arzner. Further, the film was only 'suggested by' Zola, now having elements of Gloria Swanson's old ersatz imitation, *Zaza,* so that Miss Sten could sing à la Dietrich. There is no marked difference between her Nana and her Grushenka in *Der Mörder Dmitri Karamazov* (q.v.), except that, in English, she is merely another arch coquette – and audiences had had their fill of such ladies and their final-reel repentance. Goldwyn tried twice more before giving up, and there is a certain plodding worthiness about **The Wedding Night** (1935), as directed by King Vidor; Miss Sten is a country girl who catches the attention of a happily married writer (Gary Cooper).

One who found a haven at U.A. was Howard Hughes (1905–76), a wealthy playboy with an obsessive interest in films. **Hell's Angels** (1930) had started three years earlier, but his idiosyncratic methods meant that much of it had to be refilmed with the coming of Sound – travail that today seems wasted, despite the aerial sequences – though audiences enjoy (not without derision) Jean Harlow's performance as an English girl fought over by doughboys Ben Lyon and James Hall. Hughes, wisely, thereafter contented himself with producing only, and **The Front Page** (1931), as directed by Lewis Milestone, is an account of the Hecht-MacArthur play about crime reporters as fast-talking as it was influential. A superb cast is headed by Adolphe Menjou, appropriately weaselly as the editor, with Walter Catlett, Edward Everett Horton and Frank McHugh among the newsmen; as Hildy, Pat O'Brien is likeable but indefinite, which is why in a long career he never achieved the stature of his friends Cagney and Tracy.

Hughes co-produced, with its director, Howard Hawks, **Scarface: Shame of a Nation** (1932), based on a novel by Armitage Trail, adapted by Ben Hecht, with a screenplay by Seton I. Miller, John Lee Mahin and W. R. Burnett – whose *Little Caesar,* like Tony Camonte here, had also been based on Al Capone. Since this is one of the most celebrated gangster films, it is curious how many of its aspects, if founded on fact, had already been used: the flower-shop killing in *Underworld;* the illuminated sign, 'The world is yours', in *Public Enemy;* the whistle before the murder in *M;* and the obsession with a sibling in both *Doorway to Hell* and *Born Reckless* – and as in the latter case it is a sister (Ann Dvorak) longing to get in with her brother's pals, but now the obsession is incestuous. Paul Muni (q.v.) as Camonte-Capone is both stupider and vainer than Edward G. Robinson, more open with the laugh and bonhomie, and, finally, more craven – the coward the Chief of Detectives had always claimed him to be. Originally, he was to have been killed by a rival gang, but the Hays Office insisted on his being hanged: a compromise was reached by which he is mown down by the police. Hughes fought all attempts at censorship: stories of what was excised or changed ensured the film notoriety before it opened, and it was that which caused its contemporary fame – plus the fact that it was more violent than its predecessors, and audiences had a field day recognising references to actual events.

The previous year at U.A. Roland West had made **Corsair,** deservedly his last film, about a college boy (Chester Morris) who joins the rackets to get even with his girlfriend's father – and in rejecting it the public had made it clear that it disapproved of the notion that gangsters were ordinary people. *Scarface* was more obviously crusading, contemptuous of the gangsters, with a preface from the Police Commissioner of New York demanding the control of fire arms, and the conclusion 'Let's get wise to ourselves. We're fighting organised murder.' The contribution such films made was to insist that new laws were needed, and to point out that the inability to enforce the existing ones was evidence of large-scale corruption (crooked lawyers, hung juries, suborned witnesses). That the public responded to the morality of *Scarface* naturally convinced the Hays Office that it had been right to fight for it, which reinforced a growing suspicion that a Code should be drawn up for the 'guidance' of the industry; the antics of Hughes were as much responsible as those of West and Harlow, on screen, for proving that the existing rules were insufficient.

Hughes turned his attention to other matters, aviatory and amatory. Hawks began his ill-fated tenure at M-G-M, but Milestone remained at United Artists to make **Rain** (1932) and then to take over as production chief, both moves at the behest of Joseph M. Schenck, who, despite Goldwyn, still ran the company. Milestone said later of the film that it 'had no surprise, no novelty and [Joan] Crawford wasn't up to it'; her too-blatant Sadie apart, he might have mentioned Walter Huston's fine moment of sexual tension, glint-eyed as if in the midst of a seizure. Schenck also brought Al Jolson to the company, convinced that he could restore him to favour after the failure of his last Warner films, and he assigned Milestone to direct **Hallelujah, I'm a Bum** (1933) when Harry d'Abbadie d'Arrast couldn't get on with Jolson. The film eventually cost $1¾ million – the equivalent of Jolson's equally astonishing salary – and that was partly because the actor insisted on the removal of Roland Young and Milestone, to be succeeded respectively by Frank Morgan and Chester Erskine, the latter uncredited. It was Miles-

tone who chose Rodgers and Hart to supply the songs and the rhyming dialogue; S. N. Behrman's screenplay about hoboes in Central Park bears a couple of references to the boulevard play which inspired it, and many more to the central relationship in *A Nous la Liberté* – since Milestone, like his fellow Russian Mamoulian, was alive to cinema in Europe. This weird combination of French comedy and Soviet imagery he certainly claimed as his film, and when the Depression audiences for whom it held a message failed, understandably, to find it or even to care, Schenck laid the blame on him: he was relieved of his post with the company, and was not replaced.

The history of the American cinema is littered with attempts to move away from formula: variously applauded in their time, few of them now seem superior to the well-tooled factory product. Their inception was most common when the studios had no strong yea-and-nay men, and United Artists was exceptionally vulnerable, still reeling from exhibitors' recriminations as it offered **Emperor Jones** (1933), directed by Dudley Murphy, whose previous experience, not coincidentally, had included some all-negro shorts. The title-role was played by the great negro artist, Paul Robeson (1898–1976), who had turned down the original stage production but had played it in Europe and also on revival, for financial reasons; it was because of a spiritual which he sang in it that he became singer as well as actor. His original objections to Eugene O'Neill's play had lessened when it had been pointed out that it did not follow conventional form; and it was the first serious play since 'Othello' with a black protagonist. In nine short scenes – and except for the first and the last, the Emperor Jones is alone on stage – the audience learns from his hallucinations how he fled his own country and became, with the aid of a local trader, head-man of a Caribbean island. O'Neill intended a comment on white exploitation in the area, as well as an allegory on the rise of Jean-Christophe in Haiti – a matter rendered topical by recent events in Germany. In the film both factors are virtually ignored, the latter in favour of a new first half, depicting American negroes in accepted fashion as feckless – whoring, shooting crap and knifing each other – a *coup de grâce* administered to Robeson after he had signed the contract. Once the film joins O'Neill, some purpose can be perceived, as Jones, accoutred like a marshal of Napoleon, becomes a strutting, arrogant, thoughtless oligarch, but whatever sense remains in the screenplay by Dubose Heyward (author of 'Porgy') is destroyed by Murphy, as reckless as any first-time amateur. In the circumstances, Robeson's performance, powerful and confident, cannot clarify the character; it was historically too early for films to utilise his tremendous talents, and he appeared in films fitfully and seldom to advantage. Like *Hallelujah!* this film was accepted as 'art' by a lot of people who should have known better.

The installation of a production chief had been Schenck's reponse to the demand for more films from the managers of the distribution offices and theatres in the growing circuit he had created – a problem solved when Darryl F. Zanuck entered the fold after a dispute over control at Warners. With Schenck he formed 20th Century Pictures, based on the simple expedient of formula pictures enhanced by known talent – consisting of the major independent directors and players (initially contracted for two films each), and by borrowings which were secured by the combination of Zanuck's reputation for sound film- making and Schenck's financial resources – which for this purpose would include brother Nicholas, the president of Loews. Therefore, for 20th's first film, **The Bowery** (1933), came Wallace Beery and Jackie Cooper, and from Paramount George Raft. It was a rollicking start: Zanuck's dynamism brought from a variable director, Raoul Walsh, his occasional vigour, and matters stayed bullish with **Blood Money** (1933), directed by Rowland Brown with the speed and authenticity he had brought to *Quick Millions*. An ex-lawyer (George Bancroft) makes a living going bail for the town's criminals, helped or hindered by his girlfriend (Judith Anderson), a tough Britisher who runs a speakeasy, and a society dame (Frances Dee) with a yen for low life and, as it turns out, an inexhaustible capacity for being pushed about. Like Walsh, Brown had just left Fox, and it was at this time that he reputedly crossed one of the industry's bigwigs, with the result that he had no major credits after being replaced in Britain on *The Scarlet Pimpernel* (q.v.).

Gregory LaCava directed two films for Zanuck, **Gallant Lady** (1933), notably

well-acted by Ann Harding as an unfortunate mother and Clive Brook as her drunken-outcast admirer, and **The Affairs of Cellini** (1934), a historical charade with Fredric March as the sculptor, Constance Bennett (q.v.) as his noble prey, and Frank Morgan as her jealous husband – a role he had played in 1924 in the Broadway production of the original, 'The Firebrand'. Zanuck's requirements of gusto and a sometimes misplaced sophistication were also to be found in the two historicals for which he had brought George Arliss from Warners, **The House of Rothschild** (1934), directed by Alfred Werker, and **Cardinal Richelieu** (1935), directed by Rowland V. Lee. The former impressed contemporaries, with its intimations of anti-semitism and complex financial dealings, but indulgence now is needed towards such matters as Nathan's blessing of the romance between his daughter (Loretta Young) and a gentile officer (Robert Young), or the reaction of Wellington (C. Aubrey Smith) to Napoleon's escape, 'Aaah, that blasted little Corsican is back!' The screenwriter was Nunnally Johnson (1897–1977), a former columnist, beginning a long association with Zanuck.

Johnson also wrote **Bulldog Drummond Strikes Back** (1934) for Ronald Colman, greatly superior to the latter's previous Drummond film. Stylishly directed by Roy del Ruth in London fog and lavish interiors, Colman gives Sapper's paste-board a romantic twinkle and debonair ex-army bearing. 'India should be a sacred trust' he cries in **Clive of India** (1935), based on a chronicle play which ran a year at London's Wyndham's Theatre – and the film could not have cost much more than the stage production, since major events are covered by explanatory titles or take place at night, leaving the imaginative direction of Richard Boleslawski to paper over the cracks.

The success of these films ensured Boleslawski and writer W. P. Lipscombe a bigger budget on **Les Misérables** (1935). The Valjean of Fredric March on this occasion justifies Hollywood's faith in him as a 'costume' actor, but the film belongs to Charles Laughton's Javert, moving finally when his inhuman sense of duty yields to pity. Two other popular actors to arrive were Maurice Chevalier

Hollywood before the Code

The Western, usually considered a staple of Hollywood fare, has hardly been that in the Sound period: during the five decades since the coming of Talkies it was only popular during the Forties and Fifties. During the Thirties the poverty row studios turned out Westerns, but the major companies lost interest after *Cimarron*. One reason was that the huge success of that film caused so many inferior imitations.

(before returning, disgruntled, to France) and Clark Gable, courtesy of M-G-M. Chevalier had virtually a one-man show in **Folies Bergère** (1935), directed by del Ruth, which despite the title and the production numbers by Dave Gould (who won an Oscar for them) has less to do with the Folies than with a complicated scheme filched from *The Guardsman* – a husband who tests his wife's fidelity by impersonation. The Hays Office had frowned on the plot, but did allow the surprisingly explicit relationship of Gable with Miss Young in **Call of the Wild** (1935), which in other ways, too, violates Jack London's story. However, William Wellman directed, and like all his best work it has unexpected quirks and revelations, as in Reginald Owen's pebble-bespectacled villain, an irresistible impersonation of Laughton.

At this point 20th Century amalgamated with Fox, thus completing the pattern of Hollywood studios that would remain stable for the next thirty years. Columbia (q.v.) was still emerging as an important studio, and the start of the decade had seen the formation of the other major of the period, R.K.O. Radio. Its founder was Joseph P. Kennedy, whose involvement in the industry predated his liaison with Gloria Swanson. Soon after World War I he had invested in a circuit in New England, and in 1926 he purchased the Film Booking Office of America Inc. (F.B.O.), A British-owned producing and releasing company which conentrated on low-budget features. He was disinclined to change that policy as he waited for the results of the Talkie revolution. Others, he reckoned, would want a stake in the film industry's new fortune, presenting as it did a market for new equipment and a threat to live theatre and radio. He was therefore the prime instigator of a series of mergers whereby the Radio Corporation of America (R.C.A.), in conjunction with two other electronics giants, Westinghouse and General Electric, absorbed the Keith-Albee-Orpheum circuit, the last great vaudeville chain – which, converted to cinemas, could be supplied by Kennedy's studio interests. The consequent amalgamation called itself uncertainly R.K.O. or Radio before settling on the redundant R.K.O. Radio (i.e. Keith-Orpheum flanked by two references to R.C.A.).

Put in charge of production was William Le Baron, a former journalist, dramatist and associate producer (for Paramount), who had also been vice-president of F.B.O. for some years. His first two stars were Bebe Daniels and Richard Dix, both dropped by Paramount, and individually appearing in the two films which got the company off to a flying start – Miss Daniels in **Rio Rita** (1929), based on the Broadway musical and co-starring Wheeler and Woolsey (teamed by Ziegfeld for that event and to continue successfully at R.K.O.), and Dix in **Cimarron** (1931), with Irene Dunne (b. 1904); she too was from the stage and would also become a box-office attraction for R.K.O.

Cimarron was based on Edna Ferber's massive pioneer novel, made extensively and expensively on location under the direction of Wesley Ruggles, and notable today mainly for the sincerity of its leading players. The Academy voted it its best Picture Oscar, and the profits from it enabled Kennedy to add to the conglomerate two ailing studios, the Producers' Distributing Co. (P.D.C.) and Pathé – the troubles of the last named being caused less by only marginally successful films than by lack of a chain of cinemas in which to show them. However, Pathé provided not only the space and appliances of a major studio, but talent of the order of director Gegory LaCava and stars Constance Bennett and Ann Harding – as well as Pathé News. This nucleus of players dictated to a large extent the R.K.O. product, which was quite unlike that of the other studios at this time – high-toned, semi-sophisticated and verbose, often set in Britain. Coincidentally or not, such subjects were precisely of the kind to appeal to David O. Selznick (1902–65), who replaced Le Baron in 1932, brought by Kennedy from Paramount, where his acumen had made something of a mark. Although motivated by a desire to revenge his father's rejection by the industry, he had allied to his energy far more taste than his fellow moguls and an almost faultless judgment of talent.

The films made under his aegis bear witness to his attention to detail. Although *Photoplay* thought **The Conquerors** (1932) only 'a worthy successor' to *Cimarron*, it is in fact much superior, as written by Robert Lord (from a story of Howard Esterbrook) and directed by William Wellman. It gives, said *Photoplay,* 'a pretty definite idea of everything that has happened in this country since 1870 – shows you its progress, defeats, victories, indomitable courage' – all in eighty-four minutes, including the Depression. Indeed, there are three bank crashes in all – done in Eisenstein-like montage, but a good deal wittier – and if the final one is resolved only by a message of hope that was doubtless why 'it makes you proud to be an American'. Dix, and Edna May Oliver, were retained from *Cimarron,* joined by Miss Harding and Guy Kibbee.

Though Dix's films were directed at the male half of the audience, **Hell's Highway** (1932) is a most untypical R.K.O. film as directed by Rowland Brown, a bleak, location-shot piece set among the chain gangs. **The Lost Squadron** (1932) is chiefly notable for Erich Von Stroheim, playing with relish but not humour a film director very much like himself. The director of this film is George Archainbaud, and Mary Astor is a star, Follette, who has sacrificed Dix for her career. He, Joel McCrea and Robert Armstrong play stuntmen of mutual esteem: 'He's a *grand* fellow' and 'He's a *swell* guy' they constantly exclaim.

Friends and Lovers (1931) concerns Indian Army officers, Adolphe Menjou and Laurence Olivier, both in love with Lily Damita, married to Von Stroheim – complaisant till, pushed too far, he takes a whip to her. The two officers are finally convinced that they are better off without her – a denouement considered typically British, part of the stag party syndrome wherein army camaraderie has more worth than the opposite sex. It is just possible to admire the direction of Victor Schertzinger, but there is nothing to be said for the work of Herbert Brenon on **Beau Sabreur** (1931). Returning to the author, and cadre, of *Beau Geste,* he proves incompetent in Talkies; after two further films for the company, he finished his career in Britain.

Critics did not like Wheeler and Woolsey, but they filmed regularly till 1937, when illness split them. Bert Wheeler has curly hair, a boyish face and no distinctive style ; Robert Woolsey has Harold Lloyd specs, a Groucho cigar and a way of saying 'Whooooeee' at moments of stress. **Hold 'em Jail** (1932) has them involved with a prison football game: Norman

Taurog directed, S. J. Perelman was one of the writers, and Woolsey's wooing of Edna May Oliver, a prudish but game spinster, is not unmindful of Groucho's tactics.

Occasionally R.K.O. made a gangster film, such as **Bad Company** (1931), a complicated tale as co-written and directed by Tay Garnett, with Harry Carey as the police chief and Ricardo Cortez as the gang leader – with his bust of himself, his statuette of Napoleon, his paranoia about food and cats, and his habit of flicking his cigarette stubs on the carpet for his servants to pick up (borrowed from Charles Ray during his period of glory). The film, however, was a vehicle for Helen Twelvetrees, inherited from P.D.C., a lady whose speciality was crying. Since she was not very good at that, or indeed, any of the requirements of a star, she was soon dropped. Such was not the case with Irene Dunne and Ann Harding, meeting every reversal with a smile. Though both were too ladylike to have traffic with gangsters, their vehicles were curiously similar to those of Miss Twelvetrees. In **Consolation Marriage** (1931), directed by Paul Sloane, Miss Dunne marries on the rebound and takes several reels to realise that she loves her husband (Pat O'Brien); in **If I Were Free** (1933), directed by Elliott Nugent, she leaves her caddish husband (Nils Asther) but takes just as long to find happiness with the English lawyer (Clive Brook), who has given her life a new meaning.

Ann Harding (1902–81) was beautiful, serene, and only occasionally conscious of being a big star: she played with exceptional lightness, using inflexions and pauses which make most of her contemporaries seem common place. R.K.O. made her a 'new' woman, frank about sex, but determined to do nothing about it unless the band is on her finger. A spinster in **Devotion** (1931), she sets her cap at English barrister Leslie Howard; married for the second time in **Westward Passage** (1931), she finds herself attracted again to first husband Laurence Olivier. Robert Milton directed both films, and his frequent attempts at banter are keyed to his star's performances.

The motif in all these films is female sexuality. The lady who did not resist temptation was Constance Bennett (1905–65). Considered, by her fans at least,

289

the epitome of glamour, and having had a great success as an unmarried mother, in *Common Clay,* she was kept at sinning. In **The Common Law** (1931), directed by Paul L. Stein, she falls in love with a young artist (Joel McCrea) who discovers her past before she can confess it, and there is many a reversal before she becomes his common-law wife (as we assume from the title), which is only one step to the 'approved' ending.

These frequent glimpses of sin must have made many a spectator wonder whether the path of virtue was the right one. The Silent cinema had weakened the still-prevalent Victorian moral code, but hypocritically the images of wickedness – ankle or champagne-glass – were often contradicted by intertitles. With the coming of Sound, the onus of sexual demand sometimes passed to the ladies. A Gable might be frank, or even a gentlemanly actor like Brook or Howard, but if that frankness was put into speech, he would be at best unlikeable and at worst a degenerate. It could still be pretended that women did not really enjoy sex; alternatively, the stories were based on the old myth that their bodies were their sole means of survival – so that exploiting them, or lying and cheating, was permissible behaviour. Not the least of the hypocrisies on display was the notion that even the wickedest woman could be regenerated by the love of a good man. Regeneration was less pernicious in Silents: the unhappy wives, seduced servant girls and whores from deprived backgrounds had all been made to see the error of their ways before 'The End', but now the pursuit of luxury was an end in itself. After her earlier roles it is no surprise to find Miss Bennett as a reformatory school girl desperate for a **Bed of Roses** (1933), but it is hard to believe that she could be redeemed by the love of humble river captain McCrea. She is technically pure, since her system is the common one (in movies) of getting the man (John Halliday) so drunk as to be incapable, and then climbing into his bed. Her friend (Pert Kelton) has no such qualms, and there is always the possibility – ambiguity never being absent – that McCrea's body eventually appeals more than Halliday's gewgaws.

The director was Gregory LaCava (1892–1952), whose R.K.O. work is varied. **Laugh and Get Rich** (1931) was one of several Hollywood attempts to find a co-starring team to rival Dressler and Beery: the couple here are suspicious, strict Edna May Oliver and woozy Hugh Herbert, running a boarding house. **Age of Consent** (1932) can stand with the Warner record of this period, perhaps as accurate a portrait of campus life as we have. The boys sit around in their shorts discussing girls, to the disgust of Michael (Richard Cromwell), unaware then that his own frustration will lead him into the toils of a 'friendly' waitress. **The Half-Naked Truth** (1932) is an irreverent farce with Lee Tracy as a quick-scheming P.R. man, Frank Morgan as a Broadway producer, Lupe Velez as a fake princess and, best of all, gravel-voiced Eugene Pallette pretending to be a eunuch.

LaCava's **Symphony of Six Millions** (1932) ranks with *Bad Girl* as an account of working-class life, but it is also the first serious portrait of American Jews – assuming its predecessors to have been primarily comic or sentimental. Jews in the first movies were patterned on Shylock, moneylenders or pawnbrokers – a stereotype broken when a stage player Sam Bernard, made a popular success as 'a rich, overpowering Jew', a Mr Hoggenheimer. Bernard became one of Zukor's Famous Players, around which time Broadway was laughing at the antics of Potash and Perlmutter, based on *The Saturday Evening Post* stories by Montague Glass. It was not till Goldwyn's film version ten years later, *Potash and Perlmutter* (1923), that Jews first appeared on the screen in full and admirable light – and that was due to the success of 'Abie's Irish Rose', beginning its long run the previous year. That also paved the way for *The Cohens and the Kellys* at Universal and *Kosher Kitty Kelly* at F.B.O., both in 1926, and Bernard's old success, *Friendly Enemies,* with Weber and Fields – Jewish comedians who made occasional films, as did Smith and Dale. The anomaly is that the film industry was predominantly Jewish, churning out sequels for the Cohens and Kellys but not highlighting the intensely Jewish theme of *The Jazz Singer*. The title *Symphony of Six Millions* suggests a portrait of New York, and if not applicable to the film it was doubtless justified by Fannie Hurst's original novel, in part based on her own experience. The opening sequence, in which the still-young parents discuss the futures of their children in European accents, must have struck a chord with many Americans.

The lead was played by a Jewish actor, Ricardo Cortez, so renamed because he was intended as a successor to Valentino. (It was not till the end of the decade that any studio engaged a romantic lead associated, via his stage work, with Jewish roles; he was John Garfield and the studio Warners, which had, however, had two important Jewish stars in Edward G. Robinson and Paul Muni). Cortez plays Felix, a doctor whose family persuades him to move from the ghetto to Park Avenue, to the neglect of his crippled girlfriend (Irene Dunne); unlike most screen doctors, his ideals are not in question, but LaCava, if less perceptive than Borzage, makes the most of the family gatherings and glimpses of ghetto life – matters not to be seen again in American films for almost forty years. During that time, less than half a dozen characters would be overtly Jewish, and the reasons must be speculative: I assume it to be because the Nazis brought anti-semitism to the fore and the Hollywood moguls decided – subconsciously perhaps – not to remind audiences of the differences, real or supposed, between Jews and gentiles. It could not have been because of the German market, since only Warners and R.K.O. withdrew at the time of the Nazi takeover, and Universal in 1936 – and none of the three closed their Austrian offices which could handle German distribution till after the Anschluss, at which time United Artists broke with Bayerisches-Film, which had been handling its product; Paramount, M-G-M and 20th Century-Fox maintained some form of distribution till forced to close their German offices in 1940/1.

Among directors, George Cukor was brought from Paramount and assigned to **What Price Hollywood?** (1932), after Selznick had fought front office claims that movies on this particular subject were seldom popular. Its five writers were old Hollywood hands, but it would be reckless to speculate on their sources – though, as metamorphosed into *A Star is Born* (q.v.), Colleen Moore would recognise incidents from her own life. This film is less vicious, and it is not a tragic love story, since the one who goes on the skids is not the husband of the star (Constance Bennett), but her mentor (Lowell Sherman); it does offer a portrait of a sybaritic town, peopled with parvenues prone to absurd expenditure and the values of the fan magazines. Sherman's own career, as actor and director, was ruined by drink, so he is well-cast as the unfortunate director: but the self-ironies, bragadaccio and fatalism were moulded (once again) on John Barrymore. Since the film is a compendium of all that was wrong with Hollywood in its *Photoplay* heyday, its deficiency is its avoidance of sex. There is no reference to the casting couch or the hundreds of hopefuls prepared to trade flesh for a 'chance': R.K.O. would let them admit anything but that.

It was Cukor and Selznick who brought Katharine Hepburn (b. 1909) from Broadway, for **A Bill of Divorcement** (1932), based on Clemence Dane's theatrical discussion on the problems of having a mentally sick father (John Barrymore). Hepburn is young, eager, and teetering between gaucherie and archness, yet in the often disastrous films that followed she saved the day with her directness of emotion. With misplaced confidence she would throw herself across the screen, fiddling with hair, sleeves, anything – but that same nerviness could be touching when her eyes strayed, embarrassed or hurt, looking for another focus.

In **Christopher Strong** (1933) she is the first woman to fly round the world, stealing from his wife (Billie Burke) a diplomat (Colin Clive), till then the happiest man in London. 'If I were the usual man . . . If you were the usual girl . . . We could have had our love affair and . . . not taken the thing so desperately seriously,' he says, to which she responds, 'If you were the usual man . . . If I were the usual girl . . . We could have had our love affair . . . and not taken the thing so *desperately* seriously.' She commits suicide by taking off her oxygen mask, thus transformed into the Victory of Samothrace, feathers sprouting from her arms. Because it is about an independent woman engaged in a masculine profession, this film has been requisitioned as a monument in the Women's Lib movement – but while both Hepburn and the director, Dorothy Arzner, may have held strong views on the subject it would be unwise to attribute any to Selznick, who produced, or Gilbert Frankau, who wrote the original novel.

Morning Glory (1933) starts with Hepburn wandering into a theatre lobby, and you can see that she is stage-struck by the back of her head. 'I shall never be wonderful like them,' she says, gazing at portraits of Ethel Barrymore, Maude Adams and Sarah Bernhardt, 'but I have something wonderful inside me' – and one experiences an odd frisson, since in the years since the film was made her fame has outstripped theirs. Her Eva Lovelace is magnanimous and pretentious, not qualities alien to this actress, but she has a wry humour; prattling on like a wound-up phonograph she says, 'Of course, I shall die at my zenith', and the audience roars, as the director, Lowell Sherman, intended. This dated tale remains amazingly fresh, thanks also to Adolphe Menjou as the producer who takes advantage of Eva's ambitions, and Douglas Fairbanks Jr as the dramatist who might have saved her from that fate.

Cukor's **Little Women** (1933) also remains in pristine condition, one of the few adaptations likely to please all admirers of the original novel; Hepburn is Jo, with Joan Bennett, Frances Dee and Jean Parker as her sisters, Spring Byington as Marmee, Douglass Montgomery as Laurie, Paul Lukas as Dr Bhaer and Edna May Oliver as Aunt March. The film brought Hepburn a new army of admirers, but few remained after **Spitfire** (1934) and **The Little Minister** (1934). In the former, directed by John Cromwell, she is Trigger Hawks, living in a log cabin, saying 'git' instead of 'got' and 'cain't' instead of 'can't'; in the latter, directed by Richard Wallace, she is Barrie's Lady Babbie, saying 'It's harrd fo' a lassie to keeeep up wi' a mun' – but at least the ads warned prospective customers, claiming 'something more than a motion picture – a Christmas gift for your heart'.

John Cromwell (1888–1980), a former actor, was also brought by Selznick from Paramount, and like Cukor was adept at the sort of subjects the producer favoured. He had already directed the Broadway production of Sidney Howard's **The Silver Cord** (1933), also with Laura Hope Crews, whose performance is a revelation to those who know her only from her amusing, later caricatures. the film betrays its origin by rarely straying from the family manse, and we may well wonder why everyone talks in loud voices in the hall, likely to be overheard – and the talk is dangerous, concerning a possessive mother (Miss Crews),

exposed and ousted by her daughter-in-law (Irene Dunne). Audiences are on tenterhooks to see how long it takes for the gullible to see through its monster; this is not a penetrating entertainment, but the arguments pertinent to the situation have been logically marshalled. When Miss Dunne finally turns on the old lady, calling her 'a self-centred, self-pitying, son-devouring tigress, with unmentionable proclivities on the side', it is doubtful whether all audiences understood, but the film so incensed one London suburb that it had to be withdrawn after a single performance, causing the *Daily Telegraph* to observe that it 'requires for its appreciation a certain knowledge of psycho-analysis'.

The reference is too guarded to be shocking. Since sexual frankness now constituted more than rape and seduction, how was the cinema to cope with subjects being aired in the novel and 'modern' drama? By this time the craze for Talkies was spent, Miss Harlow had given her all, and new ways were sought for enticing audiences. The executives were cautious: it was one thing to regard sex as a commodity, and another to attempt new ways to market it. The directors and writers were susceptible both to their bosses and to audiences – and in view of the apparently blameless lives of most spectators, caution was needed. But the climate was there for hints of strange psychologies and recherché habits – recognisable to the knowing, and to them part of the glamour of movies. Film-makers had become adept at suggesting odd perversions, and Cromwell made a widely-accepted version of **Of Human Bondage** (1934). Maugham's novel was no longer sensational, but by reducing it to the infatuation of a medical student it offered an experience alien to most spectators. Looked at coldly, Philip's obsession with Millie is masochistic and, to all but himself, tiresome; with Maugham's portrait of late Victorian London entirely gone, the film has to depend on the interpreters of the two roles. Bette Davis, borrowed from Warners, made her name as Millie, a self-centred harpy who refuses to see herself as other than 'a lidy': she has a flirty giggle for her other admirers, and an indifference, vehement and coquettish by turns, for Philip. However, the actress's love of detail is insufficient to counterbalance a cockney accent horrendous by today's standard. As

Philip, Leslie Howard is too commonsensical, hoping to convey passion with pensive looks. Withal, enough remains: this novel, boned, still makes an absorbing film.

The Fountain (1934) was based on a novel by Charles Morgan, whose reputation at this time perhaps exceeded Maugham's. The London *Times* – whose drama critic Morgan then was – observed that the cinema could not convey the quality of his prose, but 'the material outlines of the story remain intact': a British officer (Brian Aherne) is billeted by his German captors on a Dutch family, of whom he had known Julie (Miss Harding) while at Oxford; they fall in love again, a situation fraught with tension when her German husband (Paul Lukas) returns; but the two men find 'a peace too strong to be broken in upon by any human need'. Cromwell's direction uncovers a humourless portentousness which is apt for this particular writer, and he gets a particularly good performance from Aherne as the pipe-smoking Englishman who cares more for Keats than war: it is a character performance, but I do not think the actor knew it.

R.K.O. worked Miss Harding in such high-minded stories that the public – foolishly – began to tire of her; and the studio also borrowed Diana Wynyard for several similar items, which put *finis* to her Hollywood career. Neither was there to bail out **Jalna** (1935) – though one of the leading roles was taken by the equally sympathetic Kay Johnson, who was married to Cromwell. He tries hard with this synthetic family saga, by Mazo de la Roche, its members called Renny, Finch, Wake, Alayne, Pheasant, Eden and so on, who go about in riding boots because they're farmers. It is not surprising that R.K.O. spent most of the decade staving off bankruptcy.

The company was saved by some strokes of luck. One was the teaming (q.v.) of Fred Astaire and Ginger Rogers; another was John Ford's **The Informer** (1935), his second film for the company. Neither project interested his employers, Fox, though he had so much wanted to make **The Lost Patrol** (1934) that he had waived his salary – which suggested to the film historian Lewis Jacobs that he had 'awakened from his indifference and intended to make films about which he cared', adding that it proved he 'could make a film from the barest of materials provided

he was moved by it'. Today it is impossible to say why, or even whether, Ford was moved: the tale of men under duress has been done so often and in this same superficial way – a British cavalry unit consisting of: the idealist (Douglas Walton) who wanted to serve in the ranks because he loves Kipling; the public school drunk (Reginald Denny); the music hall artist (Wallace Ford); the religious maniac (Boris Karloff), etc. Dudley Nichols wrote it, and he also adapted *The Informer* from the novel by Liam O'Flaherty, Ford's cousin, which Ford preferred to the Western he had been offered. When Joseph Kennedy relinquished control of R.K.O., the project was abandoned, but was restarted by the new bosses on the principle that the participants were already on salary: the film was made in three weeks, at a cost of just over $200,000. Few evinced further interest till it was taken up by the New York critics, when it went on to win five Oscars, including Best Actor (Victor McLaglen) and Best Director. Ford's still-hovering reputation was finally made, and four years later Jacobs considered it 'one of the most important contributions since Sound'. All the leading American directors (Borzage, King, LaCava, Milestone, Wellman, Vidor, Capra) had made at least one such contribution – a picture of serious intent, its commercial potential of secondary consideration – but the point about *The Informer* is that there was no other American film quite like it. It is a tourist's view of Dublin – of boozy pubs, a brothel, not to mention a church or two. It is the story of a man who sells his pal to the peelers for the price of two steamship tickets – a tale of weakness and retribution, enlivened by whiffs of politics and religion. There is only a hint of romance – there was none in *The Lost Patrol* – and that was sufficiently rare as to be very impressive.

Unfortunately, like Ford's other ambitious projects, it exposes his weaknesses. There is no concern or passion, but there are the most arty of borrowed clichés:* the blind man looming in the fog; the poster blown across the street to flap at McLaglen's leg; the client done up like Mackie Messer in *Die Driegroschenoper* (q.v.). The

*Ford liked to think of himself as a 'plain' director, and when late in life a mutual friend saw him emerging from a Los Angeles art-house – he had been to see a film by Ingmar Bergman – Ford was clearly embarrassed. 'Got to keep an eye on the opposition' he growled.

The beast is, of course, King Kong in the film of that name, and the frightened lady Fay Wray. Since the film was largely composed of process shorts, the stills look somewhat artificial (illustrations from films are in fact called stills since they are shot separately, frame-enlargements from the celluloid film itself never being wholly satisfactory); but at least on the screen itself this now-aged movie continues to thrill audiences. Those of the time, if they read the show business journal *Variety*, would have seen the accompanying advertisement, indicating that Kong was a cure for the Depression blues.

ending is particularly pretentious. But though the insights are no greater than those of, say, *Public Enemy*, the combination of lofty intent, low life and Ufa lighting made them seem so. Ford himself admitted that it lacks humour, but it lacks humour precisely because of its ambitions.

Considering its heavy irony, it is only fitting that modern audiences should prefer **King Kong** (1933). The credited directors are Ernest B. Schoedsack and Merian C. Cooper, but it was masterminded by Willis O'Brien, who had worked on the monsters of *The Lost World*. Shortly after the inception of R.K.O. he was employed on a project to utilise similar processes, to be called *Creation*. Money, however, was lacking; when Selznick took over production he asked Cooper (they had worked together on *The Four Feathers*) to inspect the studio's finances, and Cooper saw what existed of *Creation* – a script and a test reel: since returning from Africa he had been trying to set up a film about gorillas, and O'Brien 'bought' it. They set to work: the screenplay is credited to James Creelman and Ruth Rose, from a story by Cooper and Edgar Wallace (whose contribution was minimal); Selznick's main contribution was to scrape money from other budgets for the cost, $650,000. Apart from pre-production work, the actual filming took fifty-five weeks. It was premiered in New York simultaneously at that city's two massive cinemas, Radio City Music Hall and the Roxy, to instant success. It is far-fetched, this tale of a film crew whose leading lady (Fay Wray) is stolen by a giant gorilla: her screams remain a byword, and her reactions are in both senses of the word hysterical. But once Kong appears, after three-quarters of an hour, the excitement doesn't let up. Kong himself was only eighteen inches high (though parts of a 'real'-size Kong were used for some sequences) and the Wray he carries was an animated doll. I cannot say that all the process work is exceptional, or that you cannot see the joins, but the tricks are loaded with imagination and the editing is particularly brilliant. We shall not see its like again, or so I said some years ago – since when the 1976 remake has come, gone and been forgotten.

There was a sequel, **Son of Kong** (1933), which, hurriedly made, is much inferior. For a follow-up, try **The Most Dangerous Game** (1932), filmed simultaneously in the same studio jungle (actually 'planted' earlier for *Bird of Paradise*), using many of the same processes. The screenplay is by Creelman, and the directors are Schoedsack and Irving Pichel. An alternative title is *The Hounds of Zaroff,* and Leslie Banks manages to be both hammy and scary as the baron whose game is hunting human beings – Miss Wray and Robert Armstrong. It is a far cry from *Chang* or *Grass* – ersatz certainly, but wholly individual.

The success of *King Kong* was instrumental in the appointment of Cooper and Schoedsack as joint production chiefs when Selznick left for M-G-M, but it must be said that R.K.O.'s most astute producer then and for some years was Pandro S. Berman (b. 1905), a protégé of Selznick. Cooper and Schoedsack did nothing else notable as a team. The latter directed, and Creelman

helped to write, **The Last Days of Pompeii** (1935) – which in fact, as a foreword admits, has nothing to do with Bulwer-Lytton's novel. It has the usual Ben-Hurish story, a historically inaccurate eruption, and a Pompeii rendered only by glass shots and some wobbly back projections. If *King Kong* is the dream factory at its most persuasive, this film is old Hollywood at its considerable worst. As both are innocuous tales, we cannot blame the Code, but it is symptomatic of the dampening of spirits discernible in the post-Code films.

The public hardly noticed, having generally regarded anything that happened on screen as occurring in some never-never land with little or no relation to real life. (In any case, *Red-Headed Woman* was regarded as much less 'real' than *Little Women,* the film most often cited as both popular and healthy entertainment.) Comment, even in the trade press, was rare; the Hays Office published its 'recommendations' in June, 1934, and the films then in production were merely toned down, with the sharper writing and directing talents continuing to try to circumvent restrictions. Nevertheless, as we shall see, the studios soon began to return to the big-budget prestige productions which drew attention to the institution of cinema-going.

With the exception of M-G-M, the studios had eschewed these during this period, having sufficient troubles with the coming of Sound, the Depression and its accompanying financial losses, and the heart-searching over censorship. One factor remained constant – the star as the keystone of the industry, but even that certainty had taken a jolt when the creatures had to talk. Old favourites had disappeared with scarifying rapidity, but the fact that they were as quickly replaced by new ones meant that they offered no real threat to the power of the moguls. Nor did the directors. Except for the rise of the cinema circuits, which only increased the power of the front offices, the industry was fundamentally unchanged since 1915, and since the recent convulsions had been so easily – in retrospect – surmounted, the mood was set fair for the future.

Now that cinemas are again as small as the original nickelodeons, we may feel nostalgic about the palaces of the late Silent and early Talkie period, ever more sumptuous and ornate. Audiences, marshalled by squadrons of ushers, entered ankle-deep in carpet. The gardens of the Alhambra were reproduced on the walls of the auditorium and the fountains of Tivoli in the foyers; ceilings contained whole galaxies and dripped chandeliers; while in the matter of gilt and marble the Paris Opéra looked dingy in comparison. Two New York theatres were the culmination of the vogue, the Roxy and, situated a block away, Radio City Music Hall (illustrated). The Roxy opened in 1927, named after the most enterprising of movie showmen, S. L. 'Roxy' Rothafel, and it was he who was called in to manage Radio City which, if slightly less lavish, was even bigger. R.K.O., the owners of Rockefeller Center and its entertainment complex, intended the Music Hall, seating 6,200, for live entertainment – to be provided by the Metropolitan Opera, which wasn't interested – while a smaller auditorium, seating a mere 3,400, would offer movies plus the supporting live show thought essential. Radio City opened with vaudeville in 1932, and promptly flopped, reopening in January 1933 with a screen-stage policy – and since the first film on the bill was *The Bitter Tea of General Yen* it is clear it was not intended to be the family cinema it later became. In March 1933 it played *King Kong* simultaneously with its smaller brother (about to change its name from the 'New R.K.O. Roxy' to the 'Center Theater'), and the following month it programmed *Cavalcade* at regular prices after its reserved-seat engagement: but not till it began to have financial troubles in the Sixties did it again show any movie that was not first-run and exclusive – and even then, long, long after other cinemas had dropped them, it retained its supporting stage-show, highlighted by its high-kicking and justly acclaimed chorus, the Rockettes.

If, in theory, the Music Hall showed films from all the major studios, there was originally a bias towards the films of R.K.O., and Disney's *Snow White and the Seven Dwarfs* was one of its biggest successes. Most films ran for only a week, necessitating up to fifty-two different stage shows every year, but towards the end of the Forties the average run was four weeks – and M-G-M seemed to have a virtual monopoly on the films supplied. In the Sixties, with the Music Hall firmly established as a tourist attraction, it became difficult to find sufficient family films – a situation that became desperate in the Seventies. In 1973 *Mary Poppins* was the Music Hall's first revival, and two years later it played for a week each four of the most popular films in M-G-M's history, *Gone with the Wind*, *2001: a Space Odyssey*, *Singin' in the Rain* and *Doctor Zhivago*. A number of films from the Thirties were revived (for one day only) to emphasise the Art Deco interior – but Radio City finally shuttered in 1978. However, it was clear that New York would not let it die and it reopened in 1979, supported by a trust fund – the aim being flexibility of programme, which may be a one-performance rock concert or a six-week revue. Film shows survive, usually only as morning revivals, and no longer supported by the Rockettes. However, that institution happily survives, along with the Music Hall's Symphony Orchestra and such seasonal events as 'The Glory of Easter' and 'The Spirit of Christmas'.

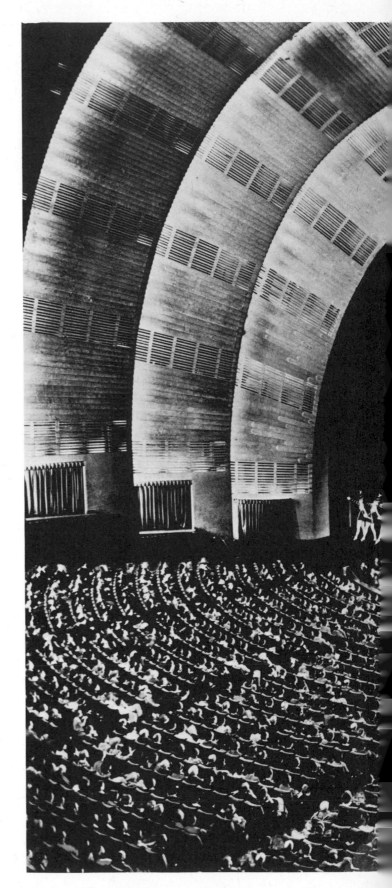

13

Film in the Third Reich

AS HOLLYWOOD settled down again after its own financial and moral crises, the situation in Europe deteriorated, till the prospect of another world war passed from a possibility to a certainty. Since most of the American movie moguls had been born in Europe and had relatives still there they occasionally allowed into their films a comment on conditions in Europe, but it would be seldom more than a comment – a pinprick of criticism directed at Germany. Few Hollywood writers felt themselves equipped for more trenchant opinion, but what Hollywood could do was provide escapist entertainments, increasingly expertly executed, to relieve a world increasingly in need of them. A desire to alleviate the world's troubles was not the prime intention of the American film-maker, nor, emerging from their Depression, did the American cinema-goer care to look too deeply into problems, his own or those of others: the front pages of the newspapers were gloomy enough.

The European situation was remote to most Americans and, however much the politicians warned, the official Nazi policies of expansion, rearmament and racial persecution seemed unlikely to result in another world conflict. But the Nazis themselves were fully aware that their immediate neighbours did not warm to their policies and methods, and the cinema was regarded as a way of dampening criticism. The leaders of the Nazi party not only adored the cinema as entertainment, but regarded it as the most powerful of all propaganda weapons. The German cinema would preach to the world the Nazi scheme of things, and the world, presumably, would understand. The leaders – or at any rate Goebbels who, as head of Nazi prop-

aganda, was officially in charge of the film industry – quickly realised, to their chagrin, that they did not have film-makers of world quality, able to compete with Hollywood; they thought, however, that by controlling the industry they could achieve this. That was typical of Nazi mentality. It is doubtful whether Goebbels, even at his most despondent over the films he commanded, ever regretted the promulgation of June 1933 – four months after Hitler was granted dictatorial powers – which forbade Jews to work in the industry. Many continued to work under pseudonyms; many had already left. A number of left-wing film-makers and others who realised that freedom of expression would be severely limited voluntarily departed also.

The German studios had been flushed with confidence as they settled down again after the disruption caused by the advent of Sound. There appeared to be an endless supply of talent to replace those directors, writers and players who had departed for Hollywood and elsewhere – a great many of whom were now being forced to return, though at least with 'international' reputations which would prove useful. With so many English-speaking people in the German studios, multilingual productions posed no problems; finance presented no problem either, for, in common with local audiences, those foreign distributors who imported German films were not looking for Hollywood-style lavishness but for tales of the everyday – provided, that is, that they were embellished with music and were mainly concerned with criminals.

Fritz Lang bowed to the current demand, and eschewed – for one film – master-criminals in favour of one despicable little murderer; but **M** (1931) was admired pre-

Fritz Lang's *M* remains one of the most famous films in the art-house repertory – partly because the direction remains startling, even today, with its clever use of sound and symbols. The title refers to the letter chalked on the shoulder of the murderer's coat – *Möder* in German – by one who suspects him. The 'M' in question is Peter Lorre, whose performance has been justly famous for fifty years.

cisely because it was recognised as a successor to those typical Lang Silents in which men were driven by unnatural impulses. Lang and von Harbou had originally planned a film on the worst crime they could think of, which they considered the writing of anonymous letters, but they then switched to child-murder; von Harbou was in fact finishing the script as the police hunted for Kürten, the Düsseldorf child murderer. The town in the film is recognisable as Berlin, whose underworld leaders co-operate with the police, baffled by lack of motive and clues. Routine checkups bring to attention a former mental patient (Peter Lorre), who in time is cornered in an attic by the underworld – and it is now difficult to take very seriously a story in which this particular subject is linked to such antiquated fictions as underworld confederacies and armies of beggars. The kangeroo court climax is too studied, with its sudden outbursts of cynical laughter, and Lorre's performance is of excessive virtuosity – though one is unlikely ever to forget his pudgy pale face and cumbersome bulk. At a time when movie villains were one-dimensional, his suggestion of inner torment evoked much praise, and Lang's

imaginative opening remains impressive: a child's balloon floating free, a toy rolling downhill, the whistling of 'Peer Gynt' on the soundtrack, and a shot of a blind beggar. Pare Lorentz in *Vanity Fair* was struck by the way dialogue was used, 'how Lang puts the audience right into his scenes by never showing the speaker – or, by thrusting his camera into a group of people, and making them so absolutely natural that the audience feels it, too, is actually seeing and hearing with the cast'. Despite its faults, the film indicates why it has remained one of the most popular items in the cinema repertory. There was a foolish American remake in 1951, directed by Joseph Losey, of which Lang remarked that it had brought him the best notices of his career.

Otto Wernicke plays Lohmann, the detective who tracks down the murderer, and Lang incorporated both actor and role in **Das Testament des Doktor Mabuse** (1933), sequel to the 1922 film, and another elongated tale of assorted skulduggery – abductions and time bombs and tick-tacky car chases. It is the antithesis of *M,* and there is nothing in the film to support Lang's later claim that he and von Harbou intended an allegory on the Nazi system of tyranny, though he may be referring to a line which says, in effect, that mastery of crime is possible when mankind is ruled by terror. The film had been made as the Nazis prepared to seize power, and Goebbels refused to allow it to be released in Germany (it was shown in Austria, and the French version was smuggled into France); when he sent for Lang to offer him the leadership of the German film industry and made no reference to the ban, Lang decided that it was time he left Germany – leaving behind his wife, who became a Nazi.

Other directors of the Silent period kept up the tradition of the grotesque, and they must have felt the subjects more topical since the Nazi Party, formerly a sinister fringe group, was now a power in the land. Richard Oswald remade his own **Unheimliche Geschicten** (1932), the source for which is several stories by Edgar Allan Poe and one, 'The Suicide Club', by Robert Louis Stevenson. Here they are reduced to a Mabuse-like confrontation between a madman (Paul Wegener) and a detective; however, the scene where it is apparent that the patients have taken over the asylum can still produce a frisson. Robert Wiene remade **Der Andere** (1930), a success of 1913, based on 'Dr Jekyll and Mr Hyde' via a play by Paul Landau. Its protagonist (Fritz Kortner) is not a mere lawyer but the state prosecutor, holding forth on humanity and one's debt to society – but, as it turns out, he is overworked to the extent that in the evenings he tears off his collar and tie, frequents whores in low bars and becomes involved in burglary and attempted murder. Kortner, a great actor, is given too little to work with to make the transformation believable, but nothing mars his performance in **Der Mörder Dimitri Karamasoff** (1931), directed by the former Soviet film-maker, Fedor Ozep, and edited by Pudovkin. Nevertheless, it is not Russian in feeling but German, and it is another reduction, using Dostoevsky to produce a ten-a-penny tale of a man who loves a whore. The style, however, is agreeable, as if von Sternberg in his later style had attempted one of the 'street' movies, making it glitter with chandeliers, guttering candles and gleaming wine bottles. As powerfully emotional as Kortner's Dimitri is the Grushenka of Anna Sten.

Nor is **Berlin Alexanderplatz** (1931) the equal of Alfred Döblin's novel, though he himself worked on the screenplay. However, if the darker anecdotes have gone, the film removes those that remain from the pretentious and consciously Joycean text to offer, if not a study of the deprived of Berlin then of its underworld. Franz Biberkopf (Heinrich George) leaves prison determined to start a new life; he becomes a street pedlar, and in the film no longer wonders whether to sell the Nazi newspaper, the *Völkischer Beobachter,* to Jews. After the pianist has casually flashed her stocking tops at him, she moves in, and just as he is drawn to felony so he gradually returns to the kind of *crime passionel* which had sent him to prison in the first place. The film was made by Phil Jutzi and it is a remarkable successor to Lamprecht's portraits of Berlin, not to mention his own *Mutter Krausens Fahrt in Glück.* Lamprecht himself deserted such subjects to make **Emil und die Detektive** (1931), and its success almost equalled that of the phenomenally popular novel by Erich Kästner on which it is based. Billy Wilder wrote the screenplay, and the film, made almost entirely on location, is shrewd, though the story itself, about a country boy who persuades a crowd of Berlin children to help him tail a crook, now seems thin. Among its virtues is another of Fritz Rasp's relishable villains, wearing his bowler hat even in bed.

Niemandsland (1931) harks back to the Silent era in its plea for peace, as directed by Victor Trivas from the rather woolly ideas of Leonhard Frank. They establish the unlikely situation of a German, a French and a British soldier joined in companionship by a deaf-mute Jewish tailor. Trivas's style, borrowed from the Soviets, is eloquent with the message that he is pushing, and his battle scenes are as forceful as those in *Westfront 1918.* The film, much discussed in its day, is now largely forgotten; but **Mädchen in Uniform** (1931) remains famous, as directed by Leontine Sagan from Christa Winsloe's play on the heady passions of pupils and teachers at an all-female academy. Sagan, a theatre director, moved to films to make this under the supervision of Carl Frölich, and she manages her overheated subject with skill and subtlety. Although the film was originally banned by the New York state censors, few reviewers had the courage to say that they recognised lesbianism in it. There is an

amazing ambiguity in the performance of
Dorothea Wieck as the teacher suspected of
corruption, a sensual and ageing woman
who keeps her own council and is perhaps
unwilling to give in to her emotions.

Also highly regarded abroad was **Ariane**
(1931), a drama which deals as charmingly
and truthfully with the battle of the sexes as
any other movie I have seen. Scripted by
Paul Czinner, the director, and Carl Mayer,
it bears out all the claims that have been
made for the latter; while the basic sourness
of its view of love is presumably that of
Claude Anet, who wrote the original
novel. It concerns an affair between an
experienced older man (Rudolf Forster)
and a student (Elisabeth Bergner) which,
since his motives are entirely selfish, goes
wrong: and when it does neither knows
how to handle the situation. Their silent last
sequence would be one of the finest emotional passages in all cinema if it had been a
little less studied – a fault of Miss Bergner's
performance generally, though she is much
more touching than might be imagined
from her later performances in English.

After the superb *Abschied* and *Voruntersuchung*, Robert Siodmak disappointed his
admirers with **Der Mann, der seinen
Mörder Sucht** (1931), which was in fact
made before the latter. Heinz Rühmann
plays a would-be suicide who, unable to
take his own life, commissions a petty
crook to kill him – till he changes his mind
after meeting a girl and then has to trace
the man. The screenplay by Ludwig
Hirschfeld, Curt Siodmak (the director's
brother) and Billy Wilder is inventive, but
the piece falls between several different
comedy styles. **Quick** (1932) fails to be
satirical on its twin settings, a health clinic
and a theatre, and is basically a vehicle for
the leaden charms of its stars, Lilian Harvey, as a lady who falls in love with a clown,
and Hans Albers (q.v.), as the clown. But
Siodmak made one of the best films of the
period – or any period – in **Brennendes
Geheimnis** (1933), a perceptive and subtle
version of a story by Stefan Zweig. Set in a
hotel on the Swiss lakes at the end of the
season, it examines the effect on a 13-year-
old boy of adultery between his mother
(Hilda Wagener) and a wealthy philanderer
(Willi Forst). The boy is all the more
disillusioned since the man had in the first
instance used him to strike up acquaintance,
and in deciding that his mother should

choose either the man or himself – not to
mention his absent father – he almost
destroys himself.

Die Koffer des Herrn O.F. (1931) is
one of the better German attempts at satire,
but it was directed by a Russian, Alexis
Granowsky. It does, however, decline once
past its premise – which concerns a sleepy
little town that decides to transform itself
into an international centre on the basis of
its one hotel housing a V.I.P. – who is in fact
imaginary. **Ich bei Tag und du bei Nacht**
(1932) is, as the title implies, a Box and Cox
tale, with Käthe von Nagy and Willy
Fritsch as the flat-sharers, hating each other
before they fall in love. Cut into the film are
excerpts from a florid movie musical playing next door to their lodging house – and it
was precisely such a film which made the
reputation of the director, Ludwig Berger.
He had just returned from Hollywood,
where Paramount had hoped he would be a
second Lubitsch. Unfortunately, after this

Paul Czinner made
his reputation in
Germany with a
number of fastidious
Silent romances; in
Britain in the Thirties
he directed some
vehicles for his wife,
Elisabeth Bergner –
mainly unwatchable
because their chief aim
was to show off her
undeniable but
mechanical talents.
Ariane, however, has a
more sensible aim and
this scene from it
shows Rudolf Forster
and Miss Bergner in the
virtuoso final
sequence, both of them
silent as audiences
wonder on the outcome
of their affair.

Film in the Third Reich

In cinema, the plays of Arthur Schnitzler will always be associated with Max Ophuls, who, born in Saarbrucken, was directing them (and other plays) at the Vienna Burgtheater in the late Twenties. One of his first films was *Leibelei*, which featured Magda Schneider as the poor girl who falls in love with a careless young officer, Wolfgang Liebeneiner. Years after Ophuls was able to recommence his career in Hollywood because people would recall this film – and among those he later made was a further adaptation of Schnitzler, *La Ronde* (q.v.).

comedy he returned to operetta, with *Walzerkrieg* (1933), about the rivalry between Strauss and Lanner.

Operetta was at first the speciality of Max Ophuls (1902–57), who had been dialogue director for Anatole Litvak, and who was given a chance to direct by Ufa. **Lachenden Erben** is a starring vehicle for Heinz Rühmann, and also a celebration of the grape, since it concerns the heir to a wine firm who falls in love with the heiress to a rival company. It is, appropriately, as light as most German comedies are heavy – and it may be because it is untypical that Ufa delayed its release for two years. In the meantime Ophuls satirised the waltztime musicals in which audiences wallowed as the Weimar Republic shuddered to its close – though **Die Verliebte Firma** (1932) is chiefly a comedy on the film industry, concerning an Alpine telegraph girl whom a daft film unit think they can turn into a star. The film has great panache, which is what also redeems **Die Verkaufte Braut** (1932), although it reduces Smetana's opera to a typical German musical of the period; the hero and heroine are horse-faced and singularly lacking in dash but, like their

rotund and supposedly comic elders, they conform to the local taste of the time.

Ophuls made his reputation with **Liebelei** (1933), based on the play by Schnitzler and set in the Vienna of cunning little alleys and tinkly cafés, of dragoon officers and their ladies – in this case Fritz (Wolfgang Liebeneiner), who tries to disembarrass himself of his noble mistress for the sake of Christine (Magda Schneider), daughter of a violinist at the Opera. It ends sadly, though the original has been much softened, to become a peg for 'Viennese' themes, romantic ardour and youthful high spirits. Ophuls's fascination with opera houses and faithless young officers, the poignancy of railway stations or falling snow, the chivalry and stupidity of duelling would appear again, but he could become only a little more accomplished than here. The film is enchanting, from Mozart at the beginning to Beethoven at the end and with the waltzes in between.

At Ufa, Erich Pommer continued to be more successful, relatively speaking, than his Hollywood counterparts in the matter of multilingual productions. His costs were lower, his ambitions less, and his understanding of European markets somewhat greater. He did not try to ape Hollywood, and a science fiction tale, **F.P.1. Antwortet Nicht** (1932) was, because of its novelty, expected to sell in those foreign markets where Ufa was not strong. Hans Albers (1892–1960) had become a star under Pommer's guidance, and here he plays a hard-drinking, hard-loving aviator who sacrifices himself for the F.P.1, which is a landing stage set down in mid-Atlantic: personally, I prefer the French version with Charles Boyer (q.v.) or the English one with Conrad Veidt. The screenplay is by Walter Reisch from a story by Curt Siodmak, and the direction by the Austrian Karl Hartl – the only one of the three still to be in Germany for the semi-follow-up, **Gold** (1934), in which Albers is a German scientist kidnapped by a mad British scientist who wants to transmute base metals into gold. It has been suggested that the unfavourable portrait of the Britisher is indicative of the increasing nationalistic fervour of films under the Nazis but it is more probably due to the fact that in the meantime English-language versions of German films, in competition with Hollywood, had become unprofitable and had been dropped. French versions continued to be made; *L'Or* starred Pierre Blanchar.

Der Tunnel (1933), though made by a rival company, was also regarded as a follow-up to *F.P.1*, as based on Bernhard Kellerman's novel about the building of a tunnel under the Atlantic, with, predictably, speculators ensuring sabotage. The director was Kurt (Curtis) Bernhardt, who had already fled the Nazis; he was preparing the French version in Paris, and his backers there arranged a passport for him to return to Munich to make the two versions. The German one was banned after the War by the Allied Military Government because some of the villains were American.

Bernhardt and Lang were not the only ones to flee the Nazis; by 1934 virtually all these directors were working in France. Ophuls, since he was born in the Saar, was able to opt for French citizenship in 1934. Like Bernhardt and Robert Siodmak (who left the country when Goebbels criticised the 'dubious morals' of *Brennendes Geheimnis*) he became successful in the French film industry before departing when it became clear that the Germans would declare war on France; Richard Oswald also left France at that time, but did not have the same success in the U.S., where he became a producer. Both Wiene and Granowsky died in France before the outbreak of war; Berger had a great success in that country with *Trois Valses* before joining Korda. Czinner and Leontine Sagan joined Korda almost immediately, the latter to make just one other (unsuccessful) film before moving to South Africa, where she remained, working in the theatre. Trivas also went to Hollywood; and among the impressive list of refugees – almost all at least temporarily domiciled in France – are the directors Karl Grune and Anatole Litvak, the animator Lotte Reiniger, the actors Peter Lorre, Ernst Deutsch, Fritz Kortner, Albert Basserman, Francis Lederer, Anton Walbrook, Oscar Homolka and Conrad Veidt, the producers Erich Pommer and Seymour Nebenzal, the composers Frederick Hollander and Franz Waxman, the cinematographers Eugen Schüfftan and Franz Planer, and the writers Walter Reisch, Carl Zuckmayer, Billy Wilder and Curt Siodmak. (The last-named paused on his way to Hollywood to work on a British version of *Der Tunnel* (q.v.). Reisch in fact wrote *Maskerade* (q.v.) in Vienna, and Jutzi worked in Vienna and Poland before abandoning direction for cinematography in 1938, shooting a few minor films before leaving the industry in 1942. Of the eminent pre-Nazi directors only Gerhard Lamprecht remained, to occupy himself with the founding of the German film archive in Berlin and a number of innocuous musicals and literary adaptations, including an uninspired *Madame Bovary* (1937) with Pola Negri.

Only one other film-maker of note remained, Werner Hochbaum (1899–1946), though the half-dozen films he made under the Nazis are seldom better than mediocre; however, of his earlier four features at least one is a masterpiece. He was dancer, actor and journalist before going into films, editing for others and reputedly making some experimental shorts before producing and directing **Brüder** (1929), about the Hamburg dock strike of 1896/7, one of the several semi-amateur left-wing movies of the late Silent period. Like the others, this one was inspired by the Soviet cinema, centring on one striking worker and his family. It tells us nothing of the trade unionism of the Kaiser's Germany, but is permeated by a feeling for socialism as it became a recognisable ideal – 'the last cry of individual man, the last movement among the masses on behalf of individual liberty, the last hope of living unregulated' as Barbara Tuchman put it in 'The Proud Tower', and in discussing this particular aspect of German history her tone is remarkably like that of Hochbaum in the film. However, it is possible that Hochbaum's prime motive was a portrait of Hamburg as potent as that of the capital in *Berlin: die Symphonie einer Grossstadt.* When the film failed to find a public it was offered to the Social Democrats, which body commissioned two propaganda shorts, of which I have seen **Zwei Welt** (1929), a persuasive exhortation to vote, amidst contrasting portraits of the poor and wealthy.

Razzia in St Pauli (1932) is arresting from the opening shot, of an accordion being played against a harbour wall, followed by the glittering sea and the superimposition of dancing feet. This is in fact a prologue, a montage celebration of a particular city, Hamburg, where we might live, laugh and love, at least for a while – to use the film's own faded romantic phrases. Its gaiety is shot through with melancholy, but it is a film above all abundantly, vividly alive. Workers arrive in a barge; a drunk stumbles home; Chinese restaurant workers blink in the dawn; and the orchestra in the Reeperbahn café starts playing at ten a.m. every day. In a room, a girl (Gena Falkenburg) adjusts a stocking while a man – client, pimp or lover? – knots his tie. He is there the following morning, too drunk to undress, and in the meantime she, Else, has had a brief fling with Matt (Friedrich Gnass). As she settles down again to sleep Hochbaum makes his point: the workers work, exploited but dedicated, and the dreaming Matts and Elses, similarly trapped, surrender to the circumstances around them. Hochbaum aligns himself with the great humanist film-makers, and because he documents rather than dramatises this is one of the best studies we have of low life. In Else's hang-out, the Kongo Bar, the bored tarts play cards, the lavatory attendant waits, and the first influx of dockers arrives, including two men who dance together (not portrayed as effeminate, as in most films of this period). They are far more believable than any other dockside people

in movies, less 'symbolic' than those in the two films which may have influenced Hochbaum, *The Docks of New York* and *Jenseits der Strasse.* He himself influenced no one, for hardly anyone saw his best films, which are the early ones. Of the several attempts at this time to get unvarnished life on the screen this late one is a culmination: Ozu was unknown, yet the similarities between Hochbaum's film and Ozu's own studies of the poor are startling, particularly in the relish of detail within rooms – and if Hochbaum is the more invigorating, that is perhaps because his images are choreographed to the score. Like Lamprecht and Siodmak, Hochbaum planned to rob the cinema of melodrama, going further than either in his portrayal of the ambiguity and unpredictability of life. It is one of the curiosities of film history that, as with the American 'realist' films, some should have been forgotten while others made or maintained their directors' reputation. It is understandable that Siodmak's *Menschen am Sonntag* appealed to contemporary audiences and has continued to be shown, but not that this exhilarating *Razzia,* once rediscovered, did not immediately join it in the international repertory.

The production company, Orbis, had financed it, since low-life tales were usually popular, and it now summoned Hochbaum to take over **Schleppzug M17** (1933) when its star and co-director, Heinrich George, quarrelled with Willy Döll, also the film's writer (and co-author of 'Mutter Krausens Fahrt ins Glück'). George, rotund and no longer in his first youth, was one of the several character players made stars by an adoring public; in this instance he accepted less than his usual fee to play a tugboat captain because that was what he had wanted to be as a boy. As a communist he welcomed the chance to work with Hochbaum, though when the Nazis came to power he changed sides with alacrity and soon joined the Party – an event which caused a hold-up in the shooting, partly due to the exodus of Jewish workers. Hochbaum took only five days to complete the film – two on location and three in the studio, but it is recognisably by the hand that had fashioned *Razzia,* with a number of similar sequences: the getting-up routine; the visits to the dives and bars; and the relationships of the captain with his wife and a whore (Betty Amman). The most

Werner Hochbaum was one of the two outstanding directors working in Germany in the Thirties. A fervent socialist, his early films had so little success that he remained virtually unknown when the Nazis came to power – and was therefore not forced to flee, like other left-wingers. Because of their failure, it is impossible to find stills for reproduction, so this picture is from his first – and only – international success, *Die Ewige Maske*, a strong psychological drama with Mathias Wieman and Peter Petersen.

remarkable sequence is a promenade through Berlin, the captain and his family contrasted with the pseudo-classical statues a mite self-consciously, but executed with a verve which was not to be seen again till the nouvelle vague.

What audiences there were, despite Herr George, found the plot lacking in incident, and Hochbaum was hardly likely to please them with **Morgen Beginnt das Leben** (1933), since the plot is even thinner than those of his earlier films. It starts with the same situation as in *Berlin Alexanderplatz*, that of a man (Erich Haussmann) leaving prison, but Germany's economic situation, not to mention Hochbaum's temperament, indicated a much less gloomy story. By mischance the man's wife (Hilde von Stolz) fails to meet him, and Hochbaum follows their subsequent adventures as he examines their individual fears before their eventual reunion. Again he offers a graphic portrait of the German capital, and if the film is less skilfully handled than those which preceded it, with a number of showy sequences, the couple in question have an ambiguity of character very rare in films of this period. The analogy with Ozu again arises, for the repeated shots of factory chimneys reinforce the view that he and Hochbaum were kindred spirits.

The film was again unpopular, and Hochbaum was professionally idle till invited to Austria to make **Vorstadt-varieté** (1934), set in and around a suburban music hall. The Austrian film industry was heavily dependent on Germany for both talent and distribution of its wares, but at the same time many of the films regarded as 'Viennese' subjects, such as *Liebelei*, emanated from Berlin. The secondary woman's role in that film had been played by Luise Ullrich, and *Vorstadtvarieté* is primarily a vehicle for this charming actress, playing a singer torn between an honest young draftsman and a dashing officer. As in all Hochbaum's films the leading characters are trapped by their circumstances, but as with the Ophuls film the original material – it was a play by Felix Salten banned for some years because of its anti-military stance – has been reworked to make it more palatable for a mass audience. Salten's bitter ending has now become a happy one, but the film continues to view the authorities with a cold eye and the world of the *heurige* with affection.

Hochbaum had a brief flutter of international recognition when **Die Ewige Maske** (1935), a Swiss-Austrian production, won one of the major prizes at the Venice festival. Otis Ferguson in *The New Republic* referred to it as 'the new *Caligari,* very intense and strange', but it is closer to *Geheimnisse Einer Seele,* also about a nervous breakdown. The victim is a hospital doctor whose principal refuses to sanction a serum he has perfected during an outbreak of meningitis, thereby sending him from depression to schizophrenia. Films on such subjects were seldom offered to lay audiences, and Hochbaum hoped to entertain them with his documentary account of the daily routine of the hospital. He also invests the subject with some of the eeriness of the German 'grotesque' films, while in adapting a novel by the Swiss writer, Leo Lapaire – with the latter's co-operation – he retains his feeling for the ordinariness of his characters.

Returning to Germany he also returned to his light vein, with *Leichte Kavallerie* (1935), a circus story whose main purpose was to introduce Ufa's new star from Hungary, Marika Rökk, and **Der Favorit der Kaiserin** (1936), a period comedy in the manner of Lubitsch, but hampered by inhibited playing. Both indicate Hochbaum's willingness to stay with subjects of no great passion, but **Schatten der Vergangenheit** (1936), made in Austria, and **Man Spricht über Jacqueline** (1937) are heavy-breathing melodramas. The first concerns twin sisters, both played by Miss Ullrich, the bad one impersonating the good one, an idea plagiarised by *A Stolen Life* in Britain a few years later. The second details the exploits of a foolish femme fatale (Wera Engels), as based on an English novel filmed five years later in that country under its original title, *Talk About Jacqueline.* The Hochbaum of the early films is only intermittently recognisable, but he compromises less in **Ein Mädchen Geht an Land** (1938), obviously happy to be back in the waterfront cafés of Hamburg. As of old he refuses to paint his characters in simple black and white, and if the put-upon heroine has little dimension as played by the pleasing but bovine Elizabeth Flickenschildt that is because the latter quality is essential to the role – since she is known to her family as 'the stevedore'. She leaves the family home – a freighter – for a series of adventures which includes a relationship with a man who is after her savings. His moral equivocation, as well as that of some of the other characters, did not go unnoticed by Goebbels, who was only too aware of Hochbaum's past and his propensity for straying from official supervision.

Hochbaum was, in consequence, commanded to make **Drei Unteroffiziere** (1939), which, as the title implies, is a study of life in a small garrison town. Three NCOs put loyalty to each other above anything except the regiment itself, till both loyalties are tested by the inevitable woman, an actress. As if realising that this would be the last film he would make Hochbaum imposes on this uncongenial material a vision that is entirely his: each of the three soldiers reflects his usual perplexity when confronted with goodness, uncertain of its value in a world usually tipped against it. The one true quality of value is love, barrier against all the world's ills, and the soldier who falls in love does so as obsessively as all Hochbaum lovers. The doomed relationship between the beloved and her elderly protector is another familiar theme, but on this occasion the hero does not sink into morbidity or rebellion because of it, since the optimistic, militaristic ending was forced on Hochbaum. To that point he had only half-heartedly endorsed the military code at the centre of the film's subject, concentrating instead on such mundane dramas as the first date made and the first date broken: and not since his early films had he celebrated so keenly the lack of glamour of dingy teashops, barracks and dusty theatres. He did not succeed, as he had hoped, in ingratiating himself with Goebbels, and although the film received the official seal of the Predikat Commission the grant which traditionally went with it – the *kunsterlische wertwoll* – was withheld.

While preparing his next film Hochbaum was officially forbidden to work in the film industry, on the grounds that in 1923 he had offered his services to the French for espionage, a charge almost certainly without foundation. After serving for a while in the army he worked pseudonymously on scripts and was preparing *Der Tanz in der Nacht* for Defa in East Germany when he died in 1946. Doubtless he had been amused to find that *Drei Unteroffiziere,* not much liked by the Party, was banned by the Allied authorities.

As the Weimar Republic died there was one left-wing film, **Kühle Wampe** (1932), which caused the stir that Hochbaum had wanted for his own similarly-inclined works – and as open Communist propaganda it was only permitted to be shown after a number of cuts. Attempting to examine the obviously common situation of a jobless family, it finds the younger generation more embittered than its elders – the boy takes his own life, but the girl, after becoming pregnant, is saved from further misfortune by the joys of worker solidarity. A mixture of arty juxtapositions and stilted dialogue, the film was initially a labour of love and later the subject of litigation among its participants, including its director, Slatan Dudow, a Bulgarian much influenced by the Soviets, and Berthold Brecht, its writer, who subsequently claimed that it was the only film with which he had been associated of which he approved. The music, by Hanns Eisler, is the sole feature of the piece to indicate either talent or professionalism.

The films with which the Nazis hoped to convey *their* message could only be better, but any improvement might escape the casual viewer. The first with which they may be associated is **Morgenrot** (1933), since Hitler ostentatiously attended the Berlin premiere only two days after becoming Chancellor. This melodrama about U-boats proclaimed the merit of dying for the *Vaterland* – though directed by an Austrian, Gustav Ucicky: however, since a mother is seen to weep for the bereaved of the other side, this is not wholly a Nazi film. Ucicky no longer had such humanist touches when he made **Flüchtlinge** (1934), whose theme was one always popular with the Nazis, the persecution of a German minority by the Russians. The Party itself distributed **Friesennot** (1935), directed under an alias by Willi Krause, a tale of oppressed Germans who rise against their Russian masters during the Revolution and return to Germany.

Communists were more likely than Jews to be found as villains, on the assumption that a Jew could not be a worthy opponent for a German; Jews usually made brief appearances as venal capitalists. Other subjects for disapproval include the previous régime, shown to be a period of racial impurity, economic instability, drugs and suicide. **S. A. Mann Brand** (1933) concerns the enmity of the Bolsheviks and the National Socialists during that time, with the Communists shown as brutal and mean-spirited – except for their leader, who is wealthy and effete. They manage to get the Nazi Youth uniform banned, just as the widowed mother of our young hero has saved up to buy him one. He is consoled, however – in what must be the funniest moment in all cinema – by a framed photograph of Hitler, given by the boy next door. Perhaps spectators were rare because they feared they would laugh: they would have seen a handsome production, due to the Nazi money poured into it and the skilled photography of Franz Koch rather than to the direction by Franz Seitz, hitherto associated with Bavarian farces.

The second Nazi film proper was a biography of Horst Wessel, the sleazy pimp whose murder was celebrated in the song the Party had adopted as its anthem. Since the facts were unsuitable, its story bore little relation to the truth, with those responsible for the murder categorised as Communists. Till the dread deed, the idealistic Wessel (Emil Lohkamp) had been in the process of converting them by preaching the higher ideals of National Socialism, and it is because of his success that he is put out of harm's way. The only considerable talent involved is Paul Wegener, as the Communist leader, and the uninspired director is Franz Wenzler. Previewed as *Horst Wessel* (1933), it was hastily re-edited and re-titled, emerging a few weeks later as **Hans Westmar, Einer von Vielenein Deutsches Schicksal aus dem Jahre 1919,** but the public took no more notice of it than it had of *S.A. Mann Brand*.

Somewhere between the standard of both films is **Hitlerjunge Quex** (1933), directed by Hans Steinhoff, with which Ufa, albeit unwillingly, joined the Nazi bandwagon. Again the plot was based on a real-life murder – of a youth killed in 1932 by Communists, though for the film's purposes he has become a boy, bewildered both by opposing political forces and weak parents – these played by Heinrich George and Bertha Drews, repeating their teaming from *Schleppzug M17*. The boy was played by an unnamed member of the Nazi Youth, an organisation presented in this film as boisterous and robot-like: but just as the unfolding events reveal the Communists to be child-murderers rather than merely slovenly, drunken and promiscuous, so the Nazis prove to be loyal, steadfast and stalwart. However, their first loyalty is

Film in the Third Reich

The hero, played by an unnamed member of the Nazi Youth Movement, in the closing sequence of *Hitlerjunge Quex*, one of the films with which the Nazi party hoped to awaken the German nation to its virtues. The films are resolutely simple-minded, and after January 1933 the propaganda became considerably more insidious – with little more success till the war years, when in patriotic fervour audiences did flock to a number of pictures condemning Germany's enemies.

always to Hitler, man and leader – and as an official creed it is witness to their mentality. The only overt propaganda in the film is the montage of Nazi marchers which concludes it, but it is worth noting that though foreign Communists are evil incarnate German Communists are either misguided or composed of the dregs to be found in any society.

With the attainment of power, proselytising by the Nazis was no longer necessary – or prudent, since it could not be suggested that the ruling party actually needed converts to its cause. Nor could the state be shown to harbour any 'dregs' stupid enough not to see its virtues – or, if they existed, they were unworthy of notice, just in case someone, somewhere, identified with them. Undoubtedly Goebbels wished that his film-makers had some revolutions to draw upon, as the Soviets had had. Instead the Nazis would celebrate the present – and, they did not doubt, the

future: but with virtually every first-class film-maker forced out of the industry it was not easy to see how these achievements could be transmitted in film.

A solution was found with the documentary, which did not require much imagination, and the occasion presented itself with the 1934 party rally at Nuremberg. At Hitler's request an approach was made to Leni Riefenstahl, a former actress who had made a formidable start as producer-director with a starring vehicle for herself, *Das Blaue Licht*. That and the subsequent films she directed indicated a penchant for handling natural phenomena, and with **Triumph des Willens** (1935) she succeeded beyond Hitler's wildest dreams. The subject genuinely fired her imagination, as she photographed and then edited the images of the Nuremberg rally – as stage-managed by the party's favoured architect, Albert Speer, under the influence of *Metropolis*: huge columns, huge swastikas on huge flags, the central podium for the speakers and party members – and the multitude within this gigantic arena an impressive witness both to the solidarity of the nation and the co-operation between Party and Government. 'The purpose of the film was twofold.' says David Stewart Hull in 'Film in the Third Reich'. 'To show the solidarity of the Party, particularly following the divisions caused by the Röhm affair; and to introduce the leaders, many of whom spoke a few words, to this pre-television society. Another, more subtle, purpose was to impress foreign audiences, and at the same time to scare the hell out of them. The film succeeded on all counts.' It is an object lesson in image-making, as banners unfurl, men march, or at camp line up for food or comb each other's hair. Their faces shine with eagerness, and it is with the same eagerness that they assemble into ranks; but as the object of their fealty becomes clear, and as the film increasingly pleads for the end of the individual – beyond the chosen few – it becomes more than mildly repellent.

A peculiar mystique, however, has grown up around this film and its companion piece, **Olympiad** (1938), a record of the Games held in Berlin in 1936 and a glowing rebuttal of the director's claim that she was not a Nazi but a film-maker. As a spokesman for the Third Reich she has a footnote in history – though it is now difficult to

308

know to what extent: the original negatives and German copies of the Nuremberg film no longer survive, and it is possible that the 'export' versions which remain were shorn of anti-Jewish propaganda (because of the high proportion of Jewish cinema proprietors who might have refused to show it). The original version of *Olympiad,* at 3 hours 40 minutes, may have included even more footage of a benignly smiling Hitler; it does have a few shots of the black runner Jesse Owens, obligatory because of his triumphs, but it is primarily a celebration of Aryan physical endeavour. The celebrated prelude – the mists of antiquity and the Greek sculptures – is now kitsch, and the handling of the opening ceremony does not begin to compare with Ichikawa's in *Tokyo Olympiad* (q.v.). In the 1972 Games, a British runner, Dave Bedford, observed that the difference between him 'and so many others is that I'm here to win, they're here to compete', but it is unedifying to watch a film permeated with the same ideal, constantly reminding us that Germany won more medals than any other country. The shots of the athletes relaxing and the symphonic arrangement of most of the other sports retain a mild virtue; Riefenstahl took eighteen months to edit the film, originally selecting the best images of fit, marshalled young men, but eventually became carried away by the rhythms she could create.

Both films, though recognised for what they were, were successful abroad, which could be said for few others made under the Nazi régime. In recent years there have been revivals of some of those directed by Detlef Sierck, as a consequence of the cult-following for the Hollywood melodramas he made after changing his name to Douglas Sirk – a following, incidentally, which both amuses and amazes him. The best of his German films is **Stutzen der Gesellschaft** (1935), a version of Ibsen's 'The Pillars of the Community' which is only adequate in direction and production values but does avoid being either literary or stagey. A dreadful, interpolated prologue shows Johan with the cowboys in the U.S., but Heinrich George is superbly cast as Consul Bernick, enduring a number of emotional ordeals as his past catches up with him. More typical of Sierck's work is **La Habanera** (1937), a vehicle for the Swedish singer popular in Germany, Zarah

Leander, who has three unlikely songs in the midst of some junketings about a grandee's ill-treated wife who conspires with a brave young compatriot to cure an outbreak of fever. Gerhard Menzel, author of *Morgenrot,* provided the plot, clearly fashioned after the current Hollywood models, but in handling it Sierck manages none of their occasional wit or drama.

In the matter of foreign success, that of *Liebelei* was soon overshadowed by that of **Maskerade** (1934), in which the Hapsburg Empire again crumbled to the strains of waltztime. As so often, the wits and gossips found in their midst an unexpected true love – that of the roué (Anton Walbrook) and the damsel demure (Paula Wessely). The London *Daily Telegraph* called the film 'superb – intelligent as to story, wittily written, magnificently acted and directed', and though contemporary opinion attributed its success to Miss Wessely, she is a little calculating in the Viennese manner.

As an actress Leni Riefenstahl had been associated with the mountaineering melodramas, so beloved by the Nazis since they emphasised courage, nationalism and the open-air life. After they came to power she was asked to direct the official records of the 1934 party rally at Nuremberg and the 1936 Olympic Games in Berlin. The latter, *Olympiad,* persuaded only the gullible that she was more interested in celebrating the human body than the party.

Another player, Willi Forst, went behind the camera to direct, and *Maskerade*, the second film he made in that capacity, has a lightness he never again achieved. The story, if delightful, was only too typical of Viennese romances, as the gossips find in their midst an unexpected true love, as the roué (Anton Walbrook), becomes enslaved of the damzel demure (Paula Wessely).

Rather it is a triumph for Walbrook, both haughty as the amorist and touchingly human as the man in love. The story is unremarkable, but serves for the expected ironies, wittily written by Walter Reisch, whose Hollywood chores would include a remake, *Escapade;* and it was photographed by a superb craftsman, the Czech-born Franz Planer, whose long and distinguished career in German films would be followed by another in Hollywood. He had photographed *Liebelei* – and would work with Ophuls again on *Letter From an Unknown Woman* (q.v.) – and though this film is stagey and slow in comparison we may suspect considerable help by both Planer and Reisch since it is so superior to the other films directed by Willi Forst.

It was his second film in that capacity, and henceforth he acted only occasionally, instead often contributing to the scripts he directed. **Mazurka** (1935) was a vehicle for Pola Negri, who had temporarily resumed her career in Germany. She plays a singer who wrongs her husband and, many years later, shoots her seducer since he is about to compromise her daughter and she does not wish history to be repeated. The actress thought her own performance outstanding, but there is nothing to detain anyone but devotees of soap opera – beyond the fact that it was first shown in London at the (original) Curzon Cinema, built by the Nazis as a showplace for their films. It opened there in 1937, one month before the Germans insisted in a new agreement with the Austrian film industry that they would only accept its product if no Jewish talent was involved. Elsewhere abroad, the Nazis were not always inclined to show their hand, and so little was known of their ownership of the Curzon that some British reviewers supposed it an Austrian film.

Forst did make most of his films in Germany, but **Bel Ami** (1939), like *Maskerade,* was made in his native Austria. A credit claims it a celebration of *belle époque* Paris, but de Maupassant's tale is merely a pretext for froufrou, all of it dowdy. As a director Forst is frivolous; excellent on occasion – in *Brennendes Geheimnis* – his own performance in the title role is poor. His anonymity is such that he could enter or leave a room without anyone noticing him, though in the case of this film one's energies are devoted to trying to follow the plot. Partly because of the setting it was one of the films the Germans foisted on the French during the Occupation; the French loathed it, but took unwillingly to the theme song. Forst was now established as a director of musicals, despite the equally lumpish *Operette* (1940), a tale of squabbling lovers: with it, he decided to give up acting, though it was because of his earlier popularity in that capacity that this was finally imported into the U.S. in 1949, to be quickly dismissed.

Reinhold Schünzel was another (former) actor who specialised in movie operettas, and the success of **Amphitryon** (1935) brought him an M-G-M contract (he directed three films for them, and made a subsequent living in Hollywood from acting). The French version, *Les Dieux s'Amusent,* made simultaneously, may well have given Giraudoux the inspiration to write his play 'Amphytryon '38'; there is a long tradition of re-telling this old Greek myth – and this particular version is only for those who believe (cf. *The Private Life of Helen of Troy*) that the Greek gods and heroes carried on like us – with such merry conceits as a Mercury on rollerskates. Willy Fritsch plays Amphitryon and Jupiter, and is rather good as the latter.

One genre had disappeared from the German cinema – the grotesque, because Goebbels knew how often these films hinted at subversion. The old tradition of the German cinema did surface for one last time with **Fährmann Maria** (1936). Death and his black-coated cohorts pursue an escaped convict, who is saved by the love of a lonely ferry-girl (Sybille Schmitz): the suggestion was whispered that this theme represented the defeat of the Nazi creed – and Goebbels, unsure, had the distribution curtailed rather than ban the film outright, which might have aroused curiosity. The director is Frank Wysbar, who also went to Hollywood, where his sole credit is a low-budget, inferior remake, *Strangler in the Swamp* (1945).

If *Fährmann Maria* is one of the more interesting films of the Nazi period, there is at least one fine film among the variable works of Helmut Käutner (1908–80), who, as with most German directors, arrived via the theatre and cabaret. His first two films are derivative, **Kitty und die Weltkonferenz** (1939), a modern tale in the tradition of *Der Kongress Tanzt,* and **Kleider Machen Leute** (1940), some variations on the theme of Zuckmayer's 'Der Hauptmann von Köpenick'. That play was anathema to Goebbels, and this film claims to be based on motifs in Gottfried Keller's 'Die Leute von Seldwyla' – both works, in any case, being akin to Gogol's 'The Government Inspector'. Käutner successfully resisted pressure to incorporate Nazi propaganda in his films while attempting to make light-hearted films on serious subjects – in both these instances, the bureaucracy of politicians, international and local. Despite his glancing touch, the humour remains pompous and Germanic, and *Kleider Machen Leute* deliberately avoids contemporary relevance, being set among the puppet-like citizens of a hundred years earlier, as drawn by Wilhelm Busch. The lead is played by Heinz Rühmann, who eventually played Zuckmayer's captain in Kautner's 1956 remake (q.v.).

Romanze in Moll (1943) is based on a story by de Maupassant, 'Le Bijou', and it is at least a great improvement on *Bel Ami;* since de Maupassant so disliked the Germans it is amusing to find that Käutner attacks his subject here in the manner of the Alsace-born Ophuls – mirrors, melodies and sweeping cameras – but he is not the stylist Ophuls was. He is even more superficial than Ophuls, and this tale of a bourgeois housewife (Marianne Hoppe) attracted to a successful composer and philanderer seems at times just out of mothballs. Fräulein Hoppe, though pleasant, does little but bring a roguish smile of triumph to the love scenes. The playing is also wan in **Die Grosse Freiheit Nr 7** (1944), but then no one is allowed to outshine its star, Hans Albers, playing an old sea-dog who sings for a living in a St Pauli bar and returns to the sea after being rejected by a much younger woman. The people are passionless and their emotions uninteresting – the besetting sins of the German films of this period; but the details of Hamburg life are lively and the colour is delightful.

Agfacolor had been first used for films in 1941, before it was fully developed, at Goebbels's behest: this is the fourth or fifth film in the process, the uncertainty coming from the fact that the film's premiere was delayed and finally given in Prague – Goebbels having commissioned the film as a tribute to the German navy and then, not surprisingly, disapproving of the result (Albers's huge popularity enabled him a measure of defiance; he had kept his Jewish wife with him till prudently deciding to send her to London).

If it compares with *Razzia in St Pauli*, **Unter den Brücken** (1945) is also strongly reminiscent of *Schleppzug M17,* being photographed almost entirely on the canals of Berlin. Almost certainly conditions in the studios were too chaotic at this stage of the War to allow filming there to proceed other than slowly: but the high percentage of shots of an unblemished Berlin may have been meant as a morale-booster to the rest of the country. Unfortunately the film was only ready as the Third Reich was about to collapse, and it disappeared till 1950 (a fate shared with Käutner's first film, withdrawn after its premiere because it seemed like a comment on the world situation; it did not reappear for over a decade). What audiences would have seen was the old German favourite of two men in love with the same girl, with not a semblance of inspired variation.

Less successful in resisting Goebbels's insistence that every script embody some aspect of Nazi ideology was Herbert Selpin. **Wässer fur Canitoga** (1939) features Hans Albers in familiar guise as a harddrinking, bawdy mining engineer, breathing Teutonic warmth, as cutely set up as Shirley Temple ever was; his qualities of leadership are not necessarily Nazi, nor his self-sacrifice – but the martial tribute sung to him after death is by a group proudly identifying itself as composed of old soldiers. The setting is Canada at the turn of the century – a fact of little significance since Selpin considered that he was making a

Western, though at this time Goebbels was increasingly concerned with criticising British imperial power, in the hope of neutralising it.

Titanic (1943) was one of his pet projects, since he considered it a chance to show the British at their most craven and greedy. Selpin was assigned to it, because he had made two other sea stories – though he preferred light comedy, with which he had made his name. His usual writer, Walter Zerlatt-Olfenius, was a fanatical Party member, and a violent quarrel between them during location work was followed by Selpin's criticism of the officers acting as extras, because they regarded filming as of less importance than dalliance with their female counterparts. He refused to retract when called to account by Goebbels and was disposed of: photographs were prepared of him hanging in his prison cell, but on sounder consideration it was thought that the public might have difficulty in accepting yet another suicide in the film industry. However, since word did leak out the film was suppressed – though an additional reason was that the scenes of panic might remind audiences too forcibly of the effect of the R.A.F. bombings; to help recoup costs it was premiered in Paris late in 1943. These facts are of more interest than the film itself, though its tedium may be relieved by a laugh or so at the expense of the German couple in steerage who show themselves so much more heroic than anyone else on board.

Goebbels was particularly keen to encourage historical subjects, since in them Jews could be exposed as capitalist plotters – and the chances of exalting military might would be less gratuitous than in *Wässer fur Canitoga.* **Das Herz der Königin** (1940), a foolish romance concerning Mary, Queen of Scots (Zarah Leander), statically directed by Carl Frölich, has points to make on the perfidy of England; **Bismarck** (1940) shows Germany's most brilliant leader outwitting the rest of Europe – in a film that is cleverly accurate, despite its omissions, though that fact cannot disguise an abysmally stodgy director at work, Wolfgang Liebeneiner, the former actor. In the sequel, **Die Entlassung** (1942), Paul Hartmann has been replaced as Bismarck by Emil Jannings and Werner Krauss is one of his enemies, von Holstein, taking as of old any honours going for this partnership. In

both films Werner Hinz plays the crown prince, and in this one he also plays his own son, who becomes Kaiser Wilhelm II, depicted as effeminate or worse in his passion for uniforms. It is even duller than its predecessor, but does show Nazi propaganda in full flood – at the end Bismarck meditates on the future of the Reich, a concept greater than any man: it will outlive him, he says, and will need another great man to take on his mantle.

A great director, Pabst, returned to Germany to make two mediocre historical films for Goebbels, **Komödianten** (1941) and **Paracelsus** (1943). As a European war became imminent he had announced that he intended to leave France and take American citizenship; he was in Austria to sell some property and collect his mother when the fall of Poland prevented him getting an exit visa. His subsequent behaviour is puzzling, and work on a number of projects, helping other film-makers, has been ascribed to him. He was later evasive on his activities; however, it should be borne in mind that not only had he snubbed the Nazis by

refusing to work for them till now, but almost every film on which his reputation rested had been at odds with National Socialist doctrine. *Komödianten* is mainly a vehicle for the accomplished Käthe Dorsch, playing Karoline Neuber who, by virtue of carting her troupe around eighteenth-century Germany, is regarded as the founder of the German theatre. That Pabst won the Best Director award at the 1941 Venice Festival can only be due to politics – or the fact that only the Axis and its allies were competing. The film is relatively harmless, but *Paracelsus* is undoubtedly nationalist, with its sixteenth-century toasts to the concept of the German Reich. Both films have a dedicated protagonist, triumphing – at least spiritually – over the petty machinations of ducal families, ignorant merchants and busybodies. They are people of destiny, rejecting 'power, wealth and honour' in the service of honour – itself to be placed with the *volk* of Nazi ideology. Since Paracelsus (Krauss) was Swiss, he is identified in this film as an empassioned promoter of the German

The Nazi historical films are among the more rewarding of the films produced in Germany at this time – at least to historians, since the stories are basically accurate, and pleasure may be taken in finding the distortions, often minor in themselves, which aim to spread the Nazi creed. The approach, otherwise, is uninspired, and they are not recommended to seekers of entertainment. Among the better ones is *Bismarck*, with Friedrich Kayssler as the Kaiser Wilhelm I and Paul Hartmann as the Chancellor.

tongue. Apart from an astonishing apparition of Death, the direction indicates no directorial interest at all: one must assume that Pabst had no control over the script, or had become entirely cynical about his own work and the Nazis. *Der Fall Molander* was made in Czechoslovakia as the Russian armies advanced, and abandoned, though shooting was completed: it was never publicly shown, and is reputedly destroyed. After the War Pabst worked for several years in Austria, but without regaining his international reputation.

One German director did make very happily the nationalistic epics beloved of Goebbels, working with a skill and passion that exposes without mercy the banal talents of his confrères. Luis Trenker (b. 1893) came from the German-speaking section of the Italian Tyrol, a mountain guide discovered for films by Dr Arnold Fanck, who gave him a leading role in *Der Heilige Berg* (1926). After several years working solely as an actor, Trenker collaborated on **Berge in Flammen** (1931) with Karl Hartl, who co-directed and wrote the screenplay from a story by Trenker – who also played the lead in this tale of Austrian-Italian enmity in the Tyrol. Universal liked the film and asked Trenker to remake it as *The Doomed Battalion,* using much of the same spectacular mountain footage and with Cyril Gardner co-directing. Then, with a subsidiary of that company, Deutsche-Universal, Trenker made **Der Rebell** (1933) in collaboration with Kurt Benhardt, playing a young Tyrolean hero who defies Napoleon. There was also an English version in which Vilma Banky replaced Luise Ullrich as the heroine. It could not be said that then or later Trenker was an attractive hero, being tightlipped in appearance. Despite the fact that these two films were in English he made no headway with American audiences, who preferred their action heroes to be more homespun: his full-blooded romanticism and obvious national pride were also incompatible with the mood of the time.

Those same qualities sat very well with the Nazi Party: Hitler and Goebbels publicly saw the film and the latter recorded his appreciation in his diary: 'Thus I could imagine the film of the future, revolutionary in character, with grand mass-scenes, composed with enormous vital energy.' That was presumably not known to Siegfried Kracauer when he came to write 'From Caligari to Hitler' in 1947, but he categorises Trenker as a Nazi director, partly on the eloquent use he made of flags. There is, however, apart from coincident ideals, no evidence that Trenker returned the admiration of the Nazis.

His next two films were mainly set and partly filmed in the U.S., and if he were indeed of the Nazi mentality it seems unlikely that he would have sought financial backing from Tobis, a company which was at this point financed from Amsterdam. A curious sidelight to the filming of the second film is that Trenker only had $30,000 available for the extensive location work, and that he was encouraged by Paul Kohner, the head of Deutsche-Universal, a company otherwise not involved: since its American owners had dropped Trenker it is ironic that their version of the same subject – *Sutter's Gold* (q.v.) – should be so infinitely inferior. Indeed, both these films are among the most remarkable of the period, and **Der Verlorene Sohn** (1934) was recognised as such at the Venice Festival, where it was awarded the Grand Prix. Despite that, and the fact that its long central section is in English, it has never been publicly shown in Britain or the U.S. This section concerns the adventures of a Tyrolean guide in America where, having failed to track down his girlfriend (Marian Marsh), he finds himself increasingly crushed by the Depression before returning home. **Der Kaiser von Kalifornien** (1936) is hardly more optimistic, concerning the ideal leader, enterprising and patriarchal, laid low by greed and political forces. If Trenker manages a happy ending to both – in this film an allegorical tribute to modern America, with the ghost riders in the sky from *Der Rebell* – it is because the romantic side of his nature always triumphed over the realistic. He was producer, director, sole writer and leading actor – and on the evidence of these two films a great film-maker, both of them towering above the majority of Hollywood's respective Depression tales and screen biographies. His films are at least visually magnificent, with some stunning montages and settings eloquently used.

However, returning to the subject of his first films as a director, alpine warfare, in **Condottieri** (1937) a number of images now begin to seem cliché – the fields of waving corn, waving flags, the mountains. Trenker, eyes and teeth agleam, preaching nationalism and love of the *Vaterland,* is a laughable figure; and though the nationalist cause came naturally to most Tyroleans it is hard not to regard this film as a sop to the Party. In fact it marked the end of the mutual enchantment, if there were any on his side: the Pope had recently issued an encyclical which had been interpreted, as intended, as a criticism of the Nazi régime, and Trenker's sequence in which his medieval hero is blessed by the Pope was regarded by Goebbels as not only gratuitous but an implied endorsement. It was cut, and the film withdrawn after a week's run in Berlin.

Trenker had begun to challenge the Nazis in *Der Kaiser von Kalifornien,* with its clear warning that self-made dictators can well end up powerless and lonely. At the time of its production he had remarked privately that he had turned down Hollywood offers because he feared for his German wife and children; now he sought foreign financing, perhaps Jewish, and he certainly had German-Jewish refugee collaborators on **The Challenge** (1938), made simultaneously with its German version, *Der Berg Ruft.* Gunther Stapenhorst produced for Korda, with a screenplay by Emeric Pressburger based on a German film of 1928, *Der Kampf ums Matterhorn,* concerning the first ascent of that mountain in 1865. Korda's cinematographer, Georges Périnal, joined forces with Albert Benitz, Trenker's usual collaborator, to bypass on this occasion the clichés of mountain photographers – and their achievement is superb, despite a limited budget of £80,000; but the scenes in the various hostelries are literally grounded, at least in the English version as co-directed by Milton Rosmer. In that, the hero is played by Robert Douglas, with Trenker as his Italian guide.

Like this film and *Condottieri,* **Der Feuerteufel** (1940) is a second-rate film made by a first-class film-maker – one with complete understanding of the possibilities of his medium. Like them, it is likeable and unforced, bringing a touch of humour to this deliberate attempt at a heroic tale. It also is much like *Der Rebell,* concerning an Alpine woodsman who leads a rebellion against Napoleon, but this time Trenker was playing with fire, since it was open

encouragement for all occupied countries to rise against the aggressor. The hero advocates peace over war, and speaks of the rights of individual nations to control their destiny. Although Napoleon, like Trenker's Sutter, is depicted as a man of some humanity, Goebbels this time could not overlook the implications, and the film was banned – except for showing to the armed forces, amongst whom it could do no harm. Trenker was immediately blacklisted, although he was allowed to act in the anti-British *Germanin,* after which he went to Italy, where he made a number of documentary shorts and a few features before returning briefly to the German industry in 1955, with *Der Flucht in die Dolomiten,* partly scripted by Pasolini (q.v.). Unlike those other veterans of the mountain film, Fanck and Riefenstahl, he had never been active in the Party, and

Luis Trenker in typical garb, playing an Alpine guide and looking very heroic against a mountain background. This picture is in fact from *Condottieri.* As an actor he is passable, but as writer-producer-director and cinematographer he achieved greatness on at least two occasions.

it is particularly ironic that he was banned with them and a number of other film-makers when in 1945 the Allies examined the probable guilt of the German film industry in supporting the Nazis. If they had looked at all his films they had not looked hard enough – nor, obviously, examined the facts. Trenker remains an enigma: branching out from the genre films which were clearly his favourites he made two magnificent films, only to retreat again. The fact that he worked in Nazi Germany perhaps inhibited him and certainly silenced him. We do not know whether he felt called upon to criticise the Nazi leadership from disillusionment or from love of humanity – though from moments in *Der Verlorene Sohn* we may suspect the latter.

Among others banned from the film industry by the Allies were Emil Jannings and Werner Krauss (Heinrich George died while interned in a Russian concentration camp), and the directors Gustav Ucicky, Wolfgang Liebeneiner and Veit Harlan. Krauss, like Trenker, was unjustly treated: his son's wife was Jewish, which was why he surrendered to Goebbels's pleas to appear in *Jud Süss* (q.v.) – the experience of which so distressed him that two years later he refused to play the lead in another propaganda historical, *Der Grosse König*. Ferdinand Marian, who played the lead in *Jud Süss,* was so riven with guilt that he committed suicide not long after he had been de-Nazified by an Allied committee. That particular film became the focal point for Allied interest in the Nazi film industry, and was banned after the War as 'the most obvious anti-semitic propaganda imaginable'. It was also the cause of its director being twice tried for Crimes Against Humanity – though he was acquitted for lack of evidence.

He was Veit Harlan (1899–1964), a former stage actor and director most noted for his soap operas, usually starring his third wife, Kristina Söderbaum, of Swedish origin. Typical of them, and of Nazi notions as to heroic and romantic ideals, is **Opfergang** (1944), concerning the re-action of Octavia (Irene von Meyendorff) when she discovers that her husband (Carl Raddatz) is having an affair with the woman (Söderbaum) next door. The wife wears tea gowns and plays Chopin; the mistress, also blonde, behaves alternately as mermaid and Diana, and then horse-woman-in-silk-hat and kitten-among-the-cushions – all the time supposed to be a 'free', close-to-nature woman. Harlan also directed a number of historical films, including **Das Unsterbliche Herz** (1939), based on a 1913 play by his father, Walter Harlan, and concerning the medieval watch maker Peter Henlein (Heinrich George); and **Der Grosse König** (1942), the last gasp of the Fridericus films, again starring Otto Gebühr and surprisingly hinting at the monarch's homosexuality. Both are unabashedly Nazi: Peter Henlein prefers work to sex, he is an idealist – unlike the merchants around him – and he wishes to die in the saddle, like the soldier with whom he compares himself, offering his life for his country. Behind the dedicated figure of Frederick in the other film is that subtle theme of Nazi ideology, that every nation is weakened when there is no strong government to stand against dissidents.

That creed is openly expounded in *Condottieri,* but it is particularly insidious in Harlan's films and certainly in **Jud Süss** (1940), where by dissidents we understand Jews, by implication a completely grasping race. The anti-semitic films did not really start till 1939, preparatory to formulating the Final Solution, and as the Germans conquered Europe these films went with them, to create a climate in which innocent people could be taken from their homes and destroyed. *Jud Süss* is accordingly vile – all the more so since it is both handsome and well-made. Harlan was at best a plodding director, but he was aided by the high traditions in art direction which remained in the German studios. He is well served here by Krauss, in a double role as the Rabbi Loew and Süss's familiar, and magnificently by Herr Marian in the title role. It is an odd experience to be confronted with a great performance of a villain, knowing that we are not supposed to hate superficially, as with most screen villains. Marian's Süss has pride, cunning, greed, intellectual power, the ability to survive personal humiliation and prejudice; unlike the earlier, creaky British version (q.v.) we meet him first as a Jew, and he is sympathetic. But he becomes loathsome. Jewry was not in 1940 what it had been in 1733 (in Stuttgart), but the film is an incitement to hate all its members.

Goebbels himself revised the script,

eventually deleting Süss's final tirade against his enemies because it included a prophecy that their cities would be destroyed by fires from heaven. It is easy to believe Harlan's later claim that none of the principals wished to be associated with the project, claiming on his own behalf that all the characters were negative; however, he was also associated with **Kolberg** (1945), the apotheosis of Nazi film-making. Goebbels intended it to rival *Gone with the Wind* (q.v.) – and as that film had provided sustenance to British audiences during the War so this was similarly intended. Kolberg was a small Prussian town which had withstood the forces of Napoleon; as Goebbels wrote to the director, the film was to demonstrate that 'a *people* united at home and at the front will overcome any enemy' – and thus, as with Trenker's films, a people's army was extolled at the expense of the official servicemen. Goebbels initiated the project in 1941 and filming began two years later, with a budget of Reichsmark 8½ million. The statistics in Hull ('Film in the Third Reich') include more than 10,000 costumes, 6,000 horses and more than 187,000 people 'involved at one time or other'. These included troops diverted from the front, while one hundred railway wagons of salt were conveyed to the location to provide snow. As usual, Goebbels declined to tamper with history, since the propaganda content was the less suspect; but the French had finally overwhelmed Kolberg, hardly a fact to stir audiences after the reversals of 1943 and 1944. The ending, often left vague during preparations, was constantly changed – and footage to the value of RM 2 million removed: it was finally clear that the only message that the film could convey was that to capitulate is to destroy a nation. Many of Goebbels's own speeches were put into the mouth of the resistance leader (Heinrich George), reiterating that the story of Kolberg is a demonstration of the popular will. La Rochelle was chosen for the premiere because it was then under siege: cans of film had to be dropped by parachute for the

Veit Harlan's *Jud Süss* must be one of the most famous of all unseen movies, renowned as anti-semitic propaganda, and therefore seldom revived. It is offensive but the one reason to see it is the performance of Ferdinand Marian in the title role. It is an odd experience to be confronted with a great performance of evil, knowing that we are not supposed to hate superficially, as with most screen villains. Marian later committed suicide, reputedly from guilt because of his association with the film – but that was only after the Allied authorities had interrogated him on the matter.

appointed date, 30 January, the anniversary of the Nazis coming to power. Virtually the only cinema still open in the ruins of Berlin was assigned to show the film, but was allowed to withdraw it after a few days. A week before the War ended Goebbels screened the film for his staff, and in the accompanying speech told them that in a hundred years' time they would be the subject of a similar film. It was revived in 1966, with newsreel footage added to point up the propaganda, but when pickets appeared outside cinemas it was soon withdrawn. It is as dreary as it is unimpressive. It is appropriate that not only is what Goebbels considered his greatest epic so completely hollow, but that few people have ever seen it.

p.320
Nils Asther and
Barbara Stanwyck in
*The Bitter Tea of
General Yen,*
a devilish bit of
Chinoiserie which
must confound
anyone who thinks
of Frank Capra as
a purveyor of
sentiment and
idealism.

Thing, poverty, success with the box lunches, reconciliation with papa; in *Dirigible,* a crash, a broken marriage, a letter that isn't read; in *Miracle Woman,* a confession, the fire, new hope; and in *Lady for a Day,* the suddenly whimsical behaviour of New York's upper crust. Mr Deeds, on trial for insanity, is saved by a confession of love; in *American Madness,* the president's marriage and his bank fail, or seem to at the same time – till the miraculous reversal. Not for nothing is one of Capra's later films called *A Pocketful of Miracles* (q.v.).

Capra and Riskin are always capable of humour, if sometimes lacking seriousness. *American Madness,* like *Miracle Woman,* moves into plot contrivance after a startlingly naturalistic start. Capra is good on the day to day activity of the bank but, even allowing for the emotional climate of the time the scenes of panic are exaggerated. He himself claims some notable firsts for the film – such as attempting to express the urgency of the bank's problems by hastening the pace faster than life, moving the performers at speed in and out of the heart of a scene, and omitting the then-current dissolve to indicate change of time or locale. Overlapping dialogue had been used before – in *Bad Girl* – but we may note a rare ability to combine humour and idiosyncrasy for greater credibility rather than less in, for instance, the characters of the piggish detective and the squeaky-voiced man at the directors' meetings.

Now, Capra decided, he wanted an Oscar: 'I would make the artiest film they ever saw ... Walter Wanger [then at Columbia] happened to be preparing a picture from Grace Zaring Stone's novel ... To me it was Art with a capital A.' In outline, **The Bitter Tea of General Yen** (1933) sounds not unlike *The Sheik,* but in practice it is a brave, romantic picture, far ahead of its time – or so one might suppose, except that it was booked into the gigantic Radio City Music Hall, and was the first film to play there. As Capra boasts, it is as much about miscegenation as eroticism; it also casts a queer light on one of the sacred cows of the era – mission work. Stanwyck plays a missionary rescued and imprisoned during a riot by a Chinese warlord (Nils Asther), and whose hostility towards him evaporates in the strangeness of her new surroundings: Beauty and the Beast interpreted in simple Freudian terms but subtle

goes awry, when, among other things, she insists that he wears garters, even if with solid gold attachments. Unhooked from her, he unhooks them and gives them to a passing hobo, who promptly demands his socks as well. The ungrateful bum was a Capra-Riskin speciality; their society people would always be, as here, stuffed shirts, and their journalists cynical but ultimately human.

When they are the heroes they will also be finally happy. Capra has an incurable belief in happy endings. If, in his own words, he and Riskin were as 'opportunist as Hearst reporters' in concocting their Depression fable, **American Madness** (1932), they at least ensured that their bank president hero (Walter Huston) 'is filled with youthful optimism and a cheerful trust in men'. All Capra's films are basically fairy stories, some by admission. All of them take their heroes to a desperate pitch before a final twist smooths things out: in *That Certain*

cinema language. Von Sternberg expressed eroticism by look; alone among players, Garbo expressed it by thought. Thinking people were rare in films, but the warlord and the missionary may be seen at least to ponder, even if, like Feyder's Carmen and Don José, their musings are closed to us. Further disrespect towards mission work is indicated in Walter Connolly's performance as the warlord's Machiavellian financial adviser, and it is not surprising that the film was banned throughout the British Empire, thus becoming – with *Miracle Woman* – Capra's only Columbia picture to lose money.

Reunited with Riskin, he again demonstrated his originality by being the first to bring one of Damon Runyon's stories to the screen, **Lady for a Day** (1933), a tract for the times concerning a Broadway pedlar, Apple Annie (May Robson), and telling how Dave the Dude (Warren William) helps her maintain the pretence, for the sake of her daughter, that she is in society. We may take it that Apple Annie is a victim of the Depression, so it is comforting that not only the pool sharks but the high-ups show their sympathy–as does Capra, his mood closer to the Hollywood Christmas-round-the-fire of the Forties than to the gold diggers currently at Warners.

His reputation was now such that Thalberg invited him to M-G-M – in exchange for a star to be loaned to Columbia; but the project, *Soviet,* was cancelled by Mayer while Thalberg was in Europe. Capra and Riskin went back to a story in *Cosmopolitan* magazine by Samuel Hopkins Adams, which came to the screen as **It Happened One Night** (1934). Robert Montgomery turned it down because he had just made a similar tale, and M-G-M substituted a rebellious Clark Gable. Myrna Loy, Miriam Hopkins and Constance Bennett refused, though the last named offered to buy the script. Claudette Colbert (q.v.) accepted,

Anyone who went to the cinema in the Thirties could not escape whacky heiresses, and there were even more to be seen after the success of *It Happened One Night.* In this case the lady is Claudette Colbert, and pursuing her is Clark Gable, who sees in her a headline story. Her initial reaction is of icy contempt, but their relationship finishes delightfully if predictably. With them is Mickey Daniels.

Jean Arthur and Gary Cooper, the incomparable partnership of *Mr Deeds Goes to Town*, which starts by reversing the situation of *It Happened One Night*. She is the reporter, he the wealthy man whose story she is already selling to her paper, which is mocking him – hence the sneers of passers-by and her own apprehensive look.

because, according to Capra, it meant $50,000 for four weeks' work, happily coinciding with her vacation from Paramount. No one would ever turn down a Capra picture again.

The contemporary reviews were warm but not ecstatic, and it was word of mouth which made it a success, as exhibitors found on rebooking. In Hollywood, also, audiences were captivated, enabling Capra to more than achieve his ambition: this was the first occasion one film took a clutch of Oscars, and till 1976 the only time any film gathered what are conceded to be the five most important – Best Film, Best Director, Best Actor, Best Actress, Best Screenplay. An Academy Award is a distinctly unreliable guide to merit, but even if this is not the best American film of that particular year it is certainly the best of the twelve nominated by the Academy (the number was later reduced to five).

Its plot was already familiar (beyond the

basic idea, which, as Capra has pointed out, is 'The Taming of the Shrew'), and has been subject since to endless variants: the pursuit of an heiress by a hard-up reporter who sees her as his next meal ticket. There were whole sequences which audiences took to their hearts: the passengers in the bus joining in a spontaneous 'Man on the Flying Trapeze'; Gable failing to stop a car with his vaunted thumb technique and Colbert succeeding with her leg; and 'The Walls of Jericho', when he hangs the blanket between the two motel beds. It is a picaresque tale, and Capra keeps the eccentricities unpretentious; the pace is fast and the playing joyous. Gable manages to suggest not only an old-sweat journalist but a 'parfit gentle knight', not giving a damn whether his lady will join him in eating raw carrots but finally touching in his stewardship; under her hoity exterior, she finally warms to a bum who is worth more than her aviator husband.

Capra borrowed both Myrna Loy and Warner Baxter for **Broadway Bill** (1934), and Baxter, often stodgy, is here a very dull dog indeed. The role is crucial, for he plays a son-in-law who turns his back on all the tycoonery for his first love, the race track; by the end he has won over his father-in-law (Walter Connolly), as well as the nice daughter (Loy). All is for the best in the best of all possible worlds. The world rejected is Higginsville, appropriately named for father-in-law: this is the first Capra-Riskin sketch of small town stuffiness, and the film furthers their search for memorable minor characters – here played by such actors as Raymond Walburn, Lynne Overman and Margaret Hamilton.

Mr Deeds Goes to Town (1936) is the crowning achievement of the partnership. If I had to choose one film to be both the best and most representative of the decade, this would be it. Graham Greene thought it Capra's 'finest film . . . and that means it is a comedy quite unmatched on the screen. For Capra has what Lubitsch, the pretty play-boy, has not: a sense of responsibility, and what Clair, whimsical, poetic, a little precious and *à la mode,* has not, a kinship with his audience, a sense of common life, a morality: he has what even Chaplin has not, complete mastery of his medium.' In the U.S. a left-wing critic, Robert Stebbins, writing in *New Theatre,* found the film 'astounding . . . a tremendous advance' for Hollywood, yet the scene he most admired, the meeting between Mr Deeds and a Depression-hit hobo, is the one which modern audiences find hardest to take – because its crusading heart is on its sleeve.

Up to that point Riskin has written a comedy of manners to stand with any in the language: of all the variations on the theme of the innocent amid the city slickers – from Ben Jonson onwards – it is the most satisfying. Mr Deeds (Gary Cooper) is no guileless bumpkin upsetting the sophisticates by chance , but a plain, honest man; his pleasures are simple (writing greeting card verse, playing a tuba, following fire engines), and he may be halfway duped: but he is a man with a sense of rightness, of resource and of pride. Cooper, by nature no one's fool, gives one of the great screen performances. The hard-boiled sob sister who both befriends and exploits him is beautifully taken by Jean Arthur (q.v.); the role may be a cipher but that is remedied by her playing. The discovery of her duplicity is followed by Mr Deeds's decision to surrender his fortune to the unemployed, and here we are in a different film – a Steinbeck 'We and Them' tale. It is not inconsistent with what has gone before, and the final court room sequence welds the essential component of comedy and social concern.

Capra won his second Best Director Oscar for *Mr Deeds,* though he thought that 'if anyone deserved Oscars Cooper and Riskin did'. Riskin, he said, wrote what he himself wanted to say, and the film's success increased his belief in what he called 'one man, one film', which the industry was prepared to accept – but only provided he was the man. He was not, as he asserts, the first American director since pioneer days to have his name above the title, for Vidor, Milestone, Borzage and deMille already had, but it is probable that only he and deMille had their names emblazoned on the marquees of cinemas. Even if statistics were available, they would be unable to prove *Mr Deeds* to be the most popular American Talkie till *Gone with the Wind,* but I think it true to say that it was both the best-thought-of and the most loved among all levels of brow.

Cohn, not a man prone to initiative – though he knew what he didn't like – had been content to let Capra have his head, and since he found himself the employer of the most admired man in the industry he agreed to buy for him a novel by James Hilton, and to allocate it $2 million, which would have paid for twenty normal Columbia features. The resulting film did not take at the first public preview, so Capra threw out the first two reels. Thus **Lost Horizon** (1937) begins in China, where Conway (Ronald Colman) 'England's man of the East, soldier, hero, diplomat' is superintending the evacuation of some Britishers: their plane is mysteriously hijacked, and they find themselves in a peaceful valley in the Himalayas called Shangri-La – for Conway, as it turns out, has been chosen to be its new ruler. He is unsure whether he wants to be, and when his final decision is not yet known in London, 'May he find his Shangri-La', they drink to him in his club, 'May we all find our Shangri-Las'.

You would have to be very cynical not to find in *Lost Horizon* the qualities of *Mr Deeds* – that it is possible to rediscover an essential beauty and goodness to life, both

Shangri-La as it appeared in *Lost Horizon*. The visual concept has dated somewhat, as has the film's view of Utopian ideals – which seemed particularly attractive in the Thirties. The film remains entertaining, because of Capra's exceptional narrative skill and Ronald Colman's charismatic performance.

bludgeoned out of existence by man in his thoughtlessness. The film offered hope in the form of fantasy. Age-old truths were to be found in Shangri-La: if not eternal life, eternal youth, and all the precepts – though it is never mentioned – of Christianity. The idea of a country without crime or war was meant to be considered against the background of events in Europe, but I cannot help feeling that cinema-goers were being sold a dud bill of goods – in theory if not in spirit. The decor by Stephen Goossens is often unfortunate, as in the interiors of the palace, looking like one of the grander Spanish *paradors;* and such things as the Utopian glade, with ducks on every pond and a squirrel to warn the bathing heroine of Conway's approach, are excruciating.

There can be no question of Capra's sincerity – though in time it would be questioned. The film was greeted with an avalanche of praise, though the more judicious critics found it expedient to ignore the metaphysics in favour of the spectacle. 'It is the second outstanding picture of the season' said *The New York Times* – the first being 'of course' *The Good Earth* (q.v.). Capra's sheer set-em-up skill is astonishing, but if even the most jaundiced must be hoping that Conway will return to Shangri-La, that has much to do with the actor concerned, 'beautiful of face and soul, sensitive to the fragile and gentle' as Capra put it. Colman's shrug as he contemplates becoming the next Foreign Secretary is an easy thing to do, but his achievement here is to listen to the High Lama (Sam Jaffe) with the intensity that must cloak the rest of the film. But not even he, nor critical praise, nor huge audiences (the film was one of the dozen or so of its time to be road-shown) could provide the miracle needed to enable Columbia to recoup its investment.

A Broadway comedy allowed Capra to plough the same furrow – Kaufman and Hart's **You Can't Take It with You** (1938), which had won the Pulitzer prize – an award that was justified, said Frank S. Nugent in *The New York Times,* not by the original but by this film version. The one-set-three-acts had become a flowing narrative; the one-dimensional characters had been clothed in flesh and blood; and it had become more serious. Nugent's review presumably pleased Capra, who had not wanted to make 'a laugh riot' but 'something deeper, something greater . . . an opportunity to dramatise Love Thy Neighbor in living drama. What the world's churches were preaching to apathetic congregations, my universal language of film might say more entertainingly to movie audiences'. The result won the Best Picture Oscar and the Best Director Oscar.

Time has proved Capra wrong, not to mention his writer Riskin, Mr Nugent and the Academy voters – even if one could still tolerate the visions of Grandpa Vanderhof as expressed by the sententious Lionel Barrymore (Henry Travers, who played the role on the stage, was surely better). He is spokesman for a household devoted to eccentric pursuits, and he himself is struggling with a capitalist (Edward Arnold) planning to enlarge his munitions factory at the expense of the family home. When the film chooses to be funny, it is hilarious; when it is serious, it is a parody of better

Capra pictures. There are, appropriately, two small salutes to Walt Disney (q.v.), for Capra's admiration for Disney transcended the usual studio rivalries; the two were certainly beholden to each other.

The heroine is Jean Arthur (b. 1905), partnered with James Stewart, and they would play together in Capra's next film, where he was perhaps a substitute for Gary Cooper. These heroes were good men but hesitant, and Miss Arthur, who had co-starred in *Mr Deeds,* was their perfect counterpart, on the surface confident and wise in city ways, but equally – or at any rate finally – devoted to the cause of right. She was Capra's favourite heroine and one of the magical comediennes of the Thirties, equally sure but delicate in drama, with a voice that is indescribable (like butter being churned, if butter had a voice) and with that warmth which seems to have died with the actresses of her generation. (Capra also adored Barbara Stanwyck, as did all the directors who worked with her.)

Miss Arthur's presence in **Mr Smith goes to Washington** (1939) is only one reason I consider it a moment in cinema comparable with *Mr Deeds,* and reviewers at the time were similarly affected. Yet there were some who noticed a deterioration, and in *The New Republic* Otis Ferguson recalled that at the time of the earlier film another critic, Alistair Cooke, had said that Capra had 'started to make movies about themes instead of people'. Ferguson himself thought *Lost Horizon* an aberration, adding that in *You Can't Take It with You* Capra 'had forgotten about people for good'. However, Graham Greene found in *Mr Smith* 'the delight – equal to the great Russians – in the ordinary human face' and considered it 'a great film, even if it is not a great story'. Capra thought the story – 'The Man from Montana' by Lewis R. Foster – both good *and* important, but it was certainly not new: Meyer Levin in *The Nation* pointed out that it was Christ and the money changers – while we may see it also as an old plot, that of the worm that turned. The screenplay is by Sidney Buchman, since Riskin had been lured away by Goldwyn, for whom however he did no credited work. Riskin's few, subsequent, non-Capra credits are not in fact very interesting, but they are still better than those of Buchman, who wrote such dire

films (q.v.) as *The Howards of Virginia* and *A Song to Remember* – the latter a cherished project of Capra's; we can only speculate what it might have been like in his hands.

Buchman's screenplay for *Mr Smith* concerns a newspaper tycoon (Edward Arnold) and a senior senator (Claude Rains) in cahoots with the Governor (Guy Kibbee); they have a land deal going, and need a junior senator who is either corrupt or a stooge. In Jefferson Smith (Stewart) they think they have the latter, till he is taken in hand by a Washingotn secretary (Miss Arthur) who, like Babe in *Mr Deeds,* rallies to him when she realises that he is a David up against the Goliath of the Senate. Capra was naive enough to think that Washington would approve of this; he believed he had struck a blow for democracy with his portrait of an idealistic senator – while Washington was only concerned with the unflattering picture of itself as a place of graft and corruption. 'Liberty is too precious a thing to be buried in books,' says Mr Smith, the lone idealist. But Capra himself is just such an idealist – the personification of the American dream, from penniless immigrant to world acclaim: he believes in the U.S.A., the land of the free. Mr Smith, like Mr Deeds, is him.

Beyond any ideas the film may have of putting the world to rights, it is marvellously well made and has an outstanding cast, even by the standards of the day; as always with Capra, each member of it has far more to express than the dialogue. Note three scenes in particular: Rains and Arnold regarding each other after they have agreed to let loose in Washington this Lincoln-Jefferson-spouting 'patriot'; Miss Arthur responding to him – part impressed, part amused; and the Press Club interviewing him, sending him up ever so slightly. No one is painted black or white; with the exception of Rains, all the villains offer a touch of humour. Mr Smith seems too naive and bumbling but, as Capra once remarked, 'Gary Cooper *is* Mr Deeds, just as Stewart is Mr Smith.' He has also said that this is his best film.

It was also his last for Columbia, and he had no intention of renewing his contract, since there still rankled (among other matters) that occasion when Cohn had taken advantage of his absence in Europe to pass off another director's film as his. Foremost among those who offered him autonomy

Claude Rains and James Stewart in *Mr Smith Goes to Washington* which was popular everywhere, except in the capital. Its timing was perfect, as when there enters the chamber 'two representatives of dictator powers who have come to see what they cannot see at home – democracy in action'. Since this turned out to be Mr Stewart rebelling at the chamber's lack of principle, Washington's reaction is not surprising.

were Goldwyn and Selznick, independents themselves, but he refused to commit himself beyond one picture at a time – and the only producer to whom that restriction was acceptable was Jack Warner, described by Capra as, 'the one non-conforming, irrepressible spirit among the studio heads'. Warner's sole stipulation was that Capra and Riskin, once again partnered, should invest $100,000 of their own money, with no requirements as to budget or subject. Capra admitted he chose his subjects to please reviewers, and had been peeved that when the New York critics' ten-best lists were combined his last three films were not included.

Meet John Doe (1941) was brought to him by its original writers, Richard Connell and Robert Presnell – the story of an out-of-work baseball player manoeuvred into becoming a national figure by preach-

ing the people's cause in a newspaper whose proprietor, a fascist with a private army, intends by this means to achieve the Presidency. As with *Mr Smith*, it seemed vitally important at that time to give a warning against fascism, but Capra and Riskin were trying to say more than that – and they were saying again what they had said better in earlier films. John Doe is the Miracle Woman, preaching Christianity for personal gain; he is Mr Deeds, innocent and unthinking; he is finally Mr Smith, rallying his intellectual resources to fight the evil which had been manipulating him. He is also played by Cooper, and the fascist yet again by Edward Arnold. Miss Stanwyck is the self-interested doll who finally, again, rallies to him, but both players, increasingly at sea with the motivation of their characters, fall back on mannerism – rare in a Capra film. His own flair leaves him, and he settles for a series of unfilmic duologues of no great interest. By that time he must have known the ending would not work: five different ones were shot, and audiences liked none of them. In his memoir, he implies that had he found the right ending he would have had a masterpiece – though he admits that he does not know whether this story ever had an ending.

Most critics liked the picture, but it was a box-office failure and Capra modestly determined to surrender some independence. By forming a company with Selznick he intended to become a fourth owner of United Artists, joining Pickford, Chaplin and Korda (q.v.). Had he been prepared to surrender all independence he could have written his own terms anywhere in Hollywood; as it was, the agreement with Selznick came to nothing since, believing that war was imminent, he joined the army. While waiting for his call-up papers he saw a play he wanted to film – one so meticulously constructed that it could not be cut without damage, and had therefore to be filmed as it stood. He envisaged a four-week schedule and a large salary to keep his family while he was away. Warners owned the rights, and Jack Warner was amenable to holding the film in storage, because it could not be released before the end of the Broadway run. **Arsenic and Old Lace** was in fact shot in December 1941, and did not premiere till almost three years later. As filmed theatre it is an exemplary job, as fast as *American Madness* and gloriously funny except where the humour has dated. No one by then could have been unaware of the subject: two dainty ladies – maiden aunts – who have made a habit of poisoning lodgers and burying them in the cellar. For all

Capra's skill and the good lines (Joseph Kesselring bore the credit for the play, but its producers, Lindsay and Crouse, are now known to have been chiefly responsible), it owes most to Cary Grant (b. 1904), playing the dramatic critic who – on his wedding day – discovers that his aunts are mass murderers slipping poison into their home-made elderberry wine. There was no actor better able to cope with the situation; William Powell or Melvyn Douglas would surely have turned the old dears in eventually, but Grant is manic enough to adjust. The Hays Office would not allow the famous last line to be used★: but if you know it, you can imagine the expression of Edward Everett Horton's face as he listens to it.

It is appropriate that the first phase of Capra's career should end thus, for he was primarily a wonderful entertainer. When he chose to be funny, which was most of the time, he was very funny and his humour has proved ageless. He also chose to demonstrate what he considered American virtues. Some have spoken of 'Capra-corn', but the seriousness of his films is more provocative of thought than are most serious films of the era. He was as much a cynic as an idealist, and the conflict which that implies is one reason that his films retain their vitality. He was not perhaps a great intellect but he was a great film technician. Do not misunderstand: I love and revere him. He has been patronised: 'Oh Capra! Of course . . .' but he is beyond patronage. He is a giant in American cinema: it was he who taught Hollywood to think.

★Which concerns the offer of a glass of poisoned elderberry wine.

15

Clowns and Korda

NOT ALL BRITISH films of the Thirties were bad, but to native cinema-goers of the time it often seemed so. The Quota Act of 1927 had worked only too well, and production rose from thirty-one features the previous year to seventy-six in 1928. A number of new companies brought into being because of the Act folded in the shake-up caused by Sound, but in 1932 British studios offered over a hundred features, together with another two score or so for the 'supporting programme'. The latter were known as 'quota quickies', brought in for as little as £4,000 – as opposed to the £30,000 which was the average cost of the very few 'first-class' first features – and many of them were backed by the American companies. Second-rate or slipping American talents arrived to 'help out' the native industry – much as they would do in Italy in the Sixties – and everyone deliberately overlooked the fact that the Quota Act had been initiated to prevent American films predominating in British cinemas.

By this time the leading Hollywood companies had abandoned local renters to establish their own distribution companies, with in some cases production facilities as well. Paramount was notably active in British production, while some local entrepreneurs made exclusive arrangements with the American-owned distributors. The latter were not very discriminating, but when a company called Real Art sold successively to Fox, First National, Radio, M-G-M and United Artists, it was still relieved that it did not have to descend to the locally-owned distributors. The structure of the British industry had reached the state of its American counterpart twenty years earlier – and with as much in-fighting. What talent there

was, however, was more mobile: though most of the entrepreneurs were temperamentally like their American counterparts – European-Jewish, though of more recent extraction – the local climate had softened them to the extent that co-operation was more readily possible.

The wholly British side of the industry remained dominated by the two rival conglomerates, B.I.P. and Gaumont-British. The founder of B.I.P., John Maxwell, had gathered into his fold not only Pathé and First National, distribution offices no longer wanted by their new American owners, but the important A.B.C. circuit – or Associated British Cinemas. From the end of 1936 onwards his companies were whittled down to one name, the Associated British Picture Corporation, or A.B.P.C. On his death in 1941 Warner Bros. bought his shares – cannily, to protect its position as a leading supplier to the circuit, and at a time when, because of the War, American interest in British industry had receded; but despite this twenty-five per cent ownership A.B.P.C. was never a vital force in British production.

Fearful of the competition provided by Maxwell, or perhaps following his example, C. M. Woolf added to his growing Gaumont circuit a number of production companies and distributors, eventually amalgamated into Gaumont-British – though the Gainsborough logo was kept out of deference to Michael Balcon, who became Woolf's Director of Productions in 1932. Balcon realised that the only British films the British public really wanted to see were those with the popular comics of stage and radio, but his recognition and encouragement of talent enabled him to make a

few modestly successful more serious pictures, an achievement seemingly denied to other local producers till the advent of Alexander Korda.

Among Balcon's better films are those directed by Victor Saville, including **Hindle Wakes** (1931), the third film version (Saville had produced the second, in 1927, directed by Maurice Elvey) of Stanley Houghton's 1912 Lancashire play, the deliberately Victorian tale of a mill girl (Belle Chrystall) seduced by the boss's son (John Stuart); he wants to marry her but she has different ideas. For all the shots of terrace houses and factories, the film is stagey, while **Michael and Mary** (1932) is even closer to Shaftesbury Avenue, with Herbert Marshall and Edna Best repeating their stage roles. He is a novelist who writes books with titles like 'Sighing Wind' and

'Dream Child', and his cosy world is shattered when a visiting blackmailer, once married to his wife, falls in a struggle and fatally hits his head. An air of smugness is increased by the dachshund charm of Frank Lawton as their son, and his habit of calling his mother 'Bubbles' and his father 'Binks'. A. A. Milne wrote the original play, and Saville achieves a certain atmosphere in the Boer War flashbacks. The professionalism of this then-popular husband and wife team, Marshall and Best may also be found in **The Faithful Heart** (1932); he courts her in a montage of flowers, Gilbert and Sullivan and an evocation of misty moonlight nights along the waterfront. She is a barmaid and he a cocky First Mate: come two wars, and he is high-ranking in the Army, having to choose between their illegitimate daughter (also played by Miss

Victor Saville's charming film of the bestselling novel, *The Good Companions,* is about three non-professionals who join a concert party and have a fine time among the footlights and make-up sticks. From left to right, Denis Hoey, Margery Binner, John Gielgud, Percy Parsons, A. W. Baskcomb, Mary Glynne, Edmund Gwenn, Jessie Matthews, Viola Compton and Richard Dolman.

Jessie Matthews performing the Rodgers and Hart number 'Dancing on the Ceiling' in *Evergreen*. She was famous as a dancer, but it is her personality which now most pleases, with her expression of petulance when she smiles, at which time her chipmunk teeth both ruin her face and enhance it.

the pet projects of Isadore Ostrer, one of Woolf's partners, who so admired the Ufa originals that several co-productions were ordered.

Saville's best film is **The Good Companions** (1933), based on the novel with which J. B. Priestley successfully revived the picaresque tradition. Almost every literate person in Britain had followed the adventures of its three protagonists: Jess Oakroyd (in the film, Edmund Gwenn), a Yorkshire factory worker who loses his job and leaves his nagging wife; Inigo Jollifant (John Gielgud), a teacher at a dank private school in the Fen Country who sets out on his travels after insulting *in vino veritas* the principal's wife; and Miss Trant (Mary Glynne), a spinster who plans to see Britain before her miserable inheritance gives out. Their fortuitous involvement with the Dinky Doos, a stranded concert party, is handled with real affection, the occasional gaucheness part of the charm. Saville catches the atmosphere which is the lot of such troupes, such as the desperation when hot weather keeps customers away and the dressing room camaraderie. The film also reminds us of that time when houses had no electricity and the Great North Road was hardly double-track.

In **Friday the Thirteenth** (1934) a London bus crashes into a shop window and, emulating Thornton Wilder's 'The Bridge of San Luis Rey', the film examines how some half dozen people came to be on it at the time. The omnibus-story film was rare: the trouble with this one is that it is increasingly apparent which of the passengers will be the predestined victims.

Featured in both films is Jessie Matthews (1907–81), a toothy, leggy star whose la-di-da accent disguised her humble background. Saville also directed her in the best British musical of the period, **Evergreen** (1934), which had earlier been a success for her when Cochran produced the stage version. As a chorus girl who tries to become a star by impersonating her grandmother, she expresses such determination, together with a surprising seam of sarcasm, that her curious talent is disarming. Her tap dancing is pleasant, but her high kicks and slow-motion jerks, to let the ospreys flow along her arms, now look absurd. Yet when she breaks into the best of the songs she is a pure spirit, certainly more effective on the screen than her rival, Evelyn Laye,

Best) and his fiancée, as in the original play by Monckton Hoffe. The charming period sequences of both films are the invention of Saville and his writer, Robert Stevenson, released from the confines of West End acceptability. However, their confidence fails with **Sunshine Susie** (1932), adapted from the German *Privatsekretarin*. Trying to unite Teutonic cheeriness and that of British musical comedy, they fall between the two stools, with Owen Nares and Jack Hulbert depressingly representing the latter and Renate Müller as the former, plump, willing and obtuse, forever emitting little tinkles of laughter. There were a number of these Anglo-German musicals,

Cedric Hardwicke, Conrad Veidt and Eliot Makeham in *Rome Express*, the quintessential train movie. Since Hardwicke's make-up gives him the appearance of the British publisher Victor Gollancz it is more than likely that the character, a phoney philanthropist, is also based on him.

though the latter was prettier and a better singer. At least, Saville could get little from this lady in **Evensong** (1934), charting the rise and fall of a diva among archdukes and temperamental managers, and based on a bestseller by Beverly Nichols, who had been secretary to Dame Nellie Melba.

I Was a Spy (1933) has a foreword by the then Secretary of State, Winston Churchill, assuring us that what follows is true: a Belgian nurse (Madeleine Carroll) finds war so intolerable that she is drawn into a spy ring with a German orderly (Herbert Marshall), plotting against a German officer (Conrad Veidt). Miss Carroll performs sanctimoniously, and though this is an implausible farrago the readers of *Film Weekly* voted it the best film of the year. And since *Picturegoer* stated categorically that **Rome Express** (1932) was 'the best British film yet made', double confidence was expressed in Woolf's new studio at Shepherd's Bush under Balcon's leadership. The director of this patent copy of *Shanghai Express* is Walter Forde (b. 1896), rattling it along at the pace the engines are

stoked: among the passengers whose paths cross and criss cross are an American film star (Esther Ralston); a suburban couple (Harold Huth, Joan Barry) escaping from their respective spouses; a golf-club bore (Gordon Harker); a philanthropist (Cedric Hardwicke) whose private life is as mean and petty as his public one is showy; and a shifty-eyed fugitive (Donald Calthrop) pursued by two mysterious men (Conrad Veidt and Hugh Williams).

Most of these films were aimed at the international market, and Balcon was encouraged to spend £120,000 – the highest budget for a British film to that time – on **Jew Süss** (1934), partly because Leon Feuchtwanger's novel (under the title 'Power') had been a sensational success in the U.S. In *The Observer* C. A. Lejeune commented that 'it could hardly have been done better', while regretting that the money had not been spent on 'a film of British industry, British agriculture or British mining' instead of one set in a German muncipality two hundred years ago – when Josef Süss Oppenheimer (Conrad Veidt) leaves the ghetto to become financial adviser to Duke Karl Alexander (Frank Vosper) of Württemberg. The complex issues of the novel – not to mention history – are reduced to a simplistic tale of a man too proud to avert his own destruction. Despite simultaneous premieres in London, New York and Toronto the defects were too numerous for transatlantic audiences, unable to accept comic-opera costumes, ludicrous emoting by all the cast except Cedric Hardwicke (as a rabbi), and the snail's pace handling of Lothar Mendes, a Ufa-trained Hollywood director.

If, despite Balcon's demands, the quality of Gaumont-British product was insufficient to ensure bookings overseas, little was to be expected from the other studios. Foreign talents appeared to succumb to the general lethargy; and since their work in Britain is so undistinguished, perhaps it was lack of confidence which caused some refugees to eschew Hollywood, where the standards were more exacting. The producer and director of *Die Strasse*, Max Schach and Karl Grune, made **Abdul the Damned** (1935) with the services of two other compatriots – all were originally from Vienna – Otto Kanturek, who photographed it, and Fritz Kortner, playing the title-role. Abdul Hamid was until Hitler the outstanding tyrant of modern times, and an analogy was clearly intended; ideas and intelligence abound, even if Abdul finally becomes the familiar megalomaniac of the German Silents. But not even Herr Kortner could surmount ineptitude as wholesale as *Jew Süss*.

Thus, though executives of the British film industry welcomed a number of cosmopolitan film-makers from Europe, whose Jewish backgrounds were often similar (albeit more sophisticated) to those of their opposite numbers in Hollywood, they were no more successful in moulding the British film for the foreign market. They found British studios lacked the intense enthusiasm of the German, probably due to the fact that only Balcon and later Korda really cared for the medium, as opposed to using it to make money. So the newcomers settled for mediocrity, compensating themselves with the artistic life of London, so much more substantial than that of Hollywood, which after the shakeup of Talkies, had again transformed the world into its own cultural suburb and,

even before *Cavalcade*, had proved itself able to make a better British film than the British. The Hollywood moguls, we might pause to consider, favoured such tales because they felt so near and so far from the velvet lawns of Empire. They were immigrants and parvenues, yet were attracted to the British (whose manners they aped in their Spanish-colonial drawing rooms) by ambition, a common language and by a taste for wealth. After Korda's first international success more American talent arrived, but they were unable in the event to help the British export either their strictly local product or their manifold imitations of Hollywood.

'British' films poured forth from Hollywood, and though packed with solecisms and accents to match were actually closer to the aspirations of British audiences than the indigenous films of the period, which mostly evoked a country of sporty gentlemen and their servants; all foreigners and the entire working class were irredeemably comic – a view also to be found in the bound volumes of *Punch*. Roy Boulting (q.v.) was once asked why he and his brother chose the cinema as a career, and he gave an answer no American or European would dream of giving. 'It was our nanny, actually' (it turned out that she had taken them to see Valentino). He gave, in fact, the *Punch* view – despite having made some of the worst-ever British movies, as late as the Seventies. The possession of a nanny does not preclude an understanding of audience requirements; George Orwell, after all, came from a household with servants, but the Britain he portrayed in 'Keep the Aspidistra Flying' and 'Coming Up for Air' is nowhere to be found in the films of the time. Concocted by immigrant and dilettante, hack and opportunist, they were as trivial in subject matter as their budgets were small.

The leading players of **No Funny Business** (1933) are three people who were three-quarters of the New York cast of 'Private Lives', one of the funniest comedies of the decade: Gertrude Lawrence, Laurence Olivier (q.v.) and Jill Esmond. Yet this tale of a divorce-bent wife and two professional co-respondents must be the unfunniest film ever made, marooning both Miss Lawrence's gift for comedy and the actors themselves – since they are usually photographed from the calves upwards, playing in uncertain profile to someone just off camera. Its producer-directors, Victor Hanbury and John Stafford, offered another Hollywood name, Victor McLaglen, in the title-role of **Dick Turpin** (1933), flailing about in a hopeless attempt to make the script comprehensible. **The Return of Bulldog Drummond** (1934) is insulting, since it turned up around the same time as Ronald Colman's second Drummond film. This one involves Drummond (Ralph Richardson) in the question of European rearmament till descending to a plot that would seem puerile even to admirers of *Fantômas* or James Bond. Walter Summers directed for B.I.P., but that company brought over an American director and players for **I Spy** (1933) – Ben Lyon to be mistaken for a secret agent, and Sally Eilers; but although Allan Dwan hurries matters along the limits of the genre are extended till they snap.

If such films were written off by spectators beforehand the thrall of cinema was such that few considered arriving only for the main feature – whose starting times were not featured in adverts, though 'Continuous Performance' was. It was not till the Fifties (in the U.S. and Britain) that audiences finally shook off the nickelodeon habit of dropping into a cinema with no regard for continuity – hence the expression, 'This is where I came in'. Among the few British films to play main attractions – other, that is, than in what the trade called 'indiscriminating halls' – were those starring the popular comic artists of the day. Both Gracie Fields and George Formby came from Lancashire, to be perplexed in their films by 'daft' city ways: it was perhaps because they did not betray their origins that they became national heroes (also in the Commonwealth, but they remained 'foreign' to Americans). Never before – and radio was also responsible – had the British been as aware of the diversity of their countrymen.

Gracie Fields (1898–1979) was unquestionably the most beloved entertainer the British have ever produced. After an amazingly successful career in music hall she made **Sally in Our Alley** (1931), directed by Maurice Elvey, from a play, 'The Likes of 'er'. The new title took advantage of her theme song, and it is no surprise to find her the darling of the *quartier,* with a bustling North Country common-sense and con-

fidence. Her boss wants to marry her and put her name above the café: 'It might look nice up there,' she agrees, 'but not down here,' and her pause before the qualification is beautifully timed. When a waiter is sacked for dancing with her at a charity ball, she offers to share her fee but does not insist when he refuses. As a screen actress she tends to play to the gallery, but has a warm sense of humour, often directed against herself, and – it is a quality rare in film stars – a huge liking for people. Basil Dean, the powerful theatre manager who also ran A.T.P. – Associated Talking Pictures – put her under contract while trying to make up his mind whether her forte was clowning or romance, her dentures and broad face being something of a dampener for the latter. She loathed filming, and simply did her duty for the audiences of the Depression with **Looking on the Bright Side** (1932), directed by Dean and Graham Cutts, the adventures of a manicurist in show business, and **Love, Life and Laughter** (1934), directed by Maurice Elvey, the adventures of a barmaid in love with a foreign prince (John Loder). Borrowing badly from Lubitsch and Clair, Dean later admitted that he grew tired 'of the caustic references by critics to the poverty of the material dished out to Britain's "£2-a-minute star" . . . the fact that much of the criticism was justified only made matters worse.'

He persuaded J. B. Priestley to write the stories for her next two films, which he himself directed, and of them **Sing As We Go** (1934) is at least ingratiating. As an unemployed millgirl forgetting her troubles in Blackpool, Miss Fields made the title song an anthem of the Depression especially with audiences in the most distressed areas who normally took their own holidays in Blackpool. Dean used extensive location footage, and although he enjoyed filming what he called *les actualités* he seems not to have realised that it was that, and the star in a recognisably demotic background, which was the reason for the film's great popularity.

Five writers were employed to assemble **Queen of Hearts** (1936), and a former Hollywood gagman and director, Monty Banks – whom the star later married – was brought in to impart Hollywood gloss; but the film is merely a long-winded farce about a seamstress with a crush on a matinee

Clowns and Korda

The singer and stage star Gracie Fields, centre, was a British institution in the Thirties, and consequently the films she made were enormously popular in the domestic market – if few of them were very good. The best is unquestionably *Sing As We Go*, and here she leads her fellow factory-workers to end the film on a high note – singing the title-song, which became an anthem for British workers during the Depression.

idol (John Loder). In two earlier films with this actor Fields had lost him to other ladies, but this time, between a number of comic routines – and an admirably perfunctory rendering of the title song – she was glamorous enough to aspire successfully. Although none of these films had been shown in the U.S., one American mogul, Darryl F. Zanuck, decided that Fields could reach an American audience, and he paid her an enormous salary to do it: but when her first film for 20th Century-Fox, *We're Going to Be Rich,* failed to impress his compatriots he was only prepared to spend miniscule amounts on her two subsequent British-made films for the company.

If bad films prevented Gracie Fields from finding American acceptance, there was little chance for George Formby (1904–61), who replaced her as A.T.P.'s chief asset. He also came to films from the halls; he played the ukelele, he had a soppy-but-happy grin, and his humour was strictly knockabout. His songs, if not his dialogue, were thick with sexual innuendo, accompanied by a leer intended to convey to audiences that their interpretation is not his. By the time he made his first film for Dean, **No Limit** (1935), the latter had learnt the lesson of *Sing As We Go,* assigning the screenplay to another leading dramatist, Walter Greenwood, and virtually duplicating the story – by sending the star to a seaside resort, in fact the Isle of Man for the T.T. races. Banks directed, but most of the A.T.P. Formby films were made by Anthony Kimmins, who also wrote them in conjunction with Austin Melford, plus a number of other writers – many of whom would work on the later Ealing comedies (q.v.). In humour seemingly borrowed from Donald McGill's saucy postcards, they put him through the usual paces – bus conductor, airman, store clerk, invariably clumsy and stupid but inevitably besting the pompous high-ups who have the mischance to cross his path; he also manages to wrest the leading lady from his rivals – usually public school smoothies like Guy Middleton in *Keep Fit,* or in most of the other films the dangerously apoplectic Garry Marsh. The Formby vehicles, if simple-minded, have energy; the best is probably **Trouble Brewing** (1939), in which George, after creating havoc at a society party – dislodging by accident a girl's skirt and on purpose, or intending to, the garter of the very grand Martita Hunt – takes a somersault across the kitchen that is worthy of Keaton.

Jack Buchanan (1891–1957) was an upper-class Formby, to the extent that they were embroiled in similar situations. Remembered as an elegant song-and-dance man, he was in fact a poor dancer, as he well knew, though his light, slightly nasal tenor can still give pleasure, as in two of the most charming songs of the period, the title tune of **Goodnight Vienna** (1932) and 'Fancy Our Meeting' from **That's a Good Girl** (1933). Herbert Wilcox directed the first of these films, laboriously, and it was he who signed Buchanan for his British & Dominions company. Since Buchanan was a Broadway star and had made two Hollywood features, Wilcox was encouraged to seek American distribution, and made a commitment to United Artists. With *That's a Good Girl,* which Buchanan also directed, established a team, to include an experienced Hollywood writer, Ralph Spence, and an American music director, Van Phillips. For **Brewster's Millions** (1935) he imported from Hollywood Lily Damita and Thornton Freeland, who had directed *Flying Down to Rio* (whose most famous number was here plagiarised as 'The Caranga'); Fay Wray arrived to make **Come Out of the Pantry** (1935) and **When Knights Were Bold** (1936), and though both were directed by a Britisher, Jack Raymond, the former is significantly set in New York. Not only were some of these films based on old farces which had been as popular in the U.S. as in Britain, but the pacing was as fast as American audiences demanded. However, those few actually submitted to the latter were instantly rejected – with good reason, for they are of poor quality. Buchanan himself is hardly an asset: unflappable, insouciant and given to facetiousness, he is much too forced, as if trying to atone for the weakness of the material.

Nevertheless, he did produce one outstanding film, unjustly overlooked (by, for instance, *Film Weekly,* which referred to the succeeding, abysmal film – **The Gang's All Here** (1939), one of his *Thin Man* imitations, directed by Freeland – as 'just about the best' Buchanan made.) René Clair directed **Break the News** (1938), having suggested to Buchanan this remake of *La Morte en Fuite*. He had not intended to make it himself, but in view of the uncertain financial climate he agreed to do it in place of the two films for which he was contracted. The material he has not only transformed into a more typical film than *The Ghost Goes West* (q.v.), but one infinitely better; its twisting narrative is genially satiric at the expense of some of his customary targets – the press and the theatre. He is most inventive at the beginning, as two chorus boys battle for the attention, professional or amatory, of the star (June Knight), a shallow publicity-hunting bitch: and it remains joyous as well as surprising when one of them, supposedly murdered by the other, becomes involved in a European revolution – one of the few truly comic revolutions of the movies. Cole Porter provided one song, and with Maurice Chevalier as co-star, almost yanking Buchanan to his level, this was the latter's best bet in his avowed attempt to win over the U.S. – but when it opened there three years later, released by Monogram, the stars were old hat and the critics grudging.

Buchanan's films were not what Joseph P. Schenck had had in mind when he contracted with British & Dominions in his desperate need to find a flow of product for United Artists (after his own Artcinema group had proved unsuccessful) – and Buchanan in this period moved first to Woolf and then to Maxwell, amicably placating Wilcox by making a guest appearance in one of his musicals, *Limelight*. Earlier, when Woolf had lost the B & D franchise, he had ordered Balcon to hire at any cost its chief assets, Buchanan and the team of farceurs, Ralph Lynn and Tom Walls, associated with film versions of plays in which they had rocked audiences at the Aldwych Theatre. Lynn and Walls succumbed, the latter continuing to double as director, at which he became reasonably proficient after an unpromising start. Lynn, over fifty at this time, continued to play juveniles, and a further deterrent to laughter is the complacent playing of both actors: but the real trouble is the material, as was usual with adaptations by Ben Travers of his own plays or when written directly by him for the screen. Audiences today are only likely to enjoy the misanthropic boom of bald, put-upon Robertson Hare in supporting roles, but just bearable is **Cuckoo in the Nest** (1933), with Lynn locked trouserless in a hotel bedroom with another man's wife, and the rest of the cast on its way to discovering that fact. Because its American director, Tim Whelan, was more amenable than Walls to Balcon's dictum on pacing, **It's a Boy** (1933) is far funnier; it also has a much more accomplished team, Edward Everett Horton and Leslie Henson, playing respectively an ageing bridegroom and a conniver who claims to be his son. Balcon hoped, vainly, that the film's reception would prove to the overweening Walls that the Aldwych team was not indispensable.

Balcon was also having trouble with a far more formidable figure, Robert Flaherty, who, unable to find backing in his own country, was working for the Empire Marketing Board (q.v.). **Man of Aran** (1934) was intended to silence those critics who regarded Gaumont-British as capable of little more than farce and melodrama. There is no plot; the only dialogue is heard in the distance; it is virtually an abstract film, an impression of the endless sea – and it is better to regard it as such, for its documentary value is nil. The climactic fight with the basking sharks was a reconstruction, for it was sixty years since the islanders had engaged in that activity – and as they had had electricity for years they did not need, as the film maintains, oil for lamps. Nor is there any mention of the twin causes of the poverty – the landlords, who escalated the rents whenever there was even a half-good seaweed crop, and the Depression, which had curtailed the subsistence money sent by relatives in the U.S. As usual, the critics called Flaherty a poet and a visionary, a view only half-shared by Balcon, who noted sourly in his memoirs that the film cost twice its original appropriation. Business was so bad on the Gaumont circuit that it took several subsequent changes of programme before receipts returned to normal.

The word 'documentary' had been coined by John Grierson (1898–1972) when discussing Flaherty: and if Flaherty was the Christ figure of the documentary movement, said John Mortimer, the dramatist (*New Statesman,* 4 May 1979), Grierson was its St Paul. The British documentary movement began in 1928, when the government set up the Empire Marketing Board under Sir Stephen Tallents, who included among its forty-five departments a film unit, organised by Grierson. Fascinated by the potentiality of film to educate, Grierson had earlier approached Tallents with a scheme to make films 'in the national interest' – by which he meant also in the Soviet manner. Certainly **Drifters** (1929), a study of the herring fishing industry, was cut to Soviet patterns and conformed to a belief in the common man. Its reception was such that Grierson persuaded Tallents to expand the unit and invite Flaherty to join it. Flaherty began **Industrial Britain** (1933), but despite a larger budget than usual was removed from the project while photographing the traditional crafts which were to provide the contrast to the 'new' Britain; Grierson completed it, assembling thirty minutes of well-composed images. The commentary, however, is only too typical of the British documentary movement, running from the trite ('You cannot afford to think of industrial Britain without thinking of its steel-works') to the chauvinistic ('It will take some other country a generation to catch up with our quality').

The Empire Marketing Board did not long survive, but the film section was transferred to the Post Office where, as the G.P.O. Film Unit, it continued to train young film-makers. The best-known of them worked on **Night Mail** (1936), produced by Grierson, directed by Basil Wright and Harry Watt, with Cavalcanti (a Brazilian who had designed and directed in the French film industry) responsible for the recording of the music by Britten and words by Auden. It is an account of the night mail from London to Edinburgh, well-edited and unpretentious, but it cannot be said to be more revealing than the documentary passages of *Rome Express*. Paul Rotha, another leader of the movement, made **Today We Live** (1936), 'A Portrait of Life in Britain Today', which contrasts in a perfunctory way villages coping with the Depression in the Rhondda valley and Gloucestershire. Rotha later observed that Grierson 'produced very good film technically but the people in them were mostly the men behind the machine; you knew nothing about them'. Nor, with one exception, did the makers of these pictures, their *de haut en bas* attitude revealed only too clearly by their commentaries, written with patronage and usually spoken with a monotonous solemnity.

It may be significant that only one of this group tried to use the spoken word as little as possible and he, Humphrey Jennings (1907–50), is its one major figure. 'Let's go down and see Humphrey being nice to the common people,' said Grierson, as recalled by a colleague, Denis Forman, who went on to remark that Jennings 'had in every sense an aristocratic mind, his sympathy not so much with the refinements of culture as with the sturdy, vigorous and romantic virtues of English working people. He had no personal contact with them and no experience of their ways from the inside and yet, like Lord Shaftesbury in an earlier century and another sphere, he was passionately sincere in his admiration for their qualities.' This interest and admiration are exemplified best in Jennings's wartime documentaries (q.v.), but his fifteen-minute **Spare Time** (1939) is a warm-hearted and eloquent study, without one false note, of the urban British at their leisures. His colleagues disapproved of it, claiming that it was not educational.

The claims made on behalf of the other British documentarists have always been extravagant, partly because many of them were also writers on film, locked in mutual admiration. They were also either unable or unwilling to work within the commercial sector of the industry, which is not necessarily to their discredit. Technically inventive, their films, partly because of the commentaries, rendered numb all but spectators interested in such aspects. Later, when the requirements of the War turned documentary into propaganda, Grierson's claims for it were rendered even more hollow*. Mortimer, who worked with him then, said, 'How wrong he was! In fact the truth told about wartime in England by documentary films was far less, and even less courageous, than the truth told about

1930s America by the box office movies which Grierson despised . . . We falsified the whole feeling of a great period of history.' With the exception noted, the comment stands against the British documentarists as a whole.

They did not lie in presenting Britain as having great gulfs in wealth and class, but it was a view which they offered unwittingly: their Britain is remote, unlike that of the Balcon films, where it is, more accurately, predominantly cosy. The Britain of the foreigner, Alexander Korda, is one of traditional values. It may be said of Korda that the British film industry needed him as much as he needed it – which was considerably. Though Britain was one of the few leading production centres in which he had not yet worked, he was an Anglophile, convinced that with a galvanising spirit like himself the British could produce movies as much in demand abroad as their other goods. His reasoning, however, had a vital flaw – and it undermined the quality of every film he made. The best Hungarian film he had ever seen, he said, was *L'Image,* made in Vienna by the Belgian-born Feyder: he may be forgiven for thinking that he and the motley-languaged crew he gathered about him could make better films than the British, but he seems never to have taken cognisance of the fact that the Feyders of this world are thin upon the ground and that, when found, work best undisturbed. His interference was partly the result of making a phenomenally successful film almost immediately: the fact that it was what he considered a wholly British subject only augmented his self-deception.

After making *Marius,* he was sent across the Channel by Paramount, dissatisfied with its British operation. Of the two contracted films one was abandoned, but the other, *Service for Ladies,* a comedy with Leslie Howard, was sufficiently liked for the company to enter into an undertaking with London Film Productions, which Korda had formed with mainly City money. Five failures left Paramount uninterested in the prospect of another, and a sixth, part-financed and released by Woolf – **Wedding Rehearsal** (1932), a supposedly frothy society comedy with Roland Young – meant that he too passed when offered **The Private Life of Henry VIII** (1933).

---

*'. . . [It] can achieve an intimacy of knowledge and effect impossible to shim-sham mechanics of the studio and the lily-fingered interpretations of the metropolitan actor.' ('Grierson on Documentary').

Charles Laughton in the film that made him world-famous, *The Private Life of Henry VIII.* He was one of the few character actors to become a major star in both American and British films, and one of the few stars constantly to change his appearance, probably emulating Werner Krauss and Emil Jannings and certainly, like them, seizing on 'show-off' roles with gusto.

It was intended as a vehicle for Charles Laughton (1899-1962), then making his American reputation, and his wife, Elsa Lanchester – a keyhole biography of the monarch, as written by Lajos Biro and Arthur Wimperis in the style of Korda's Hollywood film on Helen of Troy. Laughton's salary was the largest item in the budget which, despite extraordinary economies, escalated to a final cost of £59,000. Paramount, which held Laughton's American contract, passed again when asked for completion money, despite the offer of *The Rise of Catherine the Great* (q.v.) in outright sale. United Artists, urgently in need of quality product, invested in both, after Schenck and Goldwyn had both read the revised script – but only after assent had come from Herbert Wilcox, who had exclusive rights to supply that company with British films. A

final, desperate bid obtained a sum from Ludovico Toeplitz de Grand Ry, a former engineer who had been financing films in Italy, but his interference was such that in settlement he was offered ownership of either the finished film or that of *The Girl from Maxim's*, just completed in Paris: by choosing the latter he deprived himself of the half-million pounds that *Henry* made on its first release.

There are several reasons for the film's success of which the only interesting one is Laughton, even if he plays Henry as a crusty old buffer with a heart of gold rather than the syphilitic despot he was becoming at the time the film opens. When it announces that we shall not meet Catherine of Aragon, 'a respectable woman and therefore not very interesting', we recognise the tone not of the *Helen* film but of '1066 and All that'. Less agreeably modern – with the exception of Lanchester's Anne of Cleves – are the queens and court ladies, badly directed by Korda; the sets by his brother Vincent, though elegant, seldom resemble those Tudor residences left to us. Public concern with royal wedding and bedding – indicated by extras with warming pans – should certainly be mentioned as additional factors in the film's popularity, breaking records at Radio City Music Hall; and Laughton's Best Actor Oscar was a further distinction undreamed-of for a British film. A preview so impressed Douglas Fairbanks that United Artists rewrote its contract with Wilcox so that Korda could supply, with financial participation, sixteen further films for American distribution.

The same formula was used for Fairbanks himself, and as written by Wimperis and Frederick Lonsdale it is much more erudite: **The Private Life of Don Juan** (1934), directed by Korda, makes much play of the great lover's reputation and his middle-aged response to living up to it – but the star is unimpressive, and when the film failed he decided to retire from acting. His son, Doug Junior, misunderstands the Grand Duke Paul in **The Rise of Catherine the Great** (1934), playing him as a petulant rake, and if the china-doll Catherine of Elisabeth Bergner is hardly less likely, neither character is really suitable to the keyhole approach. Claimed to be based on the same source as *Forbidden Paradise,* the two films have little in common but the character of Catherine, this one striving, as in Von Sternberg's film, to make her an acceptable heroine. As with many Korda films, it is eventually neither one thing nor the other; his insistence on taking over so much of the direction from Paul Czinner resulted in both Czinner and Bergner refusing to work with him again. Toeplitz was also involved, and for his first film as an independent, **The Dictator** (1935), he emulated Korda by choosing an historical subject and Hollywood-British names for the leads, Clive Brook and Madeleine Carroll. His meddling caused Victor Saville to make his worst film as a director, and even the supposedly topical title is a mistake, since Benn Levy's script has nothing pertinent to say about the Hamburg doctor, Struensee (Brook), who became a protégé of an eighteenth-century Danish king (Emlyn Williams) and later cuckolded him with his English-born queen.

Korda himself, seeking that American public which had proved unresponsive since *Henry*, offered **The Scarlet Pimpernel** (1934), from an eternal bestseller by a compatriot, Baroness Orczy, which had somehow been missed by the film companies; and he brought in a team of Americans – Roland V. Brown to direct, though he was replaced by another American, Korda's editor Harold Young; Robert E. Sherwood and S. N. Behrman to assist Wimperis and Biro on the screenplay; and Harold Rosson to photograph it, instead of the customary Georges Périnal. The result is oddly anaemic: the film's success was almost certainly due to its story – a good one of its kind, about an English milord who saves French aristos from the guillotine – and the performances of Leslie Howard (1893–1943), light of eye as the foppish Sir Percy, and Raymond Massey as the spider-legged villain. As the Prince Regent, Nigel Bruce has a reference to contemporary events: 'But if a country goes mad it has the right to commit whatever horror it chooses within its own walls.'

Sherwood stayed on to write **The Ghost Goes West** (1935), and two American players, Jean Parker and Eugene Pallette, supported Robert Donat (q.v.), who had recently made his Hollywood debut; the director was René Clair, offering a notably unfunny prologue – how a laird's son loves war less than the lassies. The laird's descendant (also Donat) offers some mild fun

trying to stave off creditors, and though there are some satiric notes on the American love of publicity, matters become too desperate for a film which had announced itself as fantasy. Korda reshot much of it: enthusiastic reviews placated Clair, but when they could not agree on material two further contracted films were not made and Clair moved on to Jack Buchanan.

However, if another director from France, Jacques Feyder, was below his best for Korda, that may have been due to the exigencies of the star, Marlene Dietrich. Also crossing the Atlantic for **Knight Without Armour** (1937) was Frances Marion, to help Wimperis and Biro on the screenplay, based on a novel by James Hilton. Graham Greene, noting the budget (over £300,000, of which a huge slice went to Dietrich) anticipated 'the traditional Denham mouse' but found 'a first-class thriller has emerged', citing one scene to rank with the Odessa Steps sequence in *Potemkin* – that in the deserted railway station, reverberating with the eerie vastness of Russia, its railways a link in isolations made worse by revolution. Feyder and his art director, Lazare Meerson, convey the confusion, but in the midst of the ruins is Dietrich, as a Grand Duchess carried to safety by an English spy (Donat), opening her eyes wide to express fear. At one point, in an army outpost, she finds and dons a ball gown which must have cost almost as much as her salary.

There are no such weaknesses in **Rembrandt** (1936), which Korda himself directed, over-reverently, and which Laughton plays with too much virtuosity. Miss Lanchester and Gertrude Lawrence are the contrasting women in the painter's life, which is not to say that this is the usual Korda view of historical personages. Carl Zuckmayer's 'Scenes from the Life of an Artist' screenplay finds the painter in decline. With Laughton's concurrence the portrait is closer than most in suggesting the artist's absorption in his work.

The film failed with the public, but **Things to Come** (1936) raised Korda's prestige to its peak. He persuaded H. G. Wells to write the screenplay, and brought back from Hollywood William Cameron Menzies to direct. Later it was said that Wells prophesied the outbreak of World War II, which could not have been difficult at that time; here it begins in 1940 and lasts twenty years. In 1966, a newspaper – price £4 sterling – headlines the 'Wandering Sickness'; in 1970, the world is putting itself to rights and another dictator – played grotesquely by Ralph Richardson – is put down by an organisation for World Peace. We move forward to the City of the Future, in 2036 – and to what is most memorable about the film: the art direction of Vincent Korda, one of Alex's two brothers. Time has wrecked many of the concepts; there is an absence of ideas when it comes to plot, and the dialogue is didactic and naive – but the combination of sets, special effects (by Ned Mann and Co.) and Périnal's photography remains stunning. Naivety is also the keynote of **The Man Who Could Work Miracles** (1936), adapted by Wells from one of his own stories, with a Hollywood director, Lothar Mendes, and Roland Young in the title role – a draper's assistant who calls the world's leaders together to harangue them on the chaos they have created. Young, dropping his aitches, is not well cast, and Richardson is again disastrous, as an ageing alcoholic colonel.

If both films were widely discussed they still needed paying patrons, and *Things to Come* at least was too costly to be profitable. Nonetheless, to the outsider Korda had succeeded beyond all expectations: this one-time Hollywood dropout was publicly welcomed into United Artists, even if its principals knew privately that he was buying in on deferred terms. His other chief backer, the Prudential Assurance Co., had built him a new studio complex at Denham in Buckinghamshire, but by the time it was officially opened, in 1936, the company's losses had swelled from £30,000 the previous year to £330,000. It was not simply a question of unprofitable films; there were scripts commissioned that were never used, and actors under contract similarly idle – which was true of the Hollywood studios also, but at least they were run efficiently. Denham was not – filming seldom began before midday – and at the end of 1938 the Prudential relieved Korda of the task of running the studio. Earlier he had made a half-hearted effort to utilise its resources by doubling his output. He said that he could not make 'bread-and-butter pictures', so apart from renting out the seven sound stages to other companies he arranged for certain independents to work under the London Films banner.

Chief among these is Victor Saville, though he started with what was obviously a Korda project, **Dark Journey** (1937), an unconvincing spy story by Biro and Wimperis, relying for its appeal on its cosmopolitan background and the uncertain star teaming of Conrad Veidt and Korda's new discovery, Vivien Leigh (1913–67). She is also in **Storm in a Teacup** (1937), another hybrid, an Austrian comedy reset by James Bridie in his native Scotland, concerning a crusading journalist (Rex Harrison) who exposes the bullying of the provost (Cecil Parker) and battles for civic responsibility. This Capra imitation, co-directed by Ian Dalrymple, virtually introduced 'social concern' into the British film, and if Saville went further in **South Riding** (1938) it is because its source, 'an English landscape by Winifred Holtby', had been a bestseller. A posthumous tribute to her at the beginning is ironic, since her left-wing bias has gone, and the thrills of the Council Chamber, as promised, are abandoned for the romance between an impoverished squire (Richardson) and the new schoolmistress (Edna Best). Saville considered this his best film, but the social contrasts, if typical of their time, are objectionable: the lady bountiful (Marie Lohr) who arranges for a home help so that the brilliant, motherless young girl can write essays, thus proving that the family's dedication to the community survives after four hundred years; and the asthmatical Labour member (John Clements), stupid enough to be taken in by scoundrels, being magnanimously pardoned.

Korda did make bread-and-butter films and they are typical of the very mediocrity against which his operation was, in theory, dedicated, further demonstrating what happens to normally efficient Hollywood talents away from home. **Men Are Not Gods** (1936), directed by Walter Reisch from one of his own screenplays, offers Miriam Hopkins in a battery of close-ups as a fan caught between an Othello-playing actor (Sebastian Shaw) and his Desdemona and wife (Gertrude Lawrence); **The Squeaker** (1937), directed by William K. Howard from a novel by Edgar Wallace, has Edmund Lowe and an appallingly well-bred ingenue, Ann Todd, in a London exclusively populated by toffs in evening dress, underworld characters and Scotland Yard men. Another American, Tim Whelan, struggled with poor material in a supposed comedy, **The Divorce of Lady X** (1938), a remake of one of Korda's Paramount quickies, and **Q Planes** (1939), a thick-ear job that was part of Korda's new deal with Columbia, enabling them to meet quota requirements and him his large weekly payroll. Its cinematographer was Harry Stradling, whose credits included *La Kermesse Héroïque* (q.v.), but more importantly both films waste the talents of two actors making considerable stage reputations at the Old Vic Theatre, Laurence Olivier (b. 1907) and the variable Richardson – both playing however with authority and a seemingly effortless comic skill which few young actors today can match.

Korda also gave chances to artists like Robert Donat (1905–58), Flora Robson and John Clements, but his promotion of Merle Oberon, though understandable since he eventually married her, does not redound to his credit. Because of her, Technicolor was used for **Over the Moon** – only the second British picture in that process – and *The Divorce of Lady X*, though it failed to entail the success of either. In fact the former was a disaster: an attempt at sophisticated comedy by several Korda writers, including Wimperis, Biro and Robert E. Sherwood, and directed by Thornton Freeland (and the uncredited and by now alcoholic Howard). It was shelved – so that technically it could remain a financial asset rather than a liability. Released on the instructions of Korda's creditors in 1940, as London Films was being wound up, it was accompanied by two other films with Olivier, the equally old and dire **Twenty-One Days** and the even older **The Conquest of the Air,** the latter started in 1936 and in fact never completed. As a semi-documentary – part-written and directed by John Monk Saunders – it was, however, releasable, even if few saw it; and few saw the mayhem that is *Twenty-One Days*, despite the current popularity of Olivier and his co-star, Vivien Leigh. One who did was Graham Greene, who noted in his *Spectator* review that the screenplay by himself and Basil Dean, who directed, was culled from a particularly unfilmable story by Galsworthy. He did not make excuses, but significantly had praise only for Hay Petrie, an exceptional character actor, playing a former priest turned vagrant.

Korda's most celebrated disaster was **I, Claudius,** with Charles Laughton as the Emperor in this adaptation of Robert Graves's novel. Josef von Sternberg directed, – at the suggestion of Marlene Dietrich, who accordingly waived the last instalment of her fee for *Knight Without Armour*. When Oberon, the female lead, was injured in a car crash, Korda negotiated for the insurance due on the film, probably settling for a sum in excess of what he expected it to earn: but a secondary reason would certainly have been the lack of any rapport between Laughton and von Sternberg. Because of their reputations, this remains the most famous of the many hundreds of abandoned films in cinema history. The reputation of its producer is also involved in this interest – and the anomalies which contributed to it. Korda's love of cinema and his will to make good movies were recognised by even those colleagues who deplored his methods – and though he achieved less than his few respected Hollywood counterparts he is the only European producer to have made a similar impact on world audiences.

That fact is all the more remarkable in that the only enduring entertainments of his pre-war output are his tributes to the British spirit. Like many another naturalised citizen, his patriotism was excessive, and it must be said at once that his first 'Empire' film, **Sanders of the River**

The multi-talented Paul Robeson – law student, football player, singer and actor – made less than ten films, all but two unworthy of him. It is pleasant to hear him sing Mischa Spoliansky's authetically-based melodies in *Sanders of the River*; not so the spectacle of a great artist rigged out as a comic cannibal king, humble before the superior British.

341

The Four Feathers ABOVE is one of Korda's enduring entertainments. It was made all in colour and photographed on location in Egypt. It celebrates Korda's love of the British Empire.

(1935) has only historic value. This tribute to that 'handful of white men whose everyday work is an unsung saga of courage and efficiency' was adapted from a novel by Edgar Wallace, admired by Korda for its portrait of a supposedly ordinary District Commissioner – though only remnants remain in this tale of the two rival rulers whom he (Leslie Banks) sorts out. He tells Bosambo (Paul Robeson) that the secret of the British is that their kings are not feared but loved, which brings a sung tribute from Bosambo to his wisdom. Robeson deeply regretted making the film, having only agreed to participate on the strength of the ethnographic material – which is also what had attracted the director, Zoltan Korda (1895–1961), Alex's brother, who was making only his second film. With typical Korda inefficiency two units were sent to Africa to obtain background material, both working from different scripts. Zoltan and his co-director, Robert Flaherty, shot end-less location footage for **Elephant Boy** (1937), with more ordered results, despite the dissension seemingly inevitable on a

Flaherty project. The version of Kipling ('Toomai of the Elephants') agreed upon became a whittling down of usable footage, plus a plot filmed among the luxurious new jungles of Denham. It is not helped by blacked-up white actors, but there are enough ravishing shots of elephants bath-ing, and the like, to hold the attention; and Sabu, in the title-role, is an admirable young hero.

Fire Over England (1937) belongs to this group of films, despite a German producer (Erich Pommer), an American director (William K. Howard) and photo-grapher (James Wong Howe), a French designer (Meerson), and a Russian (Sergei Nolbandov) as co-writer with Clemence Dane. The source is a novel by A.E.W. Mason, chosen because Korda wanted to make a film about Henry VIII's daughter. As Elizabeth I, Flora Robson is as avuncu-lar as George Arliss but this is no irreverent look at royalty: it is an excuse for the swashbuckling of Olivier, as perky and determined as a young eagle. Because of expense, the Armada has to be disposed of

Korda the Imperialist

in three minutes flat, but it is anyhow only a *raison d'étre* – for Elizabeth's speech at Tilbury – meant to be relevant to current European rearmament.

The Drum (1938) is also based on a novel by Mason, a story of trouble on the North-West frontier, which on this evidence has as many holes as a piece of Gruyère. The film is unfortunate in a number of other ways: an ersatz India, with Wales doing duty for the Himalayas; direction by Zoltan Korda as stilted as the dialogue; a hero called Carruthers (Roger Livesey), who says 'Good grief, that's torn it' when his marriage proposal is accepted, and a heroine (Valerie Hobson), who wears silver lamé to a Government House reception. However, it has a rousing spirit: what matters is the skirl of the pipes as the army marches through the green hills. the following year *Gunga Din* (q.v.) would use such ingredients even better, but it does not have Technicolor.

The colour, both literal and figurative, is again superb in **The Four Feathers** (1939), partnering the same author and director,

though Zoltan's work has become more assured. The subject is conscience and Imperialism, specifically about a man who does not want to fight – by definition a man unwilling to protect the Empire. Harry Faversham (John Clements) makes the mistake of putting his own estates above Empire, and though his atonement – facing a million perils disguised as a native bearer – is excessive, few would have questioned his error in 1902, when the book was published, or, more importantly, at the time this film was made – when, it should be said, this view of military ethics did not seem as nostalgic as it essentially was. Neither film, of course, reflected revisionist thinking on Empire, which remained populated with either cannibalistic fuzzy-wuzzies or benevolent white traders and soldiers, united in their divine right to rule and protect the more docile of the former's kinfolk.

The success of *The Four Feathers* came too late to restore Korda's position with his financiers. **The Thief of Bagdad** (1940) is of the same quality, despite chaotic

The Drum ABOVE was set on the North-West frontier of India and in sheer excitement rivals the many Hollywood movies with that setting. In this picture villain Raymond Massey, second from right, confers with his cohorts.

343

changes. Ludwig Berger was replaced by Michael Powell and Tim Whelan, all of whom are credited, but the direction was also undertaken by Zoltan, Alex and William Cameron Menzies. However, from the first shot of sun-caught galleons, magic abounds. Using, with consent, the Fairbanks subtitle, 'An Arabian Nights Fantasy', this has little else in common, Biro having contributed a marvellous pastiche of such tales. One might wish less fustian in the dialogue of Miles Malleson, and a more virile hero than John Justin, with his Gielgudesque delivery; but Sabu is cute in the title-role, and Rex Ingram ★ does lots of ho-hoes as the djinni fifty feet tall. The Oscars awarded to Vincent Korda for Color Art Direction and to Périnal were richly deserved. The film was, finally, an American production, Korda having announced that since wartime conditions prevented the location-shots needed in Africa, he had transferred filming to Hollywood. In truth, with the outbreak of war and the loss of the European market, the Prudential had finally decided to cut its losses, and only with the customary Hollywood control was United Artists willing to continue with Korda's services.

That Korda's achievements, if often illusory, overshadowed those of Michael Balcon did not surprise Balcon, since he was neither interested in credit nor personal publicity. They may be regarded as the founding fathers of the British film industry, certainly with more varied and interesting pictures to their credit than the only other claimant, Herbert Wilcox.

Balcon himself said later that his programme at Gaumont-British fell into six categories: 1. the Hitchcock pictures; 2. the Jessie Matthews vehicles; 3. the Anglo-German films; 4. the comedies for home consumption; 5. the George Arliss vehicles; 6. the 'epics' made with an eye on the American market. The last two categories may be regarded as the same, for Arliss was a Hollywood star – if a fading one, which was why Balcon signed him only under protest. Gaumont's American subsidiary, distributing **The Iron Duke** (1935), must have been discouraged to find it relegated to the back pages of *Photoplay* and dismissed as

*The American black actor, not to be confused with the M-G-M director of the Silent Period.

344

'worthwhile' – which it certainly is not now: a weak romantic intrigue set around a dingily-staged Waterloo. directed by Victor Saville, with Arliss even less convincing, if possible, than in previous historical manifestations.

Among the 'epics' are **The Clairvoyant** (1935) and **The Tunnel** (1935), fast-paced but clumsy in Maurice Elvey's direction. The first, about a phoney mind-reader (Claude Rains) uses for climax the elaborate sets of the second which, predictably, makes a plea for Anglo-American unity (unlike its German original); but the presence of several Hollywood players, including Richard Dix and Walter Huston (as the U.S. president), can hardly have overcome its defects for American audiences. For them, only the title of **Non-Stop New York** (1937) could have been appealing, since it is a silly thriller with a Scotland Yard man (John Loder) climbing on the roof of an out-of-control airliner over the Atlantic. Robert Stevenson directed, and he made a much better job of **King Solomon's Mines** (1937), despite poor integration of the material shot in the studio and on location: none of the five leading players (only their doubles) went to Africa, and since the film concerns their journey through desert, bush and mountain, that is a handicap. They include Cedric Hardwicke, Roland Young, and, as their guide, Paul Robeson, singing some Spoliansky songs, as he did in *Sanders of the River*. This film is better than both that one and M-G-M's later version (q.v.) of the Rider Haggard tale.

Also, ever since *Evergreen* had played Radio City Music Hall the Jessie Matthews films had been angled towards American audiences. That particular film was emulated by **First a Girl** (1935) and **It's Love Again** (1936), both directed by Saville, concerning respectively a shopgirl who becomes a star by pretending to be a female impersonator (a remake of the German *Viktor und Viktoria*) and a stage aspirant who hopes to get ahead by impersonating a big-game hunter, Mrs Smythe-Smythe. Both are afflicted by the comic Sonnie Hale, the star's husband at the time, who was to direct her later films. In this capacity he proved no more talented and, in fact, by failing to draw out the charm that Saville had found, lost her whatever appeal she had had in the U.S. Almost all the other 'lighter' stars of stage and radio made movies, and Balcon was also successful with a husband and wife team, Jack Hulbert and Cicely Courtneidge, singly and in partnership; however, their limited but larger than life clowning, when unharnessed, is only too predictable.

The best of Balcon's clowns was Will Hay (1888–1949), if lacking in agility for American audiences. A formula was found for him with **Windbag the Sailor** (1936) when given companions equally venal, fat young Albert (Graham Moffat) and the ancient Harbottle (Moore Marriott). He lies, bluffs and cheats, and they are on to every subterfuge, openly contemptuous except when it is to their advantage. Often cast – as in his stage act – as a schoolmaster several degrees more ignorant than his boys, his finest hour was in **Oh, Mr Porter!** (1937). As the station master, he worries about the iniquities of Harbottle and Albert in giving tickets (in exchange for edibles) for trains that do not exist, and about his own sale of tickets for an 'excursion' to a gang of gun-runners who will not pay for them anyway. No British film of the decade is as worth preserving. Hay's usual writers were Val Guest, Marriott Edgar and J.O.C. Orton, and his directors William Beaudine, on the earlier films, and Marcel Varnel, on the later ones: though both were old Hollywood hands, they unquestionably slackened the pace for British audiences.

Varnel, however, took **The Frozen Limits** (1939) at full tilt, causing Graham Greene to call it 'the funniest English picture yet produced, bearing comparison with the Lloyds and Keatons of Hollywood'. Hay's writers and Moore Marriott, as an ancient prospector, are on hand, causing between them whatever hilarity is now to be had. Greene called the billed stars, The Crazy Gang, 'that rather repulsive troupe', and it must be acknowledged that they – three music-hall teams of two – do not clown at all; they twitter and squeak, thinking themselves no end of fine fellows because they don't stand on dignity. They, surely, want to make us laugh, and will try anything; but they know nothing of matters like timing and delivery.

The distribution organisation which Woolf had set up in the States never attempted to sell the British clowns (Korda, seeking world markets, did not bother with

them): but it discovered that it had a more attractive commodity than either Arliss or Matthews – a director, Alfred Hitchcock. His return to Gaumont-British after his stint at B.I.P. was not auspicious: he directed Jessie Matthews in a musical about Johann Strauss, **Waltzes from Vienna** (1934), which was not, apparently, a happy experience for anyone concerned – and that would certainly include audiences on its infrequent revivals. However, returning to crime with **The Man Who Knew Too Much** (1934), he discovered the rich vein which would make him one of the most successful directors of his generation. Most of his British films of this period are enjoyable, and having found his formula he was seldom to depart from it with profit – the apparently ordinary object which turns out to have sinister significance, and the extraordinary setting for the usual mayhem. This film begins in St Moritz, with the last words of a dying man, and ends with a gun-battle based on the Sydney Street siege;★ in between, an innocent couple (Leslie Banks, Edna Best), searching for their kidnapped child, are involved in a revivalist meeting which turns out to be a haven for crooks, and a concert at the Albert Hall which may be lethal for a visiting politician.

★Of 1911, when a small group of foreign anarchists, centred on the East End of London, took on the police and the army rather than surrender.

Graham Moffat, Moore Marriott and Will Hay in *Oh, Mr Porter* (1936), some comic adventures at a decrepit railway station. As the express approaches, they are still arguing whether the end of Official Summertime means that it is due now or in two hours' time; as the next one comes, Hay is struggling with the wheel that operates the level-crossing gate, which doesn't work: 'Why didn't you tell me?' he yells, and Marriott screams back, a refrain throughout the film, 'You never asked me.' The logic is irrefutable, the humour imperishable.

Hitchcock the Master of Suspense

Robert Donat in *The Thirty-Nine Steps*. A classic moment, perhaps, but it is hard to disagree with Graham Greene, who, introducing a collection of his film criticism in 1973, thought the story 'inexcusably spoilt' by Hitchcock. He also reiterated his earlier comments: 'His films consist of a series of small "amusing" melodramatic situations . . . very perfunctorily he builds up to [them] (paying no attention on the way to inconsistencies, loose ends, psychological absurdities) and then drops them: they mean nothing, they lead to nothing.'

The five writers who helped Hitchcock find his niche were reduced by two to fashion **The Thirty-Nine Steps** (1935) from John Buchan's novel, and if both films begin with the assassination of what turns out to be a secret agent, that at least was Buchan's device. There are other good ones: the uncurtained flat (it is being redecorated), the incessant ringing of the telephone, the figures at the corner phone booth, the revelation of the carving knife: who, with this genre, would be so ill-mannered as to ask why, if the killers got into the flat, they didn't polish off Hannay (Robert Donat) at the same time or why they were so careless as to leave that map in the victim's hands? –and what was she doing with it, anyway, in the middle of the night? Andre Sennwald in *The New York Times* thought the film superior to any Hollywood thriller, and virtually every critic liked the addition of a woman (Madeleine Carroll) to bicker with the hero in the Hollywood manner. Also more Hitchcock than Buchan are: the escape

from the train on the Forth Bridge; the interlude with the puritanical, suspicious crofter (John Laurie) and his kindly wife (Peggy Ashcroft); the Sunday pre-luncheon drinks party, with its surprising revelation; and the political rally from which the only escape is to pose as a visiting celebrity.

There is even less left of Somerset Maugham's Ashenden stories in **Secret Agent** (1936), and it is no longer a spy story, though mysteries abound – the body at the organ in the deserted church, the eeriness of the visit to the chocolate factory – and the last reels are borrowed from Lang's *Spione*. Hero (John Gielgud) and heroine (Miss Carroll) banter through the set pieces and what is supposedly Switzerland; Hitchcock later prided himself on including such 'Swiss' ingredients as chocolate and the Alps – the obvious choices of any hack Hollywood writer. Conrad's similarly-titled novel became **Sabotage** (1936), and working for the only time in his career on material by a major

346

Nevertheless, most cinemagoers will have cherished memories among Hitchcock's situations, such as that in *Young and Innocent*, when the camera sweeps down to the drummer to put into close-up that facial tic which reveals him as the murderer. In the same film, Hitchcock (in cap) appears as an extra – which he did in all his films, since this most cunning of self-publicists knew that he would be recognised.

347

The Lady Vanishes – the best of British Hitchcocks, with, behind, Cecil Parker and Linden Travers, and then from left to right, Naunton Wayne, Basil Radford, Dame May Whitty, Margaret Lockwood and Michael Redgrave.

writer, it is significant that Hitchcock makes no mention of the fact in his extensive, published conversations with Truffaut. The action has been brought forward to the present day, and there are a number of other changes, such as the transference of the episode of the time bomb from Greenwich Park to Trafalgar Square; but it is an intelligent adaptation, valid in its own right, very well played by Sylvia Sidney and by Oscar Homolka as her husband, the owner of a seedy cinema, cover for his nefarious activities. **Young and Innocent** (1937), reputedly Hitchcock's own favourite among his British films, eschews agents and anarchists for rural murder, with the Chief Constable's daughter (Nova Pilbeam) helping the wanted man (Derick de Marney) retrieve the clue which will establish his innocence. The central difficulty of

such tales – why the police don't apprehend the real murderer – never seems too relevant; and there are virtuoso sequences, such as the children's tea party fraught with menace, and the revelation of the real murderer, with its long tracking shot to close-up.

International fame invigorated Hitchcock: **The Lady Vanishes** (1938) is his most exhilarating British film, a far cry from the juvenilia of a few years earlier. When the lady vanishes, we are again in sinister Europe: only Margaret Lockwood has seen her, and apparently only Michael Redgrave believes her when she says so – though others have their reasons for feigning ignorance, such as the adulterous couple (Cecil Parker, Linden Travers) and the cricket enthusiasts (Naunton Wayne, Basil Radford) anxious to get home for the Test

Match. They are all monstrously sure of what they are doing, a rare quality in British films of the period. Through all the twists and loops – of which the best, surely, is that the hero and heroine do actually drink from the poisoned glasses – it remains cosy: but it is a film of stature which can even get away with a line like Wayne's during the final shoot-out: 'I'm half-inclined to believe there's a rational explanation for all this.'

The original novel, by Ethel Lina White, is not exceptional, and since the screenplay by Frank Launder (b. 1907) and Sidney Gilliatt (b. 1908) is brilliant, we may well ask how much, overall, Hitchcock owed to them. An answer of sorts is provided by their first script collaboration, **Seven Sinners** (1936), a remake of *The Wrecker,* a Gainsborough picture of 1929. The banter of the leads (Edmund Lowe, Constance Cummings) is obviously based on *The Thin Man;* and the fact that both *Seven Sinners* and *The Lady Vanishes* are set in and around trains is a coincidence. But both films are more tightly constructed than the preceding Hitchcocks, with each mystifying sequence leading directly to the next – though Hitchcock managed the transitions with more ease than the uninspired Albert de Courville. From this film, and in the same manner, Hitchcock used in *Dial 'M' for Murder* (q.v.) the vital clue hidden in a photograph of a reunion dinner, and there are elements of *Strange Boarders,* scripted by Gilliatt in 1938, in *Saboteur* (q.v.). To the acknowledgement that the roots of Hitchcock's 'art' lay in the British programme pictures of the period, may be added a kinship with Launder and Gilliatt, not least in a shared sense of humour.

That Hitchcock could flounder once away from his chosen genre is evidenced by **Jamaica Inn** (1939), a fact which he acknowledged by refusing to countenance any retrospective of his work which included it. He accepted the assignment between leaving Balcon and taking up his contract with Selznick, and we know from Selznick's memos that around the same time he and his British collaborators were busily engaged in destroying the same author's 'Rebecca' in their screen adaptation, till ordered to stick to the original. Daphne du Maurier's Cornwall, in the former tale, is a place of damp and mists, of hidden villages, of moors and rugged coasts; she also has a serviceable plot about a girl's growing awareness of her uncle's complicity in the wrecking of ships for booty – replaced in the film with conventional misdeeds, including a Silent screen finale in which the villain, now mad, abducts the girl and climbs the ship's rigging. Responsible for this travesty were Gilliatt and Hitchcock's usual collaborators, Alma Reville and Joan Harrison, plus J. B. Priestley, called in by Charles Laughton who wanted his part blown up – not surprisingly, for it is not in the original. In the book, the identity of the mastermind comes as a revelation, but Laughton, so obviously villainous from the start, further adds to the ruin of the film. As with *Young and Innocent,* there was a reluctance to go near the Cornish cliffs, a decision as detrimental as it might have been had John Ford decided to reconstruct Monument Valley in the studio for *Stagecoach* (q.v.). The inn itself, however – designed by Thomas N. Morahan – is considerably more picturesque than the original on Bodmin Moor, and it performs its sinister task better than do the actors.

The film was one of the three co-produced by Laughton and Erich Pommer after they broke with Korda. Of these, **Vessel of Wrath** (1938) details the events, as originally told by Somerset Maugham, which follow when a prissy spinster missionary (Elsa Lanchester) gets a fixation on a drunken beachcomber, Ginger Ted (Laughton). It retains the author's kick in the tail, 'My sister is a determined woman, Mr Gruyter. From that night they spent on the island he never had a chance,' but matters to which he merely referred – Ginger Ted's native women, the wrecking of the Chinaman's shop – are demonstrated in full splendour. Pommer directed, on locations so expensive that the film had little chance of recouping its cost.

Although Tim Whelan directed **St Martin's Lane** (1938), the look and feel of Pommer's Silent pictures has been so recaptured as to be uncanny. The combination of German romanticism and prewar London theatreland gives an odd patina to this tale of a busker (Laughton) who takes as his partner a cockney sneak thief – a role with which Vivien Leigh has trouble identifying herself. True, she goes on to become a star – selfish, vain and abnormally ambitious, with which facets Miss Leigh is quite at ease. Laughton is at his best, boasting, scheming, down and out, optimistic, and always with that ingratiating, timid beam of a smile. Clemence Dane wrote this fairy story, claimed in slightly changed form by Chaplin for *Limelight* (q.v.).

As with Korda, the combination of war and insufficient returns sent Laughton and Pommer on to Hollywood. In the meantime, Hollywood had begun to come to Britain. By 1937, when Korda and Hitchcock had proved that there was a world market for movies made there, the industry was in crisis. The two local conglomerates, Associated British and Gaumont-British, both posted losses on production, the latter to the extent of £100,000. This, already the most vulnerable branch of the industry, was further threatened when M-G-M announced the setting up of full-scale quality production in Britain, with its own studio; and there was no knowing when the other American companies might rival the better native product by moving upward from the currently sponsored quota quickies. United Artists was already heavily involved, since it distributed both London Films and those made by Wilcox's British & Dominions, and furthermore United Artists money was helping Oscar Deutsch to build up his Odeon circuit. American companies already dominated British distribution, and with their stars and know-how could certainly do so in local production if they so chose.

Britain was Hollywood's biggest market outside home territory: buying cinemas or investing in their building was not only easier and cheaper but wiser – since moves were already being made to divorce home exhibition from production and/or distribution. 20th Century-Fox had also acquired a considerable interest in the British industry, by virtue of a controlling interest in the Metropolitan & Bradford Trust, which was the majority shareholder in Gaumont-British – a fact which may throw light on the latter's decision to sell its distribution arm to pay off its production losses. The buyer was a consortium calling itself General Film Distributors, making a higher bid than Maxwell of Associated British, and consisting of Woolf, revenging himself for his forced resignation from Gaumont-British; Wilcox, who believed that United Artists was trying to oust him from his own company; Richard Norton, who had had interests in both that outfit and Korda's; and J. Arthur Rank, the only one

without industry experience, and the eventual survivor.

Rank (1888–1972) was a devout man who used the profits from his flour mills to finance religious shorts; in 1935 he joined Lady Yule, another philanthropist who believed in the 'uplifting' power of films, in backing a bucolic melodrama, **The Turn of the Tide,** directed by Norman Walker, about rival Yorkshire fishing families. It was distributed by Gaumont-British, whose unenthusiastic handling Rank blamed for its failure (seeing it today, it is hard to blame them). That whetted his appetite for battle, and since he was as patriotic as he was religious, he felt bound to prevent American financial infiltration into Britain. He was also sufficiently wise – and wealthy – to beat the foreigners at their own game, and had purchased twenty-five per cent of Universal Pictures when that company was in difficulties (q.v.) in 1936, a move that enabled G.F.D. to handle Universal's films. The G.F.D.–Gaumont agreement gave Rank not only access to Gainsborough Pictures, which had taken over all Gaumont's production commitments,* but to Gaumont's cinemas. And with the outbreak of war, when the Americans decided to withdraw their investments, he gained control of both these and Deutsch's Odeons, as well as Paramount's much smaller chain.

In the meantime, he had built a studio complex at Pinewood, not far from Denham (which he subsequently took over). Wilcox directed the first film to go on the floor, **London Melody** (1937), one of a series designed to build Anna Neagle – later Mrs Wilcox – into an international star. In it, she is discovered as a gypsy dancing in the streets and ending up, after some tussles with the diplomatic set, a big nightclub attraction. Such displays did not suggest to the principals of G.F.D. that Miss Neagle could or should play Queen Victoria, as Wilcox proposed: Woolf turned down the project, and Wilcox left G.F.D. He reached an agreement with R.K.O. to distribute, which brought in some cash from that source and by sinking his own and Miss Neagle's money into it he raised £100,000 of the budget; another £50,000 was needed, and Korda, generously, for Wilcox had

*e.g. the Will Hay films and *The Lady Vanishes* – the latter, however, distributed by M-G-M. 20th Century-Fox claimed others to fulfil quote requirements.

refused him participation, offered that amount of credit at Denham.

The result, **Victoria the Great** (1937), rode in on the fervour attached to a new outbreak of royalty, starting with a long coronation ceremony for those not surfeited with the authentic event earlier in the year. James Agate complained that beyond a glimpse of the Corn Law riots it gave no idea of Victoria's Britain, but what did he expect so soon after London had gone wild over Laurence Housman's series of playlets? – imitated here in such scenes as the quarrel, with thumpings on the bedroom door: 'It's me, the Queen . . . It's Victoria . . . It's your wife.' There is a gratuitous scene – clearly to please R.K.O. – with Abraham Lincoln divining that the intervention of the royal couple has prevented war with the U.S. The one triumph is Anton Walbrook's Albert: too romantic, no doubt, too much Strauss and too little Stockmar, it is still an interesting portrait, suggesting both the painful reserve and the quibbles of irritation, not to mention his eventual dominance. Indeed, with a signal exception, the acting is fine – H. B. Warner as Melbourne, Felix Aylmer as Palmerston, Walter Rilla as Prince Ernest – but that exception is crucial: Miss Neagle's coy and suburban Victoria. The film is so authentic-looking that it is visually indistinguishable from the sequel, filmed, by invitation, in the royal palaces, and with the embellishment of Technicolor. Agate had prophesied that the film would be popular, and it was – which may be why Wilcox did not see fit to employ an entirely new set of anecdotes. Although C. Aubrey Smith was brought in to play Wellington, **Sixty Glorious Years** (1938) gives an entirely new dimension to the expression *déjà vu,* and Walbrook's Consort, faced with Miss Neagle a second time, merely nods and pretends to listen. R.K.O., however, were so pleased that they called Wilcox and Neagle to Hollywood to film there.

In unequal exchange, Britain received various personnel from M-G-M, mounting its major operation on the outskirts of London. Louis B. Mayer cajoled Michael Balcon from Gaumont-British to head production – and then, according to Balcon's memoirs, treated him as a long-distance lackey. Certainly the project did not go as planned, for only three films emerged. The first of them, **A Yank at Oxford** (1938), directed by Jack Conway, is rightly considered an example of Anglo-American movie co-operation, and as such is treasured by all students of transatlantic interchange: it is the key film of the movement. Its most telling moment has Robert Taylor stroking the Oxford crew to victory in the Boat Race, but its prevalent tone is best expressed by an exchange between Taylor and his tutor: 'I want to major in American history' – 'There hardly seems enough of that to keep you occupied for three years.' The impact of the brash and bumptious Taylor on Oxford is followed by the realisation that we are all brothers under the skin, 'not such bad fellows after all' – which sentiments help one to overlook the fact that except for a brief shot of Magdalen Tower (which puts Taylor's college somewhere in the garden of St Hilda's) and another of the barges, it might just as well have been filmed at Culver City. As the don, C. V. France offers a superb portrait of Oxonian dottiness, and Vivien Leigh is very funny as a bookseller's wife with a set-line in vamping students.

The Citadel (1938) is based on a novel of a doctor's odyssey by A. J. Cronin, a former doctor who had seen too many doctor movies. 'I'm not going to be influenced by ignorance and superstition,' says this one (Robert Donat), struggling single-handed against both. Alas, he goes to Harley Street, but gets his ideals back in the last reel, just in time to upbraid his fashionable fellows: 'Have you heard of Louis Pasteur?' Audiences had, or so M-G-M hoped: had he not been Paul Muni (q.v.) a couple of seasons back? It is impossible to tell from this movie why the book had been so popular and widely admired: the best that can be said of it is that its clichés and half-truths have been lovingly rendered on to celluloid by King Vidor and its writers. Because of the mining sequences, the film was said to mark Vidor's return to the standard of his early films: they are not however 'equal to those in *Kameradschaft',* as Basil Wright claimed in *The Spectator,* but this section is the most successful, apart from Rosalind Russell, confusing her portrayal of the wife with Florence Nightingale.

This was, let us admit, the popular idea of a fine picture. It was as near to the truth as the majority of film-makers cared to go – and so was **Goodbye, Mr Chips** (1939), as organised by the director Sam Wood, the writers of the screenplay, R. C. Sheriff, Claudine West and Eric Maschwitz, as well as Victor Saville, who had replaced Balcon when he resigned. When the world said goodbye to Mr Chips it was also bidding farewell to a type of movie which disappeared during the War. The next study of a public school teacher, Terence Rattigan's 'The Browning Version', would take a distinctly bitter view of his lot, and when that writer was commissioned to work on the remake (q.v.) of this particular film, he could not bring himself to make his Mr Chips an honoured and much-loved old fellow. The War killed many forms of sentiment, hence increasing that of nostalgia: today we may be fond of the film precisely because it is sentimental about Chips – and the First World War, though certainly treated as if another was imminent. In James Hilton's novel, it is the war which brings Chips from retirement to achieve his ambition of becoming headmaster; there is no marriage, but that is the happiest of inventions. He meets his bride on a cycling tour, and before you know it he is in tails and she is bejewelled in a white gown (both kept, presumably, in their knapsacks): but what follows is genuinely delightful – the masters goggle-eyed that the dull Mr Chipping has caught so stunning a beauty, and she making him more approachable by asking the boys to tea and getting him to crack jokes. *Mr Chips* has heart, common sense and pathos; it manages to set its events against the background of the great world outside, e.g. 'Won't it be funny to have a king' and 'Stinks has gone to South Africa to fight the Boers' – and, worst of all but artlessly rendered, that response to a question as to what's in the papers, 'Nothing much. An Austrian archduke has been murdered in some foreign part.'

Donat, again, is much responsible for the success – he took the Best Actor Oscar that year – even if as the aged Chips he and the make-up move into caricature; as the wife, Greer Garson (q.v.) has the spirit for a girl to be found on an Alp and the graciousness to find life as a teacher's wife appealing. M-G-M was well-pleased, but in the uncertain European climate, future projects were postponed indefinitely or transferred to Hollywood.

The three productions which 20th Century-Fox made, through a subsidiary, New World, were more modest. They all starred the French actress Annabella, en route to take up a Hollywood contract: **Wings of the Morning** (1937), with Henry Fonda, and *Dinner at the Ritz,* both directed by Harold Schuster, the latter a romantic thriller with Paul Lukas and David Niven; and *Under the Red Robe,* directed by Sjöström, with Conrad Veidt as Richelieu.

Only the first is of interest, and that is because it is the first British feature in Technicolor, incorporating a brief snatch of the coronation procession. Fox had filmed the story before, in 1919, a jape about a Spanish gypsy (Annabella) disguised as an Irish stable lad – recalling 'As You Like It', obviously to its detriment. The title refers to a horse, and the cast includes 'the distinguished Irish artist and world personality', Count John McCormack, singing while the camera quite sensibly leaves him, to roam around Lake Killarney.

As it happened, 20th Century-Fox distributed Paul Czinner's **As You Like It** (1936), of which the first thing to be said, said James Agate, 'is that it has all other film versions of Shakespeare beaten to whatever is the elegant word for a frazzle'. He was an admirer of Elisabeth Bergner, though he had reservations about her Rosalind; but the reviewer in *The Illustrated London News* found that she had moulded the role 'to her own very definite personality, as every great actress has a right to do'. Those of us who are not admirers will admit that she does quite well by the text, managing the Ws with ease, faltering only on an occasional 'chepherd' or a line like 'Ah, how wery are my spihits'; but actual acting is restricted to sticking out her chin and smiling – a gallant, pixieish little Rosalind. Lazare Meerson designed appropriate settings for her: the duke's vasty castle with black-mirror floors, icing sugar walls and swans in art deco pools, and an Arden with sheep, hillocks and thatched cottages in the Raphael Tuck manner. Returning to Agate, we find him asking 'What of Shakespeare?' and the answer is that he is buried, or, rather Barried, for that eminent dramatist gets a huge credit for 'suggesting' the treatment, which presumably means that he approved the textual cuts – clearly selected to emphasise the plot at the expense of the poetry, which is not a good idea with this particular plot. However, we may

Four British star-players in two of the few films of the Thirties which made the world aware that there was a British film industry. ABOVE, Robert Donat and Greer Garson in *Goodbye, Mr Chips*, and BELOW, Leslie Howard and Wendy Hiller in *Pygmalion*. M-G-M produced only the former, but released both in the States, its interest in *Pygmalion* due partly to Howard, who was a box-office star in both countries. So was Donat, though he made only one film in Hollywood. His failure to return there led to legal wrangles with M-G-M to whom he was under contract.

enjoy Leon Quatermaine as Jacques, and Laurence Olivier, sensibly playing this Orlando as half demented.

The M-G-M trio aside, Britain's biggest international success in the second half of the decade was a version of Shaw's **Pygmalion** (1938), produced by Gabriel Pascal, who had succeeded where others had failed – for he had not only persuaded the dramatist to sell the screen rights, but also to co-operate in the filming. Pascal was Hungarian, but where his compatriot, Korda, could by general consent charm the birds off the trees, he always had a bad press. However, he also persuaded Leslie Howard to return from Hollywood to play Higgins, and to co-direct with Anthony Asquith (who since his early successes had made only one major film, *Moscow Nights*, for Korda). It does not actually seem to have been directed, but the editing by David Lean moves it faster than most British films. Apart from Shaw's words, obviously, it is the acting which counts – and above all Wilfred Lawson's incomparable Doolittle; Howard's is his standard performance of an arrogant egotist, but none the worse for that. Wendy Hiller's Eliza is particularly good at the beginning, when her apple cheeks and salty personality project her character through the Covent Garden grime; later, she retails well the doll-like speech patterns, but heavy make-up and (as far as I'm concerned) the modern clothes work against her.

Pygmalion was the first film backed by G.F.D., which next sponsored **The Mikado** (1939), still convinced that such cultural events were what world audiences wanted. So Woolf told the trade press, mentioning the years of negotiation with the D'Oyly Carte Opera Company (which held the rights), and the enthusiastic trade reception. Press and public felt otherwise, and indeed the film is a grim experience, Gilbert's humour disintegrating completely amidst the deliberately stagey sets – although the colour cinematography did win an Oscar – and the tentative direction of Victor Schertzinger, imported from Hollywood along with the Nanki-Poo, Kenny Baker.

With the outbreak of war, the importation of American directors would cease, and with the exception of the three M-G-M films, there is no evidence that they were more beneficial than most local talents – nor is there evidence that Whelan, Freeland and Herbert Brenon were more efficient because they were Hollywood-trained. Balcon, moving to take control of A.T.P. after a brief spell as an independent, turned his back completely on America. Hitherto, the films made under his aegis indicate neither a precise knowledge of audience taste nor an ability to convey to posterity the forces which had moulded that taste. Like many of the Hollywood tycoons, he didn't always know what he did want, but he always knew what he didn't want. At this time he knew that what he wanted were wholly indigenous movies, and eventually something remarkable would emerge. Meanwhile, his first for A.T.P. was **The Ware Case** (1938), a 1915 play already filmed in 1917 and 1928, concerning an impoverished baronet (Clive Brook) who murders his wife's nasty brother. Horribly old-fashioned, it still has – under Robert Stevenson's direction – its wits about it, which is more than can be said for **The Four Just Men** (1939), a loose rendering of the Edgar Wallace novel, directed zestlessly by Walter Forde.

Both men would make better films for A.T.P., though in the meantime Balcon had begun to encourage a number of younger talents, including Pen Tennyson, who was, unfortunately, killed in action a few months after making **The Proud Valley** (1940), a tale of mine disaster and unemployment in a Welsh village. Tennyson treats courteously the situation of the black American (Paul Robeson) welcomed to the village, and if the second half is muddled – the men marching to Downing Street to complain of their treatment – that is because it was filmed during the autumn of 1939, when no one knew whether or not government actions should be criticised. Nevertheless, the setting is a Britain recognisably from life and not from earlier movies, and where the weekly pay packet is a matter of much importance; the same may be said of Stevenson's **Return to Yesterday** (1940) and Forde's **Cheer, Boys, Cheer** (1939), comedies romantic and social respectively. Stevenson's film, based on a play by Robert Morley, concerns a seaside repertory theatre, the machinations to close it down, and an incognito Hollywood star (Brook) revisiting the past to find out why life has gone sour on him. Forde's film concerns a small independent brewery threatened with takeover by the aggressive manufacturer of an inferior brew. The one looks back to *The Good Companions;* the other, with its Toby-jug-collecting brewer (C. V. France) and his rival (Edmund Gwenn), pencil-moustached, reading 'Mein Kampf' and cowed by his son (Peter Coke), is a smiling forerunner of the Ealing comedies (q.v.) – and within the next year Balcon would drop the name A.T.P. in favour of Ealing Studios.

Stevenson followed Hitchcock to Hollywood, also on a Selznick contract, and with Saville departed to produce for M-G-M – not to mention the Korda family – Britain had lost its less-than-a-handful of reliable directors. One possible replacement was Thorold Dickinson (b. 1903), whose experience of most branches of theatre was an advantage; another – rare to non-existent in the British film industry – was a combined knowledge of and enthusiasm for the medium. He made his first film, **The High Command** (1937), at the instigation of Gordon Wellesley, another writer and like himself an A.T.P. alumnus. The film is a mere rigmarole – treachery in the mess, false accusations, infidelity in the jungle – but the audience half-believes it, and the images are blended with flair, another rarity in British cinema. That is, however, a quality also to be found in **Midshipman Easy** (1934), which Dickinson had produced at A.T.P., the first film directed by Carol Reed (1906–76), based on Captain Marryat's boys' story, but otherwise spoilt by Hughie Green's smug performance in the title-role. Reed's second film was a version of J.B. Priestley's **Laburnum Grove** (1936), which pleased the critic of *The Spectator*, Graham Greene: 'Nine out of ten directors would simply have canned the play for mass consumption: Mr Reed has made a film of it.' Despite that, and an interpolated excursion taken to the West End, we get but a cursory glimpse of Britain in the Thirties, and Laburnum Grove itself is the usual studio set. Reed certainly keeps the film fast moving and is well served by his stars, Edmund Gwenn, as the mild suburban man claiming to be a counterfeiter, and Cedric Hardwicke, outrageous in loud plus-fours as the shifty, hypocritical brother-in-law who is either sponging or boasting of life back in the East.

Reed, illegitimate son of the actor Her-bert Beerbohm Tree, had started humbly on the studio floor; like Dickinson, he was movie crazy, and by the time he made **Bank Holiday** (1938) was recognised as Britain's most promising young director. The film itself has no pretensions to be other than a composite picture of the seaside pleasures of the English: the beauty queen (René Ray), the cockney family (Kathleen Harrison, Wally Patch), the young couple (Margaret Lockwood, Hugh Williams) bent on a 'dirty weekend' – a double room with bath, at 18/6d a night – because they cannot yet afford to marry . . . (needless to say, she changes her mind). **A Girl Must Live** (1939), a comedy about a schoolgirl (Lockwood) fallen among show people, too strenuously apes Hollywood patterns, but **The Stars Look Down** (1939) deals with recognisable problems – as encountered by a miner (Michael Redgrave) who manages to achieve college and go on to be a Labour M.P. It is not an adventurous film; it is happier with the college boy's disastrous marriage than with politics; its account of miners' conditions calls for public ownership but is otherwise as perfunctory as that of *The Citadel* – and indeed, this film is also based on a novel by A. J. Cronin. The comparison this time with *Kameradschaft* was made by Graham Greene, not to Reed's disfavour, and he wondered whether this was not the best British film yet made.

It was not – by a long chalk, since it respects Cronin more than its audience, though that was a fault of the times. But if the British cinema remained bound to the bestseller, to literature, it was at least coming down from Cloud Cuckoo Land. The films of the clowns, and above all, Will Hay, had proved that it could be demotic and entertaining; *The Lady Vanishes, Pygmalion* and *The Four Feathers* had given it confidence, and though *Bank Holiday* was not an international success on their scale, its British reception had given Reed encouragement. If, under wartime conditions, film production were to continue, it was clear to observers that it would be in the hands of the usual bunch of mediocrities, plus himself, Balcon, and the team of Launder and Gilliat. There was no tradition to fall back on; but half a dozen films in the late thirties had given the British cinema, for the first time – *The Private Life of Henry VIII* always excepted – something of which to be proud.

16

Russia and France: Argument and Art

OF THOSE European film industries which had contributed to the 'art' of the cinema, only the French and Russian continued to hold sway in the Thirties. In the few cities where foreign-language films were exhibited there was always at least one French film to be seen – and indeed many buffs would later consider this the golden age of the French film. The Russian cinema, though second, was a long way behind, and the rest came nowhere – with the exception of Germany, and that was a special case since the Nazis were energetic in disseminating their films abroad. As the Soviets were also very propaganda-conscious, it might be supposed that they would have done the same: they tried, but to their surprise there was an audience resistance to films about tractors. The jokes made about the Russian films of the Thirtiess have basis in fact, and few of them can be recommended other than to the most ardent admirers of the Soviet régime.

It is sad that the interesting directors of the Twentiess now devoted themselves to reinforcing the faith of the masses in this régime, especially as, to judge from the results, they seem to have regarded their audience as simpled-minded to a man. Boris Barnet's **Thaw** (1931) carries a final intertitle warning its audiences to beware of reactionary forces still in their midst: otherwise this Silent is as stultifying as Dovzhenko's *Earth,* its meandering narrative subservient to the carefully composed images. Barnet was, presumably, instructed to emulate Dovzhenko – no information on this matter is forthcoming in Jay Leyda's 'Kino' or in the Russians' own histories of the period – but some of his old talent as social satirist returned with **Outskirts** (1933), which he wrote with Konstantin

Finn, based on the latter's novel and concerning the response of a small provincial town to the events of 1914–17. After an inventive and amusing start, however, Barnet, like many another, gets bogged down in propaganda, losing his sense of humour when it comes to politics. His second Talkie, **By the Bluest of Seas** (1936) is amateurish, apart from some stunning shots of the swirling Caspian; a tentative plot concerns a girl loved by two shipwrecked sailors, whose clowning is merely embarrassing.

Equally banal is **Alone** (1931), directed by Kozintsev and Trauberg, a Silent with added sound effects and a score by Shostakovich, about a Leningrad schoolteacher sent to the Altai in Siberia, where her example is such that the peasants decide to live by Soviet principles. At one point she gets frostbite and is rescued by an aeroplane – 'thanks,' says an intertitle, 'to our marvellous socialist state.' The director-producer team, not surprisingly, went on to make a trilogy about a typical party worker. Kuleshov was not so fortunate. His first Sound film, *Horizon,* about a Russian Jew returning to his native land from the U.S. was, according to Leyda, 'a fiasco'; he thereupon returned to contemporary American literature, which had provided him with *By the Law,* and came up with **The Great Consoler** (1933), based on a story by Al Jennings. Its protagonist is O. Henry, during his days in prison, and Kuleshov attempted an examination of the creative impulse by contrasting that environment with a bright spoof of one of his stories. As before, Kuleshov's admiration for the American cinema is self-evident, and in 1935 he was denounced by the Congress of Cinema Workers, ostensibly

Boris Babotchkin in the title-role of The Vassiliev Brothers' *Chapayev*, a pleasingly human hero. Since the Soviet takeover of Russia, the film industry was dedicated to propaganda, which presented the problem of heroes with weaknesses – and, if they had any, they must be very small ones. Chapayev, recently promoted to corporal, had only the failings of the 'new' Russians, being all for the new regime, but not entirely certain why.

for a film on which he was artistic supervisor. He was, however, able to make three films during the war years, and through the intervention of Eisenstein to become head of the Moscow Film Institute.

As a copy of an American genre, **The Jazz Comedy** (1934) is inept; directed by Grigori Alexandrov, Eisenstein's former collaborator, it co-stars Lyubov Orlova, who married the director – and attained a degree of popularity in his musicals – and Leonid Utyosov, who had his own 'jazz collective' in Moscow. The Russian title translates as *Jolly Fellows,* by which it was sometimes known in the West – where it was widely seen. About a shepherd who becomes involved in Moscow theatre life and society, it only serves to make Barnet's Silent comedies even more momentous in Russian cinema.

The other Soviet film widely seen in the West was **Chapayev** (1934), and in fact it became the one seemingly obligatory foreign film in the annual ten-best list of *The New York Times*. It is the only notable film of its directors, Georgi (1899–1946) and Sergei (1900–59) Vassiliev, known as The Vassiliev Brothers though they were not, in fact, related. It was a project of Lenfilm, for whom they usually worked (Sergei became the company's head in 1943), and was based on the memoirs of a widow, cleverly reconstructing the last forty-eight hours of her husband's life. He is one of Russia's new men, a cool and cunning Red commander during the Civil War which followed the Revolution, knowledgeable on Garibaldi and Suvorov but not on Alexander the Great, since he had only learnt to read two years before. He has an N.C.O.'s moustache and drinks tea from his saucer; criticised for sloppy dress, he upbraids a junior officer for the same reason. He is against Capitalism; asked whether he's for the Bolsheviks or the Communists, he answers slyly that he's for the International – and confused as to which, the second or third, he opts for whichever one Lenin is for. He is a lovely hero, very well played by Boris Babotchkin.

The plot is perfunctory, the battle scenes well-photographed but thin, and the scenes between the guerillas marred by 'meaningful' looks. Yet it is clear why the film was so

357

acclaimed – how refreshing it must have seemed after such absurd war films as *Today We Live*! It was a huge success in the Soviet Union, where response to its hero meant a farewell to the idealised heroes of Dovzhenko and the mass-heroes of Eisenstein – much to the satisfaction of the oscillating Central Committee, which had decided to condemn both directors (as well as Pudovkin) for pursuing their art at the expense of the audience.

Chapayev influenced every Russian film till the War, not excluding **Lenin in October** (1937), directed by Mikail Romm (1901–71) – quickly, to please Stalin, who commissioned it to celebrate the 20th anniversary of the Revolution. Lenin (Boris Shchukin) is found to be a nice, dear man, either writing manifestos or thoughtfully striding about, hands on hips. His landlord-bodyguard Vasili (N. Okhlopkov) is awfully nice, too – full of humour and loving care. So, come to that, are all the workers, as they plot and plan for the great day: they may not be as handsome as the workers of Eisenstein's films or the young Nazis of the films that Fräulein Riefenstahl was then making, but they have the same idealistic gleam in their eye. The Kerensky government looks exactly like the Csarist governments of other films, with Kerensky himself featured as weaselly and hesitant; one of its members, a particularly devious man, is made up to look like Trotsky. As Trotsky had been exiled (in 1929) and was not part of Kerensky's provisional government, this might merely be an *aide-memoire,* associating him with the losing side. Stalin appears briefly, smiling broadly behind Lenin as Lenin, the man of destiny, strides to take power. The storming of the Winter Palace is a reminder of past cinematic glories, and there is a cheering sequence when the military joins the workers: as hagiography this is both handsome and well-constructed – perhaps the best of the dozens of films on Lenin, few of them of more serious content than Germany's *Fridericus* cycle.

Another of the better films extolling recent heroes is **Baltic Deputy** (1937), directed by Alexander Zarkhi and Josif Heifits (b. 1905), who had studied film together, and who, as a team, directed from 1928 to 1950. The picture is dedicated to K. Timiriazev, the subject of the film though for no apparent reason given a different name – a professor of plant physiology who sided with the Bolsheviks in 1917 and thus became caught up in the great events. He is played by Nikolai Cherkassov (1903–66), who often worked with this team, but his role is merely peripheral: interest is concentrated on two ex-students – the one against him vindictive and humourless, the one for him, bearded, bespectacled and hearty. There is a further hero, a sailor (A. Melkinov), impish and bluff, a solid man of the people. The roles are nicely played, art direction and photography are superb, and in no other film has the confusion caused by the Revolution been so well caught.

Perhaps one is clutching at straws, but the propaganda of the Russian cinema, except in some literary adaptations, is so all-pervading that the films seem accompanied by the creaking bones of cowed spectators. Equally depressing is the reaction of committed left-wing audiences, laughing at every feeble anti-capitalist joke, and applauding the more heavily the more intently the piece sticks to the party line. Taken for granted most of the time is belief in the solidarity of the workers, the satisfaction of life in the commune and the beastliness of life under the Czars.

As a boy born into poverty, Maxim Gorki knew at first hand about this last, and there can be no reservations about the propaganda content of the trilogy based on his memoirs, as directed by Mark Donskoi (1901–81). Donskoi had studied with Eisenstein; he made his first film, in collaboration, in 1927. He began these films after discussions with the writer himself, who, initially uninterested, later became enthusiastic. Discussing the first of the trilogy, **The Childhood of Maxim Gorky** (1938), Catherine de la Roche wrote in *Sequence* that 'socialist realism . . . became the official aesthetic of the Soviet Cinema in the Thirties – a concept of art aiming at the expression of a constantly evolving socialist society and its ideals, wherein the artist finds self-fulfilment through participation in the life of the community.'

Donskoi does not let us lose sight of the fact that life was hard and bitter, nor of the individual's place in that society: but its importance is its evocation of time – events recalled by Alexei (i.e. Gorky) of his childhood with his grandparents. He cannot recall his mother, because she had little

meaning for him, but he remembers incidentals – a cat by the hearth, a day by the river – and such matters as his grandparents begging and the professorial neighbour chained to other convicts, being led to what strange destiny. The archaic subtitles are part of the film's charm, viz: 'On Fridays when grandfather went to Vespers, a life amusing beyond all description broke out in the kitchen.'

When the film opened in London, Richard Winnington in the *News Chronicle* thought it one of the three best films ever made, but I find it a mite self-conscious, taking its tone from the performance of the boy, Alyosha Lyarsky. I would not, however, argue about any superlatives garlanding the second part, **My Apprenticeship** (1939). The prim little boy has grown as expected into a man of integrity. In Part I, he observed; in Part II, he reads. The stupid people he encounters are particularly contemptuous of books; and in both films there is the seemingly chance association of books and prisoners, as if knowledge were imprisoned in Czarist Russia. One day, in a book, Alexei may find the answers to the problems puzzling him – problems about the nature of Russia itself, its vastness, the poverty of his own family, the viciousness of the family to whom he is apprenticed. The screen writer was I. Gruzdov, but **My Universities** (1940), like Part I, was written in collaboration with Donskoi: it is not only less good than either, but tedious by any standards. Perhaps Donskoi had tired of the project, or perhaps the War overshadowed the filming: conditions were surely affected, for there are few exteriors and the broad rivers, a motif in the earlier parts, are never glimpsed. Admittedly the action takes place in the city of Kazan, which clearly interested Donskoi less than the towns and villages featured hitherto.

Mark Donskoi's three films based on Maxim Gorki's autobiography, though of unequal merit, comprise a remarkable experience, effortlessly invoking a past time and a distant place. This scene is from the best of them, *My Apprenticeship*. Donskoi considered the trilogy the culmination of his own apprenticeship in cinema. He planned it with Gorki, but Gorki died two years before the first was completed.

Russia and France: Argument and Art

Also, N. Valbert has replaced Lyarsky, and a certain quality has gone. The story is a conventional one of tyrannical bosses and striking workers, with a particularly banal ending, as waves thunder and Alexei helps a woman give birth. 'It's coming,' he says, meaning the Revolution, and it is hard to believe that the director was the same man who shot the brief sequence in *My Apprenticeship* when a remote town learns, with a sense of awe, of the assassination of the Czar. Nevertheless, to see the three parts of the trilogy consecutively is one of the most rewarding experiences the cinema has to offer.

Russia's most famous director remained Eisenstein, so great had been the impression made by his Silent films. From that time on he was never to be professionally very happy, and except for a few hesitant intervals remained in official disfavour for the rest of his life. Stalin's disapproval of *Old and New* was followed by a European tour and, as we have seen, an abortive trip to Hollywood. Paramount was so anxious to be rid of him that the date of his departure was announced to the press, but Eisenstein left instead for Mexico, persuaded by a conversation with Robert Flaherty on the desirability of creative independence as well as correspondence with the painter Diego Rivera on the possibility of a film on Mexican life. The project became a vast panorama on present-day Mexico and its history, with financing provided – at Chaplin's suggestion – by the left-wing American novelist Upton Sinclair. However, Sinclair was unprepared for the film, now called **Que Viva Mexico!**, to become vaster day by day, and after shooting had dragged on for over a year he cut off his financial support. Since Eisenstein had been refused a visa to the U.S. he left for Russia, but with the understanding that the material he had already shot would be sent to him for editing. Sinclair, however, refused to part with it, issuing some of the footage as *Death Day,* and selling some to Sol Lesser, who used it as *Thunder Over Mexico* (1933). The best-known version is *A Time in the Sun,* assembled by Marie Seton, an Eisenstein disciple, who tried to stay as close as possible to the original plan – but her footage, culled from thirteen months' intensive filming, lasts a mere hour. The assembled film is a series of images, accompanied by guitars, of Aztec temples, cacti and mountains, a bullfight and a wedding. At one point there is a semblance of a story, with a peasant girl taken by a landowner and her young man tortured and killed – and also some references to revolution. The mood throughout is sensuous; one is always aware of the sun – though probably only someone from a cold northern country would have been so taken with the fronds of palms.

In 1935 Eisenstein began *Bezhin Meadow,* on the subject of Soviet policy for the peasants, but it was abandoned and condemned 'for its formalism and its political and sociological inadequacy'. He made a public *mea culpa,* and was later permitted to proceed with **Alexander Nevsky** (1938), deeply patriotic and topical – as one could not fail to note from its final warning, 'Those who come to us with the sword shall perish with the sword'. The invaders in the film are the Teutonic knights, in 1242, and it tells how the fisherman prince (Cherkassov) rose to defeat them before turning back to stave off the encroaching Mongols. The screenplay, by the director and Piotr A. Pavlenko, is as formalised as a primitive epic, though not without propaganda, since the rich are depicted as willing collaborators. Critics at the time thought the film a retreat to the static processional images of Lang's Nibelungen saga, but it became admired, to the extent that Richard Griffith was to write in 1948, in 'The Film Since Then', that though as spectacle it was 'nearly indistinguishable' from the work of deMille or Curtiz, it benefited from 'Eisenstein's discriminating taste and his supreme mastery of crowd scenes, and the absence of Errol Flynn'. Few today would prefer this mortician's job to the best Curtiz-Flynn movies. The battle scenes have a mechanical brilliance, but though the Teutonic knights are striking grotesques, in close-up they are seen to be mounted on rocking horses. The film is rabble-rousing, negligible as entertainment and only just redeemed by the Prokofiev score, though even that is punctuated by patriotic songs of extreme banality. Cherkassov is unconvincing as the prince, except for a brief moment as he claims he 'will not let these dogs set foot on Russian soil'.

The film silenced Eisenstein's critics, and he was appointed head of Mosfilm; in 1941 he began what was to be his final work,

Ivan the Terrible, planned in two parts and expanded to a trilogy as his enthusiasm grew. The third part was never shot, since the second, finished in 1946, was banned by the Central Committee – along with several other historical films – in case audiences drew a parallel between the characters of Ivan and Stalin. With the subtitle *The Boyars' Plot* Part 2 was offered to Western audiences in 1958, and reading the reviews one would not know how aptly titled is this *Ivan the Terrible.* Many critics were defensive, and writing in 'Kino' of Part 1 Jay Leyda observed that 'the film that does not conceal its maker's calculation has always been the least popular anywhere in the world . . . The rare film artist who defies the spontaneous, to show that the medium can invent as well as mirror, has as much to contribute to the future of cinema as do all the great artists . . . who treasure the *effect* of calculation.' He goes on to quote Eisenstein's words on this calculation: 'The grandeur of our subject called for a monumental means of presentation' and in rejecting the attempt to make Ivan accessible in modern fashion Eisenstein found 'a different tone. In him we wished chiefly to convey a sense of majesty, and this led us to adopt majestic forms.' 'Majestic forms' turn out to be a spectacular kind of village pageant, with actors congealing beneath a profusion of ruffs, baubles, cowls, cloaks, jewels and elaborate head dresses: called upon occasionally to perform, they emote in a manner considered old-fashioned even when Eisenstein was an apprentice in the industry. This is a dark, brooding film but of no serious worth. Eisenstein had had years of enforced silence, and either could not, or would not, go back to his exhilarating films about the proletariat. At least *Nevsky* moved, but in *Ivan* in searching again for historical grandeur, he confused it with the theatre – and dead theatre at that. From time to time the immense pains he took to get these posturing effects catch the imagination; but never for long. It is sad that the man who had once been the single most vital and powerful creative force in all cinema could find no better expression of his talents.

One film curio that emanated from Russia at this time was **Kämpfer** (1936), made by a group of refugees from Germany headed by Gustav von Wangenheim

(1895–1975), whose identification with left-wing theatre was such that he fled when the Nazis came to power. He wrote and directed the film, and on this evidence cinema was not his metier, for it is virtually incoherent. Nevertheless, it repays interest – as much, anyway, as any propaganda movie with no other aim. Its background is the Reichstag fire and the subsequent trial in Leipzig of a Communist named Dimitrov, who later found a haven in the U.S.S.R. He and all the 'lefties' are noble, handsome and community motivated, as in *Kühle Wampe,* while the Nazis, when out of uniform, look like the capitalists of Soviet Silent cinema; the sameness of left and right propaganda is furthered by the Maryan insistence of motherhood, and the boyish figure and hairdo of the heroine. The film, moreover, has shots of a Nazi orgy, suggesting that the men would be sexually involved with each other were they not dead drunk.

Some of the most memorable images in all cinema are provided by Eisenstein's *Ivan the Terrible,* but the film as a whole provides little in the way of entertainment or instruction. Eisenstein had been an innovative force, yet in attempting a new approach to this historical subject he made a film as rewarding as a visit to the waxworks. Cherkassov played Ivan.

Russia and France: Argument and Art

It was presumably made for distribution in Austria and Switzerland and, perhaps, for the German-speaking population of the U.S. (where it was shown as *Der Kampf*). The progress of foreign-language films between the coming of Talkies and the War, when there were only a few art houses, is curious. Almost every other country exported a film or two, but none of those I have seen – Greek, Portuguese or Finnish – deserves recalling. The most famous continental film of the decade – beyond any French or Russian Movie – was Czech, **Extase,** shown in New York in 1937. It was not seen publicly in London till 1950, yet it was known the world over to millions, and for the same reason – its leading lady, Hedy Kiesler, appeared in the nude, a fact even more widely disseminated when she reappeared in Hollywood as Hedy Lamarr. Only in stag movies, made strictly for private consumption or men's conventions known as 'smokers', did anyone appear nude on the screen, and by such standards – or those of today – Miss Keisler's appearance is chaste indeed, fleeting and hidden by trees. The shape to be discerned is undoubtedly that of an unclothed human female and her dash through the woods was to many, as Howard Dietz put it in his memoirs, 'refreshing'.

The director, Gustav Machaty (1901–63), had had a success in Germany in 1929 with *Erotikon,* but his other Czech films had not been shown abroad: that this one was has much to do with the naked gambol, but a combination of sparse dialogue, incessant and pulsating music, and accessible symbols – rearing stallions, etc. – conferred a spurious artistic respectability. A young girl marries an old man, bald and pince-nezed as usual, who falls asleep in the bathroom on their wedding night; later, while she is swimming, her horse bolts and is stopped by a lusty young lover . . . None of it was new – Woman, deprived of Satisfaction at the hearth, seeks it with a Stranger – but Machaty made of it a masturbation fantasy, schoolboyishly romantic, a hymn to primeval love.

In France, at a time when the country was increasingly unsure of itself, the industry turned out a great number of films astonishing in their confidence, all of them – and it is not paradoxical – a reflection of those times. As it became clear that dual language productions were not economic, foreign interests departed, to be followed by an incursion of refugees from Germany: in that condition of flux, the industry was exceptionally vulnerable to the country's financial crisis of 1934, which resulted in the majority of production companies being declared bankrupt. In the consequent independent atmosphere there was freedom to move away from formula, with autonomy handed to the directors, who tended to be reflective, meticulous, quasi-romantic and vitally concerned with the possibilities of the medium as an expression of narrative. Though sensibly commercial in their intentions they aimed to please the public without condescension and they also respected each other's ability. The French cinema of the Thirties is a complete body of work, its influences self-contained. Accepting that Clair's first Talkies provided an astonishing prelude, his immediate successors were of little account, but they include one enormously sympathetic figure.

Jean Vigo (1905–34) came from a journalist/anarchist background, which may have led him to avant-garde cinema. The already established director Germaine Dulac helped him, as did his father-in-law when he financed **A Propos de Nice** (1930), made in collaboration with Boris Kaufman (b. 1906), brother of Dziga-Vertov and much later a distinguished Hollywood cinematographer. This Silent, hypnotic three-reeler is an impression of Nice, and if the juxtaposition of wealthy tourists and slum dwellers no longer has much force (because it has been overused), the sum is impressive: facades, a cemetery, a game of *boule,* the Promenade des Anglais with strollers muffled up in high summer. **Zéro de Conduite** (1933) is also a short film, and impressionistic, as deeply personal as it was innovatory – recalling Vigo's own schooldays in a blend of fantasy, private jokes and public ridicule, culminating in a sequence (borrowed from the much less lethal *A Nous la Liberté*) where the boys shoot at their masters. The censors thought it subversive, and until 1945 it was banned, except for film societies.

Vigo's backer was Jacques-Louis Nouñez, who persuaded him to take on something more conventional, **L'Atalante** (1934), a scenario by Jean Guinée, which Vigo adapted with Albert

The most famous foreign-language film of the
Thirties was *Extase* (1933), an anecdote stretched to
ninety minutes about a young and frustrated wife
who meets a handsome young surveyor after taking
a dip in an old swimming-hole. Perhaps he saw her
like this, which was really more than audiences saw
of her, since for most of the time the camera stayed
well back behind the trees as she dashed through the
woods. She is Hedy Kiesler, whose husband later
attempted to buy up all copies of the film. Later still
she went to Hollywood and became Hedy Lamarr.

Russia and France: Argument and Art

Jean Vigo died young, leaving only a handful of shorts and one remarkable feature, *L'Atalante* (1934). The title refers to a barge, on which a young bride, Dita Parlo, arrives, to start a life which is not quite what she expected. Michael Simon is the old deckhand whose cabin she finds so fascinating.

Riéra. Its subject is the relationship of a newly wed couple (Jean Dasté, Dita Parlo), and the bride's reactions to her monotonous new life on the canals and rivers of France. The husband is mean-spirited but conscientious, likeable despite bouts of jealousy, while the wife, shy and bewildered, is thrilled by the prospect of Paris and flattered by a smooth-talking pedlar. These people belong in this landscape of desolate *quais* and factory chimneys – since described variously as 'realistic' and 'lyrical'. And if realism is attention to detail we can only say that Vigo has got it marvellously right. I am less sure of the passages labelled 'expressionist' – the search for the bride under water and the sequence in which he and Kaufman try to indicate sexual longing in images: but the rest is flawless. As *Le Chaland qui Passe,* retitled thus after exhibitors applauded a featured song, it was a commercial failure; as *L'Atalante* it was first shown publicly in 1940 – to become a rallying cry for a later generation of directors. Its most immediately striking qualities – the use of location, the blending of the gay and the melancholic – were established ones in French films; but it is darker than those that preceded it, due

almost certainly to Vigo's background and the leukemia which was shortly to kill him. Some have regarded his films as expressions of a social conscience, but since there are only four – the other is a short on swimming – it is more proper to regard them as experiments in self-awareness.

Vampyr, ou l'Etrange Aventure de David Grey (1932) has also been admired by cineastes, in part because Carl Dreyer adopted the formula of Universal's horror films and tried to avoid showing anything specifically horrific. But the plot is anaemic, and the film's failure prevented Dreyer from making another for ten years. Another foreigner, Fritz Lang, also had a commercial failure, **Liliom** (1934), but that, he himself thought – I think correctly – was due to the nature of the piece, which turns abruptly from drama to whimsy. The source is the Mólnar play which, set to music by Rodgers and Hammerstein, became *Carousel* (q.v.): but in Lang's version, at least, the second half is the better, being both funny and infinitely less sentimental. His first half is also good, establishing the romantic aura of the fairground, the vigorous bully of Charles Boyer

(1897–1978) and Madeleine Ozeray's touching loyalty to him.

A wistful, put-upon heroine and a sense of destiny and time passing may also be found in **La Maternelle** (1933), the most admired French film of its time. The director was Jean Benoît-Lévy (1888–1959), who spent his career alternating between educational films for schools and commercial movies, with Marie Epstein a frequent collaborator, as here. Their situations, taken from a novel by Léon Frapie, are familiar and sentimental, but their setting is realistic: Rose (Madeleine Renaud), a nursery school skivvy, adopts young Marie when her mother, the inevitable *putain,* goes off with a new man; but then Marie has a further problem when Rose receives a proposal from the school doctor. The cluttered apartment, the poorly dressed children on the stairs, even Rose scrubbing the floor, are depicted with both compassion and vitality.

Equally romantic and even more influential was **Le Grand Jeu** (1934), Jacques Feyder's first film after returning from Hollywood, written with his compatriot, Charles Spaak (1903–75). A soldier (Pierre-Richard Willm), stationed in North Africa, is struck by the resemblance between a lost soul he meets there and the coquette he left behind – both roles played by Marie Bell, though dubbed by another actress for one of them, an innovation which elicited much praise. He loves the one only as long as he can cast her in the role of the other, uncertain where the dream stops and reality begins – beautifully and erotically expressed by Feyder in a scene where Willm, thinking her asleep, removes her shoes and bends to kiss her tenderly, only to find her in command, whereupon he throws himself upon her body, luminous between her black underwear and a feathered peignoir. The accompanying realism in this case is the seedy, bug-ridden hotel kept by Charles Vanel and Françoise Rosay (1891–1974), Feyder's wife, in one of the best of her often magnificent performances. She has the eyes of a woman who has seen everything, and who would clearly rather be anywhere else; her black silk dress and her habit of spreading her legs are anything but ladylike, but her poise suggests having come to terms with the hand that life has dealt – and on the subject of the cards she is an expert. **Pension Mimosas** (1935) is closer to melodrama than tragedy, loosely adapted by Spaak from 'Phédre', with Mlle Rosay as the woman who falls in love with her adopted son. Otherwise the two films are much alike: instead of North Africa, the Côte d'Azur; instead of the legionnaires, a milieu of petty crooks; instead of the cards, the roulette wheel.

Feyder's remarkable evocation of atmosphere was achieved with the help of Lazare Meerson, his art director, and Harry Stradling, his photographer; with Spaak, they reassembled to make **La Kermesse Héroïque** (1935), the antithesis of both films – accepted then as a masterpiece and for at least two decades the yardstick by which historical films were measured. If its light-hearted approach is so much less facetious than that of Korda and Guitry (q.v.), those of us who love it must allow that the argument has faded somewhat. In a small Flemish town the Burgomaster (André Alerme) and other dignitaries await with unease the encroaching Spanish army; the Burgomaster feigns death in the hope that the Duke (Jean Murat) will pass by in deference to the mourners, but his wife (Rosay) takes command – and is too sensible, surely, to turn down the solicitations of the handsome duke. A statement is made, obviously, on the equality of women, and though few spectators then cared that the real subject of the film is the advisability of collaboration between oppressors and the oppressed it was later welcomed as such by the Nazis. It may also be said to be anti-clerical, in the person of the duke's chaplain (Louis Jouvet), a man of little faith but much appetite for gold and wine.

Since both French and German versions were made in France, Feyder decided – after *Knight Without Armour* in Britain – to make both versions of *Fahrendes Volk*/**Les Gens du Voyage** (1938) in Germany. The title refers to circus people, and Feyder's view is the usual one of the cinema – of incestuous passions, bitter rivalry, low morals, a milieu close to the underworld. Mlle Rosay is indomitable as the lion tamer, rich in humour and long-suffering wisdom; as her husband, a fugitive from justice, André Brûlé is weak, and it is possible that Hans Albers makes more of the role in the German version. The loss of Spaak is felt, for the story is trumpery. Feyder's creation of atmosphere is as vivid as ever, more

Jacques Feyder's *La Kermesse Héroïque* (1935) was once among the most famous of all films, cited by critics for its fidelity to period and its ability, then rare, to portray the people of history without either undue reverence or being patronising. Françoise Rosay, on the left, is leading the women of the town in obeisance to their temporary conquerors.

interesting than in rival movies, but we do not expect to have to make comparisons, for in the past he has towered above other directors. **La Loi du Nord** (1939) is equally disappointing; and *Une Femme Disparaît* (1942), with Rosay, is only a partial return to form. This last was made in Switzerland, where he spent the war; his last years were occupied with working in the theatre and supervising the film projects of others.

A former assistant of Feyder, Jean Gré-millon (1902–59), observed of him that even when he seemed to care only for the purely plastic qualities of film, 'one can feel him tormented by a need to offer total reality. [He needed] *to make live* the drama – with the greatest force, with the greatest presence – to make it part of the life of the

spectator.' The same may be said of Gré-millon himself, though significantly he had been making indifferent movies for nine years till Spaak wrote for him – from a novel by André Beucler – **Gueule d'Amour** (1937). The chief of several resemblances to *Le Grand Jeu* is the obsessive soldier lover (Jean Gabin), an N.C.O. in the Spahis. In the telegraph office at Cannes he meets the woman (Mireille Balin) who takes all his money, shuts the door in his face and later, when he has left the army, is unable to make up her mind about him. She becomes engaged to his unprepossessing best pal (René Lefèvre), and he has to choose between sexual love for the one and amical love for the other. Since Grémillon regarded the film simply as a commercial chore he was surprised by the subsequent acclaim. This merely adequate *femme fatale* tale does always seem more profound than it really is – despite in this instance the somewhat statuesque performances of the leads. Jean Gabin (1904–76), who managed to be in almost every notable French film of the period, was often a presence rather than an actor. Here, called upon to play a man desperately in love, a man desperate in desertion, one distracted enough to murder, he manages no more than his usual gloomy expression – but it is, as on other occasions, adequate.

Working again in Berlin for the Alliance Cinématographique Européen, the grandiose name adopted by Ufa for its French-language films, and again with Spaak – who wrote the dialogue, on a scenario by Albert Valentin – Grémillon achieved his best film, **L'Etrange Monsieur Victor** (1938). M. Victor (Raimu) is a respectable shopkeeper who allows another man (Pierre Blanchar) to go to prison for a murder he himself has committed; conscience, however, causes him to pay a stipend to the man's wife (Viviane Romance) and the matter becomes even more complicated when the man, escaped from jail, turns to him for help. Grémillon slips easily from drama to comedy, but what is most striking is that the film throbs with life. The location shots of Toulon blend with studio reconstructions – the photographic blow-up of the harbour used far more skilfully than in M-G-M's *Port of Seven Seas* (q.v.): people tumble out of bars, a girl accosts a sailor, women gossip behind clotheslines, disgruntled customers wander into M. Victor's overstocked emporium. Grémillon, like his master, believed that the care he took would be appreciated, and he *moulded* his films accordingly. In Hollywood, a few directors had managed to achieve similar results – and William Wyler was currently working with similar aims. However, part of the vitality here is provided by Raimu (1883–1946), who was temperamental, not handsome, nor renowned for intelligence; but he understood as well as any actor the demands of the camera.

Spaak worked only on the additional dialogue of **Remorques** (1941), though the screenplay was by the even more prestigious Jacques Prévert: the uneven result of this teaming may have been caused by the cessation of filming on the outbreak of war

and its resumption several months later. Gabin is a seaman with an obsessive love, this time for a lady (Michèle Morgan) who happens to be married to another. Grémillon seemed more involved than ever in his setting, a small Atlantic port, and was veering towards the non-fiction feature: in the post-war period he planned a number of semi-documentaries, with government aid, on such subjects as the Revolution of 1848 and the Munich settlement, but none came to pass. He did make several short documentaries, and the few features he subsequently made proved that he had lost interest in fiction.

Jacques Prévert (1900–77) came to films via a three-reeler, **L'Affaire est dans le Sac** (1932), written in collaboration with his actor brother Pierre, who also directed. Like other amateur ventures into films it is self-admiring but also amiable, its humour deriving from the Paris music hall; a barely discernible plot concerns the many suitors of an heiress, and the best of it features a hatter who runs around Paris stealing hats in the hope of drumming up custom.

Between them Prévert, Spaak and Henri Jeanson (1900–70) worked on every important French film at this time, so it is possible the consistency of mood or vision

Jean Grémillon's *L'Etrange Monsieur Victor* teems with life. It has one of the complicated murder plots popular in the Thirties and uses a common device of the time – a man accused of a murder he did not commit was so drunk on the evening in question that he has no memory of it. Pierre Blanchar, right, who plays the accused man, escapes from prison and turns for help to Monsieur Victor (Raimu), who unbeknownst to him – but not to the audience – is the real murderer.

Jean Gabin and Michèle Morgan as the doomed lovers in Marcel Carné's *Le Quai des Brumes* (1938), seemingly so representative of France at the time, both to foreigners and to the French themselves. At this stage of his career Gabin invariably played an outsider or a deserter, more honourable despite his status than the cheats and crooks around him who had turned the world into a place of petty corruption.

was theirs. There is reason to believe that the films of Marcel Carné (b. 1909) owe more to Prévert than to Carné himself, as Carné's work declined sharply when their collaboration ceased. Yet Carné's pre-war films are extraordinarily strong in atmosphere – which may be more the 'creation' of the director than the writer. He is the central figure of the pre-war French film-makers, and they form a school as certainly as any group of painters in art history. As a young man, before becoming assistant to Clair and then Feyder, Carné was an influential film critic. It was Feyder who enabled him to become a director by obtaining backing for **Jenny** (1936), with Rosay in the lead – that of a somewhat weary nightclub proprietress who tries to keep her profession from her priggish daughter. The role was not unlike the one she had played in *Pension Mimosas*, and Carné realised that a familiar plot would only bear retelling if exceptionally well-handled – which meant in the style of *L'Atalante* and of Feyder, by presenting the seedy suburbs of Paris in a lyrical style. His art director, Alexander Trauner (b. 1903), helped him reset that style; he had been assistant to Meerson on the films which the latter had designed for Clair and Feyder, and he had also worked with the Préverts on *L'Affaire est dans le Sac*. Incidentally, both Meerson and Trauner were foreigners (Meerson was born in Russia and Trauner in Bulgaria), which may be one reason why Trauner's studio-built Paris is such a memorable distillation.

Conversely, he made little attempt to provide a convincing London in **Drôle de Drame** (1937), and this second Carné-Prévert collaboration, though crazy in the manner of *L'Affaire est dans le Sac,* was to prove untypical. It was an original, the first *comédie noire,* derived from an English mystery novel – 'His First Offence' by J. Storer Clouston – turned into boulevard romp with murder rather than amour the motif. The French were delighted with this attack on British snobbery – and so were the British – but today the film seems small beer compared with the best of its few descendants, *Kind Hearts and Coronets* (q.v.), being also concerned with murder in high places (though strictly speaking there is only the semblance of a murder, the matter being complicated by the presence of a self-proclaimed homicidal maniac). Pratfall follows joke follows inanity, and, given the leading players, it is a pity the film looks more to event than character. They form a tremendous triumvirate: Michel Simon as an orchid-fancier who writes lowbrow thrillers under a pseudonym; Françoise Rosay as his all-gracious and all-cunning wife; and Louis Jouvet (q.v.) as their priggish episcopal cousin, a match for either in his hypocrisy.

Prévert's screenplay for **Le Quai des Brumes** (1938) has a delicate duality, assuming a contemporary urgency for a romance as mythic and as enduring as that of Tristan and Iseult. His source was a novel by Pierre MacOrlan, originally set in Montmartre in 1914 – and he has changed the hero, played by Gabin, from hoodlum to army deserter. Gabin's frequent association with uniform seems less a matter of typecasting than a continual quest for a meaning in the contemporary climate of French politics and opinion: if there was anything worth running away from it was the army, but there proves to be no matter or manner of loyalty to replace it. Without it, the will to survive is weak, and Gabin can only manage a grunt of surprise for an act of kindness. The film's title is not a quasi-romantic description of Le Havre, but the name the locals have for a particular part of it. There, Jean (Gabin) meets Nellie (Michèle Morgan), ward of the beastly Honoré (Michel Simon), who slobbers over her among the picture postcards and souvenirs of his little shop; for her, unsurprisingly, Jean gives up a passage to Venezuela. He says that were he a painter, he would paint a drowning man rather than a swimmer – to which the barman responds, impassively, 'A quoi ça sert?' – and Nellie is equally fatalistic, confessing, as she falls in love, 'Chaque fois le jour se lève, j'espère quelque chose nouvelle, quelque chose frais'. In her lover's arms she says 'C'est difficile à vivre', and she is only seventeen.

He, the stock Gabin figure, humourless and stoic, and she, with waxen features and false eyelashes, convincing neither as waif nor streetwalker, underline the film's duality – both schematic figures in an anti-romantic fantasy and yet by some alchemism real human beings. Their one night of happiness owes something to Murnau and von Sternberg, both admired by Carné and Prévert, and here there are shadows both figuratively and literally.

Hôtel du Nord (1938) is less committed, but that is part of its charm. That it is lighter is due to the substitution of Jeanson for Prévert – though the adaptation of Eugene Dabit's novel was made by Jean Aurenche (b. 1904) who would become one of the most respected writers in the industry. Though typecast, both Louis Jouvet (1887–1951) and Arletty (b. 1898) are at their most inimitable, he as the shifty fugitive from justice, with a fingernail hold on respectability and elegance, and she as his mistress, good-humouredly accepting her lot – which is, physically, one cluttered room in a no-star hotel on the Canal Saint Martin. Jean-Pierre Aumont and Annabella, as the suicide-bent lovers, do not hold the same fascination, but there are François Perier, as the young man who prefers the company of other young men to that of Annabella, and Bernard Blier, inheriting Arletty from Jouvet and startled to find that she doesn't accord him a jot of the same respect.

Perhaps Trauner's is the major contribution to **Le Jour se Lève** (1939): one might forget the story, but one could never forget the sets – the small square on the outskirts of town, dominated by the one high building in which Gabin rooms, and the lane bet-

ween the railway line and the factory. Nor could one ever forget the way Gabin looks, holed up throughout the long night, chain smoking because he is out of matches. This simple tale of love and jealousy was written by Prévert from a story by Jacques Viot, but its true subjects are the humdrum, the failed and the feeble. The arch-seducer, Jules Berry, is too weak to kill Gabin, his rival, but he does goad Gabin into killing him – in itself a sign of weakness. Gabin himself is pitiable. Life has been, he says, like waiting in the rain for a tram which, when it comes, is full. The two women have fared no better: both are promiscuous (each in her fashion) and both are somewhat pathetic – at the beginning because they are tied to Berry, at the end because they have lost Gabin. Whether such pessimism – here, as in *Quai des Brumes* – was intrinsic, endemic or acquired, the film remains remarkable for the inter-relationship between these four people. Berry is superb, with his fur collar, the cheap little brooches he gives to his girls, the wheedling, eavesdropping and fake dandy airs. Jacqueline Laurent is wilful and feminine, given to teddy bears and foolishly content to enjoy the admiration of both men. Gabin is his customary self, his relationship with Arletty an unusual one for the cinema at this time: when he proposes leaving her she responds, frowning, that they are not in love – then adding on a note of regret that with him she is able to 'breathe' a little.

The profound disillusionment was not lost on the Daladier government, which banned the film for export. A copy was, however, smuggled to North Africa, from which it reached the Allied countries in Fifties – when, because of the prestige of French movies, then denied us, it perhaps seemed better than it was. Long withdrawn because R.K.O. remade it as *The Long Night* (q.v.), its reputation growing thereby, it did not, when it resurfaced in the 50s, seem the masterpiece it was widely assumed to be. One reason was that people remembered Carné's films as being profound rather than artistic, as allegorical rather than melodramatic (or had read about them as such); they had thought them progressive and they found them dated. There were doubts as to the extent of Carné's fatalism, which was originally thought to have conveyed the spirit of the time. And, of course, we had hindsight: by

outshine most stars. The contrived nature of the piece – Jeanson was one of the three screenwriters – left the French public indifferent, despite the players and a popular theme tune, 'the Valse Grise'.

Duvivier signed a Hollywood contract, but he had an unhappy time making *The Great Waltz* (q.v.), returning to France for another collaboration with Spaak, **La Fin du Jour** (1939). Its setting is a home for retired thespians, coping with old age and each other; Jouvet is ill at ease, while Duvivier's variable response is only at its warmest with Michel Simon, as an old man with a fondness for teenage boys. His last prewar film is **Untel Père et Fils** (1940), the saga of a French family from 1870 to the present day, which had the backing of the government – presumably overlooking the fact that its characters, like most of Duvivier's protagonists, ended up dead, defeated or settling for second best.

Among other French film-makers then much admired is Sacha Guitry (1885–1957), although he was primarily a man of the theatre – the son of an actor and an actor himself as well as playwright and impresario. Coming late to the cinema, he began a prolific screen career as actor-director-writer, and since his films, whether adaptations of his stage plays or original works, were mainly to display his own talents, he infuriated a minority of observers. Abroad he was regarded as the epitome of French sophistication, so that his disregard for film convention passed for daring. He acquired international screen renown with **La Roman d'un Tricheur** (1936), and it remains his most entertaining film. As the title indicates, it is a biography of a cheat, and told almost entirely in commentary. As its hero a boy, stole eight sous, and is punished by being denied the treat of a mushroom dinner: a few hours later he is the sole survivor, not knowing whom to mourn, since, as he says, he has an *embarrass de choix*. Having decided that he owes his life to dishonesty, he embarks on a career of trickery, his actual exploits less rewarding than the bonbons: Frehel singing to army recruits; a description of Monaco, with the palace guard marching forward – and backward; a montage of lovers in a window, with discordant music when they quarrel; himself coming through a permanently revolving door in many disguises; and visual speculation on

his bride in various guises – a device used later in *On the Town* (q.v.). Guitry's younger self is played by two other actors, and when at the second transition he observes, 'I had to resign myself to the fact that although I was only thirty-four I looked forty' it is impossible not to enjoy him.

Les Perles de la Couronne was made to celebrate the coronation of 1937, an agreeable contribution to the Entente Cordiale. Italy is also heavily involved in the plot, neatly suggesting that France lies not only physically but culturally between the two countries – and in the English and Italian sequences those languages are spoken, which was then unusual. Indeed, the conception is so civilised and the narrative so freewheeling that one looks beyond the facetious tone for something which might illuminate the events mirrored: disappointingly, and typically, there is nothing. Nor is there much real wit; and, equally disappointing, the historical pageant gives way to some frippery about missing jewels. **Ils Etaient Neuf Célibataires** (1939) pinpoints Guitry's faults and virtues more engagingly. It has a funny premise, indulgently carried out. It also has a huge part for himself, but it uses the medium well, keeping several plots going simultaneously. He plays a confidence trickster who takes advantage of a new decree expelling foreigners to arrange for nine aged and improvident bachelors to accommodate wealthy foreign women who will pay heavily for husbands. One woman is furious to discover that she has married a man she once turned away as a beggar, till she finds that as an accountant he can fiddle her tax returns: we could be happy together, she says, to which he replies, 'Why not? We've never been in love.' For the most part, however, the piece is not so much cynical as simply heartless.

If Guitry's following abroad could be described as a coterie, Marcel Pagnol eventually acquired a foreign reputation which seemed about to take his films beyond the confines of the art-houses. Also from the stage and taking a primarily comic view of his fellow countrymen, he both wrote and directed, after taking a keen interest in the filming of his plays by other hands. These include not only the first two of the 'Marius' trilogy, but **Topaze** (1933), his most popular piece, handled stagily by Louis Gasnier,

a one-time Hollywood director, with Jouvet as the mild mathematics teacher who, given the opportunity, becomes a financial genius. About the same time Pagnol set up his own studio in Marseilles, since his aim was to make films of Provencal life – usually from his own material but also remodelling the novels of Jean Giono till they seemed like his own work. As director he began with assurance: **Angèle** (1934), after Giono, concerns a farm girl (Orane Demazis) seduced by the fast-talking stranger who, after their child is born, persuades her into prostitution; the family handyman (Fernandel) is sent to bring her home, and her outraged father locks her in a shed while her destiny is being resolved. That takes an excessive amount of talk – and Pagnol's refusal to contemplate 'pure' cinema earned him, in France, a similar disdain to that accorded Guitry.

However, the sun of Provence shines bright; and Pagnol's celebration of that region of France would become, in **La Femme du Boulanger** (1938), quite marvellous. There is a dead dog down a well, and there are elms preventing the sun ever getting to a neighbour's spinach; the curé is quarrelling with the schoolteacher over the remark that Joan of Arc had *thought* she heard voices. It is also the day when the new baker (Raimu) will bake his first loaves, and the villagers turn up in expectation – including the marquis (Charpin) and his shepherd, Dominique (Charles Moulin), who will collect the bread twice a week for the chateau: and when the first look passes between the handsome Dominique and the baker's young wife (Ginette Leclerc) it is a *coup de foudre*. When Dominique comes serenading, the wife slips out; and as the baker gets quickly drunk on Pernod he

Marcel Pagnol's tales of Provençal life are not as highly regarded as they once were, and he admittedly was not averse to melodrama. When his humour and powers of observation prevailed his films could be splendid, as in *La Femme du Boulanger*. The lady of the title has gone off with a young man, and her husband, the baker, has gone on strike. Discussing the matter are the squire, Charpin, left, and the cure, Robert Vattier.

373

makes one thing clear – that there will be no bread made till she returns. The story is predictable and some sequences are over-stretched, but the film preserves a way of life which disappeared first with the advent of the automobile and then with television; nowadays it is unlikely that the matter would be settled by a triumvirate of the marquis, the curé and the schoolteacher. The curé exults in his own tact; a lone spinster waits on the road to see the sinners return; and one man is desperately anxious to establish that the couple he saw on a horse seemed only a *semblance*. There are few richer films, and that is its justification: no one now could care whether this is 'pure' cinema.

Abroad, the film joined *La Kermesse Héroïque, Mayerling* (q.v.), *Un Carnet de Bal* and *La Grande Illusion* (q.v.) in encouraging new audiences for the foreign-language film. Flushed with such successes, the French film industry contemplated a larger share of the world market. Its output was only one-fifth that of Hollywood, but lower costs – the average expenditure per film was the equivalent of only $75,000 – meant higher profits; and the mainly trans-ient producers began to think in bigger terms than local product and co-productions with Germany or Italy. The majority of these entrepreneurs regarded France as a stopping-off place on their journey from Eastern Europe to America, thus hardly contributing to a settled industry, and their manifold liaisons with local film-makers had resulted in the industry being frag-mented, with production and distribution companies almost equalling the number of cinemas. The trade papers of 1938/9 announced ambitious plans, to feature internationally-known names; few of them, however, were definite projects, and the declaration of war put paid to those that were.

Though it was by chance that the struc-ture of the industry enabled directors to control their own product, they took advantage to an extent not possible in most other countries at the time. Thus the German refugee directors were able to contribute substantially to the French cinema, even though most of them were heavily indebted to the Russian-born Ger-man producer, Seymour Nebenzal (1899–1961), who had produced the last German films of Pabst and Lang. He had set up a French operation before the Nazis came to power, to enable Pabst to make the basically French *L'Atlantide,* but his biggest success in France was **Mayerling** (1936), directed by his compatriot, Anatole Litvak (1902–74), who too had found himself no longer welcome in Germany. The film is a highly romanticised account of the nineteenth-century Hapsburg tragedy; while not afraid to hint at some of its more sordid undertones, it is pictorially hand-some and drenched in atmosphere. At its centre are the lovers, the crown prince and his mistress, vividly and touchingly por-trayed by Charles Boyer and Danielle Darrieux (b. 1917). It is reputed to have inspired a number of suicide pacts among the romantically inclined, and caused Hollywood to send for Litvak.

Thus Pabst inherited **Mademoiselle Docteur** (1937), his first film in three years, but it is impossible to see why the piece should have interested two such eminent directors, unless it was the cast – Jouvet, Pierre Blanchar, Pierre Fresnay, Charles Dullin, Viviane Romance, Jean-Louis Barrault and, in the title-role, Dita Parlo. It is a trashy tale, set in Salonika during World War I, in which almost everyone turns out to be a spy. It was perhaps the uneasy European situation which raised a crop of espionage tales. French audiences had also shown a fondness for stories of faraway places, and Pabst made **Le Drame de Shanghai** (1938), as if to prove that drama in Shanghai was equally as witless as in Salonika. It concerns a Hong Kong-educated schoolgirl (Elina Labourdette), the daughter of a nightclub singer (Chris-tiane Mardayne) who is also a spy and in the power of a scar-faced member (Jouvet) of a spy ring called Le Serpent Noir. The sequences of the rallying Chinese were clearly inspired by Malraux's novel 'La Condition Humaine', but they neither raise the level of the piece nor indicate any keen interest on the part of Pabst.

Robert Siodmak, a lesser director, fared much better in France, starting with **La Crise est Finie** (1934), produced by Nebenzal. It is of a wondrous gaiety, belying the fact that both men had recently been exiled from their own country. Though the title specifically refers to a theatrical troupe which survives by putting on its own show, it also refers to the Depression – and the cast reprises the title song, clearly intended to mean in France what 'Who's Afraid of the Big Bad Wolf?' had meant in the States. The direct connection is only made when two of the troupe dress up as *flics* to recruit some men on the dole working as street musicians – which is a more definite comment on the Depression than the film's model, *42nd Street*. The finale tries for a Berkeley-like spectacle, using imagination rather than size. Till that point, Siodmak had taken Clair's style as well as his leading man, Albert Préjean, but since the piece is so entertaining it would be invidious to speak of derivation.

Both **Cargaison Blanche** (1936) and **Mister Flow** (1936) emulate Hollywood models less successfully. The former, though supposedly based on a recent magazine *reportage,* uses white slave trading as a background for the adventures of two in-and-out-of-love journalists, Jean-Pierre Aumont and Käthe de (von) Nagy; the latter is a comedy in which an aristocratic master-crook, Edwige Feuillère, gets herself involved with an innocent young advocate, Fernand Gravey. As with most of Siodmak's films, whether made in Berlin, Paris or Hollywood, subsequent events fail to measure up to the intriguing opening, which includes Jouvet fawning and cringing as an imprisoned valet who is not quite what he seems. Similarly, the best of *Cargaison Blanche* is sustained by the villainy of Jules Berry and Charles Granval.

Mollenard (1938) is virtually two different films lurking inside one. Siodmak's penchant for free spirits led him to this classic example of the anti-bourgeois film, with Harry Baur as the rumbustious, adventuresome sea captain, Justin Mollenard, and Gabrielle Dorziat as his prim, narrowminded wife. Unfortunately the skulduggery in Shanghai is no more mature than that in Pabst's movie, despite such denizens as Pierre Renoir and Dalio; and there is something about Baur's crabbed face which indicates that he could never really be a gun-runner in a B-movie. The Dunkerque sequences are very different, with a real bite, but they have difficulty in surviving the first half. Setting aside *La Crise est Finie*, this is the best of Siodmak's French films, with distinguished contributions from Eugen Schüfftan

The German director Robert Siodmak, who had been making some very fine films was forced to flee when the Nazis came to power. He settled in France – till the Germans invaded – and directed a mixed batch of films, of which *La Crise est Finie* is the best. It concerns a theatrical troupe in difficulty. Here the leading lady, Danielle Darrieux, allows herself to be taken to dinner by Marcel Carpentier, one man who could certainly help. He outlines his conditions over champagne, and Mlle Darrieux feels them too compromising.

and Henri Alekan, who trained their cameras on sets by Trauner; and from Darius Milhaud, who wrote the score, and Spaak who wrote the screenplay with the author of the original novel, O-P. Gilbert.

Pièges (1939) opens well, and for much of its length is 'French-good' – melodramatic and mysterious: but too often it is 'French-poor' – mock *Carnet de Bal*. Maria Déa is the taxi-dancer who agrees to be a police decoy to attract a mass murderer, a killer who meets his victims by advertising in the personal columns of the journals; Maurice Chevalier is the man whom the police suspect, and Pierre Renoir is his partner, suspected by audiences. There is little of the sexual obsession that American reviewers thought had been censored when the film was shown there, and modern audiences are unlikely to be titillated by just two shots of Mlle Déa's legs.

Edouard Corniglion-Molinier, the producer of *Mollenard*, was another refugee from Germany, he had earlier backed **Mauvaise Graine** (1934), written and directed by the Hungarian, Alexander Esway, who had been his assistant some years before, and also Billy Wilder, in his first attempt at direction. As in the case of *La Crise est Finie,* these exiles produced a cheerful little film, in this case borrowing from Clair (and the German musicals) the central theme of male friendship. One of the two, Jean-la-Cravatte, goes around stealing neckties – which we may recognise as a Wilder touch; and the film states bluntly that gentlemen rich enough to afford cars deserve to have them stolen, at least by such a merry and enterprising gang of thieves. This is not the only film of the period to suggest, at the end, that a new life waits overseas, a solution to the evils of Europe. Esway remained there, at one point becoming a producer in Britain, while Wilder (q.v.) went on to Hollywood.

The most successful of the emigré directors was the naturalised Frenchman, Max Ophuls, who began his French career with a new version of *Liebelei*, subtitled *Une Histoire d'Amour,* which is in fact the German film, recut and dubbed, a number of its scenes uninterestingly reshot with French principals. The German original was admired by the Italian publisher, Rizzoli, who reunited Ophuls with its writers, Hans Wilhelm and Curt Alexander, to adapt a novel by Salvator Gotta, **La Sig-** **nora di Tutti** (1933). Its heroine is a schoolgirl, Gaby Doriot (Isa Miranda), and its subject her involvement with the Nanni family – with the father (Memo Benassi), an academic, who has made her his mistress, and the son, who would like to make her his wife: when the mother dies girl and father resume their relationship, till guilt overwhelms her. The film was obviously congenial to Ophuls, for if the opera montage and the lavish use of music – by Daniel Ampitheatrof – recall *Liebelei,* certain aspects would reappear in his later work: *Letter From an Unknown Woman* (q.v.) would also feature a decent young girl caught up in a passion beyond her, and *Lola Montes* (q.v.) would use a similar framing device, for, like Lola, Gaby becomes an actress. While this is the second Ophuls film to be set in and around the film studios, **Divine** (1935) moves him to the world of live theatre, as represented by a sub-Folies Bergère outfit in Paris – his heroine is an innocent but far from divine chorus girl (Simone Berriau), whose involvement with drugs reeks of Silent melodrama: doubtless there were drug addicts in the tatty music halls of Pigalle, but the handling is absurd, due not least to the screenplay – partly contributed by Colette, on one of whose stories it is based.

Invited to the Netherlands to make **Komedie om Geld** (1936), Ophuls allowed his instinct as social satirist to take command – and the film, if uneven and often overemphatic, has extraordinary bitterness: it is the only film made by any of the emigrés which suggests that they were working off anger at their treatment by Germany (as opposed to criticising its new régime). It is possible to see analogies, as the capitalist system it attacks is represented by bankers and industrialists presumably similar to those who financed Hitler; its hero is a little man, a cashier (Hermann Bouber) whom they use and then destroy. The changes in his fortunes reflect *A Nous la Liberté, Der Letzte Mann* and *L'Argent,* but Brecht was also influential in both theme and structure; and a compère similar to that of *Dreigroschenoper* appears from time to time to sing about money.

The structure of **La Tendre Ennemie** (1936) is almost top-heavy for its hour's running time, and André-Paul Antoine's play, 'L'Ennemie', has been softened by taking some of the blame from Man's

In *Sans Lendemain*, Edwige Feuillère hires a house to impress a nice Canadian doctor so that he will agree to bring up her son. In this shot, however, she is returning to her real home. The novelletish plot is lifted by the admirable performance of Mme Feuillère and by Max Ophuls' direction – and in fact this is one of the most memorable of his tragic romances.

natural enemy, Woman, and placing it on fate. There are vestiges of Ophuls's talent for regarding society, but **Yoshiwara** (1937) demonstrates that other aspect of it, the lushly romantic. It is adapted from a popular novel by Maurice Dekobra and concerns a Russian officer (Pierre-Richard Willm), a high-born geisha (Michiko Tanaka) and the coolie (Sessue Hayakawa) who loves her madly. No better and no worse than other French romances of the time, with its uniformed men and helpless ladies, treachery and death, it at least marks a new assurance in Ophuls's work.

He later considered that he had betrayed his revered Goethe (a copy of 'Faust' was by his bedside when he died) in **Werther** (1938), which he and Wilhelm adapted for the producer Nebenzal. It is not a satisfying film since the story has been much prettified, but it is the first time, even including *Liebelei*, that all his particular qualities reach maturity – his intellect, his decorative flair and his instinct for irony and romance. Goethe's autobiographical tale concerned a young man, Werther (here, Willm) who falls in love with the fiancée, Charlotte (Annie Verney) of his best friend, Albert. When she learns of this she is both flattered and angry, and when both

Werther and she realise that they cannot change he, after taking to drink, commits suicide. In the film he does not know of the engagement, and the character has been downgraded to a shuffling Dostoyevskian official. But as the film moves further from its source and the simplicities of the first half it becomes a stronger emotional drama than most films of the time. Charlotte becomes a victim of fate, not destined for real happiness, and when the betrayed Albert confronts Werther with the dossier of his dissipation both men are almost submerged by the experience. As the moral issues grow so M. Willm gets increasingly lost, except for a brilliant moment when Werther's poetry is mocked in a brothel. There is also one quite remarkable sequence of a musical evening which in its visual handling and understanding of the past is as unspectacularly satisfying as anything in the history of cinema.

Sans Lendemain, released in the spring of 1940, must have struck a chord with French audiences, for it tells of a Woman with a Past – one who, like France, had not managed her affairs too well and thus might be said to have seen better days. She is a faded stripper who works in a Montmartre nightclub in order to bring up her son;

when an old lover (Georges Rigaud) reappears she puts herself in hock to a gang-boss for an assumed existence, and the latter sees her actions as a conscious move towards his empire of prostitution. It is more novelettish than Ophuls's films either side of it, but he is more at ease than in either, both with the sleazy settings and the chief protagonist. As played by Edwige Feuillère, who never before or again came so close to a Garboesque evocation of a doomed lady sick with love, she is one of his most affecting heroines. The film was not shown in London till 1948 (it was not released at all in the U.S.), by which time it seemed old-fashioned; we may now see it as we see *Le Jour se Lève,* where no reality impinges on the false reality which is its romantic essence.

The success of Litvak's earlier film provided the *raison d'être* for **De Mayerling à Sarajevo,** which despite its title limits its subject to a portrait of the morganatic marriage between the Archduke Franz Ferdinand (John Lodge) and the Countess Sophie Chotek (Feuillère). That an heir to the throne insisted against all odds on marrying the woman of his choice still had a certain topicality when this film went into production – but filming was postponed owing to events more pressing, and the film was finally premiered the day the Germans invaded Belgium and Luxembourg. A foreword disclaims factual accuracy, but the treatment of the romance is intelligent, even if, as is customary in such ventures, the writers – who include Carl Zuckmayer and Curt Alexander – adopt the ironic approach. 'What a pretty name!' declare the children on hearing that their parents are visiting Sarajevo, whose citizens in their loyal address express the hope that the royal visitors will find the day memorable. If the direction shows a weakness for the chandeliers of throne rooms and the drapes of boudoirs, it also manages sympathy for the humans beneath the braid – notably in Sophie's encounter after fifteen years with the emperor's head of protocol, when he assures her that he would not let pass this first chance to do her a favour, and in her first meeting with the archduke's mother who was well-practised in coping with royal amours. In this role Gabrielle Dorziat steals the film. Lodge makes less of the archduke, but he is pleasant enough, if not much like the real Franz Ferdinand.

The film opened in Paris in May 1940, six weeks before that city fell to the Germans, and clearly it was to audiences then only of limited interest. Louis Jouvet helped Ophuls after he had escaped to Switzerland, where Jouvet was acting after the fall of France, and they began to make a film of *L'Ecole des Femmes,* in which Jouvet was appearing on the stage. But there were romantic complications – both were in love with the same lady – and Ophuls left for the U.S. where he later resumed his career. Later still he returned to France to make another group of films, work that would make him world famous. Few of those made at this time were seen outside France, but they contribute to an astonishingly rich body of work.

Marcel l'Herbier had become a specialist in historical reconstruction, and his films of this time are as solid and satisfying as the sets for them designed by Eugène Lourié, who also worked with Ophuls, and the veteran Andreyev. **Nuits de Feu** (1937) is the first of three films set in Russia, an adaptation of Tolstoi's play, 'The Living Corpse', about the state prosecutor (Victor Francen) who stages his own murder when he learns that his wife (Gaby Morlay) has fallen in love with a younger colleague (Georges Rigaud). The wife loves both men but differently, and though the theme is therefore that of Shaw's 'Candida' this is merely a thumping melodrama of suspicion, injustice and revenge. **La Citadelle du Silence** (1937) concerns the daughter (Annabella) of a revolutionary who marries a prison governor (Pierre Renoir) in order to free her lover (Bernard Lancret); **La Tragédie Impériale** (1938) is a version of the fall of the Romanovs, concentrating on Rasputin (Harry Baur) and a young couple (Willm, Carine Nelson) who are the first to disdain him.

The French taste for royal romance at this time occasioned a remake of **Le Joueur d'Echecs** (1938), moving further back in Russian history to the Court of Catherine the Great (Françoise Rosay), whose patronage of the robot-making Austrian baron (Conrad Veidt) leads to mayhem; Jean Dréville directed. Raymond Bernard, who had made the 1928 version, remade a scrupulous **Les Misérables** (1933), its five hours originally shown in three separate parts. Charles Vanel brings few histrionics to his steely Javert, and the drive needed by

Jean-Louis Barrault and Viviane Romance in Jeff Musso's *Le Puritain*, which, if not as good as was thought at the time, does not deserve the semi-oblivion into which it has fallen. This seems to be the fate of films made by directors who were not prolific or who did not distinguish themselves in any other way. Musso himself made only two other films apart from this one, which is supposedly set in Dublin.

this long event is provided by M. Baur as Valjean. Baur is also the incomparable Porfiry of **Crime et Châtiment** (1935), relaxed and good-humoured, but of terrible determination. Pierre Chenil directed, drawing from Pierre Blanchar his best screen work as Raskolnikov.

These literary, historical films, made by directors equally adept at thrillers and action tales, were the commercial cornerstones of the French cinema, despite or because of their underlying pessimism. Their directors are skilful, experienced craftsmen, often veterans. Among their successors is Jean Delannoy (b. 1908), whose **Macao, l'Enfer du Jeu** (1939) is a superb example of the genre film. The basic material – from another 'exotic' novel by Maurice Dekobra – is the usual nonsense about *femmes fatales* and gunrunners, but whereas Pabst despised *Le Drame de Shanghai,* Delannoy clearly enjoys every second. The plot, which has more twists than a bedspring, involves a large cast of characters, including a stranded showgirl (Mireille Balin), a German adventurer (Erich Von Stroheim), a French journalist (Roland Toutain) and the Chinese owner (Sessue Hayakawa) of a luxurious gambling den. Marc Allégret (b. 1900), after

Fanny had specialised in farces and then melodramas, of which **Entrée des Artistes** (1938) is a good example: involved in a murder at drama school are two of the students (Odette Joyeux, Claude Dauphin), a journalist (Carette) and the professor (Jouvet).

Christian-Jaque (b. 1904) at this time seemed headed towards an interesting career; after assisting Duvivier and Guitry (uncredited, he directed most of *Les Perles de la Couronne*), he scored an international success with **Les Disparus de Saint-Agil** (1938), brilliantly invoking the enclosed, somewhat unhealthy world of the boarding school. This is not, however, a French, male version of *Mädchen in Uniform,* but a straightforward mystery, involving a drunken art master (Michel Simon) and a cordially-disliked foreign teacher (Von Stroheim): unfortunately, the plot is foolishly resolved – a fault so common that most ordinary Hollywood thrillers revive better than their more 'atmospheric' European counterparts.

The Dublin of Jeff Musso's **Le Puritain** (1937) is so Parisian as to be disconcerting: the source is a novel by Liam O'Flaherty which begins as a crime story and moves into (not very profound) psychology. A

379

religious fanatic and journalist (Jean-Louis Barrault) is in the habit of knifing prostitutes and then demanding that his paper indict society. He arouses the suspicion of the police inspector (Pierre Fresnay) while attempting to test his virtue with a whore (Viviane Romance). That he is motivated by suppressed lust seemed daring at the time, and was one reason the film was admired; this was the first feature made by Musso, who had come to films by way of writing music, and the only one of the three he made which was successful.

Far from such fictional gloom is **L'Espoir,** the one film made by André Malraux (1901–76), the novelist, historian and essayist. He began it in 1937, adapting it from his book of the same name, which details his experiences in Spain with the International Brigade. It was backed by Corniglion-Molinier, who had helped to form the air squadron attached to the Brigade. Unfinished and apparently unsatisfactory at the outbreak of war, the film was hidden away by one of the Paris staff of Pathé. When finally shown it was a failure: after the Liberation the public was in no mood for a feature-length documentary, especially one on other people's troubles. But though it is awkward, with an air of improvisation and an amateur structure, it is not only worth more than most movies on war but is an important film in its own right – not because it is anti-fascist but because its makers thought it was, as vitally certain of their cause as the great Russian Silent film-makers were of theirs. Here too amateurs play all the roles; there is no one hero with whom to identify, but a group of them; and the narrative follows no precise line but is a pattern of struggles, with newsreel footage of the Civil War intelligently blended with the material shot in Teruel. Like the film *For Whom the Bell Tolls* (q.v.), it is about the blowing up of a bridge. Dynamiting is difficult, since a machine-gun post guards the route, and bombing is no easier, as there is a fascist air base between the target and the Loyalists, who have only two slow, ancient bombers. When one plane crashes the wounded and dead are brought down from the mountains, to be joined by a trickle of sympathisers which becomes a crowd and then a multitude: it is a moving sequence precisely because up till then the film had regarded its subject with the nonchalance

associated with its heroes.

While Malraux was working on this film the French cinema was being praised for one of the few significant movies on war, *La Grande Illusion* (q.v.), which was Jean Renoir's, only great success of the decade. His work is uneven, but his films of the Thirties can now be seen as the most impressive, in sum, of any of his contemporaries. After the financial failure of *La Chienne*, he chose as more commercial **La Nuit de Carrefour** (1932), the first of Simenon's novels to be filmed. Commenting on it, Jean-Luc Godard calls it Renoir's most mysterious film, but then spoils his point by observing that Simenon has affinities with Balzac and Dostoyevsky. So he has, but this mild, tinny Maigret thriller cannot sustain such cultural respectability. However, on its way to a dénouement concerning a hoard of cocaine and some stolen jewellery there are agreeable accompaniments: the desolate crossroads and the misty country byways; the incongruity of the doctor, in white tie and tails, tending a wounded man in an oily service station; a heroine with fondness for an old Italian tune and a gauche eroticism; and Maigret (Pierre Renoir) himself, with his little black moustache and dejected countenance. The director financed the film from his own resources, and though it was released with some reels missing (lost, apparently, by Jean Mitry, who acts in the film and was later a critic) this did not prevent its being mildly successful.

Boudu Sauvé des Eaux (1932) is not a mile away from Balzac. Boudu (Michel Simon) is crossing the Pont des Beaux-Arts when he is spotted by an antiquarian bookseller, M. Lestingois (Charles Granval), who sees in him, as he says, a very successful *clochard*. He rescues him from drowning and gives him a home, which Boudu accepts with reluctance and regards with contempt, till, weeks later, his anarchic habits have brought Madame to a state of hysteria and Monsieur – who is having an affair with the maid – to sexual frustration. Madame, however, fancies Boudu, who reasons that if Monsieur can avail himself of both ladies so can he. The source material, a boulevard comedy by René Fauchois, saves the situation with a lottery ticket and a marriage, but Renoir returns to the Seine, into which Boudu throws his new bowler hat, symbol of the middle class. The film finishes with one long, last pan of the river, not at this point particularly attractive, but restful. Boudu's choice may be admirable, but is he, a man who boasts of never having said thank you to anyone, better than his benefactor, a purely disinterested philanthropist? The film's ambivalence disconcerted contemporary audiences, few of which would have preferred penniless arcadia to a comfortable bourgeoisie. It was not seen abroad publicly till the Sixties, when it became one of Renoir's most popular films. It is nice, incidentally, to learn towards the end, at his wedding, that this cuckoo in the nest is called Priapus. Priapus Boudu.

Chotard et Cie (1933) had been a stage success and its author, Roger Ferdinand, invited Renoir to film it, working with him on the screenplay. Charpin repeats his stage role as Chotard, a Marseilles grocer, whose daughter (Jeanne Boitel) dithers between two suitors, a pompous gendarme (Louis Seigner) and a dreamy poet (Georges Pomiès), who proves a disaster as a shop clerk. Renoir ruins his chance to say something about the nature of the artist and his calling by encouraging Pomiès to give the same balletic performance he gave in *Tire-au-Flanc*. This film is hardly funnier than that, but since Renoir proves – again – adept at small town satire, he may be said to be partly successful in his aim, which was to make a comedy in the American style.

Increasingly convinced that adaptations could become good cinema, he envisaged **Madame Bovary** (1934) as 'filmed theatre' – and that was what the public wanted. But in Renoir's own terms it meant a series of dialogues in long takes, allowing the performers and the material to rise to the dramatic heights of which both were capable. The screenplay he wrote from the book is exemplary, but he fails to convey the stultitude of provincial life. Nor is he helped by his Emma, Valentine Tessier, unable or unwilling to portray any taste for fantasy or hatred of her environment. With so much of the central character missing, the piece could not totally succeed, but it is good on Emma's affair with Rodolphe and her eagerness to begin a second liaison, and it has a small triumph with its Bovary, a lost, lorn, loving man as played by the director's brother, Pierre. The original ran over three hours, but was cut by the distributor to just over a 100 minutes.

A foreword to **Toni** (1935) explains that all races meet in this particular part of the Mediterranean, and it was Pagnol who enabled Renoir to make the film, at his own studio in Nice and on nearby locations. Carl Einstein helped Renoir with the scenario, based on material supplied by a friend of Renoir's who had been police commissioner at Martigues. Toni (Charles Blavette), an Italian immigrant worker, falls in love with Josefa (Céla Montalvan), who is Spanish; they are forced to marry others, but neither marriage is happy, and Toni is drawn into the affairs of Josefa, her drunken bully of a husband, and her cousin-lover Albert. These people – fortunately, given the ending – live and breathe; they follow the creed that the world is divided into the haves and have-nots, a creed which in Renoir's best work is expressed in terms of weakness versus personal dominance (as opposed to wealth and influence). He takes us gently into this rural corner of the world and he illuminates it.

Murder in the artisan class is also the subject of **Le Crime de Monsieur Lange** (1936), and it is committed when M. Batala (Jules Berry) returns to claim the publishing house which he had left in debt. In the meantime a workers' co-operative had made it profitable, and M. Lange (René Lefèvre), believing Batala dead, decides to keep it that way. His surname is a play on *l'ange,* and he looks angelic – meek, a dreamer, vague: the only positive actions he makes are to shoot Batala and to follow a buxom prostitute who accosts him when his girl has run off – both actions of which the director clearly approves. Renoir has returned to the mocking style of *Boudu,* but has become more confident in indicating his affection – for the magazine workers, their neighbours in the laundry and even for his villain, but that may be because Berry was one of the most relishable bad men in the business.

La Partie de Campagne celebrates love, youth, beauty, tranquillity and the countryside. Henriette (Sylvia Bataille) feels, she tells her mother (Jane Marken), an *espèce de tendresse* for the trees, the sky, the fields. She and her mother are gay, lively, attractive, while their men are dullards, imperceptive and, in the case of M. Dufour, gross. The canoeists who offer to entertain them while their men are fishing clearly deserve them as much as the ladies in turn

Jean Renoir is now regarded as a great director, yet
during the Thirties his international reputation was
established by only two films, *La Grande Illusion*,
ABOVE with Erich Von Stroheim to the right of the
staircase, and *La Bête Humaine*, ABOVE RIGHT, with
Simone Simon and Jean Gabin. Most of his other
films were not seen outside France, while *Partie de
Campagne*, RIGHT, with Jean Marken and Georges
Saint-Saëns, was left unfinished, and *La Règle du Jeu*
FAR RIGHT, with Roland Toutain and Renoir himself,
was cut to ribbons after a disastrous Paris showing.
When the remains of the one were assembled and the
complete version of the other finally restored, both
were seen to be among his greatest works.

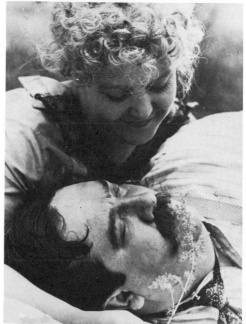

382

deserve them. But as this world goes, it cannot last. The film seems beyond analysis, or rather, should be: if not Renoir's masterpiece, it is surely flawless. It is also unfinished. Renoir wrote this adaptation of de Maupassant in 1936, and filmed it in the summer of that year, on the banks of the Loing, near Montigny – but rainy weather held up shooting till the date he was contracted to start his next film. Renoir always claimed that the piece was complete, that he had always intended to make only a 50-minute film, which was all the material could stand: but it lasts only thirty-seven minutes and has two long titles to explain points essential to the narrative. On the other hand, the producer, Pierre Braunberger, is supposed to have asked Prévert to write a full-length script featuring Renoir's material – but by the time he was ready the cast had grown too old to use. It seems unlikely that Braunberger would have backed so short a film, and one so difficult to market: at all events, it was not publicly shown. It was destroyed by the Germans during the war, but Henri Langlois of the Cinémathèque Française had saved a copy of the uncut negative. This was reshaped by Marguerite Renoir and Pierre Lestringuez and shown in Paris in 1946 as one section of a three-part film – as it was in New York, in 1950; London first saw it, without its other two parts, in 1948.

The project for which Renoir had abandoned it was **Les Bas-Fonds** (1936), based on the play by Gorki. He persuaded Charles Spaak to work on the screenplay with him, and if they have a stronger narrative than the original they do not depart too seriously from its characters: the thief (Gabin); the baron (Jouvet), embezzler and gambler; the alcoholic actor (Robert Le Vigan); the mistress (Suzy Prim) of the dosshouse; her cruel and feeble-minded older husband (Vladimir Sokoloff); her sister (Junie Astor); and the whore (Jany Holt). They do not seem Russian, and when the film was shown in London for the first time Dilys Powell in *The Sunday Times* compared it unfavourably with Donskoi's Gorki trilogy: 'theatrical, almost flimsy, a superficial comment from a different society'. Certainly life in these particular lower depths is not degrading or particularly harsh, and there is hope and understanding: when the whore lies about her past, lifting incidents from a book she has just finished

reading, the baron observes, 'It is not what she says, but why she says it.' Renoir himself described the film as a realistic poem on the loss of human dignity.

He had made it when thwarted in his wish to film *La Belle Equipe,* whose screenplay he had loved, and it should be noted that he had been drawn to *Le Crime de Monsieur Lange* because of the co-operative idea it expressed. His sympathy for the less affluent classes had not gone unnoticed by the French Communist party, which invited him to direct **La Vie est à Nous** (1936). Later, living in America, he explained his ('delighted') acceptance as an attempt to combat Nazism, but at the time, under the Popular Front, his action needed no excuses. His collaborators included Jacques Becker, Jean-Paul Le Chanois and Henri Cartier-Bresson, working under his supervision, and his own responsibility did not extend to the editing, which is significant, for the finished film is largely a compilation of newsreel material. It starts with a teacher (Jean Dasté) giving schoolchildren an impressive series of statistics on France, and then moves back to offer a history of working people in the matter of strikes, protest marches and poverty. The villains are picked out – the French fascists, stirring up trouble; the equivalent of the Hitler Youth louts, attacking a vendor of the newspaper *L'Humanité.* The answer to these and other evils turns out to be the Communist party, seen labouring on behalf of the workers in three episodes, each purportedly selected from the letters of three grateful members. A modern foreword to the film claims that it was a tremendous success, which is not suprising, since its showings were private and restricted to dedicated Communists. Its view of the party is the usual one of the great provider, but it also manages to imply that the party had failed to come up with an operative system. However, the criticism is so slight that it would not have redeemed the picture for the Nazis, who were said to have destroyed it: it survived, and was first publicly seen in Paris in 1969.

La Grande Illusion (1937), written with Spaak, was based loosely on Renoir's experiences in the War. Its setting is a P.O.W. camp, and its central characters are two officers, De Boeldieu (Pierre Fresnay), from a military family, and Maréchal (Gabin), who has risen from the ranks;

indeed, the only other officer of De Boeldieu's own class is the German commandant (Erich Von Stroheim). Class, however, is less the subject of the film than the distinctions made by temperament and tradition, as expounded in the commandant's admission of singular trust in De Boeldieu. 'For the people it's a bad thing to die in a war,' he says. 'For you and me it's a good solution.' The great illusion is that men must hate each other in war. The film's pacifism was immediately admired but not completely understood, for it was claimed that Renoir intended a plea for France and Germany not to go to war, whereas, by making one of the characters (Dalio) a wealthy and sympathetic Jew, he ensured that it would not be shown in Germany. In France it was the year's most popular film, and after running an unprecedented six months in New York it was voted the Best Foreign Film by the critics of that city. Till then, although Renoir had been respected within the industry, filmgoers, if they thought of him at all, would probably have connected him only with *Le Crime de Monsieur Lange* and *Les Bas-Fonds,* the only films of his for which they had shown any great fondness.

If, by Renoir's own confession, he longed for recognition, he could hardly have hoped to find it with **La Marseillaise** (1938), subtitled *Quelques Faits Divers sur la Chute de la Monarchie.* Made as a co-operative venture under the influence of the Popular Front, it attempted to find parallels with a return to reason in government. The aristocracy is beastly, and the workers, as Renoir himself put it, 'very simple, good-hearted people', but both are treated simplistically – the one by quibbling over dance steps or similar fripperies, and the other with cosiness. In modelling the film on *October* and *The End of St Petersburg,* Renoir saw fit to add levity; his hesitancy may have been due to the divergence of his own opinions and the more truly demotic experience of his collaborators, but certainly the end result is an inadequate response to the most momentous event in his country's history.

Renoir's second great success came with another collaboration with Spaak, **La Bête Humaine** (1938). He chose Zola's novel as being 'commercial', and perhaps hoped to emulate the pessimism so much admired in many of his confrères. However, the film remains somewhat below the level of *Quai des Brumes,* despite the expectation aroused by a foreword to explain the mental condition of Lantier (Gabin). That character is no longer, as in Zola, a passive victim of fate, and with all passions brought to the surface little is left beneath. Nevertheless Lantier's involvement with the minx Sévèrine (Simone Simon) and her older, jealous, scheming husband (Fernand Ledoux), makes for melodrama as gripping as that of the not dissimilar *La Chienne.* But the film's main strength lies in its setting, the Paris–Le Havre railway line. Renoir's realism is less poetic than Carné's, but equally memorable: the cheerless little station, the hut by the railway line where the mackintoshed lovers consummate their *amour maudit,* and the workers' dance with its haunting song, 'Le Petit Coeur de Ninon'.

La Règle du Jeu (1939) was described by Renoir as only a divertissement, and it could be somewhat autobiographical – since he plays Octave, kindly and muddled, and the character may be based on himself. Octave is one of a number of people, rich and pampered, at a house party which may be the last for all of them. Their adventures are prefaced with a quotation from Beaumarchais, to music by Mozart – actually and appropriately from 'The Marriage of Figaro'. Like that, this is a gavotte for servants and masters; it is also a masterpiece. The party is given by the marquis (Marcel Dalio), a Jew, whose wife Christiane (Nora Gregor) is Viennese, and it is perhaps because of their backgrounds that they are lightly patronised by their guests, who include the marquis's mistress, Geneviève (Mila Parély), and a famous aviator, André Jurieu (Roland Toutain), nourishing a hardly secret passion for his hostess. During the weekend, on the evening of masquerade (i.e. fancy dress), he will ask her to runaway with him, and will brawl with another suitor. Below stairs, the new servant, an ex-poacher, Marceau (Julien Carette), has fallen for the wife, Lisette (Paulette Dubost), of the gamekeeper Schumacher (Gaston Modot). He flirts, she returns his interest; and Schumacher storms through the house with a gun. Above stairs, the game is played to different precepts. It is Octave, the onlooker, who points out to André and then to Christine the rules of high society. This is a society which has codes of

One reason many people treasure the French films of the Thirties is that they contain a number of memorable performances, and of the six players on this page the adjective 'great' can safely be applied to at least three, if not all, of them. The lady is Françoise Rosay, in *Le Grand Jeu*, and the actors are, CLOCKWISE from Mme Rosay: Louis Jouvet in *Hôtel du Nord*, Harry Baur in *Crime et Châtiment*, Pierre Renoir in *Pièges*, Michel Simon in *Drôle de Drame* and Raimu in *Le Femme du Boulanger*.

behaviour but no principles: they are not vicious people, or unkind, but they are unthinking. So absorbed are they in themselves that they hardly notice Schumacher and his gun – although when the marquis apologises for the behaviour of his servants the fat lady replies, 'The poor have a right to be happy too.' The action below stairs is considerably less decorous, because its denizens do not know the chief rule of the game, which is to lie. When Christine discovers that Geneviève was her husband's mistress before her marriage, she objects to living a lie: but, Octave points out, everyone lies – government, newspapers, the radio, even the cinema. And at the end, after Schumacher has shot André – because Christine has borrowed Lisette's cloak and he mistakes them – that becomes a lie, despite the victim's eminence: a victim of fate, shot by Schumacher in mistake for a poacher. Society – this society – shrugs, and moves on to the next game.

The film had no success with spectators accustomed to the literal interpretation of all dialogue and action, but some were sharp enough to recognise its anti-fascism. Showings on the Champs-Elysées were interrupted by right-wing rioters, and the distributor, alarmed, made cuts before withdrawing it completely a few days later. The censor banned it when war broke out; the Germans ordered it destroyed. For years only hacked-about copies were in circulation, and it was in an abbreviated form that the film found its way to New York in 1950 and to London a year later. F. Maurice Speed commemorated it in his 'Film Review': 'Rather jerky little French film about a house party at which the guests behave with cruelty and complete lack of morals. All rather confusing and silly.' Such was the general reaction. It was not till the late 50s that the complete version, some of it miraculously rediscovered, was painstakingly reassembled.

The film imposes itself not because of what it says, which is unexceptional, nor because of its quasi-literary style, but because it is, withal, a personal statement in a medium which up to that time had offered very few; it has the wit, wisdom and love of humanity which inform all of this director's best work. Renoir was more richly endowed with these qualities than his contemporaries, and this film can be seen as the culmination of a remarkable period in French cinema. Technically French films had become the equal of those of Hollywood; and in the matter of maturity – of approach and subject – they surpassed any other national cinema except perhaps Japan.

This was due not to executive encouragement, except in the case of a few imaginative producers, but to an assembly of creative individuals quite as extraordinary as that working in Germany during the Silent period. There were great screenwriters, Spaak and Prévert; great art directors, Meerson, Trauner, Lourié; and great actors, Jouvet, Baur, Raimu, Pierre Renoir and Françoise Rosay. If we have an idea how much the Prévert-Carné films owe to the writer it is also clear that the Spaak scripts usually became the best work of their respective directors. Perhaps, in the end, the films said very little that is positive, always excepting the man's love of life and friends and women, as exemplified in Renoir and Pagnol; we do not doubt the cynicism of Ophuls and Guitry, so perhaps we should not doubt the pessimism that distinguishes almost every other French film-maker of this era. That is a reflection of France herself, or so we like to think, after the collapse of the Popular Front; that this pessimism was often achieved by the creation of 'atmospheric' romances and melodramas is immaterial. With or without hindsight this period of French cinema remains, as a cinema-going experience, extraordinarily potent.

17

Hollywood's Golden Age:
R.K.O., Paramount and 20th Century-Fox

THE AMERICAN movies of the late Thirties remain, by and large, vastly entertaining – expertly-wrought artefacts reflecting the confidence of the industry which produced them. Darryl F. Zanuck spoke for all the moguls when he told Henry King, his leading director, 'Henry, we have three thousand four hundred at this studio. It's my responsibility for those people to know that they have a job and it's permanent. So that's where you and I come in; we share the responsibility to give audiences substantial entertainments. We're not going to give them a lot of doctrines. We're making pictures to keep the theatres open and not to sell a lot of patent medicine.'

The convulsions which had shaken the industry at the beginning of the decade soon seemed as distant as the flickering Silents, now regarded by the trade press as items for mockery or, at best, as quaintly nostalgic. With the exception of Chaplin, all the great names of that era had been forced into retirement, belonging as much to the past as Tiffany lamps and bootleg gin; admittedly Garbo and Ronald Colman found even greater popularity in Talkies, but most of the Silent stars who elected to go on working were reduced to accepting bit roles. After the influx of stage stars and well-known stage players came a new generation of movie stars. Thus Norma Shearer and Gary Cooper had been featured above the title in the Silent era, but it was in Talkies that they became beloved; Myrna Loy, Jean Arthur, Carole Lombard and William Powell had played only supporting roles in Silents; Clark Gable, James Cagney, Spencer Tracy, Bette Davis, Katharine Hepburn, Humphrey Bogart, James

Stewart, Margaret Sullavan and Henry Fonda all came from the stage, but they were hardly names to conjure with till they appeared in movies; while from vaudeville or radio came such stars as Bing Crosby, Bob Hope, Judy Garland and Alice Faye. The studios were geared to turning out star vehicles and were interested in virtually no other sort of film. Each studio had its stable of stars, with one producer assigned to any handful: he selected the properties that would best exploit their talents and chose the writers to assemble the script. The public might not know the names of the producers, but the stockholders certainly did.

The new studio, 20th Century-Fox, counted itself fortunate indeed in acquiring Shirley Temple; Universal would almost certainly have gone out of business had it not been for Deanna Durbin; while Warner Bros. told Bette Davis that the profits from her films enabled them to build a third sound stage. Such attractions were the strongest card in the industry's battle against the rival menacing its prosperity – the radio networks. R.K.O. Radio was financially linked with N.B.C., and Paramount, in response to such heavy new investment at the start of the Talkie era, had put money into N.B.C.'S young rival, C.B.S. That percentage of the population not inside the movie houses was almost certainly tuned into the wireless, and just as the movie studios had raided Broadway so they began to poach from the radio stations. It could not, however, be said that they were either displeased or disconcerted when many radio stars – Fibber McGee and Molly, Amos n' Andy, Kate Smith among them – flopped on the screen. As late as 1938 Paramount was exhorting exhibitors, especially those in small towns, to book its films because it had stars like Bing Crosby, Bob Hope and Jack Benny, who were 'radio personalities'. And Hollywood used radio in reverse, its stars ostensibly 'guesting' in variety shows while in fact promoting their current vehicle. Until 1938 when Orson Welles (q.v.) was invited to do radio drama for C.B.S. virtually the only serious plays on American radio were recreations of movies on the 'Lux Radio Hour', with the original stars or others of like renown.

Fan magazines detailed every aspect of the stars' lives, real and imaginary, and they sold by the million. The only discordant noises came from exhibitors, who sent in contributions to the *Motion Picture Herald*'s grouse corner, 'What This Picture Did for Me', and, of course from critics – like the writer in *The New York Times* whose praise for one particular film, *The Great Waltz* (q.v.), did not preclude it from being 'a bit of a bore' – it being understood, he went on, that M-G-M 'makes the most beautiful bores in the world'. The public did not agree, keeping track of the most highly-touted films till their long-awaited local arrival. Seldom were they disappointed, and withal critics were impressed with almost as much frequency. For instance, in 1937 distributors were encouraged to road-show a total of nine films in New York (i.e. at advanced prices, running from three to fifteen weeks instead of the usual one week), and the majority of these are good on their own terms.★ Favourable notices, though welcome, were of little value beside the industry's own estimation; and as poor notices seldom kept spectators from the box-office, who needed critics? Critics in the metropolitan areas wilfully encouraged the highbrows to patronise the latest European movie – though since the end of the Silent era that was less than ever a commercial threat. Hollywood no longer aped the continental film, though it did purchase remake rights to a few. Apart from waning stars and the difficulty of finding the right vehicles for popular ones the only problem for producers was

★*The Good Earth, Lost Horizon, Captains Courageous, The Life of Emile Zola, The Hurricane, The Firefly, Souls at Sea, The Road Back* and *High, Wide and Handsome.*

whether the additional cost of Technicolor was justified.

The improvement in the Technicolor system was unquestionably the most important technical advance of the decade, but was regarded with almost total indifference by most people in the industry; and only cursory consideration, if that, would have been given to using it for the nine films listed in the footnote. Nowadays, because almost all of the films of the period were in black and white, television networks prefer to air them, if at all, at off-peak times, thus banishing a whole generation of exceptional talents – players, writers, directors, designers and cameramen.

If the over-riding flaw of the films of this period is lack of realism, we may yet admire the simulation of Paris or Venice on the studio lot; William Wyler said that it never occurred to anyone involved with *Dodsworth* (q.v.) to film the European sequences *in situ*. The only contemporary subjects were taken from novels or plays already successful, and reconstructions of the past were as far as Hollywood was prepared to go towards what was often its declared aim, to 'elevate' the medium and educate audiences. Forgotten along with the Silents were the sex stories of the pre-Code era and the modestly-budgeted conversation pieces (and it had always been clear which conversations were most worth catching), to be replaced by films of the utmost respectability. Hollywood, which had once offended the nation's morals, was now its spokesman on such matters. Banished from movies was a vast spectrum of American life – factories, drinking-dens, the poor: in movies, immigration was no longer a factor, and not to be mentioned were the ethnic origins of any of the characters. Faced with the gentle realities of suburban or rural life, they had all been American for generations; and indeed the only part of the American past to be mentioned – bar a trip or so to the Barbary Coast – was the time of the pioneers. As the decade reached its halfway point Hollywood again could afford to finance the pioneer tales and historical epics which had been the surest crowd-pullers in the Silent days.

So although the pre-Code films tell us much about American life at the time, those that followed were set in some sort of idealised land, of lawns and mansions, of spacious and clean tenements – a land where stenographers had a change of attire for every scene, and very often a maid as well. Racial tension, like sex, was virtually non-existent, and after an era of unemployment, near-starvation, large-scale crime and civic corruption the palliatives served up were welcome to a population trying to regain an even keel. The American films of the late Thirties tell us little beyond what audiences liked, or were thought to like. The U.S. recovered, but the rest of the world darkened. Europe rearmed, while the U.S. remained in isolation; but even in Europe cares were momentarily stilled as audiences watched Mickey Mouse and Garbo and Fred and Ginger. Entertaining audiences was what the studios understood, and as one examines the films they made one can see how seldom they deviated from the star vehicle. And what stars they were! They captivated audiences then, and they have captured the imagination since. Of all the stars who have emerged since the War, perhaps less than a dozen have left any lasting impression. Their films have become more realistic, as they were bound to do, but I doubt whether posterity will regard them as fondly as those of the Thirties.

R.K.O. was the studio responsible for the immortal musicals which Fred Astaire made with Ginger Rogers. Astaire (b. 1899) had been a Broadway star; Miss Rogers (b. 1911) had come from Broadway to play second leads in pictures. R.K.O. put them both into **Flying Down to Rio** (1933), directed by Thornton Freeland, planning to bolster a star who was not shining as brightly as the studio had once hoped, Dolores del Rio: they were merely accessories – he a buddy of the male lead, Gene Raymond, and she a brassy-tongued band singer. But they had one speciality dance together, 'The Carioca', and on the strength of rave notices for that they were teamed in **The Gay Divorcee** (1934), adapted from Astaire's most recent New York and London success. There were misgivings about his looks, not deemed to be sufficiently romantic, but it was hoped to duplicate his stage popularity in films. In the case of

Rogers, it was *faute de mieux*: she could sing and dance, if in neither case with his style, and had an aptitude for the sassy dialogue required of such pieces. This one, concerning marital misunderstanding, was typical stage fare, and remained such as directed by Mark Sandrich (1900–45), a former gag-man who would go on to handle half the Astaire-Rogers films. The Cole Porter score was jettisoned, with the exception of 'Night and Day', but one of the new numbers, 'The Continental', won the newly-designated Oscar for Best Song. Also from the play came Eric Blore and Erik Rhodes, respectively as a leering waiter and effeminate professional co-respondent, to be joined as comic relief by Edward Everett Horton, dithering as Astaire's best pal, while Rogers's sidekick, Alice Brady, is an ageing lady 'on' to men. (These three actors would support Astaire in other films of the series, but Miss Brady's role would be reinterpreted by Helen Broderick or Luella Gear.) Despite vast sets with which Van Nest Polglase turned Brighton into a science fiction version of Palm Beach, the effect is intimate, and that became the keynote of the films that followed.

It was not intended as a series, but **Roberta** (1935), a starring vehicle for Irene Dunne, had two other roles of equal importance, a bandleader and a showgirl who poses as a Polish countess. Astaire and Rogers were cast, and Jerome Kern's score was rich enough to allow them some numbers, including 'I Won't Dance'. Randolph Scott is the American bandsman who helps Miss Dunne revive her Paris couturier-house – a matter handled by William A. Seiter more seriously than warranted, probably because the original had been a Broadway success, but Dunne and Astaire are individually so captivating that the twin romances sit easily together.

There would be, with one exception, no more dual love stories. Thereafter the films devoted themselves to Astaire wooing Rogers in flippant and debonair manner, her recalcitrance keeping him at elbow length till the last reel – except for the dances, proof to us and to him, if not to her, that they were meant for each other. These dances – among the supreme pleasures of the cinema – adhere to no formula, sometimes taking place on stage or on dance floor, but also in natural surroundings when arising directly from the plot. The stories and dialogue are weak, but the charm of the principals is such that we are restless only when the numbers are few and far between – as in **Top Hat** (1935), though when they appear they are superb: 'No Strings', which starts as a simple expression of high spirits; 'Isn't This a Lovely Day?', the greatest wooing dance in movies; the title song, with Astaire immaculate before a male chorus; and a balladic pas de deux, 'Cheek to Cheek'. Since at this stage the studio wished only to repeat the success of *The Gay Divorcee,* the plot is homogenised farce: Mark Sandrich directed, Irving Berlin wrote the score, and both did better with **Follow the Fleet** (1936) – Berlin if only because he contributed seven songs instead of five. Two of them are sung by Harriet Hilliard, as Ginger's sister, and we might like them and her more – not to mention Scott as Astaire's sailor buddy – if they did not keep us from the main couple.

Swing Time (1936) is the only occasion when Astaire and Rogers had a first-class director, George Stevens (1904–75), and it is the peak of their partnership. Both the settings and Miss Rogers's gowns have been simplified, so that she entirely complements Astaire instead of diverting attention from him, and it is the only film of the series with an elegance to match his own. We find him, dapper and white-tied, against a black marble floor, and as he finishes 'Never Gonna Dance' he and Rogers go into 'The Way You Look Tonight' and reprise 'The Waltz in Swingtime', changing styles and rhythms, offering more of their skills, and for longer, than in any other of their films – proving in this case that one cannot have too much of a good thing. Jerome Kern wrote the superlative score – only for Gershwin perhaps to surpass it in **Shall We Dance?** (1937), directed by Sandrich. In this case 'They All Laughed', 'They Can't Take That Away from Me', 'Let's Call the Whole Thing Off', and the rest divert attention from a particularly tedious plot about a musical comedy queen and a ballet dancer reported to be married. Miss Rogers had continued to make straight films, and for almost as long Astaire had fretted about being merely

half of a partnership. At first R.K.O. felt that the team was too great an asset to be disbanded, but finally they agreed to let him make a film without her, **A Damsel in Distress** (1937). The Gershwins wrote another superb score and Stevens again achieved visual elegance, for an inconsequential plot (from a novel by P. G. Wodehouse) about an American stage star hired as an under-footman to woo, for the sake of a bet, a British heiress (Joan Fontaine). It is admirably suited to Astaire's throwaway style of acting, the self-conscious charm of which is rescued by the modesty and uncertainty often evident in great performers (in his case betrayed by the nervous twist of his hand at an emotional moment or the pause at a sentimental phrase in a song); Fontaine dances only a few twirls, so that audiences could not make comparisons, and the comic team of Gracie Allen and George Burns were the billed co-stars. It is a film oddly neglected, for surely no one looks at Ginger when Fred is on screen.

Reunited in **Carefree** (1938), they managed to live up to the title despite the internal evidence of R.K.O.'s ever-faltering finances, the too infrequent dancing and a lumbering plot about a psychiatrist, Astaire, trying to cure the vacillating fiancée, Rogers, of Ralph Bellamy (who as usual loses the girl). Sandrich directed, and the Berlin score has two strong numbers: 'Change Partners' and 'I used to Be Color-blind'. For the first time no special score was commissioned for **The Story of Vernon and Irene Castle** (1939), which also differs from the others in being a show-business biography and having a sad ending, causing Frank S. Nugent to remark in *The New York Times* that the stars were so identified with light comedy that this was 'practically as disconcerting as it would be if Walt Disney were to throw Mickey Mouse to the lions'. The separation of the team, announced before the film appeared, further obscured its merits, which include a lively ragtime sequence and H. C. Potter's lighthearted direction. Astaire's contract was due to expire and he planned to freelance; but he told R.K.O. that if he returned to the studio it would not be for a resumption of the partnership.

That partnership had been largely responsible for the survival of the

The Screen's Great Dance Team

Roberta, RIGHT, followed *Flying Down to Rio* and then came *Top Hat,* ABOVE RIGHT, which, if not the best of the Astaire-Rogers musicals, is the most famous since the title immediately brings to mind Astaire's ever immaculate appearance. The invigorating dances culminate in 'The Piccolino' which a huge chorus repeats several times until the camera cuts to Fred and Ginger – first to their feet, till, drawn inexorably by the rhythm, they rise tip-tapping to the camera. They appeared next in *Follow the Fleet,* ABOVE, one of the best remembered of their efforts and which was succeeded by their best film together, *Swing Time,* FAR RIGHT.

company, at the peak of its popularity with *Top Hat* and *Follow the Fleet* bringing it into profit – $684,000 – for the first time since 1930. That was in 1935, when Floyd Odlum bought a half-share in the company, convinced that there could be further profits if there were more business sense at the top; with Sam Briskin in charge of production profits rose to almost $2 million two years later. However, the other co-owners, R.C.A. and Rockefeller Center Inc., did not care for the policy of B-pictures and a few quality films. In the search for more prestige, they brought in George Schaefer as president and Pandro S. Berman became head of production, encouraging major talents to come to R.K.O. – a policy that continued after Berman had left for M-G-M in 1940, with Joseph I. Breen in charge of production and Sol Lesser as executive producer.

Unfortunately R.K.O.'s finances seldom permitted the major talents to remain for long. There was only one important director under long-term contract, George Stevens, and he rose by merit from B-movies to some of Hollywood's most memorable entertainments. Other leading directors came and went, as was the case at Columbia – often seeking a temporary berth after disaffection at Paramount, M-G-M or 20th Century-Fox. A similar situation prevailed with the stars: of the chief R.K.O. stars only Astaire, Rogers and Katharine Hepburn were under exclusive contracts, while others, such as Irene Dunne, Cary Grant (b. 1904) and Barbara Stanwyck, were free to film elsewhere. These particular three were so much in demand that they did not need the protection of a long-term contract, but whereas at Columbia Harry Cohn avoided such binding terms from meanness, the R.K.O. management was in a constant state of insecurity, undoubtedly due to Odlum's indecisive leadership.

The studio publicity department explained the breaking-up of Astaire and Rogers as due to her desire to be known as a dramatic actress. As such, she was really only competent at playing working-class girls, even if in **Having Wonderful Time** (1938) she does not attempt a Bronx accent – but neither does Douglas Fairbanks Jr, in the role John Garfield had played on stage. Arthur Kober, adapting

his own play, was required for the film to eliminate the Jewishness of these working folk on vacation in the Catskills; but, as directed by Alfred Santell, it is still a more truthful account of working-class life than was customary. The **Fifth Avenue Girl** (1939) is Miss Rogers: it is a Cinderella story, but that role is assigned to Walter Connolly who, discovering that his family could not care less whether he is alive or dead, decides to pass off an out-of-work shopgirl as his 'companion'. The writer, Allen Scott, worked on some of the Astaire-Rogers musicals but none of his other credits suggest a film as interesting as this. The script is very funny but it is Gregory LaCava's direction which adds distinction: unlike the other tales of mad Park Avenue families, this one is aware that the rich *are* different; their lovable eccentricities are more kindly handled than the communist-spouting speeches of the chauffeur, but there is no doubt which side LaCava was on.

He and Scott approach the very different family of **Primrose Path** (1940) with appropriate wit – Pa (Miles Mander), one-time classics professor and now a hopeless drunk; Granny (Queenie Vassar), whose vicious tongue is directed at Pa; and Ma (Marjorie Rambeau), an easygoing woman whose Goodtime Charlies make up for Pa's shortcomings. The film does move towards fairy tale in the manner of such predecessors as *Man's Castle* (q.v.); but LaCava never loses sight of the quotation from Menander which prefaces the action, 'We live not as we wish to, but as we must.' His source was a play by Robert L. Buckner and Walter Hart, acted on Broadway by Betty Field, an actress of far more range than Miss Rogers, whose chief contribution is a new brunette hairstyle. She won an Oscar for **Kitty Foyle** (1940), but there is nothing in the film to explain why: she gets a vast number of close-ups, and is always pretty enough to justify them, but neither in performance nor accent does she suggest a girl from the wrong side of the tracks – which is what the film is supposed to be about. Since the flashbacks – just then a wildly popular device – give no indication of the period, which was the early Thirties, the film falls even flatter, and is not helped by Sam Wood's direction or the emasculation wrought by Dalton

Trumbo on Christopher Morley's novel.

As we have seen, R.K.O. was happiest fashioning vehicles for its female stars. If, to the studio, Miss Rogers (away from Astaire) was at one end of the social scale, Katharine Hepburn was at the other. In **Alice Adams** (1935) she is not best pleased that the Adams family is not well off. Alice is 'a pushing sort of person', as someone puts it, and when her mother says of her that she has been 'snubbed and picked upon by every girl in town', we can hardly blame them. There is no doubt that Hepburn understands Alice: she shows her as pretentious and artificial but she also brings out her fundamental loneliness and bravery; Fred MacMurray, as her wealthy suitor, is somewhat awed by her, which is not, even with Hepburn, the way one expects the rich to react to shabby gentility. The dinner party scene, with Alice desperately delving into French to divert attention from the slatternly maid (Hattie McDaniel) is so funny as to make Booth Tarkington's original (unhappy) ending unthinkable. Hepburn had been determined to film this book, but found no R.K.O. director interested except George Stevens, stuck till then with Wheeler and Woolsey comedies: by insisting that he direct, she started him on his fine career – and if here he indulges her a little we can hardly blame him.

It was George Cukor who suggested to her a film of Compton Mackenzie's picaresque novel, **Sylvia Scarlett** (1935), and star and director are self-indulgent to the point of embarrassment, presumably hoping for a modern 'Twelfth Night'. The wayward story slips from comedy to melodrama, but most of it is for connoisseurs of the bizarre, notably the moment of Hepburn's decision to play a boy, and her chunks of dialogue with the curly-headed, pipe-smoking artist (Brian Aherne) with whom she has fallen in love. Cukor has said that he and Hepburn were so appalled by the reception at the preview that they offered the producer, Pandro S. Berman, to do a film for no salaries – to which he responded tersely that he wanted neither of them ever to work for him again.

R.K.O. would have been better off – at least financially – without the next three Hepburn films. **Mary of Scotland** (1935) falls into every pitfall available to the historical film: it is reverent and anachronistic (it offers tartans long before they were known and the soundtrack throbs with Jacobean melodies), and though it distorts and simplifies it manages to be both confusing and dull. The source is a play by Maxwell Anderson – his blank verse eliminated by Dudley Nichols, whose companion play about Elizabeth I was to make a better film (q.v.) for Warners. Hepburn merely postures and John Ford bungles even the big scenes, handling the confrontations with Knox, the murders of Rizzio and Darnley and Mary's trial both perfunctorily and pretentiously. 'I'm a sight tonight and I wanted to look my best,' are Mary's first words on entering Holyrood; 'Ah, Darnley, still hanging on?' asks Bothwell – and with such dialogue Fredric March's interpretation is clearly ludicrous. The fact that the characters behave like modern people also mars **A Woman Rebels** (1936), which concerns a strong-minded Victorian 'gel' who becomes a crusading journalist – an interesting idea in an area neglected by film-makers, but the writers, Anthony Veiller and Ernest Vajda, have burrowed into Victorian fact and fiction without understanding either. However, Hepburn more than makes up for her earlier Mary Stuart: as directed by Mark Sandrich, here she is always charming, and as she ages she looks remarkably like herself twenty years later (a rare occurrence in the annals of movie make-up).

She flutters and sobs energetically enough in **Quality Street** (1937), but in view of the nature of the piece – a James Barrie sub-'Cranford' trifle – her obvious pleasure in her own pantomime is disconcerting. No one else so misjudges their roles, yet despite her overplaying and the ceaseless background music one is always aware of a civilised and even cultured director at work – George Stevens – though his skills are really more than the film deserves.

The American public, remembering the last Hepburn expedition into Barrie, was not tempted, but her box–office standing was temporarily restored by **Stage Door** (1937), considered by most reviewers to be even better than its Broadway original, by Edna Ferber and George S. Kaufman, as adapted by Morrie Ryskind and Anthony Veiller. The setting is a theatrical boarding house where the girls lounge

Adolphe Menjou with Ginger Rogers and Katharine Hepburn as stage hopefuls in Gregory LaCava's *Stage Door*, which remains a delight at least to those who relish bitchy wise-cracks. Rogers, reverting to her 'Anytime Annie' persona, gets the best lines, such as this one to a girl – not Hepburn – about to dine with a producer, 'Don't eat the bones and give yourself away.'

between auditions, into which coven comes Miss Hepburn, a wealthy daddy's girl, kind and clear-sighted despite her affectations. Unexpectedly she does not fall on her face but becomes a star – this at the expense of Andrea Leeds, fretting about losing the role she considered herself born to play. The ardour of both these characters is nicely balanced by the cynicism of the three other leading girls in the boarding house, Ginger Rogers, Lucille Ball and Eve Arden. Leeds was nominated for a Best Supporting Oscar, proof that that sort of 'sobbing woman' playing was prized above the splendid work of the Misses Ball and Arden; and the director, Gregory LaCava, was reported as crying whenever in later years he watched her suicide scene. He shot as few takes as possible, which accounts for the honesty and high spirits, as well as an occasional unconvincing moment.

In **Bringing Up Baby** (1938) Hepburn is a 'madcap heiress' (as they were usually described), with Cary Grant a palaeontologist who has the misfortune to get in her way; their joint adventures culminate in jail for singing 'I Can't Give You Anything but Love' to a leopard at midnight in a neighbour's garden. Hepburn's manner alone carries off the illogicality of it all, while Grant gallantly plays straight man. Obsession is their métier: she with him, he with an ancient bone – and obsession can be very funny in comedy. Their playing has brought the film some status in recent years but at the time it was not particularly well received by either press or public. Eileen Creelman wrote with some fairness in *The New York Sun*: 'The film is rather frantically funny, relying on improbable situations and slapstick. Mr Grant and Miss Hepburn, when in doubt, fall flat on their faces, fall over logs, knock each other down. Once was enough . . . The film is much too long, stretching its title joke to 102 minutes.' Howard Hawks directed, and the film was Hepburn's last for the company, which was conscious of the fact that two comedies in a row had failed to reinstate her in public favour.

In view of the fact that Hepburn had always been a thorn in their flesh, it is probable that the R.K.O. executives regarded her most fondly for having promoted George Stevens. After *Alice Adams* he made **Annie Oakley** (1935), Barbara Stanwyck's first vehicle under her R.K.O. contract. A foreword warns that the true story of its heroine is more incredible than most films, but the events of this one are virtually negligible, as if waiting for the Irving Berlin score to liven up matters (the 'book' of 'Annie Get Your Gun' is so similar as to suggest the same source material). Stevens has settled for good performances and an impeccable period atmosphere: the meticulousness which was always the centre of his craft is particularly apparent in the sequence of the group photograph – and in making Annie when famous somewhat blowsy. His work on *Swing Time, Quality Street* and *A Damsel in Distress* established his position as the studio's best contract director, and **Vivacious Lady** (1938) confirms his gift for comedy. A college professor (James Stewart) is reluctant to admit that the showgirl (Ginger Rogers) with him is his newly-wed wife: they have difficulty, therefore, in consummating the marriage, and though that is never mentioned, it is proof that by this time Hollywood writers were exhausting every situation in which a handsome young couple might find themselves. Miss Rogers is light of touch without ever becoming a comedienne, which throws most of the burden on to Stewart, who fortunately can cope with it.

Stevens was assigned to the studio's most expensive production to date, **Gunga Din** (1939), which uses Kipling's poem only as a starting point. Ben Hecht and Charles MacArthur came up with a story about three army buddies (Cary Grant, Douglas Fairbanks Jr and Victor McLaglen) and their Indian bearer (Sam Jaffe). Stevens's handling is exemplified in the two ambush sequences, one wittily choreographed and always entirely possible, the other particularly exciting. Those were what made it a popular success; but as with *Cavalcade* one wonders what Americans made of its Imperial concepts. At this time Britain was increasingly looked to as the one free and strong country in Europe, and it may be that Hollywood only wanted to express admiration: these and similar films imply that because the British Empire was so admirable Americans should follow the noble precepts which had helped to build it. Bluntly put, these were that white is right and black is not – which was something most Americans could accept. The faithful Gunga Din is the representative of all those millions to whom the British were paternal, and bets were further hedged by making the group-villain a sect devoted to killing.

'British' subjects were usually given to Hollywood's most prestigious or sensitive directors, and Stevens does excellently on **Vigil in the Night** (1940), which R.K.O. hoped would duplicate the success of *The Citadel,* also based on a novel by A. J. Cronin. 'The world's most famous doctor rips the veil from the hidden lives of bitter women who knew men too well,' said the publicity department, ill-preparing us for a tale of a doctor (Brian Aherne) who sports a pipe, three-piece tweeds, a dashing but comforting moustache and a twinkle in his eye when confronted by eager young nurses. It is he whom Carole Lombard sends for after a bus crash, and afterwards over cocoa – she refuses the sherry offered – he talks to her only of his plans for the new hospital, which may seem strange conduct for a

man alone at night with this particular actress, even though she enacts the role as if she were a reincarnation of Florence Nightingale. Yet if Stevens cannot make his stars flesh and blood, he is good elsewhere: rare among American directors of the time he allows no caricatures of the British, and he shows an understanding of their national character; and since the life of the hospital is as convincingly portrayed as in any movie then or since, the whole is preferable to the film of *The Citadel*.

With a title like **Penny Serenade** (1941) the battle is half won, and it matters not whether it refers to the sentiment on display or the adopted child at the centre of the story. As Irene Dunne recalls, with the aid of phonograph records, the ups and downs of her marriage with Cary Grant, Stevens tries for a blend of comedy and real-life hurt and pain, never getting far from the promise of the title: but the balance he achieves, with Morrie Ryskind's adroit screenplay and the tact of his players, is still miraculous.

The film was in fact made at Columbia, and for a number of reasons – not least the presence of Miss Dunne – we may pair it with Leo McCarey's **Love Affair** (1939).

Douglas Fairbanks Jr as one of the three comrades-in-arms who keep the Union Jack flying in India in *Gunga Din*. It is a splendid adventure film, though its attitudes are now somewhat bewildering, as when Cary Grant says ''Ow can I get a nice little war going?'

Irene Dunne and Charles Boyer in Leo McCarey's *Love Affair* which magically succeeds as romance while played in a comic vein which ought to have deflated it, as when she says, under the stars, that her father's philosophy was 'Wishing will make it so. Just keep on wishing, and cares will go. Dreamers tell us dreams come true,' adding, after the briefest of pauses, 'Of course, my father was a drunk.'

In *Penny Serenade* Stevens had treated his more serious sequences with the rigour of the best French cinema of the time, but both he and McCarey attained 'that genius of sentimentality' which Stravinsky noticed in 'La Bohème', 'so perfectly matched to the dramatic subst-ance and so superbly deployed that even I leave the theatre, when I can get a ticket, humming my lost innocence.' *Love Affair* is one of several good films of the time concerned with great and difficult romances, with a screenplay by Delmer Daves and Donald Ogden Stewart. The film begins as an amusing shipboard romance between Miss Dunne, a sophisti-cated New York 'kept woman', and Charles Boyer, playboy of two conti-nents. Parted after their journey, they do not meet again till she is hopelessly crip-pled: he does not know that was why she did not keep their rendezvous, or indeed of her accident – and since she is seated, and with no intention of telling him, the audience is reasonably on tenterhooks for a happy ending. (And it was said, inciden-tally, that the Hays Office allowed Miss

Dunne to play a kept woman since the accident could be seen as just retribution.) Of course the playing helps: Boyer's com-bination of the debonair and the doglike was never more attractive, and if Miss Dunne flutters and gurgles and arches her eyebrows over every misfortune there still isn't a single consonant or vowel that she cannot elevate into a whole continent of wit.

John Cromwell was also adept at mak-ing doubtful material believable, and the playing of Carole Lombard and Cary Grant in **In Name Only** (1939) further helps it on its way. As a married man and the woman for whom he wants a divorce, their reactions are always right – hers of frequent despair and his of encourage-ment and frivolity. Graham Greene in *The Spectator* noted that this was one of the few American films in which the 'other woman' was the heroine, admiring also the picture of misery engendered by divorce and such moments as the seedy hotel manager suggesting a cigarette or a drink or something more with Miss Lom-bard. Such matters, however, cannot quite rescue the material from soap opera: even in movies the course of true love was seldom more bumpy.

R.K.O. found an interesting director in Garson Kanin (b.1912), a minor Broad-way figure brought to Hollywood by Goldwyn, who did not use him. At R.K.O. he directed a B-movie, *A Man to Remember* (1938), which was sufficiently well-received for him to do **The Great Man Votes** (1939). The screenplay by a contract writer, John Twist, concerns politics, for which reason the budget was restricted to $200,000; but as the 'drunk old bummer' who holds the crucial vote and is therefore promised the job of Com-missioner for Education ('If it's good enough for the mayor's brother-in-law, it's good enough for you'), Kanin was allowed to use John Barrymore – persona non grata at the studio since his disappear-ance in mid-film some years before. Barrymore's histrionics overwhelm an otherwise pleasing combination of politi-cal satire and 'Little Orphan Annie', but Kanin's next two films, **Bachelor Mother** (1939) and **My Favorite Wife** (1940), proved 'Hollywood's youngest director', as *Photoplay* called him, adept at handling light-hearted situations – classic comedy built on deceit and predicament. The protagonist is put in an impossible situation, which entails lying, and that leads to further intricacy. In the first of these a shopgirl (Ginger Rogers) is landed with an orphan baby which no one will believe is not hers; in the second a newly-married husband (Cary Grant) is unable to pluck up courage to tell his second wife that his first (Irene Dunne) is back from the dead. Delicate situations are handled surely but in the airiest manner, and the playing is considerably more inventive than the dialogue. In view of the fact that Kanin did not direct after the War (apart from two failures in 1969) it is sad that neither of his other films of this time quite works: **They Knew What They Wanted** (1940), from Sidney Howard's once famous play, already filmed in 1928 and 1930, with Lombard now as the mail-order bride, and **Tom, Dick and Harry** (1940), with Miss Rogers beset by suitors. Both heroines are so mercenary that their last-reel conversion to true love is unbelievable. Censorship wrecked the Howard piece, reducing the mutual attraction of wife and foreman (William Gargan) to one night of passion followed by contrition; the unpleasing suggestion that love rests solely on physical attraction remains, despite the ending, perhaps because Charles Laughton is tediously Italian and hence unconvincing as the husband. Miss Rogers as the small-town girl determined to marry a millionaire – presumably an admirable goal in the post-Depression U.S. – plays even a calculating hussy with too much calculation; marrying the boss's son (David Niven) in *Bachelor Mother* she is perfect, but that is New York fairy tale.

So is **The Devil and Miss Jones** (1941), and Jean Arthur is also perfect. She plays a store clerk who meets an old man (Charles Coburn) at Coney Island, and feeling sorry for him encourages him to get a job in the store, not knowing that he is the boss. That is the sort of situation Hollywood talents could make workable – in this case including Sam Wood (1883–1949), directing without pretension just before embarking on more ambitious projects.

A lesser director, Leigh Jason, nevertheless made one of the quintessential movies of the time, **The Mad Miss Manton** (1938), an inconsequential and inventive murder mystery, with the pleasing team of Henry Fonda, as a New York editor, and Barbara Stanwyck, as the sleuthing but empty-headed heiress who is, till the last reel, the bane of his existence. Many of the star pairings of this era are marvellous, but William Powell hardly hits it off with Ginger Rogers in **Star of Midnight** (1935) and not at all with Jean Arthur in **The Ex-Mrs Bradford** (1936), both *Thin Man* (q.v.) imitations directed by Stephen Roberts; the second is particularly poor. We may wonder what Depression audiences made of the impeccably-tailored Powell in these enormous apartments in glass and white. It was probably the aftermath of the Depression which caused so many movies like **Joy of Living** (1938), which questioned material values; there were also too many with this particular plot, about the poor little rich girl who starts to wake up and live after just one night's binge. In *Joy of Living* she is Irene Dunne, supposedly Broadway's greatest star, teaming neatly with free-living Douglas Fairbanks Jr; the songs are by Jerome Kern, and the direction by Tay Garnett emphasises how much the best screwball comedies owed to the McCareys and LaCavas.

The customary cross-pollination between the poor and the wealthy is less in evidence in **Lucky Partners** (1940) and **My Life with Caroline** (1941), perhaps because both were based on French originals by, respectively, Guitry, and Louis Verneuil and Jacques Barr. They also mark a turning point in American film comedy: the careless spirit of the Thirties lives on, but the wit has gone. Ginger Rogers is in the first, involved in complications over a lottery ticket. A British actress, Anna Lee, is in the second, a rare instance in a Hollywood film of an inadequate star player. Both films star Ronald Colman as a man of affairs, in the process making him somewhat tiresome, but it is hard to feel sorry for him since he had not long before turned down both *Rebecca* (q.v.) and *Intermezzo* (q.v.). He also co-produced, with the director, Lewis Milestone, who observed that these were movies 'you did if you hoped to stay in pictures, in the expectation that the next film might give you a chance to redeem yourself'.

Perhaps the R.K.O. comedy most revived is that which the Marx Brothers made between assignments at M-G-M. This is **Room Service** (1938), a successful Broadway play for which the studio, in its erratic policy, paid the then-record sum of $225,000, and for which the Marxes were paid $250,000 for four weeks' work. The history of the film is confusing, from Groucho's claim that R.K.O. needed them because there were no suitable players under contract, to the statement that it was intended as a vehicle for them. They were not players easy to fit into existing material, and as Morrie Ryskind's screenplay adheres faithfully to the original, that may have been written with them in mind (its authors, John Murray and Allen Boretz, had not long since arrived at R.K.O. under contract). Groucho is the frantic producer of a theatrical troupe stranded in a hotel, Chico the show's director and Harpo a handyman. Weaknesses in the supporting cast indicate late budget restrictions, as does the fact that, under William A. Seiter's unimaginative direction, it is little more than a filmed play.

Another newcomer to the studio was Lily Pons, acquired during the Hollywood onslaught on American opera houses after the success at Columbia of Grace Moore (q.v.). It finally gave up hopes of her with **Hitting a New High** (1937), a title in no way descriptive of the film as directed by Raoul Walsh. She reveals no reason to indicate why R.K.O. tried once, let alone three times in all, yet the obvious desperation is interesting: having failed with her in romance, they dropped her in to farce, as a cabaret singer pretending to be a Rima-like bird-girl in an attempt to get a chance in opera, with considerably less footage allotted her than to supporting players Eric Blore and Edward Everett Horton.

Also welcomed to Hollywood were the Britishers, Herbert Wilcox and Anna Neagle, whose two films on Queen Victoria had been successful for R.K.O. However, directed by Wilcox in **Irene** (1940), Neagle, like Anna Lee, proved deficient in the star personality expected in such glossy Hollywood products. Since her singing and dancing are amateurish, and since a fine supporting cast has nothing to support, it is not surprising to find *The New York Times* later lamenting: 'Miss Neagle has now appeared to very dubious advantage in screen versions of *Irene* and *No, No, Nanette*, and they say that she is next to play the late Marilyn Miller's role in a translation of *Sunny*. If she continues at this rate, the fine nostalgic flavor of American musical comedy will soon be completely dissipated. It is all very depressing indeed.' After similar notices for *Sunny* the pair returned to Britain.

Another English player, Charles Laughton, was signed to an R.K.O. contract, and in **The Hunchback of Notre Dame** (1939) he is a more memorable Quasimodo than Lon Chaney, acting with one eye (the other is in the middle of his cheek: his make-up man deserved an Oscar), limping and making the guttural sounds of a deaf mute. He evokes pity, whether in the pillory or gazing at Esmerelda – less a fiery gypsy dancer than a shy Irish colleen as played by Maureen O'Hara, who must have dismayed William Dieterle; but he moves the old tale at a fast clip. Later offered a producer-director contract under a new studio policy to encourage well-known names to join it, Dieterle made **All that Money Can Buy** (1941), sometimes known as *The Devil and Daniel Webster* after the story by Stephen Vincent Benét upon which it is based. It concerns a man (James Craig) who sells his soul to the devil (Walter Huston), and for once, intoned the English critic James Agate, 'Hollywood has boldly ventured into something that is neither vulgar nor silly'. He and others were undoubtedly impressed by the artistic approach, which includes the title credits, not designating the actual functions of any of the personnel, and lighting effects which were common when the director was working in Germany, often on similar plots. This one is Americana, and is therefore whimsical rather than eery – but it is equally humourless and lacks the twist in the tail which might justify the malarkey. Craig, a nice man who otherwise played mainly leads in Bs at Metro, can spark no interest, and sin for him is merely a bad attack of thoughtlessness and a mistress (Simone Simon).

Of the two films directed by Rowland V. Lee for R.K.O. **The Toast of New York** (1937) is also concerned with matters financial and moral, but both he and the writers (Dudley Nichols, John Twist and Joel Sayre) demonstrate the usual Hollywood confusion at having to deal critically with capitalism: they are detailed but not explicit on the financial finaglings of Jim Fiske, demoting him from one of the most evil of the robber barons to a mere scoundrel. Fiske's penchant for uniforms and his private army are treated as harmless eccentricities, and although he Pays at the End he is played by Edward Arnold, specialising then in 'lovable' tycoons. Later, when Hollywood managed to condemn a capitalist, it made him primarily a fascist, as in two of the characters Arnold played for Capra; and though the film sets out to show that Fiske's quest for power was as unprincipled as that of modern dictators, it is clearly less interested in that than in his relations with the actress (Frances Farmer) who is his 'protégée'.

Among the few other R.K.O. films of serious content is **The Plough and the Stars** (1936), which John Ford remained to make after *Mary of Scotland*: and since both films share with *The Informer* an impression that everything happens at night we must assume that to be Ford's approach to his more important endeavours. Despite the success of *The Informer*, this version of Sean O'Casey's play was completely compromised: in return for being allowed to import some Abbey Theatre players, Ford was compelled (or so he claimed) to use a star, Barbara Stanwyck, and though she agreed to wear no make-up, it must be said that her accent is uncertain. A happy ending was tacked on, and, after Ford had left, the studio removed all references to the fact that the Clitheroes (Stanwyck, Preston Foster) were married. Dudley Nichols's screenplay has chopped the play into three separate entities – the comic Irish (Barry Fitzgerald), the romantic Irish (Stanwyck) and the fighting Irish (Arthur Shields) – while Ford's poetic Dublin looks even more precious than hitherto when intercut with newsreel footage of the 'Troubles'.

R.K.O. had another way of using existing material, which though not uncommon in Europe was rarely a Hollywood practice – and that was to buy up foreign productions and intercut their most spec-tacular scenes with newly-shot material. **The Woman I Love** (1937) is therefore mainly *L'Équipage*, complete to the Honegger score, with the same director, Anatole Litvak (whom the success of *Mayerling* had brought to Hollywood); but whereas Annabella, Jean-Pierre Aumont and Charles Vanel had made something touching of this wartime triangle drama, it becomes merely coarse as enacted by Miriam Hopkins, Louis Hayward and Paul Muni. **The Soldier and the Lady** (1937), trade-shown as *Michael Strogoff*, is a revamp of a French-German co-production of the previous year, with the same star, Anton Walbrook. When he swiftly left Hollywood R.K.O. lost interest in the film, since his performance was its strongest asset; the trade was unimpressed, knowing that all the genuinely spectacular sequences had been bought – if matching the new material directed by George Nicholls Jr.

R.K.O.'s most signal failure of the decade was its involvement with Technicolor. In 1932 the Technicolor Corporation had finally achieved the three-colour process which offered the whole prism. One of the few industry executives interested was R.K.O.'s head of production, Merian C. Cooper, who failed to get the New York office either to invest in the Technicolor Corporation, then ailing, or to film *Flying Down to Rio* in the system. As distributors, however, they were to handle a Disney 'Silly Symphony', **Flowers and Trees** – for which Disney had enthusiastically scrapped the existing black and white footage to re-do it in colour. R.K.O. had not been encouraging, and Disney only proceeded when Sid Grauman, after a minute's trial, agreed to book it into his Los Angeles theatre to support *Strange Interlude* . Probably everyone at the premiere had seen an experimental colour short, either in (two-tone) Technicolor or in one of the other myriad colour processes; but the enthusiastic reaction to this 'Silly Symphony' indicated that future Disney cartoons in monochrome were inconceivable: the Silly Symphonies went into colour immediately, and Mickey Mouse followed two years later.

Meanwhile, Disney failed to get backing from his usual distributor, United Artists, for a full-length cartoon version of *Babes in Toyland*, and he appealed to Cooper, who was unable to persuade the R.K.O. board that a full-length cartoon was a viable proposition. Cooper remained one of the few powerful industry figures farsighted enough to agree with Disney about colour, and in order to exploit the process he formed Pioneer Pictures – in conjunction with John Hay Whitney and Cornelius V. Whitney, with some financing from Technicolor. The Technicolor Corporation had granted Disney exclusive rights to three-tone Technicolor, partly from pique at industry indifference, and it was not until July 1934 that Pioneer tried out a short, **La Cucaracha**. That won an Oscar as the year's best short subject, but the industry waited to see audience reaction to Pioneer's first feature, and that had to be delayed till Cooper's R.K.O. contract was up. Nevertheless, as with *La Cucaracha*, R.K.O. distributed, the nominal producer was an R.K.O. man, and the studio's penchant at the time for English literary tales was reflected in the material.

The film, rechristened **Becky Sharp** (1935), found audiences siding with the industry. They had not long adjusted to Sound and were content. Insufficient patrons were curious to see the film, and since the popularity of the Disney shorts was enormous it was clear that colour should be confined to animation. It could not be said that *Becky Sharp* is the better because of it. It begins imaginatively, after white and grey titles, with a girl's head popping through a grey curtain, but otherwise the sole sequence of note is that in which the officers hurry from the Duchess of Richmond's ball, their red cloaks swirling. Rouben Mamoulian (who took over direction when Lowell Sherman died, reputedly throwing out a month's footage) may have given thought to the pallette, but he reveals no understanding of what is one of the greatest novels in the language. We look vainly for Thackeray's amusement at the foibles and follies, the superficialities and snobberies of that high society he christened 'Vanity Fair', finding instead the pallid progress of a saucy gold digger. Becky was not subtle, but Miriam Hopkins signals every scheme and manoeuvre as if she were a lighthouse, less an adventuress than a spoilt young woman with a yen for men.

This actress's brittle manner fitted her best for roles of bitchy persuasion, but she insisted on playing for sympathy, and in the most predictable way, alternating half-smiles and half-tears – using so much effort that she was incapable of making any one line relate to another, ruining Becky as a comic character. Cedric Hardwicke's Lord Steyne, cold and grey, is a major performance, with such authenticity of feeling that he overshadows Nigel Bruce, as Jos, and Alan Mowbray, as Rawdon, both otherwise capable. Alison Skipworth has some moments as Miss Crawley and William Stack is good as Pitt, but Frances Dee as Emmy and Colin Tapley are not, predictably, Thackeray's ninnies at all. But then the twenty years of his novel have been reduced to just eighty-three minutes.

Pioneer and R.K.O. tried again with **The Dancing Pirate** (1936), but if the lack of star names was a contributor to its failure it seemed to confirm that colour in itself was not a box-office attraction – and it was also still very costly. At 20th, Zanuck used it for the ending of *The House of Rothschild* and one reel of *The Little Colonel* (1935), while *The Trail of the Lonesome Pine* (q.v.), in fact the second Technicolor feature, was a mild success for Paramount. By virtue of having become Disney's distributor R.K.O. handled the first really successful Technicolor attraction, *Snow White and the Seven Dwarfs* (q.v.), but that was regarded as a freak, and it was not until audiences had endorsed Warners' *Adventures of Robin Hood* (q.v.) that most studios began to abandon caution. R.K.O. was not among them: twice bitten it remained shy, holding out till well after the War.

At Paramount there were recurring threats of bankruptcy and boardroom shuffles. On returning from M-G-M and *The Merry Widow* Lubitsch was appointed head of production by the new management, till it was decided that the films made under his supervision, while. successful enough, were more costly than necessary. He was succeeded in 1936 by William Le Baron, reckoned to be the company's most astute Associate Producer (since his return from R.K.O. in 1932), and under his skilful control Paramount's financial troubles receded.

During that period Lubitsch had prepared one film, **Desire** (1936), borrowing Frank Borzage from Warners to direct it – and it is apparent from the outset that it has affinities with *Trouble with Paradise*. The opening is pure Lubitsch: Marlene Dietrich (released from Von Sternberg at last) glides into the Place Vendôme in quest of a pearl necklace for which she has no intention of paying. Having accomplished her coup, she has to get the necklace past Customs, and behind her is Gary Cooper, an engineer from Detroit, an all-too-convenient innocent: but it is one thing to slip the necklace into his pocket and another to retrieve it. Nothing in the film is as good as its opening scene – and if a reformed Dietrich settles for Detroit, that is part of the general fantasy. Borzage leaned more towards the romantic than Lubitsch, and the stars complement each other as dreamily as in *Morocco*, she self-assured in Travis Banton gowns, he ingenuous in double-breasted suits, and in awe of Europe.

A world of make-believe was the whole *raison d'être* – a point missed by C. A. Lejeune in her celebrated put-down of **Angel** (1937): 'The first moment that Miss Marlene Dietrich sweeps up to the reception desk of a Paris hotel, you feel sure that you are looking at a mystery woman. It is something about the highlight on her lip-rouge, the way her eyes peek from side to side, and the dashing way in which she tosses off the signature "Mrs Brown" in the register. You know, of course, that she isn't Mrs Brown, but beyond that you have no notion who she may be, except possibly Miss Marlene Dietrich, practising acting. In point of fact, she is the wife of a British Cabinet Minister, who is currently representing his country in Geneva. Oh, you move in exalted circles in *Angel*, and meet the most wonderful people.' This critic was not the only one to quote one of the more fatuous exchanges: 'What's worrying you, darling?' asks Dietrich, 'Is it France?' He shakes his head. 'Jugoslavia.' Lubitsch knew that this was risible: the jig is to keep us entertained by a tale which never reaches the far borders of probability. He not only takes advantage of Hollywood convention but piles it on. Thus the country mansion has, as Lejeune says, 'yards of mullion round the windows', and the

lady's wardrobe surpasses most in lavishness and tasteful tinsel. Dietrich is more puppet-like than ever; Herbert Marshall and Melvyn Douglas, as husband and would-be lover respectively, were never more urbane or gentlemanly.

Lubitsch made **Bluebeard's Eighth Wife** (1938) to fulfil a promise to Claudette Colbert, whose special gift for hesitant or unexpressed scepticism was seldom better exploited. It also demonstrates why he preferred directing Gary Cooper to any other actor. Cooper plays one of the richest men in the world, wanting, in a Côte d'Azur store, only the top of a pair of pyjamas, while she wants only the pants: that is the start, and the scene ends with her cure for insomnia – spelling Czechoslovakia backwards. As with such references in *Angel*, audiences were expected to contrast the facetiousness with the situation current in Europe: and in treating in equally unmindful fashion the real theme of the film – which is

Lubitsch grew so weary of being praised for his famous 'touch' that he branched into new forms of comedy on leaving Paramount in 1939. His later Paramount films are notable for their artificiality, as might be guessed from this scene from *Angel*, with Herbert Marshall, Marlene Dietrich and Melvyn Douglas.

403

Carole Lombard. In her playing of comedy, beauty and elegance were matched by a perfect sense of movement, timing and delivery – and as much might be said of Irene Dunne, Jean Arthur, Claudette Colbert, Myrna Loy, Constance Bennett and, on occasion, Katharine Hepburn and Barbara Stanwyck. They were real, they were unreal, they were extraordinary: few actresses since have approached them in skill – and whether they acquired it or were born with it, why are today's actresses so much less blessed?

the non-consummation of a marriage – Lubitsch was playing for time, till the real issues had to be faced. On *Angel* his writer was, as customary, Samson Raphaelson, working from a play by Melchior Lengyel, who would collaborate on *To Be or Not to Be* (q.v.); *Bluebeard's Eighth Wife* was written by Billy Wilder and Charles Brackett – teamed for the first time – but equally clearly Lubitsch dictated the tone (so different from Sam Wood's 1923 version of the same tale, with Gloria Swanson). However, the finale, in a mental home, may be recognised as the sort of thin ice on which Wilder would skate for the rest of his career. Later both he and Lubitsch made films about the War which were both more realistic *and* more entertaining than most films on the subject; before that they would collaborate on *Ninotchka* (q.v.) which, if still shirking the real issues, took a pungent enough look at Russian communism. Lubitsch was canny: when *The Man I Killed* failed to make anything like the same impact as

Milestone's *All Quiet on the Western Front* he stuck to furbelows and baubles, retaining control of his career while the eclectic Milestone was forced to take industry assignments. *Ninotchka* was made at M-G-M because he wanted to make a film with Garbo; he did not return to Paramount.

That company's penchant for comedy may be explained by the presence among their star players of Miss Colbert (b. 1905) and Carole Lombard (1908–42). Colbert was equally adept at dither or serenity when faced with impossible situations, whereas Lombard was possessed of an uncontrollable impulse towards the erratic and the extravagant. They were respectively in the two films said to have begun the memorable cycle of Thirties comedies, *It Happened One Night* and *Twentieth Century* (q.v.), both made at Columbia. This cycle has been variously described, but *Webster's* definition of 'screwball' provides the only appropriate adjective: 'One conspicuous for dizzily fantastic ideas or wildly irrational behaviour' – which surely describes Colbert in that particular movie and Lombard in most that she made. The films have been called 'sophisticated', since their normal milieu is boudoir or night club, and 'slapstick', because their characters take pratfalls; but though their *attitudes* are sophisticated, there is a paucity of verbal wit. To judge from audience response, the funniest moments are those which do not translate into print, as when, in Leisen's *Easy Living* (q.v.), Jean Arthur boasts that the boys' magazine for which she works has a million readers and Edward Arnold riposts pompously, 'You haven't got me' – and that is a particularly successful example of a screenwriter working in the much-admired tradition of *The New Yorker* magazine. Though the spectacle of debutantes and lounge lizards acting crazy can be dispiriting when poorly done, the fact that the best of these films have not yet received the recognition that is their due★ is probably because we cannot quote from them as we can from Mae West or the Marx Brothers.

Mitchell Leisen was Paramount's best comedy director after Lubitsch. While an

★ I once saw on the same day Coward's oft-revived play 'Present Laughter' and LaCava's totally neglected *She Married her Boss* (q.v.), which is at least five times as funny.

artisan seldom crosses a Lubitsch drawing room, in the films of Leisen the penniless are in constant conflict with the well-to-do. After making his debut on *The Eagle and the Hawk* he achieved both commercial and critical success with **Death Takes a Holiday** (1934), an Italian piece of whimsy revamped by Maxwell Anderson, whose artificial situations made it the *L'Année Dernière à Marienbad* (q.v.) of its day. Leisen increased in confidence, and **Hands Across the Table** (1935) is a delightful film. When Lombard first sees Fred MacMurray he is playing hopscotch in a hotel corridor; told they cannot enter a nightclub in day clothes they start to strip; and, discovered trouserless in her apartment, he claims he is her husband, which she caps by denying it. It is a tale of like meets like: both are intent on marrying money. The first millionaire she meets is a crippled aviator (Ralph Bellamy), but both his lust for her and his physical condition are ignored by the director. Leisen tolerated no experiments in taste or sentiment, such as we associate with his best-known writers after they turned director, Preston Sturges and Billy Wilder. Because of their later renown, and because they provided him with his two masterpieces, **Easy Living** (1937) and **Midnight** (1939) respectively, it is tempting to suggest that he was only as good as his material – yet we are aware of a sureness of control comparable to that of Lubitsch.

In *Easy Living* a typist (Jean Arthur) is riding on the top of a Fifth Avenue bus when a fur coat drops on her head, and soon the whole of New York has jumped to the conclusion that she is the mistress of the thrower, a tycoon (Edward Arnold). In *Midnight* an American showgirl (Miss Colbert), having left her last bangle in a Monte Carlo pawnshop, arrives in Paris looking for a millionaire; she had one once, she tells the cab driver (Don Ameche), till his father offered to buy her off. 'Didn't you hit him?' he asks. 'How could I?' she replies. 'My hands were full of money.' Miss Arthur's Cinderella, to her astonishment, finds herself installed in New York's best hotel; Miss Colbert's finds herself posing as a countess so that John Barrymore can woo away his wife (Mary Astor) from her latest 'admirer' (Francis Lederer). Both

Mitchell Leisen's two great comedies of the Thirties, *Easy Living*, LEFT, with Luis Alberni and Jean Arthur, and *Midnight*, ABOVE, with John Barrymore, Don Ameche, Rex O'Malley and Claudette Colbert. Neither was particularly well received: *Variety* said of the former, 'Slapstick farce, incredible, and without rhyme or reason, is Paramount's contribution to the cycle of goofy pictures', while *Midnight* was disregarded, overshadowed by events in Europe. Both films were the product of a Hollywood looking askance at the world, and compelled to lighten it in its own manner.

films are heartless and convoluted, and may be seen as tracts for the times: but whereas there was no longer the need for the obligatory reference to the Depression by the time *Midnight* was made, in the earlier film we may compare the bums' invasion of the automat with the seventeen trunks the tycoon's wife takes to Florida.

Leisen directed Lombard and MacMurray again in **Swing High, Swing Low** (1937), a new version of 'Burlesque', partly written by Oscar Hammerstein and partly reset in Panama. The playful first half is well balanced by the dramatic second, whose shots of MacMurray stumbling about a back-projected Manhattan prefigure a number of later movies featuring drunken jazz musicians. Leisen failed with the team of Jack Benny and Gracie Allen (plus George Burns) in **The Big Broadcast of 1937** (1936), despite a large team of writers, but with an equally ordinary screenplay he transformed **Artists and Models Abroad** (1938), with Benny leading a cast which seems to be happily improvising. The plot concerns a third-rate theatrical troupe stranded in Paris, and the musical numbers include two, in street and hotel room, which achieve spontaneous group outbursts into song, usually thought to be absent from musicals till *On the Town* (q.v.). We may also thank Leisen – fashion conscious though he was – for realising that most movie-goers were bored by fashion parades, and that consequently the best way to treat such occasions was to send them up. **Remember the Night** (1940) is the last screenplay by Sturges that he did not direct himself, and its tone is close to his subsequent films (David Chierichetti's excellent book on Leisen indicates that he shot considerably less than Sturges wrote.) Barbara Stanwyck plays a girl who not absentmindedly leaves a jewellery store without paying for the goods and is prosecuted by MacMurray; he gets her out on bail for Christmas, and a series of surprisingly credible circumstances has them spending it together.

Audiences took this stream of comedies for granted: Wesley Ruggles made one after another, written from **The Gilded Lily** (1935) onwards by the adept but uninspired Claude Binyon (till he left for Columbia in 1940). This is a superficial romantic comedy, justified by the presence of Miss Colbert. She is a stenographer at first, but she gets to be a famous cabaret singer – which was exactly what audiences expected. They went to see the Colbert fashions, the Colbert figure, the Colbert smile; they went to see Colbert sad and Colbert witty; they wanted less to appreciate than to revel in the familiar and much-loved Colbert personality. This film actually calls for nice Claudette to go high-hat, but the dénouement is so fixed that audiences will go on loving her. Miss Lombard worried less about wardrobe – and less about being loved: in **True Confession** (1937) she plays a girl who confesses to a murder she didn't commit in order to throw the limelight on her husband (Fred MacMurray), an unsuccessful lawyer. Recognition for the films themselves was not lacking: Graham Greene later described this one as the 'year's funniest film' and *The New York Times* placed **I Met Him in Paris** (1937) among the year's best films. The latter, a revamp of *Design for Living*, leaves Colbert, Melvyn Douglas and Robert Young stranded with witless material, so that *True Confession* is, despite a weak ending, the only one of Ruggles's later films that can now be strongly recommended.

Leo McCarey's reputation for comedy could rest solely on **Ruggles of Red Gap** (1935), from the novel by Harry Leon Wilson (who also wrote 'Merton of the Movies') which had been filmed twice in the Silent era. The conversion of the perfect (British) servant, Ruggles, into his own (American) man was said to be a psychological study or a comment on democratic values, but the film is now best regarded as a vehicle for several star comics – which McCarey, emulating his own *Six of a Kind*, surely intended. And though Charles Laughton gives a performance of resource and delicacy in the title-role, stoically accepting the vulgarity of his new employers, he almost loses the film to Roland Young, whose bemused aristocrat, tempted by ladies, booze and the habits of Mr Floud, is a lovely creation. Equally good are Charles Ruggles as Floud, a simple man of the frontier, Mary Boland as his socially ambitious wife, forever bearing down and forbearing his peccadilloes, and Zazu Pitts as the widow who courts the manservant.

The film's reception encouraged McCarey to produce and direct another piece for several middle-aged players, **Make Way for Tomorrow** (1937). A penniless elderly couple (Beulah Bondi, Victor Moore) must be separated till their five children can club together enough cash to buy them a new house. The New York son is played by Thomas Mitchell and his wife by Fay Bainter, both adept at portraying likeable, dependable people, and they remain likeable, more or less, as she grows increasingly irritated by Ma's ways and he comes to the decision to put her in a home. Frank S. Nugent in *The New York Times* praised the film's 'humanity, honesty, warmth', but the situation is contrived: five children – one with a maid – and not one spare double room? – and surely Pa, not senile, could have found a job? Nugent also thought the film 'courageous' to provide no final solution, but if that was meant to leave no dry eye in the cinema McCarey and his sensitive screenwriter, Vina Delmar, elsewhere refuse to milk tears. The sentimental journey taken by Ma and Pa to their honeymoon hotel is perhaps excessive, but there is a Jewish character, rare in films at this time, a friendly storekeeper (Maurice Moscovitch). Nugent listed the film as among the year's best, alongside *The Life of Emile Zola, The Good Earth, Stage Door, Captains Courageous, They Won't Forget, I Met Him in Paris, A Star Is Born, Lost Horizon* and *Camille*: in other words, Hollywood entertainment at its most appealing. McCarey's is the only film on the list to reflect ordinary life, since the others are set in either an unusual milieu or an exceptional one – except *They Won't Forget* (q.v.), which is too melodramatic to be taken seriously.

That *Make Way for Tomorrow* also reflected credit on Paramount was of no consequence when it failed outside the urban centres, and McCarey was sacked. Paramount's stockholders were more interested in deMille, whose films continued to be expensive but profitable. One of them, **The Crusades** (1935), was described by *Film Weekly* as 'alternatively thrilling and inept', but the thrills are confined to the taking of Acre, which takes up less than ten minutes of the film's two hours. Needless to say, it features the Coeur-de-Lion (Henry Wilcoxon) of

legend (if mildly misogynist), finally inspired by the Moslem concept of peace – clearly meant as a message for audiences of the time. This could possibly be the most historically inaccurate film ever made. At least any superlatives applied to deMille's next film, **The Plainsman** (1936), should be complimentary. Graham Greene thought it 'perhaps . . . the finest Western in the history of films.' The form had been in abeyance for some time, except for the poverty-row Westerns churned out for addicts, and these were so despised that Paramount's attempts to revive the genre with King Vidor's *The Texas Rangers* and Frank Lloyd's *Wells Fargo* were carefully categorised as 'pioneer epics'. In returning to the Western deMille made his first good film in more than a decade, and we may echo Greene's surprise, also wondering whether the for once excellent dialogue was an accident and whether deMille was not inspired by players of the quality of Gary Cooper and Jean Arthur – as a Wild Bill Hickock and Calamity Jane helping to make the frontier safe. In the lesser **Union Pacific** (1939) Barbara Stanwyck and Joel McCrea aid the joining together of the two transcontinental railroads in Utah; and with **Northwest**

Beulah Bondi and Victor Moore in Leo McCarey's *Make Way for Tomorrow*, one of his rare serious films and an unusual one for Hollywood, since its subject is old age.

Mounted Police (1940) deMille, despite a move into Technicolor, was back to his now customary low standard, with Cooper helping the British to suppress the rising of Louis Reil – a subject chosen to indicate solidarity with the Empire.

Apart from *The Texas Rangers*, Vidor's other film for Paramount was also an exploration of America's past, So Red the Rose (1935), a Civil War story about a Southern belle (Margaret Sullavan), coquettish and self-willed like all such ladies in fiction. Her adventures are banal, but Vidor responds when a chance is offered – the reading of a letter from the Front, a mother searching for the corpse of her son on the battlefield. The screenwriters included Lawrence Stallings and Maxwell Anderson, and since, like Vidor, they had made memorable cinematic statements on war much was expected of this film. Its failure became legendary, and later comforted those who had passed up or missed the chance to buy the rights to *Gone with the Wind* (q.v.). When that film became successful the industry remembered *The Birth of a Nation* and decided that the public was only interested in the Civil War as an epic. This one is notably confused on the crucial issue, the freedom of the slaves, who move rapidly from Massah-lovin' to rabble rousing and are then quickly forgotten. It is as if the harsh truth must not intrude on the daydream which this film really is – more Louisa M. Alcott than Stephen Crane – and audiences resented its dishonesties more than those on more trivial subjects.

Frank Lloyd, after *Wells Fargo*, again delved into American history for Paramount: Maid of Salem (1937) tells of the seventeenth-century witch trials in Massachusetts – perfunctorily handled, with more attention paid to boy-meets-girl. Fred MacMurray is miscast as a devil-may-care Irishman, and Claudette Colbert is too modern as one of the accused; it is also difficult to accept the strictures on her bonnet frills when her face is caked in make-up. At the end, his evidence frees her, and the judges merrily declare that the whole business has been a temporary aberration – a view compounded by Lloyd, who never achieves a persuasive picture of hysteria and panic. Lloyd's once-high reputation plunged still

further with If I Were King (1938), the screenplay for which – by Preston Sturges – was of little help in reviving the oft-told tale of François Villon (Ronald Colman).

Paramount's best action director was Henry Hathaway (b.1898), who progressed from B-Westerns to some of the studio's most important films. His first A-feature was Now and Forever (1934), which is fine as long as it concentrates on con man Gary Cooper and his mistress (Carole Lombard), but not so good when it shifts to his child (Shirley Temple). Lives of a Bengal Lancer (1935) was described by *Photoplay* as 'one of the best [films] ever to come out of the Paramount studios' – reviewing it after *Clive of India*, *The Good Fairy*, *Ruggles of Red Gap* and *David Copperfield*, which prompts the reflection that two tributes to the British Empire in one month seem excessive, especially among the assorted studies of British eccentricities. As a portrait of the Raj it is romanticised, and the climax – the siege and the tortures – belong to a lesser film; but the barrack scenes – the bantering hostility between Cooper and Franchot Tone, their fathering of the new recruit (Richard Cromwell) and their mutual interdependence – reflect with affection the peculiar psychology of regimental life.

Hathaway's inclination towards romanticism was allowed full play in Peter Ibbetson (1935), from George du Maurier's novel about two lovers who, though parted, see each other as young and together only in their dreams – an unusual subject for this time, though Paramount had filmed it in 1921 with Wallace Reid. The studio rebought the property in 1931, after Deems Taylor had turned it into an opera for Jeanette MacDonald, who did not play it; the film then became a (straight) vehicle for Fredric March, but he left the studio before production started. Robert Donat and then Brian Aherne both accepted but did not take up the role, which Hathaway eventually persuaded Gary Cooper to play; during these delays Irene Dunne ceded the lead to Ann Harding, whose ethereal presence immeasurably aids Hathaway's purpose. As against its complete rejection by the American public, it had a cult following in Paris, where it was quaintly described by André Breton as 'a triumph of surrealist thought'. It is likeable if absurd, with such solecisms as a railway station called 'London', and a shot of Tower Bridge, unfinished when the novel was published – and in any case the film is set a quarter of a century earlier.*

Hathaways's **The Trail of the Lonesome Pine** (1936) was Paramount's first Technicolor film, and it is difficult to say whether the subject was chosen to fit the colour or vice-versa; James Fox Jr's novel had been filmed before, in 1916 and 1923, and it must have been old hat then – with hill families feuding, like the Hatfields and McCoys, till the railroad comes and the handsome stranger (Fred MacMurray) steals the girl (Sylvia Sidney) from the mountain boy (Henry Fonda). The colour – mainly outdoor – gave it a cachet, but the unwieldy Technicolor cameras seem to have inhibited both cast and director to the point of petrification. Hathaway was clearly much happier returning to black and white with **Souls at Sea** (1937), with Cooper and George Raft, and **Spawn of the North** (1938), with Fonda and Raft: but his vigorous handling of squalls and brawls does not entirely compensate for script deficiencies.

Technicolor was supposed to enhance **Men with Wings** (1938), which William Wellman returned to Paramount to direct – and this lachrymose, longwinded and fictionalised study of the early days of aviation needed all the help it could get. Though it was not a return to the form of *Wings*, Wellman did manage to get back into form with another film from that era, **Beau Geste** (1939); his remake follows the Silent version to a T, improving on the sinister opening, though losing perhaps a little with the mutiny. Its most significant difference is the substitution of Gary Cooper for Ronald Colman – the latter the ideal Beau, whereas Cooper is the ideal Cooper, which is not the same thing. Wellman directed Colman in another remake, **The Light that Failed** (1939), also a tale of British heroism, but of such pessimism that it was curious of Paramount to offer it as Britain prepared for war. It was based on Kipling's first novel, and one representing his own

attitude towards literary London: Helder (Colman) returns to London from the Sudan, and becomes corrupted as his war paintings make him famous. The heroics at the end suggest that Paramount wanted another *Bengal Lancers*, but the pessimism of the book is too strong for them. The miscasting of Colman accentuates the unsatisfactory nature of the piece: Helder drinks like Sidney Carton and is similarly disillusioned (on the wound that caused his blindness, 'If a man starts cutting you across the head, don't duck, let him keep cutting'), but he cannot convince you that he is a man without integrity. What he could do, movingly, is a line like the one on learning of his blindness, 'We've got it badly, little dog, just as badly as we could get it.'

Lewis Milestone's stint at Paramount included **Anything Goes** (1936), a fast-moving musical farce with Bing Crosby singing a score somewhat different from the Broadway original: the jettisoning of the old in favour of the new was common practice in filming musicals, but when the original songs are among Cole Porter's best it becomes ludicrous. When Paramount offered no further assignment, Milestone got hold of **The General Died at Dawn** (1936), and secured for the screenplay Clifford Odets, who had just made his name with 'Waiting for Lefty'. Lubitsch, then head of production, was not enthusiastic, but Milestone was allowed Gary Cooper in the lead – and Cooper was the company's most popular male star. As a soldier of fortune he meets up with Madeleine Carroll, a lovely lacquered lady who is to lead him to his doom on an Oriental train. As it chugs through the rain to its meeting with machine guns it is reminiscent of the Shanghai Express that Dietrich once took, and these intrigues need the vitality of the earlier film. Milestone does manage some good atmospherics, notably in a Shanghai hotel where several seedy schemers (Dudley Digges, Akim Tamiroff, Porter Hall, J. M. Kerrigan) clasp each other as birds of a feather. Odets's dialogue is quite wrong for the matters in hand, as when Cooper says to Carroll, facing death: 'We could have made beautiful music together. We could have made a circle of light and warmth.'

Rouben Mamoulian made one film for

---

* Conversely, the Customs House in *Desire* is a replica of the one that still stood there, on the French-Spanish border, as late as 1962.

Paramount during this time: **High, Wide and Handsome** (1937), which many think of as the 'pipe-laying musical' – telling as it does of the Pennsylvania farmers who, having discovered oil (in 1859), lay a pipeline rather than see the railroad tycoons take their profits. Kern (music) and Hammerstein (words) wrote it in the same celebration of Americana which had resulted in 'Show Boat' and 'Sweet Adeline' – from the film versions of which came Irene Dunne, to play a circus girl who marries a farmer (Randolph Scott). Her song 'The Folks Who Live on the Hill' is staged with wrinkles in the backcloth and fake apple blossom; and the film as a whole fails to substantiate claims for the director's reputation.

Fritz Lang went to Paramount for one film, **You and Me** (1938), his third in the U.S., but failed to repeat the critical success of the first two (q.v.). That he made so few films at this time was due to his determination to select his own material – but on this occasion he chose badly. He wanted to make a film following Brecht's method of *Lehrstück* – 'a play that teaches you something' – and the resulting message is certainly simple-minded, with Sylvia Sidney proving to a bunch of crooks that 'only the biggest saps in the world think crime pays dividends'.

The success of Ben Hecht and Charles MacArthur as suppliers of material to Hollywood was such that their agent, Leland Hayward, arranged a unique contract with Paramount – to write, produce and direct four films, albeit on limited budgets, with complete independence. Lee Garmes, one of the studio's most experienced cameramen, was sent to help them – for the Long Island studio had been reopened for the purpose. The general impression, however, of **Crime without Passion** (1934) is one of amateurism, and while fashion still demanded a 'European' look and patina for self-important subjects, it is startling to find that the two newspapermen who wrote 'The Front Page' have gone so wild. Their film begins with three ladies in flowing robes pretending to be Furies, and concludes with them after they have brought Nemesis to Claude Rains. Pretension proliferates: a close-up of a drop of blood, a *boutonière* grasped as a victim falls to her death . . . Contemporaries,

however, were impressed: it was thought to be witty, presumably because of Rains's high-handed approach to women and to his profession, the law.

The second film, **Once in a Blue Moon**, was so bad that release was delayed for two years; **Soak the Rich** (1936) was an even greater flop. Reviewers, however, were for a second time favourable – to **The Scoundrel** (1935), doubtless because Noël Coward at last deigned to make his film debut and the eminent critic Alexander Woollcott agreed to be in the supporting cast, both playing members of New York's literary set. Coward is a publisher loathed by his authors, and he himself has no illusions, planning to marry 'the only person I've ever met who is emptier and more superficial than I am'. Obviously this is not the poetess (Julie Haydon), for she is offered 'one month of happiness and six months of farewells'. 'I'm old-fashioned,' she tells him. 'You're the dawn of time,' he reassures her, but she is soon just another life he has wrecked. He dies in a storm at sea, but returns like the Flying Dutchman – and for the same reason. This mixture of cynicism and the supernatural eked out a miserable week at Radio City Music Hall, but later, with *Caligari*, it became the life-blood of New York's art cinemas. British audiences break up when Coward has a plain if emotional line, e.g. 'Julia – *don't* – be tiresome', and it must be said that when he reappears as a spirit his clipped delivery makes every line seem even more banal.

Paramount's experiment with Hecht and MacArthur confirmed the impression left by Griffith years before, that creative film-makers, however talented, could not be left without supervision. Lubitsch had made a firm bid against that industry rule, but Hecht and MacArthur managed to lose all the ground he had gained. Studio control of the stars was no less onerous, yet most of them could say that at Paramount at least their talents were well displayed. As we have seen, the popularity of Cooper and Colbert was maintained by their work under the studio's leading directors, and before we leave this studio we might glance at four performers who did not command those of the first rank.

To move from Coward to Shirley Temple (q.v.) is not quite to move from the sublime to the ridiculous; she was far more famous than he, and their renown, like that of Garbo and Chaplin, far transcended the show business gossip column. She made two films for Paramount as that fame was beginning – and in **Little Miss Marker** (1934) received solo star billing: but it has little in common with her later films for Fox and does not even seem designed for the same audience. Its source is a story by Damon Runyon, and it is a Damon Runyon picture before it is a Temple vehicle: Runyon – according to Garson Kanin – was the only contemporary writer respected by the Hollywood moguls, and this film, directed by Alexander Hall, is certainly respectful of him. It is about a bookie called Sorrowful Jones, who finds himself saddled with someone else's small child; the bookie is expertly played by Adolphe Menjou, with Lynne Overman, Charles Bickford, Dorothy Dell, Warren Hymer and Sam Hardy among the lugheads looking after the child.

There are three star players whose names will always be associated with Paramount: Bing Crosby, Bob Hope and Dorothy Lamour. Miss Lamour's speciality was the jungle romance, a genre for which Paramount thought Technicolor especially suited. The studio's second film in the process was **Ebb Tide** (1937), a dull version of the South Seas story by Robert Louis Stevenson and Lloyd Osbourne, directed by James Hogan. Frances Farmer in fact wore the sarong in this, but in just one film – her first, *The Jungle Princess* (1936) – Lamour had made that garment her own, and she donned it again for **Her Jungle Love** (1938), with Paramount venturing into colour for only the third time. If you can follow the film attentively, which is difficult, you will find that it cannot decide whether it is set in Malaya or the South Pacific. George Archainbaud directed. Another Silent veteran, Alfred Santell, made **Aloma of the South Seas** (1941), a later demonstration of studio cynicism, with shoddy special effects and dialogue which refers to the ocean as 'the big water' and a volcano as 'the fire god'. As a primitive native girl Lamour says 'Oh pooh' in times of crisis, and is otherwise the only person involved who has her tongue in her cheek. She made some half dozen of these films,

which raises the question as to whether any other woman in film history was set to such idiotic tasks.

Bob Hope (b. 1904) came from vaudeville and Broadway; he was primarily a gag-man, but his expressions of cowardice and self-delight carried him through a large number of films. The public adored him, to the extent that by the end of the War he was already a national figure, although without achieving much critical regard – in which respect he is unlike most of the major screen clowns. His early films revive extremely well. They have funny lines and situations, suggesting that his writers enjoyed inventing for the vain scaredy-cat whom he plays so superbly; and they are, unlike most vehicles for comics, extremely well made – one might compare those that Paramount produced with W. C. Fields. For instance, consider the art direction, of the pathetic *Aloma of the South Seas* alongside that of **The Cat and the Canary** (1939) or **The Ghost Breakers** (1940), whose creepy old dark houses are masterpieces of the designer's skill. The former is a straightforward remake of Paul Leni's funny-creepie – made funnier now, because Hope, as a vaudeville performer, is allowed some jokes – and it is just about the best film with which to experience secret passages and sliding panels and portraits with removable eyes. Elliot Nugent's direction allows no burlesque, and the same is true of George Marshall's work on *The Ghost Breakers*, also with Paulette Goddard, and also the remake of a Silent film. **Louisiana Purchase** (1941) is based on a stage musical with book by Morrie Ryskind, who ten years earlier had been one of the writers of 'Of Thee I Sing', the first musical to win the Pulitzer Prize – despite which the movie companies had always avoided it, since its subject is political corruption. So it is here, but this was filmed because Buddy de Sylva, who had produced it on Broadway, had since become Chief of Production at Paramount (in succession to William Le Baron). From the show came Victor Moore, as the incorruptible senator, and also Irene Bordoni and Vera Zorina to aid Hope (replacing William Gaxton, who had teamed with Moore in both the stage shows), who is blackmailed into corrupting him. Aided by Irving

Cummings, who in any case always directed at a plod, de Sylva decreed a literal version of the show, even to the 'business' for the lead comics. Eliminating most of Irving Berlin's score is inexcusable: to keep the book and throw out the songs★ was one of the many unfathomable decisions which litter Hollywood history.

Bing Crosby always gave the impression of being one of the nicest fellows ever to step before a camera. He sang in a relaxed manner, called crooning to distinguish it from the stentorian voices of the ballad-singers who were prevalent when he started. Gradually he found complete audience acceptance in the light comedies he made for Paramount in the Thirties, his songs interspersed throughout the love-doesn't-run-smoothly plots. Perhaps because of his lazy manner they have little impetus; his clowning is game rather than accomplished, and he tried whenever he could to offset the soulfulness of most of the songs he was given to sing. He enjoyed working with comics and wisely handed **Doctor Rhythm** (1938) to Beatrice Lillie, in fine fettle as a woman who hires him, a medic posing as a cop, to prevent her niece (Mary Carlisle) from running off with a fortune hunter; Frank Tuttle directed, supposedly from a story by O. Henry. **The Birth of the Blues** (1941), ostensibly about the formation of the first all-White Dixieland band, is not really about jazz, nor the event mentioned in the title: however, it is unpretentious and is one of the first features that not only acknowledges but clearly likes what it refers to as 'darkie music' – perhaps because the director, Victor Schertzinger, was also a composer. Crosby's admiration for Louis Armstrong had got that player included in two earlier Crosby vehicles, and it is a pity he is not in this (except in a montage); Edward 'Rochester' Anderson is the only coloured entertainer on hand, as a caustic family retainer. The leading lady is Mary Martin, briefly under contract to Paramount – and her failure to find popularity in films is astonishing: she now seems, after Judy Garland, the best female in musicals of the time – so much warmer, more vibrant, more pure fun than the Grables, Huttons

★ Berlin's Hollywood contracts thereafter gave him total control over the use of his material.

and Lamours. She, Crosby and Jack Teagarden have a number together, 'The Waiter, the Porter and the Upstairs Maid' which, though indifferently staged, is as delightful as anything in the genre.

The conditions prevailing at 20th Century-Fox were happier than at R.K.O. and Paramount, and since there were no financial troubles as the industry recovered from the Depression, there were no executive shifts. Darryl F. Zanuck was the youngest head of any of the major studios, and considered the most enlightened; but his policy was no different from that of any of the other tycoons, for it also revolved round the stars. However, virtually all the studio's most important pictures were directed by either John Ford or Henry King, filmmakers of proved accomplishment. Significantly, they were also veterans, having wielded the director's megaphone for almost a decade before the coming of Talkies. The industry, including Zanuck, was not a great believer in youth – at least, behind the camera; and one of the reasons Hollywood and its films changed so little between the end of the Depression and America's entry into the War was its lack of interest in new blood. Indeed, between the arrival of theatre directors with the coming of Talkies and the graduation of directors from television almost three decades later only a handful of important new film-makers arrived – usually from Broadway or abroad.

John Ford's Oscar for *The Informer* gave him more clout at 20th Century-Fox, his home studio, and in **The Prisoner of Shark Island** (1936) he made one of his best films, handling with quiet verisimilitude sequences of great tension. Nunnally Johnson wrote the screenplay, and as in many another good film the story is from the byways of history, concerning the Dr Mudd (Warner Baxter) who splinted the leg of John Wilkes Booth, broken as he fled the scene of his crime. Mudd was convicted in the hysteria which followed Lincoln's assassination and sentenced to life imprisonment on what, so a title informs us, is the American equivalent of Devil's Island. The facts have been simplified, omitting both Mudd's recognition of Booth and the savage treatment he received before his trial; but the cinema has rarely done so well by its old standby, the miscarriage of justice.

Zanuck's most pressing need was for suitable vehicles for Shirley Temple, an unexpected gift to film-goers and his stockholders. Thus, after returning to R.K.O. for his Scottish and Irish pictures, Ford directed her in **Wee Willie Winkie** (1937), which changed the sex of Kipling's young hero to accommodate her. She brings peace to the North-West Frontier between some red-blooded scenes concerning the sergeant (Victor McLaglen), and Ford's portrait of Frontier life is as romantic and heroic as the American West of his later films. He responds to India as Hathaway did in *Lives of a Bengal Lancer,* but again away from his home lot **The Hurricane** (1937) confirms a new mastery in his approach. The camera is placed with a clear eye for the strongest possible evocation of time and place, and in such a way as to enhance both players and subject. Bert Glennon was the cinematographer and in fact, working for Goldwyn, Ford was able to use a number of his preferred collaborators, including Dudley Nichols (who adapted a story by Nordhoff and Hall). The film was one of the expensive 'natural disaster' movies of the time, and it remains watchable: a slight tale of colonial injustice holds our interest till the winds start to blow – concerning a separated native couple, Jon Hall and Dorothy Lamour, who are expertly supported by Mary Astor, Raymond Massey and Thomas Mitchell – and the climax itself is tremendous.

If, on such occasions, Ford begins to justify such hyperbole as 'the indomitable poet of the American cinema' (Gavin Lambert and Lindsay Anderson in *Sight and Sound*), he is anything but on either **Four Men and a Prayer** (1938) or **Submarine Patrol** (1938). The former concerns four brothers (Richard Greene, David Niven, George Sanders, William Henry) trying to discover why their father (C. Aubrey Smith) was cashiered from the Indian Army; in the second a playboy (Greene) joins the Navy as a grease-monkey, and it does have a certain bite when confined to the activities of the crew. War films were reckoned to be anathema at the box-office, but, said the *Motion Picture Herald*, with 'war on the front pages of every newspaper showmen shouldn't be afraid of this one'.

Ford's irritation with both assignments increased when Zanuck would not approve his next project, a Western script he had bought (nor would Selznick, so Ford never made the contracted film with him); but Walter Wanger, producing independently for United Artists, agreed to do it. The film was **Stagecoach** (1939), and it was a watershed. Gary Cooper had turned down the leading role so Ford cast John Wayne, an actor from B-Westerns – and with Wayne he was restricted to a medium budget. Nevertheless he went to Monument Valley for locations (for the first time), and if the film in that regard and others now seems stale, that may be because it is one of the most imitated films ever made. Wayne became a leading star, and Westerns again became the staple they had not been since Silent days. This one was not exactly new, for Ernest Haycocks had based his novel on Guy de Maupassant's celebrated tale, 'Boule de Suif'. It is the tale of a mixed group of people suddenly thrown together, including a prostitute (Claire Trevor) hounded out of town, a drunken doctor (Thomas Mitchell), a pregnant woman (Louise Platt), and a pompous bank manager (Berton Churchill) absconding with the cash. Nothing much happens till the Indians attack, and then, as Ford later admitted, the film would have ended if they had had the sense to shoot the horses.

Ford's next project, **Young Mr Lincoln** (1939), was sanctioned by Zanuck because a play on the subject ('Abe Lincoln in Illinois') had been a Broadway success; Ford wanted to do a story foreshadowing Lincoln's later greatness, and worked closely with Lamar Trotti on the superficial script, which is almost saved by the likeable portrait by Henry Fonda in the title-role. The images have been so carefully composed as to be almost petrified. Ford was ever prone to preciosity, especially when he took it upon himself to be 'artistic': there is a huge difference between the shots of shutters in *Wee Willie Winkie* and those in *The Fugitive* (q.v.), one commercial and the other ostensibly 'art', and in the same way the evocation of the American past is much less pretentious in *Stagecoach* than in *Lincoln,* on

John Ford's tendency towards artiness when confronted with a 'serious' issue was effectively curbed on *The Grapes of Wrath*, which stands as the peak of his career. The film is impressive not because it is about people on the starvation line but because it never patronises them, and only rarely makes concessions to melodrama or to sentiment. The players are Jane Darwell, Henry Fonda and Russell Simpson.

which Ford made the same distinctions. There are elements of both in **Drums Along the Mohawk** (1939), where the conventional early Technicolor shots of banked clouds are preferable to the self-consciously 'Fordian' compositions; similarly the piece is strongest on such matters as the Indian attacks, weakest when attempting a statement on war. Trotti and Sonya Levien wrote the screenplay, from a novel by Walter D. Edmonds, and the besieged pioneer couple are Fonda and Claudette Colbert.

However, these films had increased Ford's standing to the point where, if unable to select his subjects as freely as Capra did, he could at least select from the properties available those with which he felt the closest affinity. Zanuck's offer of **The Grapes of Wrath** (1940) enabled him to prove again that he was a fine director given a good script and under the right conditions – and that Hollywood could make a great and serious film if it had the right book upon which to build. John Steinbeck's novel had been a best seller: but in view of Nunnally Johnson's superb screenplay we need not consider studio motivation. It stands today, four decades after it was made, as a document of social history, and presents an America that would not be seen on the screen again for another two decades. The novel starts

in the Oklahoma dust-bowl, and the film opens as an anonymous 'they' have sent in tractors to mow down the shacks serving as homesteads. In reality, the sharecroppers had farmed their lands unwisely and when the droughts came were forced to mortgage everything they had; whereupon the banks forced them out because they considered they knew more modern ways to farm the land. Actually, the film is not about Oklahoma, except to start the Joad family on its odyssey, but about the exploitation they found in California. The migrants there were not treated as human beings; and they hardly regarded themselves as such.

One of the achievements of the film is its avoidance of a statement on human dignity. The Joads do not particularly suffer, or smile through their tears; all they ask is for work in order to eat. The famous ending, with its affirmation of the refusal to be 'licked', comes a mite falsely, but it is the right sentiment, and a better ending than Steinbeck provided. I cannot see in the film any indignation or concern on the part of its makers, but that was not then considered part of their job – which was to make *us* concerned. At the end, the Joads arrive at a decent camp administered by the Department of Agriculture. 'Why aren't there more like it?' asks Tom (Fonda), and the caretaker (Grant Mitchell) replies 'You figger it out. I can't.' Fonda's grave face and his loping walk were never better used; as Ma, Jane Darwell's strength and smile are perhaps too comforting, but her eyes convey her suffering and her indifference to it now. She won a Best Supporting Oscar, and the Academy also voted one to Ford as Best Director; but they did not like the film enough to place it above *Rebecca* (q.v.) or the lightweight *Philadelphia Story* (q.v.), which were voted respectively Best Picture and Best Screenplay. Nevertheless, the controversy it stirred up was entirely favourable to Hollywood, even if the industry's conversion to current affairs was a little tardy, and as ever based on prior acceptance in another medium.

Ford returned to Wanger and United Artists to make **The Long Voyage Home** (1940), a modernisation by Dudley Nichols of four one-act plays by Eugene O'Neill, set on a homeward-bound British merchant vessel. The photographer was Gregg Toland, whose uncluttered, clear images for *The Grapes of Wrath* here give way to Ufa-style artiness, a weakness to which Ford was prone. However, this is still the best American film about life at sea. It is meandering: whores come aboard and smuggle in liquor; there is a raid by a German aircraft and a funeral at sea; the whores are paid off and the men get drunk – a flawed sequence, but redeemed by its feeling for the fragmentary and romantic nature of such occasions. The captain is Wilfred Lawson, and the motley crew includes two Svenskas (John Wayne, John Qualen) and inevitably several Irishmen (Thomas Mitchell, Barry Fitzgerald, Arthur Shields). The use of Irish airs in Ford's Irish films is oppressive, but he makes the shanties work; and if the use of 'Harbour Lights' is anachronistic this song surely expresses the sweet-sour oil-salt smell of ships and ports and being at sea.

Tobacco Road (1941) as a play – by Jack Kirkland, adapted from the novel by Erskine Caldwell – had, as a foreword tells us, opened in New York City in 1933 and was still running. The chief reason for that – and some said the only one – was its sexual content, and the Hays Office allowed only hints of that in the film, as when young Pearl runs away from Lov (Ward Bond), who 'wasn't doin' nothin' to her but tiein' her up with some rope' and he replaces her with a sister (Gene Tierney) too grown-up for his tastes. People sit around scratchin' and arguin', as one might expect in a film in which Charley Grapewin gets top billing: the burden of it falls on him and Elizabeth Patterson, as his wife, making sympathetic comedy out of 'poor white-trash'. Ford, reflecting the original play, finds nothing in poverty but quaintness.

His supposed sympathy for the proletariat brought Ford to **How Green Was My Valley** (1941). 'The majesty of plain people and the beauty which shines in the souls of simple, honest folk are seldom made the topics of extensive discourse on the screen' was the way Bosley Crowther began his review in *The New York Times*, going on to describe it as 'one which may truly be regarded as an outstanding film of the year'. It went on to win a handful of Oscars, including Best Picture and Best

Director. Richard Llewellyn's novel had been read by millions, and it cost a packet to build his Welsh village on the backlot. The only Welshman in the cast is Rhys Williams, in a minor role, but despite only occasional attempts at the right accent by the rest of the cast you know where you are because – this being a Ford movie – the soundtrack throbs with appropriate airs. Philip Dunne's adaptation of the novel – which is of the 'trouble-at-t'-mine' school – retains its framework, that of a middle-aged man recalling his boyhood in such phrases as: 'For singing is in my people as sight is in the eye.' The boy is played by 'Master Roddy McDowall'; Donald Crisp is the father, Sara Allgood is the mother, Maureen O'Hara the daughter, and there is a heap of sons, all of whom work down the mine. Since the material is so inferior to the Steinbeck – though it was not thought so at the time – it is interesting to find Ford descending to its level, if effectively, as in the sequences calculated to invoke family love. He is at his best with the boy (as movies often are), but this family defeats even his loving treatment, much too self-satisfied despite a generation-gap quarrel over socialism and the daughter's improbable marriage.

Until Ford came into his own Henry King had been Zanuck's automatic choice for his prestige pictures. King made the studio's first Technicolor feature, **Ramona** (1936), which was the fourth screen version of that old and highly sentimentalised account of the plight of an Indian couple – and if the first part (fiestas and such) is artificial, it improves mightily once the drama begins, partly as a result of the expansive performance of Jane Darwell, and partly because it is not till then that King responds to both the drama and the colour, making them, as they should be, inseparable. Loretta Young in a black wig is Loretta Young in a black wig; and we do wonder why the Christian and Westernised Indian chief (Don Amche) doesn't simply don Western dress to avoid trouble. King remade two other famous films (both inferior to his best films of that time), **Way Down East** (1935) and **Seventh Heaven** (1936), and though the material was equally dated, his response, when stirred, is sound, going for full-blooded romance by way of exquisite framing and romantic lighting. But you wonder why they bothered – especially in the latter case, with the Hays Office requirements making equivocal the profession of the heroine, played by Simone Simon with overmuch sophistication. It is also hard to accept James Stewart as a Parisian sewer-rat; but if the lecherous C.O. at the end has become a shining (if wounded) subaltern, there is gain in the role of Chico's chum (J. Edward Bromberg, chameleon among character actors), whose love of cats and hatred of Diane suggests some darkling thought.

Lloyds of London (1937) was one of the factual historical dramas of which Zanuck was so fond, and is mainly notable for the revelation of a new leading man, Tyrone Power (1913–58), who became after Shirley Temple the studio's most important property: willing rather than gifted, he was put into the studio's biggest projects and therefore continued to benefit from King's expertise. Miscast as an ambitious schemer buying politicians in **In Old Chicago** (1938), King simply gets him offscreen as quickly and often as possible. The role was meant for Clark Gable (the advent of Power meant that Zanuck became less dependent on Metro when he had a male lead to cast, and an additional blessing was the advent of Alice Faye, playing here the role intended for Jean Harlow), and the film itself is a part-copy of *San Francisco* (q.v.), with a similarly contrived plot, to be resolved by a disaster – the Great Fire – which also provides a spectacular climax. It is, however, a gutsy, gusty entertainment: the Chicago of 1871 knee-deep in mud, carriages tearing through, pretty ladies with parasols, and men with walrus moustaches in lush, over-padded interiors – all this, and Mrs O'Leary's cow.

The same three players, Power, Faye and Don Ameche, were reunited for **Alexander's Ragtime Band** (1938), and it has been suggested that their obvious liking for each other is one reason for its almost-total success; but King himself claimed credit for responding warmly to his material – a show-business story built around people he had known in New York. Two dozen or so songs by Irving Berlin, old and new, dictated the form of the story, a panoramic one from ragtime

to radio, via the First World War. The form was innovatory for a musical, the combination in this genre of comedy and drama had been untried for several years; and more than any film so far it confirmed the reputation of what was then Hollywood's youngest studio.

King's craftsmanship and always responsible approach to his material are further evident in both **Jesse James** (1939), another excursion into Technicolor, and **Stanley and Livingstone** (1939), both confirming Zanuck's penchant for the historical spectacular. There are considerable distortions of fact in both films – particularly regrettable in the case of Nunnally Johnson's screenplay for *Jesse James,* for the James brothers were virtually the only ones among the famous outlaws to have had any degree of political importance; indeed, Johnson uses none of the horrifying facts (even the details of the assassination are wrong), offering a bland tale of injustice and turning the James boys into Robin Hood-motivated badmen. 'He ain't a knight fightin' a bad railroad,' someone says, 'he's a wild animal.' But as played by Mr Power the only animal he resembles is a domestic cat. In *Stanley and Livingstone,* Spencer Tracy and Cedric Hardwicke play the famous explorers, journalist and medical man respectively, and both are on their best form: no audience would ever snigger at the manner in which the famous line is spoken. When the piece sticks to the facts, it is dull, and when it telescopes and hypes them, towards the end, it becomes banal; but all in all, as B. R. Crisler said in *The New York Times,* it 'represents rather a fine renunciation of cheap dramatics by a studio which occasionally in the past has shown an inclination to overindulgence'.

Zanuck next came up with **Little Old New York** (1940), whose title and the presence of Alice Faye (q.v.) were meant to suggest a follow-up to *In Old Chicago.* The less than robust rivals for her favours are Fred MacMurray and Richard Greene, the latter as Robert Fulton, who built the first steamboat in 1807. King's handling of the boat-building sequence attests to his response when enthused, as he was throughout two better studies of the American past, **Chad Hanna** (1940) and **Remember the Day** (1941). The former, in Technicolor, is a tale of circus folk in the 1840s, written by Nunnally Johnson from a story by Walter D. Edmonds, with Fonda, Darwell, Guy Kibbee and two conventional Hollywood ladies, Linda Darnell and Dorothy Lamour; the latter is one of several films spawned by the success of *Goodbye, Mr Chips,* with Claudette Colbert as the aged teacher remembering earlier days and the sportsmaster (John Payne) who went to war and did not come back. It belongs in the vanguard of memory films of the time, all touching on the First World War (it was released at the time of Pearl Harbor): with girls in gingham dresses strolling on lawns, the first Model T Ford, and stern or benign fathers in wing collars.

Henry Hathaway joined 20th and made **Johnny Apollo** (1940), a film untypical of both, about a college boy (Power) who turns mobster after considering the disparity between the prison sentences handed out to his father (Edward Arnold) and another gangster (Lloyd Nolan). In this case, both period detail and Power were poor – the film was a deliberate attempt by Zanuck to put Power into the sort of role which had made Cagney famous. To that end one of the writers of the screenplay – the other was Philip Dunne – was Rowland Brown, who had made two of the best gangster films: undoubtedly we owe to him the chilling details – the stiletto kept inside the trouser-leg, the sequence in the mortuary – which make this less an attempt to revive an old genre than the first *film noir* of the Forties. Of **Brigham Young** (1940), Hathaway said later, 'It was a very difficult film to make – all those goddam wagons.' The word *Frontiersman* was added to the title to forewarn audiences that they could not expect a film about legalised harems – and though Young (Dean Jagger) admits to twelve wives, we see only one (Mary Astor). Unhappily also visible is a completely untruthful tale of the Mormons' trek to escape religious persecution, the usual pallid romance, between Power and Linda Darnell, and a repeat of the climax of *The Good Earth* (q.v.).

Its writer was Lamar Trotti, whom Zanuck considered an expert on the American past. He was also responsible for the screenplay of **Hudson's Bay** (1940), which Irving Pichel directed, concerning two French explorers (Paul Muni, Laird Cregar) and the Court of Charles II (Vincent Price). Muni displays misplaced enthusiasm with dialogue like this: 'Before yoy take a contri wiz your hand yoy most take eet wiz ziz' (placing hand on heart); while John Sutton asks, quite seriously, 'How's Nell?' Zanuck's historical films are among the most useless ever made. Scott Fitzgerald thought **Suez** (1938) would put the cinema back three years, and that seems an optimistic estimate. Zanuck's penchant for building pictures round a concept – event, place, person – was never more foolhardy than here, as de Lesseps (Power) loses his beloved Eugenie (Loretta Young) to Louis Napoleon (Leon Ames); just about everyone turns up, from Disraeli to Liszt and Victor Hugo. The director, Allan Dwan, said he was drawn to the film for its 'human story. Whether the canal was built or not was of no importance to me.' He also mentioned that the de Lesseps family sued, in France, but the case was thrown out because 'this picture did such honour to France'. France, possibly; 20th Century-Fox, decidedly not.

It is not surprising that the majority of these films concerned the New World, since there was a revulsion in the U.S. towards events in the Old one, as war threatened once again. As the subject became increasingly discussed, Hollywood produced a number of films on World War One, but the public did not want to see Zanuck's **The Road to Glory** (1936), based on a four-year-old French film which he had bought, *Le Croix de Bois*. Howard Hawks returned to direct, and eventually a new screenplay was commissioned from Joel Sayre and William Faulkner, borrowing much from Humphrey Cobb's novel, 'Paths of Glory'★ (and the line about blindness from *Mata Hari*). Warner Baxter and Fredric March are entirely serious, but the finale with white-bearded Lionel Barrymore, meant to represent a last act of supreme heroism, founders in bathos. Indeed, although this film is much grimmer than Hawks's *The Dawn Patrol*, it is not in the same league.

The purpose of **The Mark of Zorro** (1940) was not so much to recreate old

★ 'Some Time in the Sun' by Tom Dardis confirms that Faulkner had owned a copy.

California as to allow Tyrone Power to swashbuckle, which he does with zest, unembarrassed by the tight pants and the necessary show of effeminacy. Basil Rathbone is, for once, conventional as a villain, and the film belongs to J. Edward Bromberg as the greedy and incompetent governor, strutting about like a turkey-cock. Gale Sondergaard* is his vain wife and Linda Darnell an effective heroine. Rouben Mamoulian's direction is almost flawless, but another remake of a famous Silent, **Blood and Sand** (1941), is over-long and unduly earnest. Power has Valentino's role, and the women in his life are Miss Darnell and Rita Hayworth, the latter particularly decorative in Technicolor – which seems to have taken most of Mamoulian's attention.

Since most of Mamoulian's later films are unsatisfactory, the sheer excellence of *The Mark of Zorro* may be due to the team built up by Zanuck, or to the man himself in his capacity of taskmaster, examining every inch of film and chivvying everyone around him. Another poor director, Bruce Humberstone, made an exceptional film at this time, **I Wake up Screaming** (1941), based on a murder novel by Bruce Fisher. With *The Maltese Falcon* (q.v.) this film launched the vogue for what we now call the Hollywood *film noir* – an over-studied but enjoyable series. As with *Johnny Apollo,* the studio created an exceptionally sleazy New York – the all-night cinema, a florist's shop, the bare precinct; and the often shifty detectives of the old gangster films become in Laird Cregar a figure of such sadness and evil that Humberstone does not need the camera to emphasise the huge expanse of waistcoat, the Oscar Wilde lips and hooded eyes. Elisha Cook is the cringing, fawning lift-boy with a hang-up on the dead girl (Carole Landis), a former hash-slinger whose heart of stone had finally put the ticket to Hollywood in her purse – but the film is even more enjoyable if you wonder exactly what she had done for him and Cregar. The keynotes of the *film noir* – pathology, seediness and melancholy – were merely revivals from the gangster film era, to be noted and enjoyed now that the pace of films had so slowed down.

* Ten years later, both artists were among those black-listed for supposed communist affiliations; Bromberg's family believe he died because of it.

The studio also had a brief fling with the most famous detective of all, and **The Hound of the Baskervilles** (1939) is the most taking of the Holmes stories, with the ghostly cur roaming Dartmoor baying for blood. This was the sixth film version, and the first time Basil Rathbone and Nigel Bruce played Holmes and Watson, but what most concerned Fox was that it provided an English gentleman role for Richard Greene, unconvincing as anything else. Graham Greene noted a number of changes from the book, including the fact that Holmes had been given a sense of humour, and its welcome prompted a sequel (the later B-series with Rathbone was made by Universal), **The Adventures of Sherlock Holmes** (1939), with Alfred Werker replacing Sidney Lanfield as director; both films, though medium budget, are handsome and reasonably intriguing.

Under Two Flags (1936) was another much-filmed piece, with Frank Lloyd this time in charge of Ouida's novel. In a Foreign Legion station, 'the white man's most distant outpost', a tough major (Victor McLaglen) is in love with the local bar-owner, Cigarette (Claudette Colbert) till the advent of a sergeant (Ronald Colman). 'Do you speak Arabic?' someone asks him. 'Oh, fairly well,' he says, with familiar nonchalance. Lady Venetia (Rosalind Russell) arrives on the scene, displaying a most unladylike desire to inspect the barrack room. She falls for the sergeant, certain that she has met him before, and without batting an eye goes on to discuss 'one of the most popular officers in the Guards' who shielded his younger brother and disappeared.

The subject of the British abroad also featured in **The Rains Came** (1939), from a more recent best seller, by Louis Bromfield, and Clarence Brown was borrowed from M-G-M to direct. No one gets the accents right, including Marie Ouspenskaya and Tyrone Power as Indians, and though the Indian character and the British presence are much discussed, the film actually says nothing, while the plot, about a bored socialite (Myrna Loy) finding redemption in healing, is tired. However, the flood and earthquake are impressive, as huge pieces of masonry hurtle about the screen: and if, for the director's convenience, the special effects generally take place at night, the disasters are all the more frightening for taking place in darkness.

With the outstanding exception of *The Grapes of Wrath,* that was the closest 20th came to a serious film on a contemporary subject, but mention might be made of **Dante's Inferno** (1935), directed by Harry Lachman, and **It Had to Happen** (1936), directed by Roy del Ruth, both concerned with a backstreet boy whose ambition turns sour on him at the end. In the former Spencer Tracy is the carnival barker who tramples on everyone till he is a powerful entrepreneur; in the latter George Raft is the immigrant who becomes one of the underworld powers behind the governor. That a wealthy and married society lady (Miss Russell) stands by him when he is indicted with fraud is one of the interesting themes which this film merely plays with. The other film is notable for its recreation of Dante's hell, building from the sequences of the Silent film of the same name to create a Bosch-like splendour.

The success or failure of most 20th Century-Fox films had become relatively immaterial with the rise of Shirley Temple (b. 1928). Her popularity in fact began during the Fox regime, after her singing one song in **Stand Up and Cheer** (1934), a musical intended to make audiences feel less despondent about the Depression. Presumably it did, for the public took her to its heart, and for the next three years she surpassed even Clark Gable as the biggest box-office draw in films – a fact which makes even more curious much of the dialogue of her early films, nudging audiences by constantly referring to her as adorable, lovable, cute, etc. 'Curly Top, you're a bundle of joy-/Curly Top, you're like a wonderful toy/You're so full of sunshine, folks all agree,' sings John Boles in **Curly Top** (1935).

Her pictures were often new versions of the Silent vehicles of Baby Peggy and Mary Pickford, but instead of growing up to adolescence in the last reel for the fade-out kiss Temple was usually given an elder sister to take care of that department; because audiences liked to see the tot sing and dance, many of her films are concerned with show business. She was constantly surrounded by ageing vaude-villians, and her movies are sometimes

worth seeing for them or for the equally ageing supporting players. Some are worth viewing for themselves, at their best when proposing the Dickensian view of a child struggling against a malevolent universe, and at their worst when she is restoring happiness to others or melting stony hearts – including on occasion Honest Abe and Queen Victoria. **Captain January** (1936), directed by David Butler, is one of the former, while – were it not for little steelheart of the golden locks – **Heidi** (1937) would rank with the very best films made for children. Taken from Johanna Spyri's popular tale, the child suffers a vicious aunt (Mady Christians), a crabbed old hermit of a grandfather (Jean Hersholt) and, with her crippled companion (Marcia Mae Jones) a governess (Mary Nash) of such double-dyed villainy that she plans to sell Heidi to the gypsies. The director was Allan Dwan, working with Raymond Griffith

The entire world in the Thirties seemed to agree with 20th Century-Fox that Shirley Temple was the most adorable child on earth, but today audiences find her an acquired taste. It was inevitable that she would play *Heidi* and that by any standard is an admirable film.

as producer, and Dwan paid him this tribute: 'He understood pictures because he had been in them and knew all the problems. And he was excellent at gags . . . He had an effervescent attitude.' They also worked on **Rebecca of Sunnybrook Farm** (1938), which is enjoyable, due mainly to the presence of Helen Westley, magisterial in pince-nez and floral prints, bridling at each suspected infringement of her dignity. This actress also decorates **Stowaway** (1936), as does Alice Faye, but more prettily; and as directed by William A. Seiter the excitement promised by the title is still conveyed to every child in the audience.

Of the other Temple films, two are worth seeing for their villainesses: Jane Withers in **Bright Eyes** (1934), a pampered, vicious infant who delights in pulling dolls apart, and Miss Nash again, as the headmistress in **The Little Princess** (1939). Neither the addition of Technicolor nor the fact that Temple, approaching adolescence, had become an adequate actress could prevent the film from falling below expectations. Zanuck had refused to lend her for *The Wizard of Oz* (q.v.), thus doing the world an enduring favour; but when that film triumphed he put Temple into a similar Technicolor fantasy, **The Blue Bird** (1940), with Walter Lang as director. The story is less engaging, but there is a tremendous sequence of a forest fire raging amid a huge storm, and it is only inferior in one great respect – its heroine, who lacked not only the wistfulness but almost everything else that made Judy Garland so effective. **Young People** (1940), directed by Dwan and inspired by *Babes in Arms* (q.v.), reminds us that Garland had arrived in films, although Temple, leggy now, was no better a singer or dancer than she had ever been. The public refused to flock to either film, and though the studio defensively attributed the well-known failure of *The Blue Bird* to its exorbitant cost, only a tentative step was taken towards renewing the child's contract. Her run had been phenomenal – and that is the right adjective in both senses: she appeared when Hollywood and audiences needed her, in reaction to the sleazy sex stories washed away by the new Code, and with a smiling confidence which suggested that if she had heard of the Depression it did not bother her. But the fact that the public deserted her almost overnight on the advent of a more talented youngster – not to mention Deanna Durbin (q.v.) – suggests only a freak attraction.

In the same category belongs Sonja Henie, an Olympic skating champion who came into films and skated. Years later Zanuck observed that 'stars confine you to the standard thing,' but if in deploring the star-system he contradicted much of his career he had demonstrated, with these 'standard things', that he knew plenty about packaging a young lady who, once she took off her skates, was devoid of interest. Her early films have ridiculous plots – mere opportunities to get her on to ice – and an excellent array of supporting talent whose excessive fondness for the Sonja character was also borrowed from the Temple films. Henie's two best movies are both with Tyrone Power and directed by Sidney Lanfield; **Thin Ice** (1937), in which, for once, the skating is imaginatively staged and choreographed, and **Second Fiddle** (1939), with its half dozen songs by Irving Berlin – and if he was not at his most inspired who could blame him, since neither artist could sing or dance? The War might have revitalised Henie's career, since her Norwegian accent enabled her to play a refugee in **Sun Valley Serenade** (1941), directed by Bruce Humberstone in an uneasy compromise between the wholly visual and the wholly aural – because its rival attraction is Glenn Miller's orchestra, for whose sake it is occasionally revived today.

Judy Garland made her feature debut at 20th in **Pigskin Parade** (1936), directed by David Butler, a college musical only otherwise remarkable for the presence of a left-wing student (Elisha Cook Jr) – who is, of course, an object of scorn. The leading players are Stuart Erwin, Patsy Kelly and Jack Haley. Garland, billed ninth, does sing three songs, but the studio was not sufficiently interested to ask M-G-M – who did not know what to do with her – whether it could keep her; nor was it then interested in the lady billed sixth, Betty Grable, who later became one of its biggest stars.

The singing star at 20th Century-Fox

was Alice Faye (b. 1915), whose popularity soared once Zanuck decided she need no longer look like Jean Harlow; indeed, the more gentle appearance suited one of the screen's most amiable personalities and the best of the light vocalists. She did not have to be packaged like Temple or Henie, but her films – unpretentious, undemanding entertainments – show a similar care: **King of Burlesque** (1935), directed by Lanfield, with Warner Baxter reprising his role in *42nd Street* and Faye and Jack Oakie in the roles they would play again in *Hello, Frisco, Hello* (q.v.), a partial remake; **Sing, Baby, Sing** (1936), directed by Lanfield, in which Faye is a singer promoted by a no-good agent (Gregory Ratoff) because she's supposedly being wooed by a drunken movie-star (Adolphe Menjou, parodying John Barrymore); **On the Avenue** (1937), directed by Roy del Ruth, singing the Irving Berlin score and, according to the billing, 'supporting' Dick Powell as a Broadway composer-producer star and Madeleine Carroll as the richest girl in the world, who is lampooned by him; and **You Can't Have Everything** (1937), directed by Norman Taurog, as an aspiring playwright whose work is pinched by a musical comedy writer (Don Ameche). Indeed, she is not only a playwright, but an intense young intellectual – a role never played less convincingly nor more charmingly, while Ameche responds with pleasing insouciance. They are an underrated team, he enthusiastic and sometimes unfeeling, she loving and patient. In **Hollywood Cavalcade** (1939) he is a prop-boy who becomes a director after discovering her, and she later gives him the chance of a come-back, directing her first Talkie. The Mack Sennett reconstructions, directed by Mal St Clair, are accurate, but otherwise only the old tunes provide an authentic period touch; the rest is sluggishly directed by Irving Cummings, wasting a good idea, a good title, Technicolor and Buster Keaton, cast as a custard-pie-throwing Silent comic (which he emphatically was not).

This was one of the panoramic musicals engendered by the success of *Alexander's Ragtime Band* (though audiences waiting for Faye to become a *singing* star were disappointed), another was **Rose of Washington Square** (1939), directed by

Gregory Ratoff. Intended as a dramatic musical, it concerns a stage star (Faye) in love with a gambler (Tyrone Power). Al Jolson appears as the heroine's confidant and 'the greatest star Broadway's ever known', singing yet again a medley of his famous songs, and giving a real charge to Nunnally Johnson's dialogue: 'The only girl on Broadway who'd rather listen to her own voice than her own heart!' and 'This is your song. It was born just for you. Sing it and they'll never forget it or you.' The song is 'My Man', and no one could have missed the allusion to the woman who had made it famous in the U.S., Fanny Brice. Song and situation recur in *Funny Girl* (q.v.), when they were so poorly rendered that no one could say, as here, 'It's like taking her heart in her two hands and holding it out in front of her.' Also to the same formula, and as

Tyrone Power and Alice Faye in typical mood when they were the biggest stars on the Fox lot: *Rose of Washington Square*. Since the film was recognisably based on the life of Fanny Brice, the usual disclaimer in the credits of 'any resemblance to real persons' is writ large instead of being tucked away at the bottom of the screen.

genial as they are predictable, are **Tin Pan Alley** (1940), directed by Walter Lang, and **The Great American Broadcast** (1941), directed by Archie Mayo – indeed, the plots and casts are virtually identical, though the World War One footage in the former is stridently pro-British.

Zanuck was as adept at copying others as himself, and **Swanee River** (1939) was an attempt to repeat the success of M-G-M's Strauss musical and Paramount's *The Great Victor Herbert*; moreover, he realised that the Old South and the Negro minstrel shows would look splendid in the Technicolor he was increasingly using – and they do, partly because the Technicolor Corporation insisted on supervising, restraining the palette to pastel shades. Otherwise, as directed by Sidney Lanfield, the story of Stephen Foster (Ameche) is reduced to 'And then I wrote . . .', blaming his alcoholism on his frustrated yearning to be a serious composer rather than on his being a Northerner writing in Southern idiom at that time of conflict. Jolson, appearing as Christy the minstrel man, is given one self-indicting line, 'If there's anything I hate in a man it's an inflated ego,' while Ameche, not an actor of much resource, has charm to spare and a light touch. His d'Artagnan is the one saving grace of **The Three Musketeers** (1939), a 'musical comedy version' directed by Dwan, though the songs of that otherwise unfunny team, The Ritz Brothers, playing the lackeys, have a certain daffy splendour.

Ameche's screen partnership with Miss Faye was interrupted with **Down Argentine Way** (1940), when illness necessitated her replacement by Betty Grable, who plays an heiress with a bare midriff given to singing in Manhattan bars. This otherwise dreary racetrack tale, directed by Irving Cummings, was also notable for introducing the Argentinian-born Carmen Miranda, even if her numbers were filmed in New York and interpolated into the completed film. Beyond her elaborate costumes, nothing in the film justified the use of Technicolor, at this point only used in Hollywood for subjects considered of pictorial beauty. Public response supported Zanuck's faith in the system, and he stepped up production to one Technicolor film a month, often with subjects which did not, by the standards of the other studios, seem to require it. Within two years Technicolor was synonymous with the 20th Century-Fox musical, though with the increase in colour films the Technicolor Corporation was no longer able to supervise each production as it would have liked. The system was no longer discriminately used, as may be seen in **Moon Over Miami** (1941), where the by now *de rigeur* night club settings are part paint-box and part chocolate-box. The film itself, directed by Lang, is the 'standard thing', the second version of the studio's perennial about three fortune-hunting girls – and quite the dullest, apart from a few minutes by Ameche as a drunk millionaire and a bright song-and-dance at the beginning, choreographed by Hermes Pan, whose work with the studio would be much less distinguished than that with Fred Astaire, either before or later.

18

Hollywood's Golden Age: Universal, Warner and M-G-M

AT UNIVERSAL the problem was less to find the right star vehicles – the studio had no major names – than to keep the bailiff from the door. Not paying huge star salaries kept the overheads down, but it also meant that exhibitors were not inclined to book Universal pictures – which was one reason the studio continued, reluctantly, to make the potentially profitable horror films. Amongst these, and its programmers, Universal leavened each season with a couple of big pictures; and the Laemmles' assets included two or three directors capable of drawing leading players from other studios.

The success of earlier four-handkerchief efforts by John M. Stahl brought Claudette Colbert to the studio for **Imitation of Life** (1934), and Irene Dunne returned for **Magnificent Obsession** (1935), both of which make the earlier films seem as austere as legal textbooks. The first is taken from a novel by Fannie Hurst on racial integration and the second is based on an 'inspirational' novel by Lloyd C. Douglas. Neither would seem to appeal to anyone of mature mind for more than a few minutes – and that certainly applies to the remade versions of the Fifties – but Stahl works lightly and directly, keeping well back at the tricky moments and having sensible, humorous people (Ned Sparkes, Charles Butterworth) to support the stars. *Imitation of Life* concerns the partnership between a young widow (Colbert) and her coloured maid (Louise Beavers) who become wealthy as co-owners of Aunt Delilah's Pancake Mix. They live together, but one sits beside the chauffeur and the other behind; one goes downstairs and the other

up, and while the one upstairs throws a party the one in the basement sits listening to the noise. Presumably such conventions would have been observed, even if the film had had a stronger basis in reality, and it is sympathetic towards its lovable, stereotyped mammy and the daughter who, wanting to pass for white, is comforted with the dry philosophy: 'You've got to get used to it, so you might as well start now.' Everyone is desperately keen to do the right thing, which is also true of *Magnificent Obsession,* with its drunken playboy (Robert Taylor), accidentally responsible for the death of a doctor and the blinding of his widow (Miss Dunne). Taylor, his bounce kept down, is convincing except when, having redeemed himself, he is revealed as a Nobel prize-winner; while Dunne, though she is seen reading Braille with only one hand, actually did so herself after several weeks of instruction by experts. In **When Tomorrow Comes** (1939) she is equally convincing whether bending to examine a magazine while warbling the Liebestraum or delivering the one good line, 'I'm so hungry I'd eat anything that didn't bite me first'. The plot, however, is strained – about a waitress involved in a *coup de foudre* with a pianist (Charles Boyer), before discovering he is married – and showed that Stahl had lost conviction. He had left the studio after the change of management and had been assigned to a programmer on his return; he left again after this film, and continued to decline.

As did James Whale, an erratic but often talented director. Stahl was at one time capable of the same kind of alchemy as Borzage and McCarey, and the achievements of this small group contrasted sharply with the results of the Warner craftsmen, who could only hope their zest and attention to detail would paper over any cracks. Whale, like Mamoulian, belongs to a third group who, capable of mismanaging and misjudging their material to a degree, are yet by virtue of their taste and a penchant for copying directors with a strong personal style able to make an occasional good film. However, even in Whale's best films there is little evidence of strong control. *Photoplay* praised the direction of **By Candlelight** (1934), but its fairground sequence is taken from von Sternberg and the rest is pastiche Lubitsch. Hans Kräly's name appears among the four screenwriters (working from a German play adapted by P. G. Wodehouse), and the idea is Lubitschesque: a valet (Paul Lukas) masquerades as his master in order to emulate his philandering, not knowing that the lady concerned is in fact the lady's maid (Elissa Landi). But Whale misses the point, which is that two nice people make a fairy tale come true by emulating two not very nice people, and the rout is completed by the stars, he elephantine in a role ideal for Boyer (not then a star) while she seems to be playing exclusively for audiences in Shaftesbury Avenue.

Whale was one of the few homosexual directors to fail with actresses, but in **One More River** (1934) Diana Wynyard is an exception. With her aristocratic tones and delivery she at first seems only of the period, but then she advances ahead of her time, throwing away words and stepping on those of others, changing tempo within speeches as her thoughts change and using her whole body to convey meaning. She cannot, however, pull the film through: from a portrait of the English as forelock-tugging yokels it descends to domestic trivia, going to extreme lengths to put the wife (Miss Wynyard) in a compromising situation – in a broken-down car near Henley – and then keeping her chaste. R. C. Sherriff wrote the screenplay from a novel by Galsworthy, and the film was presumably meant for those who followed the headlines-making society divorces of the period.

Showboat (1936) was Universal's second version of the Kern-Hammerstein operetta, based in turn on Edna Ferber's novel about the old Mississippi and the showboat daughter (Irene Dunne) who marries the gambler (Allan Jones). Whale clearly enjoyed recreating old-time melodramas, and in general the anachronisms – e.g. those shots illustrating 'Ol' Man River' – can be forgiven as the cast sweeps into Kern's almost intact score. 'Ol' Man River' is sung by its greatest interpreter, Paul Robeson, for whom Kern wrote a new song, 'I Still Suits Me'. From the original cast Helen Morgan does her incomparable, moving 'Bill' and 'Can't Help Lovin' dat Man'. Only Mr Jones is poor: if it were a perfect world, the ideal man would have been Howard Keel from the later M-G-M version (q.v.). That gave us a better ending, and Technicolor; this is at its best with the moonlit river and the lovers on the top deck singing 'You Are Love': they don't do the verse, but then it's not a perfect world.

The Road Back (1937) was suitable for Universal inasmuch as its source was a novel by Erich Maria Remarque, taking off from *All Quiet on the Western Front*; its screenplay is by another war veteran, R. C. Sherriff, with Charles Kenyon, and, like the earlier film, it has a non-star cast. It starts in the trenches, and moves via the Armistice to the Revolution, which it handles gingerly; devolving into a study of post-war restlessness, it takes on a seriousness which the propagandist fervour of the earlier reels lacked. The art direction makes a convincing Germany, and reminds us that decor was Whale's strength. Whale copies Pabst for the murder; and though the subsequent trial turns on the old plea that the boys were taught to kill, it remains powerful, concluding with a montage of Europe rearming: it would be two years before another American film acknowledged that fact.

The film was a failure, thus not redeeming the situation at the studio, whereby the new management was hostile to most of the people who had worked for its predecessor. At Warners, Whale made **The Great Garrick** (1937), with Brian Aherne in the title-role and described as 'a play for the screen by Ernst Vajda' – and though derived from 'She Stoops to Conquer' closer in spirit to the period farces which still cluttered the world's stages. The credits also boasted

'A James Whale Production', a distinction granted by the studios only to directors of eminence, e.g. Capra, Lubitsch – but the film itself gave no reason why Whale retained it. He had no recourse but to take on two Bs at Universal before moving to M-G-M on a three-picture contract negotiated before Thalberg died. It was Thalberg's intention that he make *Goodbye Mr Chips,* but he was put, instead, on **Port of Seven Seas** (1938), a condensed version of Marcel Pagnol's *Marius* trilogy, which someone had seen as a vehicle for Wallace Beery: acting his head off, he never comes within a million miles of Raimu. As the film consists mainly of the wrangles with Panisse (Frank Morgan) it is clear that the screenwriter, Preston Sturges (chosen because he spoke French), wanted to preserve the original, but the finished film indicates no understanding of it. It is not all Whale's work, for Sam Wood did some re-takes; Whale's contract was annulled, and he went to United Artists for a fair version of *The Man in the Iron Mask* (q.v.), returning to Universal for **Green Hell** (1940). Frank Nugent called it 'the worst picture of the year', confident that the succeeding eleven months would provide none worse; in Britain, C. A. Lejeune, somewhat kinder, thought it 'the funniest melodrama since *Her Jungle Love*'. As Joan Bennett wears a series of gowns more suited to a Buckingham Palace garden party the film does not live up to its name, offering in fact, an all-too-desirable jungle. 'Funny, it's the little things you remember,' says John Howard, preparing to die. 'It must be spring now in Devonshire,' says George Sanders. In Devon then the people were accustoming themselves to likely invasion. Whale's war drama, *They Dare not Love* (1941), indicated further that he was no longer in touch with this planet; he retired on its completion.

William Wyler belongs to the contrasting school of directors, a group of strong and meticulous craftsmen capable of forging films at least technically perfect. He left Universal mainly due to the management troubles there; his last film for that studio, **The Good Fairy** (1935), is an excellent example of his work, but has a flaw that a director of his temperament could not disguise. That flaw springs from the nature of the material, a play by Molnár about a marvellously innocent girl whose desire to do good leads her into a variety of situations with men whose own desires are primarily sexual. The Hays Office refused to sanction the material as it stood, and the adaptation by Preston Sturges was necessarily extensive: but if it was not to give offence, and the girl's naivety retained, there was no alternative but also to retain the excessive verbiage used by Molnár to set up his situations – at least, there was no alternative for Wyler, though he responds best to the Sturges interpolations and to the star, Margaret Sullavan. Since Wyler married her (however briefly), we need not wonder about the perfection of her performance. In no other film, however, does she so well demonstrate her ability to find that point at which she could express her own personality or star quality while still offering maximum fidelity both to the script and the rules of human behaviour. This is true of all the best performers and some, like Clark Gable, found that truth without it being anything but their star quality and were hence effective even if not greatly gifted. It was and is a delicate balance, poised between elements of personality, technical knowledge, exhibitionism and a gift for acting – which is perhaps why Miss Sullavan, then in her early twenties, demonstrates it so well. Some performers upset the balance as they age, if their technical mastery increases or their personality strengthens with success – and then they need a strong director. Bette Davis is one such example, with her tendency to demonstrate that she definitely is *not* coasting through her role. Another is Katharine Hepburn, anxious always to flaunt the admired Hepburn personality. The balance may have been achieved instinctively or with the help of directors. Miss Sullavan did not lose her understanding of it as she aged: but if in some cases it was due to youth that would be ironic, since cinema-goers of the time thought of the Hollywood stars as ageless.

Another of the magical names, Carole Lombard, made two films for Universal, playing in both a wilful, tantrum-throwing, zany, rich girl. **Love before Breakfast** (1936), directed by Walter Lang, has a story-line described by *The New York Times* as 'thin to the point of emaciation' and that is part of its charm; it is not one of the great screwball comedies, but it is the one most about nothing. **My Man Godfrey** (1936) is one of the classics of the genre. William Powell is the derelict, 'a forgotten man' in the film's parlance, dragged from his shack under the Queensborough Bridge to be Lombard's trophy at a society scavenger hunt. Taken on as the butler, he has to cope with her lovesickness, the schemings of her sister (Gail Patrick), the non sequiturs of her mother (Alice Brady), and mother's simian 'protégé' (Mischa Auer); Eugene Pallette is the bewildered father. To see Miss Lombard pursuing Godfrey – she is a lady to whom nothing has been denied – is to see heaven, but the film's serious implications are best ignored, as devised by the director, Gregory LaCava, and the writers, Morrie Ryskind and Eric Hatch. By now the worst of the Depression was over, but the film cheats: the derelict turns out to be the scion of one of the best Boston families, gone to pieces after his marriage failed, and *his* cure for the times is to turn shantytown into the ritziest nightspot in town.

The film was a great success, but was finished a few weeks too late to save the Laemmles. During 1932 and 1933 the company had chalked up losses of over a million dollars, and after a small profit in 1934 – mainly due to *The Invisible Man* – it went into the red again in 1935 to the tune of $677,186. The situation was not helped by the year's major productions: *Magnificent Obsession,* though popular, had been expensive, and *Showboat* was delayed in production; while the public did not care for **Diamond Jim** (1935), despite its excellences, which include the vitality of Edward Sutherland's direction and a screenplay without extreme blacks and whites by Preston Sturges. No film better captured the vulgarity and achievement of the nineteenth-century tycoons and, as Diamond Jim Brady, Edward Arnold has the requisite dynamism. However, he was a burly, middle-aged character actor, whom, unaccountably, most Hollywood studios thought a star, and he would soon appear on the exhibitors' list of those they considered box-office poison. Unfortunately he was cast in **Sutter's Gold** (1936), on which the Laemmles placed their chief hopes.

This epic on the man who had discovered gold in California – the subject also of Trenker's *Der Kaiser von Kalifornien* – was based in part on Blaise Cendrar's novel 'L'Or', which Eisenstein had planned as his first American film and which Universal had bought from Paramount. The Laemmles made a second mistake in offering the direction to James Cruze, on the ground that he had made a 'classic' pioneering epic, *The Covered Wagon.* However, his more recent films had been potboilers, and his work on this one is of such ineptitude that long explanatory titles are needed. During production, Laemmle negotiated a loan of $750,000 from an investment group headed by the Standard Capital Corporation and Charles R. Rogers, offering as collateral his controlling stock and the films currently in progress. A further $300,000 was negotiated a few months later, as delays extended the shooting of both *Sutter's Gold* and *Showboat,* and one month later, in March 1936, Rogers decided to exercise the option, thus purchasing Universal for himself and Standard Capital for a mere $4,500,000. Laemmle not only lost the theatres and distribution companies throughout the world but also the studio – not too great a deprivation, for he was nearing the end of his life. Junior Laemmle was less expectedly ousted, having been held responsible for all the company's successful films since *All Quiet on the Western Front.* Rogers, however, had had considerable experience as a producer, if only of programmers (for Paramount and R.K.O.), and automatically was appointed vice-president in charge of production. He was replaced two years later – a contributory factor was the ambitious *Top of the Town* (1938), usually referred to as 'Flop of the Town' – by Cliff Work, from the R.K.O. circuit, who owed his appointment to Universal's new president, Nate Blumberg, arriving from the same source. It is, however, a child of fourteen who was finally responsible for taking the studio out of the red.

Deanna Durbin (b. 1921), Canadian-born of British parents, had a remarkable soprano voice and, this being the high era of the studio talent scout, had appeared in a short for M-G-M, with Judy Garland, and had sung on radio. She was brought to Universal by producer Joe Pasternak and director Henry Koster, both formerly with the company's now defunct European branch and started in the U.S. with the medium-budget films with which Rogers hoped to keep the studio ticking over. **Three Smart Girls** (1937) featured a bevy of popular supporting players, including Alice Brady and Mischa Auer in virtual repeats of their roles in *My Man Godfrey,* and is a comedy about divorcing parents reunited by their children: Miss Durbin was the youngest of these, and after a few days' shooting her part was built up and the original budget of $150,000 doubled. On first release the film took $2 million at the box-office, and when her succeeding star vehicles did as well, or better, Rogers's cares were over.

Miss Durbin occurred when not only Universal but the audiences of the world needed her; they responded with an affection afforded few stars since Mary Pickford – another innocent – and it was the last time they would be cheered and heartened by innocence. In the U.S. the Depression had weakened belief in the old fundamental values; Europe was seething with refugees, with racial intolerance, and with the unthinkable prospect of populations destroyed by aerial bombardment. The movies offered a panacea, allaying both the miseries of the past and the horrors to come. Innocence was not really endemic to Hollywood and audiences understood this: that was part of the fascination. The films that Koster and Pasternak fashioned for Durbin were fairy tales, but no one thought they were made up by dreamers or mystics. If today they are not better known it is perhaps because those who have seen only the later work of Pasternak and Koster are disinclined to investigate the rest. Deanna was not, as Graham Greene pointed out, 'the innocent centre', but 'everything is innocent all round her'; she was (in her own words, later) a 'Little Miss Fix-It', but unlike Pickford or Temple she was a meddling, bossy brat who in other circumstances would be a pain in the neck. Those around her either fawned on her or distrusted her and, just as they are observed with asperity, so her misplaced sense of charity saves her from winsomeness. That her meddling was in the interests of others, and carried out with such verve, was one reason she seemed to audiences

the ideal daughter or sweetheart; and if the time was right for her extreme self-confidence it was also right for the smattering of popular classics she sang – all of which conveyed a picture of wholesomeness; indeed, for the cinema-goers whom J. P. Mayer interviewed when researching his 'Sociology of the Film' she was the most consistently admired and emulated star.

In **One Hundred Men and a Girl** (1937), directed by Koster, she finds work for on the dole musicians, an endearing entertainment but for Stokowski's stilted performance as himself; Adolphe Menjou is her father, saying 'Fairy tales never come true', and at one point we find her rushing through a song she didn't want in the first place while glancing hungrily at the food she had had to abandon: 'Don't go, you're too original and charming,' coos Alice Brady, but the response of her husband, Eugene Pallette, is 'Shut up, you brat'. In **Mad about Music** (1938), directed by Norman Taurog, she finds and pesters a surrogate father in the shape of Herbert Marshall; in **That Certain Age** (1938), directed by Edward Ludwig, she is a pest to a journalist (Melvyn Douglas) till she hears of his

Of the many films in which Deanna Durbin appeared the one most fondly remembered is *One Hundred Men and a Girl*. That a fifteen-year-old child should have had such a clarity in singing and masterly musicianship was remarkable, but matched by a similar instinct for acting is nothing short of miraculous.

experiences in the Spanish Civil War and develops a crush on him. In **Three Smart Girls Grow Up** (1939) she is involved in her sisters' romances, and in **First Love** (1939) she is a modern Cinderella. These two are the best of the Durbin vehicles, with Koster confidently in command of the make-believe and the reasonably witty scripts. Indeed, the latter is something of a triumph, since a modern 'Cinderella' is not very appealing, but from *Ella Cinders* to whatever is the latest version of the Perrault story, this is easily the best: and I would match its crazy family with any other zany movie family of the time.

Koster's crisp approach, particularly on these last two films, contrasts with that of William A. Seiter, who simply refuses to find any comedy inherent in the pleasant scripts of **It's a Date** (1940) and **Nice Girl?** (1941), so that apart from the star's presence they are chiefly notable for Pasternak's astuteness in weening her into adult roles. In the former she develops a crush on a man (Walter Pidgeon) of her mother's age, resolutely refusing to see that he prefers her mother (Kay Francis); in the latter, tired of being taken for granted by the boy (Robert Stack) next door, she again throws herself at an older man (Franchot Tone), intending to lose her virginity – though the word is never mentioned. Now in romantic roles, she was to be plagued by dull leading men till she retired, but she has Charles Laughton as co-star in **It Started with Eve** (1941); he is supposedly dying, so for his sake she poses as the fiancée of his son (Robert Cummings). Koster directed, and the situations are well explored by the writers, Norman Krasna and Leo Townsend. An 'Ambersons-gloom' mansion counterbalances Durbin's sunniness and Laughton's cuteness, but it was the last time Pasternak found the balance for her: he could not agree with Universal how the adult Durbin was to be handled, and moved to M-G-M.

The Rage of Paris (1938) is the one picture under her Universal contract made by Danielle Darrieux; pert and roguish, she is suspected of being a gold digger by her fiancé's friend, Douglas Fairbanks Jr. Pasternak produced and Koster directed, confirming his light touch at this time, and it was written by Bruce Manning and Felix Jackson, both of whom worked on the Durbin films. They also wrote the exemplary screenplay which is the basis of the second version of **Back Street** (1941), directed by Robert Stevenson. It is the story of the Other Woman from a different angle – hers. Helping to jerk the tears so expertly are Charles Boyer as the man, handsome and loving but unwilling to give up his career, and Margaret Sullavan as his mistress, who starts out flighty and self-possessed but ends up lonely and bitter.

It was Pasternak who revitalised the career of Marlene Dietrich, returning her to Blue Angel mood, vulgar and hoydenish, in **Destry Rides Again** (1939), prototype of all those Westerns with heroes slow on speech and quick on the draw. Universal had filmed Max Brand's novel with Tom Mix in 1932; this time Pasternak decided to capitalise on the opportunities for comic relief. It is the first comedy Western, parent of the facetious Westerns with us to this day and superior to all of them. In a long career George Marshall never elsewhere achieved such mastery – moving the story at a fast pace, balancing the fun and the tension, and single-mindedly embellishing the evils of Bottleneck. As the town's real boss, the saloon queen Frenchie, Dietrich has a genuine mocking nastiness and cheap allure, surprisingly well matched by James Stewart as Jefferson Destry, the 'innocent' gunman – in its own right a fine performance. Equally well partnered by John Wayne, as an easy-going all-American lieutenant, she does for the South Seas in **Seven Sinners** (1940) what she had done for the Old West: but where that was satirical this is parody, cheerfully tossing in all the clichés of the genre. The director, Tay Garnett, has fun at the expense of von Sternberg, with a camera style that finds the shadows of shutters over everything (though that is true of all Hollywood excursions into Maugham territory) and Dietrich as of yore decked in sequins and ostrich feathers. In no other post-von Sternberg film is she allowed to do her thing so much and so well, whether striding along the waterfront in black lace which looks like a petticoat or descending the stairs in naval drag intoning, cigarette in lips, 'You Can Bet the Man's in the Navy'. Garnett's handling is as confident as Marshall's, and both films are superior to anything made by either Howard Hawks or Raoul Walsh, who in recent years have monopolised most discussions of the Hollywood action film – which is doubly odd, because both Marshall and Garnett made films just as awful as the worst of Hawks and Walsh.

The other memorable star player at Universal at this period was also a Paramount alumnus, W. C. Fields, returning to films, after a long illness, and a new popularity due to a radio programme he shared with Charley McCarthy, the dummy, and Edgar Bergen, the ventriloquist: they are with him in **You Can't Cheat an Honest Man** (1939), but though the Fields–McCarthy feud offers little Fields is often very funny – disguised as Buffalo Bertha, a bearded bare-back rider, confessing to the bailiffs that his real name is Gretchel Schickelgruber, or meeting the Bel-Goodies (glorious Fieldsian name!) and telling an interminable story about his exploits at Lake Titicaca, proceeding unperturbed each time his mention of snakes sends Mrs Bel-Goodie into hysterics. Fields himself provided the film's story, under a pseudonym, and the credited director is George Marshall – though when he could no longer control his antipathy towards Fields he was replaced by Eddie Cline. Cline directed the rest of the comic's films for Universal, but fared no better; as Fields's biographer, Robert Lewis Taylor, remarked: 'With the hapless Cline he set marks of highhanded truculence that the movie industry may never see equalled.' The famous collaboration with Mae West can be seen not working in **My Little Chickadee** (1940), when the camera catches her unhappiness. Beyond that, they are an ill-suited team, she as studied as he is casual. The screenplay, credited to both of them, mainly concerns her marrying him after being compromised by a masked bandit, and his wan but not hopeful attempts to consummate the marriage. The best of it are his asides, ad-libbed on set in an attempt to steal the film from her.

'What is he up to now?' is the first line of **Bank Dick** (1940), spoken by Fields's film mother-in-law (Jessie Ralph), who despises him just a bit more than does his wife (Cora Witherspoon); the latter could not be less interested when he becomes a hero by capturing a robber – and then is

actively annoyed, for she has a grudge against the bank concerned. His elder daughter (Una Merkel) for her part reacts to praise of him with indifference tempered by surprise, but the younger one makes with mother and grandmother a trio united in loathing. 'Shall I bounce a rock off his head?' she asks: 'Respect your father,' says mother, adding quickly, 'What sort of rock?' That Fields knew he was best in domestic situations is clear: his most-admired earlier films, *It's a Gift* and *The Man on the Flying Trapeze*, are among the half dozen for which he provided the stories: *Bank Dick* is his only solo writing credit (his first screenplay credit is the one with Miss West), and it is prodigal with humour. Misanthropic in life he may have been but as an entertainer he saw comic possibilities in everything – most of all in the role of a tippling middle-aged man who alone regards himself as a success. His pseudonym on this occasion was Mahatma Kane Jeeves, which should have prepared some for the surrealist capering of **Never Give a Sucker an Even Break** (1941), lurching as it does from non sequitur to outright implausibility. It starts in a film studio, that much is clear; later, when his whisky bottle falls out of a plane, Fields dives after it and lands in a mountain eyrie, where a girl tells him she has never seen a man before – which spurs

It seemed like a good idea at the time to team W. C. Fields and Mae West in *My Little Chickadee,* and both magnificos co-operated on the script. During the filming the antipathy between them increased to the extent that they had to be photographed separately whenever possible – and as a result the picture is spotty and devoid of both genuine humour and spontaneity.

him into instant action. He had courted widows and spinsters for money but never girls, for the odds were too great: but this he can't resist, inventing a kissing game appropriate to her age and the occasion, called 'Squiggleum' – which is funnier than it sounds, as is a further Pooh-like hum, 'Chickens Have Pretty Legs in Kansas'. There is a descent in a basket, a scene in a Russian village, a fight with a gorilla and, as in *Bank Dick,* a hilarious Keystonian chase at the end – though this time it has no connection with the plot.

Arriving temporarily at Universal was Alice Faye, for **You're a Sweetheart** (1937). With her Zanuck sent director David Butler, for a pleasant musical about a Broadway star and a waiter (George Murphy), with whom she becomes involved in a publicity stunt. Butler returned to helm the two films Bing Crosby made for Universal, and, as with Miss Faye, suited the material to the star's usual style rather than that of the studio. **East Side of Heaven** (1939) is also agreeable, despite a homosexual *double entendre* rare at this time, when Joan Blondell sobs at hearing the Crosby-Mischa Auer lovey-dovey dialogue, not knowing they are talking to a baby.

Among Universal's other light fare is **The Boys from Syracuse** (1940), which throws out several Rodgers and Hart songs but is otherwise a reasonable facsimile of the Broadway original. The studio's scant faith in it is indicated by the short running time and the lower-case cast headed by Martha Raye and Allan Jones – but then it is based on 'The Comedy of Errors'. Shakespeare also looms over **Tower of London** (1939), the story of Richard III (Basil Rathbone), plus a sinister headsman (Boris Karloff) purloined from Harrison Ainsworth's novel of the same name. It is no worse than, say, *Suez,* but more irritating because it edges towards both the swashbuckler and the horror film, worthier forms than the feeble retelling of historical fact. Both films cannot hide budget limitations. The directors were, respectively, Edward Sutherland and Rowland V. Lee. Lee also made the much better – and more serious – **The Sun Never Sets** (1939), directing and producing, with Douglas Fairbanks Jr and Basil Rathbone as two British brothers devoted to the Foreign Service, who manage to outwit a man planning to dominate the world by undermining the Empire. His nationality is not given, nor is he played with an accent by Lionel Atwill but his name is Hugo Zorif, which has a Germanic ring, and most spectators could have guessed the nationality of those likely to be involved in scientific research in Africa. The heroes' grandfather is C. Aubrey Smith: indispensable in such tales.

'Three hours of Entertainment that was Three Centuries in the Making! Since there has never been a motion picture like [it] its exhibition to the public will differ from that of any other screen attraction . . . Premieres of these engagements will not only be outstanding events in the film world, but significant civic occasions': thus Warner Bros. announced **A Midsummer Night's Dream** (1935) – which in fact lasts just 132 minutes. Renowned for their introduction of Sound, and recognised for their social dramas, the Warners felt it incumbent on them to advance the art of the cinema once more – offering the Bard, no less, in the first of his plays to be filmed since the Pickford-Fairbanks *Shrew.* Max Reinhardt, a legendary theatre man, was brought to direct – with the aid of the film-experienced William Dieterle, a fellow-countryman: the result is like one of those funfair machines with a mechanical hand manipulated to pick up objects visible within the glass case – useless things stuffed in because they're supposed to be pretty, or because people are supposed to want them. The film's visual conception, meant to be charming and impressive, is now just dowdy, be it a Court of Athens more suitable for chorus girls or the cobwebby, dewdropped forest peopled with the biggest army of fairies ever to escape from the pictures of Arthur Rackham, prancing in muslin, gliding in waist-length peroxide wigs – often viewed through Vaseline (on the lens) to pick up extra highlights. There is one magical moment: Oberon riding off at dawn with his black cloak billowing out behind him – and if there is anything else to admire it must be the confidence apparent in the whole mistaken enterprise, plus the irreverent, capable way the verse has been chopped up into four-word sentences. The text was mangled partly to use

Mendelssohn's score; but the cast cannot manage even these speeches: like many American players in Shakespeare they intone so carefully that their depleted energy allows only two expressions – a frown to denote anger and a mouth turned up at the corners to signify happiness. Victor Jory's stern-jowled Oberon is capable; the hysterically-giggling Puck of Mickey Rooney (q.v.) is at least bearable. As Snout, Hugh Herbert over-uses his giggle, but the best of the rustics is Bottom as tackled by James Cagney – bombastic, cheery and light of foot.

Despite the failure of reviewers to echo the publicity department, the film found sufficient public for M-G-M to proceed with *Romeo and Juliet* (q.v.). Warners, with prestige still in mind, offered **The Green Pastures** (1936), a not particularly courageous act in view of the play's 640 performances in New York and no less than five national tours. However, foreign returns were uncertain – in Britain the play was unknown because the Lord Chamberlain had banned it – so the film was so budgeted that its cost would be recovered by reasonable patronage in the U.S. The play had won the Pulitzer Prize, and *The New York Times* had pronounced it 'Marc Connelly's naive, ludicrous, sublime and heartbreaking masterpiece'. The film, said the same paper, 'still has the rough beauty of the home-spun, the irresistible beauty of simple faith'. Its subject is heaven, and it consists of selected events in the Old Testament as pictured in the imagination of a piccaninny Sunday School. It was the first all-Negro film since *Hallelujah!,* and there is no other quite like it. But apart from the performance of Rex Ingram as De Lawd, authoritative and with an uncanny glow of holiness, it is now difficult to see why the piece was so much admired. It is no longer possible to appreciate the Bible in *faux-naïf* terms, an interpretation by a professional playwright of the slangy idiom of the Southern negro. Warners thought Connelly so important that he was given co-director status with William Keighley, but the actors are not so much directed as marshalled.

Both films are listed among the credits of Hal B. Wallis, who had risen from publicity director to Executive Producer in Charge of Production, replacing Zanuck, in 1933. Though answerable to Jack L. Warner, he was allowed reasonable autonomy and was probably responsible for all the best Warner films of this period, either in his executive capacity or as individual producer of many of them, notably including most of the Bette Davis vehicles (q.v.). The studio owed its greatest prestige to him, as producer of the series of biographical films directed by William Dieterle, usually starring Paul Muni (1895–1967). After working together on **Doctor Socrates** (1935), a likeable and fast-paced piece about a kindly small-town doctor 'used' by gangsters, star and director were reunited for **The Story of Louis Pasteur** (1935), for which Muni won an Academy Award. Muni's zest and penchant for impersonation convinced many that he was a great actor, and it was to find something worthy of him that Warners had undertaken the project. It was, for the time, sober and conscientiously done, as the press recognised, but few liked **The White Angel** (1936), with Kay Francis impersonating Florence Nightingale. However, **The Life of Emile Zola** (1937) pleased everyone, winning also a Best Picture Oscar. Muni is Zola; Gale Sondergaard and Joseph Schildkraut are the Dreyfuses, all teeth and tightness respectively; Robert Barrat is the puzzled Esterhazy; and Henry O'Neill, Picquard. For a while it is as trying as *Suez* – Cézanne as Zola's best friend, Zola meeting his inspiration for 'Nana', Anatole France flitting across the screen – but as a brief guide to the Dreyfus affair it is altogether admirable. The ads called it 'One of the few great films of all time', a claim taken seriously by the press – and today we might still admire the concise attempts to pierce the mentality of the General Staff. We may writhe when the defending attorney says 'Once before the centuries reversed the judgment – that too was a closed case' but the use of Anatole France's statement, 'He was a moment in the conscience of time' is still moving.

Juarez (1939) can hold its own with any historical film yet made: it also telescopes and distorts, but the screenplay – by John Huston, Wolfgang Reinhardt and Aeneas MacKenzie – knits its various strands into a dramatic whole, all the more remarkable in that it divides our attention between Juarez (Muni) and Maximilian (Brian Aherne), without even an engineered meeting. The dialogue is archaic but never absurd; the writers have positively embraced the whys and wherefores, and the exposition is good drama and goodish history as it outlines Louis Napoleon's reasons for intervention and the situation in Mexico. After the fantastic establishment of a Hapsburg palace on that alien shore, the situations become more conventional, with on one side the growing misery of the head that wears a crown and on the other the idealist dreaming of unification. Dieterle is as assured with the intermittent battles as with the confrontations, and Tony Gaudio's photography is memorable, notably in the shot of the hunched and victorious Juarez with his supporters, or the final shot of a slumped Carlotta (Bette Davis). Miss Davis has the least of the three major roles, but from the start she conveys both great love and her desperation; her eyes really do seem to shoot balls of fire when she berates Napoleon (Claude Rains). Aherne's Maximilian is correct – weak, well-intentioned – but not a very resourceful performance; nor is Mr Muni's unsmiling but benevolent 'father of the people'.

Despite the customary praise from the critics, the film did only fair business. The Warners were unwilling to abandon a series which had brought them so much prestige, and virtually every figure in modern history had become a candidate for the studio's treatment. Beethoven was one of them, but the project was cancelled after the returns were in on *Juarez* – and as a result Muni left the studio. Edward G. Robinson replaced him in **Dr Ehrlich's Magic Bullet** (1940) and **A Despatch from Reuter's** (1941), in the former as the German doctor who discovered a cure for syphilis and in the latter as the founder of the news agency. In returning to the humanist-scientist origins of the series, *Ehrlich* has a certain weight, and would have been better if it had been less mealy-mouthed both as to the nature of syphilis and the faith of Ehrlich, especially as the postscript is a reprimand to his countrymen for the treatment of modern Jews; but if *Reuter's* indicated that Warners had lost courage both in subject matter and treatment, it found Dieterle also disin-

terested, concluding the series on a conventional note.

These film biographies had been particularly pleasing to the Warner board, satisfying its craving for respectability and its preference for star vehicles. Warner Bros. advertised itself in the trade press as the studio of stars, whereas that, as far as the public was concerned, was M-G-M. Warners was the only other company with which the public associated a particular commodity, and that commodity was the 'social conscience' drama. Wallis was not particularly interested in the form, though he had produced *I Am a Fugitive from a Chain Gang,* and while the studio did not entirely abandon it the message conveyed was usually subsidiary to displays of star personality and the customary ingredients of 'action' drama.

As we have seen, Warners' crusading films had begun to fail at the box-office, and **Black Fury** (1935) did little better, after Hays Office interference had made a butchery of the original script, on the grounds that it might cause anarchy in the Pennsylvania coalfields where the film is set. The subject is trade unionism, but after establishing that a rabble-rouser (J Carroll Naish) arrives to create a strike at the behest of a company of professional strike-breakers, the rest, under the direction of Michael Curtiz, is incomprehensible. The dissatisfied star, Paul Muni, referred to the result as 'Coal Diggers of 1935', and as Radek, an ebullient Slav miner, he is saddled with lines like 'Joe Radek, he like everybody and everybody like Joe Radek'.

Since Warners so longed to be M-G-M, it was able to return to the genre after Metro's prestige success with *Fury* (q.v.). **Black Legion** (1936) concerns a nice guy played by Humphrey Bogart (1900–57) who becomes bitter when passed over for promotion, allowing his resentment to grow till he is sucked into the Ku Klux Klan. An attempt is made to examine his mentality, and in the film's most revealing moment he poses before the mirror with his new gun: but the conclusion seems to be that he and his fellows are petty and cowardly, less fanatics than mere tools of the racketeers who run the Klan for profit. Archie Mayo directed, and Mervyn LeRoy both produced and directed **They Won't Forget** (1937), which also sets up its situation with skill before falling apart – and only partly because, as in most Warner movies, detectives are incapable of detecting and doctors of performing autopsies. It is the more ambitious of the two films and is set recognisably in the South – which indeed is its *raison d'être*. Two Northerners, a man accused of murder and his lawyer (Otto Kruger), find that they are no match for Southern bigotry, particularly as practised by an ambitious district attorney (Claude Rains), who rather than ride to glory on a 'Nigra' prefers a white suspect to a black one. The film's refusal to disclose the guilt or innocence of the accused is its trump card, for it demands that audiences respond instead to the prospect of his being lynched; but the clues that he is in fact guilty become increasingly hysterical. There were similar faults in LeRoy's early films, but his direction on this occasion is sloppy and the acting dreadful – with the exceptions of Clinton Rosemond as the Negro janitor and Elizabeth Risdon, who provides a fine portrayal of tragic grief as the accused man's mother. Robert Rossen and Abem Finkel wrote the screenplay, from a fictionalised account of the Leo M. Frank affair – which is why the disclaimer as to 'any resemblance to persons living or dead' appears before the studio logo. Lincoln's claim, 'A nation conceived in liberty and dedicated to the proposition that all men are equal' provides a foreword, but the film, despite contemporary admiration, is unworthy of it.

The next few Warner films in this genre are best considered as crime films or star vehicles, but **Confessions of a Nazi Spy** (1939) proved that the old crusading spirit was not dead. Jack L. Warner had been the only Jewish studio head to support the industry's Anti-Nazi League, and his view is stressed in this film: 'In six centuries the world fought its way from Medieval barbarism. In six short years the Nazis have darkened it again.' He ran no risk of Warner films being banned in Germany, for by this time few American films reached there, but there was the possibility of this one being banned by countries not wishing to offend Germany, and it became the subject of a dispute between the U.S. Government and the German Embassy. The Government stressed Hollywood's right to free speech, and pointed out that the film was based on a trial in which three people were convicted of spying for the Germans.

The small interest that occasioned has become in the film 'blazing headlines' and the hectoring, laughable commentary is grandiloquent in its chauvinism, rabidly anti-appeasement and anti-isolationist: but the film's exciting account of espionage and justice is matched by another of inter-related Nazi propaganda activities, and the intolerance they helped to promote. Technically it manages to be both derivative and adventurous, borrowing from the newsreel approach of 'The March of Time' and M-G-M's 'Crime Does Not Pay' series, against a background of the annexation of Austria and Czechoslovakia. Anatole Litvak directed, from a screenplay by Milton Krims and John Wexley, based on articles by a former F.B.I. agent, Leon G. Turrou – played here, under a different name, by Edward G. Robinson. It is heartening to see a Jewish actor in this role, holding the tension between the factual and the melodramatic without histrionics. His opponents are headed by Paul Lukas, as a fascist fanatic; by George Sanders, moving into Teutonic caricature; and notably by Francis Lederer, as a shifty little man who dreams of glory.

It cannot be termed 'social concern', but **Oil for the Lamps of China** (1935) is as good as any film that ever came from Warners. 'This fine, sincere story of an idealist's unwavering faith in his job will remain long in your memory,' said *Photoplay,* and if that was all there was to it it would deserve the neglect into which it has fallen. It is a tale of a working-life – admittedly a remarkable one – spent in China. The epidemics and revolutions of other movies about China are kept in the background, and the piece mainly progresses by way of the colleagues, good and bad, of the central character (Pat O'Brien), and if he is sometimes foolishly loyal that is because he has a wife and child and therefore needs a salary. Alice Tisdale Hobart wrote the original novel and the film is not free of 'bestsellerdom' – such as O'Brien's meeting with the woman (Josephine Hutchinson) he marries; but there is such common sense and such lack of 'rigging' that it commands

Pat O'Brien, left, in *Oil for the Lamps of China*, based on a popular book of the Thirties. It was because of the book's success that Warners filmed it, but there is no other film quite like it in Hollywood history, for it is simply an account of one man's career: and although the setting is exotic, what happens to him is very much what happens to professional men in Oshkosh or New York.

admiration. LeRoy proves on this occasion that he could direct, and O'Brien my contention that all good actors have an especially fine performance in them. Miss Hutchinson at first seems to be one of those actresses whose sole virtue is the smile that relieves her plainness, but she has a contained emotion that is increasingly telling.

White Banners (1938) also belongs to the unsung near-masterpieces in Warners' past, and even when it comes apart at the end (like *Magnificent Obsession* it is based on a novel by the sanctimonious Lloyd C. Douglas) it remains likeable. The direction by Edmund Goulding is exemplary, initially teasing in its account of a schoolmaster (Claude Rains), his family and the stray old lady (Fay Bainter) they take into their home. Since he makes them as ordinary as they are amusing, Goulding demonstrates remarkable skill at superior soap opera.

Both these films were among the few made at Warners which were aimed at both men and women. So were the films of Errol Flynn (q.v.), but by and large the studio's product could be divided into vehicles for Kay Francis and Bette Davis, destined for the women, and the vehicles for Robinson, Cagney and O'Brien, meant for the men. At the end of the decade the pattern changed slightly, with the loss of Francis and O'Brien and the arrival of both John Garfield (q.v.) and George Raft; and the percentage of male dramas increased when it was clear that the studio would have to give in to critics and public and no longer confine Bogart to supporting roles. The masculine films are the more stereotyped, featuring the know-it-all-kid, the learned-it-the-hard-way philosophy and the fight-against-the-odds finish. They were churned out so quickly that many of the scripts are cannibalistic, but a number of them remain enjoyable, such as **San Quentin** (1937), directed by Lloyd Bacon, in which O'Brien is a prison governor whose 'psychological' approach to inmates is tested when he has to handle Bogart, who happens to be the brother of his girlfriend (Ann Sheridan). The plot is virtually the same as that of the earlier *Mayor of Hell,* of which **Crime School** (1938) is a straightforward remake, made by Warners' B-unit and directed by Lewis Seiler, with the Dead End kids (it was a vehicle for them) and Bogart, in fine form as the humanitarian governor. A few months later M-G-M's *Boys Town* (q.v.) was to make the country aware of the problem of juvenile delinquency; this film shows as much concern and has as little credibility.

Several of Robinson's films are notable for more than his performances in them, and both **Bullets and Ballots** (1936) and **Kid Galahad** (1936) remain effective melodramas. The former, directed by William Keighley, has nothing to do with elections, proving perhaps that the title had found favour. Robinson is an undercover man who infiltrates the rackets – and if this does not give a true picture of such matters the myths remain satisfying. The plot is less so, but the villain is Bogart, embarking on his career of needling Robinson and Cagney, his lot here being one of constant frustration. His thunderous expressions are to be savoured, and he and Robinson cross notably in the opening sequence of *Kid Galahad*: handy with gun and flick-knife, he shows off by cutting off the pants of a bellhop (Wayne Morris), who promptly slugs a prizefighter – whereupon Robinson resolves to promote the boy into a champion. 'He don't want no girl,' snarls Robinson, predictably furious when the boy falls in love with his sister (Jane Bryan) but remarkably understanding when his own moll (Bette Davis) also falls for Sunny Jim. Michael Curtiz directed this best of Thirties boxing movies.

A Slight Case of Murder (1938) is based on a play by Damon Runyon and Howard Lindsay. It had not been one of the glories of the American theatre: that the film *is* one of the glories of the screen reflects credit on the scriptwriters, Earl Baldwin and Joseph Schrank. Robinson is a one-time bootlegger settling into respectability when his house-party is intruded upon by the bodies of four late enemies. The farce that ensues is not, as it has been said to be, a satire on gangster movies, but Robinson is certainly guying Little Caesar, with boundless vanity and occasional sneers and elegant flicks of the cigar. His wife is the marvellous Ruth Donnelly, uncertain in her bid for 'class', and also in gratifyingly large roles are Edward Brophy and Allen Jenkins, as Robinson's henchmen. Not to be overlooked is the daughter's fiancé (Willard Parker), a six-foot-plus state trooper who quails at the thought of confronting the corpses. Lloyd Bacon directed, and in his **Brother Orchid** (1940) Robinson is again a mugg who wants to go straight – to get 'class' in 'London, Paris, Rome, all them places'. Dunned and broke, he returns to find his ever-lovin' broad (Ann Sothern) the owner of a nightclub, and his Number Two (Bogart) in charge of his gang. Self-preservation later finds him in a monastery, where he gets the rackets going again; but despite felicities this is not quite as funny as the earlier film.

As far as James Cagney was concerned, **G–Men** (1935) was his best picture since *The Public Enemy* – according to *Time Magazine,* while *Liberty* thought it 'as masculine as a bank robbery'. He plays a failed lawyer who becomes a government agent to avenge a pal's death: his quarry is Barton MacLane, burly villain of every other Warners movie and seen here at his best. En route to the climactic shoot-out there is some Warner crusading in the form of a police plea for Senate help (to make bank robberies federal offences, to have G-men armed), and as directed by William Keighley it is a fast ride. That steam-engine Warners pace was soon to be lost, but Howard Hawks uses it in **Ceiling Zero** (1935), one of a series of films teaming Cagney and Pat O'Brien, the former as treacherous but lovable, finally coming to heel, and O'Brien equally dynamic but nevertheless pugnacious and longsuffering. In this one they spend most of their time in the control room, an indication that the original Broadway play was of that slice-of-life school popularised by Elmer Rice: Frank Wead wrote both that and the screenplay, borrowing from *Air Mail*, on which he also worked.

In view of the lack of originality prevailing at Warners at this time and the fact that he was required to make half a dozen similar movies every year, it is not surprising that Cagney walked out on his contract. Because the Warner stars were the most rebellious, Jack L. Warner was forced, eventually, to be the most magnanimous of the tycoons – which may not have been difficult for him, as he was considered as charming outside the studio as he was dictatorial – and ignorant – within it. Cagney duly returned for **Boy Meets Girl** (1938), directed by Bacon from the Broadway play by Sam and Bella Spewack about two scriptwriters; it was one of his happiest teamings with O'Brien, playing mutually dependent kidders, moving in a whirlwind of wisecracks in what was a thinly disguised sketch of Hecht and MacArthur. The result is less satiric than *Once in a Lifetime,* despite a baby star who is a has-been at eight months and a vain cowboy star (Dick Foran) also suffering from audience rejection. Ralph Bellamy is a studio executive, doubtless recognised by some – painstakingly tolerant of his writers, servile and sycophantic to those above him, hostile to those below, dedicated, moronic, self-conscious, referring to 'we intellectuals' and occupied in trying to edit out chunks from a film, 'Young England'.

In **Angels with Dirty Faces** (1938),

435

Humphrey Bogart, all gritted teeth and nervous glances, is a superb villain in *Angels with Dirty Faces,* and James Cagney, as a good guy gone to the bad, is even better. The New York critics named him the year's Best Actor, presumably because he is so alive, so true, and so thrilling to watch.

Cagney and O'Brien are East Side buddies as kids: grown up, the former gets in with Bogart, a crooked lawyer who is in cahoots with George Bancroft, in turn in league with every corrupt V.I.P. in town. Meanwhile O'Brien has become a priest, with a trilby that he sports over one eye or, on important occasions, carries. He is tolerant of Cagney, as is Ann Sheridan, their mutual old flame, but then she too has been through the mill. Also on hand are the Dead End kids from *Dead End* (q.v.), and dull delinquents they are, but Cagney's handling of them is enterprising. He agrees to go to the Chair as a craven coward so as to dampen their hero worship, and if the morality is dubious it may be said that Curtiz tears through the tale with little pause for reflection.

There are also assumptions about law and order in **The Oklahoma Kid** (1939), with Cagney as a bad man who is acceptable as a hero because he's on our side, for which reason he may also take the law into his own hands. This is the first of the two Westerns he made during his career, and neither he nor Bogart, in black as the villain, is at home on the range. Lloyd Bacon directed, and Rosemary Lane, in the expected gingham, is a rather more

spunky heroine than usual. **The Fighting 69th** (1940), directed by Keighley, was at least smartly timed, and the American public responded as to no other war drama in recent years. It is based on fact – on a New York regiment also known as 'the fighting Irish' – and the plot involves two of its most famous sons, the poet Joyce Kilmer (Jeffrey Lynn) and Father Duffy (O'Brien), whose statue stands near Times Square – and which appears at the end of this film, with O'Brien and Cagney superimposed upon it. The latter plays his customary braggart, hot-headed and undisciplined: 'I don't go for that Holy Joe stuff,' he tells Father Duffy, who of course becomes his best friend. Dying, he tells him, 'Father, I just been talking to your boss.'

He plays a boxer in **City for Conquest** (1940), risking his sight in the ring so that his kid brother (Arthur Kennedy) can play his concerto at Carnegie Hall – *the* concerto, one that 'captures the hum of a great city'. The kid waxes emotional over the sacrifice, but there is some atoning tension in the scenes between Cagney and Sheridan, as the dancer he loves, and Sheridan and Anthony Quinn, as the rotter she takes up with. Elia Kazan is an East Side boy who becomes a mobster, muttering 'I never figgered on this' as he lies shot; and the studio's virtues are in evidence, as well as its occasional vice of sermonising. As directed by Anatole Litvak, it was considered one of the best pictures made about New York – a feat it manages solely by means of back projection, plus no doubt the borrowings from *Dead End* (q.v.) and *Golden Boy* (q.v.).

Before looking at Cagney's partnerships with the other tough-guy stars, and some of their films, we might pause at **The Strawberry Blonde** (1941), a remake of a Gary Cooper vehicle, *One Sunday Afternoon,* made by Paramount in 1933. The new film was occasioned when the Broadway success of 'Life with Father' again indicated interest in the days when the century was young. The gentle story gets lost among the bustles, sleeve-garters and barbershop quartets, but that is mainly because Raoul Walsh handles it as though it were farce. When a dentist (Cagney) loses the belle he loves (Rita Hayworth) to his buddy (Jack Carson), he marries on the rebound but continues to nurture his passion through years of marriage: but with Olivia de Havilland at her most appealing as the wife this seems nonsense, and the point is further weakened because the Hays Office would not allow Cagney to be unfaithful, even in thought.

The British version of **Each Dawn I Die** (1939) has a foreword explaining that the conditions depicted therein are not those of British prisons – but those conditions, apart from the usual humane governor (George Bancroft) seem not unlike those of a holiday camp. Nor does the title seem appropriate, for far from each day being a living death there is a thrill a minute as directed by Keighley. And, of course, the screenplay cheats, since the convicted hero is innocent: 'Framed! – because they knew I was going to show them up for the grasping rats they are!' – and he is framed, incidentally, with a whisky bottle and a crashed car, a device of earlier gangster films and still being used as late as *The Thomas Crown Affair* (q.v.). George Raft is the fellow con sworn to bring Cagney's enemies to book because he is the first man not to want moolah for a favour rendered.

Cagney is not in **Invisible Stripes** (1940), but Raft is, playing – as so often – an ex-con up against it. Forced unwillingly back into crime, he robs banks to buy a garage for his kid brother (William Holden), to prevent him joining the numbers racket. In time he and Bogart are mowed down in the garage, and there is an epilogue in which the kid renames the garage in commemoration. 'Who's the brother?' asks a passing cop. 'A sort of silent partner?' 'You could say that,' replies Holden. Warners must have hoped that audiences had forgotten that the garage was financed by hold-ups in the mid-West: thus crime does pay if you have a considerate elder brother. Bacon directed.

Such topsy-turvy moralising was sanctioned by the Hays Office, whose requirements had compromised the gangster film proper: however, the success of *Angels with Dirty Faces* dictated another attempt – and, of course, the era of Chicago warfare was now history. At the time **The Roaring Twenties** (1939) attracted little attention, but if actually not the best of the cycle, it does pack the most in, with its marvellous montages of booze,

bottles, bootlegging and bombings, of old cars, gangs, revelry and shoot-outs (many pinched from earlier films). It starts in the trenches, with Cagney, Bogart and Jeffrey Lynn, and follows their fortunes till Black Tuesday and after: Bogart is all bad, Lynn is all good, and Cagney would be good if bootlegging weren't so congenial a way to earn a living. Priscilla Lane as a would-be singer does some songs of the period, which is otherwise poorly evoked; but the dialogue is superb. It was written by Jerry Wald, Richard Macaulay and Robert Rossen, whose intermittently romantic view is shared by the director, Raoul Walsh. The epilogue this time has Cagney dying on the snowswept steps of a church, cradled in the arms of a raddled cabaret singer (Gladys George), who answers the inevitable passing cop: 'He used to be a big shot.'

Raft and Bogart are long-distance truck drivers in **They Drive by Night** (1940), based according to the credits on 'Long Haul' by A. I. Bezzerides but borrowing much from *Bordertown* (q.v.), with Ida Lupino as the floozie wife who murders her husband (Alan Hale) in a vain bid to win the hero. As directed by Walsh, this is formula film-making at its best, its quality partly due to the playing, notably Ann Sheridan as an itinerant hash-house waitress, and partly to the outstandingly slangy screenplay by Wald and Macaulay – which gives her the best lines. 'Classy chassis,' says one trucker, and another ventures that he would be prepared to pay in instalments. 'You couldn't even afford the headlights,' she tells him.

It is not an agreeable experience to watch Bogart support Raft, a much inferior actor. Since he had returned to films in 1936 in *The Petrified Forest* (q.v.) – he had made his reputation in the Broadway original – Humphrey Bogart had been one of the most critically admired of the Warner players. He finally became a star in **High Sierra** (1941): the crook as tragic hero, never more *purely* done than in this adaptation of a novel by W. R. Burnett, scripted by him and John Huston and directed by Walsh. The role was turned down by Paul Muni because he was angry over the abandonment of his Beethoven project, by Raft because he did not want to die at the end, by Cagney because he resented being asked third, and

Humphrey Bogart and Mary Astor in John Huston's exemplary screen version of *The Maltese Falcon*, the third and best of Warner's attempts to film Dashiell Hammett's novel. It was one of several films of that time which Bogart made by default, the roles having been turned down by other actors: but reading Hammett's description of Sam Spade, it is difficult to believe that the role was intended for anyone else, for Bogart had established a screen character equally rueful, unsurprised and cynical.

by Robinson because he didn't care to do the location work. None of them could have been as good as Bogart, part-Galahad, part-Capone, preparing from his mountain cabin what will be his last caper: a good man gone bad going to his end. There is an edge, a force, a danger to him that Raft always lacked.

It is also not an agreeable experience to see Bogart in a film as poor as **The Wagons Roll at Night** (1941). The wagons roll quickly under Ray Enright's direction but otherwise it is tired, perhaps because it had first seen service as *Kid Galahad,* swopping the boxing arenas for a circus tent, with Bogart as the boss. **Manpower** (1941), a vehicle for Edward G. Robinson, is a ragbag of bits from two of his early films, *Tiger Shark* and *Two Seconds,* now set among a crew of high-voltage cable repairmen. He is again the unlikely candidate for marriage, proposing to a penniless girl (Marlene Dietrich), and Raft is the buddy who falls in love with her: once more he is the decent man who gets drunk and goes mad at the end. However, the credits note an 'original screenplay', by Wald and Macaulay, of the same zesty level as those they did for

The Roaring Twenties, They Drive by Night and *Torrid Zone,* in which Cagney and Sheridan cross wits with each other. Wald produced and Macaulay wrote *Across the Pacific* (q.v.), also notable for the punchy dialogue, but as their credits before and after their collaboration are of little interest we must assume this a specially felicitous union, especially when, as here, they had Walsh to hand over their material in good shape to the cutting room.

That particular film reminds us that Warners' tough guys would soon be fighting Nazis and Nippons; but as this series of crime melodramas died it produced its one undisputed classic, **The Maltese Falcon** (1941), Huston's version of Dashiell Hammett's novel. John Huston (b. 1906), the son of Walter Huston, was first assigned to screenwriting by William Wyler when directing his father, but did not make his mark till he joined Warners and worked on *Jezebel* (q.v.). He wrote the screenplay for this third version of the Hammett book, staying faithful to it, and was assigned to direct it on a modest budget. He says that nervousness caused him to sketch a plan for every shot, and as we know that most American film-makers prepare a project by screening anything made earlier that may be relevant to it we may suppose his sketches were made after viewing Paramount's 1935 version of another Hammett private eye novel, *The Glass Key,* directed by Frank Tuttle. After noting that both films were tailored for the same star, George Raft (who refused this one) and that the 1942 version of *The Glass Key* (q.v.) is different in feel and appearance – if better – than the earlier one, it is apparent that both Huston and Tuttle had the sense to allow Hammett's style to dictate theirs, so that spareness of setting and camera movement counterbalances the intricacy of plot and the deviousness of everyone involved in it. Bogart leads a magnificent cast: Mary Astor as Miss Wunderly, consciously lady-in-distress, girlishly anxious but for a suggestion of greed around the lips; Peter Lorre as Joel Cairo, frizzy-haired and smelling of gardenia, as querulous as he is treacherous; Elisha Cook Jr as the 'bodyguard', overcoated to the floor; Jerome Cowan as the murdered partner, somewhat shifty; Gladys George as the falsely-grieving widow; Barton MacLane and Ward Bond as the cops; Lee Patrick as the loving secretary; and Sydney Greenstreet, above all, as Mr Gutman, vast, jovial and deadly, though minus the black ringlets with which Hammett endowed him.

Warners had another tough star in John Garfield (1913–52), acquired from Broadway. A gutter-brat vitality suggested an heir to Cagney, but while he often played the same big-headed punk he was less a man of action than a chip-on-the-shoulder guy caught in the cross-winds. He made his film debut in *Four Daughters,* based on a novel by Fannie Hurst, which was so successful that it spawned a number of sequels; **Daughters Courageous** (1939), also directed by Michael Curtiz, utilised much of the same cast for a not dissimilar story, based on a Broadway play. Garfield is a young bum, as penniless as he is uncouth, but he is acceptable as a suitor in this democratic bourgeois family till the daughter concerned (Priscilla Lane) realises that he is a younger edition of her returned prodigal father (Claude Rains). That respectability triumphs is the sole concession to reality.

The advent of Garfield gave Warners another chance to recycle old material, but both **They Made Me a Criminal** (1939), directed by Busby Berkeley (promoted from his role of choreographer), and **Castle on the Hudson** (1940), directed by Anatole Litvak, are inferior, sanitised versions of their progenitors, *The Life of Jimmy Dolan* and *20,000 Years in Sing Sing* respectively. However, in the former Garfield is more convincing than was Douglas Fairbanks Jr as an unprincipled prizefighter, and the opening sequences show his involvement with a fast-living crowd with the old panache; but once he has been framed for murder and is on the lam the film becomes conventional. He is also on the run for most of **Dust Be My Destiny** (1939), but the director, Lewis Seiler, is unable to disguise the fact that Warners' later protest movies have become flaccid. No couple ever behaved as foolishly as Garfield and Miss Lane do here – but then even Warners seldom stacked the chips so high. When retribution comes she pleads: 'If you convict him I'll have to believe the way he does – that there's no hope for people like us.' Two scenes prove the old realism not quite dead: tramping the highways has so frayed their nerves that they quarrel, agree to part, then cannot go through with it; and, marrying for the money before a movie audience, they are hustled and ignored the instant the ceremony is over, and he is ordered to get out of them (striped) pants pretty damn quick.

Garfield lacked Cagney's charm but his wry, alert expression suggested that he would be well cast as the aspiring, ordinary guy and in **Saturday's Children** (1940) he dreams of becoming an inventor or of voyaging to the Orient. The piece has other points in common with *Bad Girl* – Maxwell Anderson's original play had won the Pulitzer Prize in 1927, and First National had filmed it two years later – but in the intervening period poverty in urban areas was no longer so desperate (if it ever was) that a man would maim himself for the compensation money. Warners deserve credit for acknowledging that there were people who led humdrum lives; the only other studio to do so was R.K.O., but their 'plain folk' films were comedies in the Capra manner. Both studios showed that they could be serious on such subjects, but *Saturday's Children* does not indicate that either Warners or the director, Vincent Sherman, were very interested.

Before leaving the films designed mainly for the men in the audience we should look at two of the studio's occasional horror movies – in the case of **The Walking Dead** (1936) for its enterprising plot. A syndicate of businessmen pin the murder of a judge on a man (Boris Karloff) he once convicted, first ensuring that he has no alibi; he is charged and found guilty, but as he is electrocuted defence witnesses come forward and a doctor (Edmund Gwenn) brings him back from the dead to seek out the guilty. The tale is superbly packaged by Michael Curtiz, who makes its sixty minutes pass as ten. He was not normally a B-picture director, but was given this assignment because of his success with *Doctor X*. A sequel to that finally appeared, **The Return of Dr X** (1939), again a combination of reporters, sinister doctors, unexplained deaths and urgent operations, this time directed by Vincent Sherman. Humphrey Bogart despised his role as the bloodsucking doctor, but with scarred white face and pince-nez, and a white streak in his hair, he is an alarming figure.

The outsider in Warners' menagerie of stars is Errol Flynn (1909–59), and it is tempting to think that his films were designed for the small boy in all of us. He was often felicitously teamed with Olivia de Havilland (b. 1916), as delicate and beautiful as he was dashing and handsome. When he played Robin Hood to her Maid Marian he said 'I do love you, you know,' and we did not need to be told years later that he meant it. He was born in Australia of Irish parentage and after some years as a small-part actor arrived at Warners just as the studio despaired of getting a British lead for their version of Rafael Sabatini's pirate tale, **Captain Blood** (1935). His looks were still cloddish, his dash less than he would muster thereafter, his Australian accent intermittently apparent and harassed by 'Heave-ho m' hearties' dialogue. As the heroine, Olivia de Havilland is not as pretty as she would later become, and as the villain Basil Rathbone is only a shadow of what he could be: indeed, it is a stale piece except for the battles. It is impossible to

say how many set-ups were used, and how much stock footage (e.g. from the Silent *Sea Hawk*) was incorporated, or how much is owed to the editing: but the screen is alive with action at every corner and, like all of Curtiz's action films, stirring. The Curtiz-Flynn romances as a whole are the most enduring of screen spectaculars: they have wit and brawn and glitter; they deploy their crowds with a vigour and a prodigality we are unlikely to see again; they are devoted to action and adventure and have no desire to be other than a showcase for Flynn's gallantry.

He lost his gaucheness without gaining much in thespian ability, but most of the time that didn't matter: in **The Charge of the Light Brigade** (1936) he is a dedicated soldier, far-sighted, resourceful and steely-minded. These are the things that matter in a film which positively dotes on the military and the panoply of Empire (even if, as C. A. Lejeune noted, nine times out of ten the Union Jack is upside down). It was harshly thought of at the time for distorting history, but the foreword explains it is fiction. Was it the Charge that prompted its making? – or had Warners looked at the profits of *Lives of a Bengal Lancer* and commissioned an Indian Army epic of their own? Or did they rummage through Imperial history for a subject, find two, and decide to combine them? The plot owes much to G. A. Henty, and has the ring of Victorian adventure, building splendidly from India to that insane assault on the Russian cannon. Tennyson's poem is naively superimposed on the images, and the effect is oddly moving – not just because the battle is magnificently re-staged but because the old ringing phrases retain their power. Miss de Havilland is again the heroine, unaccountably preferring Flynn's brother (Patric Knowles) to him.

The Adventures of Robin Hood (1938) is even better: indeed, it is the Curtiz-Flynn masterpiece, though to be accurate the direction was shared with William Keighley. The cinematography was also shared: Sol Polito, who worked so memorably on these films, was joined by Tony Gaudio, and they used Technicolor – with spectacular result. It is Hollywood English; some of the chases are reminiscent of B-Westerns; and even

Seen today on television, *The Adventures of Robin Hood* is merely good entertainment, but in the cinemas for which it was designed it is magnificent, frequently bringing forth cheers and applause. Here are Olivia de Havilland as Maid Marian and and Errol Flynn as Robin.

this subject might take a little more sophistication; but I still think it one of the most splendid entertainments ever devised. If Flynn's bravura is a little gauche, he has nonchalance, nobility and a concern for the Saxons that we take for real. Miss de Havilland's Maid Marian melts before him, and to these best among heroes and heroines one must add the best, or worst, of villains: Basil Rathbone as the terse, humourless Sir Guy; Claude Rains as the smiling, devious Prince John; the boastful, cowardly Sheriff of Melville Cooper; and the merriest of men: Eugene Pallette as Friar Tuck, Alan Hale as Little John, Herbert Mundin as Much, the miller's son, Patric Knowles as Will Scarlet. Carl J. Weyl won an Oscar for the decor, and an award might as well have gone to whoever devised the magical duel at the end.

The climax of **The Sea Hawk** (1940) is equally magnificent, with Henry Daniell, most underrated of villains, replacing Rathbone; and if elsewhere Brenda Marshall is no substitute for de Havilland she *looks* Spanish, which is the point. Technicolor is absent, but this is again a perfect schoolboy romance, with the Queen Elizabeth of such tales – this is another adaptation of Sabatini – animated with vivacity by Flora Robson. When he proposes to rob the Spanish treasure troves she says, 'You go with the express disapproval of the Queen of England but take with you the grateful affection of Elizabeth,' but matters move differently at the end, when she speaks of 'the ruthless ambition of one man,' adding that England will fight tyrants now 'and for generations to come' – which we may regard as Hollywood's equivalent of Bundles to Britain, reassuring and touching, if of little use to the War Effort.

Flynn is badly cast in two Westerns, **Dodge City** (1939) and **Virginia City** (1940). Both have splendid shots of movement across the wide open spaces, the former, photographed in Technicolor by Sol Polito, being one of the first films to demonstrate how liberating that process was to imaginative cameramen. It also has perhaps the most spectacular barroom brawl on record, plus Miss de Havilland. *Virginia City* is a story of espionage during the American Civil War, with uneasy performances by Miriam Hopkins as a dance hall queen and

441

Humphrey Bogart as a half-caste bandit. Like Flynn, both are miscast, and we might also note the backstage loathing between Flynn and Curtiz, and that of both towards Miss Hopkins – while Bogart despised Flynn, a fact that had much to do with his opinion of Flynn's prowess in such parts. Like his rival *jeune premiers,* Tyrone Power and Robert Taylor, Flynn was not a natural man of the West. As a swashbuckler he has dash and fervour, but his other heroics look false, particularly in the egalitarian world of the Western. 'I quite understand your point of view, men,' he says in **Santa Fe Trail** (1940), but he patently doesn't; he was never one of the 'lads', as he called them, which was why Warners realised that he could not be an everyman hero as Gable or Cooper could. Warners made him quizzical, mocking, polite but amused in lovemaking, and one remains conscious of the real Flynn, wanting to be ruthless, arrogant, drunken. *Santa Fe Trail* is also a Civil War Western, and in both that and **They Died with Their Boots On** (1941) he starts out as a West Point cadet. Indeed, in the latter he is General Custer, given to extravagant uniforms, self-glorification and, between the War and Little Big Horn, liberal drinking. In the earlier film Ronald Reagan plays Custer, and the abolitionist John Brown (Raymond Massey) is a subsidiary character. Flynn and his colleagues are supposed to be sympathetic towards his cause, but it is Miss de Havilland who puts it into words: 'Why can't they free the slaves before it's too late?' These were her last two films with Flynn, and this one was his last with Curtiz. They quarrelled, and Raoul Walsh directed *They Died with Their Boots On* – which is equally vigorous, suggesting that those really responsible for the Warner action films were the men in the cutting room.

Curtiz had also directed Flynn in two comedies, **The Perfect Specimen** (1937) and **Four's a Crowd** (1938). This studio was not strong in comedy, but both begin on that Hollywood premise of the period, the eccentricity of the very wealthy – respectively, an old lady (May Robson) bringing up her son (Flynn) to be the perfect specimen, and a bad-tempered tycoon (Walter Connolly) who becomes involved in the schemes of a P.R. man

(Flynn). The former is a variation of *It Happened One Night,* with Joan Blondell as a reporter; Rosalind Russell is the obligatory reporter in the other film, with de Havilland and Knowles making up the 'crowd'. Connolly has the best line, 'Posterity. What's posterity ever done for me? Why should I do anything for posterity?'

In **Green Light** (1937) Flynn is an agnostic young surgeon who, after taking the blame for the death of a saintly old lady, goes to the wilds to research a cure for spotted fever and when the real culprit flies out to save his life finds God. None of the Warner virtues is evident, as directed by Frank Borzage, and the film's sole point of interest is its inferiority to *White Banners*, taken from what is presumably an equally mawkish novel by the same writer.

Flynn appears only intermittently in **The Prince and the Pauper** (1937), Mark Twain's twee story of a guttersnipe who invades a Tudor palace and changes places with Prince Edward – roles played by the young Mauch twins. The film was a vehicle for them, but Warners also clearly wanted to show the world a British coronation ceremony when that was the topic of the day: it is inadequate, however, and William Keighley's direction lacks all sense of fantasy. Edmund Goulding directed **The Dawn Patrol** (1938), and while his sensitivity confined him otherwise to women's pictures, the scenes here of the mess indicate that quality – and with Flynn, Rathbone and David Niven all superior to the players in the original version, this is much the better film. However, critical prejudice against remakes and public indifference meant that it failed at the time. Warners remembered that when Britain's entry into the War started another spate of war dramas, and did not put Flynn – who usually played Britishers – into any of them. However, in acknowledgement of the War, Flynn cast away his doublet and hose after *The Sea Hawk,* and was called upon to be more responsible thereafter.

The European War persuaded Warners to back a pet project of Jesse L. Lasky, an independent producer since leaving Paramount, and **Sergeant York** (1941), a biography of the World War I hero, was very popular. As the film has it, he (Gary Cooper) is a drunken layabout till he has a vision and finds God: refused deferment as a conscientious objector, he one day has another vision which enables him to go ahead and kill lots of Germans; a coda at the end suggests that he wanted more than glory. Ploddingly directed by Howard Hawks, this mixture of hayseed drama ('Figger on goin' to thet there shindig nex' Sat'dy ev'nin', Miss Williams?'), heavenly choirs and shoot-outs is now only bearable for one of Cooper's best performances.

On Warners' lighter side was Joe E. Brown, a likeable comic but never a major one. His chief asset was his face – a huge mouth and a bemused expression. Most film comic roles, from Max Linder onwards, were about inefficient people who succeed only by luck, but Brown was often cast as a man of some eminence, proclaimed by dandyish clothes – loud checks and stripes, Argyle socks, glaring bow ties. Indecision and naivety, however, did not correlate with his position, and he could be put upon and manipulated. He had a gift for knockabout, and his films are generally persuasive. Two of his best are **Alibi Ike** (1935), directed by Ray Enright, from Ring Lardner's tale about a star baseball player who cannot help lying, prevaricating or just making excuses; and **Bright Lights** (1935), directed by Busby Berkeley, in which he is a burlesque star who neglects his wife (Ann Dvorak) to court an heiress.

Jolson returned, with wanton single-mindedness, to make two pictures as himself, in both of them a Broadway headliner trying for a comeback. In **Go Into your Dance** (1935) he has to conquer a reputation for unreliability and excessive ego, and in **The Singing Kid** (1936) he has lost his voice. The first, directed by Archie Mayo, is the better, somewhat resembling *Wonder Bar,* with an excellent cast including Helen Morgan and Ruby Keeler (then Jolson's wife); the second, directed by William Keighley, is notable for a large and unusual production number which begins on stage and finishes amid the traffic. Jolson loathed doing it, complaining that the other artists had too much footage; and refused to make the third film for which he was contracted. As ever, he is referred to as 'the world's greatest entertainer'. 'From what I hear,' says Miss Keeler, 'in more

ways than one.' One cannot imagine Fred Astaire passing either of those lines; Chevalier might have sanctioned both, but never in conjunction. Jolson seems to have believed that arrogance and vanity were virtues, and in his case perhaps they were.

The other Warner musicals are not up to their predecessors. The fortune hunters of **Gold Diggers of 1935** (1935) are not girls, but Adolphe Menjou, Glenda Farrell and Grant Mitchell, out to fleece Alice Brady, Hugh Herbert and other rich suckers. The setting is a hotel at a luxury resort, but there are no jokes about honeymooners: sex is no longer a laughing matter. The film does, however, have Busby Berkeley's best work (he also directed): the opening number, bright and cynical, tossed around by the hotel staff; an Astaire-Rogers-type duet for Dick Powell and Gloria Stuart; and two huge productions at the end, one with crinolines, candelabra and a hundred gliding grand pianos, and the other the 'Lullaby of Broadway'. Berkeley is a vulgarian, but these vignettes of Broadway are hypnotic – a clock going round, the milkman on his way, the 'babies' preparing for bed, and that gigantic night club with its serried rows of pounding feet.

The success of the Astaire-Rogers films however was proving to the studio that the effort and lavish expenditure needed for such numbers was unjustified, and the numbers in **In Caliente** (1935) and **Gold Diggers of 1937** (1936) are very simple. The former has 'The Lady in Red' and 'Muchacha' ('Muchacha, I've gotcha, and I'm hotcha for you'), and the latter some casual numbers for Powell and Joan Blondell, plus a finale, 'All's Fair in Love and War', which marks a nadir – though perhaps Berkeley was not responsible for the notion that bombs and guns are amusing. Lloyd Bacon directed both films on the principle that at 90 m.p.h. such nonsense is mildly diverting, and in both Miss Farrell is a gold digger. *In Caliente* is again set in a luxury hotel, and has a farcical plot about a hard-boiled New York editor obsessed with a dancer (Dolores del Rio). *Gold Diggers* starts out with stranded showgirls and vintage lines ('When they start shelling out jobs in a men's washroom a new day is dawning' says one blonde), but turns out to be about putting

Fredric March and Olivia de Havilland in *Anthony Adverse* (1936), which is what happened to Warners after it abandoned stories of the everyday for the bestseller. That said, it is a treat, galloping along under Mervyn LeRoy's direction, and cramming in as much as possible of Hervey Allen's widely discussed novel of a foundling who has a thousand and one adventures before coming into his rightful inheritance.

on a show. **Varsity Show** (1937), directed by Keighley, is some travail about collegiates putting on a Broadway show with the help of alumnus Dick Powell – whose co-stars are, according to the billing, 'Fred Waring and his Pennsylvanians'. Berkeley's finale is ingenious, and the film contains a stunning black speciality act, Buck and Bubbles.

Hollywood Hotel (1937) is also rubbishy, but it is cheerful, often funny and gleamingly professional as it charts the progress of Mr Powell from sax player with Benny Goodman to his apotheosis as singer on Louella Parsons' radio hour. Berkeley directed the film and arranged the numbers, functioning in the latter capacity only on **Gold Diggers in Paris** (1938), which Enright directed. The stars are Rudy Vallee and Rosemary Lane, not backed by the usual splendid supporting cast; it is but a pale, pale shadow.

Warners lost interest in musicals and released only one, *Naughty but Nice* (1939), in the period 1939–42. They bought **On Your Toes** (1939), and tossed out the superb Rodgers and Hart score

with the exception of 'Slaughter on Tenth Avenue' and its hit tune, 'There's a Small Hotel', the latter heard only in the background. The result, as directed by Enright, is an odd comedy about a hoofer (Eddie Albert) caught up with the exponents of Russian ballet. Another curiosity with music is **Blues in the Night** (1941), clearly meant to be significant since Anatole Litvak's direction and Robert Rossen's screenplay attempt both realism – only Priscilla Lane has conventional movie looks – and dimension. Excited by negro jazz, some white boys (Richard Whorf, Billy Halop, Elia Kazan) form a combo, making an odd buck or so, and while they are 'giving' with a number called 'Hang on to Your Lids, Kids' we cannot guess that they're about to meet up with wild and woolly melodrama in a New Jersey roadhouse, with the hero (Whorf) finally stumbling around Times Square, unshaven and begging for a drink. That was not so much a cliché then: in 1946 Richard Winnington referred to this as 'the only swing [sic] film I've ever liked'. The only memorable ingredient is Harold Arlen's title tune, sung by a negro chorus; the hero later turns it into a piano concerto.

Among the Warner Bros. ladies Kay Francis endured some heart-pulsing melodramas, after unashamedly playing Lenin's secretary in **British Agent** (1934), directed by Curtiz, a weird concoction fashioned from the memoirs of H. Bruce Lockhart, 'our man' during the Bolshevik Revolution, played here by Leslie Howard. **Living on Velvet** (1935) concerns a flyer (George Brent) who becomes a charming eccentric after killing his family in a crash; one enchanted evening he spots Miss Francis during a party and whisks her away from Warren William to live on Long Island, where he converts their back yard into an airstrip – which for her is the last straw. Frank Borzage directed under his Warner contract, and it finds him again at low ebb. **Stolen Holiday** (1935), directed by Curtiz, is based on the Stavisky affair, and if it is possibly surprising to find that as the basis for a story of love and self-sacrifice it *is* surprising to find the Eiffel Tower lurking just behind Le Bourget. Miss Francis as usual wears some four dozen creations by Orry-Kelly, with the excuse this time that she is head of a fashion house, financed by the man (Claude Rains) whose mistress she probably is. When his empire crumbles she signs away her every penny to pay the people he swindled, and is comforted by a nice British diplomat (Ian Hunter).

Hunter and Errol Flynn are her leading men in **Another Dawn** (1937), and William Dieterle directed this modern division of the Bengal Lancers movie in which Flynn, as flirtatious as he is daring, makes a pass at the Colonel's lady. 'But I wish I was Judy O'Grady,' she says as she kisses him. Caught in a sandstorm, she observes, 'We can't go on meeting like this,' and later she cries to her husband, 'There must be some solution'. 'Yes, there is. To play the game according to the rules.' She decides to leave them both: 'You will go on, building a nation . . .'

Miss Francis is a pitiful figure in Hollywood history, her prolonged decline engineered by Warners while the fan magazines speculated on how long she could cling on. She hardly deserved to be a major star, being less an actress than a clothes-horse, smiling and self-conscious; in the three consecutive films she made with George Brent it is depressing to watch him trying to be devil-may-care and her attempting to match him flippancy for flippancy. Her comic approach consists of opening her eyes wide and speaking quickly: in **First Lady** (1937) she is the soft centre. She is also a far cry from dowdy, beloved Eleanor – a not irrelevant point, since the film's source, a play by George S. Kaufman and Katherine Dayton, had been occasioned by the acute interest in Washington caused by the arrival of the Roosevelts. Central to the plot is the enmity between Francis and Veree Teasdale, whose husband (Walter Connolly) is also running for the presidency – and this ill-matched couple have one of the longest and funniest sequences of the decade, as he attempts to listen to his favourite soap opera during one of her tirades. The director is Stanley Logan, who made only a handful of films, and the screenwriter Rowland Leigh, but the tone is recognisably that of Kaufman.

It was one of two stage comedies – from a rich Broadway season – that Warners filmed at this time. Jacques Deval's

Tovarich (1937) had been anglicised by Robert E. Sherwood, and Casey Robinson wrote it for the screen: it still concerns a White Russian couple (Claudette Colbert, Charles Boyer) in Paris, subsisting by light-fingering at the *charcuterie* till forced into domestic service, which they tackle happily if not skilfully. Their employers, a pompous banker and his scatterbrained wife, are deliciously rendered by Melville Cooper and Isabel Jeans; Miss Colbert is at her considerable best and Boyer, if not the world's most natural light comedian, has grace and wit. Directing, Anatole Litvak demonstrates how quickly a European film-maker could subdue his own style to that of the Hollywood factory.

Warners' great female star was, of course, Bette Davis (b. 1908), a New England girl who was managing a modest career on stage till signed for pictures; she played conventional leading ladies – unconventionally when possible – up to *Of Human Bondage*. She has an equally colourful part in **Bordertown** (1935), directed by Archie Mayo – that of the young wife of a middle-aged café proprietor (Eugene Pallette), relieving her boredom with a Mexican lawyer (Paul Muni). She loathed most of the films she was called upon to do – but is, for instance, stylish in **Front Page Woman** (1935), and much more convincing than in *Of Human Bondage*, despite the fox furs and flower-pot hats easily suggesting the drive of an ace reporter. As the rival with whom she is in love George Brent is lively for once, Curtiz directs as if matching the rhythm of the typewriters in the newsroom and that, with some goodish lines, helps him to disguise the film's essential triviality.

It is Davis who is **Dangerous** (1935), discovered as a haggard tramp on the sidewalk. 'Say, weren't you Joyce Heath?' asks someone. 'What a vitally tempestuous creature she was!' says someone else, and since she *is* Joyce Heath, and since a young architect (Franchot Tone) remembers her – 'Only two people could have played that part, Jeanne Eagels and Joyce Heath' – he sets out to rehabilitate her. The yarn has surprises, and Alfred E. Green's direction an attention to pertinent detail, but contemporary interest was centred on Miss Davis, who won an

Oscar for her performance: she puts an intensity and an equivocation into the role that it hardly deserves, missing nothing of the woman's destructiveness or her callousness. Thus she revolutionised star acting in Hollywood. If the great comediennes were arrogant and indifferent to their audiences that was the basis of their style; and those who played bad ladies, such as Crawford and Shearer, were incapable of shadings: Davis was arrogant, but instead of demanding audience love or loathing she asked for understanding. Character actors of genius who were also stars – Werner Krauss, Charles Laughton – had tapped this vein, but most stars were encouraged to be relatively unambitious: the instinct and intelligence of a Cagney or Garbo enabled them to put flesh and blood on thin characters, but Davis went further, by continually – almost perversely – rejecting the standard ways of expressing emotions, and by deliberately giving those emotions greater and more varied play. She established a personality with strength, drive, a sense of reality and a brittle sense of humour – and over the next forty years she continued to utilise these qualities, with the added ability of being able to subdue them and substitute others less admirable, as Hepburn, for instance, would not or could not subdue her hauteur and 'radiance'.

In **The Petrified Forest** (1936) Davis transformed herself into an adolescent; the drive is there in the form of an ardour for literature, but the dreaminess is new. She can make credible a line like 'You know, that guy' – François Villon – 'writes wonderful stuff.' She has changed herself, whereas Leslie Howard, no less convincing despite equally sticky lines, gives his usual performance – part quizzical, part lost, filling out the unlikely role of a vagabond philosopher. The third memorable player is Humphrey Bogart, his theatrical entrance reminding us that the role was not new to him; but he understood the medium well enough to throw away the rapping comments of contempt and sarcasm. Also excellent are Genevieve Tobin and Paul Harvey, finding in adversity – they are held up in an Arizona gas station – a mutual marital loathing. Indeed, the performances are the saving of Robert E. Sherwood's drama, directed by Mayo as filmed theatre.

Satan Met a Lady (1936) is *The Maltese Falcon* revamped, and nothing in it prefigures the marvellous remake of four years later; the falcon itself has become a hunting horn, and Mr Guttman has metamorphosed into Alison Skipworth. Warren William is as much Casanova as private eye, for matters are entirely frivolous, the heavy pantomiming suggesting that Dieterle did each scene in one quick take. Davis, soignée and crisp, takes her reversals with a smile.

Like Cagney, she quarrelled about scripts, and after her walk-out returned to make **Marked Woman** (1937), which is certainly better than most of her films up till then. Like many another Warner melodrama this was concocted from fact, the long-delayed arrest of Lucky Luciano, on sixty-one charges of compulsory prostitution: the girls under his control turned against him, and two of them penned their confessions for *Liberty Magazine* – the basis of the screenplay by Robert Rossen and Abem Finkel. However, the film was closely watched by the Hays Office, which insisted that the girls become dance hostesses, and for further safety made them share an apartment. The only time money changes hands it is due to a misunderstanding on the part of Davis's innocent sister (Jane Bryan) – the ever-present sibling of Warner movies. It is left to the cast to suggest the unspeakable, and to Lloyd Bacon to supply the pace, which he does; the best scenes are those between Davis and Bogart, particularly forceful as an attorney, a character based on Thomas E. Dewey.

A reformed gangster's moll whose past comes back to haunt her is the subject of Davis's next film, **That Certain Woman** (1937), written and directed by Edmund Goulding from *The Trespasser,* which he had made with Gloria Swanson in 1929: his evident fondness for the dated material cannot really excuse it. Well received in its time, **It's Love I'm After** (1937) seems thin today, with insufficient laughs in Casey Robinson's script and too heavy a touch in Mayo's direction; as the spatting theatrical lovers Bette Davis and Leslie Howard are never flamboyant enough. Davis's performance, however, is unlike any of her others before – puffing on a cigarette (a mannerism for the future), icily sarcastic but humourless. Howard is believable as a philanderer, but not as an overweening egotist. The film is anyway stolen from them by the relatively inexperienced Olivia de Havilland, as a dewy socialite with a crush on Howard, and then from her by Eric Blore as Howard's valet. It would have benefited – a rare fault at Warners – by tighter editing.

Jezebel (1938) is a magnolia-scented tale about a spoilt Southern girl (Davis) who schemes to get back the fiancé (Henry Fonda) she has lost. The standard plot is nevertheless enjoyable, since we can never anticipate Davis's reactions, always one of her virtues, if unquestionably helped on this occasion by the director, William Wyler. He takes perhaps too much care over this portrait of antebellum society, with its fads and duels and codes of honour and de darkies singin' on de old plantation, his majestic style now seeming too rich for an intrinsically meretricious tale. As Buck – Rhett to Davis's Scarlett – George Brent has all the animation of a penguin, but Fonda is fine as the obstinate, determined beau. Fay Bainter won a Best Supporting Actress for her performance as the aunt and Davis, consecrated by a second Oscar, settled into a decade of unrivalled admiration with critics, with the public, and within the industry.

The vehicles Warners fashioned for her, however, are essentially second-rate if beautifully carpentered and written above the average – qualities inherited from their sources, usually well-meaning lending library fiction. Litvak directed **The Sisters** (1938), a family chronicle that takes in a number of political rallies, the 'Frisco 'quake, a bordello sanctioned by the Hays Office and run by Laura Hope Crews, and the failing marriage of Errol Flynn and Davis, the latter as a determined woman hopelessly in love. 'There's a kind of quiet assurance about you which bewilders me,' says he, a remark which sums up both characters and both players. Edmund Goulding directed and Casey Robinson wrote both **Dark Victory** (1939) and **The Old Maid** (1939), the latter from a novel by Edith Wharton – one of the very few to be filmed, after a Pulitzer-prizewinning Broadway version. *Dark Victory* concerns a rich bitch who falls in love and goes blind, acquiring niceness and bravery with marriage and

knowledge of The End. This was a property which had been around Hollywood for years, and Davis fought to play it. The result 'turned out to be my favorite and the public's favorite part I have ever played'. In the other film, she is the Old Maid, an independent girl who brings up her own child in the orphanage she runs, pretending to the child and the world that she is the daughter of her flighty and malicious cousin (Miriam Hopkins). Goulding is particularly at home here, the camera gliding among the plush and crinolines, but the film would be nothing without Davis. She takes every scene from Hopkins, though that lady, as usual, does everything but chew the scenery.

Davis's approach to her work is apparent in **The Private Lives of Elizabeth and Essex** (1939), even if her claim (in her memoirs) to have studied 'the Holbein portrait of the Queen' does not invite confidence in her research. She shaved her head and plucked her eyebrows, and also against studio advice insisted on farthingales of the correct width. She was thirty, and Elizabeth was in her sixties; she is short not tall; and she has the wrong-shaped head. Nor does she have the

Bette Davis, left, in *Jezebel*, at the time audiences were discovering that they loved her wilful or downright wicked. She is a Southern belle who shocks the town and loses her fiancé, Henry Fonda, by wearing red to the season's most important function; also shocked is Fay Bainter, as her giddy but worried aunt.

Queen's long fingers, but she uses her hands to brilliant effect, fondling her fan or the gewgaws at her neck, at moments of emotion helplessly clawing the air. She is glimpsed first as a shadow and even thus conveys the blazing sun the Queen was to her court and the endless source of mystery to her people. The Technicolor sets and costumes (Anton Grot and Orry-Kelly respectively) are, if not accurate, resplendent, and that is the other reason the film is memorable. Apart from some mistaken malarkey in the Irish bogs Michael Curtiz keeps the series of conversation pieces moving briskly; and if Warners chose to simplify a relationship which has intrigued historians from that day to this they were only following in the steps of a formidable number of novelists. The source, in fact, is a blank verse play by Maxwell Anderson, which the Lunts had once done – and it would seem to have been a very bad one. Or perhaps the screen writers are to blame for the climax, in which the Queen secretly visits Essex (Errol Flynn) in the Tower (offering the throne, which he gallantly refuses because his 'ambitions might harm the people'), or for the dialogue, which descends from the authentic to such lines as 'As a queen, yes, but as a woman? – do I mean nothing to you?' Flynn's stock schoolboy hero is useless here. Davis had unwillingly accepted him as co-star and neither she nor Curtiz seems to have given him the slightest help.

However, in **All This and Heaven Too** (1940) she for once has a leading man to her measure, Charles Boyer. Their skill and magnetism lead us through a wayward plot about a nobleman (Boyer) who murders his unstable wife (Barbara O'Neill) because he is in love with the governess (Davis). Casey Robinson adapted the popular novel by Rachel Field, based in turn on an incident in the family which owned the chateau of Vaux-le-Vicomte. Anatole Litvak handles the period detail with ease but is defeated by the framing story – which concerns marriage with an American pastor (Jeffrey Lynn), but a future with Mr Lynn can be no one's idea of bliss, least of all Miss Davis's.

The ending is also the weakest ingredient of **The Letter** (1940), and as Nemesis waits in the moonlight, imposed by the Hays Office, it is the only weak aspect of the film. Warners again borrowed Wyler from Goldwyn, and he does disguise the fact that Maugham's play, from one of his own stories, is one of the old warhorses – originally performed by both Gladys Cooper and Katharine Cornell in 1927 and filmed two years later with Jeanne Eagels: it could never have been done as well as this version. It is one of Maugham's studies of infidelity in the Malay peninsula, and in Howard Koch's brisk screenplay might be called serious fun: towards the climax we anticipate a trenchant statement on the nature of love and death (why she killed her lover, why she loved him, why she deceived her husband, whether she should die), and that is because Davis continually suggests that this is more than melodrama. It is one of her great performances – a woman of both abiding respectability and sensuality, of calculation and sensibility. Wyler gets her to use long silences and mordant stares, with an occasional blink of the big eyes, and she is never likeable or pitiable. The equivocal relationship with her defending counsel (James Stephenson) is brilliantly done; and other equally good performances include Herbert Marshall as the husband (he was the lover in the 1929 version) and Bruce Lester as that particular type of earnest young Englishman found in the Colonies. Amidst the studio jungle – with the moon as his motif – Wyler offers a vivid and correct impression of British Malaya, stiff and snobbish; and when confronted with Chinatown and the Eurasian wife (Gale Sondergaard) he soft-pedals. That he should view this society with more bite than the not dissimilar one in *Jezebel* is proof of Maugham's superiority, if sometimes only slight, to the majority of writers adapted for the cinema.

The Great Lie (1941) is also a film with class, which is clear because it starts with the thunderous chords of the Tchaikovsky Piano Concerto in B Flat Minor. It caused such a run on records and sheet music that this piece was featured in several films thereafter – and it opened up American films to the use of classical music. Mary Astor is a concert pianist; she is also a bitch. 'I hate her' are Davis's first words on the subject, and the film gives us plenty of opportunities to share that feeling, as they squabble over George Brent and a baby. Davis is all urgency and intelligence; Astor, behind the vanity and gay laugh of a spoiled career women, suggests someone desperately unhappy with herself. The latter has only featured billing, but Davis allowed her as many close-ups as herself. Goulding's direction is exactly right for the screenplay by Lenore Coffee – above average for this writer – from a novel by Polan Banks; and did it occur to anyone that there never would have been a Great Lie if Mr Brent had demanded to see the birth certificate.

Pausing between such histrionics Davis did two comedies, **The Bride Came C.O.D.** (1941) and **The Man Who Came to Dinner** (1941), both directed by William Keighley. The former proved that though she and Cagney could play slapstick they needed material worthy of them. The latter is not great art, but is a reminder of the golden age of Broadway comedy, for the material has been but little adapted. Kaufman and Hart's play is the apotheosis of the comedy of insult, as personified by Monty Woolley (in his stage role), bon vivant and litterateur, rude and insufferable. The character is based on Alexander Woollcott; the vain and bad-tempered actress on Gertrude Lawrence, though a miscast Ann Sheridan makes her into a vamping Hollywood blonde; Banjo (Jimmy Durante) is Harpo Marx; and Beverly Garland (Reginald Gardiner) Noël Coward. Also subject to Woolley's whims and insults are his dedicated secretary (Davis), the apoplectic and increasingly unwilling host (Grant Mitchell), the latter's wife (Billie Burke), and, best of all, the frozen-faced nurse (Mary Wickes). Woolley, often dull in films, is here roaringly good.

'Til We Meet Again (1940) is about a heroine with an incurable disease. Also like *Dark Victory*, it was directed by Edmund Goulding, with George Brent in the male lead. The heroine is not Davis but Merle Oberon, whom Jack L. Warner had contracted in expectation of replacing Davis as the studio's chief dramatic lady – which is one of those industry misjudgments to take the breath away. Goulding gets from her at least an approximation of acting, and indeed this is a good entertainment for those who like to listen to consistently elevated dialogue, viz. 'You can find eternity in a moment' and 'Everything you say has a note of farewell in it'. At moments of desperation Merle is prone to rush out and plead with the sky, 'Not just yet'. She wears some sumptuous gowns and looks healthy, if pale. Pat O'Brien is a detective; as the Countess, Binnie Barnes isn't a patch on Aline Mac-Mahon in *One Way Passage*, of which this is a remake. Nor is anything else.

That Warner Bros. abandoned their sharp social documents for glossy romances has much to do with the account ledgers at M-G-M. In 1934 the Warners restricted themselves to carefully budgeted films, yet still managed to end in the red for the fourth successive year. M-G-M, after spending lavishly on what went on the screen, managed the highest profits of any of the Hollywood companies. Until the War M-G-M outstripped its rivals at the box-office, reaching an unprecedented $14½ million in 1937 – which was even better than the sum racked up in the Talkie boom year of 1929. To get more, M-G-M spent more: when the average cost of a programme picture was $100,000 Loews might designate a budget of one million dollars or more for a vehicle for Garbo or Gable. Thus, as the other studios prepared their spectacles, so M-G-M more than ever eschewed the sort of subject which excited controversy but no action at the box-office; in 1935, two M-G-M films of social concern did manage to slip through, but they were the last. Neither, significantly, looks or feels at all like an M-G-M production.

Robin Hood of Eldorado (1935) is based on a novel by Walter Noble Burns, who had earlier provided the basis for the studio's film *Billy the Kid*: that had not been a success, but this one had affinities with *Viva Villa!*, and that recommended it to the company. Its subject is the dispossession of the Mexican population when the Americans overran California, and it is offered with a real sense of grievance; it was William Wellman's first film for the company, and the fact that his name appears on the writing credits – when it was commonplace for directors of his calibre to work on their screenplays anyway – indicates more than the usual involvement. It is a true story – subsequently retold in a number of minor films

– of Joaquin Murieta (Warner Baxter), who becomes an outlaw after the Americans rape his wife and steal his smallholding. His plight is charted from a sunny fiesta to a final welter of blood, and with one exception – Bruce Cabot as his pursuer – the Americans are portrayed as crafty, scruffy and dirty. The violence, circumspectly handled, is more effective than in many films of the Seventies; there are some weaknesses, however, in the latter section, notably the performance by Ann Loring as the revolutionary leader. Mr Baxter merely looks old and troubled. He was cast in this role because of his popularity as the Cisco Kid, but that fact did not recommend this more serious film to audiences; nor did the title.

Fury (1936), on the other hand, commended itself by its cliff-hanging plot, about a nice young man (Spencer Tracy) arrested on circumstantial evidence and the victim of mob violence. This was Fritz Lang's first film for the studio, after a year on salary, working from a story by Norman Krasna; he wanted it to look like a newsreel, which it frequently does, but after the quiet construction of the trap around Tracy in the first half the latter section seems overpitched, with huge close-ups of the citizenry and Tracy behaving like a manic Emil Jannings. It was its Germanic quality as much as its indictment of mob rule that brought it contemporary renown; today it is easier to react to the statement by the district attorney (Walter Abel) that in the last forty-nine years there had been 6,010 outbreaks of violence, and that only 675 people had been brought to justice. According to Lang, Louis B. Mayer was initially puzzled by the film and its press reception, then began to loath its positiveness, furious at the inference that the U.S.A. was not composed of decent family men. Despite the réclame, the film was never reissued. Wellman paid for his aberration by being assigned to a routine love story, **Small Town Girl** (1936), and then went to work for Selznick; Lang, brought originally to M-G-M by Selznick, was punished by having his contract abrogated – and he also went to work for one of the independents, Walter Wanger (q.v.).

That Selznick was at M-G-M was partly to do with the fact that the Mayer-Thalberg relationship was disintegrating. It was considered that Thalberg's quest for quality, together with his knack of estimating box-office potential, were mainly responsible for the pre-eminence of M-G-M: accordingly, Mayer was anxious to appease him; but as time went by Thalberg hankered to be free of anyone who in the final resort had the yea or nay – and, for Mayer's part, Thalberg's failing health was a source of anxiety. Thalberg approached Nicholas Schenck with a view to forming his own company, the films to be released, like the M-G-M films, through the parent company, Loews. Schenck agreed, though insistent that Thalberg complete his contract first – but Thalberg died of pneumonia before that was achieved. It was against this background – Thalberg's health and his quarrels with Mayer – that Mayer approached Selznick to join Metro. Though unrestricted, he was, as he predicted, unhappy at Culver City, though the films he produced for the company were prestigious and generally held in esteem. His two versions of Dickens were notably successful.

His conscientious approach to **David Copperfield** (1935) is typical. From R.K.O. he brought George Cukor, who had directed *Little Women* for him, and from Britain he summoned Hugh Walpole to do the adaptation and Freddie Bartholomew to play the boy David – in resistance to Mayer, who wished to cast Jackie Cooper. Lord David Cecil has described the book 'not as a clear, shapely whole, but as a gleaming chaos', and it is that chaos which Selznick and his collaborators appreciated, cramming in as much as possible. The 'gleam' is partly M-G-M, but it is also partly 'Phiz', from the opening onwards – a shot of a determined Betsy Trotwood stumping through the windy garden of Mrs Copperfield. As in the original, the best part is David's childhood, and if Creakle's establishment and the friendly waiter have both gone the Orfling is there in the person of Elsa Lanchester, and there are superb minor interpolations, such as that sinister moment when Mr Murdstone wheels away David's mother as she tries to wave goodbye to her son. The second half concentrates on David's first marriage and the Wickfield-Heep-Micawber machinations, held together by Frank Lawton, a usually uninteresting actor. To call the casting inspired is to underrate it (cf. the 1969 version, with half the British acting aristocracy): W.C. Fields as Micawber; Edna May Oliver as Betsy Trotwood; Basil Rathbone as Mr Murdstone, an unfeeling man rather than a villain, and Violet Kemble Cooper as his sister, venting her feelings with 'Of all the boys in the world I believe this one is the worst'; Jessie Ralph as Peggotty; Roland Young as Heep; Herbert Mundin as Barkis; Lennox Pawle as Mr Dick; and Maureen O'Sullivan and Madge Evans as David's two loves, respectively and rightly fluttery and insipid.

A Tale of Two Cities (1935) is similarly blessed: Miss Oliver as Miss Pross; Walter Catlett as Barsad; Henry B. Walthall as old Manette; Donald Woods as Darnay; and Reginald Owen as Stryver. Mr Rathbone is, alas, a lip-smacking St Evremonde and Blanche Yurka a ludicrous Mme Defarge but there is great good fortune in the Carton. The charm and the noble gesture come naturally to Ronald Colman; any competent actor might have managed the drunkenness and the manner of *laisser-aller*, but he invests both the poseur and the disinterested friend he pretends to be with a dignity which makes the final sacrifice very moving. Jack Conway directed; the clever adaptation is by W.P. Lipscomb and S.N. Behrman. 'For more than two hours it crowds the screen with beauty and excitement,' wrote Andre Sennwald in *The New York Times*, overlooking the fact that the crowds seem to be Silent film footage and Paris is a matter of process-shots.

The two films differ little in quality: one was directed by a man who has a great number of fine films to his credit and the other by one who made a handful of good ones and many mediocre ones – and that is a tribute to the M-G-M production machine. When M-G-M lost by death and defection (for Selznick soon left) its two boy wonders the machine should have foundered, but in terms of subject matter, quality and technique there is little to choose between the Metro films of 1933 and those of 1940. Both Thalberg and Selznick had negative as opposed to positive creative ability; they seldom knew what they wanted, unless in

terms of an existing film, but they knew what they didn't want, and left it to their writers, directors and craftsmen to find the solution. A young writer from Paramount, Joseph L. Mankiewicz (b. 1909), became, as a producer, one of the heirs of Thalberg: when much later he became a writer-director his films have both consistency and intelligence, but one must search for these qualities in the earlier films he produced, which range from the untypical *Fury* to *Reunion in France*, a Joan Crawford vehicle which is bad even by the standards of Joan Crawford vehicles. Little more individuality is evident among the directors – Clarence Brown, Sam Wood, Victor Fleming, King Vidor, Robert Z. Leonard, Frank Borzage, W. S. Van Dyke, Richard Thorpe, Cukor and Conway, who were all associated with M-G-M at this time. We can say that Thorpe's films were seldom interesting, and that Van Dyke's usually were: both were notable for printing the first take, but whereas in Van Dyke's case his films have spontaneity and vigour – he was known as 'One-Take Woody' – the reverse is true of Thorpe. Lubitsch made two films at Metro which are undeniably Lubitsch films, but where in the case of Borzage are the qualities of his early films? Julien Duvivier came from France to make *The Great Waltz* which if in no sense personal at least has the same imaginative approach of his other films – except that the best stuff in it (according to Selznick's memos) was shot, uncredited, by Fleming.

In this context, we might look at one of the studio's most successful films, **The Good Earth** (1937), a tale of a Chinese peasant couple through poverty, wealth, famine, revolution, marital disorder and death. Thalberg bought Pearl S. Buck's highly-regarded best seller in 1932 (the film is dedicated to his memory). The credits list a play based on it, and just three of the writers who worked on the screenplay in the intervening years – Talbot Jennings, Tess Schlesinger and Claudine West. Frances Marion also worked on it; her ex-husband, George Hill, was originally scheduled to direct, and when he was sent to China to get footage she was sent to keep an eye on him (he was an alcoholic: back in the U.S., aware that he was to be removed

Paul Muni in *The Good Earth*, in the California valley M-G-M leased for the film's production. Karl Freund deserved the Oscar he won for his photography, his spare and beautiful images often compensating for the lack of heart in the performances.

from the project, he shot himself after a story conference). Victor Fleming took over, but when he became ill was replaced by Sidney Franklin, the credited director; and, according to *The Hollywood Reporter*, Sam Wood was working on crowd scenes and Fred Niblo – the studio's once-supreme director, now retired – had returned to get the 'atmosphere' shots. Franklin was much less interested in directing than producing – he did not direct again for more than twenty years – and it may be that he merely assembled the actors, checked their make-up, and turned them over to be photographed by Karl Freund, who was returning to cinematography after directing some half dozen features.

Credit must also be due to the special effects man, Arnold Gillespie, who simulated the plague of locusts by photographing ground coffee swirling in a glass tank; to Margaret Booth, champion of editors, and to her protégé, Slavko Vorkapich, who did the impressive montages. However, the leads deserve little praise, though Luise Rainer uses her two expressions, smiling and woebegone, to good

effect and Paul Muni is 'strong' without being interesting. It would be impossible now to accept Hollywood stars pretending to be Chinese peasants, and we would jib at the superficiality; but that it works at all is what the magic of the movies was all about.

The reason for the subservience of producer and director is simple: the most important element in a film was the star, and M-G-M boasted they had 'more stars than there are in heaven'. More, they were, according to M-G-M publicists, the public's favourites. The public went to see M-G-M films because M-G-M stars were in them, and those films had to be good enough to ensure that the fans stood in line the next time Clark Gable or Myrna Loy turned up at the local Bijou or Strand. A star was worth, according to Joe Pasternak, ten million dollars, and on the title page of the monthly magazines a cartoon Leo glowed with pride at the success of M-G-M players in M-G-M films. Both Thalberg and Mayer were ardent believers in stars; and the greatest of theirs remained Garbo. Her films of this period are those we know best, and some of us have watched them countless times, embarked on what is always a voyage of rediscovery.

She was cast in **Queen Christina** (1933) at her own insistence, the first time she hadn't played a lady with a past. It is hard to say whether, coming from that long line of courtesans, she had the measure of Christina, but it is clear that – with the exception of Bette Davis – she is light years ahead of her contemporaries in the matter of royal interpretation. When she tells the mob that it is her business to govern one does not question it; one notes the dignity with which she receives her lover before the court, a secret smile playing at her lips; and one wonders, in her abdication speech, to what extent she is sincere. However, in view of her projection of love, one sympathises with the studio's reluctance to cast her as anything but the amorous lady. The celebrated scene in which she memorises the room in which she has slept with her lover is hauntingly beautiful, but note the subsequent scene where, vaguely impatient and pleased to have her lady-in-waiting see that she is happy, she is otherwise locked in a private exultation that we cannot enter. To say that she is playing a woman who has discovered love and happiness is, in view of the image she presents, to reduce her performance to triteness. With genius or at least good judgment Rouben Mamoulian keeps her at the centre of the film, but otherwise fails again to justify his reputation – the crowd scenes would not do justice to a third-rate fit-up company. Cora Sue Collins as the child queen could not have grown up as Garbo's stand-in, let alone Garbo, and John Gilbert's pop-eyed, insipid lover works only at room temperature. The high-style romanticism is of its era, but despite lapses the dialogue remains good – at least it seems so as spoken by Garbo; the cadences of her voice, the way she alights on one word or syllable, ignoring others, are unmistakably modern and right.

Although the expensive *Christina* made a handsome profit Garbo's popularity in the U.S. had begun to fade. Loews studied her American reviews and her undiminished European popularity in conjunction with her salary; they sighed, and not very happily continued to carry her as a prestige asset. In return for letting her play the Swedish queen she was thrown back into the sort of story from which she sought to escape: **The Painted Veil** (1934), Maugham's tale of adultery in Hong Kong, more than somewhat transformed. For her the trip to the cholera-infested town becomes an act of regeneration rather than retribution; there is a happy ending, but most to be regretted is the elimination of the bitchy, accurate study of local society – the book's *raison d'être* – and the flashbacks, indicating why the Colonies were populated with these particular people. To accommodate Garbo, the wife has become Austrian; Maugham's opening, one of the most striking in all his work, gives way to her meeting with the man she will marry. As the film takes off into the upper realms where Garbo was made to dwell, there is no point in considering it on any realistic level; M-G-M's Chinese festival is to the real thing as Cartier to a Woolworth brooch. She takes the advances of her lover (George Brent) in playful manner, a woman of sunny disposition and common sense; but there remain darker corners, as in the multi-syllabic 'No' to her husband's question as to whether she had slept, the reply of a woman who has spent the time deep in her own thoughts. The dialogue is simple, alone an echo of Maugham; these people talk intensely but rationally, usually in one long take. Richard Boleslawksi's direction is exemplary: The film could be shown to students to demonstrate how to make this kind of story.

The original also overshadows **Anna Karenina** (1935), making of it a parody of real life, never entirely false but also never exact. As an example of M-G-M film-making it can hardly be faulted, with Clarence Brown's discreet set-ups, with its featureless, elegant Cedric Gibbons decor, and with some sterling performances – Reginald Denny as Yashkin, Reginald Owen as Stefan, May Robson as the Countess Vronsky; but though a couple of the later scenes between Anna and Vronsky come off the only true echo of Tolstoy is in the two sequences where Anna visits Stefan and Dolly. The dialogue (Clemence Dane, Salka Viertel, S. N. Behrman) is passable. Garbo's Anna is her least endearing performance but fascinating not only in its revelation of range but for the economy with which she makes her points. She smiles indulgently at Stefan, sadly at Kitty, reassuringly at Dolly; her second look at Vronsky records complaisance, her greeting to Karenin that the marriage is dead. The great care taken – over, for instance, pronunciation – is dissipated by the playing of the men in Anna's life. As the son, Freddie Bartholomew is beyond redemption; as Karenin, Basil Rathbone acts with a permanent sneer and no dimension; and though Fredric March, with Prussian haircut and moustache, is good as Vronsky the soldier, he is lost as a lover. Consequently Garbo hardly lavishes as much love on him as on some of the others, with the result that this film is not high in the Garbo canon.

Handicapped by the well-meaning, semi-sensitive dolts who planned her career or, rather, marketed her as merchandise, she existed serenely in their centre, trying to put love and spirit and 'body' into the grand passions in which they embroiled her. **Camille** (1937) is often said to be her best film, and certainly George Cukor was more tasteful and tactful than her other directors. The sets, of quilted satin, are vulgar even for a demi-mondaine, and the same may be said of Laura Hope Crews and Leonore Ulric as the cronies of this one, Marguerite Gautier (Garbo); while Robert Taylor's Armand is of such unworthiness as to give the old drama an extra poignancy. However, as the baron, Henry Daniell is invaluable: there is little here but good speaking and style, but his coldness counterbalance's Taylor's puppyish warmth; and of the players one must also except Jessie Ralph, whose Nanine provides Marguerite's only prop in a fickle world. Garbo herself is more yearning, more sardonic, more world-weary than ever, projecting the feeling that she knows she owes her place in the world to the bestowing of physical favours: she can give up Armand because she is accustomed to losing men. *Camille* has the most exultant love scenes of her Sound films, as for instance when she grasps Taylor by the shoulder-pads to draw his lips hungrily to hers; and it is this quality of love which makes her death scene so memorable.

When she has other people on the screen to whom she can respond, her whole body is aglow: her humanity reaches out to them and consequently to us. If one sometimes becomes aware of her limitations when she is acting to the camera alone she is sublime with a partner, and in **Conquest** (1937) Charles Boyer is one of her best (in the Sound period, only Gable is as strong, though Melvyn Douglas complements her admirably). The film itself is one of the stranger Hollywood manifestations, costing over $2 million at a time when Garbo was a box-office risk. Anti-climactic and over-ambitious, both a love story and a study of Napoleon, it is satisfactory as neither, and would be forgotten along with *Suez* and *Marie Antoinette* (q.v.) were it not for the presence of the stars. Everyone has worked conscientiously – Garbo's films were regarded more critically than those of any Hollywood artist except Chaplin and Capra – but the result is like an early nineteenth-century memorial tomb, heavy and intricately decorated. Nevertheless, the stars move through M-G-M's marble halls as to the manner born, and contemplating either of them our spirits lighten, particularly in the ballroom scene which is their second meeting

– when he and we glimpse her in the throng, alone of the ladies in translucent white, throwing her head back to laugh. Her most sombre mood is one of resignation, not the desperation of Anna Karenina or the shame of Marguerite Gautier. As Marie Walewska, Polish mistress of the Emperor, she is less at ease than as some of the loose ladies she had played in earlier films; and on this occasion Clarence Brown cannot quite hide her occasional gaucheness. Boyer is magnificent: the film retains Napoleon's paunch, but nothing could have prevented this actor from projecting the romantic aura that was uniquely his at the time. His eyes have a manic glitter, his gestures the pettiness of egotism, but he carries the 'destiny' and can, when required, evoke the great man foolishly in love; without help from the writers, he manages to suggest in the final sequences that Walewska's love has now only little but practical value. Few American films of the Thirties offer so rounded a performance.

American audiences, however, proved indifferent, which gave M-G-M pause. Garbo herself had made it known that she wanted to play comedy – she had asked to do both *Tovarich* and *Idiot's Delight* (q.v.) – and Lubitsch that he wanted to direct her: **Ninotchka** (1939), the result, commissioned from Billy Wilder, Charles Brackett and Walter Reisch, starting from the premise that three Soviet commissars, in Paris to recover some White Russian jewels, are so taken with Western hedonism that another commissar (Garbo) is sent to fetch them back. The anti-Russian, anti-Communist jokes are at best good-natured, but it is otherwise virtually flawless, *au fond* the old story of the plain Jane country cousin first at odds with, and then succumbing to, the glamour of the big city. Lubitsch manages few of his visual jokes – and they are mostly to do with the reactions of the three commissars to compliant cigarette girls – but then this is primarily a vehicle for Garbo; and this time her predominant, enthralling quality is her vulnerability. Arriving in Paris, she is sceptical, caustic and supremely self-controlled; but we know that she is in a lion's den. Wisely, the writers do not predicate a character change (or if they did she doesn't play it),

454

Garbo in the Thirties

Garbo in two of her historical warhorses which made audiences weep in the Thirties – and still do. UPPER LEFT, with Ian Keith in *Queen Christina*, LOWER RIGHT, with Robert Taylor in *Camille* and, LOWER LEFT, a glimpse of her dancing the Chica-Choca in *Two-Faced Woman*, the 'gayer GRANDER *GREATER* Greta' promised by the trailer.

455

and she smiles little after she surrenders. 'Garbo laughs' was the slogan, but we remember less the one scene of laughter than the mordant way with the caution 'Don't make an issue of my womanhood'. Melvyn Douglas's suave *boulevardier* is the perfect counterpart; accustomed though we are to the two top-billed players ending in a clinch, there is still something startling about this man falling in love with this woman, and Douglas, an underrated actor, is clearly as surprised as we.

There was at the time a poignancy about the Paris of *Ninotchka*. Throughout the decade Hollywood purveyed a city – albeit via back-projection – in which glamour and romance were the *sine qua non*, but by the time this film came out the real Paris was at war; by the time it had completed its release Paris was Occupied. The European market was closed to American films, and since there was little prospect of a Garbo picture recovering its cost in the U.S. alone M-G-M relinquished a long-held plan to turn her into Madame Curie; moreover, *Ninotchka* had been her most popular film in years, proving not only that she could play comedy but that this was the way the public wanted to see her. Hoping for a Lubitsch-like lightness, Behrman, Viertel and George Oppenheimer adapted an old play by Ludwig Fulda (filmed in 1920 as *Her Sister from Paris*, with Constance Talmadge), and **Two-Faced Woman** (1941) was introduced to cinema patrons thus: 'Who is the screen's rhumba queen?' – 'Who is still your favourite top-ranking star?' – 'Who no longer wants to be alone?' – 'A gayer GRANDER *GREATER* Greta . . . Every other inch a lady – with every other man.'

This trailer, if she saw it, must have confirmed her view – which was not without foundation – that M-G-M wanted to kill her off. *The New York Times* called her 'as gauche and stilted as the script' and referred to her 'obvious posturings, her appallingly unflattering clothes', while *Time* magazine found it 'almost as shocking as seeing your mother drunk'. The film itself does not deserve such abuse but because its reception signalled her desertion from us we may regard it no more favourably. She is consistently good, but is, however, diminished by the total effect of the

Chica-Choca, the negligees, the candid man-poaching and lines more suitable to Joan Blondell, e.g. 'I like men. Especially rich men.' Her co-star, again Melvyn Douglas, later said she 'didn't have an ounce of humour in her', but that in *Ninotchka* Lubitsch had utilised her 'utterly charming sense of childish play . . . all her *eccentricities*, if you like, for comic effect'. This was something George Cukor now failed to do, as Garbo attempted to recapture her straying husband by impersonating her sister; and what fun there is is lessened by the scene – interpolated to appease the Legion of Decency and others – in which Douglas accidentally learns of her plan. He is good, as are Roland Young, Ruth Gordon and Constance Bennett – a lady who must bear some responsibility for the loss of Garbo from the screen, for the latter trusted her to choose her wardrobe for her, and Bennett ensured that her own chic gowns would easily upstage Garbo's. Garbo originally retired only for the duration of the War but, ever timorous, lacked the courage to face the cameras again: as new generations discovered her in revivals, it mattered less. In 1940 Malcolm Muggeridge wrote (in 'The Thirties'): 'It is difficult to realise that ten years hence Greta Garbo will seem as sadly strange as Lillian Gish does now': it says much about both Garbo and the evolution of the cinema that that has never happened.

If Garbo stood supreme and apart, it was generally conceded that Norma Shearer was the Queen on the M-G-M lot. The reverse of Garbo, all technique and no feeling, she set her seal on some varied heroines – Elizabeth Barrett Browning, Shakespeare's Juliet and Marie Antoinette. Eyes glistening with tears of joy or happiness, she ought in every case to be inappropriate, but in fact she tackles all three roles with perception as well as high-spirited charm. Two of the three films are surprisingly durable. **The Barretts of Wimpole Street** (1934) had been a highly successful Broadway and London play – by Rudolf Besier – and no film ever did less to hide its origins. Sidney Franklin's direction, however, like the playing, is animated by its own dynamism: whatever the quality of the material, it is impossible to look away – for every member of the audience must be waiting for the monstrous father to get his come-uppance. In that role Charles Laughton is a master of morose expressions, testiness and forbidding silences; as the impetuous Mr Browning Fredric March is as self-conscious as he is debonair. **Romeo and Juliet** (1936) is remembered for its over-age lovers, but at least this best of the pre-Olivier Shakespeare films can be discussed seriously, as its rivals could not. Leslie Howard is Romeo, and whether by coincidence or design the lovers' contemporaries are all played by actors who had been in films since the early Twenties. The director, Cukor, has said 'It's not desperate enough. Zeffirelli got that very well' (i.e. in his later version, q.v.); he also said that neither he nor Oliver Messel fought the art department strongly enough, and indeed Messel's designs are coated with M-G-M icing sugar: the Capulet and Montague retinues suggest unlimited time with needle and thread. We long for simplicity; but there is compensation in the vigour of the handling.

As romance – Hollywood's equivalent of the historical novel – **Marie Antoinette** (1938) is not quite boring, and the dialogue (by Claudine West, Ernst Vajda and Donald Ogden Stewart, based 'in part on the book by Stefan Zweig') not actually laughable, but that is all. The first part does touch on the ramifications of dynastic marriages, the peculiar milieu of the Court of Louis XV and the anomalous position of the King's mistress. Later, Marie Antoinette is seen to meddle in politics to a minute degree, and she is given a conscience – on being offered the famous diamond necklace: 'What, when people are starving?' Yet she purchases it, and thus causes the Revolution! Robert Morley plays Louis XVI as a booby, and makes the character touching. John Barrymore is excellent as Louis XVI and Tyrone Power dull as Fersen, the Queen's lover; others include Joseph Schildkraut (indispensable in Hollywood historicals) as the Duc d'Orleans and Gladys George as the Dubarry. William Daniels's camera takes the chill off the marble halls without diminishing their grandeur, and when he has a difficult scene – as when the mob arrives to cart off the king and queen – he shoots it from slightly above, the only way to do it. The

director was W. S. Van Dyke, a last-minute replacement for Sidney Franklin, reputedly because he shot faster. However, the move was seen by some as an attempt to dishearten Miss Shearer, who by virtue of being Thalberg's widow controlled a huge portion of Loews stock. It was seldom thought that Thalberg – this film had been one of his pet projects – indulged his wife, for her popularity was enough to justify her own whims; but despite that popularity and because of executive hostility she made plans to retire.

Of her five last films two were highly successful versions of Broadway plays. **Idiot's Delight** (1939) was written by Robert E. Sherwood in 1936, and visualised a Europe on the verge of World War Two. Brooks Atkinson has called the play 'a playfully highminded antiwar comedy', and it won a Pulitzer Prize; but *Time* magazine – on the film – comes closer: 'The fact that [it] has nothing very important to tell its audience by no means indicates that it is bad entertainment.' Between the highmindedness – a debate between a pacifist (Burgess Meredith) and an armaments manufacturer (Edward Arnold) – there is a plot about the latter's Russian mistress (Shearer) and the American hoofer (Clark Gable) who swears she once played the bill with him in Omaha. Sherwood's screenplay does away with the play's mystery by offering that past time as prologue – either because audiences were not expected to take a whole film of highmindedness or because Miss Shearer wanted to look and behave naturally before donning the blonde page-boy wig and accent as used by Lynn Fontanne in the play – she rather saw herself as the Lynn Fontanne of the screen. As directed by Clarence Brown, this half hour is delightful, with Laura Hope Crews as a tippling clairvoyant and Gable having the time of his life as a third-rate vaudevillian. M-G-M had bought the play for Garbo – attracted by highmindedness again: but it does provide one of the studio's rare excursions into the contemporary world.

Not so **The Women** (1939), as presented, say the credits, 'for 666 performances of its triumphal run at the Ethel Barrymore Theatre'. Clare Booth Luce's all-woman play is two hours of bitchiness and sentiment, and of doubtful value; but from the first good line – 'I hate to tell you, dear, but your skin makes the Rocky Mountains look like velvet' – it takes wing. Cukor takes his cue from what he sees as the key character, Sylvia (Rosalind Russell), for it is her machinations and gossip which move the plot about; and she is very funny. Shearer is so soignée, so generous-hearted and 'lovely' that it is hard to believe in her as a mouse-like creature who loses her husband; but she has two or three telephone calls with him – after his defection – which deserve to be anthologised. As Crystal, the perfume-counter clerk who steals him, Joan Crawford, like Russell, overdoes it, and one correspondingly enjoys her eventual discomfiture. Among the others are Mary Boland, as the much-married countess, hopefully crying 'L'amour, l'amour toujours l'amour'; Paulette Goddard as the predatory, wisecracking showgirl; and Joan Fontaine as a little ninny.

Shearer plays a Countess in **Escape** (1940), becoming involved with Robert Taylor, who has come to Germany to look for his mother (Nazimova), who has disappeared inside a concentration camp. After *The Mortal Storm* (q.v.), this was the studio's second comment on the evils of Nazism, and it further deserves respect as a superb example of the Hollywood production factory, as directed by Mervyn LeRoy. The plot, from a once-famous book by Ethel Vance, is not without coincidence, but is a cliff-hanger nevertheless.

Joan Crawford had waited more than a decade to step into Shearer's shoes, and it is therefore ironic that just at the time Shearer left, Crawford's contract was not renewed. Her films of this period are as delirious as those of her other periods, but **Forsaking All Others** (1934), directed by W. S. Van Dyke and written by Joseph L. Mankiewicz from a failed Broadway play, proves that she could not play comedy. Around her, Clark Gable and Robert Montgomery do the daffy things of screwball comedy, but she, steely-jawed, is merely game. There is at least one convulsive moment in **The Bride Wore Red** (1938), directed by Dorothy Arzner: Crawford, a Trieste cabaret singer, has been offered a vacation by a mysterious benefactor, but despite the newly-acquired virginal veil she is lonely – when

along come the villagers, in Tyrolean dress, to serenade her with one of their Neapolitan songs. At that instant you may appreciate the full force of the slogan in the ads, 'The Kind of Glamorous Production Only M-G-M Makes'. More than the other Crawford films, this one reveals Mankiewicz as the complete cynic. There are her vehicles, and there are movies, and though the two seldom resemble each other the gap is narrowed by **A Woman's Face** (1941), adapted by Donald Ogden Stewart and Elliot Paul from a play, 'Il Etait une Fois' by François de Croisset (already filmed in Sweden, with Ingrid Bergman (q.v.)). For one thing, Cukor has kept the star under control: given her head, she gives her all, but here she is almost as sober as her supporting cast – Melvyn Douglas, Conrad Veidt, Albert Basserman and Reginald Owen. The story is incredible, but everyone behaves logically, though the two halves of the film still refuse to make a whole: the business of this woman's face has nothing to do with her later role as a governess – except that we're asked to believe that a woman once badly scarred can loathe the world so much that she could turn child-murderer. But that is M-G-M: they would let Crawford blackmail (as here), they might let her play Lady Macbeth, but they would never let her murder a child – even this one (Richard Nichols), who fully deserves such a fate.

By the time M-G-M let Shearer and Crawford go they had found a new 'lady' star, Greer Garson (b. 1914), an Irish-born London stage actress, who after her appearance in *Goodbye, Mr Chips* was rushed to Hollywood to star in **Pride and Prejudice** (1940). It is a truth universally acknowledged that M-G-M's Olde England has little in common with the world of Jane Austen: at the time the two collided the life of a film was reckoned at ten years, but since television became the circulating library of old movies Miss Garson remains Elizabeth Bennett to many who have never read the book. She spars neatly, but if her words are not coquettish her manner is – to the extent that we may not be entirely grateful that it is she rather than Miss Shearer who, fancying herself in crinolines, had persuaded M-G-M to buy Helen Jerome's stage version. Darcy was originally intended for Clark Gable, but he refused to consider another costume role and Laurence Olivier was eventually chosen. The strictures applied to his co-star emphatically do not fit him – darkly, smoulderingly handsome and if arrogant and distant, not ·unlikeable, despite his refusal to use an ounce of charm. He is one of the players Miss Austen might have acknowledged, along with Edmund Gwenn's Mr Bennett and Melville Cooper's pompous Mr Collins. Mary Boland is a vulgar Mrs Bennett, even for Mrs Bennett, but she is marvellous: and we may think similarly of Edna May Oliver's too-broad Lady Catherine. The screenplay by Aldous Huxley and Jane Murfin is a clever condensation of the book, with stretches of the original dialogue, and since the film gets so much right – Mr Collins shooing away the chickens as he rushes to see Lady Catherine – one may forgive it such conventions of period movies as ladies chattering behind fans. The producer, Hunt Stromberg, and the director, Robert Z. Leonard, had done service on the Mac-Donald-Eddy movies (q.v.), but on this occasion they clearly warmed to their task.

Anyone not put off by the title, **Blossoms in the Dust** (1940), deserves to actually watch the film, which consists of one hundred minutes of treacly Technicolored uplift. Miss Garson plays Edna Kahly, who turns into a society gadfly, laughing on the outside and crying on the inside, after losing her child; and though she remonstrates when her husband sneaks a replacement into the house in no time at all she is running an orphanage. Bankruptcy is later threatened, but since the outcome is not vouchsafed us we may assume that it interested neither the writer, Anita Loos, working from a supposedly true story, nor the director, Mervyn LeRoy – the same Mervyn LeRoy who had once made *Little Caesar*.

Fortunately for sanity, the Marx brothers were also working at M-G-M – due to the enthusiasm of Thalberg, who supervised **A Night at the Opera** (1935) but died during the preparation of **A Day at the Races** (1937). However both, at his suggestion, were tried out as stage shows – so that what went into them was not necessarily what the Marx brothers did best, but what the public best liked

them doing. These preparations also enabled the director, Sam Wood, to shoot their routines in one take. Groucho considered these their two best films because they were the most commercially successful, and for the same reason he defended Thalberg's insistence on the songs and sub-plots for the juveniles – which buffs are united in deploring. Even at their lowest ebb – a song called 'By Blue Venetian Waters', danced amidst fountains by one Vivien Fay – they are worth bearing, for Groucho still has more insults to throw at Margaret Dumont – who never loved him more. In *A Day at the Races* she is in full bloom, a hypochondriac bridling with pride as she announces 'Dr Hackenbush tells me I'm the only case in history. I have *high* blood pressure on my right side and *low* blood pressure on my left side.' There are those who doubt his qualifications – he is in fact a horse doctor – but she never does.

A Night at the Opera is the more brilliant of the two films, with the Marxes' most celebrated sequence, the cramped cabin, and Groucho interpreting Harpo's horn-blowing as 'Two more hard-boiled eggs', one of their unspoken conspiracies. Running amok during 'Il Trovatore' Harpo is a wild sprite defying the pursuers who would encage him; but the old anarchic spirit is missing, later to decline still further; and it is hard to identify the one-time sex maniac with this pied piper to a bunch of piccaninnies in *A Day at the Races*. In **At the Circus** (1939) one cannot imagine him stealing cutlery, let alone sporting a blackjack. The film comes alive only when Groucho's insults are recognisable Marxist theory; the butt of them, Miss Dumont, does get fired from a cannon, and at the end of the film an orchestra floats out to sea – which is, with good reason, the only thing people remember about it. The writer was Irving Brecher and the director Edward Buzzell, who were also responsible for **Go West** (1940), which is the Marxes' 'Timon' or 'Cymbeline'. They no longer create anarchy, lords of their own domain, for the script suggests that Brecher had been studying The Three Stooges. If he had seen any of the Marxes' previous movies it could only have been the one he wrote – on this evidence he simply would not have understood *Duck Soup*. The final

459

chase is aboard a train, to remind us that Buster Keaton was a gag-man at M-G-M at this period: but, he recorded, the Marx brothers failed to connect with him. Bad notices and their concomitant, increasing studio indifference, determined them on retirement. One last film is a partial return to form: **The Big Store** (1941), directed by Charles Reisner. It is not particularly Marxian – the chase might have been written for any comic team – but it does cast Groucho as a detective, and he is more or less at his best, despite unmemorable lines; also, Miss Dumont – absent in the previous film – returns for a last measure of derision. Tony Martin sings 'The Tenement Symphony', which is schmaltz of a certain order.

While the Marx brothers were then of limited appeal, Jeanette MacDonald and Nelson Eddy were the world's singing sweethearts. Mention them today and strong men faint while others smirk: and confronted with their all-too-public declarations of love – 'Ah, Sweet Mystery of Life!' – who can blame them? That song features in their first film together, **Naughty Marietta** (1935), a version of an old Victor Herbert operetta which finds the director W. S. Van Dyke at his least enthusiastic; but he also handled **Rose Marie** (1936), an enjoyable film by any standards. Also from an old stage piece, it has the definitive version of the 'Indian Love Call', warbled by the lovers on a lake in the Rockies. Later she sings it as he, a Mountie, escorts away her brother (James Stewart), and strains of it interrupt her interpretation of Act III of 'Tosca'. Finally they carol it reunited on her sick-bed. Louis B. Mayer was so impressed by Grace Moore's success at Columbia that both these films had originally been planned for her – so the famous teaming was accidental, since MacDonald was cast in both by default. The title role of *Rose Marie* had been adapted to suit either – and had therefore become a temperamental and self-centred opera singer, and it is at her expense that Van Dyke offers the first number. He keeps the proceedings light and airy, and MacDonald abets him gleefully throughout, never demanding sympathy: even the cumbersome Eddy cannot dampen the fun.

There are excellent moments to be found in these films – though not in all of them, and certainly not in **Maytime** (1937), which concerns a penniless singer (Eddy) in Paris, a prima donna (MacDonald) and her Svengali-like mentor (John Barrymore). More cloying than the plot is a sub-plot which frames it – set in a cherry orchard of such ostentation that if you missed the credits you would still know it was an M-G-M film. It finishes with petals falling thick and fast, while ghosts of Eddy and Jeanette warble 'Will You Remember?' – the only song left from Sigmund Romberg's original score. Frank S. Nugent in *The New York Times* called the movie, 'the most joyous operetta of the season, a film to treasure', but then he liked the opera fashioned from Tchaikovsky's Fifth. The film does feature a chunk of 'Les Huguenots' – one of the few times that Hollywood, ransacking the classics for their 'heavier' singers, used a rare opera. **The Firefly** (1937) is also based on an aged piece and its 131-minute running time is witness to M-G-M's confidence in it: but instead of concerning a yachting trip to Burma, as in Friml's operetta, it is about a runaway prima donna who becomes a double agent during the Peninsular War. Eddy has been replaced by Allan Jones, not quite an improvement, but he has 'The Donkey Serenade' – if not the best song then the best *handled* song in the series. Snatches of it break into the action, swelling against the images, till finally he gives vent to voice: it may not be the song one most wants to hear (again), but the skill with which it is deployed is undeniable.

Robert Z. Leonard directed both films and also two other warhorses, **The Girl of the Golden West** (1938) and **New Moon** (1940) – the latter remembered as the one in which Eddy and chorus press on through swampland, oblivious of conditions, singing, 'Give Me Some Men Who Are Stout-Hearted Men'. The former, from Belasco's play, already filmed three times, boasted not Puccini but a new Romberg score. *New Moon* was his 1927 operetta (filmed by Metro in 1930), with the stars more judiciously cast – French countess and freedom fighter, as opposed to (untutored) saloon queen and dashing bandit. They are a husband and wife team on modern Broadway in **Sweethearts** (1938), utilising an old Victor Herbert score and Technicolor, the studio's first film in that process. **Bitter Sweet** (1940) also has Technicolor and Van Dyke's direction, plus a certain respect for Noël Coward's songs, even if these are no longer distributed throughout the cast. MacDonald, otherwise increasingly arch, kicks up her heels to recall her Lubitsch days in 'Ladies of the Town'. Despite barely diminished public response the formula was shifted with **I Married an Angel** (1942), a Rodgers and Hart modern fantasy from Broadway, directed by Van Dyke, but the decision had already been made to discontinue the series, owing to all-round personal differences. The two stars had given great pleasure to cinemagoers, few of whom would have dreamed that one day their films would be considered greatly inferior to those of that other popular musical couple, Astaire and Rogers.

Of the same genre is **The Great Waltz** (1938). 'See this film for its musical charm, its infectious lyrical quality, and its joyous spirit,' said *Film Weekly*, doubtless deluded into finding these qualities in a film claiming the 'spirit' of the music of Strauss the younger. The musical sequences are cleverly staged, in particular the crowds drawn to the empty restaurant where Strauss is conducting one of his waltzes, and the drive through the Vienna Woods, where the clip-clop of the horses inspires him to a certain composition . . . The score is played with such verve, with the editing choreographed to it, that the sheer contrivance is disarming. The rest is distinctly not 'joyous' – operetta plot No. 1, in which the marriage of composer (Fernand Gravet, as rechristened) and waiflike wife (Luise Rainer) is threatened by the bounteous diva (Militza Korjus, pronounced 'gorgeous' said the ads): what makes it especially trying is that 'Schanni' isn't even moderately considerate to his wife – yet it turns out that *she* was his inspiration, for as the Viennese sing back at him, on the balcony of Schönbrunn, it is her likeness which is superimposed over the belvedere. The credited director, Julien Duvivier, is absolved from blame, for most of the film is known to have been by other hands.

As the title implies, **The Great Ziegfeld** (1936) was the other mighty M-G-M musical, though it was originally a Universal project, sold because of financial difficulties. Billie Burke was to have played herself, Ziegfeld's second wife, but Myrna Loy replaced her: William Powell is Ziegfeld, and Miss Rainer his first wife, Anna Held – and, except in her celebrated telephone scene, excellent, with all the characteristics associated with a great and silly lady of the theatre. The splendid cast also includes Fanny Brice and Frank Morgan; but the film lasts just over three hours – the longest Sound film made up to that time – and as directed by Robert Z. Leonard it seems like it. Nevertheless, it made a profit on substantial expenditure, and won a Best Picture Oscar. There is only one song in the last hour, and the famous number, 'A Pretty Girl is Like a Melody', with the kitsch and classical interpolations, is really the climactic moment.

Customarily the M-G-M musical *ended* with the spectacular number – in terms of size dwarfing those of other studios and often built around the Terpsichorean talents of Eleanor Powell. **Rosalie** (1937) replaced Gershwin's 1928 score with a new one by Cole Porter while retaining the 'book' (but then the film's producer and writer, William Anthony McGuire, had contributed to that), a fable about a Puritanian princess and a West Point cadet. Miss Powell and Nelson Eddy make a deadly duo, he wooden and she twinkling her perception of the joke to every member of the audience – presumably because Van Dyke did not give her the same attention as her other directors.

As with their early Talkie progenitor, neither **Broadway Melody of 1936** (1935) nor **Broadway Melody of 1938** (1937) has much to do with the real Broadway – no exteriors, no grit and grin, no hint of the harshness of *42nd Street*: just two more backstage tales with excuses to get into white-tie-and-tails for the big numbers. The songs again are by Arthur Freed (q.v.) and Nacio Herb Brown. The director of both is Roy del Ruth, and in both Robert Taylor is a Broadway producer and Miss Powell a stagestruck youngster. The first of them wastes Jack Benny; it has an excellent 'impromptu' number danced by Buddy and Vilma Ebsen on a Manhattan rooftop, and another as magical as any in movie musicals – 'I've Got a Feeling You're Fooling', tip-tappy toes on a night club floor, all

Irving Berlin's song, 'A Pretty Girl is like a Melody', as featured in *The Great Ziegfeld*. It is absurd, of course, but it is impossible not to feel a frisson as the camera finally moves back to reveal this set, decorated in its moving kitsch.

join in and everybody sing. In the second film two of the numbers foreshadow the best of the musicals which Freed later produced: a dance in a rainstorm (done by George Murphy) and an ad-lib dance in a freight car very much like the 'Good Morning' sequence also in *Singin' in the Rain* (q.v.). Coming between the two, **Born to Dance** (1936) has the same writers as the earlier film, the same director, and so many of the original players – Powell, Una Merkel, Ebsen, Frances Langford and Sid Silvers – that the decision not to call it 'Broadway Melody of 1937' is inexplicable. Cole Porter's score includes 'I've Got You Under My Skin' and 'Easy to Love', the latter crooned by an unembarrassed James Stewart as the sailor hero. These films, if not easy to love are easy to take – and if we are fonder of **Broadway Melody of 1940** (1940), it is because of Fred Astaire, more precise and more ethereal than ever. The score is again by Porter, the direction by Norman Taurog, and the construction even smarter than Astaire's R.K.O. movies, keeping the dancing couple – she is Miss Powell, and Murphy is his partner and rival – romantically but not choreographically apart till the finale.

The chief joy to be found in these pictures is, however, the youngster billed eighth in *Broadway Melody of 1938*, a stagestruck child being promoted by her grandmother (Sophie Tucker); she has an extraneous number built around a photograph of Clark Gable, 'You Made Me Love You', whose lyric contains the words 'As far as I'm concerned you'll always be the top' – which is the way many Hollywood-watchers feel about *her*: Judy Garland (1922–69). The daughter of vaudeville parents, she had been with M-G-M, idle, till Roger Edens, of the studio's music department, arranged the Gable song for her to sing at a party for the star. She was to be profitably teamed with Mickey Rooney (b. 1920), another child of vaudeville, in movies since childhood, as he climbed to a popularity which would outstrip even Gable's, always playing the know-it-all wise guy with the tender heart, junior version. **Thoroughbreds Don't Cry** (1937), directed by Alfred E. Green, was designed to demonstrate the opposing talents of him and the studio's other boy actor, Freddie Barth-

olomew – replaced, in the event, by Robert Sinclair. As the girl trying to attract their attention Garland is a miracle: dumpy, plain, given to puppy-fat, her playing is relaxed and her singing has a sense of self-mockery remarkable in a child. 'I'm going to be a great singer, I'm going to be a great actress,' is her second line, and she plays it for laughs.

Stage-struck again in **Everybody Sing** (1938), she gets into a show with the family chef, Allan Jones, and the Russian maid, Fanny Brice; and her duet with the latter, though a poor song, makes clear that you are watching two of the century's legendary artists. 'Are all families as crazy as this?' she asks, and the answer is No, only in movies. Edwin L. Marin directed this one.

The family in **Love Finds Andy Hardy** (1938) is something else. The Hardy family started in a B-picture, *A Family Affair* (1937), with Rooney, and Lionel Barrymore as the father; in *You're Only Young Once* (1938) Lewis Stone and Fay Holden took over the roles of the older Hardys, which they would play in all the sequels. Family series – the Joneses at 20th, Blondie at Columbia – were common on the lower half of double bills, but Louis B. Mayer so loved these two films that the budgets were increased to A-picture level, and the public responded warmly for some years. The Hardys hopefully reflected America to itself: they were comfortably off – father was a judge – and both parents were founts of wisdom and virtue. Andy (Rooney) got into scrapes, but father's advice prevailed in the end; he flirted with other girls, but always returned to Polly (Ann Rutherford). There was a touch of humour, a touch of sentiment, always well handled by George B. Seitz, an unobtrusive director In this case, William Ludwig's screenplay is both funny and sympathetic – and Rooney is unquestionably a most gifted performer. Several strands of plot include Garland's crush on him, which, of course, he doesn't notice. She is, admittedly, appealing, but her delicacy of approach, with an instinctive use of the right glance and the right inflexion, constitutes a formidable talent – never more than in a haunting and witty lament, 'In-between'.

Her own 'in-between' stage presented a problem, for she was too young for

Judy Garland as the world fell in love with her. ABOVE in *The Wizard of Oz*, having proceeded far enough along the yellow brick road to meet the Scarecrow, Ray Bolger, and not suspecting the troubles in store, which include the Witch (Margaret Hamilton). RIGHT, in *Babes in Arms*, with Mickey Rooney, one of the series designed to showcase their talents in every direction.

romance and too old for the customary child-star roles, though she did have a Shirley Temple-like role in **Listen, Darling** (1938), directed by Marin, bringing romance to mother, Mary Astor, in the shape of Walter Pidgeon. Then came **The Wizard of Oz** (1939), for which Mayer had wanted Miss Temple: in fact, Goldwyn sold the property – Frank L. Baum's book – because he too had been unable to wrench that child from Zanuck. As fantasy was a risky proposition (there had been earlier versions in 1910 and 1925), it is clear that Loews were persuaded by the takings of *Snow White and the Seven Dwarfs* (q.v.); but it was the intention of Arthur Freed to launch Garland as a star – it was his first film as producer, though the official credit went to Mervyn LeRoy, who supervised. Victor Fleming directed – until taken off to complete *Gone with the Wind* (q.v.), at which point King Vidor (uncredited) filmed the Kansas sequences, including 'Over the Rainbow'. The screenplay stays close enough to the book, with witches, flying monkeys, and those equally fantastic figures who are the companions of Dorothy (Garland) on the journey to Oz – the Scarecrow (Ray Bolger), the Tin Man (Jack Haley) and the Cowardly Lion (Bert Lahr). The start is only middling, and the move into Technicolor not magical; but as Dorothy breaks into a gay little dance, 'We're Off to See the Wizard', it achieves enchantment. Garland seems to believe in the magic, which is complete but for the decor – notably Oz, the Emerald City, an art-deco monstrosity with fake glitter, and the calendar-art land of the Munchkins. Frank Morgan is the wizard, Billie Burke and Margaret Hamilton the good and bad witches respectively, and the score is by Harold Arlen and E. Y. Harburg – all factors in its being, apart from Disney, the most popular film for children ever made; it was a huge success then, and in terms of re-issues and television showings the most successful film M-G-M ever produced.

Babes in Arms (1939) had been a Rodgers and Hart Broadway musical about the offspring of touring vaudevillians putting on a show of their own: with the score trimmed and the book reworked into a sentimental valentine to show business, it remains a very taking film, justifying two follow-ups, **Strike Up the Band** (1940) and **Babes on Broadway** (1941), also both produced by Freed and directed by Busby Berkeley. Their purpose is to exploit the talents of Garland and Rooney, with wistful ballads for her and clowning for him, impromptu duets round a piano, or the two of them leading a well-drilled chorus in the slam-bang finales. They appear to be enjoying themselves hugely, and so does the audience (though when these films were shown in post-war France, the critics were appalled by their popularity, certain it was undermining French culture); the plots, virtually indistinguishable, fill the spaces well enough, and if there is a flaw it is their smugness: 'Gee, it's more than just a show. We're doing it for all the kids in America,' says Rooney. We might jibe at some patriotism – a song called 'God's Country' – but what to make of the last of

the trio, with its message of love for Britain? James Agate found it 'patronising', but there is a lump in my throat as Garland sings 'Don't give up, Tommy Atkins . . . There's a whole world behind you shouting, "Stout fella".'

She pined for Rooney again in **Andy Hardy Meets Debutante** (1940), and while M-G-M was not the studio to resist public demand – hence the dependence on teams – her growing popularity and Freed's desire to showcase her talent found her solo in **Little Nellie Kelly** (1940), George M. Cohan's old play, which Freed bought for her. Audiences may have loved this tale of feuding New York Irish in 1922, but it was stale by this time. Garland has a double role, mother and daughter: touching as mother, she is just another cutie as the younger Nellie – at least as directed by Norman Taurog. She is better served by Robert Z. Leonard in **Ziegfeld Girl** (1941); the studio had debated a Ziegfeld sequel for years, but this has little in common with the earlier picture, less a backstage story than a woman's magazine serial punctuated with songs. It focuses on three hopeful showgirls, and the lacquered personalities of Hedy Lamarr and Lana Turner throw Garland's talent into relief. She was certainly well-versed in playing stagestruck girls, and one may wonder how much these roles – longing for the big time, to play the Palace – contributed to the confused state of her later life.

At about this time there arrived at M-G-M another of the nonpareils, Margaret Sullavan. 'Hers is a shimmering, almost unendurably lovely performance,' said Frank S. Nugent in *The New York Times* of her work in **Three Comrades** (1938), for which she also won the New York critics' Best Actress Award. Following *Little Man, What Now?*, this was the second German subject in which she was directed by Frank Borzage. The source is a novel by Erich Maria Remarque, about three war veterans (Robert Taylor, Robert Young, Franchot Tone), one of whom falls for a girl (Sullavan) dying of tuberculosis. 'I'm not alone any more,' she says, giving to such lines an extraordinary poignancy for all their sentimentality: 'There are so many drifters. We may all drift together and some day we may find pleasant seas.' Borzage takes an equally romantic view. 'Get drunk, get very drunk and love your comrades,' says one of them, but perhaps there we recognise the hand of F. Scott Fitzgerald, whose only screen-writing credit this is (shared with Edward E. Paramore). He considered himself betrayed by the producer, Mankiewicz, but while the latter indeed rewrote his dialogue it was because Miss Sullavan could not speak it and because the front office had decreed that the Nazi angle be soft-pedalled – to the extent that the word 'Nazi' is not mentioned, nor the hoodlums identified.

Despite the altered European situation **The Mortal Storm** (1940) also hedges: says the wife (Irene Rich) of the professor (Frank Morgan) whom we understand to be Jewish: 'Now that these people have come to power, what about people who think differently – people who are . . . (pause) non-Aryan?' Germany is portrayed as a nation of thugs, where people are carried off and never seen again – and as in the case of *Confessions of a Nazi Spy* the German Embassy again protested. The film was much admired perhaps because it was made in a neutral country, and it was cheering to those Americans with relatives still in Germany; but if mild compared with the truth it is still too melodramatic. Miss Sullavan is the professor's daughter, in love with a young man (James Stewart) brave enough to defy the storm troopers. The source is a novel by Phyllis Bottome – and Borzage's participation, despite the credits, was minimal. Victor Saville took over production from Sidney Franklin, who left to prepare *Mrs Miniver* (q.v.). He found Borzage, he said, 'in great difficulties', and directed all but a week of it, refusing credit since, as a British Jew, he feared he might be thought parti pris. Yet Loews, of course, was a Jewish firm. Because both films are so mealy-mouthed – and because the settings are so patently false – it is impossible to find them impressive on contemporary problems, though *Three Comrades* is a touching romance. Even on their appointed subjects, sincerity is not enough.

The Shopworn Angel (1938) is an enjoyable attempt to tell a conventional story in realistic fashion. H. C. Potter directed, Mankiewicz produced, Waldo Salt wrote the screenplay, and one would not have to know their later work – Salt wrote *Midnight Cowboy* (q.v.) – to see this as a wry tale for sophisticates, 'La Dame aux Camélias' updated. The 1929 version starred Nancy Carroll and Gary Cooper. Like Carroll, Miss Sullavan specialised in suffering, and Metro regarded James Stewart as their answer to Cooper – but this version is hard and sharp, and very different to the earlier one in mood. The lady is a hard-boiled dame, and her protector (Walter Pidgeon) very understanding; she is selfish, dissolute and greedy, and it is her unwillingness to love the soldier (Stewart) that gives the piece conviction.

Sullavan's special qualities are particularly apparent in **The Shining Hour** (1938), for she is pitted against Joan Crawford. Of stardom, Clive Brook said once, 'We became rubber stamps – trademarks – recognised as Clive Brook, Ruth Chatterton, Ronald Colman, or whatever trademark we are sold under;' and as Crawford was trademarked as the Tough Go-It-Alone Girl, so was Sullavan as the Little Woman Bravely Coping. Like Fay Bainter, here playing her sister-in-law, she could be artificial; but even then she at least resembles a real woman, which Crawford never did. The latter plays a dancer from the wrong side of the tracks who marries a Wisconsin farmer (Melvyn Douglas), with catalytic effect upon his family (Sullavan, Bainter, Robert Young). Mankiewicz produced, Borzage directed, allowing us nary a glimpse of the cattle about which we hear so much (the Borzage of *The River* had long gone); the original play was by Keith Winter, adapted by Jane Murfin and, of all people, Ogden Nash.

For Miss Sullavan and **The Shop Around the Corner** (1940) the Culver City sound stage was turned into the Budapest of dreams, cream pastries and gypsy violins; and though peopled by Hollywood actors its conviction, unlike *The Mortal Storm*, is complete. Lubitsch was the alchemist responsible, together with Samson Raphaelson, who wrote the screenplay from a play by Miklos Laszlo. The result does not belong to any tradition of screen comedy: the only movies it at all resembles are other Lubitsch films, but in leaving innuendo behind he continues to regard his characters with delighted anticipation – the hero (James Stewart) and heroine (Sullavan) working in the same shop, mutually antagonistic, both of them, unknown to the other, dreaming of a pen pal. Frank Morgan plays the boss, a sad figure when he loses his wife and a ferocious one when he fires people. It is the film's underlying sadness which prevents this caprice from outstaying its welcome, but then it was made by the most adroit judge of effect and taste in Hollywood history.

Innocence – of a sort – is also at a premium in **Waterloo Bridge** (1940): 'Such things don't happen!' says her friend when Vivien Leigh tells her that her husband (Robert Taylor) has returned from the dead to save her from a life of sin – and it is the best possible comment on the whole film. The British at war wallowed in it, not minding such solecisms as Gloucester Cathedral doubling for a Mayfair parish church. As directed by Mervyn LeRoy the film is vastly inferior to the earlier version, and the subject has slightly shifted – to that of a particular English society and a dancer destroyed as she seeks to enter it. That she becomes a whore from expediency is hard to believe, what with the demand for chorus girls in the shows for the boys on leave, but there she is, welcoming the boys at Waterloo in beret and black silk dress, Taylor is in such a state of euphoria that he does not notice her outfit, and the game is only up when his C.O. (C. Aubrey Smith) tells her she will be an honour to the regiment. 'Has there been anyone else?' asks her fiancé's mother (Lucile Watson), in response to her tears, and we are cheated of the obvious reply ('Hundreds') by a cool line, 'Oh Lady Margaret, you are naif!' She would not have been the first lady of the manor who had been a lady of the evening, but for American audiences, even at this time, British hypocrisy had to triumph over true love. Miss Leigh suffers prettily against 'Swan Lake' and a medley of British airs: as an actress she was only technically accomplished, but she has a springlike aura stemming from the knowledge that she was beautiful and very clever.

Waterloo Bridge is one of the few Robert Taylor vehicles that has not slid into oblivion. Another of his films, **Stand Up and Fight** (1939), is a nineteenth-century

adventure tale with a note of seriousness – about setting the slaves free: 'People have been arguing that point for years. Maybe there'll be a war about it one day.' There were graver problems at Metro than the questioning of historical attitudes – the problem of Taylor, for instance: how to package this handsome and wooden star so that he appealed to men as well as women. Thus this particular formula movie: he as a ne'er-do-well growing up in the two-fisted milieu of the old West, with Florence Rice in a crinoline and Wallace Beery as the gosh-darn-it manager of her stage line; Van Dyke, directing, was clearly not interested in the narrative. **Billy the Kid** (1941) is a remake in Technicolor by David Miller of the early Talkie, again romanticising the saga: Billy (Taylor) has a grudge against society because his father was shot in the back; when treated kindly he becomes an upstanding citizen – till compelled to revenge his benefactor (Ian Hunter). Gene Fowler's screenplay tries for the frontier feeling – an awareness of sudden swift death, a loyalty to friends and benefactor. The effect, for a film of the time, is liberating, but Taylor and Brian Donlevy (as the Pat Garrett character) were both dull actors.

Johnny Eager (1941) was another attempt to give Taylor a more robust image, for he plays a tough gangleader –

Margaret Sullavan and James Stewart, right, in Lubitsch's enchanting *The Shop Around the Corner.* To call her vulnerable and skittish, or him gawky and down-to-earth, is to underrate them both; it is easier to 'place' Frank Morgan, centre, as the boss, crusty but with a heart of gold.

467

William Powell and Myrna Loy with Asta the dog in *The Thin Man*, the first of a popular series. Their diamond-hard playing still delights: Miss Loy said later that she based her characterisation on Lillian Hellman, the mistress of Dashiell Hammett, on whose novel the film was based.

and if this is odd casting, it is less so than that of Lana Turner as a sociology student. We may understand her leaving her staid life for love of him, but her claim to a knowledge of 'Cyrano de Bergerac' is one of the least convincing speeches in screen history. Mervyn LeRoy directs this good example of the late gangster film, well performed by Edward Arnold, Barry Nelson and Glenda Farrell. Van Heflin plays Taylor's self-pitying friend and lodger with a crush on him a mile high and a mile wide – the first overt Hollywood portrait of a deviate, presumably slipping past the notice of Louis B. Mayer (and winning for Heflin a Best Supporting Oscar).

Mayer did not like Westerns or gangster films, and **The Last Gangster** (1937), despite its title, is basically a mother love drama. Edward G. Robinson plays a hot-shot gangster who loses his wife (Rosa Stradner) to a smarty-pants reporter (James Stewart) while in jail and has to see her again when their son is kidnapped. Edward Ludwig directed, from a screenplay by William A. Wellman and Robert Carson, suggested by events in the life of Al Capone. As with Capone, Robinson is caught for tax evasion, and Capone's

rumoured homosexuality expressed by Robinson's complete indifference towards his wife.

In **The Earl of Chicago** (1940), Robert Montgomery is also a gangster – one who inherits an English peerage and begins to take his tenantry seriously. Richard Thorpe directed, from a screenplay based, say the credits, on the 'philosophy' of a book of the same name; according to the producer, Victor Saville, Montgomery was responsible for both style and story. The 'philosophy' is contained in a speech by the valet (Edmund Gwenn): 'Our class never let yours down, and your class never let ours down.'

Montgomery had played the role at his own insistence, as he had earlier played the psychotic in the film of Emlyn Williams's play, **Night Must Fall** (1937), directed by Thorpe. Presumably as a relief from comedy parts he acted both roles in the same odd manner, repeating the performance yet again in **Rage in Heaven** (1941). This is another picture which, as directed by Van Dyke, has particular reverence for M-G-M's England, and is clearly one of the psychological dramas which flowered in the wake of *Rebecca* (q.v.). But are the intimations of homosexuality in the original novel by James Hilton, or are they the invention of Christopher Isherwood, who with Robert Thoeren wrote the screenplay? The presence of this theme in yet another M-G-M film suggests a concerted effort in the writers' bungalow to offer an affront to the front office and the moralising Mayer – but in this case less hidden than usual, since Montgomery pushes his best friend (George Sanders) at his wife (Ingrid Bergman) after secretly gazing at a photograph of him and then goes, literally, mad with jealousy. The result is a very curious melodrama.

The studio's leading light comedian was William Powell, his career given a new impetus by the film for which Van Dyke is best remembered, **The Thin Man** (1934). While directing Powell and Myrna Loy in *Manhattan Melodrama* he envisaged them as Nick and Norah Charles, Dashiell Hammett's amateur private detective and his wife, and since Powell had played Philo Vance several times the studio thought this a safe enough investment. Van Dyke was given a B-picture schedule of sixteen days, and that was all he wanted. 'We managed to achieve,' said Miss Loy later, 'what for those days was an almost pioneering sense of spontaneity.' Today the film is just another murder mystery, but Powell and Loy are nonchalant, debonair, take-it-or-leave-it – and it is startling to realise that their chief interests are sex, money and booze: she says, surveying the drunks at their Christmas party, 'I love you because you know such lovely people,' and he explains thus his refusal to take up a murder case, 'I'm much too busy making sure you don't waste the money I married you for.' Albert Hackett and his wife, Frances Goodrich, added a few such lines to Hammett's, and the result is a film much more modern than the 1950s T.V. series based on it.

For much of its length **After the Thin Man** (1936) is better still: the banter is light, the plot pleasingly complicated and the work of Powell, Loy and Van Dyke as accomplished; but it goes on too long – 110 minutes as opposed to ninety-three. In **Another Thin Man** (1939) the red herrings are as compulsively confusing, but as the weaker plot indicates the Hacketts have based their screenplay on the second of the series rather than on Hammett. The credits of both films insist that they are based on 'an original story' by that writer, but the pretence is not kept up in **Shadow of the Thin Man** (1941) – nor from now on do the titles acknowledge that the 'thin man' of the original was the actual murderer. This is a shadow indeed: the Hacketts have ceded to Irving Brecher and Harry Kurnitz, who do not observe whodunnit rules. Later, in **The Thin Man Goes Home** (1944), directed by Richard Thorpe (Van Dyke had died), and **Song of the Thin Man** (1947), directed by Edward Buzzell, Norah and Nick would be bowdlerised, partly because the studio traded on Miss Loy's image as 'the perfect wife'.

Reckless (1935) was planned by Selznick as a Joan Crawford vehicle in the manner of *Dancing Lady*, a basically serious tale told in wisecracks; Powell was set to co-star, and at the last minute Crawford was jettisoned in favour of Jean Harlow, whose romance with him was very much in the public eye. Opportunism was further rampant in that the plot was based on the case of Libby Holman, a Broadway star widely suspected of having murdered her husband. In the film the star's career suffers when her playboy husband (Franchot Tone) shoots himself; Powell is the old standby. It is more enjoyable than **Wife vs Secretary** (1936), which, as directed by Clarence Brown, is no more than a vehicle for Loy, Harlow and Clark Gable – names which promise more than they actually deliver. Harlow's popularity had grown to the extent that her old image no longer suited M-G-M, so her hair was darkened for her to play the perfect secretary. Gable is tempted by her in a Havana hotel room, but resists while Loy foolishly suspects the worst. The credits of **Libeled Lady** (1936) are preceded by a shot of Powell, Loy, Harlow and Spencer Tracy walking towards us, a sign of Metro's prodigality in the matter of stars. Loy is the lady of the title, Tracy the libelling editor, Harlow his fiancée, Powell the colleague Tracy persuades to marry Harlow, with the object of getting her to sue Loy for alienation of affection. Jack Conway's direction seems confident that the players will make the oscillating fun seem more homogenous than it is.

The Powell-Loy comedies were inevitably about marital relations. He was the more gifted of the two, an accomplished farceur; her personal charm tended to disguise the fact that she was really only effective at one sort of cool, guarded, sarcastic humour. **I Love You Again** (1940) and **Love Crazy** (1941) are both screwball comedies, directed by Van Dyke and Conway respectively. In the former Powell, recovering from amnesia, is appalled by every facet of his past life except his wife (Loy), whom he persuades not to divorce him; in the latter, to prevent her from divorcing him he feigns madness – which requires him at one point to don female attire. Because of this impeccable drag act and its more inventive slapstick, *Love Crazy* has the edge. It also has the advantage of Gail Patrick as an old flame, Jack Carson in one of his best big-headed roles and, above all, Florence Bates as the mother-in-law, eyes agleam with venom.

In common with other late screwball comedies **It's a Wonderful World** (1940) has tremendous contrivance as written by Ben Hecht and Herman J.

Mankiewicz (q.v.: Joseph's brother), going to great lengths to keep hero and heroine scrapping till the last reel. Van Dyke must take much of the credit – if not for his pacing, as fast as ever, then for the inventiveness of the playing: James Stewart as a private eye out to establish his innocence, and Claudette Colbert as the poetess unwillingly involved with him, companions in loathing, one or other of them clinging to the other, by turns, like leeches. The prototype is *It Happened One Night*, and the middle part is a good deal funnier, even, than that: as ever Miss Colbert's eyes are glazed when there is news she doesn't wish to hear, but she reveals a stronger determination than ever to turn everything to her own advantage.

The film is certainly wittier than M-G-M's most renowned comedy of the period, **The Philadelphia Story** (1940), a version of 'The Taming of the Shrew' – or, rather, the prig. At the time it broke records at Radio City Music Hall, and resuscitated the career of Katharine Hepburn. She had scored a personal success on Broadway in Philip Barry's original play and had cannily purchased the screen rights. Warners offered $225,000 for them, but that did not include her; M-G-M took a chance, offering her $175,000 for the play and $75,000 for her services. Clark Gable was supposed to have propped her up at the box office, but refused the assignment. Cary Grant replaced him, on condition that he got top billing and that his fee of $137,500 was paid to British War Relief. In the subsidiary role of the snooping reporter James Stewart won a Best Actor Oscar (clearly a compensation for not having won for *Mr Smith Goes to Washington*). George Cukor directs with the utmost discretion, using mainly two-shot, and letting relaxed playing give the maximum to the lines and situations. The point is supposed to be that Tracey (Hepburn), a Philadelphia blue-blood, is humanised after some digs from her ex-husband (Grant), a drunken romp with the reporter and a lecture from her playboy father: but we are shown no transformation. Much is said about her, but beyond one aside (correcting 'my house' to 'our house' for the sake of her fiancé) there is no indication that she has changed an iota. The strength of Hepburn's personality disguises the fact that her role hardly exists, and the few real laughs go to lines devoid of wit, like her description of Philadelphia, 'It's an interesting place, full of relics, and how old are you, Mr Connor?' and the rest of the dialogue consists of such flat aphorisms as 'The prettiest sight in the world is watching the privileged classes enjoying their privileges.' Donald Ogden Stewart won an Oscar for his screenplay – having, in his own words, merely copied out Barry's text, and from neither is there a hint of comment: from Fairbanks Sr's two-reelers to *Fifth Avenue Girl* Hollywood had promulgated a satiric view of the rich, but beyond the bemusement of the reporters there is none here.

Hepburn wanted to stay at M-G-M, and it was Garson Kanin who provided the excuse, having, as he said, 'discovered the formula for a Hepburn success . . . a hoity-toity girl is brought down to earth.' **Woman of the Year** (1942) concerns a woman political pundit and a sports columnist (Spencer Tracy). Kanin was drafted, so handed the idea on to his brother, Michael, whose subsequent screenplay with Ring Lardner Jr won an Oscar. Other civilised talents involved included Joseph Mankiewicz, as producer, and George Stevens, brought in to direct. It is a film which doesn't pall, and in this, the first teaming of the stars, they were never better – she priggish and self-centred, he the rough diamond, practical and tolerant. Married, he moves in: 'I won't be much trouble,' he tells her maid, who agrees: 'Yes, that's what she said.' War-time sentiment dictated the subsequent descent into bathos; the writers should have found something stronger than the words of the wedding service to trigger Hepburn's inevitable act of repentance. That takes the form of a maladroit attempt to prepare breakfast, under Tracy's baleful gaze, and it is one of the classic sequences of screen comedy.

Tracy's progress at M-G-M had been cautious. As the Portuguese fisherman in **Captains Courageous** (1937), after an uncertain start, he takes over the film, giving it a grandeur in the dull middle reaches which reverberates after his death and makes the film oddly touching. Instituted as a result of the success of *Mutiny on the Bounty* (q.v.), Kipling's story offers

Harold Rossen a chance for some fine seascapes and Victor Fleming the opportunity for a robust adventure; with some years lopped off his age, the spoilt brat regenerated by the sea becomes Freddie Bartholomew, and he is finely supported by Melvyn Douglas (as his father), Lionel Barrymore and Mickey Rooney.

For the performance Tracy received a Best Actor Oscar – and the chore of partnering two of the studio's lady stars, Luise Rainer and Joan Crawford, in **Big City** (1937) and **Mannequin** (1938) respectively. The director of both was Borzage, much below the form of an earlier film with Tracy, *Man's Castle* (q.v.). Tracy is a cab driver involved in a taxi war in *Big City*, written by Dore Schary and Hugo Butler, probably after first planning the trailer – a mixture of fisticuffs and Luise 'soffering'. She also does a reprise of her telephone scene from *The Great Ziegfeld*, and since she plays Tracy's immigrant wife he tries to pretend that he is in love with her; in *Mannequin* he tries to persuade us that he is dotty over Miss Crawford. The writers (story by Katherine Brush, screenplay by Lawrence Hazard) aspire to nothing higher than displaying the slender talents of this lady – though there are signs that they also wanted to entertain anyone who might have simply stepped out of the rain: they have given Tracy a good role, but sadly the presence of Tracy in a Crawford film does not guarantee depth or intelligence. To anyone not reared on the Hollywood movie it must be an odd experience to see these two together, both working conscientiously to give some semblance of meaning to the script, he emerging as reasonably real and she as her usual unreal self. He is the shipping magnate who loves her truly; Alan Curtis is the rotter she marries. The title is inaccurate: she starts out as a factory worker (the opening is reminiscent of *Bad Girl*), and subsequently becomes a chorus girl. (Connoisseurs may argue whether this is the first movie appearance of the rose-covered cottage so memorable in *Random Harvest* (q.v.).)

After such films **Boys Town** (1938) seemed fresh, and since M-G-M seldom produced anything with any contemporary significance they made quite a fuss about it. Norman Taurog directed, very

simply, this tribute to one of the country's most admired men, Father Flanagan, who had founded a home for stray boys in Nebraska. In that role Tracy won his second consecutive Oscar, and he uses a sardonic and quietly self-righteous sense of humour on dialogue which must have been difficult to speak. 'How much time I got?' asks a condemned man: 'Eternity begins in forty-five minutes,' says Tracy Flanagan, ineluctably. Such matters inspire him to turn his home over to derelicts and to start saving boys: 'It's worth a shot, isn't it?' Yes: but since the screenplay (by Dore Schary and John Meehan, from a story by Schary and Eleanor Griffin) can think of nothing to say about either Flanagan or Boys Town it offers instead (a) his greatest critic financing his scheme, and (b) the rebellious Whitey (Mickey Rooney) reforming and leading the boys of Boys Town to capture the crooks.

It was singularly popular at Saturday matinees, but the same could not be said

Woman of the Year marked the first appearance together of Katharine Hepburn and Spencer Tracy, whose opposing qualities made them very effective. It was pleasing to learn, years later, that they appreciated these qualities in each other, or at any rate perhaps behaved together in private as on the screen: at any rate their off-screen devotion to each other added another folk-tale to the many that surround Hollywood.

of **Northwest Passage** (1940), which concerns Rogers' Rangers, an expeditionary force attached to the British army (the time is 1759), and their efforts to destroy a band of marauding Indians. They suffer starvation, mosquitoes and sickness; they carry their boats overland and form a human chain to cross a river – and so on. There is only one good actor in the cast – Tracy as Rogers – and even he cannot fill 125 minutes with little to do but look authoritative. Nor is there distinction in King Vidor's direction – a deficiency little helped by his own comment: 'We only filmed the book's first part, which was really a prologue to the main action in Part II. The second part was never made because of the producers' lack of courage. In the first part Rogers was a tremendous hero, but the second part showed his going to pieces, his disintegration, and I guess they feared that audiences of that time wouldn't accept it. Anyway, we kept enlarging the first half so much that it became a full-length picture, and it was always anticipated that I would continue on to the second part.' Jack Conway shot the truncated ending; Laurence Stallings and Talbot Jennings wrote the screenplay, from Kenneth Roberts' best-selling novel. The location shooting, in Technicolor, was a considerable undertaking for the time, and Vidor, in priding himself on the lack of process-shots and backdrops, could only do so by forgetting the back-projections and studio sets.

By this time Tracy was held in the same esteem as Paul Muni at Warners, whose biographical format M-G-M bettered by simultaneously making *two* films on Thomas Edison, **Young Tom Edison** (1940), directed by Norman Taurog, with Mickey Rooney in the title role, and **Edison, the Man**, directed by Clarence Brown, with Tracy struggling to surmount cliché, hagiography and an acreage of face-whiskers. Unlike the Rooney film it was a success, but cynics noted that the Associate Producer was called Orville O. Dull. Tracy otherwise resisted the sort of prestige roles associated with Muni. He even fought against doing **Dr Jekyll and Mr Hyde** (1941), and was mortified when both film and performance were badly received by reviewers, it being axiomatic that remakes were inferior to the earlier versions. That was not in fact

so in this case, and, as directed with astonishing force by Victor Fleming from a screenplay by John Lee Mahin, it is superior both in setting forth Jekyll's theories of moral ambiguity and in its atmosphere. The intimations of sadism and the erotic fantasies during the transformations would have been daring in Hollywood in 1931, when the far less restricted Mamoulian version was made; while this is M-G-M's best London, a place of railings and beckoning steps, vistas of lamplight and damp trees dripping in the fog through which Hyde flashes like a bat. It is not till late in the film that we actually witness the transformation of Jekyll into Hyde, which, as it turns out, is dramatically the right place for it. Except that he does not attempt an English accent, Tracy is perfect: as Jekyll, he has only a demoniac glint and a twist to his mouth; as Hyde, he is all make-up, barnstorming to blazes, which is really the only way to play the part. Ingrid Bergman is inviting enough as the light lady, and forlorn later, if never a Cockney drab. As the ingenue, Lana Turner has to listen to a fellow diner who asks 'Has anyone read that poem by that new chap, Oscar Wilde?' and she deserves no better.

The failure of *Young Tom Edison* gave M-G-M an unpleasant jolt, since at that time Mickey Rooney was, according to American distributors, an even more potent box-office draw than Gable. At first the least of the studio's three boy stars, he soon overtook the other two – Jackie Cooper and Freddie Bartholomew – in popularity. He was top-billed with them in a vehicle for the trio, playing New York schoolmates in **The Devil is a Sissy** (1936), an early example of studio shamelessness, directed by Van Dyke. Rooney's great popularity sprang from the Andy Hardy films and his partnership with Judy Garland, but he also made the best of the several screen versions of **The Adventures of Huckleberry Finn** (1939), directed by the otherwise uninspired Richard Thorpe. Mankiewicz produced, with fine Missouri locations and a likeable cast – Elizabeth Risdon as the widow Douglass, Rex Ingram as the slave Jim and Walter Connolly and William Frawley as the two rogues; the role of Huck fits Rooney like a glove, by turns rebellious, mischievous and enthusiastic.

Rooney also appeared in **Ah, Wilderness** (1935) as the younger son, with Lionel Barrymore and Spring Byington as his parents, Wallace Beery as tippling Uncle Sid and Aline MacMahon as Cousin Lily. The older boy (Eric Linden) returns home drunk, but that would seem to be the only vice around these parts, since his left-wing leanings are merely a reflection of youth's rebelliousness. M-G-M had earlier filmed two of Eugene O'Neill's more sombre plays, so this one was a natural for the studio; Louis B. Mayer loved such subjects, and Clarence Brown proves his skill as a director at this time – as he would illustrate again in **Of Human Hearts** (1938), a less cheerful look, despite the title, at America's past. It is Americana, and it is significant that no other country has a similar word – though doubtless a number of them could produce a similar body of work. The word suggests pride and cosiness, and yet for most of its length the plot here concerns either poverty or ingratitude. Walter Huston is the poor parson and Beulah Bondi his wife, settling on the Ohio River, the views of which recall Silent photography at its peak. James Stewart is the son, forgetful of his mother while at war. By the time Lincoln (John Carradine) reminds him of his filial duty the film has started to fall apart. But then perhaps it was a little too compromised and conventional to begin with.

H. M. Pulham, Esq. (1941) also concerns the American past, but is, in keeping with the changed attitudes of the last two or three years, more nostalgic and consequently not entirely faithful to John P. Marquand's original book, despite its physical presence under the credits, complete with dust jacket 'by the author of "The Late George Apley"'. The earlier book was an anatomy of a man's life, but this is merely an account of a Boston gentleman (Robert Young) forced by family pressures to leave the hurly-burly of a Manhattan advertising office and the girl (Hedy Lamarr) he loves. Bostonian philosophy is expressed rather vaguely by his father (Charles Coburn): 'You get it in a good book. In Scott. In Thackeray. In what I understand of Shakespeare.' As directed by King Vidor the film is better than *Kitty Foyle*, but much inferior to *The Magnificent Ambersons* (q.v.), also manifes-

tations of American interest in its old families.

It is a film to suit M-G-M's changed image; **China Seas** (1935) is more typical of the studio's more raffish reputation while Thalberg was alive. Clark Gable is the captain, hard drinking ashore and at sea given to reminiscing about the rivers of England. 'Limey' he is called by China Doll (Jean Harlow), who has pursued him to this corner of the East. He becomes engaged to a patrician English widow, Sybil (Rosalind Russell), but finds that he would rather wait for China Doll to come out of jail than leave the China seas for Sybil and his beloved English rivers. There is a pirate attack and a mutiny, a subplot about a stolen necklace involving Akim Tamiroff and Ed Brophy, and such ballast as Robert Benchley as a drunk writer, Lewis Stone as a one-time coward, and C. Aubrey Smith as the captain. As the villain Wallace Beery for one does not mug nor is he lovable, while Gable, still boyish, dominates the action and justifies his huge popularity. The director was Tay Garnett and the writers were Kevin McGuinness and Jules Furthman – whose hand we recognise in the rich irrelevancies, including the lady who has 'sailed the China seas for thirty years and never lost a spangle' and the cheery farewell of the maid (Hattie McDaniel): 'Goodbye Miss Dolly. You sho' been mighty good to me even if they does hang you.' *Photoplay* thought the film 'not sufficiently adroit in its handling to make coarseness and brutality even slightly palatable' – the sort of high-handed reaction which prevented this highly enjoyable entertainment from receiving the recognition it deserved.

There were no such reservations about the studio's other lavish sea drama, **Mutiny on the Bounty** (1935), which made a million dollars' profit on an investment of almost two million – the studio's most costly project since *Ben-Hur*; it also won a Best Picture Oscar. There was respectability here – and history, as taken from the popular books by Charles Nordhoff and James Norman Hall. 'It is superlatively thrilling' said *The New York Times*, not without reason, of the adventures of H.M.S. *Bounty* and the clashes between First Mate Fletcher Christian (Gable) and the inhuman Captain Bligh

473

San Francisco, not without reason, is one of the most self-absorbed of cities, and it relishes the movie which M-G-M made of the famous earthquake and fire of 1906. Still today, in the revival houses, when the organ breaks into the song that Jeanette Macdonald sang in the film, the whole audience joins in without prompting. Clarke Gable and Spencer Tracy spend the last part of the film looking for that lady, and at this point seem to be climbing Twin Peaks, where they will find her comforting the displaced population with a hymn.

(Charles Laughton). But neither the screenplay – by Talbot Jennings, Furthman and Carey Wilson – nor Frank Lloyd's direction can disguise the fact that the tale is anti-climactic. It is not surprising that the inferior remake (q.v.) had difficulty in finding an ending.

Because of that remake the film remained for years as hidden as *China Seas*, but there never was a close season for **San Francisco** (1936), so that Judy Garland could years later bring down the house when she did a take-off of Jeanette MacDonald singing on amidst the ruins. The earthquake sequence is as stunning as the Odessa Steps sequence in *Potemkin*, due to editor Booth and effects man Gillespie, who devised magnetic rods to support the buildings, which fell apart when the current was cut off. The plot, however, does not evoke *Potemkin*, an on-again off-again affair between a saloon owner (Gable) and a singer (MacDonald), which could have been on-again or off-again many more times (or less) without anyone giving a damn, but it swings forward with confidence under Van Dyke's direction. 'Magnificent and vulgar' says a title in the film of the Barbary

Coast, and we may feel the same way, as Gable spars with his dog-collared boyhood buddy (Spencer Tracy) or strides through the ruins, trouser leg coyly ripped, bow tie askew, a smudge of blood on his forehead, looking for Jeanette, who is finally found trilling 'Nearer My God to Thee' as the population resolves to build a new – and greater – San Francisco.

Saratoga (1937) is Harlow's final film with Gable, with a script so complicated that it gives them no chance for their treasurable slanging matches – though by this time the Code was working with a vengeance, forbidding the old sexual tangling. She looks tired; perhaps knowledge of her imminent death cast a pall on the proceedings – she is said to have died suddenly, but in one scene Walter Pidgeon helps her to a cigarette and when three or four fall out he ignores them: the fact that director Conway did not retake it suggests that speed of completion was of the essence. The stand-in who completed her part is so obviously that (back to the camera, hidden by dark glasses or picture hat) that it is difficult to concentrate. The plot, naturally, is about horses, with Gable as a bookmaker with an eye to the main chance. **Parnell** (1937) became famous as Gable's only flop of the period, but it certainly did not deserve the critical lambasting that it received. John M. Stahl directed, from a reasonably accurate and well-constructed screenplay by John Van Druten and S. N. Behrman, based on a recent Broadway play. Since at this time public opinion still held that the private lives of public figures should be above reproach,* the film withholds some important details: but after constantly referring to Parnell as 'the uncrowned king of Ireland' it has him echoing Edward VIII in speaking of 'every man's right to have the woman he loves standing beside him'. The chief weaknesses in the film are its leading players, allowed to be in awe of playing Victorian Britons: Gable lacks his usual fire and Myrna Loy, as Kitty O'Shea, performs in equally restrained and dignified manner.

Another Gable vehicle, **Test Pilot** (1938), was once admired for its aero-

* A number of British politicians resigned after scandalous revelations in the 1960s; in the U.S. in 1980, ten years after the Chappaquidick affair, Senator Edward Kennedy gained widespread support in his bid for the Presidency.

nautics: in *The Nation* Mark Van Doren confessed that he staggered out of the cinema, unable to persuade himself that some of the aerial sequences were faked: 'there is no use denying it, [this is] a terrifying affair; and since that is what it tried to be it must be acknowledged a success'. Today it is notable for the curious and heated courtship of Loy by Gable, her devotion to him and that of Tracy as his mechanic; the latter's presence and Victor Fleming's direction give it class. 'Entertain me! Thrill me!' says Walter Connolly at the start of **Too Hot to Handle** (1938): he is the boss and Gable a newsreel cameraman – one not averse to faking shots, which is nothing to what Special Effects get up to here. In fact, the fakery is so evident and the climax up the Amazon so far-fetched – even for this sort of tale – that it fails to thrill. But it entertains, as crackingly handled by Conway and played by Gable, Loy and Pidgeon as his rival.

Since Gable spent most of 1939 on loan to Selznick making *Gone with the Wind* (q.v.) it is a pity that his return was marked by **Strange Cargo** (1940), a film which marked his final teaming with Joan Crawford. The producer, Mankiewicz, Frank Borzage and Lawrence Hazard (adapting a novel by Richard Sale) had last worked together on a Crawford vehicle, and that is what this chiefly is, if not typical. The first scene, set on the quayside of Devil's Island, is stupendous: Gable is a convict who dreams of Paris, and Crawford, though referred to as 'one of the girls from the café', a whore from Marseilles; she carries a parasol and has a cigarette hanging from her mouth. Later they are involved in an escape attempt, with Albert Dekker and Paul Lukas – and Ian Hunter, a stranger beatifically smiling among the convicts. For a while it seems that we are watching an adventure story into which someone had the taste – bad or good – to add God; and when we reach a thirty-minute patch in an open boat without drinking-water, it is clear that something is being said about the human condition. There is much talk of death,

Hunter is the Conciliator, and when they die they die happy. As Joan says, 'When it came to their end, they suddenly found *sumthen tuh hang on tuh.*'

In fact, Gable's presence in *Gone with the Wind* seems to have confused M-G-M, for the films he made immediately following it are all poor. He has his Rhett Butler status of entrepreneur in both **Boom Town** (1940) and **Honky Tonk** (1941), plus his old image of ladies' man, a bit of a heel (who'll reform) and a hell-raiser. Rivalry among the oil fields with Tracy makes the former picture bearable for a while, but its sermonising on capitalism – of which it definitely approves, despite the evidence presented therein – is inept; and Hedy Lamarr is tiresome as the industrial spy who tries to win him from Claudette Colbert. *Honky Tonk,* also directed by Conway, has Lana Turner as a sparring sex partner, but she is not even a grade school imitation of Harlow; as the saloon queen who loses him, Claire Trevor is much more his sort of woman – and of course a better actress.

Gable is more his old self in **Comrade X** (1940), directed by King Vidor from a script by Ben Hecht and Charles Lederer and based on an original by Walter Reisch, who had worked on the similar *Ninotchka*. The cracks here are less funny and more vicious – for at this time the U.S.S.R. was fair game (Russia had a non-aggression pact with Germany): 'The problem of taking the masses from boogie-woogie is a difficult one,' says Lamarr as a tram driver, a poor substitute for Garbo. Gable is a fearless American correspondent, involved at one point in a chase more suitable for a comic. Gable took pratfalls; he played con men; he was brusque and short tempered; he lied and cheated; in this film his fedora is seldom worn correctly and his braces dangle from his pants. He was not without vanity, but he was the most human of the great romantic stars – which was something that of those who came after him only Burt Reynolds (q.v.) understood, and Gable, in direct contrast, was far more instinctive.

19

Hollywood's Golden Age: Columbia and United Artists

COLUMBIA in the Thirties was, as we have seen, mainly notable for the films of Capra, bringing that studio to the point where it joined Universal and United Artists as the lesser of the eight acknowledged majors. Harry Cohn was even more of an opportunist than the other tycoons, and liked to employ waning stars and directors or those in dispute with the other studios, for he was then able to pay them less than their usual salaries. He offered only short commitments, which satisfied both parties. Few either stayed or returned, for Cohn – known as White Fang – was the most foul-mouthed and abusive of the studio dictators, and those who clashed with him did not, if they could help it, do so again. His only important star at this time was Jean Arthur, though both Irene Dunne and Cary Grant signed non-exclusive contracts, the advantage to them being that with less competition they got the pick of the star roles. Columbia did attract a number of leading directors, for the successful ones tended to be the most independently-minded; and they had noted Capra's claim that once he had convinced Cohn that a particular project was the one he wanted to make, and the only one, he was allowed tc proceed without interference. And that was rare in Hollywood.

Before Capra's rise to fame one leading director, Howard Hawks, had already tested Cohn's non-intervention, and he was to make three more films for Columbia during the decade. After his success with *The Dawn Patrol* at Warners Cohn invited him to direct **The Criminal Code** (1931), one of the studio's rare attempts then to escape from supporting features; it was also more serious than most Columbia films, but Cohn hoped to emulate M-G-M's success with *Big House*. Based on a Broadway play by Martin Flavin, it concerns a humane prison warden (Walter Huston) and a prisoner (Phillips Holmes) whom he puts on trust. Hawks handles it over-deliberately, and its quality is due mainly to Huston, a little theatrical but as ever confirming Stanislavsky's opinion that he was one of the best living actors.

Hawks's next Columbia film, **Twentieth Century** (1934), belonged with a number of recent plays exposing and exploding the egos of show folk. Himself parodied in 'The Royal Family of Broadway', John Barrymore here parodies Jed Harris, producer of 'The Front Page', the authors of which, Hecht and MacArthur, wrote this screenplay (though using as their source an unproduced play). Barrymore's hamming, for once conscious and therefore enjoyable, is well complemented by Carole Lombard as a bitchy actress whom he discovers and puts into a dreadful Southern play (all dreadful plays in movies are set in the South); the years pass and she has a bad case of her Master's temperament as they squabble on the Twentieth Century Express among a motley group which includes a religious maniac (Etienne Girardot). The introduction of this character is so clumsy as to suggest a new plot starting, and though Hawks juggles his people in and out of staterooms the pacing is frenetic but not assured.

More nonsense has been written about Hawks than any other figure in Hollywood history. At Columbia he made his two best pictures – not because he needed to express some 'Hawksian ethos' but because he had the sort of material to which he could respond. **Only Angels Have Wings** (1939) was written by Jules Furthman and concerns a group of American flyers in a banana republic. They are joined by Jean Arthur – and what would she be doing down there if she wasn't a stranded showgirl? Their boss is Cary Grant – finding new levels of charming boorishness – whose henchmen include Thomas Mitchell, not prepared to acknowledge that his flying days are over, and Richard Barthelmess, more hangdog than ever as a one-time coward hoping for a new break; the latter's wife is Rita Hayworth, a relic of Grant's past and the only anaemic player in the film. It is otherwise a confident piece of film-making; the aerial shots vary, but otherwise the atmosphere is very strong. Hawks has a dangerous control over the witty script, but it is Miss Arthur who lifts it, as the seemingly tough, confident girl who finds that she is neither when she realises that she is carrying a torch for the tough, confident man.

His Girl Friday (1940), Hawks's masterwork, was written by Charles Lederer from 'The Front Page', and evolved from an attempt by Hawks to demonstrate to friends that the play had the best modern dialogue ever written, when, since no actor was available, a girlfriend read the part of Hildy. Thus in the film Hildy has become the ex-wife (Rosalind Russell) of Walter Burns (Grant), who not only wants headlines from her but to have her back in his arms. No lie or trick is too low: Grant offers two dozen expressions and they all mean deceit. The marvellous quality about their playing – and neither was ever more adroit – is her cold-eyed acceptance of his cunning, which in itself amounts to a *rapprochement*. What is also there, whether consciously or not, is the glamour of people like Hildy and Burns: they are one step ahead, the haves – as opposed to the have-nots, such as the stolid fiancé (Ralph Bellamy) and the condemned man; and the other reporters also are absolutely true to that generation of American humorists. The timing throughout – unlike that in *Twentieth Century* – is brilliant.

Superlatives may also be applied to **Man's Castle** (1933), Frank Borzage's first independent production. The pub-

licity stressed its resemblance to *Seventh Heaven,* and love now flowers in a shanty-town on the Hudson instead of in a Paris garret. Borzage takes his customary romantic attitude towards life among the down and outs, probably in this case because no other was suitable in view of the Depression: yet when Bill (Spencer Tracy) meets Trina (Loretta Young) starving and contemplating suicide he subtly suggests that for women at least there is an alternative to the river. Tracy's gifts of warmth and caring were never better used, and it is surprising that Cooper, Cagney and Muni were all considered for the role before him. Miss Young never again acted so delicately, and they are beautifully supported by Glenda Farrell, Walter Connolly and Marjorie Rambeau. Jo Swerling wrote the screenplay, from a play by Lawrence Hazard, and its wry/funny dialogue includes the same endearments for the girl as in *Bad Girl,* 'whozis' and 'stoopid'.

Loretta Young and Spencer Tracy in *Man's Castle,* directed by Frank Borzage. 'From these characters and this background the Old Master charms something like beauty and when it is all over and you are out in the street you wonder how he has done it' said *Picturegoer.*

477

Irene Dunne and Cary Grant in *The Awful Truth*, one of the insouciant screwball comedies of the time. It was in films like this (to take a phrase associated with a later movie, the lugubrious *Love Story* of 1970) that being in love means never having to say you are sorry.

Swerling also wrote **No Greater Glory** (1934) for Borzage, from Ferenc Molnár's 'The Boys of Paul Street', and we may well wish that they had left this 'immortal novel' – as the credits have it – between its covers. This tale of boys engaged in their own messy war games had been filmed in Hungary in 1928 and had a renewed topicality with the Nazis in power and the U.S. apparently terrified of a Communist takeover: hence the strong anti-militarist tone, with its deliberate echo of *All Quiet on the Western Front*. 'A film with a propagandistic flavour,' said *The Times* (London). 'The objections to it are many and obvious, but [it] is a quite magnificent film, sure of its approach' – presumably meaning that it hammers away at the obvious, like many another well-intentioned Hollywood 'message' film basically unsure of its audience. Harry Cohn's objections were many and obvious and when the public apparently agreed with him the film had no prospect of recovering its slight investment – especially as several countries, including France, banned it. Borzage left Columbia in such disgrace that in signing with Warners he had to forfeit the independence he had had for almost a decade.

It was the other way round with Leo McCarey and **The Awful Truth** (1937), remade as a vehicle for Irene Dunne. Arthur Richman's 1922 play had been filmed by P.D.C. in 1925, and then by Pathé in 1929 with its Broadway star, Ina Clair; when Pathé was in turn absorbed by R.K.O. all its story properties were sold to Columbia for a mere $35,000. Capra was at loggerheads with Cohn, who sought out McCarey to prove to Capra that in the matter of comedy Columbia was not dependent on him alone – to the extent that he found himself paying McCarey not the peanuts he expected (because of the failure of *Make Way for Tomorrow*), but $100,000 (as opposed to Miss Dunne's $50,000 and Cary Grant's $40,000). McCarey brought in Vina Delmar to improve Dwight Taylor's existing script; he made the film under budget; and won the 1937 Oscar for Best Direction. The film itself is arguably the supreme example of the 'life is a game' school of comedy. Grant and Dunne are both rich, pampered and handsome; they are also relentlessly facetious, with no objective in life other than to trump the other's ace as they embark upon an improbable divorce. 'You didn't hurt both hands?' she says, only to look disappointed on learning that he had not; or, having expressed regret at picking up the phone – it was his fiancée – doing so again with alacrity and a smile broader than a Cheshire Cat's.

She Married her Boss (1935) is also clever and delightful. The title refers to Claudette Colbert, and her boss is Melvyn Douglas; the marriage she so much desired brings with it, however, his self-dramatising sister (Katherine Alexander) and his spoilt brat of a child (Edith Fellows). Sidney Buchman wrote it, getting his biggest laughs from what is left unsaid – such as non sequiturs and interrupted sentences. The director, Gregory LaCava, responds at such times but loses control whenever Buchman's invention fails him. Buchman is credited on the screenplay of **Holiday** (1938), along with Donald Ogden Stewart, but according to George Cukor, who directed, the latter alone was responsible for this version of Philip Barry's play. Filmed originally by Pathé in 1931 with Ann Harding, the property was another which Columbia purchased in its job lot, and Katharine Hepburn came to the studio because she wanted to make it, bringing her cronies with her. Cary Grant partners her again, and as with *The Philadelphia Story,* which would reteam them with Cukor, the screenplay is as verbose and superficial as the direction is unobtrusively skilful. The subject is the intrusion of a poor man (Grant) as fiancé into a wealthy family and, joined by Jean Dixon and Edward Everett Horton as his bohemian friends, the bemused attitude towards the excesses of the rich is better expressed than in the later film: but in neither do Barry, Cukor or Stewart have anything pointed to say on the subject.

John Ford also made one film for Columbia, **The Whole Town's Talking** (1935), for which the studio borrowed Edward G. Robinson, in a double role as meek clerk and infamous gangster – and as each impersonates the other at various times (and we are never in doubt as to his identity) it calls upon all his ingenuity. The twists outnumber the laughs, and the plotting is so ingenious – screenplay by Swerling, from a novel by W. R. Burnett – that it would be churlish to point out a gaping hole at the climax. A good cast includes Jean Arthur as the girl.

Lewis Milestone's one film for the studio is **The Captain Hates the Sea** (1934), so much like *Transatlantic* as to support the adage that most American films were copies; but in this case the passenger list is more colourful and the director more proficient. It isn't, in fact, the sea that the captain (Walter Connolly) hates, but the passengers: a tippling writer (John Gilbert); an ex-cop turned detective (Victor McLaglen); a nouveau riche lady (Alison Skipworth); an ex-whore (Wynne Gibson), whose husband is paranoic about her past; a South American general (Akim Tamiroff); a lady (Helen Vinson) posing as a Boston librarian; and a number of assorted crooks.

Rosalind Russell and the director Dorothy Arzner arrived at Columbia to make **Craig's Wife** (1936), based on a play by George Kelly which was later remade with Joan Crawford. Its subject is a houseproud wife, and the best of her several moments of comeuppance occurs when the husband (John Boles), finally exasperated, smashes her favourite vase.

In this version it is an act of defiance, and Miss Russell accepts it as such; in the other, it is an act of rebellion, and in one of the best sequences in all Crawfordiana one waits for the lady to descend the stairs and spot the breakage. Cool and unruffled as Russell is, she is not quite as enjoyable as Crawford.

The film has dated less than the once-admired **Golden Boy** (1939), based on Clifford Odets's play – which was, said Brooks Atkinson, 'a metaphor of cultural corruption in a materialistic society'. It was mauled on its way to the screen, but Odets cannot be exonerated, for, though uncredited, he did actually write the film version, according to Rouben Mamoulian, its director. William Saroyan also worked on it at one point, and might thus share the blame for such lines as 'Poppa, you don't understand. I gotta do what I gotta do' and 'I'm good for only one thing slugging Slugging my way to the title.' 'Music and fighting don't mix,' says Joe Bonaparte (William Holden), and at the end he faces a future without either, untainted by his contact with the underworld but taking with him the girlfriend (Barbara Stanwyck) of his promoter (Adolph Menjou) – and no one has a tear for *him.* Due partly to Lee J. Cobb's over-the-top performance the scenes of home life are particularly embarrassing.

Incredibly, the plays of Odets and the others presented by the Group Theatre were considered to be too highbrow for cinema audiences, and when Ben Hecht imitated Odets in **Angels Over Broadway** (1940), he diluted his message with Runyon-flavoured whimsy. A clerk (John Qualen) embezzles $3,000 and then decides to commit suicide, so he elects – as we all might – to spend his last hours in a night club where he falls in with a penniless con man (Douglas Fairbanks Jr), an unemployed dancer (Rita Hayworth) and a drunken playwright (Thomas Mitchell). Hecht's ideas of dramatists' dialogue make Odets seem reticent: drunk? – 'an understatement by three bottles and a thousand tears'; his wife? – 'The only place I felt at home was in your heart. You were the only light that didn't go out on me.' Fairbanks tries for an Allen Jenkins accent from time to time, and has one sentimental speech: 'What happened to the Poles, the Finns, the Dutch?

479

They're little guys. They didn't win,' to which Hayworth replies, 'They will, some day.' Hecht wrote and directed, with Fairbanks as associate producer, and with Lee Garmes again on camera – as in Hecht's earlier ventures with Charles MacArthur: it is also incredible that he was undeterred by neither those nor this, and tried yet again with the even more pretentious *The Specter of the Rose* (1945), a ballet story.

Josef von Sternberg made two films for Columbia, signed at the behest of B. P. Schulberg, who had found a temporary home there after being ousted from Paramount. It was Schulberg who assigned him to **Crime and Punishment** (1935), which had the misfortune to open in most cities just after the French film of the same novel. Graham Greene called it 'this gleaming lunch-bar chromium version' and, warming to his theme, 'vulgar as only the great New World can be vulgar,' but it is not that bad. Its virtues are negative ones: the lack of music, except for an occasional violin; the simple sets (clearly reflecting the budget); and the direct way with the plot – which, though cut to eighty-eight minutes, is still too long. As Raskolnikov the too-old Peter Lorre repeats his performance in *M*; Edward Arnold is no more than capable as the Inspector; and as the whore Marian Marsh seems to have wandered in from a B-Western. There are echoes of von Sternberg's better dramas, but he eschews, alas, chiaroscuro – not that light and shade is the way to interpret Dostoevsky, but darkness can at least evoke gloom and evil, both needed here. Also miscast is Grace Moore as a teenage princess, in **The King Steps Out** (1937): von Sternberg had been invited to embellish her few natural charms when audiences failed to respond to her second Columbia film as they had to her first, *One Night of Love*. Star and director, both noted for their unruly temperaments, worked in mutual antagonism, but despite her performance, which lacks the required daintiness, this is a good example of farce-operetta, with music by Fritz Kreisler – one of several tales of the youth of the Empress Elizabeth, here wooed incognito by Franz Joseph (Franchot Tone). As an apoplectic innkeeper Herman Bing is very funny, and Raymond

Walburn has perhaps the only explicitly homosexual line in an American movie in three decades: after telling the ballet girls not to flirt with the soldiers he adds, to the startled ballet master, 'And I trust you won't, either.'

The receipts of neither film endeared von Sternberg to Cohn, and his Hollywood career was almost over, as was that of Schulberg, though the latter produced a handful of films for Paramount and again for Columbia before he also was rejected by the industry. Another former Paramount glory, Frank Lloyd, arrived, having persuaded Cohn that a remake of a famous Silent film, **The Howards of Virginia** (1940), could constitute Columbia's reaffirmation of its faith in democracy – a statement thought necessary in view of the War. Unfortunately Lloyd agreed to direct, proving that *Cavalcade* was long in the past. Adapted from the first part of Elizabeth Page's 'The Tree of Liberty', it starts with Cary Grant as a shabby backwoodsman and never gets more likely – nor does it miss a cliché as it moves him, via the War of Independence, from log cabin to colonial mansion.

The dramatist Robert Sherwood was another who resided temporarily at Columbia, to produce just one film, **Adam Had Four Sons** (1941) – which he had no hand in writing. This is another family saga, indifferently directed by Gregory Ratoff and this time concerning the viper in its bosom. She is the bad girl (Susan Hayward), whom everyone thinks is good, while the good girl (Ingrid Bergman) takes the rap. Being clearly so sensible, Bergman is well cast; beyond the fact that she must be the nicest governess four boys ever had, she has the instinct of her compatriot, Garbo, for the right gesture – as with her hunched-up stance over the banisters during the operation on the mother (Fay Wray). Archer Winston commented in *The New York Times*: 'Miss Bergman is such a wholesome and healthy-looking individual that it seems too much to hope that she could be an actress of taste and sensitivity also. But that is what she establishes . . . beyond any question.' This was the second American film of the Swedish-born Bergman (b. 1915), and with the acquisition of this refreshingly natural actress Hollywood reached a milestone in its progress to maturity. She was not under contract to Columbia, and it was a star at the other end of the scale, Rita Hayworth (q.v.), who would help Cohn complete the transformation of Columbia into a major studio.

At United Artists Chaplin was the only founder member still active, and the gestation period of his films had increased to almost five years. **Modern Times** (1936) was over a year on the studio floor, and the final budget reached $1½ million. Though it was patently derived from *A Nous la Liberté*, Chaplin claimed at the time 'an impulse to say something about the way life is being standardised and channelised, and men turned into machines', while in his autobiography he takes pains to claim credit for his 'original idea'. Critics pointed out the resemblances to Clair's film, but few dreamed of finding fault, and the Tramp's adventures with the automatic feeding machine and the conveyor belt were considered satiric rather than anti-capitalist. The film's original introduction, an equation of 'humanity' with a flock of sheep, was revealingly removed by Chaplin from the reissue prints; and since the film is no longer either pointed or funny it is fortunate in having a sustaining element in the relationship of the Tramp and the gamin, played by Paulette Goddard, with whom Chaplin was at that time living and had supposedly married. In the film she is a minor, and if they behave as man and wife there is nothing to which the Hays Office might have taken offence: it is possible that the relationship is a kind of autobiographical comment on Chaplin's sexuality (not unknown to the public, after the revelations of his first two wives) – though it is certain that the sentimental aspect of two derelicts protecting each other also appealed to him. At one point they are sitting on a grass verge in a cosy suburb when a policeman moves them on – the poor never win; yet the triteness of this is counterbalanced by the fact that till he meets the girl his dearest wish is to return to prison, where the police keep him well fed and comfortable. His ambivalent attitude towards the rich is extended to Authority, and it is a strength which helps the film survive – plus the Tramp's beautiful movements, skilfully choreographed from the tip of his hat to the open ends of his boots.

As Thornton Delehanty said in *The New York Post*, there was no doubt that the film was 'the season's motion picture event' – but that was as nothing to the advent of **The Great Dictator** (1940): 'No event in the history of the screen has ever been anticipated with more hopeful excitement,' wrote Bosley Crowther in *The New York Times*. 'No picture ever made has promised more momentous consequences.' Not only was Chaplin to *speak* on the screen for the first time (*Modern Times* had one gibberish song among the music and sound effects) but he had taken on no less an adversary than Hitler. In a dual role, he plays a Jewish barber, a man very like the Tramp, and Adenoid Hynkel, dictator of Tomania – a vain little man, given to protocol, vainglory, ranting and bluster; he has an aide, Garbage (Henry Daniell), and a fellow dictator, Benzino Napaloni (Jack Oakie) who, like him, is planning to invade Osterlich. When he finally does so the Jewish barber is mistaken for him: forced to make a speech, he makes a plea for freedom and an end to tyranny. That speech was Chaplin speaking to the world, and it was the object of much admiration: it is long but patently sincere – which is its justification. Chaplin had been told so often that he spoke for all mankind: one cannot decry him for taking this opportunity to prove it. The film is today often poorly received, since its attempts at both sentiment and humour are grotesquely over-contrived; but at the time Chaplin's courage in offering a political tract in comic strip form only confirmed his supposed genius.

Of the other original United Artists, Mary Pickford did emerge from semi-retirement to produce two films for a company she formed with Jesse L. Lasky, but neither was successful. Her relative inactivity and that of Chaplin left them free to interfere with board decisions, and the comings and goings at United Artists – beyond the major suppliers, Korda, Goldwyn and Selznick – were as frequent with this company as at R.K.O. and Columbia. Among the motley crew welcomed was Arnold Pressburger, an emigré attempting a foothold in Hollywood and bringing a fresh eye to bear on

Fredric March, Margaret Sullavan and Glenn Ford in *So Ends Our Night* (1940), directed by John Cromwell for producers David L. Loew and Albert Lewin, and released by United Artists. Based on a novel by Erich Maria Remarque, the film gets as close as Hollywood dared to the situation in Europe, following a group of people hounded from their native land because their race, religion or creed did not suit Hitler. The script uses the word 'Jew' instead of the expression 'non-Aryan', which Hollywood preferred when dealing with this subject. When Ford says, 'Let's drink to the beauty of the world, we have a right to that,' Sullavan replies, 'We have no rights to anything, we are refugees.' And there is a moving gesture a moment later, when a stranger offers them a cake because he hates what is happening in his country.

The Shanghai Gesture (1941). The source was a play by John Colton, a specialist in the exotic (he had dramatised 'Rain'), and in the sixteen years since its Broadway presentation it was reputed to have been turned down by the Hays Office thirty-two times, in as many adaptations. The setting of the original was the Shanghai brothel of Mother Goddam, whose main attraction is her half-caste, drug-addicted daughter Poppy. As adapted by the director, Josef von Sternberg, and his collaborators, this has become the gambling den of Mother Gin Sling (Ona Munson), among whose thrill-seeking clientele is Victoria (Gene Tierney), who finds 'it has a ghastly familiarity, like a half-remembered dream'. She is really Poppy, and she makes a play for her mother's lover (Victor Mature) by quoting 'Omar Khayyam' at him, to which he responds with the information that he was born under a full moon near the sands of Damascus. Every character is either corrupt or equivocal, and the best of them is Walter Huston, in the impossible role of the girl's English father. It was not, with reason, a film that appealed to either the industry or the public, and since that was increasingly true of von Sternberg's films Hollywood producers were no longer prepared to countenance his arrogance. An exception was Howard Hughes (q.v.), and von Sternberg did contribute to other people's

films without credit till **The Saga of Anatahan** (1952), which he wrote, produced, directed and photographed in Japan: its failure was complete, and his later involvement with film was confined to teaching the subject in California.

Another Silent veteran berthed briefly at U.A. was Ernst Lubitsch, who remade his own 1925 *Kiss Me Again* as **That Uncertain Feeling** (1941), with a script by Donald Ogden Stewart, who had thought of nothing to help this tired tale of a wife (Merle Oberon) who leaves her husband (Melvyn Douglas) for an egotistic musician (Burgess Meredith). Of the principals, only Douglas has the required style. Korda was to an extent involved in the production, as he was married to Miss Oberon and was establishing himself as an American supplier to U.A. He and Lubitsch co-produced *To Be or Not To Be* (q.v.) before the latter moved on to 20th Century-Fox, and meanwhile he designed **Lydia** (1941) primarily as a vehicle for Oberon. The director was Julien Duvivier, exiled from France because of the War, and though its inspiration was clearly his *Carnet de Bal* the only points in common were a ball in the past and a woman who recalls old lovers: instead of visiting them she dreams of youthful romances in flashback.

Another veteran producer, Edward Small, made some uneven films for U.A., but there is some merit in his four versions of Dumas. **The Count of Monte Cristo** (1934), was directed by Rowland V. Lee and has a cheering performance by Robert Donat in the title role. **The Man in the Iron Mask** (1939) suffers from Louis Hayward's colourless performance in the lead and from James Whale's faltering handling, but the combination of Lee and Hayward is pleasing in **Son of Monte Cristo** (1940): as ersatz Dumas, its plot resembling the current crop of European resistance movies, it has no right to be the most successful of the three movies. Small persuaded Douglas Fairbanks Jr to finally take on the mantle of his father in **The Corsican Brothers** (1941), and in his first full-blooded swashbuckling role the actor proves himself a true heir, handsome and dashing; but Gregory Ratoff, directing, is less at home than Lee with the conventions of the genre.

Yet another Silent veteran, Hal Roach,

eventually arrived at United Artists, but since he kept autonomy during the years in which M-G-M in fact distributed his product it is not unreasonable to consider him with these other independents. Roach was not the only producer to try to keep alive the spirit of Silent comedy, but he was the most successful, turning out two-reelers with, among others, Charley Chase, 'Our Gang' (a group of children) and Laurel and Hardy. Stan Laurel (1890–1965) was born in Lancashire and gravitated to films via the British music hall and American vaudeville. Oliver Hardy (1892–1957) was born in Georgia and had started in films as a bit player before his bulk typed him as a villain – it being the fashion for fat men to be the butts in the comedies which he mostly made. They were both under contract to Roach and had appeared together before *Putting Pants on Philip* (1927) teamed them for the first time. Their Silent shorts contain their most brilliant work; speech slowed them up, and the years took toll of their inspiration, which was mainly that of Laurel, the creative partner. Their early shorts are variable, but **Laughing Gravy** (1931) triumphantly supports the view that they were great screen comics. James V. Horne directed these misadventures set in a grim boarding house and their private world was never better exemplified as they try to protect their beloved mutt from a weasely, hard-hearted landlord. No matter how much Stan's woolliness infuriates Ollie or how much they bicker and fight, at times of crisis their delight in each other is a stirring thing. They were seldom more in accord than in that orgy of suburban destruction, **Big Business** (1929), while Ollie's exasperation with Stan is best sampled as they manoeuvre a piano up a vast flight of stairs in **The Music Box** (1932).

Pardon Us (1931), directed by James Parrott, was one of their spoofs on other movies, in this case *Big House*, whose set was still standing on the M-G-M lot. In return, Metro demanded a feature, so a compromise length was reached of fifty-five minutes. Their second full-length film, **Sons of the Desert** (1934), is better sustained as directed by William A. Seiter. Adapted from one of their Silent shorts, *We Faw Down* (in itself a remake of an earlier Roach short, *Ambrose's First False-*

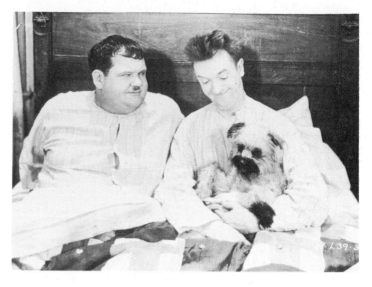

hood), it has them living it up at a masonic convention, on the lam from their wives – and when they are married, the ladies concerned make the spouses of W. C. Fields seem like angels of sweetness and light. **Bonnie Scotland** (1935) does begin in that country, but as a take-off on *Lives of a Bengal Lancer* most of it is set on the North-West Frontier: hardly more organised than *Pardon Us*, it should be seen for their dance to 'A Hundred Pipers', which is touching, graceful, inventive, absurd and marvellous. The best thing in **Way Out West** (1937), also directed by Horne, is their soft-shoe shuffle to 'The Trail of the Lonesome Pine'. They were comic relief in a number of feeble operettas, the best of which is **Swiss Miss** (1938), in which they are mousetrap salesmen; the same director, John G. Blystone, also made the most integrated of their features, **Blockheads** (1938). Borrowing from several of their early shorts (and those of Harry Langdon, who worked on the script), it makes them old war buddies, reunited – too late, for Ollie has just married Minna Gombell, his 'dove' and 'cooey lamb', nice enough but suspicious. 'How often have I told you not to bring your tramp friends around here?' she asks, to which he replies 'But Toots – Stan is different.' Of course: how could she have understood their special relationship?

That was their last picture for Roach

Laurel and Hardy in *Laughing Gravy*, a two-reeler which alone would justify their immortality. The dog in Stan's arms provides the title, for that is his name – and it is the sort of whimsical touch with which their best films are studded.

Constance Bennett with Alan Mowbray in *Merrily We Live*, one of the many comedies of the time dealing with crazy families. They were invariably wealthy, and audiences were doubtless greatly relieved to find the rich viewed as completely irresponsible.

and M-G-M. Laurel had been increasingly unhappy, demanding more creative control (to placate him, some of the later features were labelled 'A Stan Laurel Production'); but after **Flying Deuces** (1939) for Boris Morros, released through R.K.O., they returned to Roach – now releasing through United Artists – for two further features. When they could not get backing for an independent feature they signed contracts with M-G-M and 20th Century-Fox – but were allowed no creative say in the eight remaining American films they made. Their personal relationship was always cordial, but in the Roach days there had been the possibility of a split. In that eventuality Langdon was cited to take Laurel's place, and Roach did team him and Hardy in **Zenobia** (1939), the latter as a kindly doctor who unties a knot in an elephant's tail and is therefore sued by Langdon for alienation of affection – a promising idea suffering from a lame script and poor production values; Gordon Douglas directed.

Roach's cavalier approach to production values was less apparent in his first feature without Laurel and Hardy; but because two leading stars were involved M-G-M was more concerned with **Topper** (1939) than with most Roach products. Its source was a novel by Thorne Smith, and its subject ghosts – as impersonated by Cary Grant and Constance Bennett, materialising to the embarrassment of the Toppers (Miss Burke, Roland Young). Comic ghosts appealed to Roach, while the racy tone of Smith's humorous novel had caused other producers to neglect it. Unfortunately the adapters found nothing to substitute for the raciness, nor do they explore the potential of the situation. However, it is funnier than **Topper Takes a Trip** (1938), which lacks more than Mr Grant. Both films were directed by an old comedy hand from Paramount, Norman Z. McLeod, but **Topper Returns** (1941) was done by Roy del Ruth. Miss Bennett was gone – replaced by Joan Blondell – and so had the spirit of Thorne Smith: it is another 'old dark house' comedy-thriller in the manner of *The Cat and the Canary* – and as such, not unsuccessful. McLeod also directed **Merrily We Live** (1938), and that has affinities to *My Man Godfrey*, with another scatty woman (Billie Burke) trying to help the down and outs by making one of them (Brian Aherne) her chauffeur. He tames her temperamental daughter (Miss Bennett), and turns out to be a novelist. The film, though not one of the half dozen best screwball comedies, has foolishness and fun.

Foolishness is all with **One Million B.C.** (1940): the idea of making a serious film set in pre-history was then so outlandish that it could only have come from a former gag-writer like Roach (who had employed D. W. Griffith at the planning stage, till they quarrelled). There is a background of Montague and Capulet-like warring tribes – with Victor Mature and Carole Landis as the lovers – and to sustain interest the dinosaurs are wheeled on: the special effects man was king, but his effects, if numerous, are derisory.

Roach produced one excellent serious picture, **Of Mice and Men** (1939), but only in lieu of paying damages to Lewis Milestone, who had successfully sued him over a contract. Like many other people, Milestone had been impressed by John Steinbeck's novella and the Broadway play made from it; the screenplay – credited to Eugene Solow, though Milestone claimed it as his own work – is remarkably faithful, beginning in gloom and foreboding and then courting tragedy as it studies some itinerant farmworkers during the Depression. Within the dual themes of the deeply loyal friendship between the simple-minded Lennie (Lon

Chaney Jr) and bright-as-a-button George (Burgess Meredith), and the relationship between the boss's son and his bored wife (Betty Field), there is an honest portrait of life down on the farm: the camaraderie in the bunkhouse; the gossip in the wash-room; the silent, vast meals; the beer-swilling Saturday night hops in town. Lonely old men spend their affection on dogs, and the crippled, bespectacled Negro (Leigh Whipper) long ago became accustomed to being denied the bunk-house. Milestone's love of the piece is apparent and it is his best film after *All Quiet on the Western Front*. Meredith and Chaney never had better roles, and Miss Field is the definitive floozie – not loose, just bored and empty-headed, courting disaster by hanging round the men.

Of the other independents Walter Wanger (1894–1968) was reputedly the best-liked and best read of Hollywood executives, and one of the few of his generation with a college background; he gained theatre experience with, among others, Harley Granville-Barker. Jesse Lasky brought him to Paramount in 1929 in charge of production, and after brief spells at Columbia and M-G-M he returned to that company, which at that time was so desperate for producer talent that they acceded to his terms – to work within the company as an independent. The first of the ten contracted films was **The President Vanishes** (1934) which, despite its source in a Rex Stout story, is less a thriller than an attack on fascism, profiteering and war-mongering as directed by William Wellman. A Presi-dent does vanish, rather than be drawn into a European war. However, we sus-pect the complicity of the Greyshirts, and it is they who provide the chief interest, along with their crazed leader (Edward Ellis), who was prophetically christened Lincoln (George Lincoln Rockwell would be the American Nazi party leader in the Fifties). But the film is far from its pro-totype, *Gabriel Over the White House*, as a political statement.

Wanger invited LaCava, his director on that film, to rejoin him for **Private Worlds** (1935), one of the few serious movies of the time to lose little over the years, even if Claudette Colbert is described as 'one of the finest doctors in the country'. Written by Lynn Starling and LaCava, from a novel by Phyllis Bottome, it does not shrink from the details of life in a psychiatric clinic – and if these now seem mild none is notably dishonest. A later film on the same sub-ject, *The Cobweb* (q.v.), goes further in suggesting that the staff are as dotty as their patients, but their problems engage us: for Colbert, it is frigidity and over-work; for Charles Boyer, the new head, prejudice against women in medical work and how to cope with his neurotic sister; and for Joan Bennett, her own inadequacy in relation to her husband (Joel McCrea).

When United Artists decided that it needed product an offer was made to Wanger, recognised as one of the best 'quality' producers; as an incentive he was promised larger budgets and complete autonomy unless he wanted to spend over $750,000. His first film for the company was **You Only Live Once** (1937), and he offered the direction to Fritz Lang – an obvious contender, since *Fury*, for another 'social protest' movie. Its stance is simple: ex-convicts have the dice loaded against them. It has been suggested in recent years that the film is a version of the Clyde Barrow-Bonnie Parker saga, but there are only fleeting resemblances – at the end, when Jo (Sylvia Sidney) and Eddie (Henry Fonda) are fugitives, living in a motor car. Lang does not substantiate Eddie's claim of innocence, but the film does demand our sympathy – puzzlingly so, for surely the Hays Office would not have allowed the sentimentalisation of a couple of killers? The film is clearer in its portrait of a society which cannot forget or forgive, even if it allows us only two incidents of prejudice. Fonda's perform-ance is no help in clarifying the intentions of its makers – intense and passionate, but hardly suggestive of a criminal mentality. Thus the film works best as a tragic love story, at what Lang called the theme running through all his work – 'this fight against destiny, against fate'. His direc-tion has moments of Germanic showiness (prison bars and their shadows; swirling fog for the confrontation with the padre) not inappropriate to the preposterous material. Yet Lang's view of the U.S. is mordant, and in a sense he made the only real Depression films: in them, the coun-try is like a soft-centred chocolate which, when bitten into, turns out to be rock hard and sour. America did not like this view of itself for, despite glowing notices, the film was a commercial failure.

History Is Made at Night (1937) is the quintessential Thirties movie, with its dotty title, which Publicity ensured was equated with the *Titanic* disaster: spectators not drawn to it would surely have been converted by the shipwreck footage in the trailer for forthcoming attractions. Then there are Jean Arthur and Charles Boyer, in evening dress throughout, though in his case the wayward plot has him posing as a head waiter. Since neither was ever better, and since Frank Borzage achieves a unifying romantic mood in episodes melodramatic or facetious, the story does not matter. The cinema has become more realistic in the intervening years, but posterity may prefer lovely confections like this to the entertainments currently offered. The writers were Gene Towne and Graham Baker, also responsible for *You Only Live Once*; they also wrote **Stand-In** (1937), from a story by Clarence Budington Kelland, and Tay Garnett directed. 'Howling laugh-material for the movie colony's selected few,' said *Photoplay*, 'But will probably mean little to the average audience.' Audiences seeing it today, clued in on Hollywood, greet it with roars of approval – but then *Photoplay* found Leslie Howard 'never so colourless': I think him brilliant here, as a wizard accountant sent out to save (or sell) an ailing Hollywood studio. His unexpected aides are a confident stand-in (Joan Blondell) and an alcoholic director (Humphrey Bogart); the latter's 'In Hollywood, when you turn the other cheek, they kick it' is virtually the only critical line, for the humour is affectionate, deriving from three main sources: Howard's ignorance of movies, Blondell's worldliness ('Life has only one great moment left for me – when they make Shirley Temple president of a bank'), and the pretensions of the star, Cherie ('Why, even I was a cigarette girl in a night club in Dallas – would you believe that?').

Blockade (1938) is a story 'of adventure and love' says a foreword, 'not intended to treat with or take sides in the conflict of ideas' – for its subject is the Spanish Civil War. And these words were added by Wanger to answer criticism that the film trivialises that war. This paltry account of spies and counterspies was ineptly written by John Howard Lawson (later blacklisted), and directed similarly by William Dieterle – though he gets a half-decent performance from Madeleine Carroll as a White Russian. Henry Fonda almost convinces one that he's the one Spanish farmer able to quote Byron. Deliberately more escapist is **Algiers** (1938), the first important American remake of a renowned European film of the Talkie period, causing much less outcry and derision than later examples – partly because Wanger bought the U.S. rights to Duvivier's *Pépé le Moko*, so comparisons could not be made (it was not shown in the U.S. till 1941). John Cromwell, directing, insisted that the original could not be improved, and settled for a carbon copy: footage of the Casbah was freely borrowed, and a new one was built on the Goldwyn lot. The casting was as close as could be with, for instance, the police informer (Charpin) played by an equally roly-poly actor (Gene Lockhart). The intensity of Boyer and the beauty of Hedy Lamarr make the love scenes agreeably exaggerated: she is exactly right, even if, as Cromwell maintained, she was no actress (the performance was apparently put together in the cutting room). Lawson wrote the screenplay, and James Wong Howe photographed; the final effect is mechanical and, like most copies, disjointed.

Slightly Honorable (1940) was an attempt to add a serious note to a whacky murder mystery in the shape of corrupt senators and a war-trained killer, but director Tay Garnett is at a loss with the shifts in the material. **Sundown** (1941) is marvellous hokum, a horse opera set in Kenya, where George Sanders tangles with native Gene Tierney and dies for King and Country, and with an epilogue in a bombed London cathedral. Henry Hathaway directed, emphasising the absurdity of the dialogue. The film was financially very successful, but was released after Wanger had left United Artists following long battles with the board over money. His early films for the company had been deemed too costly, and certainly there were large losses on the Technicolored *Vogues of 1938* – though these were more than made up for by the significant earnings of *Trade Winds,*

Algiers and *Stagecoach*. His next few films were unsuccessful or, like *The Long Voyage Home* and *Foreign Correspondent* (q.v.), slow to turn a profit. The company declared Wanger $300,000 in debt to it, while he himself reckoned that at least $1 million due to him was frozen abroad because of wartime currency restrictions. Finally the board purchased his unit for $100,000, eventually making good profits on his more recent films. He was permitted to take with him the pre-production plans for *Eagle Squadron*, which the company did not wish to make, and the screenplay of *Arabian Nights* (q.v.). Both films were undistinguished but profitable, which may explain why less than a handful of Wanger's subsequent films are of interest.

In the quarrels between Samuel Goldwyn and United Artists the dissatisfaction was mainly on the part of the producer. In 1937 he and Korda, whom he considered the only other producer contributing to the company's profits, were thwarted of buying out the interests of the founders. Goldwyn subsequently charged the new president, Maurice Silverstein, with sanctioning too many poor pictures, thereby damaging the prestige of his own and defeating the very purpose of the company as originally defined. Those who worked for him have assured us that he wanted only the best; but he was said by others to have been vain, vindictive, publicity-seeking, devious, arbitrary, petty and tyrannical. He once told Garson Kanin: 'Directors are a dime a dozen. You know how many directors are in Hollywood? And most of them looking for work. But executives, producers – real producers, not these jerks [who] call themselves producers . . . Don't you see that when you're a producer, you *hire* directors. Producers hire directors, and sometimes they *fire* directors. Did you ever hear of a director hiring a producer? Did you ever hear of a director *firing* a producer?' In 1935 he hired a director, William Wyler, whose eight films for him are virtually the only Goldwyn products worth serious consideration. After the critical success of the earliest of them Wyler was allowed almost complete autonomy – which included the producer's absence from the set during shooting. Goldwyn recognised

Wyler's standing with the critics and hence assigned him to his more important projects – Wyler's first three films for him were based on much-admired Broadway plays – though his acumen in acquiring properties was due less to an understanding of them than his ability to keep his ear to the ground. His male stars (Colman, Cooper, Cantor) were all proven successes, while his female stars (Sten, Hopkins, Oberon, Virginia Mayo) do not inspire confidence in his judgement. Leaving aside the Wyler films, it is clear that his own taste ran to Americana or grandiose projects like **The Goldwyn Follies** (1938), in fact planned since Ziegfeld's death, and an attempt to establish himself as the movie equivalent. George Marshall directed Ben Hecht's witless script, set in a film studio, and the jumble of artists on display, presumably reflecting Goldwyn's own taste, include the Ritz Brothers, Edgar Bergen, Kenny Baker and Vera Zorina – whose 'classical' ballets, choreographed by her then-husband, George Balanchine, are at best embarrassing. George Gershwin contributed the score, unfinished when he died, and one of its best songs, 'I Was Doing All Right', is relegated to the equivalent of a bit role.

The Adventures of Marco Polo (1938) was originally the idea of Douglas Fairbanks, planning a lighthearted film on the famous traveller. Unfortunately Goldwyn commissioned a script from Robert E. Sherwood, who had no gift for the form required. John Cromwell directed for one week, and Wyler refused to take over after reading the script and seeing the rushes: Archie Mayo finally directed, dully, and Gary Cooper is Polo. When Goldwyn found that Oberon was not succeeding with the American public and wanted to find a vehicle for her to be teamed with Cooper, Leo McCarey cynically rehashed 'The Taming of the Shrew' and sold it to him for $50,000: and twenty-seven writers in all worked on **The Cowboy and the Lady** (1938), including Robert Ardrey, Frederick Lonsdale, Robert Riskin and Dorothy Parker. McCarey had refused to direct and Wyler, who unenthusiastically began it, was replaced by H. C. Potter – himself replaced (since he had another assignment) by Stuart Heisler, at that time an editor. Both films are amongst the worst that Cooper ever made.

Barbary Coast (1935) and **Come and Get It** (1936) are better, and typical Goldwyn concepts, tying flimsy stories to re-creations of America's past. The former was turned into a screenplay, for a daunting sum, by Hecht and MacArthur, and is about a saloon queen (Miss Hopkins), her boss-man lover (Edward G. Robinson), and an idealistic young prospector (Joel McCrea). The second film was in fact adapted from a novel by Edna Ferber by Jane Murfin and Jules Furthman, a story of Wisconsin timber men set over two generations: an ambitions foreman (Edward Arnold) lets go the girl (Frances Farmer) he loves, only to fall much later for her daughter (also Miss Farmer). In both there is compensation in the mise-en-scène of Howard Hawks, notably his Barbary Coast, a city of permanent mists, gaslight gleaming malignly and the hulls of ships looming threateningly above scurrying figures. *Come and Get It* is credited to both Hawks and Wyler, after Hawks was forced off the set, because Goldwyn, who had been in hospital, objected to what he had shot – on the principle, apparently, that he had rewritten some scenes and was not an accredited writer. Wyler – who was working on *Dodsworth* (q.v.) – resisted the assignment, but there was nothing in his contract to protect him. He did not consider it one of his films, and observed that the first half hour – all Hawks – is the best of it, citing also the superb logging sequence directed by Richard Rosson.

Wyler's films for Goldwyn, along with the Capra movies, were regarded as the summit of Hollywood achievement in their time; and though their seriousness now seldom seems justified, his fastidious and instinctive direction remains a pleasure. Any individual scene is correct as to tempo, imagery and intensity, slotting easily between those preceding and following it. Like Cukor and George Stevens, his art lies in his response to his material rather than any insistence on individual themes or idiosyncrasies, and, indeed, his chief pleasure was to tackle something he had not done before. As with most people in the industry at that time, he believed the material the most important element in the constitution of any movie. Since, therefore, his own personality cannot be found in his films, they have been decried, and it has been claimed that he was immeasurably aided by Gregg Toland (1904-48); but Toland's photography varied, and was always at its best under the stronger directors. He was expected to contribute as much to the end result as the cast, and it is significant that both photography and playing are of high standard with Wyler, Stevens, Cukor, Fleming and Capra, while they are variable with Borzage, LaCava, McCarey, Vidor, Ford and Hawks, who were less interested in psychological detail (as rendered by players or visuals) than in mood and pacing. All had in mind the same result: to take the audience into the heart of the matter, and send them out content.

Wyler's first film for Goldwyn was **These Three** (1936), adapted by Lillian Hellman from her own Broadway play, 'The Children's Hour' – and bought by Goldwyn, reputedly, not recognising nor understanding the subject of lesbianism. But since its real subject is scandal and the havoc created by the lies of a vindictive child it was easy enough for the screenwriters to change the accusations to heterosexual fornication – though robbing the piece of some of its force, it being unthinkable that a child could have imagined her teachers locked in embrace. In the film the child (Bonita Granville) accuses one teacher (Hopkins) of having an affair with the fiancé (Joel McCrea) of the other (Oberon). The Hays Office had no intention of passing the play for the screen, and it is doubtful whether exhibitors or audiences would have tolerated it. 'I have seldom been so moved by any fictional film,' wrote Graham Greene. 'After ten minutes of the usual screen sentiment, quaintness and exaggeration, one began to watch with incredulous pleasure nothing less than a life: a genuine situation, a moral realism.' I cannot imagine anyone today being moved by this transference to the screen of a well-made play, which continues to bury its situation in sentiment and exaggeration. Wyler removed that when he remade it, with the original title (q.v.), but with that Hollywood scaffolding gone all credibility went too, revealing the piece as soap opera with pretensions to tragedy.

Goldwyn's reputation rests more firmly on **Dodsworth** (1936), though he had shown no interest in Sinclair Lewis's novel till Sidney Howard's dramatisation had been successful in New York. Sam and Fran Dodsworth are wealthy products of the mid-West who find their marriage falling apart during their first trip to Europe. His complacency receives a jolt, but his common sense and receptivity see him through. Fran, however, her ambitions hitherto stifled by the ethics of the country club set, finds herself so enchanted by what she conceives to be continental sophistication that she loses Sam to another woman. Movie audiences had not been asked to contemplate the prospect of middle-aged people finding each other attractive since the days of the deMille comedies, and this film was far from lighthearted: indeed the bedtime row while husband and wife undress may be the only time a man in his garters has been used for drama instead of farce. Wyler, afraid perhaps that audiences would not be interested in such material, takes it at a speed of knots, so that today it seems melodramatic, sustained for a while only by Walter Huston's portrait of Sam, a friendly, uncomplicated man, alternately exasperated and amused by Fran's surrender to all things European. Ruth Chatterton surprisingly fails to give Fran dimension, and she emerges as a conventional villainess, while Mary Astor as Sam's comforter looks wistful or understanding on cue. However, the material eventually rises to Huston's level, and this remains one of the most entertaining dramas of the period.

On the other hand, **Dead End** (1937) has dated as badly as all the other sociological studies which arrived in Hollywood via Broadway. Since the film was crusading in purpose – with every one of the $140,000 that Goldwyn had paid for the rights – it was safe for *The New York Post* to editorialise, informing Congress that it should have been shown to the committee that crippled the Wagner Housing Act. Critics praised, and Miss Hellman's screen play misses none of the excitement which had endeared Sidney Kingsley's play to theatregoers. It might be more acceptable had Wyler been allowed to film on location, as he had wanted, but Richard Day's famous set remains an emotion in itself, portraying that part of Manhattan where the apartments of the wealthy look down upon the deprived. A would-be architect (Joel McCrea) takes many words to realise that he loves not the rich girl but Drina (Sylvia Sidney) from his own block; she is footsore from picketing, and it is typical of the film's approach that we know not why. Babyface Martin (Humphrey Bogart) is a Dead End Kid gone wrong, and his girl (Claire Trevor) has become a lady of the streets (in the original she also had syphilis). 'What chance have they got against all this?' says McCrea of the kids, but unlike the more romantic *Man's Castle* the film finally tells us nothing about the Depression.

It was because of Miss Sidney that Wyler directed a film of Emily Brontë's masterpiece, **Wuthering Heights** (1939). Wagner had planned a version for her and Charles Boyer (both of whom knew they were wrong for the roles), and had commissioned a screenplay from Hecht and MacArthur – which he was not sorry to sell, at Wyler's insistence, to Goldwyn. Although the latter was to claim it his favourite film he would not let work proceed till persuaded that it was an ideal vehicle for Merle Oberon. The resulting film uses only the first half of the book, omitting the vengeance worked out on a second generation. There is something of Heathcliff in every wild-spirited romantic hero created since then, but the original is a complex man – finally motivated by a dual emotion, consuming love for Cathy and deep hatred for Hindley. Laurence Olivier manages both emotions effortlessly, though without touching on one whole side of Heathcliff, that coal-black, earthy, surly, dangerous eagle spirit. He attempts at the outset a touch of Mummerset; as the gentleman Heathcliff, he speaks with an Old Vic accent, if softly – but was even then an actor of such persuasion that a frown suggested self-torture and a sardonic smile a bent for physical cruelty. Wyler had continually to hold him in check; had he not, Miss Oberon would have been swept away. Her declaration, 'I *am* Heathcliff,' is done with all the elocuted passion of a deb on her first day at finishing school. The lack of the Yorkshire Moors is almost as detrimental, but Wyler and Toland cleverly use the California mock-up. It is a measure of the film's success that a British

Geraldine Fitzgerald and Laurence Olivier in William Wyler's *Wuthering Heights*. Olivier himself has said that the only thing that stands up is the Isabella of Miss Fitzgerald – no one could say it of Merle Oberon's Cathy – but the whole is watchable and intermittently powerful.

version, made in 1972 *in situ*, in colour and with the right accents, neither challenged this nor made a dent in the cinema consciousness.

Wyler had begun as a director of Westerns, and the successful resurrection of the genre caused him to go back to his roots – plus the fact that **The Westerner** (1940) was a suitable vehicle for Gary Cooper, playing a stranger 'from nowhere in particular' bound for 'nowhere special'. He meets a rascally self-appointed judge (Walter Brennan), and their confrontation, mutually wary, suspicious and respectful, is a classic Western situation. The judge is a historical character of little note called Roy Bean, later impersonated by Paul Newman (q.v.): both films dwell on his passion for Lily Langtry and his arbitrary manner of justice, and this one, essentially more serious, is also funnier – but the story (by Stuart N. Lake, written for the screen by Jo Swerling and Abe Burrows) is weak enough to suggest that it was considered secondary to the setting. Experienced action directors, when in doubt, would accelerate the pace, but Wyler is so deliberate that possibly he hoped the film would seem more signifi-

cant than it is. Brennan is not an opponent to the measure of Cooper, but Academy voters may have been so surprised not to see him in his usual country bumpkin role that he won his third Supporting Oscar in successive years.

Wyler's most commercially successful films had been the two he made at Warners with Bette Davis, but directing her in **The Little Foxes** (1941) was 'a gamble', according to *Life* magazine, since she was its sole box office asset. The *Life* article went on to discuss the studios' few prestige pictures, which must have pleased Goldwyn mightily – but since the piece is merely puff we may suspect that it was written in conjunction with his publicity department, which traditionally stressed that he was more interested in art than in money. In fact, Miss Hellman's much-praised play was basically the sort of melodrama which movies had done since they began, though disguised by sombre and long-winded comments on the nature of greed. The characters divide into those that are evil (the Hubbard family) and those that are good (everyone else), but they speak intelligently, and the expected stabs-in-the-back and worms-turning are handled with ingenuity. Wyler excelled at strong emotional situations, and Toland's gliding camera finds many of them happening on the circular staircase which Wyler decided to make the pivot of the action (as Welles would do, with the same photographer, a few months later, in *The Magnificent Ambersons*, q.v.); and if the mansion is too grand – it should be decaying, as Davis herself pointed out – that is because Goldwyn interfered. From the Broadway production Patricia Collinge, Dan Duryea, Charles Dingle and Carl Benton Reid give memorable performances. As the husband Herbert Marshall could not be bettered, finding strength at last to pay back Regina for a lifetime of misery. As Regina Miss Davis is the only point of controversy: Wyler wanted the character to have 'great charm, humour, sex', but Davis, having reluctantly seen Tallulah Bankhead's stage performance, believed that that was the only way to play it – inhumanly. As she watches her husband die (the situation had been used in *Gabriel Over the White House*) her face expresses malevolence, satisfaction and fear – such as no other actress could have achieved. It may be, however, that Wyler was right, since the film's ending goes for little: Regina's self-absorption does not even suggest that she will notice her loneliness much.

The film made a great deal of money – but not because of an interpolated romance between the daughter (Teresa Wright) and a reporter (Richard Carlson): it is presumably because of this new subplot that Miss Hellman has said that she dislikes the picture, and we may suppose it the work of Arthur Kober, Dorothy Parker and Alan Campbell, who are credited with additional dialogue (though Wyler does not recall anyone but Hellman working on the screenplay).

The director, said *Photoplay*, 'plays restraint against shopworn dramatics for magnificent effect [and] the film rolls from the cameras as almost perfect cinema, telling the story with direct and brutal simplicity' – but the magazine was speaking not of Wyler, of whom it would also be true, but King Vidor. The film in question is the remake of **Stella Dallas** (1937), and the adapters, realising that the material had dated, have made father and daughter a good deal more sensitive, and Stella, at the beginning, merely a dreamy girl. Of its type, it is good; this is not the way people behave together, but there are a number of felicities on the ways of soap opera people, as at that moment when daughter takes over from mother the business of re-dyeing the parting in her hair. Barbara Stanwyck is Stella, splendid in the part – and as always under a good director avoiding cliché.

She and Gary Cooper almost salvage **Ball of Fire** (1941), which is enjoyable rather than particularly funny – as was its intention. Stanwyck plays a burlesque queen and Cooper one of seven professors – since the starting point for the writers, Billy Wilder and Charles Brackett, was *Snow White and the Seven Dwarfs* (q.v.). Unfortunately the sages are a cute bunch, at their worst in Richard Haydn's standard performance, and Howard Hawks gets little more fun from the gangsters – though as their chief Dana Andrews was not the man to help him. Instead Hawks concentrates on the stars, and Stanwyck is wonderfully believable as a hard-boiled dame in love with the last man she would

have dreamed of, while Cooper, if overdoing his 'shucks, me' act, gives the impression of being a very nice man indeed.

R.K.O. Radio released both this film and *The Little Foxes*, since Goldwyn had finally broken away from United Artists; after a series of court battles he sold his stock to the board for $300,000 – only half of what it was worth, since he wanted to be rid of his contract to supply pictures. Among the producers likely to replace him the company looked to Sol Lesser, but in 1941 he also left to join R.K.O., where he returned to an old pastime, that of producing Tarzan pictures. In fact he produced only one notable film during his time at United Artists, **Our Town** (1940), one of the so-called prestige pictures noted by *Life* magazine, but of less value than any Tarzan movie. The people of *Our Town* are meant to be ordinary – 'no one very famous ever came from here, least, as far as we know'. As the commentator drones on about 'something eternal here, and it has something to do with human beings . . . there's something eternal about every human being' it is clear that on screen Thornton Wilder's dialogue becomes even more banal, Mom-and-applepieist. The result is a soppy version of Andy Hardy despite Sam Wood's direction, which has a number of grace notes in its Hollywooden way.

A greater blow to United Artists than the defection of Goldwyn was the loss of David O. Selznick, when he ceased production in 1940. (In fact he signed a new agreement in 1941, buying a quarter interest in the company for $1,200,000, and later there was litigation between him and the board, which objected to his selling properties for which it had forwarded the preparation money.) He had arrived there in 1936, finding a natural berth for his independent company, Selznick International. His first backers were Thalberg and Norma Shearer, but the bulk of the financing came from the Whitney family. John Hay Whitney (chairman) had also backed Merian C. Cooper when he formed Pioneer Pictures to exploit the use of Technicolor; Cooper now joined the new company, and although the name 'Pioneer' was dropped that company owned both *A Star is Born* (q.v.) and *Nothing Sacred* (q.v.), which were part of the programme of Selznick International. As Whitney also owned stock in Technicolor Inc, Selznick was expected to give a lead in that direction to other studios whose attitude was, at best, hesitant. A Technicolor programme was drawn up, but financial requirements indicated a first film to be issued with the least possible delay, so that **Little Lord Fauntleroy** (1936) was after all made in monochrome.

John Cromwell directed and, shorn of Mary Pickford's curls, the story is endurable: a small American boy becomes heir to an English earldom and melts the heart of the old earl (Sir C. Aubrey Smith) who greatly resents his American mother (Dolores Costello Barrymore, as she is billed). It is worth remembering that its author, Frances Hodgson Burnett, was a true Anglo-American (born in Manchester and brought up in Tennessee, and later resident for long periods in both countries): a reappraisal of her work in recent years has indicated that the little lord is not that contemptible – and the only note that jars in this version is the tugging of the forelocks, though that is historically correct. Selznick's partiality for the story was conditioned by the fact that his young Copperfield, Freddie Bartholomew, was considered a draw at the time, and that his priggish good manners and smug behaviour are just what is required here. And Sir C. Aubrey played aristocratic curmudgeons so often that one takes him for granted, but he is quite touching in his conversion.

To Selznick's generation the novels of the Victorians and Edwardians (like their paintings) were the height of respectability. **The Garden of Allah** (1936), was based on one by Robert Hichens, its ingredients including mysticism, self-sacrifice, religious preaching, cardboard characters and the sort of dialogue better engraved on tombstones. The fact that the film is at all watchable is due to the Technicolor ('designed for the screen by Lansing C. Holden'), and the spectacle of Marlene Dietrich (Garbo refused the role) and Charles Boyer mooning about in the desert. Since both are fleeing from monastic propriety it is impossible to believe in either character or their Great Love – but at least Boyer endeavours to invoke some conscience and feeling as directed by

Richard Boleslawski. Dietrich, auburn-haired, a deathshead with her plucked eyebrows, is as rewarding as ever.

Equally romantic but a brighter prospect is **A Star Is Born** (1937), Selznick's return to the theme of *What Price Hollywood?*, here credited to William Wellman, who also directed, and Robert Carson, with a screenplay by Dorothy Parker, Alan Campbell and Carson. The 1954 version (q.v.) improves upon it, but the second halves of both films are much alike, with certain key scenes – the visit of Niles to the sanatorium, the encounter at the race track, the night court – virtually identical. The weakness of this earlier version is at the beginning, when Esther (Janet Gaynor) announces her intention of becoming a movie star, and is taken so seriously that her grandmother provides the rail fare to California – though, once she arrived there, this fairy tale turns sour. She eventually gets a job as a waitress at a party given by a drunken director (Owen Moore) and meets an equally drunk big-time star (Fredric March), who gets her a screen test because he is both drunk and sentimental. They fall in love, but as her career waxes his wanes. Miss Gaynor is merely sweet and touching and quaint; it is curious that both she and Judy Garland played this role towards the end of already long screen careers. March is excellent in a role probably based on Owen Moore,* underplaying, and here more of an actor and less of a star than any of his peers. There are two improbabilities – that the press agent (Lionel Stander) should be so rude to him while his wife is the studio's leading star, and that March's suicide stems from believing her stardom more important than their happiness. That, of course, is a Hollywood point of view, as is the slapstick honeymoon in a trailer, predicated on the assumption that movie stars are simple people at heart, longing to get away from fame and the Cocoanut Grove. Otherwise the film underlines the cruelty of Hollywood, only hinted at in earlier films on similar subjects. Like the remake, it is worth seeing; the 1976 version is not, and not merely because its milieu has been changed from movie studio to rock-concert platform.

* However, as Colleen Moore recognised this as partly her story, the character may be based on her first husband, John McCormick.

A Star Is Born was Selznick's third movie and only the sixth in Technicolor. Its cost was $1,400,000 and that of *The Garden of Allah* $2,700,000. Since a year later *The Goldwyn Follies* cost $2,100,000 against the estimated $1½ million it would have cost in black and white we may conclude a round million for a monochrome *Star*, and even at that price it was a doubtful proposition. Selznick's subsequent Technicolor ventures, *Nothing Sacred* (q.v.) and a very likeable version of Mark Twain's *The Adventures of Tom Sawyer* (1938), directed by Norman Taurog, likewise caused no stampede to the box-office, and the tide did not begin to turn till four colour films – *The Goldwyn Follies, Robin Hood, Kentucky* and *Sweethearts* – were listed among the top ten grossing films of 1938. But in the meantime Selznick had abandoned colour, thus exemplifying the perversity of Hollywood: of his first six films, only two were in black and white – and they were the two which would have benefited most from colour.

We can get some idea of what **The Prisoner of Zenda** (1937) would have been like in Technicolor, since M–G–M's remake is a carbon copy – though this version will be around long after the latter has rotted away. Selznick said that he purchased Anthony Hope's 'old-fashioned fairy tale and melodrama' partly because he believed the public to be ready for 'a great and clean love story', rendered topical by the romance of Edward VIII and Mrs Simpson, but mainly because Ronald Colman was under contract. He may never have made a more prescient move, for Colman is perfect as the gallant English gentleman forced by chance to impersonate the dissolute Ruritanian king. (The concept of this mythical Balkan kingdom originates in Hope's novel.) The others in the cast are his equal, this being a film in which each role is marvellously cast: Madeleine Carroll, meltingly beautiful as the princess; Douglas Fairbanks Jr as Rupert of Hentzau, the jesting soldier of fortune; Raymond Massey as Black Michael, unable to hide either his superciliousness or his furies; Mary Astor as his mistress, serenely but desperately plotting his overthrow; Sir C. Aubrey Smith, the epitome of proud-backed, aged counsellors; and David Niven as the carefree young

Madeleine Carroll and Ronald Colman in Selznick's version of *The Prisoner of Zenda* – and this was exactly the sort of still taken in the hope that it would grace the covers of fan-magazines around the world. So it should have done, for this is one of the magical films of which Hollywood was then capable.

aide. The screenplay is by John L. Balderston, the photography by James Wong Howe, and the sets by Lyle Wheeler, but the supreme achievement is that of the director. John Cromwell brought intelligence to some pleasant romances and here achieves what Selznick intended, a fine, holding tale of love and derring-do, no more serious (hence its strength) than Hope's novel. Nevertheless, W. S. Van Dyke was brought in to restage the duel, and George Cukor (thought the best man to handle it) did the renunciation scene – lopped from Rex Ingram's silent version because exhibitors then refused an unhappy ending.

Nothing Sacred (1937) has a golden reputation among fanciers of Thirties comedies, and the idea is fancy enough: poor little poor girl Carole Lombard gets a trip to New York and achieves fame by her flamboyant bravery in the face of what she claims to be imminent death. It might be a companion picture to *Mr Deeds Goes to Town*, being one of the few comedies of the era to justify the adjective sometimes applied to them, 'satirical', but Capra's film is funnier and warmer. Ben Hecht* wrote the script, William Wellman directed, and they must take the blame for

* The profusion and variable quality of Hecht's output was later thought to be due to his employing a team of ghostwriters.

Ingrid Bergman and Leslie Howard in *Intermezzo: a Love Story*. Miss Bergman had appeared in a Swedish version of this story, which Selznick bought, he said, in his belief 'that a duplicating job on it could be done, with a somewhat faster tempo . . .'

sequences which fail to build. But the real weakness is Fredric March as the opportunistic reporter, offering only a general willingness in place of the wit and style of William Powell or Don Ameche. In contrast **The Young in Heart** (1938) is admirably written, by Paul Osborn, from a novel by I.A.R. Wylie, and well directed by Richard Wallace. Its sentimentality is deplorable, but the comic moments, if few, are treasurable. Its moral values seemed correct at the time, and if we may now prefer confidence tricksters to be unregenerate, the reformation of this group is the whole point. They are played by Roland Young, almost startlingly in command of his technique, Billie Burke and Douglas Fairbanks Jr, equally good, and Janet Gaynor, too obvious a candidate for reform.

Made for Each Other (1939) was written by Jo Swerling and directed by Cromwell: *Time* magazine didn't know whether to credit them, Selznick or the stars (Lombard and James Stewart) 'for the indisputable fact that this mundane, domestic chronicle has more dramatic impact than all the hurricanes, sandstorms and earthquakes manufactured in Hollywood last season . . .' He is a young New York lawyer called John; she is called Jane; and their problems include a nagging mother, a cancelled honeymoon and dinner for the boss after the maid has walked out. Years later, Garson Kanin

and Ruth Gordon, remembering this picture, sat down and wrote *The Marrying Kind* (q.v.), also about the trials and tribulations of the first year of marriage (a frequent subject in the Silents): but they got it right; this film does not. There *is* a hurricane, or at least a snowstorm; the marriage has fallen apart, baby is ill with pneumonia, and wouldn't you know that the only vaccine is in Salt Lake City and all the planes are grounded?

Intermezzo: a Love Story (1939) is the remake of a Swedish picture, recommended to Selznick by his story editor, Kay Brown, together with its female lead, Ingrid Bergman. He dallied with Loretta Young; Ronald Colman and then William Powell turned down the male lead, and he planned to start it with Miss Young and Charles Boyer; but he came back to Bergman. Leslie Howard took on the male role because Selznick allowed him to be Associate Producer – in fact an appeasement for Howard's reluctant involvement with *Gone with the Wind*. Wyler was to have directed, but there were delays and *The Westerner* intervened. Since the result is so much better than any other film directed by Gregory Ratoff we must acknowledge the photography by Gregg Toland (Wyler's choice) and Selznick's own painstaking concern. The American film is twenty-two minutes shorter than the Swedish one, and it is much to Selznick's credit that he thought it sufficient thus – at sixty-six minutes, the shortest major Hollywood picture in thirty years. A celebrated violinist (Howard) asks his daughter's music teacher (Bergman) to accompany him on tour: extemporising after a concert, he tells her they should have been playing 'Rustle of Spring', and it is an apt analogy, for Miss Bergman is springlike. This radiant, sensible, demure girl is the most innocent of home-breakers. We do not smile that they have separate rooms in that unlikely Riviera hotel; we do not demur when, like Camille, she renounces him for love. Of course it is dishonest, with the understanding wife (Edna Best) waiting to welcome him home. Audiences fantasised with the lovers, grew sentimental, later, when they heard the theme tune on the wireless, and welcomed, reassured, the downfall of adultery.

These romances, like Hollywood's

screwball comedies, did not survive the war, and few later attempts to imitate them were successful. Almost the last of them was **Rebecca** (1940), which although directed by Alfred Hitchcock – his first American film – is primarily a love story. It does, however, have suspense and a murder, though that was changed to an accident to conform to the Hays Office regulations (which by insisting that all crimes must be expiated before the final fade-out would in this case have necessitated an unhappy ending). Daphne du Maurier's novel had taken both Britain and the U.S. by storm, and since many people can quote, still, its opening line, they probably agree with James Agate that it is not well written but impossible to put down. It is a story both preposterous and endearing, though it has dated now, for we have lost our fascination with stately homes and the rich who live in them. Yet the girl who marries into one is the perennial Cinderella (she is also Jane Eyre); the hero's dead first wife and her faithful (living) housekeeper are the ugly sisters, and he, Prince Charming, is revealed as a murderer. This Cinderella is discovered on the Côte d'Azur, the mousy companion to a vulgar, celebrity-hunting American (Florence Bates). That lady's reaction when she learns that the girl has nabbed one of the best catches in England makes one of the most entertaining sequences in all movies, and from then on audiences are hooked. Joan Fontaine was born to play the girl, and Laurence Olivier manages shading as the moody, aloof husband. With the exception of the bounder, played by George Sanders, no other character has any existence outside this genre, but at least they are well-acted – except for Judith Anderson's too villainous housekeeper.

Hitchcock's summons to Hollywood was further evidence of the revived prestige of the director, coinciding as it did with the rising eminence of Wyler and the re-emergence of Ford, all of them being accorded the respect shown to Capra. Though others had wielded power on occasion, the producer remained god, and the film that is Hollywood's masterpiece is a demonstration of Selznick at the peak of his powers.

The making of **Gone with the Wind** (1939) is a consistently interesting affair.

Margaret Mitchell's novel about the Deep South and the Civil War, modelled on 'War and Peace', had been published in 1936. Encouraged by Whitney, Selznick bought it, still in galley, for $50,000 – a record price for a property not an established success. Jack L. Warner had taken an option, as a subject for Bette Davis, but had dropped it when she left for Europe. Other producers watched curiously – aware that the film would have to be very expensive – and thinking Selznick less and less foolish as the book became the rage of the nation. Its success solved the major problem, since it became increasingly clear that the public would insist on seeing *all* the story, thus entailing a commitment to a very long film. At one point a two-part movie was contemplated; the final running-time was 3 hours 43 minutes, plus intermission. This meant – with the essential re-creation of Atlanta in the 1860s – an unprecedented cost, which finally totalled $4,250,000. The Selznick publicity fanned the flames, and by the time the film was ready a Gallup poll had certified that over fifty-six million Americans could not wait to see it.

The premier choice for Rhett Butler was Clark Gable, but Mayer, still smarting from Selznick's defection, was considered unapproachable. Goldwyn refused a bid for Gary Cooper; Warners, approached for Errol Flynn, offered him

Joan Fontaine and Laurence Olivier in *Rebecca*, and this is one of the more memorable moments from a memorable film. It is deeply romantic, but she has just mistaken his proposal of marriage, assuming he wanted only a secretary.

in a deal to include Bette Davis, who desperately wanted to play Scarlett – but not to Flynn's Rhett. Selznick returned to Ronald Colman, actually announced for the role because he was under contract, and also dickered with the idea of Warner Baxter; but it was progressively more apparent that the public would consider no Rhett but Gable. Mayer refused every overture till May 1938 when he offered to buy the property, plus all pre-production work and Selznick's services as producer. The matter was resolved thus: it remained a Selznick International picture, but M-G-M contributed Gable and an investment of $1¼ million (Selznick, short of money after his expensive and unprofitable programme, was tempted to sell outright, but Whitney supplied the extra finance needed) – for which they got fifty per cent of the profits and distribution rights. As Selznick's contract with United Artists did not run out till the delivery of *Made for Each Other*, he was not anxious to begin production – and à propos of that there was the vexed and popular matter of the casting of Scarlett O'Hara.

The first name announced was Tallulah Bankhead. Miriam Hopkins was also considered, but the only serious early contender was Norma Shearer – till she canvassed her fans and found that they did not want her to play this baggage. Other established actresses considered were Carole Lombard, Irene Dunne, Claudette Colbert, Margaret Sullavan and Joan Crawford (Mayer's choice); among the unknowns and little-knowns were Paulette Goddard, Ann Sheridan, Lana Turner, Susan Hayward and Lucille Ball. By the time production was due to start – at the end of 1938 – the choice had levelled down to Joan Bennett, Jean Arthur, Loretta Young and Katharine Hepburn – the last-named the choice of George Cukor, signed at the start to direct the film (she was also, almost certainly, the actress the author had in mind when she wrote her final draft); but neither Selznick nor Gable wanted Hepburn, and nor, to judge from the response to her recent films, did the public. At the last minute, as the cameras started turning – on the burning of Atlanta (which was the left-over set of *King Kong*, needing to be cleared so that other sets could be constructed) – Selznick's brother, Myron, an

agent, turned up with the English actress, Vivien Leigh, whose tests were to prove so exciting – because, as Cukor recalled later, 'there was an indescribable wildness about her,' as if 'possessed of the devil'.

She was signed in January 1939 (noticeably, in the flight across the burning Atlanta, Scarlett either has her head turned from the camera or her arm across her face; but the close-ups are marvellously integrated). Filming proper began at the end of that month and stopped two weeks later with the removal of Cukor due to 'disagreements'. Elaborating many years later Selznick said that Cukor could not respond to the spectacle, but speculation within the industry at the time centred upon Gable's dissatisfaction. He had been unwilling to play the role and since the failure of *Parnell* was apprehensive of donning period costume; he was also said to be unhappy that Cukor was paying less attention to his performance than those of Miss Leigh and Olivia de Havilland, though Cukor is on record as saying that Gable made no complaint direct to him.★ Of the four M-G-M directors mentioned to take over, Jack Conway, Robert Z. Leonard, King Vidor and Victor Fleming, the last-named was the obvious choice, since he had had two recent 'spectacle' successes, *Captains Courageous* and *Test Pilot*, the latter with Gable, who regarded him as a friend. He was, however, working on *The Wizard of Oz*, at that point the most important Metro film in production, but Gable's preference prevailed. (Vidor took over that film for the final weeks of shooting and in this game of musical chairs Cukor went to M-G-M to make *The Women*, thus releasing Lubitsch to begin *Ninotchka*.) All that Cukor shot is in the film: the birth of Melanie's baby; the marauding soldier at Tara; and the death of Bonnie. Sam Wood directed, according to Selznick, 'three solid reels' when Fleming was felled by overwork and these are dotted throughout the film. Although the sole writing credit went to the dramatist Sidney Howard, others who contributed, apart from Selznick himself, were Oliver

★ Cukor later said privately that he believed that he had a moral advantage over Gable, since he knew that Gable as a young man in Hollywood had been the lover of one of the best-known leading men of the day; and they did dispute once on the set – when Cukor insisted on Rhett's crying at the death of his child.

Garett, Ben Hecht, John Van Druten and Scott Fitzgerald. Ernest Haller is the credited photographer, but Ray Rennahan and Lee Garmes also worked on it.

But the glory for this Hollywood monument should finally go to Selznick, Cukor and William Cameron Menzies, credited as Production Designer. They spent two years preparing it, and because the film is so consistent in its alternation from close-up to long-shot (much more so than in most films of the time) we may assume they 'blocked' the script in this way. Menzies was given carte blanche on the physical look of the film, as we know from his detailed story-board designs, but it was presumably in consultation with Cukor that he decided to set so many conversations before windows, beyond which Atlanta burns or merely raindrops fall. And of course anything that Selznick did not suggest he had to approve, down to the smallest detail.

The film remains visually splendid, but its silhouette-and-sunset pannings back to Tara – complemented by Max Steiner's pounding musical theme – more than anything else now render it old-fashioned. Another factor that keeps the film of its time is the character of Scarlett, but that is mainly because she was the prototype of every subsequent soap opera heroine of any ambition. Just as Miss Mitchell took from Becky Sharp elements of her character she most understood – such as her scheming – so later writers have quarried Scarlett for her most sensational aspects: her dealings with men, her wilfulness, her taking to drink, her denial of the marriage bed to Rhett, her losing her child by falling downstairs. It is clear, however, why the adventures of Scarlett enthralled a generation of readers and picturegoers: in war, she grew from silly girlhood to capable womanhood. First glimpsed as a girl whose sole realities are the total admiration of beaux and having her own way, she is deprived of both at once when Ashley Wilkes (Leslie Howard) tells her that he is to marry another; she reacts by marrying the man who happens to be nearest to her, his early death, later, in battle, being of no consequence. She still pines for Ashley, but is pursued by Captain Butler – best described as an adventurer, if not a war-profiteer, but always very gallant, especially where Mrs Wilkes, Melanie, is concerned. He knows Melanie to be worth a dozen Scarletts, with her courage, understanding, kindness and gentleness – as opposed to Scarlett's one admirable quality, her tenacity. Nevertheless he marries Scarlett, but cannot tame her or control her; even more clear-sightedly, at the end he walks out on her.

If audiences were satisfied that Scarlett gets her just deserts they were fascinated to find that even Gable could not tame this shrew – just as they applauded her vow not to let war defeat her, and sympathised when she, as a volunteer nurse, refuses to help at the amputation of a leg. *Gone with the Wind* is, in fact, two films: although the war between the States is its *raison d'être,* and it was this which helped it towards its enormous popularity that is only the background to Scarlett's adventures – and if we question the worth of the characters the film's portrait of war becomes its greatest achievement. This is not very well done, despite the dead and dying in hospital or in the square outside, despite the gunfire, the fires, the deserters, the casualty lists, the destruction everywhere. But an odd sentence touches the nerve, as when Rhett says, 'Take a good look, my dear. One day you can tell your children how you saw the South disappear in one night,' or Aunt Pittypat's sad 'It's like the ending of the world.' What is moving is the very breadth of the tale, its attempt to show the end of an era – and Hollywood's faith in itself as a chronicler of such things. For compulsive viewing the first half will stand with anything put on film. It is also, quite often, funny – modern audiences love Scarlett's disdain for her widow's weeds at the ball, and Prissy's claim that, after all, she 'don' know nuthin' 'bout birthin' babies, Mssss Scarlett'.

The second half is the Reconstruction. After an opening which retains the broad canvas of the earlier part it devolves into a study of an incompatible marriage. I do not think Miss Mitchell understood much of such matters as the refusal of marital rights; and that we remain attentive says much for the first part and the superb performances of the four principals – two of whom had not wanted to be in the film in the first place.

No film has caught the popular imagination as *Gone with the Wind* did, and it continues to do so. ABOVE, Scarlett running through the grounds of Tara. BELOW, Scarlett with her 'Mammy', Hattie McDaniel, ABOVE FAR RIGHT, Scarlett and Melanie as nurses in the hospital of Atlanta. BELOW FAR RIGHT, Olivia de Havilland as Melanie with Leslie Howard as Ashley Wilkes, her husband.

Leslie Howard was as uninterested as Gable was unwilling, which does not contradict Olivia de Havilland's statement years later that everyone concerned embarked upon the film as upon no other, with the thought that it would be their one claim to immortality – a touching belief, as well as telling us much about Hollywood at the time. She herself brings so much warmth and beauty to a character too good to be true that we cannot despise her as Scarlett docs. As for Miss Leigh, apart from an invincible spirit she has a cat-like beauty in repose, both disarming and inscrutable. Despite her later claim that she could find nothing of herself in Scarlett, biographical accounts suggest a number of common qualities – ambition, wit, selfishness, temperament (it was her differences with Fleming which led to his near-nervous breakdown), loyalty, and a coquettish way with men. She overdoes the 'Fiddle-de-dee' Scarlett of the beginning, but the mature Scarlett deserves all the praise showered upon her. She won the Best Actress Oscar; the Best Supporting Oscar went to Hattie McDaniel for her splendid Mammy, Scarlett's unimpressible nurse. As Scarlett's father, Thomas Mitchell was similarly honoured, and the film took the expected fistful of Oscars.

Its achievements are thrown into relief when one starts to enumerate its faults – and length is not one of them, despite longueurs in the second half. Apart from the tale itself, which will be ever tinged with purple, there is only one major flaw – the large number of shots through glass and other trick shots, too many of them unconvincing (late in production Selznick realised that much more of the film should have been filmed on location). The movie has been castigated for taking no stand on the race problem, but that is beside the point; more pertinently, as some contemporary critics pointed out, it did nothing to illuminate the events which were essential to its telling.

Of the several accounts of the filming there have been no less than three full-length books, one by Gavin Lambert (which is ironic, for at the time – the early Fifties – he was editor of *Sight and Sound,* and it was a film which his contributors, if they mentioned it at all, despised). What vexed those who regarded themselves as the guardians of 'serious' cinema is that both the industry and the public regarded it as 'the greatest film ever made' – yet it could be advertised as such on its revivals in the Seventies without fear of contradiction. In 1975 David Robinson in *The Times* pointed out that truth, noting that no one says that it is the *best* film ever made. Certainly none of the later colossi so beloved of the industry (*Quo Vadis?, Ben-Hur, Doctor Zhivago,* q.v.) is ever likely to win such universal respect; and it requires no prescience to say that there will never be another film quite like it. It was for many years the most financially successful film ever, only dropping down the lists when the rise in seat prices automatically increased the profits of more recent films; but recent adjustments, bringing 1939 seat prices into line with current prices, indicate that it has still been seen by more people than any other film to the present day. And that is without taking into account its first American telecast (in November 1976, on two nights, with an estimated seventy-nine minutes of commercials), when it broke all viewing records. In 1978, when it was leased to T.V. for a twenty-year period for $20 million, it was already the only film, with the exception of Disney's cartoons, to be consistently and successfully reissued as a major movie world-wide – on some occasions saving M-G-M from bankruptcy. (Selznick had sold his interest in the film to Whitney during the War to profit from capital gains; Whitney sold it to M-G-M in 1944.) Its only notable failure was in Paris, in 1950, when it arrived at the end of the backlog of Hollywood movies which had piled up during the war years, and it had perhaps been too keenly awaited for too long; but it subsequently became as firm a favourite in France as elsewhere. For a great many people it was part of their War; it ran in London throughout the Blitz, and for four years thereafter. Its timing was right. It is old-fashioned now, but still powerful entertainment. It is the Sistine Chapel among movies, with all the weaknesses, virtues and vastness that that implies. It is the apotheosis of the Hollywood film.

Clark Gable and Vivien Leigh in the second half of *Gone with the Wind.* The film has virtually never been shown without an interval, dividing the story at the obvious point, and most people seem to think the first half the better. The strength of its situations – the coming of the War between the states – and the conviction with which they are told, carry us through to the very end of the film, as well as, today, lulling us into acceptance of their essential melodrama.

INTERMISSION

IN 1978, a writer in *The New Yorker's* 'Talk of the Town' column (issue of 6 March) decided that 'any inventory of the things that have stuck in a nation's collective mind is going to be odd and unpredictable', citing as examples 'the movies of certain decades (the Thirties and Forties) but not of other decades (the Fifties and Sixties) . . . our present decade might have very little to contribute.' We might therefore look at an American newspaper poll of a few months earlier, when readers voted on their ten best American films of all time. The final list read:

1. *Gone with the Wind*
2. *Star Wars*
3. *The Wizard of Oz*
4. *The Sound of Music*
5. *Jaws*
6. *The Godfather*
7. *Ben-Hur* (1959)
8. *Rocky*
9. *The African Queen*
10. *One Flew Over the Cuckoo's Nest*

That the list includes five films from the Seventies does not necessarily mean that the public has a short memory; but how many of those five films will be in a similar list in ten years time? More revealing is the poll of October 1975, when the Broadcast Information of the U.S. asked industry executives and their spouses for their favourite films, which turned out to be, in order, *The Best Years of Our Lives* (which tells us much about them), *Casablanca*, *Gone with the Wind*, *All About Eve* and *The Wizard of Oz*, none less than thirty years old. Is, incidentally, *The Wizard of Oz* genuinely more loved than *Snow White and the Seven Dwarfs*, or is its annual presence on T.V. a factor in its popularity?

As the golden years of Hollywood died, one New York cinema polled its patrons as to their favourite movie. The result:

1. *Mrs Miniver*
2. *Gone with the Wind*
3. *How Green Was My Valley*
4. *Goodbye, Mr Chips*
5. *Rebecca*
6. *Wuthering Heights*
7. *The Good Earth*
8. *Boys Town*
9. *The Philadelphia Story*
10. *Mr Deeds Goes to Town*

The same year, 1942, in Britain, the readers of *Picturegoer* came up with their list:

1. *Goodbye, Mr Chips*
2. *Mrs Miniver*
3. *Gone with the Wind* (not then seen outside first-run theatres)
4. *Rebecca*
5. *How Green Was My Valley*
6. *The Good Earth*
7. *Citizen Kane*
8. *Snow White and the Seven Dwarfs*
9. *Wuthering Heights*
10. *Ben-Hur* (1925)

In 1951, when *Picturegoer* conducted a second poll, the only pre-war film to figure on the list was *Gone with the Wind*, which was first: but then, such statistics depend on local factors, and it is doubtful whether, at that time, more than a handful of *Picturegoer* readers had seen the Silent *Ben-Hur*. Around the same time – in 1950 – *Daily Variety* polled its readers to commemorate a half-century of films. The best Sound film, said its readers, was *Gone with the Wind*, followed by *The Best Years of Our Lives*. Asked specifically for Silent films, they chose *Birth of a Nation*, followed by *The Big Parade* and *The Kid*.

Since these may well have been the only Silent films they remembered, we should turn to one of the best critics of the time, Richard Winnington, who listed his choice of the world's 'greatest films', worked out in conjunction with Gavin Lambert and Lindsay Anderson. There were nine; they couldn't agree on a tenth: *The Childhood of Maxim Gorki*, *The Grapes of Wrath*, *Earth*, *Road to Life*, *Zéro de*

Conduite, *Le Jour se Lève*, *Ladri di Biciclette*, *Un Chapeau de Paille d'Italie* and *City Lights*. In 1958, the organisers of the Brussels Film Exhibition polled 117 film historians in twenty-six countries for their selection of the twelve greatest films ever made:

1. *Battleship Potemkin*
2. (equal) *The Gold Rush*
   Ladri di Biciclette
4. *La Passion de Jeanne d'Arc*
5. *La Grande Illusion*
6. *Greed*
7. *Intolerance*
8. *Mother*
9. *Citizen Kane*
10. *Earth*
11. *Der Letzte Mann*
12. *Das Kabinet des Dr Caligari*

The list is as relevant as if a list of the best plays in English was found to consist of pre-Shakespearian drama, and the 1952 *Sight and Sound* poll of critics and film historians also did little but indicate the extent of reputation:

1. *Ladri di Biciclette*
2. (equal) *City Lights*
   The Gold Rush
4. *Battleship Potemkin*
5. (equal) *Louisiana Story*
   Intolerance
7. (equal) *Greed*
   Le Jour se Lève
   La Passion de Jeanne d'Arc
10. (equal) *Brief Encounter*
    Le Million
    Le Règle du Jeu

Ten years later, the *Sight and Sound* poll retained only a few of the pre-war titles: *La Règle du Jeu*, *Greed* and *Potemkin*, but had added two more from that period, *Citizen Kane*, which was first, and *L'Atalante*. Ten years on, in 1972, *La Règle du Jeu*, *Potemkin* and *Kane* all remained, the last named still in first position; *La Passion de Jeanne d'Arc* had returned to the list, and *The General* had found its way on to it.

Any reader who has borne with me to this point may suspect that I am more partial to the public's choices than to the critics'. They are certainly more honestly chosen: I understand a liking for both *Mrs Miniver* and *How Green Was My Valley*, much as I dislike them, but I cannot understand a taste for *Earth* or *Road to Life*, which seem to me equally worthless as representations of life in this century. It is certainly true that critics and some buffs prefer to look back on the elevating, the innovative and the socially-crusading. They have tended to despise the merely entertaining, and are certainly subject to fashion, so that neither Clair nor de Sica commands the admiration they once did; they find it safer to vote for *Potemkin*, kept firmly in the repertory for many years.

Fortunately, at the present time, film appreciation is under constant scrutiny, with the Hollywood entertainment film at last receiving its due – and often very much more than its due. I have watched friends stumble glassy-eyed with boredom out of *Intolerance* and *Caligari*, and have found veterans, once enthralled by Pudovkin and Chaplin, puzzled as to why they should now appear so dowdy and dull. To me, the supreme artists of the Silent era are Keaton and Sjöström, whose work I am confident will still engage attention a century hence; and I trust posterity will continue to find excitement in the work of Eisenstein and Pudovkin, of Pabst and Lamprecht, of Ozu, and enjoyment in much of Von Stroheim and Harold Lloyd. Posterity, I think, will find richness from the first decade of Talkies: Lubitsch, Clair, Carné, Renoir, Trenker, Ophuls; much of Ford, Hochbaum, Borzage, Feyder, LaCava, Grémillon, Wyler, Siodmak, Cukor, Hitchcock, Duvivier, McCarey, Henry King, Wellman and Hawks; a number of screwball comedies and some Hollywood romantic pictures; the early Warner melodramas; above all, in the presence of a generation of players which has not been equalled since.

Few of these films represent their period accurately in terms of what it was, but they reflect the aspirations and hopes of the people who watched them, if not always of the people who made them, and they have an emotional vitality recognisable to the patrons of the Renaissance painters, or the first readers of Dickens, Thackeray and George Eliot. The Lumières had only recorded, but Méliès entertained, and since then the chief function of the film has been to entertain. Between Méliès and *Gone with the Wind* a mercifully large body of films managed to achieve something more: the record may be incomplete, the portrait uncertain, the light it throws on humanity somewhat biased – but the richness of human behaviour and misbehaviour had been trapped in celluloid.

And then came 'Rosebud'.

Acknowledgments

AMONG those who have worked with me on this book there has been a remarkable unanimity on its content. We were also agreed that nothing would be taken for granted, which has meant not only viewing the films but researching contemporary opinions and/or personal reminiscences of the film-makers involved. The published sources consulted during ten years' work include not only countless newspapers and magazines but virtually every book ever published on film, so vast in fact that I have restricted my bibliography to recommendations for further reading; this appears at the end of Volume Two.

I have to thank many people who have generously enabled me to see rare films, and those who have guided me to relatively unexplored corners of film. That I avoid a proliferation of names does not lessen my gratitude. There are many individuals in the British Film Institute who have given of time and trouble, and if I single out only John Gillette I know that his colleagues will understand why: he and I have not always been in agreement, but whenever my own spirits have flagged at the prospect of yet another film (say, the fourth within one day) I have before me the example of John and his unstinted enthusiasm for good cinema.

I have been fortunate in finding that quality also in the two editors of this history, Keith Roberts and Richard Cohen. Keith died, in his early forties, and I would like to think that this book is a small memorial to him. It is certainly a tribute to the patience and care of Richard Cohen, on whose desk the manuscript luckily landed, and the rest of the team that worked with him. The consultant editors were Barbara Noble, an English lady in her seventies who had worked for several years within the film industry, and Bruce Goldstein, an American in his twenties who can already look back on a decade of running repertory cinemas in New York and elsewhere. I have had other important editorial contributions from Christine Pye and Rosalind Main, while Margaret Fraser has designed the book with much enthusiasm and good judgment. Our only problem was length, trying to pare away discussion of those films and film-makers we considered important; and I doubt whether any of us ever worked on a happier book.

I have also to thank the film companies for their co-operation in allowing us to reproduce stills, chief among them being Atlas, Columbia, E.M.I., Lenfilm, London Film Productions, Metro-Goldwyn-Meyer, Mosfilm, Paramount, Rank, R.K.O. Radio, Svensk Filmindustri, 20th Century-Fox, United Artists, Universal and Warner Bros. Invaluable help in this matter has also been provided by the National Film Archive, Fred Zentner of the Cinema Bookshop and the Museum of Modern Art.

Index

Figures in italic indicate illustrations

Index

508

Index

510

Index

Index

Index

Index

Index

Index

Index